"In the rapidly burgeoning, cumulative progress that characterizes our field today, this is the compendium that everyone needs. Graduate students and researchers alike will feast on this collection."

Professor Keith E. Stanovich, University of Toronto, Canada

"This authoritative handbook defines the science of reading, reviewing the huge advances in knowledge over the last thirty years in a dazzling display of scholarship. No one interested in the psychology of reading can do without it."

Professor Uta Frith, Institute of Cognitive Neuroscience,
University College London

"At last! The handbook we've all been waiting for – graduate students and seasoned researchers alike – an authoritative, state-of-the-art source-book encompassing all the central topics in the science of reading, with an author list that reads like a Who's Who of basic reading research. The breadth and depth of each of so many seminal reviews confirms the status of reading science as one of the 'trophies' of modern cognitive science. I expect this will remain the definitive work for years to come."

Professor David L. Share, Department of Learning Disabilities,
University of Haifa, Israel

**Blackwell Handbooks of Developmental Psychology**

This outstanding series of handbooks provides a cutting-edge overview of classic research, current research and future trends in developmental psychology.

- Each handbook draws together 25–30 newly commissioned chapters to provide a comprehensive overview of a subdiscipline of developmental psychology.
- The international team of contributors to each handbook has been specially chosen for its expertise and knowledge of each field.
- Each handbook is introduced and contextualized by leading figures in the field, lending coherence and authority to each volume.

The *Blackwell Handbooks of Developmental Psychology* will provide an invaluable overview for advanced students of developmental psychology and for researchers as an authoritative definition of their chosen field.

**Published**

*Blackwell Handbook of Infant Development*
Edited by Gavin Bremner and Alan Fogel

*Blackwell Handbook of Childhood Social Development*
Edited by Peter K. Smith and Craig H. Hart

*Blackwell Handbook of Childhood Cognitive Development*
Edited by Usha Goswami

*Blackwell Handbook of Adolescence*
Edited by Gerald R. Adams and Michael D. Berzonsky

*The Science of Reading: A Handbook*
Edited by Margaret J. Snowling and Charles Hulme

*Blackwell Handbook of Early Childhood Development*
Edited by Kathleen McCartney and Deborah A. Phillips

*Blackwell Handbook of Language Development*
Edited by Erika Hoff and Marilyn Shatz

# The Science of Reading: A Handbook

Edited by

**Margaret J. Snowling and Charles Hulme**

BLACKWELL PUBLISHING
350 Main Street, Malden, MA 02148-5020, USA
9600 Garsington Road, Oxford OX4 2DQ, UK
550 Swanston Street, Carlton, Victoria 3053, Australia

First published 2005 by Blackwell Publishing Ltd
First published in paperback 2007 by Blackwell Publishing Ltd

7   2013

*Library of Congress Cataloging-in-Publication Data*

The science of reading : a handbook / edited by Margaret J. Snowling and Charles Hulme.
    p. cm. — (Blackwell handbooks of developmental psychology)
  Includes bibliographical references and indexes.
  ISBN 978-1-4051-1488-2 (alk. paper)
  ISBN 978-1-4051-6811-3 (paperback: alk. paper)
1. Reading.   2. Reading—Research.   3. Reading, Psychology of.   I. Snowling, Margaret J.
II. Hulme, Charles.   III. Series.
LB1050.S365 2005
428.4—dc22

                                                                          2005001421

A catalogue record for this title is available from the British Library.

Set in 10.5 on 12.5 pt Adobe Garamond
by SNP Best-set Typesetter Ltd., Hong Kong
Printed and bound in Singapore
by Ho Printing Singapore Pte Ltd

The publisher's policy is to use permanent paper from mills that operate a sustainable forestry
policy, and which has been manufactured from pulp processed using acid-free and elementary
chlorine-free practices. Furthermore, the publisher ensures that the text paper and cover board
used have met acceptable environmental accreditation standards.

For further information on
Blackwell Publishing, visit our website:
www.blackwellpublishing.com

# Contents

# Contributors

Judith A. Bowey
School of Psychology
University of Queensland
St Lucia
Queensland 4072
Australia
email: j.bowey@psy.uq.edu.au

Brian Byrne
School of Psychology
University of New England
Armidale NSW 2351
Australia
email: bbyrne@pobox.une.edu.au

Markéta Caravolas
Department of Psychology
University of Liverpool
Liverpool L69 7ZA
UK
email: M.C.Caravolas@liverpool.ac.uk

Max Coltheart
Macquarie Centre for Cognitive Science
Macquarie University
Sydney NSW 2109
Australia
email: max@maccs.mq.edu.au

Anna Maria Di Betta
Neurosciences Research Institute
School of Life and Health Sciences
Aston University
Birmingham B4 7ET
UK
email: a.m.dibetta@aston.ac.uk

Linnea C. Ehri
Graduate Center of the City University
  of New York
Program in Educational Psychology
CUNY Graduate Center
365 Fifth Ave.
New York, NY 10016
USA
email: LEhri@gc.cuny.edu

Jack M. Fletcher
Center for Academic and Reading Skills
  Department of Pediatrics
University of Texas Health Science
  Center at Houston
7000 Fannin UCT 2478
Houston TX 77030
USA
email: Jack.M.Fletcher@uth.tmc.edu

Ram Frost
Department of Psychology
The Hebrew University
Jerusalem 91905
Israel
email: frost@mscc.huji.ac.il

J. Richard Hanley
Department of Psychology
University of Essex
Wivenhoe Park
Colchester CO4 3SQ
UK
email: rhanley@essex.ac.uk

Charles Hulme
Department of Psychology
York University
York YO10 5DD
UK
email: ch1@york.ac.uk

Connie Juel
School of Education
Stanford University
485 Lasuen Mall
Stanford, CA 94305-3096
USA
email: cjuel@stanford.edu

Barbara J. Juhasz
Department of Psychology
University of Massachusetts
Amherst, MA 01003
USA
email: bjjuhasz@psych.umass.edu

Brett Kessler
Psychology Department
Washington University in St. Louis
Campus Box 1125
One Brookings Drive
St. Louis, MO 63130-4899
USA
email: bkessler@wustl.edu

Walter Kintsch
Department of Psychology
University of Colorado
Boulder, CO 80309-0344
USA
email: wkintsch@clipr.colorado.edu

Heidi Kloos
Center for Cognitive Sciences
Ohio State University
211 G Ohio Stadium East
1961 Tuttle Park Place
Columbus, OH 43210
email: Kloos.6@osu.edu

Régine Kolinsky
UNESCOG (CP 191)
Université libre de Bruxelles
50 Av. F. D. Roosevelt
B-1050 Brussels
Belgium
email: rkolins@ulb.ac.be

Matthew A. Lambon Ralph
Department of Psychology
University of Manchester
Manchester M13 9PL
UK
email: matt.lambon-ralph@man.ac.uk

Nicole Landi
Learning Research and Development
   Center
University of Pittsburgh
Pittsburgh, PA 15260
USA
email: nil3@pitt.edu

Jacqueline Leybaert
LAPSE
Université libre de Bruxelles
50 Av. F. D. Roosevelt
B-1050 Brussels
Belgium
email: leybaert@ulb.ac.be

Christopher J. Lonigan
Department of Psychology
Florida State University
One University Way
Tallahassee, FL 32306-1270
USA
email: lonigan@psy.fsu.edu

Stephen J. Lupker
Department of Psychology
University of Western Ontario
London
Ontario N6A 5C2
Canada
email: lupker@uwo.ca

Eamon McCrory
Department of Psychology
Institute of Psychiatry
De Crespigny Park
London SE5 8AF
UK
email: eamonmccrory@hotmail.com

José Morais
UNESCOG (CP 191)
Université libre de Bruxelles
50 Av. F. D. Roosevelt
B-1050 Brussels
Belgium
email: jmorais@ulb.ac.be

Kate Nation
Department of Experimental Psychology
University of Oxford
South Parks Road
Oxford OX1 3UD
UK
email: kate.nation@psy.ox.ac.uk

Jane Oakhill
Department of Psychology
University of Sussex
Falmer House
Brighton BN1 9RH
UK
email: J.Oakhill@sussex.ac.uk

Andrew Olson
Department of Psychology
University of Birmingham
Edgbaston
Birmingham B15 2TT
UK
email: a.l.o.olson@bham.ac.uk

Richard K. Olson
Department of Psychology
University of Colorado, UCB 345
Boulder, CO 80309
USA
email: rolson@psych.colorado.edu

Karalyn Patterson
MRC Cognition and Brain Sciences Unit
15 Chaucer Road
Cambridge CB2 2EF
UK
email: karalyn.patterson@mrc-
    cbu.cam.ac.uk

Bruce F. Pennington
Department of Psychology
University of Denver
2155 S. Race St.
Denver, CO 80210-4638
USA
email: bpenning@nova.psy.du.edu

Charles A. Perfetti
Learning Research and Development
    Center
University of Pittsburgh
Pittsburgh, PA 15260
USA
email: Perfetti@pitt.edu

Beth M. Phillips
Florida Center for Reading Research
City Centre Building Suite 7250
227 North Bronough St.
Tallahassee, FL 32301
USA
email: bphillips@fcrr.org

David C. Plaut
Departments of Psychology and
    Computer Science and Center for
    the Neural Basis of Cognition
Carnegie Mellon University
5000 Forbes Ave.
Pittsburgh, PA 15213-3890
USA
email: plaut@cmu.edu


Alexander Pollatsek
Department of Psychology
University of Massachusetts
Amherst, MA 01003
USA
email: pollatsek@psych.umass.edu


Cathy J. Price
Wellcome Department of Imaging
    Neuroscience
University College London
Institute of Neurology
12 Queen Square
London WC1N 3BG
UK
email: c.price@fil.ion.ucl.ac.uk


Katherine Rawson
Kent State University
Department of Psychology
P.O. Box 5190
Kent, OH 44242-0001
USA
email: krawson1@kent.edu


Keith Rayner
Department of Psychology
University of Massachusetts
Amherst, MA 01003
USA
email: rayner@psych.umass.edu

Cristina Romani
Department of Psychology
Aston University
Aston Triangle
Birmingham B4 7ET
UK
email: c.romani@aston.ac.uk


Philip H. K. Seymour
Department of Psychology
University of Dundee
Dundee DD1 4HN
UK
email: phks@edenfield65.freeserve.co.uk


Catherine E. Snow
Harvard Graduate School of Education
Larsen 3
Cambridge, MA 02138
USA
email: snowcat@gse.harvard.edu


Margaret J. Snowling
Department of Psychology
York University
York YO10 5DD
UK
email: m.snowling@psych.york.ac.uk


Joseph K. Torgesen
Florida Center for Reading Research at
    Florida State University
227 N. Bronough St., Suite 7250
Tallahassee, FL 32301
USA
email: torgesen@fcrr.org


Rebecca Treiman
Psychology Department
Washington University in St. Louis
Campus Box 1125
One Brookings Drive
St. Louis, MO 63130-4899
USA
email: rtreiman@wustl.edu

Guy C. Van Orden
Department of Psychology
Arizona State University
Tempe, AZ 85287-1104
USA
email: guy.van.orden@asu.edu

Frank R. Vellutino
Department of Psychology
State University of New York
1535 Western Avenue
Albany, NY 12203
USA
email: frv@csc.albany.edu

# Preface

"To completely analyse what we do when we read would almost be the acme of the psychologist's achievements, for it would be to describe very many of the most intricate workings of the human mind"

(Huey, 1968).

The science of reading is mature and healthy as the contributions to this volume make clear. Together they provide an assessment of how far we have come in meeting the challenge laid down by Huey more than a century ago. Different chapters illustrate how some old issues remain alive, how new questions have been raised and how some problems have been solved. Many of the issues discussed here would undoubtedly have been familiar to Huey. Discussions of how skilled readers recognize printed words rapidly, of how eye movements in reading are controlled, the factors limiting reading comprehension, and arguments about how best to teach reading, all featured prominently in early studies of reading. These are important topics and ones that remain current, as several chapters in this book attest. There is little doubt that the technical advances made in many of these areas would be a source of pleasure to Huey and his contemporaries in the field of reading research. On the other hand, a number of issues dealt with in this book would probably have seemed totally foreign to people in the field of reading a century ago. For example, studies imaging the brain while it reads, studies examining the molecular genetics of reading disorders, and computational models of different aspects of the reading process would have seemed like science fiction a hundred years ago.

This Handbook provides a state-of-the-art overview of scientific studies of reading. The book is divided into seven sections. Part I deals with word recognition processes and is concerned largely with theories developed in studies of fluent adult reading. Such theories have heavily influenced (and been influenced by) studies of reading development, which are dealt with in Part II. Efficient word recognition processes are necessary, but not sufficient, for reading comprehension (Gough & Tunmer, 1986) and the chapters in Part III go beyond single word processing to consider reading comprehension processes in both adults and children, with an emphasis on the problems that may be encountered in children learning to comprehend what they read. Studies of reading and reading development have until recently been concerned only with reading English. Gough and Hillinger (1980) suggested that learning to read was an "unnatural act"; if that is true there is growing evidence that learning to read in English is a *particularly* unnatural act! Part IV of the book brings together work exploring how reading and reading development may differ across languages. This section highlights a number of issues and confronts the question of whether we can hope for a universal cognitive theory of reading and reading development – such a hope seems closer than some may have believed.

One justification for much research in psychology is that it helps us to understand, and in turn to prevent and to treat, disorders in psychological processes. The chapters in Part V look at our understanding of developmental and acquired disorders of reading and spelling. An important question here is the extent to which common forms of explanation may be valid for both acquired and developmental disorders. Part VI of the book examines the biological substrates of reading. It brings together work on brain imaging, which has revealed with new clarity the brain regions involved in different aspects of reading, with work on the genetic basis of dyslexia. The final section of the book, Part VII, examines how scientific studies of reading can contribute to improving the teaching of reading both in normally developing children and children with dyslexia.

We hope that the overviews of research presented here will be of value to psychologists and educationalists studying reading, their students, and to practitioners and others who want to find out about the current status of The Science of Reading.

# Acknowledgments

We would like to thank Mark Seidenberg who played an invaluable role in helping to shape the form of this book in the early stages of its development.

We have learned a great deal from editing this book and would like to thank all our contributors for their excellent chapters, which made our task so easy and pleasurable.

Maggie Snowling and Charles Hulme

# PART I

*Word Recognition Processes in Reading*

# Editorial Part I

Word recognition is the foundation of reading; all other processes are dependent on it. If word recognition processes do not operate fluently and efficiently, reading will be at best highly inefficient. The study of word recognition processes is one of the oldest areas of research in the whole of experimental psychology (Cattell, 1886). The chapters in this section of the Handbook present an overview of current theories, methods, and findings in the study of word recognition processes in reading.

What do we mean by recognition here? Recognition involves accessing information stored in memory. In the case of visual word recognition this typically involves retrieving information about a word's spoken form and meaning from its printed form. The first two chapters, by Coltheart and Plaut, outline the two most influential theoretical frameworks for studies of visual word recognition.

Coltheart outlines the history and evolution of dual-route models of reading *aloud* (i.e., how the pronunciation of a printed word is generated). These dual-route models posit that there are two routes from print to speech: a lexical and nonlexical route. Broadly the lexical route involves looking up the pronunciation of a word stored in a lexicon or mental dictionary. In contrast, the nonlexical route involves translating the graphemes (letters or letter groups) into phonemes and assembling the pronunciation of a word from this sequence of phonemes. Such a process should work just as well for nonwords as for words, just so long as the word follows the spelling pattern of the language (a nonlexical reading of YACHT, will not yield the pronunciation for a kind of boat with a sail on it). This idea is embodied in an explicit computational model (the DRC model) that Coltheart describes in detail. It may be worth emphasizing that this highly influential model is a model of how adults read aloud; it is not concerned with how the knowledge allowing this to happen is acquired. A major focus of the model is how different disorders of reading aloud, which arise after brain damage in adults, can be accounted for.

Plaut gives an overview of a different class of models of reading aloud that employ connectionist architectures (models that learn to pronounce words by training associations between distributed representations of orthography and phonology). One particularly influential model of this type is the so-called triangle model (Plaut, McClelland, Seidenberg, & Patterson, 1996; Seidenberg & McClelland, 1989). This model abandons the distinction between a lexical and nonlexical procedure for translating visual words into pronunciations; instead the same mechanism is used to convert words and nonwords into pronunciations, based on patterns of connections between orthographic inputs and phonological outputs. One other critical difference between the triangle model and the DRC model is that the triangle model explicitly embodies a learning procedure and thus can be considered a model of both adult reading and reading development. It is clear that these are very different conceptions of how the mind reads single words. Both approaches deal with a wide range of evidence. Arguably, the DRC model is more successful in dealing with the detailed form of reading impairments observed after brain damage in adults, while the ability to think about development and adult performance together in the triangle model is a considerable attraction. There is no doubt that differences between these models will be a source of intense interest in the coming years.

Lupker's chapter moves on to review a huge body of experimental evidence concerned with how adults recognize printed words. Many of these experiments investigate what is a remarkably rapid and accurate process in most adults, by measuring reaction time, or by impairing performance by using masking (preventing participants from seeing a word clearly by superimposing another stimulus immediately after the word has been presented). Any complete model of word recognition ultimately will have many phenomena from such experiments to explain. These include the fact that people perceive letters more efficiently when they are embedded in words, that high-frequency (i.e., more familiar) words are recognized easier than less familiar words, and that recognition of words is influenced by previously presented words (seeing a prior word that is related in form or meaning helps us to recognize a word that follows it). One conclusion that emerges powerfully from Lupker's review is the need for interactive models in which activation of orthographic and phonological information reciprocally influence each other. This is an issue that Van Orden and Kloos take up in detail, presenting a wealth of evidence that converges on the idea that there is intimate and perpetual interaction between representations of orthography and phonology (spelling and sound) during the process of recognizing a printed word.

Moving on from the recognition of isolated words, Rayner, Juhasz, and Pollatsek discuss eye movements in reading. Eye movements provide a fascinating window on how word recognition processes operate in the more natural context of reading continuous text. It appears that the pattern of eye movements in reading is heavily influenced by the cognitive processes subserving both word recognition and text comprehension. The majority of words in text are directly fixated (usually somewhere in the first half of the word). For readers of English the area of text processed during a fixation (the perceptual span) is about 3 or 4 letters to the left of fixation and some 14 or 15 letters to the right of fixation. This limit seems to be a basic one determined by acuity limitations, and useful information about letter identity is extracted only from a smaller area, perhaps 7 or 8 letters to the right of the fixation point. It appears that only short, frequent, or highly predictable words are identified prior to being fixated (so that they can be skipped). However, partial information (about a word's orthography and phonology but typically not its meaning) about the word following the fixation point often is extracted and combined with information subsequently extracted when the word is directly fixated. These studies are consistent with the view that the speed and efficiency of word recognition processes (as well as higher-level text-based processes) place fundamental constraints on how quickly even skilled readers read text.

Arguably the central question in the study of word recognition in reading is the role of phonology. All of the chapters in Part I address this issue explicitly. It appears that a consensus has been reached: phonological coding is central to word recognition, though opinions are divided on many details of how phonology is accessed and its possible importance in providing access to semantic information.

# 1

## Modeling Reading: The Dual-Route Approach

**Max Coltheart**

Reading is information-processing: transforming print to speech, or print to meaning. Anyone who has successfully learned to read has acquired a mental information-processing system that can accomplish such transformations. If we are to understand reading, we will have to understand the nature of that system. What are its individual information-processing components? What are the pathways of communication between these components?

Most research on reading since 1970 has investigated reading aloud and so sought to learn about the parts of the reading system that are particularly involved in transforming print to speech. A broad theoretical consensus has been reached: whether theories are connectionist (e.g., Seidenberg & McClelland, 1989; Plaut, this volume) or nonconnectionist (e.g., Coltheart, Curtis, Atkins & Haller, 1993), it is agreed that within the reading system there are two different procedures accomplishing this transformation – there are dual routes from print to speech. (The distinction between connectionist and nonconnectionist theories of cognition is discussed later in this chapter.)

### In the Beginning . . .

The dual-route conception of reading seems first to have been enunciated by de Saussure (1922; translated 1983, p. 34):

> there is also the question of reading. We read in two ways; the new or unknown word is scanned letter after letter, but a common or familiar word is taken in at a glance, without bothering about the individual letters: its visual shape functions like an ideogram.

However, it was not until the 1970s that this conception achieved wide currency. A clear and explicit expression of the dual-route idea was offered by Forster and Chambers (1973):

> The pronunciation of a visually presented word involves assigning to a sequence of letters some kind of acoustic or articulatory coding. There are presumably two alternative ways in which this coding can be assigned. First, the pronunciation could be computed by application of a set of grapheme–phoneme rules, or letter-sound correspondence rules. This coding can be carried out independently of any consideration of the meaning or familiarity of the letter sequence, as in the pronunciation of previously unencountered sequences, such as flitch, mantiness and streep. Alternatively, the pronunciation may be determined by searching long-term memory for stored information about how to pronounce familiar letter sequences, obtaining the necessary information by a direct dictionary look-up, instead of rule application. Obviously, this procedure would work only for familiar words. (Forster & Chambers, 1973, p. 627)
>
> Subjects always begin computing pronunciations from scratch at the same time as they begin lexical search. Whichever process is completed first controls the output generated. (Forster & Chambers, 1973, p. 632)

In the same year, Marshall and Newcombe (1973) advanced a similar idea within a box-and arrow diagram. The text of their paper indicates that one of the routes in that model consists of reading "via putative grapheme–phoneme correspondence rules" (Marshall & Newcombe, 1973, p. 191). Since the other route in the model they proposed involves reading via semantics, and is thus available only for familiar words, their conception would seem to have been exactly the same as that of Forster and Chambers (1973).

This idea spread rapidly:

> We can . . . distinguish between an orthographic mechanism, which makes use of such general and productive relationships between letter patterns and sounds as exist, and a lexical mechanism, which relies instead upon specific knowledge of pronunciations of particular words or morphemes, that is, a lexicon of pronunciations (if not meanings as well). (Baron & Strawson, 1976, p. 386)
>
> It seems that both of the mechanisms we have suggested, the orthographic and lexical mechanisms, are used for pronouncing printed words. (Baron & Strawson, 1976, p. 391)
>
> Naming can be accomplished either by orthographic-phonemic translation, or by reference to the internal lexicon. (Frederiksen & Kroll, 1976, p. 378)

In these first explications of the dual route idea, a contrast was typically drawn between words (which can be read by the lexical route) and nonwords (which cannot, and so require the nonlexical route). Baron and Strawson (1976) were the first to see that, within the context of dual-route models, this is not quite the right contrast to be making (at least for English):

> The main idea behind Experiment 1 was to compare the times taken to read three different kinds of stimuli: (a) regular words, which follow the "rules" of English orthography, (b) exception words, which break these rules, and (c) nonsense words, which can only be pronounced by the rules, since they are not words. (Baron & Strawson, 1976, p. 387)

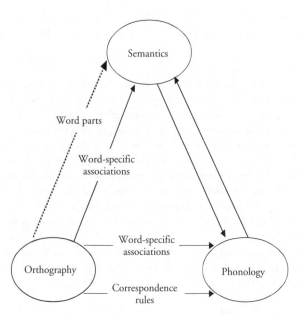

**Figure 1.1**    An architecture of the reading system (redrawn from Baron, 1977).

Baron (1977) was the first to express these ideas in a completely explicit box-and-arrow model of reading, which is shown in figure 1.1. This model has some remarkably modern features: for example, it has a lexical-nonsemantic route for reading aloud (a route that is available only for words yet does not proceed via the semantic system) and it envisages the possibility of a route from orthography to semantics that uses word parts (Baron had in mind prefixes and suffixes here) as well as one that uses whole words.

Even more importantly, the diagram in figure 1.1 involves two different uses of the dual-route conception. The work previously cited in this chapter all concerned a dual-route account of reading aloud; but Baron's model also offered a dual-route account of reading comprehension:

> we may get from print to meaning either directly – as when we use pictures or maps, and possibly when we read a sentence like *I saw the son* – or indirectly, through sound, as when we first read a word we have only heard before. (Baron, 1977, p. 176)
>
> Two different strategies are available to readers of English for identifying a printed word. The phonemic strategy involves first translating the word into a full phonemic (auditory and/or articulatory) representation, and then using this representation to retrieve the meaning of the word. This second step relies on the same knowledge used in identifying words in spoken language. This strategy must be used when we encounter for the first time a word we have heard but not seen. The visual strategy involves using the visual information itself (or possibly some derivative of it which is not formally equivalent to overt pronunciation) to retrieve the meaning. It must be used to distinguish homophones when the context is insufficient, for example, in the sentence, "Give me a pair (pear)." (Baron & McKillop, 1975, p. 91)

The dual-route theory of reading aloud and the dual-route theory of reading comprehension are logically independent: the correctness of one says nothing about the correctness of the other. Further discussion of these two dual-route theories may be found in Coltheart (2000). The present chapter considers just the dual-route approach to reading aloud.

A final point worth making re Baron's chapter has to do with the analogy he used to illustrate why two routes might be better than one (even when one is imperfect – the nonlexical route with irregular words, for example):

> A third – and to me most satisfying – explanation of the use of the indirect path . . . is that it is used in parallel with the direct path. If this is the case, we can expect it to be useful even if it is usually slower than the direct path in providing information about meaning. If we imagine the two paths as hoses that can be used to fill up a bucket with information about meaning, we can see that addition of a second hose can speed up filling the bucket even if it provides less water than the first. (Baron, 1977, p. 203)

An analogy commonly used to describe the relationship between the two routes in dual-route models has been the horse race: the lexical and nonlexical routes race, and whichever finishes first is responsible for output. But this analogy is wrong. In the reading aloud of irregular words, on those occasions where the nonlexical route wins, according to the horse race analogy the response will be wrong: it will be a regularization error. But what is typically seen in experiments on the regularity effect in reading aloud is that responses to irregular words are correct but slow. The horse race analogy cannot capture that typical result, whereas Baron's hose-and-bucket analogy can. The latter analogy is equally apt in the case of the dual-route model of reading comprehension.

## "Lexical" and "Nonlexical" Reading Routes

This use of the terms "lexical" and "nonlexical" for referring to the two reading routes seems to have originated with Coltheart (1980). Reading via the lexical route involves looking up a word in a mental lexicon containing knowledge about the spellings and pronunciations of letter strings that are real words (and so are present in the lexicon); reading via the nonlexical route makes no reference to this lexicon, but instead involves making use of rules relating segments of orthography to segments of phonology. The quotation from de Saussure with which this chapter began suggested that the orthographic segments used by the nonlexical route are single letters, but, as discussed by Coltheart (1978), that cannot be right, since in most alphabetically written languages single phonemes are frequently represented by sequences of letters rather than single letters. Coltheart (1978) used the term "grapheme" to refer to any letter or letter sequence that represents a single phoneme, so that TH and IGH are the two graphemes of the two-phoneme word THIGH. He suggested that the rules used by the nonlexical reading route are, specifically, grapheme–phoneme correspondence rules such as TH $\rightarrow$ /$\theta$/ and IGH $\rightarrow$ /ai/.

## Phenomena Explained via the Dual-Route Model

This model was meant to explain data not only from normal reading, but also facts about disorders of reading, both acquired and developmental.

Reaction times in reading-aloud experiments are longer for irregular words than regular words, and the dual-route model attributed this to that fact that the two routes generate conflicting information at the phoneme level when a word is irregular, but not when a word is regular: resolution of that conflict takes time, and that is responsible for the regularity effect in speeded reading aloud. Frequency effects on reading aloud were explained by proposing that access to entries for high-frequency words in the mental lexicon was faster than access for low-frequency words. From that it follows, according to the dual-route model, that low-frequency words will show a larger regularity effect, since lexical processing will be relatively slow for such words and there will be more time for the conflicting information from the nonlexical route to affect reading; and this interaction of frequency with regularity was observed.

Suppose brain damage in a previously literate person selectively impaired the operation of the lexical route for reading aloud while leaving the nonlexical route intact. What would such a person's reading be like? Well, nonwords and regular words would still be read with normal accuracy because the nonlexical route can do this job; but irregular words will suffer, because for correct reading they require the lexical route. If it fails with an irregular word, then the response will just come from the nonlexical route, and so will be wrong: *island* will be read as "iz-land," *yacht* to rhyme with "matched," and *have* to rhyme with "cave." Exactly this pattern is seen in some people whose reading has been impaired by brain damage; it is called surface dyslexia, and two particularly clear cases are those reported by McCarthy and Warrington (1986) and Behrmann and Bub (1992). The occurrence of surface dyslexia is good evidence that the reading system contains lexical and nonlexical routes for reading aloud, since this reading disorder is exactly what would be expected if the lexical route is damaged and the nonlexical route is spared.

Suppose instead that brain damage in a previously literate person selectively impaired the operation of the nonlexical route for reading aloud while leaving the lexical route intact. What would such a person's reading be like? Well, irregular words and regular words would still be read with normal accuracy because the lexical route can do this job; but nonwords will suffer, because for correct reading they require the nonlexical route. Exactly this pattern – good reading of words with poor reading of nonwords – is seen in some people whose reading has been impaired by brain damage; it is called phonological dyslexia (see Coltheart, 1996, for a review of such studies). This too is good evidence for a dual-route conception of the reading system.

The reading disorders just discussed are called acquired dyslexias because they are acquired as a result of brain damage in people who were previously literate. The term "developmental dyslexia," in contrast, refers to people who have had difficulty in learning to read in the first place, and have never attained a normal level of reading skill. Just as brain damage can selectively affect the lexical or the nonlexical reading route, perhaps also learning these two routes is subject to such selective influence. This is so. There are children who are very poor for their age at reading irregular words but normal for their age at reading regular words (e.g., Castles & Coltheart, 1996); this is developmental surface dyslexia. And there are children who are very poor for their age at reading non-words but normal for their age at reading regular words and irregular words (e.g., Stothard, Snowling, & Hulme, 1996); this is developmental phonological dyslexia. Since it appears that difficulties in learning just the lexical and or just the nonlexical route can be observed, these different patterns of developmental dyslexia are also good evidence for the dual-route model of reading.

## Computational Modeling of Reading

We have seen that the dual-route conception, applied both to reading aloud and to reading comprehension, was well established by the mid-1970s. A major next step in the study of reading was computational modeling.

A computational model of some form of cognitive processing is a computer program which not only executes that particular form of processing, but does so in a way that the modeler believes to be also the way in which human beings perform the cognitive task in question. Various virtues of computational modeling are generally acknowledged – for example, it allows the theorist to discover parts of a theory that are not explicit enough; inexplicit parts of a theory cannot be translated into computer instructions. Once that problem is solved and a program that can actually be executed has been written, the modeler can then determine how closely the behavior of the model corresponds to the behavior of humans. Do all the variables that influence the behavior of humans as they perform the relevant cognitive task also affect the behavior of the program, and in the same way? And do all the variables that influence the behavior of the program as it performs the relevant cognitive task also affect the behavior of humans, and in the same way? Provided that the answer to both questions is yes, studying the behavior of the computational model has demonstrated that the theory from which the model was generated is sufficient to explain what is so far known about how humans perform in the relevant cognitive domain. That does not mean that there could not be a different theory from which a different computational model could be generated which performed just as well. If that happens, the time has come for working out experiments about which the theories make different predictions – that is, whose outcomes in simulations by the two computational models are in conflict.

Of all cognitive domains, reading is the one in which computational modeling has been most intensively employed. This began with the interactive activation and competition (IAC) model of McClelland and Rumelhart (1981) and Rumelhart and McClelland (1982). This was a model just of visual word recognition, not concerned with semantics or phonology. The latter domains were introduced in the much more extensive computational model developed in a seminal paper by Seidenberg and McClelland (1989). One influence their paper had was to prompt the development of a computational version of the dual-route model: the DRC ("dual-route cascaded") model (Coltheart et al., 1993; Coltheart, Rastle, Perry, Langdon, & Ziegler, 2001).

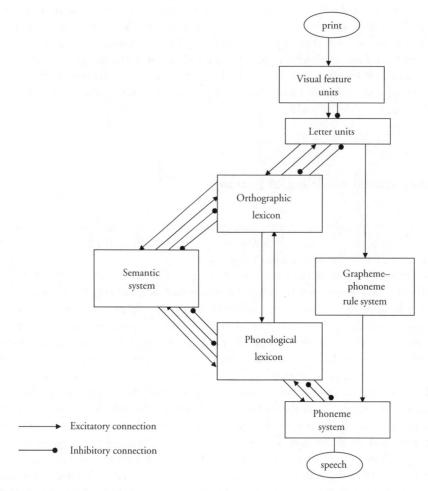

**Figure 1.2**   The DRC model.

## The Dual-Route Cascaded (DRC) Model

The DRC is a computational model that computes pronunciation from print via two procedures, a lexical procedure and a nonlexical procedure (see figure 1.2).

The lexical procedure involves accessing a representation in the model's orthographic lexicon of real words and from there activating the word's node in the model's phonological lexicon of real words, which in turn activates the word's phonemes at the phoneme level of the model. Nonwords cannot be correctly read by this procedure since they are not present in these lexicons, but that does not mean that the lexical route will simply not produce any phonological output when the input is a nonword. A nonword such as SARE can produce some activation of entries in the orthographic lexicon for words visually similar to it, such as CARE, SORE, or SANE; this in turn can activate the phonological lexicon and hence the phoneme level. Such lexically generated activation cannot produce the correct pronunciation for a nonword, but there is evidence that it does influence the reading aloud of nonwords. For example, a nonword like SARE which is similar to many entries in the orthographic lexicon will be read aloud with a shorter reaction time (RT) than a nonword like ZUCE which is similar to few (McCann & Besner, 1987).

The nonlexical procedure of the DRC model applies grapheme–phoneme correspondence rules to the input string to convert letters to phonemes. It does so in serial left-to-right fashion, initially considering just the first letter in the string, then the first two letters, then the first three letters, and so on, until it gets past the last letter in the input. It correctly converts nonwords from print to sound, and also regular words (those that obey its grapheme–phoneme correspondence rules). Irregular (exception) words are "regularized" by the nonlexical procedure – that is, their rule-based pronunciations, which will be incorrect.

Processing along the lexical route occurs as follows:

Cycle 0: set all the units for visual features that are actually present in the input string to 1; set all others to zero.

Cycle 1: every visual feature set to 1 contributes activation to all the letters in the letter units to which it is connected. The connections are inhibitory when the letter does not contain that feature, and so the activation contributed is negative; the connections are excitatory when the letter does contain that feature, and so the activation contributed is positive.

Cycle 2: what happens on Cycle 1 again happens here. In addition, every letter unit contributes activation to all the word units in the orthographic lexicon to which it is connected. The connections are inhibitory when the word does not contain that letter, and so the activation contributed from letter unit to word unit is negative; the connections are excitatory when the word does contain that letter, and so the activation contributed from letter unit to word unit is positive.

Cycle 3: everything that happens on Cycle 1 and Cycle 2 happens again here. In addition:

(a)  Feedforward: each unit in the orthographic lexicon contributes activation to its corresponding unit in the phonological lexicon.

(b)  Feedback: every word unit in the orthographic lexicon unit contributes activation back to all the letter units to which it is connected. The connections are inhibitory when the word does not contain that letter, and so the activation contributed from word unit to letter unit is negative; the connections are excitatory when the word does contain that letter, and so the activation contributed from word unit to letter unit is positive.

Cycle 4: everything that happens on Cycles 1, 2, and 3 happens again here. In addition:

(a)  Feedforward: every unit in the phonological lexicon contributes activation to all the phoneme units to which it is connected. The connections are inhibitory when the word's pronunciation does not contain that phoneme, and so the activation contributed from word unit to phoneme unit is negative; the connections are excitatory when the word's pronunciation does contain that phoneme, and so the activation contributed from word unit to phoneme unit is positive.

(b)    Feedback: every unit in the phonological lexicon contributes feedback activation to its corresponding unit in the orthographic lexicon.

Cycle 5: everything that happens on Cycles 1, 2, 3, and 4 happens again here. In addition: every phoneme unit contributes activation back to all the word units in the phonological lexicon to which it is connected. The connections are inhibitory when the word does not contain that phoneme, and so the activation contributed from phoneme unit to word unit is negative; the connections are excitatory when the word does contain that phoneme, and so the activation contributed from phoneme unit to word unit is positive.

And so it goes. As processing cycles progress, inhibitory and excitatory influences continue to flow upwards and downwards in the way described above until the reading-aloud response is ready. How is this readiness determined? As follows. In the description of processing cycles given above, the first cycle on which the phoneme system receives any activation is Cycle 4. At the end of cycle 4, some phoneme units will be activated, but extremely weakly. As processing continues, activation of some of the phoneme units will slowly rise. Quite often, early in processing, some of the phoneme units activated will be incorrect ones. But over time as phoneme activations continue to rise it is the correct phonemes that are the most activated. A reading response is considered to be ready when phonemes have reached a critical level of activation (set to .43 when the model is being used for simulating human reading aloud). The pronunciation generated by the model is taken to consist of the most highly activated phoneme within each of the eight sets of phoneme units (one set per position) that comprise the phoneme system. The processing cycle on which that state of affairs occurs is the DRC model's reading-aloud latency for the particular letter string that was input.

Processing along the nonlexical route does not begin to operate until cycle 10. Without this time lapse after the lexical route begins to operate, the model would have serious difficulty in reading aloud irregular words. When cycle 10 is reached, the nonlexical route translates the first letter of the string into its phoneme using the appropriate grapheme–phoneme rule, and contributes activation to the phoneme's unit in the phoneme system. This continues to occur for the next 16 processing cycles. The grapheme–phoneme conversion (GPC) system operates from left to right, so eventually will move on to consider the second letter in the string as well as the first. Every 17 cycles, the GPC system moves on to consider the next letter, translate it to a phoneme, and activate that phoneme in the phoneme system. So with the letter string DESK, the GPC system has no input until cycle 10, deals with just D until cycle 27, deals with just DE from cycle 28 to cycle 44, then DES until cycle 60, DESK until cycle 76 and so on.

Computations on the lexical and nonlexical route occur simultaneously – that is, information from the visual feature level is thought of as flowing simultaneously through the lexical and the nonlexical routes and converging on the phoneme system from these two sources. Whenever the input is an irregular word or a nonword, the two sources of activation conflict at the phoneme level. If the system is to produce correct pronunciations for irregular words and for nonwords, it will have to have a way of resolving these conflicts in favor of the correct pronunciation. Nevertheless, the model reads aloud irregular words and nonwords with high accuracy, so these conflicts are almost always resolved in a way that results in a correct pronunciation (via the interplay of inhibition and activation at various levels of the model). This depends on a judicious choice of values for the parameters of the model, such as the strengths of the inhibitory and the facilitatory connections between components of the model. If the lexical route is too strong relative to the nonlexical route, all words will be read correctly but there will be nonword reading errors. If the lexical route is too weak relative to the nonlexical route, all regular words and nonwords will be read correctly but there will be errors in reading irregular words. A delicate balance between the strengths of the two routes is needed if the model is to perform well with both nonwords and irregular words.

## What the DRC Model Can Explain

One way in which Coltheart et al. (2001) evaluated the DRC model was to compare its reaction times to particular sets of stimuli to the reaction times of human readers when they are reading aloud the same stimuli. Do variables that affect human reading-aloud reaction times also affect DRC's reading-aloud reaction times? Many examples where this was so were reported by Coltheart et al. (2001). For both human readers and the DRC model:

(a)  High-frequency words are read aloud faster than low-frequency words.
(b)  Words are read aloud faster than nonwords.
(c)  Regular words are read aloud faster than irregular words.
(d)  The size of this regularity advantage is larger for low-frequency words than for high-frequency words.
(e)  The later in an irregular word its irregular grapheme–phoneme correspondence is, the less the cost incurred by its irregularity. So CHEF (position 1 irregularity) is worse than SHOE (position 2 irregularity), which is worse than CROW (position 3 irregularity).
(f)  Pseudohomophones (nonwords that are pronounced exactly like real English words, such as brane) are read aloud faster than non-pseudohomophonic nonwords (such as brene).
(g)  Pseudohomophones derived from high-frequency words (e.g., hazz) are read aloud faster than pseudohomophones derived from low-frequency words (e.g., glew).
(h)  The number of orthographic neighbors a non-pseudohomophonic nonword has (i.e., the number of words that differ from it by just one letter), the faster it is read aloud.
(i)  The number of orthographic neighbors a pseudohomophone has does not influence how fast it is read aloud.
(j)  The more letters in a nonword there are the slower it is read aloud; but number of letters has little or no effect on reading aloud for real words.

The DRC model was also used to simulate acquired dyslexias. Surface dyslexia was simulated by slowing down rate of access to the orthographic lexicon: this lesioned DRC made regularization errors with irregular words, more so when they were low in frequency, just as is seen in surface dyslexia, whereas its reading aloud of regular words and non-words remained normal, as in the pure cases of surface dyslexia (Behrmann & Bub, 1992; McCarthy & Warrington, 1986). Phonological dyslexia was simulated by slowing down the operation of the nonlexical route: this lesioned DRC still read words correctly, but misread nonwords, especially if they were nonpseudohomophones, as in the case of phonological dyslexia.

Thus, the DRC model can explain an impressively large number of findings from studies of normal and disordered reading, far more than any other computational model of reading. Nevertheless, Coltheart et al. (2001) drew attention to a number of limitations of the current implementation of the DRC model: its procedure for performing the lexical decision task was crude, it was not applicable to the pronunciation of polysyllabic words or nonwords, it did not offer any account of one popular paradigm for studying reading (masked priming), the difference between word and nonword reading RTs by the model was probably implausibly large, the amount of variance of word reading RTs that the model could account for, though always significant, was disappointingly low, and the implemented model has nothing to say about semantics. A new version of the DRC model that will correct these and other shortcomings of the existing model is under development.

## Connectionist and nonconnectionist modeling

This chapter distinguishes between connectionist models of reading (such as the models of Seidenberg & McClelland, 1989, and Plaut, McClelland, Seidenberg, & Patterson, 1996) and nonconnectionist models of reading (such as the DRC model). The description of the DRC model in Coltheart et al. (2001) uses the term "connection" and the model in fact "contains" about 4.5 million connections, in the sense of the term "connection" used by Coltheart et al. (2001). However, in the DRC model, connections are just expository devices used for talking about how the modules of the model communicate with each other. One could expound this in other ways without using the term "connection." In contrast, in connectionist models, the connections are often thought of as neuron-like, the models are referred to as neural networks, and terms like "biologically inspired" or "neurally plausible" are often applied. Here a connection is something that is physically realizable as an individual object, in contrast to the DRC model in which there is no such sense to the term.

A second major difference between connectionist and nonconnectionist modeling, at least as those trades have been practiced up until now, is that connectionist models have typically been developed by applying a neural-net learning algorithm to a training set of stimuli, whereas the architectures of nonconnectionist models have typically been specified by the modeler on the basis of the empirical effects that the model is meant to explain.

The Seidenberg and McClelland (1989) connectionist computational model of reading is often presented as an alternative to the dual-route model. Indeed, claims such as "The dual-route model has been more recently questioned by a plethora of single-route computational models based on connectionist principles" (Damper & Marchand, 2000,

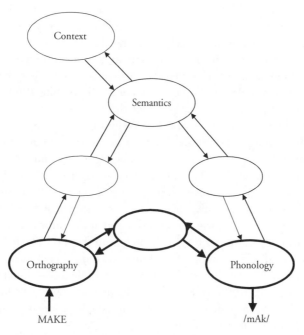

**Figure 1.3**   The Seidenberg and McClelland (1989) model. (The implemented model is in bold-face type.)

p. 13) are common in the literature. But that was not the view of the authors themselves. They were clear about this: "Ours is a dual route model," they stated (Seidenberg & McClelland, 1989, p. 559).

This is perfectly evident from their diagram of their model (Seidenberg & McClelland, 1989, figure 1, reproduced as figure 1.3 here): it explicitly represents two distinct routes from orthography to phonology, one direct and the other via meaning, and explicitly represents two distinct routes from orthography to semantics, one direct and the other via phonology. One of the two routes for reading aloud (the one via semantics) can only be used for reading words aloud; it would fail for nonwords. The other (nonsemantic) route for reading aloud is required if the stimulus is a nonword. This model has come to be called the triangle model, perhaps because of the reference in Seidenberg and McClelland (1989, p. 559) to "the third side of the triangle in Figure 1." More than one subsequent model has been referred to as the triangle model despite being different from Seidenberg and McClelland's model. So far there have been seven different triangle models, an issue discussed later in this chapter.

What is it that has led to this widespread misunderstanding? The answer is clear: a failure to distinguish between the following two claims:

(a)   It is possible for a single processing system to correctly read aloud all irregular words and all nonwords.
(b)   The human reading system possesses only one procedure for computing pronunciation from print.

Seidenberg and McClelland (1989) did make claim (a). But they did not make claim (b); indeed, as the quotation in the previous paragraph indicates, they repudiated claim (b). That is why theirs is a dual-route model of reading aloud.

This seminal model turned out not to be able to offer a good account of how people read nonwords aloud because its accuracy on this task was far less than the accuracy that human readers show (Besner, Twilley, McCann, & Seergobin, 1990). The suggestion (Seidenberg & McClelland, 1990, p. 448) that this was because the database of words on which the model was trained was too limited and did not contain enough information for nonword reading to be learned from it was shown to be incorrect by Coltheart et al. (1993). They developed a GPC rule-learning algorithm and applied it to the Sei-denberg–McClelland training set. The rule set that this algorithm learned from that training set was then used with 133 nonwords from Glushko (1979). Whereas the Seidenberg and McClelland model scored only 68% correct on a subset of 52 of these nonwords, the DRC read 97.9% of these correctly. This shows that the information needed to learn to be an excellent nonword reader is actually present in the model's database, and so "the poor performance of the PDP model in reading nonwords is a defect not of the database but of the model itself" (Coltheart et al., 1993, p. 594). Hence, as noted by Plaut (1997, p. 769) and (Plaut et al., 1996, p. 63), the Seidenberg and McClelland model did not succeed in providing evidence that it is possible for a single processing system to correctly read aloud all irregular words and all nonwords.

Nevertheless, it might well be possible to devise a single processing procedure that can correctly read aloud all irregular words and all nonwords. Plaut et al. (1996) sought to devise such a procedure via training a connectionist network similar in overall architecture to that of the network of Seidenberg and McClelland shown in figure 1.3 (it was, for example, a dual-route model in just the same sense that Seidenberg and McClelland viewed their model as a dual-route model, though training was carried out on only one of the two routes), but differing from the Seidenberg and McClelland model in a number of ways, including in the forms of orthographic and phonological representations used in the network. Input units, which were distributed representations in the Seidenberg and McClelland model, became local representations (each representing a grapheme). Output units, which were distributed representations in the Seidenberg and McClelland model, became local representations (each representing a phoneme).

Plaut et al. (1996) actually presented three different though related models – that is, a second, third and fourth triangle model, the first triangle model being that of Seidenberg and McClelland (1989):

Model 1: purely feedforward, 105 grapheme units, 100 hidden units, 61 phoneme units.

Model 2: as for Model 1 but with feedback from phoneme units back to hidden units: an attractor network.

Model 3: as for Model 1 but adding (unimplemented) external input to the output units, so as to mimic what could happen if there were an implemented semantic system activated by orthography and in turn activating phonology. This approach, discussed further below, was pursued in an attempt to simulate acquired surface dyslexia.

How well do these models read nonwords? Model 1 (which after training scored 100% on reading the 2,972 nonhomographic words in the training set) did quite well on nonword reading (see table 3 of Plaut et al., 1996), almost as well as human readers. However it still fails with items like JINJE, the reason being that there is no word in the training corpus that ends with the final grapheme of this nonword. It follows that careful selection of nonwords which exploits such gaps in the training corpus would produce a set of nonwords on which the model would score at or close to zero. Human readers would be vastly superior to the model on such nonwords. Results with nonword reading by Model 2 were similar, though its nonword reading was slightly worse than that of Model 1. The JINJE problem remained.

Given this work by Plaut et al. (1996), what are we to say about the two claims mentioned above? These claims were:

(a)   It is possible for a single processing system to correctly read aloud all irregular words and all nonwords.
(b)   The human reading system possesses just one procedure for computing pronunciation from print.

Although nonword reading was better by the PMSP models than by the SM model, the PMSP models still do not read nonwords correctly in the sense of "as well as human readers do," since it is not difficult to devise nonwords that human readers read well and the PMSP models read wrongly: there is no sense in which reading JINJE to rhyme with "wine" (as the PMSP models do) could be regarded as correct. So claim (a) remains without support. And no current model of reading aloud makes claim (b). Hence at present it is reasonable to regard both claims as false.

However, the work on simulation of surface dyslexia using Model 3 has an interesting implication for these claims. Indeed, in general simulation of disordered rather than normal reading it has been particularly crucial in recent years for comparative evaluation of computational models of reading. Hence much of the following discussion of dual-route modeling will focus on the application of such models to the explanation of disordered reading.

## Simulating disordered reading with the triangle models

*Simulating acquired surface dyslexia.* Acquired surface dyslexia (Marshall & Newcombe, 1973; Patterson, Marshall, & Coltheart, 1985) is a reading disorder, caused by brain damage, in which there is selective impairment of the ability to read irregular words aloud with relative sparing of regular word and nonword reading. Many cases are not normal at regular word and nonword reading; I will focus here, as did Plaut et al. (1996), on two particularly pure cases, KT (McCarthy & Warrington, 1986) and MP (Behrmann & Bub, 1992). Both showed virtually normal accuracy in reading aloud regular words and nonwords, but were impaired at reading irregular words, especially when these were low in frequency (KT: high frequency 47%; low frequency 26%; MP: high frequency 93%; low frequency 73%).

Computational models are meant to be able to explain impaired reading as well as normal reading: that is, it should be possible to artificially lesion these models so that their patterns of preserved and impaired reading correctly match such patterns seen in various forms of acquired dyslexia. Plaut and colleagues therefore investigated whether there was any way of lesioning any of their three models that would lead to impaired irregular word reading with preserved regular word and nonword reading.

This was investigated by studying the effects of deleting various proportions of the connections in the implemented orthography-to-phonology pathway, or various proportions of the hidden units, in Model 2. This was not successful in simulating the more severe patient KT: any lesion that produced accuracies of around 26% for low-frequency irregular words also produced very poor performance with nonwords, whereas KT was perfect at reading nonwords. It was therefore not possible to simulate acquired surface dyslexia just with the implemented part of the model.

So Plaut et al. turned from Model 2 to Model 3, which has an unimplemented component (semantic input to the phonological output level). With sufficient training, Model 3 does well with irregular words, regular words, and nonwords. What is crucial here, though, is the competence of the implemented (orthography-to-phonology) part of Model 3. When it is trained without semantics (this is Model 1), it learns to read irregular words perfectly and nonwords very well. But this is not the case when it is trained with concurrent semantic input. Low-frequency irregular words are never learned perfectly by the direct orthography-to-phonology pathway here: for this pathway operating on its own, accuracy for low-frequency irregular words is about 70% after 400 epochs of training and then declines down to about 30% correct after 2,000 epochs. Performance with high-frequency irregular words is almost perfect at 400 epochs, but further training progressively worsens performance with these words, down to about 55% at epoch 2,000. Regular word and nonword performance is almost perfect at epoch 400 and remains at that level with further training to epoch 2,000.

If training is stopped at 400 epochs, and semantic input to the system is then deleted, performance is good with regular words, nonwords, and high-frequency irregular words, but somewhat impaired with low-frequency irregular words; that matches the surface dyslexic pattern shown by MP.

If training is stopped at 2,000 epochs, and semantic input to the system is then deleted, performance is good with regular words, and nonwords, impaired with high-frequency irregular words, and very poor with low-frequency irregular words; that matches the surface dyslexic pattern shown by KT.

The suggestion here is that the cause of acquired surface dyslexia is semantic damage, and that the more the patient had relied on semantic input for reading aloud premorbidly, the more severe the surface dyslexia will be when semantic damage occurs. The implication is that, even if it is possible for a single processing system to correctly read aloud all irregular words and all nonwords, most human readers do not possess such a system.

Because there are patients with severe semantic damage who can read irregular words with normal accuracy (e.g., Cipolotti & Warrington, 1995; Lambon Ralph, Ellis, & Franklin, 1995; Schwartz, Saffran, & Marin, 1980a; see also Gerhand, 2001), Plaut et al. (1996, p. 99) had to suppose that some people learn to read without any support from semantics and so can read all irregular words without recourse to semantics. But in other work using the triangle models this supposition has been abandoned:

> It is important to note that, because this version of the triangle model assumes a causal rela-
> tionship between semantic impairment and surface dyslexia, its adequacy is challenged by
> any observations of semantically impaired patients whose reading does not reveal a surface
> dyslexic pattern. (Fushimi et al., 2003, p. 1656)
>
> A degraded semantic system will inevitably impair the ability to "know" a letter string
> . . . as belonging to the repertoire of real words. (Rogers, Lambon Ralph, Hodges, &
> Patterson, 2004, p. 347)

According to Model 3 as it is applied to the analysis of surface dyslexia, intact human readers possess two routes from print to speech. Let's call these, theory-neutrally, Route A and Route B. Properties of these routes are:

(a)   Route A can correctly read aloud all known words (regular or irregular) but cannot read nonwords aloud correctly.
(b)   Route B can correctly read aloud all regular words and all nonwords, but will misread X% of irregular words.

This connectionist dual-route model of reading aloud differs from the nonconnectionist dual-route DRC model of reading aloud (Coltheart et al., 2001, discussed below) only with respect to the value of X. According to Plaut et al. (1996), premorbidly X can on rare occasions be zero (the patients referred to above who are normal at irregular word reading but have severe semantic impairments) but typically is not and can be at least as high as 64% (patient KT's overall error rate on irregular words). According to the DRC model, X is always 100%.

So, while it is of course logically possible that the system humans use for reading aloud has a single-route architecture, there are no theoretical proposals embodying such an architecture that can escape refutation from available data from studies of normal and impaired readers. All the models are dual-route models. Current and future theorizing is and will be about the details of what these two routes are actually like.

## Simulating acquired phonological dyslexia

Harm and Seidenberg (2001) used another connectionist triangle model in work attempting to simulate acquired phonological dyslexia. In their view, this form of acquired dyslexia is always caused by a phonological impairment. Therefore, after training their model until it was performing well in reading words and nonwords, they lesioned the phonological component of the model by adding random noise each time the units in that component were being updated. This harmed nonword reading more than word reading and so simulated phonological dyslexia. However, this explanation of acquired phonological dyslexia predicts that cases of acquired phonological dyslexia without the presence of a phonological impairment will not be seen, and this prediction is incorrect. Dérouesné and Beauvois (1985), Bisiacchi, Cipolotti, and Denes (1989), and Caccappolo-van Vliet, Miozzo, & Stern (2004) have all reported cases of acquired phonological dyslexia with preserved phonological processing.

As we have seen, the development of connectionist triangle models of reading has been considerably influenced by attempts to simulate acquired dyslexia; and this approach has also been applied to the simulation of developmental dyslexia.

*Simulating developmental dyslexia.* Harm and Seidenberg (1999) developed a model in which to simulate developmental reading disorders. Their particular triangle model differed from all earlier triangle models in a number of ways:

(a)    Learning in the phonological units was assisted by the presence of a set of cleanup units attached to the phonological units.
(b)    The phonological units represented phonetic features, not phonemes.
(c)    The orthographic units represented letters, not graphemes.
(d)    Positional coding of orthography was relative to the vowel in the input string, rather than absolute.

After training, the model achieved satisfactory levels of performance in reading the irregular words in the training set, and also in reading nonwords (though again performance seemed slightly inferior to human nonword reading).

Harm and Seidenberg (1999) were specifically interested in attempting to simulate developmental dyslexia. Having shown that their triangle model was capable of learning to read adequately, they then investigated ways of impeding its learning that might result in either of two different subtypes of developmental dyslexia, one in which nonword reading is selectively affected (developmental phonological dyslexia) and another in which irregular word reading is selectively affected (developmental surface dyslexia; Harm and Seidenberg preferred the term "reading delay dyslexia" because they believed that the reading of children with developmental surface dyslexia is just like the reading of younger children who are learning to read normally).

Because Harm and Seidenberg (1999) believed that developmental phonological dyslexia is always caused by the child having a phonological processing deficit, their approach to simulating developmental phonological dyslexia involved lesioning their model's phonological system. This was done in two different ways:

(a)    Mild phonological impairment: a slight degree of weight decay was imposed on the phonetic feature units throughout training.
(b)    Moderate phonological impairment: in addition to the weight decay, the cleanup units were removed from the network, as were a random 50% of the interconnections between the phonetic feature units.

Both types of lesioning did impair the model's ability to learn to read nonwords. But when this impairment was more than mild, the ability of the model to learn to read words was also impaired. Hence what could not be simulated here was pure severe developmental phonological dyslexia (where "pure" means that word reading is in the normal range and "severe" means the impairment of nonword reading was more than mild). That raises the question: does one ever see pure severe developmental phonological dyslexia in human readers? A number of such cases have been reported (see e.g. Campbell & Butterworth, 1985; Funnell & Davison, 1989; Holmes & Standish, 1996; Howard & Best, 1996; Stothard et al., 1996). Hence these data from developmental cognitive neuropsychology provide a challenge for the Harm and Seidenberg (1999) connectionist model of reading.

Developmental surface dyslexia ("reading delay dyslexia") was simulated in the work of Harm and Seidenberg (1999) by reducing the number of hidden units in the network from 100 to 20, and also by reducing the network's learning rate. Both types of developmental damage to the network harmed the learning of irregular words more than the learning of nonwords; but in both cases the learning of nonwords suffered too. Thus it was not possible to simulate "pure" developmental surface dyslexia (i.e., impaired irregular word reading with *normal* nonword reading). However, pure developmental surface dyslexia is seen in human readers (Castles & Coltheart, 1996; Hanley & Gard, 1995; Goulandris & Snowling, 1991). Hence again these data from developmental cognitive neuropsychology do not provide support for the Harm & Seidenberg (1999) connectionist model of reading.

## Conclusions

Reading theorists have reached unanimity concerning the existence in the human reading system of two separate procedures for reading aloud – that is, dual routes from print to speech. One of these processing routes is usable only when the stimulus to be read is a real word; it cannot read nonwords. The other route can read all nonwords and regular words; there is still some dispute concerning how well it reads irregular words.

These dual-route models differ in terms of whether they are connectionist models such as the triangle models or nonconnectionist models such as the DRC model. At present the data favor the nonconnectionist approach. The DRC model does a good job of simulating patterns of acquired dyslexia, which the connectionist models have not succeeded in doing. Nor have the connectionist models succeeded in accounting for developmental reading disorders, whereas the DRC model is compatible with everything we currently know about these disorders. Finally, none of the connectionist models can explain all of the phenomena from studies of normal reading listed above (see the section "What the DRC Model Can Explain"), whereas all of these can be simulated by the DRC model.

# 2

# Connectionist Approaches to Reading

## David C. Plaut

Reading is a highly complex task involving the rapid coordination of visual, phonological, semantic, and linguistic processes. Computational models have played a key role in the scientific study of reading. These models allow us to explore the implications of specific hypotheses concerning the representations and processes underlying reading acquisition and performance. A particular form of computational modeling, known as connectionist or neural network modeling, offers the further advantage of being explicit about how such mechanisms might be implemented in the brain.

In connectionist models, cognitive processes take the form of cooperative and competitive interactions among large numbers of simple neuron-like processing units. Typically, each unit has a real-valued activity level, roughly analogous to the firing rate of a neuron. Unit interactions are governed by weighted connections that encode the long-term knowledge of the system and are learned gradually through experience. Units are often organized into layers or groups; the activity of some groups of units encode the input to the system; the resulting activity of other groups of units encodes the system's response to that input. For example, one group might encode the written form (orthography) of a word, another might encode its spoken form (phonology), and a third might encode its meaning (semantics; see figure 2.1). The patterns of activity of the remaining groups of units – sometimes termed "hidden" units – constitute learned, internal representations that mediate between inputs and outputs. In this way, the connectionist approach attempts to capture the essential computational properties of the vast ensembles of real neuronal elements found in the brain using simulations of smaller networks of more abstract units. By linking neural computation to behavior, the framework enables developmental, cognitive, and neurobiological issues to be addressed within a single, integrated formalism. One very important advantage of connectionist models is that they deal explicitly with learning. Though many of these models have focused predominantly on simulating aspects of adult, rather than children's, reading, many of the models do explicitly consider the process of learning (e.g., Plaut, McClelland, Seidenberg, & Patterson,

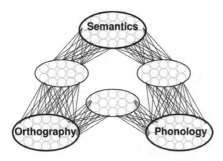

**Figure 2.1**  A connectionist network that relates orthographic, phonological, and semantic information in word reading and other lexical tasks, based on the "triangle" framework (Harm & Seidenberg, 2004; Plaut et al., 1996; Seidenberg & McClelland, 1989).

1996; Seidenberg & McClelland, 1989). In essence, such models instantiate learning as a process as a slow incremental increase in knowledge, represented by increasingly strong and accurate connections between different units (e.g., the letters in printed words and the phonemes in spoken words to which they correspond).

Another critical feature of many connectionist systems is that after learning they show the ability to generalize (e.g., to pronounce novel words which they have not been trained on). Finally, and related to this, such systems often show graceful degradation when damaged. Removing units or connections in such systems typically does not result in an all-or-none loss of knowledge; rather, damage results in a gradual degradation of performance. These three aspects of connectionist models have clear parallels in human reading behavior – children gradually learn to read more and more words in an incremental fashion over a long period, such learning brings with it the ability to generalize to novel items children have not been taught, and in cases of brain damage there are often graded declines in performance with inconsistent performance at different times. The fact that connectionist models display such parallels to human reading behavior has generated considerable excitement at the prospect that such models may offer new, explicit, and detailed accounts of how reading is implemented in the human brain.

## Principles of Connectionist Modeling

Before turning to how specific connectionist models have been applied to various reading-related phenomena, it will be helpful to consider the implications of the underlying computational principles more generally. These can be grouped into issues related to processing, representation, learning, and network architecture.

### Processing

A standard connectionist unit integrates information from other units by first computing its *net input*, equal to a linear sum of positive- and negative-weighted activations from

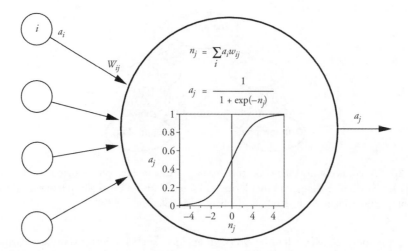

**Figure 2.2**   The operation of a standard connectionist unit (indexed by $j$), which computes a net input $n_j$ as a weighted sum of activations $a_i$ from other units (indexed by $i$), and then computes its own activation $a_j$ as a smooth, nonlinear (sigmoid) function of its net input (where $\exp(\cdot)$ is the exponential function).

sending units, and then setting its own activation according to a nonlinear, monotoni-cally increasing (sigmoid) function of this net input (see figure 2.2). In some networks, unit activations change gradually in response to input from other units instead of being recomputed from scratch each time.

Both the linear integration of net input and the nonlinear activation function play critical roles in shaping how connectionist networks behave. The fact that the net input to each unit is a simple weighted sum is at the heart of why networks exhibit similarity-based generalization to novel inputs (e.g., being able to pronounce a pseudoword like MAVE based on knowledge of words like GAVE, SAVE, MATE, etc.). If a unit is pre-sented with a similar pattern of activity along its input lines, it will tend to produce a similar net input and, hence, a similar response. This fails to hold only if the weights for those inputs that differ between the patterns are very large, but such large weights develop during learning only when necessary (e.g., when handling exceptional cases; see the section on learning below).

If all processing in the network were strictly linear, however, the types of mappings it could learn would be severely limited (Minsky & Papert, 1969). The nonlinear activa-tion function allows individual units – and hence the network as a whole – to preserve some types of similarity in its response while ignoring others. The sigmoid activation function asymptotes for large positive or negative net inputs, but produces roughly pro-portional responses for small and moderate net inputs (see figure 2.2). If networks start out with relatively small weights, most units' activations will fall in the linear range of the sigmoid function, and the network as a whole will give similar responses to similar inputs. However, when aspects of a task require responses that are not predicted by input similarity (e.g., pronouncing SEW like SO instead of SUE, or mapping CAP and CAT to completely different meanings), learning must develop sufficiently large weights to drive the relevant units into their nonlinear (asymptotic) range, where changes in net input have little if any effect on activation. In this way, a network can remain largely linear for systematic or "regular" aspects of a task, while simultaneously exhibiting non-linear behavior for the unsystematic or "irregular" aspects.

Understanding how a connectionist network operates above the level of individual units requires consideration of how patterns of activity across the various groups of units interact and evolve over the course of processing a given input. A very useful concept in this regard is the notion of an *attractor*. At any given instant, the current pattern of activity over a group of units in the network (or over the network as a whole) can be represented in terms of the coordinates of a point in a multidimensional *state space* that has a dimension for each unit. As the pattern of activity changes during processing, the corresponding point in state space moves. In many networks, unit interactions eventually reach a state in which the activation of each unit is maximally consistent with those of other units and the pattern as a whole stops changing. The point in state space corresponding to this final pattern is called an attractor because interactions among units in the network cause nearby points (i.e., similar patterns) to be "pulled" towards the same final attractor point. (The region around an attractor that settles to it is called its *basin* of attraction.) The stability of attractor patterns gives networks a considerable degree of robustness to partially missing or noisy inputs, or to the effects of damage.

## Representation

As described thus far, a typical connectionist network processes an input through unit interactions that cause the network to settle to an attractor, in which the resulting pattern of activity over output units corresponds to the network's response to the input. An issue of central relevance is the nature of the representations that participate in this process – the way that inputs, outputs, and groups of intermediate units encode information in terms of patterns of activity. Some connectionist models use *localist* representations, in which individual units stand for familiar entities such as letters, words, concepts, and propositions. Others use *distributed* representations, in which each such entity is represented by a particular pattern of activity over many units rather than by the activity of an single unit. Localist representations can be easier to think about and to manipulate directly (Page, 2000), but often permit too much flexibility to constrain theorizing sufficiently (Plaut & McClelland, 2000). By contrast, distributed representations are typically much more difficult to use and understand but can give rise to unanticipated emergent properties that contribute in important ways to the explanation of cognitive phenomena (see e.g. Hinton & Shallice, 1991).

Given that, as explained above, similar patterns tend to have similar consequences in connectionist networks, the key to the use of distributed representations is to assign patterns to entities in such a way that the similarity relations among patterns captures the underlying functional relationships among the entities they represent. For groups of units that must be interpreted directly (i.e., inputs and outputs), this is done based on independent empirical evidence concerning the relevant representational similarities.

However, except for the simplest of tasks, it is impossible to perform the relevant mappings without additional intermediate units, and it is infeasible to specify appropriate connection weights for such units by hand. Accordingly, distributed connectionist networks almost invariably use learning to discover effective internal representations based on task demands.

## Learning

The knowledge in a network consists of the entire set of weights on connections among units, because these weights govern how units interact and hence how the network responds to any given input. Accordingly, learning involves adjusting the weights in a way that generally benefits performance on one or more tasks (i.e., mapping from inputs to outputs).

Connectionist learning procedures fall into three broad classes based on how much performance feedback is available. At one extreme are *unsupervised* procedures, such as Hebbian learning (as it is typically applied; Hebb, 1949), that make no use of performance feedback and, instead, adjust connection weights to capture the statistical structure among activity patterns. At the other extreme are *supervised* procedures, such as back-propagation (Rumelhart, Hinton, & Williams, 1986), that assume the learning environment provides, for every trained input pattern, a fully specified "target" pattern that should be generated over the output units. Between these two extremes are *reinforcement* procedures, such as temporal difference methods (Sutton, 1988), that assume the environment provides potentially intermittent evaluative feedback that does not specify correct behavior but rather conveys the degree to which behavioral outcomes were good or bad.

When performance or evaluative feedback is available, it is relatively straightforward to use it to adapt connection weights to improve performance. If the activation of an output unit is too high, it can be reduced by decreasing positive incoming weights and the corresponding sending activations and by increasing (in magnitude) negative weights and sending activations (see the equations in figure 2.2); the reverse is true if output activation is too low. Changing the sending activations involves reapplying the same procedure to their incoming weights and incoming activations, and so on. Specific algorithms differ in how they compute feedback and how they distribute information on how to change weights.

Many applications of distributed connectionist modeling to cognitive phenomena use back-propagation despite its biological implausibility (Crick, 1989). This is partly because, unlike most alternatives, the procedure is effective at learning difficult mappings, including those with complex temporal characteristics (Williams & Peng, 1990). It is also the case that the time-course and ultimate outcome of learning with back-propagation is highly similar to the properties of more biologically plausible supervised procedures, such as Contrastive Hebbian learning (Ackley, Hinton, & Sejnowski, 1985; O'Reilly, 1996; Peterson & Anderson, 1987). Thus, one can interpret back-propagation as a computationally efficient means of learning internal representations in distributed connectionist networks in a way that approximates the properties of performance-driven learning in the brain.

## Network architecture

The *architecture* of a network – the pattern of connectivity among and within groups of units representing different types of information – can have an important impact on the behavior of a connectionist model in its acquisition, skilled performance, and impairment following damage. The strong emphasis on learning in the development of connectionist models has led some researchers to conclude that the approach disavows any built-in structure within the cognitive system. A more accurate characterization would be that the effectiveness of learning in connectionist networks makes it possible to explore the degree to which built-in structure is necessary to account for some empirical phenomena. The modeling framework itself allows for the expression of a wide variety of network architectures, ranging from those with extensive built-in structure to those with minimal structure.

Connectionist models often contrast with alternative formulations in terms of the *kinds* of distinctions that are instantiated in the architecture of the system. A classic example is the traditional separation of rule-based and item-based mechanisms in "dual-route" theories of word reading (Coltheart, Rastle, Perry, Langdon, & Ziegler, 2001) and inflectional morphology (Pinker, 1999). Because the processing mechanisms within a connectionist system are homogeneous – involving massively parallel unit interactions throughout – the underlying theories rarely isolate different types of *processing* into separate systems or pathways. Rather, architectural divisions typically reflect different types of *information* (e.g., orthographic, phonological, semantic). Given that such distinctions often correspond to modalities of input or output, they can be supported directly by data on neuroanatomic localization of the corresponding neural representations.

## Realist Versus Fundamentalist Approaches

Before turning to an overview of connectionist models of reading, it is worth distinguishing two broad approaches to cognitive modeling, because they often have rather different goals. The *realist* approach tries to incorporate into a model as much detail as possible of what is known about the real system in the belief that complex interactions of these factors are necessary to capture the relevant phenomena. The *fundamentalist* approach, by contrast, holds that a model should, as much as possible, embody only those principles that are claimed to account for the relevant phenomenon and should abstract out extraneous details. In evaluating any given modeling effort, it is important to identify the specific goals of the work; some models are intended to provide comprehensive accounts of detailed behavioral data, whereas others are intended more as demonstrations of specific computational arguments. Often the most effective modeling approach over the long term is to begin with fundamentalist models to elucidate the key underlying

principles, and then gradually move towards more realist models as the theoretical implications of additional details become understood.

## Connectionist Modeling of Reading

Most connectionist models of reading have focused on single word processing as it is generally thought that, above the lexical level, written language engages largely the same
mechanisms as spoken language. In the review that follows, these models are characterized in terms of whether their representations for words are localist (one unit per word)
or distributed (alternative patterns of activity for each word) and whether they focus on
the task of word recognition (deriving a lexical or semantic representation) or oral reading
(deriving a pronunciation).

### *Localist models of word recognition*

One of the earliest and arguably most influential connectionist models of reading is a
localist, nonlearning model – the interactive activation and competition (IAC) model of
letter and word perception (McClelland & Rumelhart, 1981; Rumelhart & McClelland,
1982). The model consists of three layers of units – letter feature units, letter units, and
word units. The model was designed to recognize four-letter words, so there is a separate
set of feature units and letter units for each of four letter positions. The activation of each
unit can be thought of as reflecting the network's confidence in the hypothesis that the
entity represented by the unit (e.g., a T in the first position, or the word TAKE) is part
of the correct interpretation. The weights on connections between units reflect the degree
to which one hypothesis is consistent or inconsistent with another. Within each level,
units representing inconsistent hypotheses (e.g., a T versus a P in the first letter position,
or the words TAKE and TRIP) have negative connections between them. Between levels,
units representing consistent hypotheses (e.g., a top horizontal letter feature and the letter
T, or a T in the first position and the word TAKE) have positive connections between
them, whereas units representing inconsistent hypotheses (e.g., a P in the first position
and the word TAKE) have negative connections between them. Connections throughout
the system are bidirectional, allowing both top-down and bottom-up information to
influence unit activations.

   A primary goal of the model was to explain the *word superiority effect* (Reicher, 1969;
Wheeler, 1970), in which the perception of a briefly presented letter is more accurate
when it occurs in a word compared with when it occurs in a random consonant string
or even in isolation (see Lupker, this volume). In the IA model, this effect arises due to
partial activation of word units that provide top-down support for the letters they contain.
The model was also able to explain the *pseudoword superiority effect* (e.g., Carr, Davidson,
& Hawkins, 1978; McClelland & Johnston, 1977), in which letters occurring in pronounceable nonwords (e.g., MAVE) are perceived better than in consonant strings or in
isolation (although not quite as well as in words). Although pseudowords are not fully
consistent with any of the units at the word level in the model, they are partially consis-

tent with many words. The presentation of a pseudoword typically generates weak activation of word units sharing three of its four letters; these units, in turn, conspire to
provide top-down support for the letters in the pseudowords. In this way, the IA model
provided an early demonstration of how even a localist model can generalize on the
basis of similarity, through the use of what are essentially distributed representations for
pseudowords.

In subsequent work, McClelland (1991) (see also Movellan & McClelland, 2001) elaborated the model to use units with an intrinsically noisy or stochastic activation function
to bring the model in line with empirical evidence for statistical independence in how
people integrate multiple sources of information (Massaro, 1988). More recently,
Grainger and Jacobs (1996) generalized the interactive activation framework to address a
broader range of tasks and issues related to word recognition.

## Distributed models of word recognition

Mozer (1991) developed a connectionist model of object recognition and spatial attention, called MORSEL, that was applied to the specific task of recognizing words. In the
model, an attentional system forms a spatially contiguous bubble of activation that serves
to select a subset of the bottom-up letter feature information for further processing by a
hierarchically organized object recognition system. Each layer in the recognition system
(called BLIRNET) consists of units with spatially restricted receptive fields that form conjunctions of the simpler features in the previous layer. At the top of the system are posi-
tion-independent units that respond to specific triples of letters (following Wickelgren's
[1969] proposal for representing spoken words). In this way, words were represented by
a pattern of activity over multiple letter triples (e.g., #HO, OUS, USE, SE#, for the word
HOUSE) rather than by the activation of a single word unit (as in the IA model).
Although there was no learning in the system, it was still successful at activating the
correct set of letter triples for a fairly large vocabulary of words. When presented with
multiple words, it usually selected and recognized one of them accurately but, like human
subjects, would occasionally misrecognize the attended word due to letter migrations from
the unattended word (Mozer, 1983). Moreover, when one side of the attentional mechanism was impaired, the damaged model exhibited all of the major characteristics of
neglect dyslexia, the manifestation of hemispatial neglect with written words as stimuli
(Mozer & Behrmann, 1990).

Although MORSEL used distributed word representations, it did not employ learning. Other distributed models have cast the problem of word recognition as mapping
from the written forms of words to their meanings (rather than to higher-order orthographic representations, as in MORSEL), and have used learning to develop weights that
accomplish this mapping. Note, however, that, apart from morphological relationships,
the relationship between the surface forms of words and their meanings is largely arbitrary. In other words, similarity in form (e.g., CAT, CAP) is unrelated to similarity in
meaning (e.g., CAT, DOG). This is the most difficult type of mapping for connectionist networks to learn, given their inherent bias towards preserving similarity. In fact, some
researchers questioned whether it was even possible for distributed networks to accom-

plish this mapping without word-specific intermediate units. Kawamoto (1993) used a variant of Hebbian learning to train a distributed network to map among orthographic, phonological, and semantic representations (see also Van Orden, Pennington, & Stone, 1990). However, because the network lacked any hidden units, it could learn a vocabulary of only a few words. Nonetheless, Kawamoto was able to show that the model provided a natural account of a number of phenomena related to lexical semantic ambiguity resolution (see also Kawamoto, Kello, & Jones, 1994).

To address the more general challenge, Hinton and Sejnowski (1986) trained a Boltzmann Machine – a network of stochastic binary units – to map between orthography and semantics for a larger (although still small) set of words. Although training was difficult, the network was able to develop distributed representations over intermediate hidden units that accomplished the mapping. They also found that, with mild damage, the network occasionally responded to a word by giving another, semantically related word as a response (e.g., CAT read as DOG) – a *semantic error* reminiscent of those made by patients with *deep dyslexia* (Coltheart, Patterson, & Marshall, 1980).

Following Hinton and Sejnowski (1986), Hinton and Shallice (1991) used back-propagation to train a recurrent network with hidden units to map from orthography to semantics for 40 words falling into five concrete semantic categories. Orthographic representations were based on position-specific letter units; semantic representations consisted of subsets of 68 hand-specified semantic features that captured a variety of conceptual distinctions among word meanings. When the network was damaged by removing some units or connections, it no longer settled normally; the initial semantic activity caused by an input would occasionally fall within a neighboring attractor basin, giving rise to an error response. These errors were often semantically related to the stimulus because words with similar meanings correspond to nearby attractors in semantic space. Like deep dyslexic patients, the damaged network also produced errors with visual similarity to the stimulus (e.g., BOG read as DOG) and with both visual and semantic similarity (e.g., CAT read as RAT), due to its inherent bias towards similarity: visually similar words tend to produce similar initial semantic patterns, which can lead to a visual error if the basins are distorted by damage (see figure 2.3).

Plaut and Shallice (1993) extended these initial findings in a number of ways. They established the generality of the co-occurrence of error types across a wide range of simulations, showing that it does not depend on specific characteristics of the network architecture, the learning procedure, or the way responses are generated from semantic activity. They also showed that distributed attractor networks exhibited a number of other characteristics of deep dyslexia not considered by Hinton and Shallice (1991), including the occurrence of visual-then-semantic errors, greater confidence in visual as compared with semantic errors, and relatively preserved lexical decision with impaired naming. They also extended the approach to address effects of concreteness on word reading in deep dyslexia. They trained a network to pronounce a new set of words consisting of both concrete and abstract words. Concrete words were assigned far more semantic features than were abstract words, under the assumption that the semantic representations of concrete words are less dependent on the contexts in which they occur (Saffran, Bogyo, Schwartz, & Marin, 1980).

As a result, the network developed stronger attractors for concrete than abstract words during training, giving rise to better performance in reading concrete words under most

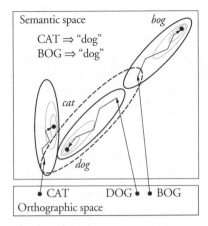

**Figure 2.3** How damage to an attractor network can give rise to both semantic and visual errors. Points within each rectangular area correspond to specific patterns of activation over orthographic or semantic representations; neighboring points corresponding to similar (overlapping) patterns. The arrows reflect the way in which these patterns change over the course of processing. The solid ovals represent the basins of attraction in the normal network; the dashed ovals represent alterations of these basins due to damage (based on Hinton & Shallice, 1991).

types of damage, as observed in deep dyslexia. Surprisingly, severe damage to connections implementing the attractors at the semantic level produced the opposite pattern, in which the network read *abstract* words better than concrete words. This pattern of performance is reminiscent of CAV, the single, enigmatic patient with *concrete word dyslexia* (Warrington, 1981). The double dissociation between reading concrete versus abstract words in patients is often interpreted as implying that there are separate modules within the cognitive system for concrete and abstract words. The Plaut and Shallice simulation demonstrates that such a radical interpretation is unnecessary: the double dissociation can arise from damage to different parts of a distributed network which processes both types of items but develops somewhat different functional specializations through learning (see also Plaut, 1995a).

### *"Dual-route" models of reading aloud*

Much of the controversy surrounding theories of word reading centers not around how words are recognized and understood but how they are read aloud. In part, this is because, in contrast to the arbitrary nature of form-meaning mappings, the mapping between the written and spoken forms of words is highly systematic; words that are spelled similarly are typically also pronounced similarly. This property derives from the fact that written English follows an *alphabetic principle* in which parts of written forms (letters and multiletter graphemes like TH, PH) correspond to parts of spoken forms (phonemes). The sharp contrast between the systematic nature of pronunciation and the arbitrary nature of comprehension has led a number of researchers (e.g., Coltheart, 1978; Marshall &

Newcombe, 1973) to propose separate pathways or "routes" for these two tasks, each employing very different computational mechanisms: a *sublexical* pathway employing grapheme–phoneme correspondence (GPC) rules for pronunciation, and a *lexical* pathway involving a word-specific lexical look-up procedure for comprehension (characterized much like the IA model in later formulations; see e.g. Coltheart et al., 2001; Coltheart, this volume). Complications arise, however, because the pronunciation task itself is not fully systematic; roughly 20% of English words are *irregular* in that they violate the GPC rules (e.g., SEW, PINT, YACHT). So-called "dual-route" theories propose that pronouncing such words also depends on the lexical pathway.

Although traditional dual-route models implement the sublexical pathway with symbolic rules (Coltheart, Curtis, Atkins, & Haller, 1993; Coltheart et al., 2001), it is perfectly feasible to build a dual-route mechanism out of connectionist hardware. For example, Zorzi, Houghton, and Butterworth (1998) describe simulations in which direct connections from letter units to phoneme units support the pronunciation of regular words and nonwords, whereas a separate pathway, composed either of hidden units or localist word units, supports the pronunciation of irregular words (see also Ans, Carbonnel, & Valdois, 1998). Although the mechanisms employed for the two pathways are more homogeneous than in more traditional, rule-based implementations, the models nonetheless retain a categorical distinction between words that obey spelling-sound rules and words that violate them.

## Distributed models of reading aloud

The first researchers to take on the challenge of training a single connectionist network to pronounce all English words were Sejnowski and Rosenberg (1987), who developed a system called NETtalk. Orthographic input was presented to NETtalk by sweeping a 7-letter window over a large text corpus (the Brown corpus; Kucera & Francis, 1967), successively centering the window on each letter in the text. For each letter position, the system was trained to generate the single phoneme corresponding to the central letter in the window. This allows each successive letter to be processed by the same set of units, so the knowledge extracted in processing letters in any position are available for processing letters in every other position. At the same time, the presence of other letters in the surrounding slots allows the network to be sensitive to the context in which letters occur. This is necessary not only for pronouncing exception words but also for handling multiletter graphemes (e.g., TH, PH, SH). For these, the system was trained to generate the appropriate phoneme for the first letter and then silence for the remaining letters. The alignment of phonemes to letters was specified by hand.

Although impressive as a first attempt, the performance of NETtalk when judged in terms of entire words pronounced correctly was much poorer than skilled readers. In follow-up work, Bullinaria (1997) showed that performance in a NETtalk-like system could be improved dramatically by allowing the network to discover the best letter-phoneme alignment by itself. This was done by evaluating the network's output against all possible alignments, and training towards the one that yields the lowest overall error. This pressures the system to converge on alignments that are maximally consistent across the entire training corpus, yielding perfect performance on words and good generalization to pronounceable nonwords.

The need for strictly sequential processing on even the shortest words raises questions about the psychological plausibility of the NETtalk approach. One way to address this concern is to propose that skilled readers attempt to process as much of the input as they can in parallel, then redirect fixation and continue. In this view, unskilled reading may be strictly sequential, as in NETtalk, but as skill develops, it becomes much more parallel. To explore this possibility, Plaut (1999) trained a simple recurrent (sequential) network to produce sequences of single phonemes as output when given position-specific letters as input. The network was also trained to maintain a representation of its current position within the input string. When the network found a peripheral portion of the input difficult to pronounce, it used the position signal to refixate the input, shifting the peripheral portion to the point of fixation where the network had had more experience in generating pronunciations. In this way, the network could apply the knowledge tied to the units at the point of fixation to any difficult portion of the input. Early on in training, the network required multiple fixations to read words, but as the network became more competent it eventually read most words in a single fixation. The network could also read nonwords about as well as skilled readers, occasionally falling back on a refixation strategy for difficult nonwords. Finally, a peripheral impairment to the model reproduced the major characteristics of letter-by-letter reading in pure alexic patients (Behrmann, Plaut, & Nelson, 1998b). Specifically, when input letter activations were corrupted with noise, the model exhibited a clear effect of orthographic length in its number of fixations (a loose analog to naming latency), and this effect interacted with lexical frequency such that the increase was much greater for low- compared with high-frequency words.

An alternative approach to word reading, first articulated by Seidenberg and McClelland (1989), casts the problem as learning to map among orthographic, phonological and semantic representations for entire words in parallel (see figure 2.1). The approach does not deny the existence of sequential processes related to both visual input and articulatory output, but emphasizes the parallel interactions among more central types of lexical information. In support of this general "triangle" framework, Seidenberg and McClelland (1989) trained a connectionist network to map from the orthography of about 3000 monosyllabic English words – both regular and exception – to their phonology via a set of hidden units (i.e., the bottom portion of the framework in figure 2.1, referred to as the *phonological* pathway). The network was also trained to use the same internal representation to regenerate the orthographic input, providing a means for the network of distinguishing words from nonwords based on the accuracy of this reconstruction. Orthographic input was coded in terms of context-sensitive letter triples, much like the highest-level representations in MORSEL. Phonological output was coded in terms of triples of phonemic features. To determine the network's pronunciation of a given letter string, an external procedure constructed the most likely phoneme string given the feature triples generated by the network. This string was then compared with the actual pronunciation of the stimulus to determine whether the network made a correct or error response. After training, the network pronounced correctly 97.7% of the words, including most exception words. The network also exhibited the standard empirical pattern of an interaction of frequency and consistency in naming latency (Andrews, 1982; Seidenberg, Waters,

Barnes, & Tanenhaus, 1984; Taraban & McClelland, 1987; Waters & Seidenberg, 1985) if its real-valued accuracy in generating a response is taken as a proxy for response time (under the assumption that an imprecise phonological representation would be less effective at driving an articulatory system). However, the model was much worse than skilled readers at pronouncing orthographically legal nonwords and at lexical decision under some conditions (Besner, Twilley, McCann, & Seergobin, 1990). Thus, although highly successful in many respects, the model failed to refute traditional claims that localist, word-specific representations and separate mechanisms are necessary to account for skilled reading.

Plaut et al. (1996) showed, however, that the limitations of the Seidenberg and McClelland model stem not from any general limitation in the abilities of connectionist networks, but from its use of poorly structured orthographic and phonological representations. The triples-based orthographic and phonological representations used by the original model fail to capture the relevant similarities among written and spoken forms of words adequately, essentially because the contribution that each grapheme and phoneme makes is overly sensitive to the surrounding context. When more appropriately structured representations are used – based on graphemes and phonemes and embodying phonotactic and graphotactic constraints – network implementations of the phonological pathway can learn to pronounce regular words, exception words, and nonwords as well as skilled readers. Furthermore, the networks also exhibit the empirical frequency-by-consistency interaction pattern, even when naming latencies are modeled directly by the settling time of a recurrent, attractor network.

Although Plaut et al. (1996) demonstrated that implementations of the phonological pathway on its own can learn to pronounce words and nonwords as well as skilled readers, a central aspect of their general theory is that skilled reading more typically requires the combined support of both the semantic and phonological pathways (see also Hillis & Caramazza, 1991; Van Orden & Goldinger, 1994), and that individuals may differ in the relative competence of each pathway (Plaut, 1997; Seidenberg, 1992). The division-of-labor between these pathways has important implications for understanding acquired surface dyslexia, a neuropsychological disorder in which patients pronounce regular words and nonwords normally but "regularize" exception words, particularly those of low frequency (e.g., SEW read as SUE; see Patterson, Coltheart, & Marshall, 1985). Plaut et al. (1996) explored the possibility that surface dyslexia might reflect the natural limitations of an intact phonological pathway that had learned to rely on semantic support that was reduced or eliminated by brain damage. They approximated the contribution that the semantic pathway would make to oral reading by providing phonological representations with external input that pushed them toward the correct pronunciation of each word during training. A semantic impairment was modeled by weakening this external input. Plaut and colleagues found that, indeed, a phonological pathway trained in the context of support from semantics exhibited the central phenomena of surface dyslexia following semantic damage: intact nonword reading and regularization of low-frequency exception words (see Lambon-Ralph & Patterson, this volume). Moreover, as explored in additional simulations (Plaut, 1997), individual differences in the severity of surface dyslexia can arise, not only from differences in the amount of semantic damage, but also from *premorbid* differences in the division of labor between the semantic and phonological pathways.

The relative strengths of these pathways, and the overall competence of the reading system, would be expected to be influenced by a wide variety of factors, including the nature of reading instruction, the sophistication of preliterate phonological representations, relative experience in reading aloud versus silently, the computational resources (e.g., numbers of units and connections) devoted to each pathway, and the reader's more general skill levels in visual pattern recognition and in spoken word comprehension and production. On this view, the more severe surface dyslexic patients had greater premorbid reliance on the semantic pathway as a result of one or more of these factors.

A remaining limitation of the Seidenberg and McClelland model that was not addressed by Plaut et al. (1996) concerns the ability of a distributed network lacking word-specific representations to perform lexical decision accurately. The focus of work with the Seidenberg and McClelland model was on demonstrating that, under some conditions, lexical decisions can be performed on the basis of a measure of orthographic familiarity. Plaut (1997) demonstrated that lexical decisions can be made more accurately when based on a familiarity measure applied to semantics. A feedforward network was trained to map from the orthographic representations of the 2,998 monosyllabic words in the Plaut et al. (1996) corpus to their phonological representations and to artificially created semantic representations generated to cluster around prototype patterns over 200 semantic features. After training, the network was tested for its ability to perform lexical decision based on semantic *stress* – an information-theoretic measure of the degree to which the states of semantic units differed from rest. When tested on the pronounceable nonwords from Seidenberg, Plaut, Petersen, McClelland, and McRae (1994), there was very little overlap between the semantic stress values for nonwords and those for words: an optimal decision criterion yielded only 1% errors. Moreover, the distributions of stress values for words varied systematically as a function of their frequency. In a second test, the network produced reliably higher semantic stress values – and thus poorer discrimination from words – for the Seidenberg, Petersen, MacDonald, and Plaut (1996) pseudo-homophones compared with their controls. Thus, the network exhibited accurate lexical decision performance overall, along with an advantage for higher-frequency words and a disadvantage for pseudohomophones, as found in empirical studies.

More recently, Harm and Seidenberg (2004) have developed a full implementation of the "triangle" framework (see figure 2.1) and used it to examine a number of issues related to the division-of-labor in the reading system. Although the focus of the work is on the comprehension of written words via the direct versus phonologically mediated pathways, the underlying principles apply equally well to the computation of phonology both directly or via semantics. First, to approximate preliterate language experience, the network was trained to map bidirectionally between phonology and semantics for 6,103 monosyllabic words (see also Harm & Seidenberg, 1999, for a computational examination of the relevance of preliterate experience to reading acquisition). The phonology of each word was encoded in terms of eight slots of 25 phonetic features, organized into a CCCVVCCC template. In constructing semantic representations, words were first categorized by their most frequent word class (Francis & Kucera, 1982). For uninflected nouns and verbs, semantic features were generated using the WordNet online semantic database (Miller, 1990). Adjectives, adverbs and closed-class words were hand-coded according to preexisting feature taxonomies (e.g., Frawley, 1992). Inflected words were assigned the features of their base forms plus specific inflectional features. In total, 1,989 semantic features were generated to encode word meanings, with words averaging 7.6 features each (range 1–37). Once the preliterate network was reasonably accurate at understanding and producing spoken words (86% and 90% correct, respectively), the network was then trained on the reading task. Orthography was encoded using letter units organized into vowel-centered slot-based representation (analogous to phonology). After extended training, the model succeeded in activating the correct semantic features for 97.3% of the words and the correct phonological features for 99.2% of the words.

The trained model exhibited the appropriate effects of word frequency, spelling-sound consistency, and imageability in pronouncing words, and was as accurate as skilled readers in pronouncing pseudowords. Harm and Seidenberg's (2004) primary goal, however, was to address the longstanding debate on whether reading is necessarily phonologically mediated. An examination of the division-of-labor in activating meaning from print over the course of training indicated that the network relied heavily on phonological mediation (orthography-phonology-semantics) in the early stages of reading acquisition but gradually shifted towards increased reliance on the direct mapping (orthography-semantics) as reading skill improved. Even at the end of training, however, both pathways continue to make important contributions to performance. This is especially true for homophones (e.g., ATE, EIGHT), which cannot be comprehended solely by the mediated pathway. Harm and Seidenberg demonstrate that the model's performance with homophones matches the findings from a number of empirical studies (Jared & Seidenberg, 1991; Lesch & Pollatsek, 1993; Van Orden, 1987; see also Van Orden & Kloos, this volume).

## Conclusion

Connectionist models instantiate a set of computational principles that are intended to approximate the core properties of neural computation. Early efforts to apply these models to reading employed localist representations for words and hand-specified connection weights. More recent efforts have focused on learning internal distributed representations that effectively mediate the interaction of orthographic, phonological, and semantic information. Because such systems lack word-specific representations and separate pathways for regular versus irregular items, they stand in sharp contrast to traditional dual-route theories of word reading. Existing models are still limited in the size and diversity of the vocabulary they handle and the range of empirical issues they address. Nonetheless, these systems illustrate how a common computational framework can provide insight into reading acquisition, normal skilled reading, patterns of reading impairment following brain damage, and even possible approaches to remediation of developmental (Harm, McCandliss, & Seidenberg, 2003) and acquired (Plaut, 1996) deficits.

## Note

The preparation of this chapter was supported by NIH grant MH55628.

# 3

# Visual Word Recognition: Theories and Findings

## Stephen J. Lupker

The topic of "visual word recognition" may have the largest literature in Cognitive Psychology and, therefore, a chapter on the topic must be selective. This chapter will first place the relevant issues in a historical context and then review the basic visual word recognition phenomena within the context of current models. It will then be argued that any successful model of visual word recognition needs to incorporate the assumption of "interactivity," that is, that the various components of the visual word recognition system (i.e., orthographic, phonological, semantic) mutually activate and inhibit each other while a word is being processed (see also Van Orden & Kloos, this volume). (Hereafter, the term "word recognition" will be used as shorthand for the term "visual word recognition.")

What is "word recognition"? At least until the appearance of Seidenberg and McClelland's (1989) connectionist model of reading, word recognition was typically thought of as the process of going from a printed letter string to the selection of a single item stored in lexical memory. Lexical memory, or the "lexicon," is a mental dictionary containing entries for all the words a reader knows. Thus, word recognition was essentially synonymous with the terms "lexical access" or "lexical selection." Such a definition, of course, assumes that words are represented as lexical entries in memory. Seidenberg and McClelland's model explicitly denied the existence of such representations, arguing instead that representations were distributed across sets of simple subsymbolic processing units. To the extent that models of this sort have been successful, they have forced theorists to contemplate the possibility that some of the standard assumptions about the architecture of the word recognition system should be altered.

What appears to be an equally important aspect of Seidenberg and McClelland's (1989) model was that it contained a straightforward outline for how semantics should be integrated into the word recognition system. That is, semantic information was assumed to be represented no differently than other types of information (i.e., orthographic and phonological) and all of these mental representations were assumed to follow the same rules of activation. As such, this model represented what I would argue was the first complete model of word recognition. This is a crucial point because, as will be argued in this chapter (see also Balota, Ferraro, & Connor, 1991), any successful model of word recognition will need to have a mechanism for explaining the impact of semantics, both the impact of the semantic context within which a word is processed and the impact of the semantic attributes of the word itself (Whaley, 1978).

## Historical Context

Most of the early models of word recognition (e.g., Gough, 1972; Massaro, 1975; Morton, 1969; Smith & Spoehr, 1974; Theios & Muise, 1977) relied on two assumptions. First, the human information processing system involves a series of processing stages that work in a serial, nonoverlapping fashion. Information only flows one way, that is, forward, through the system and, further, each stage is essentially completed before the next begins. The term "thresholded" is used to refer to the assumption that each stage must be completed before the next one can begin. The idea is that a stage is ready to pass information on to the next stage only when the activation at the initial stage reaches a threshold. In contrast, models proposing that information passes between stages as soon as information at one stage begins to be activated are referred to as "cascaded" (McClelland, 1979). The second assumption was that the word recognition system is a fairly autonomous system, that is, it works only with the information stored within it, in particular, the information that can be referred to as lexical information (Forster, 1981). (Theios & Muise's, 1977, model, contained in figure 3.1, is a typical example of this type of model.)

At the risk of overgeneralizing, these models proposed that there is initially a perceptually based process that leads to the activation of sublexical units (typically letter units). The activation of these sublexical units allows the formation of some sort of "prelexical" code. This code activates those word (i.e., lexical) units that are more or less consistent with it. Ultimately, one of these units is selected or accessed. Only at that point does meaning start to become activated. The specific assumption that meaning activation strictly follows lexical selection is referred to as the "form-first" assumption (Forster & Hector, 2002).

One major problem that the early models faced was explaining why there often seemed to be observable effects of "higher-level" information on "lower-level" processing. The classic example is the word superiority effect (Reicher, 1969; Wheeler, 1970). The word superiority effect refers to the fact that letters (i.e., lower-level information) are more accurately reported when presented in words than when presented in nonwords. The experimental task involves the rapid presentation of a letter string often followed by a mask in order to make perception difficult. One letter position is cued for report. To prevent guessing from differentially influencing responding, two alternatives are presented for the identity of the cued letter on each trial. If the letter string had been a word, both alternatives would create a word (e.g., if the word had been WORD and the final position had been

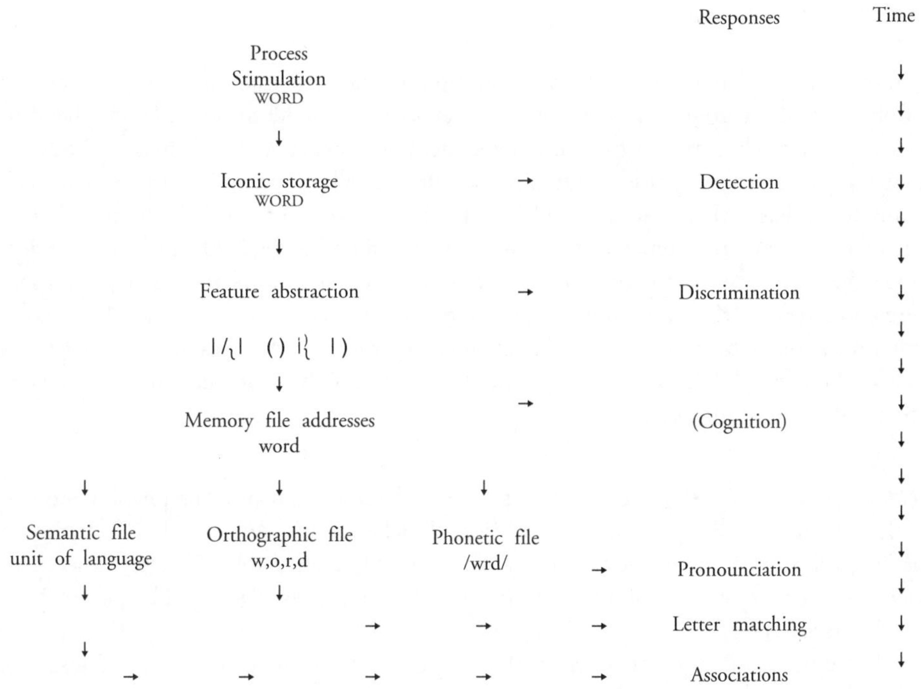

Responses        Time

Process
Stimulation                                               ↓
WORD                                                      ↓
↓                                                         ↓

Iconic storage          →              Detection          ↓
WORD                                                      ↓
↓                                                         ↓

Feature abstraction     →              Discrimination     ↓
                                                          ↓
|/ι| () ι} ι)                                             ↓
↓                       →                                 ↓

Memory file addresses                  (Cognition)        ↓
word                                                      ↓

↓          ↓            ↓                                 ↓
                                                          ↓

Semantic file    Orthographic file   Phonetic file        ↓
unit of language    w,o,r,d           /wrd/    →   Pronounciation   ↓
↓                ↓                                         ↓

                 →          →          →   Letter matching    ↓
↓

→        →        →        →        →   Associations

**Figure 3.1**   Model of word recognition (Theios & Muise, 1977).

cued for report, the alternatives might be D and K). If the letter string had been a nonword, both alternatives would create a nonword (e.g., VCRD with D and K as alternatives for the final position). The standard result is better performance in the word condition than in the nonword condition (e.g., Johnston & McClelland, 1973; Maris, 2002; Paap, Chun, & Vonnahme, 1999; Paap, Newsome, McDonald, & Schvaneveldt, 1982).

The problem for models based on the principles of autonomy and thresholded processing is obvious. How can the existence of a mental representation for a word (e.g., a lexical unit) influence the processing of letter information if that mental representation itself is not accessed until the identity of the letter in question is known? Do changes have to be made to the functional architecture of the models to explain these findings, or is it only necessary to change a single assumption of the model? Alternatively, can these effects be explained in terms of some process (e.g., decision) not actually described by the model itself? It now seems clear that it was the impetus provided by these types of questions that led to the explosion in word recognition research witnessed since the early 1970s. (For a discussion of these issues in auditory word recognition, see Norris, McQueen, & Cutler, 2000, and the invited commentaries.)

## The basic phenomena

Although a complete model of word recognition will need to account for an extensive set of phenomena, at present, it is premature to expect any model to do so. Some phenomena will ultimately turn out to be task dependent and, hence, not informative about the nature of the word recognition system per se. Others will only arise in such restricted circumstances that their impact on models of the process will necessarily be limited. What, then, are the basic phenomena that all models should address? Clearly, this list is subjective. The main criteria for inclusion are replicability and the likelihood that the phenomenon reflects the basic architecture of the word recognition system. This second criterion appears to be especially challenging. For three of the four phenomena listed below, there are already arguments in the literature that these phenomena arise outside the word recognition system.

*The word superiority effect.* Based on its historical import, an obvious phenomenon to include would be the word superiority effect (Reicher, 1969; Wheeler, 1970). It should be noted, however, that some researchers have recently argued that this effect may actually have more to do with phonology than with lexical processing (e.g., Hooper & Paap, 1997; Maris, 2002).

Unlike the word superiority effect, the next three effects all arise in speeded response tasks, that is, tasks in which participants are instructed to respond as rapidly and accurately as possible, and response latency is the main dependent variable. The two standard tasks of this sort are naming, where participants simply have to pronounce a presented word, and lexical decision, where subjects have to decide whether a letter string is a word in the language (e.g., CAT vs. SLINT).

*The word frequency effect.* The second phenomenon is the word frequency effect (Becker, 1976; Forster & Chambers, 1973; Monsell, 1991; Monsell, Doyle, & Haggard, 1989). Words that are seen more often are responded to more rapidly. Once again, however, this effect is controversial. Balota and Chumbley (1984) have argued that this is a decision phenomenon and, hence, may have little to do with the word recognition system. Further, some researchers (e.g., Morrison & Ellis, 1995) have suggested that observed frequency effects are at least partly due to confounding frequency with age-of-acquisition – that words learned at younger ages are more rapidly processed and, due to the fact that higher-frequency words are typically learned at younger ages, frequency effects may be, to some degree, age-of-acquisition effects.

*The semantic priming effect.* The third phenomenon is the semantic priming effect (Meyer & Schvaneveldt, 1971; see Neely, 1991, for a review). The experimental task involves the presentation of two words. The first, the "prime," establishes a context. Typically, no response is required to the prime. The second word, the "target," requires either a naming or lexical-decision response. Targets (e.g., DOG) that are related to the semantic context provided by the prime (e.g., CAT) are responded to more rapidly than targets that are not (e.g., NURSE) although there is some controversy as to whether all types of seman-tic context (e.g., category, antonym) produce priming effects (Lupker, 1984; Shelton & Martin, 1992; Williams, 1996). It should also be noted that there is general agreement that at least some of the observed priming effects are due to processes outside the word recognition system (although see Plaut & Booth, 2000, for an attempt to explain seman-tic priming solely in terms of lexical processing).

*The masked repetition priming effect.* The fourth and final phenomenon is the masked repetition priming effect (Evett & Humphreys, 1981; Forster & Davis, 1984). In the masked priming technique, a prime word is briefly presented followed immediately in the same physical position on the computer screen by the target. The presentation of the prime and target in this way means that the target masks the prime such that participants typically report that no stimulus other than the target had been presented. The prime and target are in different cases so that there is very little figural overlap between them (e.g., dog-DOG). Targets are responded to more rapidly if the prime and target are the same word.

There are undoubtedly some phenomena that are noticeable by their absence from the above list. Some are absent because they form the core of the eventual discussion about interactivity (e.g., ambiguity effects, homophone effects). Others are absent because the stability of the effect is still being challenged. Among these are neighborhood effects and form-priming effects. A word's "neighborhood" is defined as all the other words that share letters at all but one letter position (Coltheart, Davelaar, Jonasson, & Besner, 1977). Thus, the word PINE has as neighbors, LINE, PANE, PILE, and PINT, among others. A number of researchers have reported that words with large neighborhoods are processed more rapidly than words with small neighborhoods (Andrews, 1992; 1997; Sears, Hino, & Lupker, 1995; although see Forster & Shen, 1996, and Grainger, 1990). In addition, a number of researchers have reported that words without higher-frequency neighbors are processed more rapidly than words with higher-frequency neighbors (Grainger, 1990; Grainger & Jacobs, 1996; Grainger, O'Regan, Jacobs, & Segui, 1989, although see Sears, et al., 1995; Sears, Lupker, & Hino,1999; and Siakaluk, Sears, & Lupker, 2002). Form priming refers to priming that arises when the prime and target have similar forms (e.g., tile–PILE). Although it seems likely that form priming effects do exist, the experimental conditions under which they exist is still unclear in both masked prime (Forster, Davis, Schoknecht, & Carter, 1987; Segui & Grainger, 1990) and unmasked prime (Colombo, 1986; Lupker & Colombo, 1994; Martin & Jensen, 1988) experiments. Other effects are absent because they appear to be restricted to the naming task (e.g., regularity, length). These effects do not appear to represent characteristics of the word recognition system per se and would be better dealt with in a discussion of the processes involved in naming.

Finally, there are a number of effects that are based on responses to nonwords in the lexical decision task, such as the nonword legality effect (Rubenstein, Lewis, & Ruben-stein, 1971a; Stanners & Forbach, 1973), the pseudohomophone effect (Coltheart et al., 1977; Dennis, Besner, & Davelaar, 1985), and the nonword neighborhood size effect (Coltheart et al., 1977). While an argument can be made that it is precisely when the word recognition system fails that we can learn most about it, these types of effects seem to have more to say about task specific processes, in this case, in lexical decision, than about the word recognition process per se.

## The Models

### Search models

*The bin model.* Search models best represent the way in which one can build a model based on the assumption of thresholded, autonomous processing. According to search models, readers recognize a word by comparing a prelexical code against a set of lexical codes until a match is obtained. The search is not through all of lexical memory but rather, some process designates a section of lexical memory as the optimal search area and the search is confined there. The model that best exemplifies this idea is Forster's bin model (1976; 1989).

According to Forster's (1976) model, the lexical system involves three peripheral access files and a master file, each containing information about all the words in our lexicon. The three peripheral files are orthographically-, phonologically- and semantically-based and each serves as a means of getting to word entries in the master file where all the information about the word is contained. It is relevant to visual word recognition to focus on the orthographic file in which each word in our lexicon contains an entry (this is also true for the other two peripheral files). In each entry in the orthographic file are two things, an "orthographic access code," which is a description of the orthographic properties of the word, and a pointer to the location for that word in the master file.

When a word is viewed, a perceptual process turns that word into a prelexical code that is format compatible with the access codes in the orthographic file. The orthographic file is then searched by comparing the prelexical code with the orthographic access codes. As noted, this search is constrained to a section of the orthographic file. In particular, the orthographic file is organized into bins that contain similar orthographic access codes. So, for example, the words CAT and CAN would probably be in the same bin. In essence, the search is constrained to the bin that is most likely to contain the word being viewed.

The idea of bins may be better understood by drawing a partial parallel to looking up a word in a dictionary. When using a dictionary, one checks the words at the top of each page and only looks at the individual items on the page if it is a page that the word is likely to be on (e.g., the word COMET is virtually certain to be on the page with the heading COMBO–COMFORT). Each bin is like a page in the dictionary and the reader goes directly to the bin most likely to contain the word being viewed. The parallel is not perfect, however, because the words in the bin are not ordered alphabetically, as they are on a dictionary page, but in descending order of frequency. Thus, the entries in the bin are searched in descending order of frequency.

If the search through the designated bin turns up a close match with one of the entries, the location of this entry is flagged while the search continues, looking for other close matches. If a match is close enough, the entry is opened and the pointer to the master file is used to access the word's entry in that file. This process engages a second analysis, referred to as "post-access check," which compares the properties of the stimulus with the properties of the word in the master file. If this comparison is successful, the word has been successfully recognized. Note also that if none of the words in the bin are success-fully recognized in the initial search, close matches that had been flagged but not had their entries opened are then evaluated (Forster, 1989; Forster, Mohan, & Hector, 2003).

In terms of the four basic phenomena, the model has no difficulty explaining the fre-quency effect and the masked repetition priming effect. The more rapid processing of high-frequency words follows directly from the fact that the bins are searched in descend-ing order of frequency. Masked repetition priming arises because the prime begins the word recognition process and, if the target is a repetition of the prime, its processing has a head start. In particular, it is assumed that the prime begins to open the correct entry in the orthographic file. Thus, the entry opening time for the target is shortened, pro-ducing more rapid processing. In contrast, the model does not have any obvious way of explaining the word superiority effect.

The other phenomenon, semantic priming, can be explained in terms of cross-refer-encing in the master file, at least according to the original version of the model (Forster, 1976). Entries for semantically related words are directly linked in the master file. Thus, after the prime DOG has been recognized, the CAT entry in the master file can be easily accessed. As a result, the post-access check of the properties for CAT against the proper-ties of the stimulus can be started without bothering with the search process.

This proposal concerning the (limited) impact of semantics on the word recognition process has a number of implications. One is that, because semantically primed words do not engage the search process, there should be no frequency effect for those words. In fact, Becker (1979) has demonstrated that the frequency effect is smaller when words are semantically primed. A second implication is that semantic priming effects should only exist when the prime's entry is successfully accessed in the master file. Thus, semantic priming effects from primes that are masked in order to avoid recognition (e.g., Carr, McCauley, Sperber, & Parmelee, 1982; Fischler & Goodman, 1978; Hines, Czerwinski, Sawyer, & Dwyer, 1986; Marcel, 1983) are problematic for the model. Finally, because the only impact of semantics on lexical processing is due to the structure of the master file, the model cannot explain any effects of semantics on word recognition with the exception of semantic priming effects. As will be discussed subsequently, there are a number of such effects.

*The activation-verification model.* Paap et al.'s (1982) activation-verification model (see also, Paap, Johansen, Chun, & Vonnahme, 2000) is also a search model; however, it differs from Forster's (1976) in that, although it is an autonomous model, it invokes cascaded processing. In the model, first letter units and then word units are activated in a serial, but cascaded, fashion (so that information passes through the system before initial pro-cessing is complete). Letter activation occurs in position-specific channels and is concep-tualized as a feature matching process. Thus, there is some probability that an incorrect but featurally similar letter will be activated at each letter position. Activity at the letter level continuously feeds into the lexicon with the activation of any lexical unit being a function of the activity levels of that word's constituent letters.

It is the activity levels in the lexicon that determine which set of word candidates is selected for further processing. The nature of that further processing is crucially dependent on whether the reader has also been able to establish a "refined perceptual representation of the word" (Paap et al., 1982, p. 574), which is the situation in normal reading. In this case, the set of candidates is serially verified against the perceptual representation (this is the search process). If there is a sufficient match between a candidate and the perceptual representation at any point, the candidate is accepted and the verification process is terminated. As in Forster's (1976) model, the verification process is frequency-based (higher-frequency words are verified first). Further, if there is a semantic context (i.e., a prime), words semantically related to the prime will enter the candidate set and be verified first. If a refined perceptual representation cannot be established, as in perceptual identification tasks, it is not possible to carry out the verification process. Thus, a probabilistic selection is made from among the candidates based on the activation levels of those candidates.

In terms of the four basic phenomena, this model has had its greatest success explaining the word superiority effect (see Paap et al., 1982). The model can also explain both frequency effects and semantic priming effects. Frequency effects arise due to the serial, frequency-based verification process, whereas semantic priming effects are due to the inclusion of semantically related words in the candidate set. Masked repetition priming effects are more problematic for the model. Presenting a masked prime that is identical to the target will activate target representations at both the letter level and the lexical level. The most important determinant of processing speed, however, is the search process, which only begins once the candidate set has been established. The prime's activation of the target's representations may increase the probability that the target will be in the candidate set; however, it should not change its position in the search order. Hence, unless additional assumptions are added, the prediction would be that a masked repetition prime would not have any effect on target processing.

Two additional points should be made about the model. First, in data-limited tasks, tasks in which it is hard to establish a refined perceptual representation, the verification process cannot be carried out. Thus, there is no mechanism for producing a frequency effect. Indeed, there does not appear to be much evidence for frequency effects in word superiority effect experiments (Manelis, 1977; Paap & Johansen, 1994; Paap & Newsome, 1980). Second, as is true of Forster's model (1976), this model has no means of explaining any semantic effects other than semantic priming effects.

## Activation models

*The interactive activation model.* Activation models represent the other end of the continuum from the search models in terms of cascaded and autonomous processing. The preeminent activation model is McClelland and Rumelhart's (1981) interactive activation model. This model represents the first real implementation of activation and inhibition processes. It also forms the core of a number of other models in the literature (e.g., Coltheart, Rastle, Perry, Langdon, & Ziegler, 2001; Grainger and Jacobs, 1996).

The interactive activation model was specifically intended to be a model that would explain the effects of higher-level information on lower-level processing, in particular, the word superiority effect. In the model, there are three levels of representation: feature,

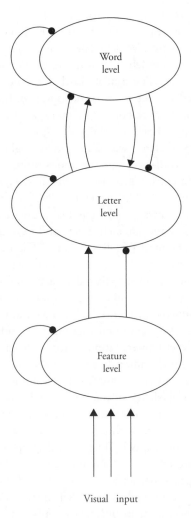

**Figure 3.2** Interactive activation model (McClelland & Rumelhart, 1981).

letter, and word. When processing begins, there is a continuous flow of activation upstream from feature-level representations to letter-level representations to word-level representations, as well as downstream from word-level representations back to lower-level representations ("feedback activation"). There is also a flow of inhibition between representations at the same level. Lexical selection is achieved when the activation in a lexical representation exceeds a threshold. (See figure 3.2 for a graphic description of the interactive activation model.).

As McClelland and Rumelhart (1981) argue (see also Rumelhart & McClelland, 1982), this type of system can readily account for the impact of higher-level representations on lower-level representations and, hence, it can explain the word superiority effect. It can also explain frequency effects due to the fact that the resting level activations of word-level representations are frequency dependent. Thus, once activated, representations for high-frequency words will reach their activation threshold more quickly than representations for low-frequency words. Masked repetition priming effects would be explained in terms of the residual activation left in a word's representations as a result of the brief exposure to the masked prime. The model also has the potential to explain semantic priming effects as well as effects due to semantic aspects of the word itself, for example, the fact that imageable words are responded to more rapidly than nonimageable words in lexical decision tasks (e.g., Bleasdale, 1987; de Groot, 1989; James, 1975; Kroll & Merves, 1986). These types of effects would be due to "higher-level input" (i.e., semantic information) impacting word-level representations through feedback activation.

The proposal of a fully interactive system, like that in the interactive activation model, has had its critics (e.g., Massaro, 1988; Paap et al., 2000). However, many modelers have found the idea of interactivity attractive. In the dual-route cascaded model (Coltheart et al., 2001), for example, the basic interactive activation system is used to describe the actions of the first part of the model's "lexical route." The model also has a number of additional structures. In particular, the system containing word-level representations (the "orthographic input lexicon") is directly linked to a phonological output lexicon. The phonological output lexicon contains phonological codes of words known to the reader and it is linked to the phoneme system, which allows translation of the phonological codes into speech. There is also the second route in the model, the "nonlexical route," which connects the letter-level representations directly to the phoneme system. Finally, there is a semantic system, which indirectly connects the orthographic input lexicon and the phonological output lexicon (see Coltheart, this volume, for further discussion). In theory, this system, through feedback operations, would provide a means of explaining both semantic priming effects and effects due to the semantic nature of the word itself.

A second well-known extension of the interactive activation model is Grainger and Jacobs's (1996) multiple read-out model. The main goal of the multiple read-out model was to explain neighborhood effects (and any interactions with word frequency) in both lexical decision and perceptual identification tasks. In order to explain these effects in lexical decision, two new features had to be added: first, a time-based criterion mechanism was added to explain how participants make negative, "nonword" decisions. Second, the assumption was made that positive, "word" decisions could be based on something other than a word-level unit reaching an activation threshold. In particular, positive decisions can be made if there is a high overall level of activation at the word level (i.e., if that activity level exceeded a criterion, it would be taken as sufficient evidence that a word had been presented). The model has had some success at explaining neighborhood effects (although see Sears et al., 1999, and Siakaluk et al., 2002). What the model does not have, however, is any real mechanism for explaining semantic effects. Given the level of precision at which this model is attempting to predict lexical decision latencies, and given the clear impact of semantics on this process (as will be described later), this omission would seem to represent an obvious problem for the model.

*Parallel distributed processing models.* The models discussed so far contain different assumptions about cascaded processing and the autonomy of lexical processing, but they all agree on one assumption. The core process in word recognition is isolating (i.e., "select-

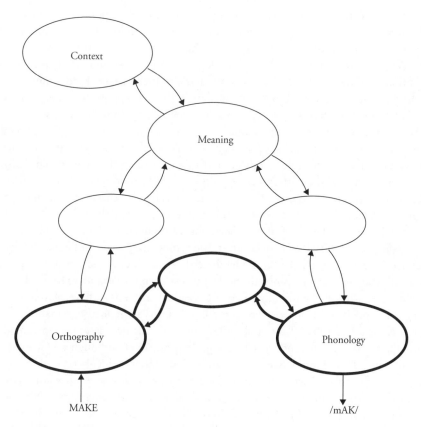

**Figure 3.3**   Triangle framework (Seidenberg & McClelland, 1989).

ing," "accessing") the relevant lexical unit. However, there are now a number of models in the literature that propose there is no such thing as a lexical unit. Instead, these models are based on the idea that what makes up our lexical system are sets of distributed, sub-symbolic codes representing the attributes of the words we know. The word recognition process is the process of activating the appropriate sets of these codes. The models are referred to as parallel distributed processing (PDP) models and they are typically represented with a triangle framework (see figure 3.3 and Plaut, this volume).

The first of these models was proposed by Seidenberg and McClelland (1989). The basic idea is that the word recognition system involves three types of mental representations (orthographic, phonological and semantic representations). Units of each type are assumed to be connected to units of the other types, producing the triangle representation (see figure 3.3). The appropriate connections between sets of units have to be learned, just as a young reader must learn to read. Within the model, learning is essentially an error correction process. When presented with a word, the units at all levels begin to activate (and inhibit) each other, resulting in a pattern of activation across all the units. These activation patterns, which initially will be quite inaccurate, are compared with the correct patterns and then weights between units are adjusted in order to make processing more accurate the next time. This process continues with each new exposure to the word. As a result, over time, activation in one set of units comes to produce the appropriate activation in the units in the other pools (e.g., orthographic processing of the visually presented word CAT allows the activation of the phonological units for the phoneme sequence [kat]). In addition, as shown in figure 3.3, these models also incorporate "hidden units." These units help define the relationships between units in the main pools (for an explanation of why hidden units are necessary see Hinton, McClelland, & Rumelhart, 1986).

The nature and number of representations in each domain (orthographic, phonological, semantic) are often model specific. For example, in the Seidenberg and McClelland (1989) model, the orthographic units are not intended to represent psychologically real concepts; nonetheless, the pattern across units does give rise to sets of letter triples (e.g., MAK). Due to this fact, although the model had considerable success in explaining word recognition data, it also had some serious limitations, particularly in its ability to name nonwords (Besner, Twilley, McCann, & Seergobin, 1990; Fera & Besner, 1992; Coltheart, Curtis, Atkins, & Haller, 1993). In contrast, the orthographic units in Plaut, McClelland, Seidenberg, and Patterson's (1996) model directly represent either letters or letter combinations, allowing some of the problems noted by Besner and colleagues to be fixed. Semantic units, which, until recently (e.g., Harm & Seidenberg, 2004), have played a smaller role in the models' development are typically assumed to represent semantic features (Hinton & Shallice, 1991; Plaut et al., 1996; Plaut & Shallice, 1993), even though the features themselves are often not specified (e.g., Masson, 1991; although see Cree, McRae, & McNorgan, 1999; Harm & Seidenberg, 2004; and McRae, Seidenberg, & de Sa, 1997).

In terms of the four basic phenomena, the model can clearly account for frequency effects. Indeed, the frequency of exposure to a word is the main determinant of the values of the connection weights for the word's units. Further, because the model is an activation model, it should also be able to explain masked repetition priming. That is, the briefly presented masked prime would activate some of the prime's units, allowing for more rapid processing of the target if that target is a repetition of the prime. With respect to semantic priming, modeling work by Masson (1991, 1995), Cree et al. (1999), Plaut (1995b), Plaut and Booth (2000), and McRae et al. (1997) has demonstrated that these types of models can produce semantic priming effects, at least when the concepts share semantic features. In particular, according to these models, the processing of related targets (e.g., DOG following the prime CAT) is easier because the two concepts share semantic units. As a result, some of the semantic units for the target will have already been activated when the target appears, speeding target processing. Notice that the interactivity inherent in these models, specifically, the feedback processes presumed to occur between the semantic units and the "lower-level" orthographic and phonological units, plays essentially no role in this explanation. As will be discussed below, explanations in which these feedback processes do play an important role may provide an even better way of explaining semantic priming effects.

Explaining the word superiority effect is more of a challenge for the model. It would seem like the feedback processes at work in the model should, as with the interactive activation model, produce a word superiority effect. A key distinction here, however, is that it is the feedback from word units in the interactive activation model that produces the word superiority effect. Those units do not exist in PDP models. However, as Plaut et al.

(1996) note, units in network models tend to organize themselves into stable patterns called "attractors." These patterns of units that group together to become attractor units may function somewhat similarly to word units, providing the necessary feedback. Thus, it is possible that, with the correct assumptions, the model could also explain the word superiority effect.

The various models discussed above all have their strengths and weaknesses based on their ability to account for the basic phenomena. At present, there is no clear winner. The proposition to be argued in the remainder of this chapter, however, is that other evidence indicates that any successful model of word recognition will need to assume that there is an interactive flow of activation among the processing structures (see also Stone & Van Orden, 1994; Taft & van Graan, 1998; Van Orden & Goldinger, 1994). That is, not only does activation flow forward from activated units to other sets of units, but also, once those units start to become activated, they send activation back to the appropriate units at other levels (see Van Orden & Kloos, this volume). The term "feedback" is used to refer to the flow of activation back to units that were initially activated (i.e., the ortho-graphic units when the word CAT is read). As noted, the interactivity notion is embod-ied to various degrees by the activation models and is a direct contradiction of the autonomy assumptions that tend to characterize the search models. The framework for this discussion will be the triangle framework, which is most clearly an attribute of the PDP models. In theory, it would be possible to refer instead to a model like Coltheart et al.'s (2001), as it also has the triangle structure embedded within it (i.e., with its ortho-graphic input lexicon, phonological output lexicon, and semantic system). However, the units in the first two of these systems are lexical, while some of the effects to be discussed below (e.g., Stone, Van Hoy, & Van Orden, 1997) are based on sublexical units, making it more difficult to see how those effects fit within this framework.

## The Orthographic-Phonological Interaction

### *Feedback from phonology to orthography*

In visual word recognition tasks, the units initially activated are the orthographic units. Thus, evidence for feedback activation would come from experiments demonstrating that phonological activation affects the activation in those orthographic units. For example, Stone et al. (1997) and Ziegler, Montant, and Jacobs (1997) have shown that words that have multiple possible mappings from phonology to orthography (i.e., words like GAIN, which could have been spelled GANE) produce longer lexical decision latencies than words like TENT which have only one possible mapping (see also Perry, 2003). Words like GAIN are referred to as "feedback inconsistent" because the mapping from phono-logical units to orthographic units are one-to-many. Words having one-to-one mappings, between phonology and orthography, like TENT, are referred to as "feedback consistent." The explanation for these findings is that, with inconsistent words, feedback slows the activation of the correct orthographic code because at least some of that feedback is mis-directed to the incorrect orthographic code (e.g., ANE), creating competition.

The effects reported by Stone et al. (1997) and Ziegler et al. (1997) were not large and their reliability has been challenged by Peereman, Content, and Bonin (1998). One could argue, however, that the reason the effects were small was because the manipulations were weak. The feedback directed to the incorrect orthography (i.e., ANE) does not activate a strong competitor for GAIN because neither GANE nor ANE are words and, hence, neither is strongly represented within the orthographic units. The use of homophones allows for a much stronger manipulation. Homophones are words that have different spellings but the same pronunciation (e.g., PAIN and PANE). According to a feedback account, if either is presented visually, the activation of /pAn/ would lead to activation being fed back to the orthographic codes for both PAIN and PANE. The result should be strong competition, leading to a delay in responding. That is, there should be a homophone disadvantage in tasks based on orthographic processing (e.g., lexical decision).

The available data are firmly supportive of this prediction. Rubenstein et al. (1971a) were the first to report a homophone disadvantage in lexical decision in comparison to a control condition. While there was considerable controversy about this finding (e.g., Clark, 1973) and some failures to replicate (e.g., Coltheart et al., 1977), more recently the pattern has emerged very clearly (Davelaar, Coltheart, Besner, & Jonnasson, 1978; Pexman & Lupker, 1999; Pexman, Lupker, & Jared, 2001; Pexman, Lupker, & Reggin, 2002).

Early accounts of homophone effects were based on the idea that visual word recognition was phonologically mediated. Part of the reason was that, originally, these effects were only found when processing the lower-frequency member of the homophone pair (e.g., PANE). The explanation was that both PAIN and PANE activated the phonological code /pAn/ and it then led to the selection of the lexical unit for the higher-frequency member of the homophone pair (i.e., PAIN). Further processing allowed the discrepancy to be noted, at which point the lexical selection process was restarted. The result, of course, was longer latencies for low-frequency homophones. The Pexman et al. (2001) paper is especially important in this regard. Here the nonwords in the lexical decision task were pseudohomophones (nonwords that sound like words when pronounced; e.g., BRANE). These nonwords produced longer word latencies and not only did the homophone effect increase for the low-frequency words, but there was also a significant homophone effect for the high-frequency words. This should never happen if the homophone effect were due to selecting the higher-frequency member of the pair first in lexical search because that event should not be altered by changing the type of nonword being used. In contrast, this result is quite consistent with the claim that these effects are feedback effects.

## Feedback from orthography to phonology

The key issue for word recognition is the impact of phonology on orthographic processing. However, for completeness, it is important to discuss the impact of orthography on phonological processing. Research directly relevant to this issue is fairly extensive (e.g., Borowsky, Owen, & Fonos, 1999; Dijkstra, Roelofs, & Fieuws, 1995; Ziegler, Muneaux, & Grainger, 2003); I will focus on two of the earlier papers. A key finding suggesting that orthographic feedback has an impact on speech perception was reported by Seidenberg and Tanenhaus (1979) (see also Donnenwerth-Nolan, Tanenhaus, & Seidenberg, 1981). Seidenberg and Tanenhaus presented participants with a cue word (typically auditorily) followed by auditorily presented target words. The subject's task was to respond as soon as one of the target words rhymed with the prime. Although accurate performance in this task must be based on an evaluation of the phonological code, there was a clear impact of the orthographic relationship between the cue and target. That is, participants were much faster to respond when the two words were spelled the same (e.g., GREED–DEED) than when they were not (e.g., BEAD–DEED).

This effect indicates that orthographic information is automatically activated when a spoken word is heard. It also indicates that orthographic information plays a role in the processing of subsequently presented spoken words. Although it might be the case that participants evaluate the spelling of the words in these experiments in spite of the fact that they are explicitly told to do something else, a more reasonable explanation is that orthographic information was automatically activated when the cue word was processed, and it fed back to the phonological codes for similarly spelled words. Thus, those words were more activated and, hence, easier to process.

A second finding suggesting the impact of orthographic feedback on speech perception was reported by Ziegler and Ferrand (1998). As those authors note, effects like those reported by Seidenberg and Tanenhaus's (1979) derive from the processing of an initial stimulus. Many strategies are available to participants in such a situation, allowing a number of alternative explanations for the findings. Ziegler and Ferrand investigated an on-line effect using an auditory lexical decision task. The key variable was whether the target word had only one or multiple possible spellings. That is, as before, because the word TENT has only one way that it could possibly be spelled, its phonology-orthography mapping is referred to as "consistent" while the word GAIN, which could have been spelled GANE, has an "inconsistent" phonology-orthography mapping. The results showed more rapid latencies for consistent words than for inconsistent words. The explanation offered is that words like GAIN, when presented auditorily, activate incorrect orthographies (e.g., GANE) reducing the support the phonological code /gAn/ receives through feedback activation. Thus, its activation is slowed.

## Interactions with Semantics

### Facilitative effects of feedback

To provide a satisfactory explanation of any effect, there needs to be at least an implicit assumption about how an experimental task is performed. More specifically, it is necessary to take a position on what units are important in each task. The following discussion will focus on interactions involving semantic and both orthographic and phonological units. We have argued that the interaction between semantics and orthography manifests itself in effects in lexical decision (Hino & Lupker, 1996; Pexman &

Lupker, 1999), whereas the interaction between semantics and phonology manifests itself in effects in naming (e.g., Hino & Lupker, 1996; Pexman, Lupker, & Reggin, 2002). In short, the process of making a lexical decision is driven mainly by activity within the orthographic units, while the naming task is mainly based on activity within the phonological units.

The first effect to be discussed is the ambiguity effect in lexical decision. The standard finding is that words with more than one meaning (e.g., BANK) have shorter latencies than words with a single meaning (e.g., EVENT – Borowsky & Masson, 1996; Hino & Lupker, 1996; Hino, Lupker, & Pexman, 2002; Hino, Lupker, Sears, & Ogawa, 1998; Jastrzembski, 1981; Jastrzembski & Stanners, 1975; Kellas, Ferraro, & Simpson, 1988; Millis & Button, 1989; Pexman & Lupker, 1999; Rubenstein, Garfield, & Millikan, 1970; Rubenstein, Lewis, & Rubenstein, 1971b). This result has a ready explanation in terms of feedback. An ambiguous word has a single set of orthographic units linked to multiple semantic units. When these semantic units are activated, they provide feedback to the correct set of orthographic units, supporting and increasing their activation. As a result, activation rises faster in the units of ambiguous words, producing an ambiguity advantage. A similar expectation holds for the naming task. That is, higher levels of semantic activation provide increased activation from the semantic units to the phonological units. As a result, naming latencies should be shorter for ambiguous words. Again, this result seems to hold (Gottlob, Goldinger, Stone, & Van Orden, 1999; Hino & Lupker, 1996; Hino et al., 2002; Hino et al., 1998; Lichacz, Herdman, LeFevre, & Baird, 1999; Rodd, 2004; although see Borowsky & Masson, 1996).

These effects are based on a many (sets) to one (set) feedback relationship from semantics to either orthography or phonology. However, any variable that affects the semantic richness of concepts (i.e., the amount of activity created at the semantic level) should produce a processing advantage in both lexical decision and naming tasks. For example, words that are highly imageable are assumed to have a richer semantic representation than low-imageable words, and, thus, there should be a processing advantage for such items. (Although a distinction can be made between the concepts of imageabilty and concreteness, the distinction seems somewhat artificial.) In fact, a processing advantage for more highly imageable low-frequency words has been consistently found in lexical decision tasks (e.g., Bleasdale, 1987; de Groot, 1989; James, 1975; Kroll & Merves, 1986). (See Schwanenflugel, Harnishfeger, & Stowe, 1988, for an argument that the active semantic variable here is better described as "context availability" rather than imageability/ concreteness.) More recently, similar effects have been found in naming in both English (Cortese, Simpson, & Woolsey, 1997; Strain, Patterson, & Seidenberg, 1995) and Persian (Baluch & Besner, 2001), but again only for the more slowly processed words (cf. Ellis & Monaghan, 2002).

The reason that these effects tend to be restricted to words of low frequency is that low-frequency words are processed more slowly and feedback operations take time. A set of orthographic units must begin to be activated, the activation has to flow forward to the semantic units, a set of semantic units must be activated and, finally, activation has to feed back to the orthographic units (in lexical decision) or forward to the phonological units (in naming) soon enough to actually have an impact. Thus, only words that are more difficult to process would be expected to show an effect.

Pexman, Lupker, and Hino (2002) provided another examination of these ideas by selecting two sets of words that differed in semantic features. This was done using norms for 190 concepts that McRae et al. (1997) derived by asking participants to list the "physical (perceptual) properties . . . functional properties . . . and encyclopaedic facts" (p. 104) for those concepts. The prediction was that words with more features (a richer semantic representation) should produce more activation flowing from semantics to both the orthographic and phonological units. In line with this prediction, Pexman et al. (2002) found that words with more semantic features produced shorter latencies in both lexical decision and naming tasks.

A final point to make is that this type of framework also provides a rather straightforward explanation for semantic priming effects (Meyer & Schvaneveldt, 1971; Neely, 1977, 1991). Feedback activation from the prime's semantic units goes not only to the prime's orthographic units but also to any orthographic units connected to those same semantic units. Thus, the orthographic units for DOG will be partially activated by the prime CAT. As a result, if DOG is presented as a target, activation of its orthographic units will reach the necessary threshold more rapidly. This type of explanation is not very different from that offered by classic "spreading-activation" models that were based on the assumption that words are represented as lexical units (e.g., Collins & Loftus, 1975). In such models, the presentation of CAT as the prime causes activation to spread from its semantic representation to the semantic representation for DOG and then back to the lexical unit for DOG, making DOG easier to process. As noted earlier, however, this type of idea differs noticeably from the explanations offered by Masson (1991, 1995), Cree et al. (1999), Plaut (1995b), Plaut & Booth (2000), and McRae et al. (1997). In these accounts, semantic priming is due to the fact that the prime establishes a position in semantic space by activating a set of semantic units similar to those of the target. Moving from the activation pattern created by the prime to that created by the target is then easier if the target and prime are related (and, hence, share semantic units) than if they are not.

An explanation of semantic priming based on changing activation patterns in semantic space (like those proposed by Masson, 1991, 1995, and others) is only a viable explanation, however, if it is assumed that responses in both lexical decision and naming tasks are based on the results of semantic processing (i.e., the time it takes for the system to settle at the semantic level). This seems to be an unlikely assumption, particularly when one considers the naming task. Rather, a feedback explanation would seem to be a more parsimonious explanation for the effects of semantic priming in both tasks (also see Becker, Moscovitch, Behrmann, & Joordens, 1997, and Cree et al., 1999, for the argument that explanations based on changing position in semantic space are more applicable to semantically based tasks).

## Inhibitory effects of feedback

To this point, discussion of the interaction between semantics and orthography or semantics and phonology has been noticeably different from the discussion of the interaction between phonology and orthography. In the one case, the argument has been that a richer semantic representation creates stronger feedback to a single set of orthographic or phonological units, producing more rapid processing. In the other case, the argument has been that a single phonological representation feeds activation to two sets of orthographic units, producing competition and, hence, a processing cost. Both of these predictions are based on the nature of the links between units and the presumed nature of the processing required for the task (e.g., an evaluation of orthographic codes in lexical decision). However, there is nothing special about these particular links. Any linkages between units allow for an analysis and predictions.

The type of relationship between orthography and phonology that produces a homophone effect (i.e., two sets of orthographic units are linked to one set of phonological units) has a parallel in the relationship between orthography and semantics and in the relationship between phonology and semantics. In particular, when considering words that have synonyms, there are two sets of orthographic (phonological) units being mapped into one set of semantic units. Thus, when that set of semantic units is activated, it will feed activation back not only to the correct set of orthographic (phonological) units but also to the set of orthographic (phonological) units appropriate to the synonym, producing a competition. The prediction is that there should be a processing cost in both lexical decision and naming. The results in both Dutch (Pecher, 2001) and Japanese Katakana (Hino et al., 2002) support this prediction.

## Two Other Emerging Issues

### Representing ambiguous words

As Joordens and Besner (1994) note, models based on distributed representations make a clear prediction about the semantic processing of ambiguous words. They predict that there will be competition at the semantic level between the sets of units for the different meanings, producing a processing cost. Thus, ambiguous words should be more difficult to process than unambiguous words, completely the opposite of what is typically reported in lexical decision and naming experiments (Borowsky & Masson, 1996; Gottlob et al., 1999; Hino & Lupker, 1996; Hino et al., 1998; Hino et al., 2002; Jastrzembski, 1981; Jastrzembski & Stanners, 1975; Kellas et al., 1988; Lichacz et al., 1999; Millis & Button, 1989; Pexman & Lupker, 1999; Rubenstein et al., 1970; Rubenstein et al., 1971b). When considering just these two tasks, a feedback explanation within a PDP framework gets around the problem if one assumes that lexical decision responses are based on activity at the orthographic level and naming responses are based on activity at the phonological level. Thus, semantic level competition has little impact in either task (see also Borowsky & Masson, 1996, and Kawamoto, Farrar, & Kello, 1994, for other ways of addressing this problem). The question still lingers, however, as to whether there is any behavioural evidence for this rather key prediction of PDP models.

There are now three sets of results in the literature supporting this prediction. First, Rayner and colleagues (e.g., Duffy, Morris, & Rayner, 1988; Rayner & Duffy, 1986) reported that in some circumstances, ambiguous words receive longer fixations. Second, Gottlob et al. (1999) and Piercey and Joordens (2000) have reported an ambiguity disadvantage in a relatedness-judgment task in that subjects found it more difficult to decide that a word (e.g., MONEY) was related to an ambiguous word (e.g., BANK) than to an unambiguous word (e.g., DOLLAR). Finally, Hino et al. (2002) have shown that ambiguous words take longer to classify (on negative trials) in a semantic categorization task (i.e., BANK – is it a living thing?).

On closer inspection, however, this evidence appears to be quite weak. As Duffy et al. (1988) note, their results are perfectly compatible with a decision-based explanation. That is, it is possible that all meanings of the ambiguous word are activated simultaneously (and without competition) and that the delay in gaze duration is due to the time taken to select the intended meaning for the sentence. In a similar vein, the effects reported by Gottlob et al. (1999) and Piercey and Joordens (2000) can be explained by assuming that all meanings of the ambiguous words are activated without competition but there is then a competition between response tendencies. When the stimulus is MONEY–BANK, the financial meaning of BANK produces a drive to respond "yes" (the correct response), while the river meaning of BANK produces a drive to respond "no." Indeed, recent work by Pexman, Hino, and Lupker (2004) has shown that when there is no response competition, there is no effect. That is, when the correct response is "no" (e.g., TREE–BANK vs. TREE–DOLLAR), there is no ambiguity disadvantage. Finally, Hino et al.'s (2002) effect in the semantic categorization task has been shown to be category dependent. That is, it arises when the category is broad (e.g., living things) but not when the category is narrow (e.g., animals, vegetables) (Forster, 1999; Hino, Lupker, & Pexman, 2001). These results also point toward a decision-based, rather than a semantic-processing, explanation.

One issue that might be relevant here is that there are essentially two types of ambiguous words (see Klein & Murphy, 2001, 2002). One type is words that have completely unrelated meanings; for example, BANK. The fact that this word has at least two meanings – 'a place where you keep your money and the edge of a river' is an accident of history. These types of words are called *homonyms* and, presumably, the various meanings are represented separately in semantic memory. There are also words that have multiple senses that have evolved from a single meaning; for example, the word BELT. The fact that this word means 'the strip of material that you have around your waist', 'a thin area of land', 'a hard blow', and 'a drink of an alcoholic beverage' is not an accident of history. These senses all evolved from the basic meaning of BELT. These types of words are called *polysemous* and the different senses may not be represented separately in semantic memory. If so, there could be different processing implications for the two word types; in particular, only homonyms may produce any real competition during semantic processing.

Klein and Murphy (2001, 2002) examined the question of how different senses of a word are represented in memory using their "sensicality judgement" task. In this task subjects see adjective-noun pairs, like SHREDDED PAPER, and their task is to decide whether this combination of words makes sense. Klein and Murphy reported that participants were much faster and more accurate in responding to the second of two adjacent word pairs when the two pairs tapped the same sense of the polysemous noun (e.g., WRAPPING PAPER followed by SHREDDED PAPER) than when the two pairs tapped different senses of the polysemous noun (e.g., DAILY PAPER followed by SHREDDED PAPER). A similar pattern emerged when they considered homonyms. That is, participants were faster and more accurate in responding to the second word pair when the pairs tapped the same meaning of the noun (e.g., COMMERCIAL BANK followed by SAVINGS BANK) than when the pairs tapped different meanings of the noun (e.g., CREEK BANK followed by SAVINGS BANK). Based on these results, Klein and Murphy suggested that the separate senses of polysemous words appear to be represented separately in semantic memory and, in fact, they are represented essentially the same way that the separate meanings of homonyms are.

In contrast, Azuma and Van Orden (1997) and Rodd, Gaskell, and Marslen-Wilson (2002) have argued that there is an important distinction between homonyms and poly-semous words that has processing implications for lexical decision tasks. Rodd et al. selected a set of words in which the number of senses (few vs. many) varied orthogonally with the number of meanings (one vs. more than one). Although words with multiple senses showed shorter latencies than words with few senses (in line with previous research), words with multiple meanings produced slightly longer latencies than words with one meaning, although this effect was quite small and nonsignificant. Further, these results only emerged when the nonwords were pseudohomophones (as did the relevant results in Azuma and Van Orden's, 1997, experiments). If a number of assumptions are made about how participants perform the lexical decision task, Rodd et al.'s inhibitory effect of mul-tiple meanings supports the PDP model prediction about the semantic processing of ambiguous words. However, their findings have not yet proved replicable (Hino & Lupker, 2003; Hino et al., 2001; Pexman, Hino, & Lupker, 2002) and there appears to be no other example of an ambiguity disadvantage of this sort ever reported in the literature.

## Prelexical coding

So far, little has been said about the nature of the prelexical code that is used to access the core components of the word recognition system. Indeed, research on this issue is sparse. In all of the models that exist as simulations, assumptions about this code have had to be made. Even in those situations, however, the assumptions have been driven mainly by modeling convenience. Nonetheless, as Andrews (1997) has argued, these assumptions are important. For example, most models are based on the idea that this code allows at least partial activation of all word units in which the orthography is similar to what is contained in this code. In order to produce legitimate simulations of the word recognition process, it is necessary to specify which set of words is activated in this fashion and to what degree. A second, more concrete, example of why this is important is the fact that it was a change in the assumptions about the orthographic codes that the prelex-ical code contacts that allowed Plaut et al.'s (1996) model to account for the nonword naming data that Seidenberg and McClelland's (1989) model could not. The nature of the prelexical code is, of course, constrained by the nature of the orthographic code because the only purpose of the former is to activate the latter.

Most of the standard models of word recognition (e.g., Grainger & Jacobs, 1996; McClelland & Rumelhart, 1981; Paap et al., 1982) assume a "channel specific" coding scheme for the prelexical code. That is, each letter in a word is immediately assigned to a channel and then identified within that channel. So, when SALT is being read, there would be some activation of word units for HALT, MALT, WALT, SILT, and SALE, those words overlapping in three of the four channels, but much less, if any, activation of SENT, SLAT and SAT. However, extant evidence, suggests that this assumption is incorrect. Humphreys, Evett, and Quinlan (1990), for example, have shown that shorter letter strings can prime longer words (e.g., oitk–WHITE) in a masked prime, perceptual identification task (see also Perea & Carreiras, 1998; and de Moor & Brysbaert, 2000). Such effects have forced researchers, more recently, to adopt "relative-position" coding schemes (e.g., Coltheart et al., 2001); however, the problem does not appear to be fully solved even with those schemes. For example, data suggest that letter strings containing transposed letters (i.e., SALT–SLAT) are actually more similar to one another than letter strings matching in N-1 positions (e.g., SALT–HALT). For example, transposed letter nonwords (e.g., JUGDE) are harder to reject than one-letter different nonwords (e.g., JUDPE) or control nonwords (e.g., SLINT) in lexical decision tasks (Andrews, 1996; Chambers, 1979; Holmes & Ng, 1993). In addition, Forster et al. (1987) showed that masked priming effects for transposed letter primes (e.g., anwser–ANSWER) were as large as those for repetition primes (e.g., answer–ANSWER) and larger than those for one-letter different primes (e.g., antwer–ANSWER). Finally, Perea and Lupker (2003) have reported significant facilitation in a masked semantic priming experiment with transposed letter primes (e.g., jugde–COURT) and little, if any, priming with one letter different primes (e.g., judpe–COURT) (although see Bourassa & Besner, 1998, for a demonstration that these latter effects can become significant if the experiment has enough power). Taken together, these results suggest that, for example, the letter string JUGDE has more potential to activate the lexical structures for the word JUDGE than the nonword JUDPE does, a conclusion that is quite inconsistent with the assumptions of virtually all of the models of word recognition discussed in this chapter. Future empirical work should be directed at a better understanding of the nature of these prelexical codes (see e.g. Davis, 1999, Ratcliff, 1981, and Whitney, 2001, for some possibilities) and that knowledge should then be used to modify current models.

## Parting Thoughts

Since the early 1970s, tremendous strides have been made in terms of understanding the visual word recognition process. A major trend that has emerged during this time period has been a movement toward word recognition models that assume considerable interactivity among the various types of lexical and semantic structures. This is not to suggest that the more autonomous conceptualizations of word recognition, such as those described in the search models, can never make a comeback. Nor is it to deny that certain local components of the word recognition system may work on more autonomous principles (e.g., the establishment of prelexical codes; see Norris et al., 2000). The picture is far from complete and future work is likely to capitalize on insights not only from experimental cognitive psychology but also from the neuroscientific study of reading development and reading disorders.

## Note

Much of the author's research discussed in this chapter was supported by Natural Sciences and Engineering Research Council of Canada Grant A6333. I would like to thank Penny Pexman, Yasushi Hino, Manuel Perea, and Sachiko Kinoshita for their splendid contributions to that research and for their comments on earlier drafts of the chapter. I would also like to thank Ken Forster and Ken Paap for their helpful comments on sections of this chapter in which their models were discussed.

# 4

# The Question of Phonology and Reading

## Guy C. Van Orden and Heidi Kloos

Picture a 6-year-old puzzling out the printed word *island*. For this child, the printed form of the word is not entirely familiar and requires effortful decoding. First the child says /i . . . i/, then /iz/, then /land/, then /iz land/, and all of a sudden she gets it right: she correctly reads *island* aloud. English is notorious for words like *island*, with spellings that only partly reveal how they are spoken. Nonetheless, the way a word is spelled almost always reveals something of how to say it aloud, something of its phonology. This fact illustrates the alphabetic principle, which has long lead scientists to wonder about the role of phonology in reading. For instance, does a printed word's phonology play a role in deriving meaning from the word?

A central question of reading is whether understanding individual written words always depends upon prior access to their phonology: Do mental representations of phonology mediate the comprehension of written words? This question is based on the idea that reading can be taken apart as the links of a chain of mental events. Think again of the 6-year-old child and the word *island*. Reading *island* aloud, the effect, seems to depend on an intermediate representation of *island*'s phonology, its cause. Presented with the visual stimulus *island*, the child's mind first forms a representation of the word's spelling. The spelling representation will be decoded, or puzzled out, to create a representation of phonology. In turn, the mental representation of *island*'s phonology activates the motor program of its pronunciation, and the child says *island* aloud.

The child portrayed as reading *island* aloud illustrates the classic view of stimulus → mediating representations → response: the idea of a causal chain between the stimulus word *island* and its pronunciation. It is from this vantage point that the question of phonology and reading is posed. Both the printed word *island* and *island*'s pronunciation appear in some sense to be outside the child's head, but she constructs phonology inside her head. Phonology is intermediate, both in the sense of a middle position in time or space and in the sense of a mental causal link between the printed word and its pronunciation (cf. Fodor, 1981; Kihlstrom, 1987; Markman & Dietrich, 2000).

Debate about whether comprehension of individual words requires intermediate phonology began in the nineteenth century and continues today. But decisive evidence, one way or the other, has eluded reading scientists. This chapter uses examples of the conflicting evidence to understand why the evidence has failed to settle the debate. The first half of this chapter describes homophone studies and priming studies. Both kinds of studies discover phonology effects that are contingent on task demands. They illustrate how task contingent evidence, instead of settling the debate, simply fuels it. The second half of the chapter describes evidence of a complex interaction between printed and spoken language. Complex interactions could explain why previous evidence was so sensitive to task demands.

## How Evidence Fuels the Controversy

Do representations of phonology mediate comprehension in skilled reading? An influential theory – the dual-process theory – defined itself in an answer to this question. Proposed by Marshall and Newcombe (1973) and refined by Coltheart (1978), this important theory set the stage for a contemporary science of reading (see Van Orden, Pennington, & Stone, 1990, 2001, for reviews).

### Dual-process theory

As the name suggests, dual-process theory includes two processes by which words can be identified in reading. One process involves rules for how to map elements of spelling onto elements of phonology. This process parses a word's string of letters into its elementary units of spelling, called graphemes. Then grapheme–phoneme rules are applied to map graphemes onto elementary units of phonology, called phonemes. Finally, the phonemes are combined to form a representation of the word's phonology, which can pick the word out in a phonological lexicon.

The other process is called direct access. Direct access takes a visual representation of the word as input and assigns it to an abstract placeholder in the mental lexicon. Identification of a word happens in one step going from a visual representation to an entry in the mental lexicon. It is called direct access because it creates a shortcut that bypasses the grapheme–phoneme rules. To link each word's visual representation to a lexical entry requires word-by-word associations. The links develop as a reader becomes familiar with words.

The two processes, grapheme–phoneme rules and direct access, should distinguish between skilled and unskilled readers. An unskilled reader should identify words by applying grapheme–phoneme rules, like a child who has just learned to read. Skilled readers should bypass grapheme–phoneme rules as direct access becomes available. Skilled readers should only use grapheme–phoneme rules when they confront an unfamiliar word such as *pharisee* (Doctor & Coltheart, 1980).

In this dual-process view, learning to read depends crucially on learning the alphabetic principle, of which grapheme–phoneme rules is one hypothetical approximation. Skilled reading, in contrast, is predicted to occur without mediating phonology. Evidence from homophone errors and priming studies does not corroborate this clear-cut prediction, but neither is the prediction ruled out, as explained next.

## Homophone errors

In a semantic categorization task, a homophone target such as *break* is sometimes miscategorized as a *part of a car* (Van Orden, 1987). This error stems from the fact that *break* shares identical phonology with *brake*. At face value, such homophone errors clearly demonstrate mediating phonology; words are confused because they share the same phonology.

Dual-process theory predicted that skilled readers would read familiar words via direct access. Yet skilled readers make homophone errors to homophone words irrespective of their familiarity. Homophone errors are no less likely when frequently read homophones like *break* appear as targets than when targets are relatively unfamiliar homophones, like *peek* for the category *part of a mountain*. Insensitivity to word familiarity would appear to falsify the direct-access hypothesis of skilled reading, but the story is not that simple.

If a categorization task includes more broadly specified categories such as *object*, then familiar homophone targets such as *break* produce no more errors than control items (Jared & Seidenberg, 1991; Van Orden, Holden, Podgornik, & Aitchison, 1999). Familiarity now matters. Semantic categorization to broadly specified categories produces homophone errors to low frequency homophones like *peek* but not to high frequency homophones like *break*. This finding is inconsistent with the previous results, but consistent with the direct-access hypothesis. Direct-access should be available for words that are frequently read and direct access would preclude homophone errors.

On the basis of homophone errors' absence, one could argue that the readers are not using phonology (Jared & Seidenberg, 1991). That is, the null effect of homophone phonology, when familiar homophones are judged against broadly specified categories, could imply that no phonology link exists in this case. If so, then the link between phonology and comprehension of printed words is at best partial and certainly not obligatory for skilled readers.

This logic may seem too arbitrary or simplistic. Too many reasonable alternatives present themselves for how a change in task demands may eliminate a phonology effect but not eliminate phonology (Bosman & de Groot, 1996; Lesch & Pollatsek, 1993). For example, the effects of phonology as a cause of homophone word comprehension may be concealed in contexts where performance rises to ceiling, as it usually does to highly familiar words (Lukatela & Turvey, 1994a; Van Orden et al., 1999). Perhaps overly familiar homophone words are coded too efficiently to reveal a phonology effect under the conditions of the broadly specified categories (cf. Unsworth & Pexman, 2003). Or perhaps phonology interacts in complex ways with task demands and other sources of information and the question is altogether too simply framed (Van Orden, Holden, & Turvey, 2003).

Clearly, the evidence provided by homophone errors leaves the causal status of phonology as a mediator between print and meaning undecided. As a consequence, homophone errors do not answer the question of phonology and reading to the satisfaction of all reading scientists. Special circumstances of task demands are required to produce homophone errors to familiar homophones. But a phonology effect based on special circumstance is not persuasive; it will not dissuade scientists who trust the direct-access hypothesis. In the same vein, special circumstances of task demands are required to make homophone errors go missing, and the consequent null phonology effect will not dissuade scientists who trust that reading includes mediating phonology.

## Priming studies

The direct-access hypothesis has a constant traveling companion: the assumption that mediating phonology is delayed with respect to direct access (as Frost, 1998, points out; however, see Paap, Noel, & Johansen, 1992). According to this assumption, word identification via an assembly process of grapheme–phoneme rules takes more time than the direct visual associations of direct lexical access. Thus, for example, skilled readers may not base their response in a lexical decision task on phonology representations because direct access recognizes a familiar word, as a word, prior to assembly of phonology. Perhaps studies that address the delayed-phonology hypothesis may decide the status of phonology in reading.

How soon after seeing a printed word does phonology become available? One way to answer this question is with a combination of backward masking and priming. Masking concerns the length of time that items are visible. Priming concerns how one letter string may affect another, how a prime such as *REEZ* may affect identification of a target such as *rose*, for instance. The target word *rose* appears for a fraction of a second before it is replaced by the prime *REEZ*. *REEZ* serves as a mask of *rose* because it limits the amount of time available to derive *rose* phonology, and it serves as a prime because it shares partial phonology with *rose*, the consonants /r..z/. The prime *REEZ* itself is also briefly presented before being replaced by a visual pattern mask such as #####. The pattern mask ends visibility of *REEZ*. Backward masking strictly limits the time that *rose* and *REEZ* are visible, which limits the time available to derive phonology. If phonology becomes available rapidly, then the interaction of *REEZ* and *rose* phonology should benefit identification of *rose*, compared to a control condition.

The backward priming paradigm revealed that phonology is available very soon after seeing a word. Berent and Perfetti (1995) demonstrated that consonant phonology of pseudoword primes such as *REEZ* is available 20–40 ms after the pseudoword becomes visible (cf. Lee, Rayner, & Pollatsek, 2001; Perry & Ziegler, 2002; but cf. Lukatela & Turvey, 2000). Colombo, Zorzi, Cubelli, and Brivio (2003) established that both consonant and vowel phonology of printed Italian are available under the same conditions of brief visibility. And Lukatela, Frost, and Turvey (1998) demonstrated that the phonology of pseudohomophones such as *KLIP* is available within a 29 ms window of visibility (see also Berent & Van Orden, 2000, 2003; Lee, Rayner, & Pollatsek, 1999; Perfetti, Bell, & Delaney, 1988; Rayner, Sereno, Lesch, & Pollatsek, 1995; Xu & Perfetti, 1999).

Rapidly available phonology is at least consistent with the possibility that phonology is a mediating cause in word comprehension (Frost, 1998; see also Frost, this volume).

Yet it is one thing to demonstrate that phonology is rapidly available and another thing to demonstrate that phonology has priority over direct access. Ziegler, Ferrand, Jacobs, Rey, and Grainger (2000) conducted an incremental priming study to explore the latter issue. Incremental priming allows a continuous manipulation of how one letter-string may affect another, how a prime nonword may affect a target word, for instance. The beauty of incremental priming is its precise control over when primes are available. The duration or intensity of priming words can be changed incrementally from a range in which primes do not benefit the identification of target words to a range in which they do. This adds a dimension of control that is missing in most other priming studies (Jacobs, Grainger, & Ferrand, 1995).

Ziegler and his colleagues examined the relative priority of phonology versus direct access using forward masking and they conducted the experiment in French. Forward masking rearranges the order of events compared to backward masking. A forward-masking trial briefly presents a mask (#####), which is quickly replaced by a prime, which is in turn replaced quickly by a target word. The target word remains visible until the participant responds.

The experimental manipulation consisted of three priming conditions that differ in similarity between prime and target. In one condition the primes were similar to targets in spelling and identical to targets in French phonology (e.g., pseudohomophone *nert* for target word *NERF*). This condition was called the O+P+ [O plus, P plus]condition, O+ implying similar orthography between prime and target, and P+ implying similar phonology. Their second condition O−P+ [O minus, P plus]presented primes that were dissimilar in spelling but identical in phonology (e.g., pseudohomophone *nair* for target *NERF*). And their third condition O+P− presented primes that were similar to targets in spelling but dissimilar in phonology (e.g., nonword *narf* for target *NERF*).

In all three prime conditions, lexical decisions to targets showed facilitation from priming compared to a no-prime control condition. A facilitation effect equals the degree to which the prime reduces the latency of the target "word" decision-time, compared to a baseline. In the facilitation calculus of Ziegler et al. (2000), the slower response time in the O−P+ condition minus the faster response time in the O+P+ condition estimates the facilitation effect of spelling similarity – the direct access effect. Likewise, O+P− minus O+P+ estimates facilitation due to similar phonology – the mediating phonology effect.

With a prime duration of 29 ms, the facilitation calculus revealed a greater magnitude of facilitation due to similar spelling compared to facilitation due to similar phonology. Similar spelling outdid similar phonology and so direct access must have priority over mediated access from phonology (see also Ferrand & Grainger, 1992, 1993, 1994). Other studies using masking and priming paradigms have found comparable patterns that sometimes include null effects of similar phonology, which seems to reinforce the case for priority of direct access (Brysbaert & Praet, 1992; Davis, Castles, & Iakovidis, 1998; Shen & Forster, 1999; Verstaen, Humphreys, Olson, & D'Ydewalle, 1995). Again however the story is not so simple; the pattern of facilitation changes if a different task is used.

In a comparable word naming study, Ziegler et al. (2000) observed results that contradict the pattern from lexical decision. In word naming, similar phonology appears to outdo similar spelling at all prime durations and the pattern becomes statistically reliable at a prime duration of 42 ms (see also Montant & Ziegler, 2001). In this case, the results suggest that mediated access from phonology has priority over direct access. So which task demands are most comparable to the demands of natural skilled reading – forward masking or backward masking, 29 ms or 42 ms, lexical decision or naming, or none of the above? The story only gets murkier. How one may interpret Ziegler et al.'s (2000) lexical decision results rests on debatable assumptions about similarity and activation, and a possible confound, which is discussed next.

The facilitation logic depends on whether similarity has been straightforwardly added in or subtracted out of relations between primes and targets. This may not be the case for the O+P– lexical decision primes. The O+P– condition was supposed to entail a reduction in similar phonology between primes and targets compared to the O+P+ condition. The contrast between the conditions was meant to isolate the facilitation due to the more similar phonology of the O+P+ condition: O+P– response times minus O+P+ response times estimated facilitation due to more similar phonology. However, in the O+P– "priming condition the consonantal skeleton is typically maintained"; for example *n..rf – N..RF* (Ziegler et al., 2000, p. 687). This creates a confound whereby O+P– and O+P+ priming can be almost identical at very short prime durations. As a consequence, the magnitude of facilitation due to similar phonology is systematically underestimated.

Consonant phonology is more quickly available than vowel phonology in languages with predominantly ambiguous vowel spellings (Berent & Perfetti, 1995; Lee et al., 2001; Perry & Ziegler, 2002). The earliest moments of activation emphasize reliable correspondences between consonant spelling and phonology, and the O+P– primes share these reliable correspondences with their targets. This means that O+P– primes are comparable to the O+P+ primes in their potential for facilitation in the earliest moments of activation. As a consequence, phonology priming is underestimated at the shortest prime durations, such as the 29 ms duration. The contrasted conditions O+P– versus O+P+ could only be expected to diverge at longer prime durations, as vowel phonology comes into play. This confound undermines the contrast in the 29 ms condition that seemed to favor similar spelling over similar phonology. The confound renders the lexical decision outcome equivocal; it no longer favors direct access.

Priming manipulations that contrast degrees of similarity are often problematic. How does one discount the similarity in phonology that is inherent when items are similar in spelling? Some accounts claim that the first instants of word comprehension include multiply active patterns of phonology that, over time, settle into a single pattern (e.g., Kawamoto & Zemblidge, 1992; Van Orden et al., 1990; Van Orden & Goldinger, 1994). Consequently, items such as *plaid* and *plain* would activate virtually identical "clouds" of phonology in the first milliseconds, but they are not identical in spelling and do not settle into the same phonology. Other accounts assume that the first milliseconds of word comprehension include incompletely specified phonology. This assumption also allows that similar spellings may activate identical phonology at the outset of word comprehension (e.g., Berent & Perfetti, 1995; Frost, 1998).

Finally, how does one insure that similarity along a phonology dimension is ever comparable in magnitude to similarity along a spelling dimension? Do null effects of similar phonology stem from weak manipulations of similarity? Sometimes yes; other times nobody knows (Frost, Ahissar, Gotesman, & Tayeb, 2003). Again, how one interprets the idiosyncratic task conditions that produce the evidence determines how one interprets the evidence, and there are inestimable degrees of freedom for interpretation of task demands. Like homophone errors, the evidence from masked priming studies leaves the causal status of phonology representations in skilled reading undecided. Some special task demands yield reliable effects of phonology variables, and others do not.

## Giving Up Ether

Ideally, robust phonology effects would be found in all laboratory reading contexts. Ideally, laboratory methods should reveal a blueprint of reading that is independent of the laboratory tools used in the investigation. With respect to this ideal, a phonology effect that cuts across all reading contexts would satisfy the requirements (Jacobs & Grainger, 1994). Mediating phonology would then become an accepted component in the architecture of word comprehension. But so far no one has discovered a generally robust phonology effect in skilled reading, as the previous sections illustrate. The consequence is a perennial debate about phonology and reading.

Homophone errors and priming studies illustrate why the question of phonology has not found a satisfactory answer. Evidence that favors phonology is the product of special task demands, and evidence that favors direct access is also the product of special task demands. Idiosyncratic findings from idiosyncratic task conditions simply fuel the long-standing controversy about phonology and reading (cf. Frost, 1998; Pollatsek & Rayner, 2003; Van Orden et al., 1999; 2001). And yet, although no particular phonology effect can be found to familiar words in all contexts, a phonology effect of some kind can be found in most contexts. In some cases, the task contexts that yield a null effect of one phonology variable also yield a positive effect of a different phonology variable (Berent, 1997; Berent & Van Orden, 2003). Thus neither direct access nor mediating phonology can claim unequivocal empirical support.

The dilemma that phonology effects present leaves the contest between mediating phonology versus direct access in stalemate. As a consequence, the question of whether phonology mediates comprehension in reading is never answered to the satisfaction of reading scientists. Capricious phonology effects do not dissuade scientists who believe that skilled reading is a visual process of direct access (e.g., Coltheart, 2000; Daneman & Reingold, 2000; Davis et al., 1998; Shen & Forster, 1999; Verstaen et al., 1995). Null effects do not dissuade scientists who believe that reading is a linguistic process that includes mediating phonology (e.g., Frost, 1998; Liberman, 1992, 1999; Lukatela & Turvey, 1998; Rayner, Pollatsek, & Binder, 1998).

One idea about how to resolve the dilemma would be to add more factors into the equation. Plausibly, reading scientists could isolate factors such as task demands or participant strategies. However, simply manipulating more factors to collect more data is likely to further complicate matters, as more and higher-order interactions with context arise (Gibbs & Van Orden, 1998; Stone & Van Orden, 1993; Van Orden et al., 1999,

2001). If all factors interact, then attempts to isolate any single factor will meet the same fate as phonology factors.

Perhaps another way can be found around the stalemate, one that circumvents the conventional reductive logic that guides mechanistic explanations. It may help to look elsewhere, to other science that has successfully abandoned mechanistic explanation, science that has already confronted and moved past a comparable dilemma. For example, the present dilemma of reading scientists is analogous to the dilemma of nineteenth-century physicists concerning the concept of ether. Ether, at that time, defined an absolute frame of reference for all movement. To sustain this belief physicists accumulated many ad hoc assumptions. To explain why ether's motion does not disturb matter, they assumed that ether does not interact with matter. But to explain why the velocity of light changes when it passes through glass or water, they were forced to assume that ether does interact with matter. "In other words, there is an interaction between ether and matter in optical phenomena, but none in mechanical phenomena! This is certainly a very paradoxical conclusion!" (Einstein & Infeld, 1938, p. 120).

For reading scientists a context independent architecture of reading takes the role of ether, and task demands take the role of matter. When reliable phonology effects are observed, pro-phonology scientists assume the architecture of reading did not interact with task demands. But to explain null effects of phonology, the architecture must have interacted with task demands, which concealed the effects of phonology. Anti-phonology reading scientists accumulate inverted assumptions. When null phonology effects are observed, then the architecture of direct access did not interact with task demands. But to explain positive effects of phonology, the architecture of reading must have interacted with task demands, which produced the sham phonology effects. Both camps resemble nineteenth-century physicists in their paradoxical conclusions about reading and task demands.

One hundred years of stalemate warrants rethinking the traditional assumptions about reading. The assumptions are in conflict with actual reading phenomena. Phonology factors interact with other word factors and their pattern of interaction changes with changing task demands. All effects of all reading factors are in motion, so to speak, with respect to each other and with respect to the task contexts in which they are observed. One may take this flexible catalog of interaction effects at face value – no absolute frame of reference presents itself. Reading scientists may follow the lead of physicists and give up altogether a baseless idea of an absolute frame of reference.

## Summary and conclusion

The role of phonology in skilled reading remains unclear. Looking across this now vast literature, the appearance and disappearance of phonology effects does not divide neatly among processes of word comprehension. The appearance and disappearance of phonology effects are only captured in reliable high-order interactions among reading histories of participants, word factors, and the special circumstances of task demands. Apparent phonology effects and other reading effects are context sensitive by their very nature. Such context sensitivity is symptomatic of complex interactive systems. The next sections review evidence that more pointedly suggests that phonology and other processes always join in a complex interaction.

## Spelling and Phonology in an Interactive System

The role of phonology in skilled reading can be considered in terms of interactive processes. The question is now asked with respect to variables that modulate the performance of an interactive system, rather than with respect to isolated causal factors. One prominent variable is ambiguity.

Notice how many ways the same ambiguous phoneme /eɪ/ can be spelled in *Kay*, *weigh*, *made*, and *pail*, or how many ways the same ambiguous vowel spelling *ai* can be pronounced in *plaid*, *raid*, *said*, and *aisle*. Such ambiguity has consequences for performance. For instance, if a presented spelling can be pronounced in more than one way, then it yields a slower naming time compared to an unambiguous spelling, all other things equal.

Ambiguity is not your standard causal factor. Ambiguity effects cannot be localized in spelling or phonology taken separately. Ambiguity is only defined in a relation between the two. Thus empirical tests for ambiguity effects are tests about how phonology is related to other aspects of language, such as spelling. The next sections of this chapter describe empirical findings that demonstrate ambiguity effects.

### *Simulations of interactive processes*

Before turning to the experiments, briefly consider some previous simulations of interactive processes. Simulations of interactive processes among spelling, phonology, and semantics have changed the way scientists look at the structure of language (e.g., Grossberg & Stone, 1986; Jacobs, Rey, Ziegler, & Grainger, 1998; Kawamoto & Zemblidge, 1992; Masson, 1995; McClelland & Rumelhart, 1981; Plaut, McClelland, Seidenberg, & Patterson, 1996). They have focused scientists' attention on ambiguity and the statistical structure of language (Plaut et al., 1996; Saffran, 2003; Van Orden et al., 1990), and they introduced the possibility of feedback in word comprehension.

Consider the ambiguous spelling of the homograph word *wind*. *Wind* has two legitimate pronunciations: it can rhyme with *pinned* or *find*. In an interactive model, spelling nodes representing *wind*'s spelling activate nodes that represent the two pronunciations of *wind*, and these two pronunciations both feed back activation to their common spelling. This creates two competing feedback loops, which characterizes how ambiguity is expressed in an interactive model. Ambiguity breeds competition between multiple potential outcomes, which takes time to resolve (see also Lupker, this volume).

Kawamoto and Zemblidge (1992) simulated the competition between homograph pronunciations as it unfolds across a naming trial. The model included feedforward and feedback connections among letter, phoneme, and semantic node families. The connections modulate node activity very roughly as synapses may modulate the activity of neurons. In the Kawamoto and Zemblidge model, connections were excitatory between node families but mostly inhibitory within node families. For instance, letter nodes excite phoneme nodes and phoneme nodes excite letter nodes, but competing phoneme nodes inhibit each other. Consequently, phoneme nodes compete directly with other phoneme nodes and indirectly with letter or semantic nodes. A phoneme node competes indirectly by activating some particular letter or semantic node that can compete directly. Thus every node interacts with every other node, either directly or indirectly.

Simulations have been successful as guides for how to look at language. They are less successful as models of actual psychological processes. Despite highly unintuitive and yet reliable predictions, actual simulations are perpetually challenged by the details of human performance (e.g., Spieler & Balota, 1997; Treiman, Kessler, & Bick, 2003). It is the assumptions behind the simulations that seem to capture a reliable picture of language, but painted in somewhat broad strokes.

## Ambiguity at the scale of whole words

Homographs like *wind* have a dominant pronunciation (the more regular pronunciation that rhymes with *pinned*) and a subordinate pronunciation (the less regular pronunciation that rhymes with *find*). In an actual word naming experiment, some readers will produce the dominant pronunciation and some will produce the subordinate. Also, when the dominant pronunciation is produced, it yields faster naming times, on average, than the subordinate pronunciation. One way to think about this pattern is that the two pronunciations compete in the course of a word naming trial prior to an observed pronunciation.

In a simulated naming trial, *wind*'s subordinate pronunciation is less strongly activated, at least initially, but nevertheless can win the competition. To do so it must accrue sufficient activation, within the time course of the trial, to overcome activation of the dominant pronunciation. This implies an on-line qualitative change from dominant to subordinate phonology. The qualitative change occurs at an exchange point in what is called a bifurcation. Kawamoto and Zemblidge (1992) simulated the bifurcation of a homograph pronunciation, from statistically dominant to subordinate, as a transcritical bifurcation.

The dominant pronunciation of *wind* has a stronger feedback loop between letter and phoneme nodes, a stronger and more stable local attractor. The subordinate pronunciation has the weaker or less stable attractor between letter and phoneme nodes, but has the more stable attractor between phoneme and semantic nodes. The feedback loop between phoneme and semantic nodes takes some time to grow in strength and lend sufficient support to *wind*'s subordinate pronunciation. Enough support makes *wind*'s subordinate pronunciation a winner. This outcome occurs when a reader or model is sufficiently more familiar with the subordinate pronunciation's semantic variants, which counters the inherent disadvantage of the subordinate pronunciation's less-regular relation between spelling and phonology.

Initially *wind* activates the two pronunciation patterns, and the dominant pattern is initially favored. However, slowly accruing activation in a semantic and phoneme feedback loop lends increasing support to the subordinate pronunciation. Within the time of a naming trial, activation in the phoneme-semantic feedback loop grows to a sufficient degree that it turns the tide in the competition. The tide turns at the bifurcation point. Within the time between the appearance of *wind* and a pronunciation, semantic-phoneme activation and the subordinate's letter-phoneme activation overtake the otherwise dominant pronunciation. At the bifurcation point, semantic-phoneme feedback puts *wind*'s subordinate pronunciation over the top, and the dominant pronunciation exchanges stability with the less-regular subordinate pronunciation. Subsequently, the model produces the subordinate pronunciation.

So why do some readers produce the dominant pronunciation and others the subordinate? Different readers, or models, may sample language differently. Each reader has a unique history of covariation among words' spellings, phonology, and semantics. Pronunciations can have strong or weak ties to semantics based on different readers' different familiarity with different words. At any particular time, some readers will quickly produce the dominant more regular pronunciation, and other readers, sufficiently more familiar with subordinate variants, will more slowly produce the subordinate pronunciation.

*Wind*'s homograph spelling is one ambiguous spelling, one pocket of ambiguity, within a reader's accumulated sample of English. Yet *wind* is only ambiguous if that reader's history includes samples of both interpretations of *wind*. A reader's sample of a language delimits the potential for ambiguous or unambiguous relations. The aggregate statistical pattern of relations that makes up a reader's language is specific to the reader's history and changes throughout a lifetime of reading.

## Multiple scales of ambiguity

Homograph ambiguity exists at multiple scales. In a homograph, every letter has associations with different pronunciations. For example, the homograph *wind* is ambiguous at a micro scale because its grapheme *i* is ambiguous. This ambiguity is amplified at a meso scale of *wind*'s ambiguous spelling-body *-ind*, and is further enlarged at a macroscale of the ambiguous whole word. In this way of thinking, local ambiguity is infectious, in a manner of speaking. A local ambiguity, like *wind*'s ambiguous grapheme *i*, infects every larger scale of spelling that has a history of multiple pronunciations.

Words infected with more ambiguity have slower naming times. Compare the homograph *wind* with the word *pint*. *Pint*'s spelling is also ambiguous but not to the same degree as *wind*. *Pint* is infected with ambiguity up to the scale of its spelling-body *-int*, but *pint* does not entail whole-word ambiguity. The difference explains why homograph pronunciations are slower than pronunciations to ambiguous control items that are not homographs (Gottlob, Goldinger, Stone, & Van Orden, 1999; but cf. Hino, Lupker, & Pexman, 2002). This outcome would be observed even if every letter of *wind*, taken one at a time, were no more ambiguous than the individual letters of *pint*. *Wind* has a slower naming time even when contrasted with precisely constructed *mint* and *pint* controls equated for spelling body ambiguity (Holden, 2002).

Connectionist models track in the same matrix all the scales at which spelling relates to phonology. They illustrate how all these relations can be co-instantiated; different levels of representation are not necessary for the different scales to be effective. Models with recurrent feedback connections, in addition, track multiple scale relations in all directions. Stronger feedback loops like those of dominant relations correspond to relatively more stable attractors in the network. One can find dominant and subordinate relations at each scale, which means that dominant and subordinate relations may be nested across scales. In other words, there are relations within relations, attractors within attractors.

Now everything is in place to discuss feedforward ambiguity effects, and then feedback ambiguity effects, that have been demonstrated empirically. Ambiguity effects can be identified at the scale of spelling-bodies and graphemes and feedback effects can be identified at all the same scales.

## Feedforward ambiguity at the scale of spelling-bodies

The more regular dominant pronunciation of the spelling body -*int* rhymes with *mint* (consider *lint, tint,* and *hint*). The subordinate pronunciation of -*int* rhymes with *pint*. *Pint* takes longer to name than *mint* because *pint*'s rime is the subordinate pronunciation of the body -*int*. When *pint* is the word to be named, a mispronunciation of -*int* to rhyme with *mint* strongly competes with *pint*'s correct pronunciation. This competition is so close that a mispronunciation of *pint* can be elicited even from skilled readers. For example, participants can be trained to respond rapidly, in time with a beat, in a word naming task, but in doing so they commit errors of pronunciation including the kind of error in which *pint* is mispronounced to rhyme with *mint* (Kello & Plaut, 2000). More slowly emerging semantic features must combine with *pint*'s correct pronunciation to counter the dominant rhyme with *mint* (Farrar & Van Orden, 2001). In this case, *pint*'s rhyme with *mint* is not a word and would not have coherent semantic associations (cf. Lesch & Pollatsek, 1998, however).

When *mint* is the word to be named, the subordinate mispronunciation that would rhyme with *pint* competes with *mint*'s correct pronunciation. Just as for homographs, the two pronunciations compete in the course of a naming trial prior to an observed pronunciation, and the competition takes time to resolve. Thus naming times to *mint* should be slower than to words with unambiguous body-rime relations. Compare the spelling body -*int* with -*uck*, the spelling body of *duck*. *Duck*'s spelling body is unambiguous; it supports only one pronunciation (consider *luck, buck, muck,* and *puck*). The /uk/ rime also reliably covaries with the -*uck* body. Together they form an invariant relation between body and rime, and rime and body. Indeed, words like *mint* are more slowly named than words like *duck* (Glushko, 1979). A word like *mint* is more widely infected with ambiguity than a word like *duck*.

## Feedforward ambiguity at the scale of graphemes

Pockets of more or less ambiguity are also found at the microscale of graphemes and phonemes (compare Zorzi, Houghton, & Butterworth, 1998). English vowel spellings are almost always ambiguous. But some English consonants have invariant relations with phonology. The consonant grapheme *d*, at the beginning of a word, is always associated with the phoneme /d/, and the /d/ phoneme is always spelled *d*. Overall, in English, consonant spellings covary more reliably with their pronunciations than do vowel spellings. Consequently, in English, consonant phonology is resolved earlier than vowel phonology. For example, the relative ambiguity of consonant and vowel spellings predicts when their phonology will become available in masked priming experiments: consonant phonology coheres before vowel phonology (Berent & Perfetti, 1995; Lee et al., 2001; Perry & Ziegler, 2002).

For a visually presented word, the mapping from spelling to phonology is the feedforward relation and the mapping from phonology to spelling is the feedback relation. For auditory presentations this is reversed. The mapping from phonology to spelling is feedforward and the mapping from spelling to phonology is feedback. The previous examples all concerned ambiguity from spelling to phonology. Ambiguity effects also generalize to the inverted mapping from phonology to spelling, as feedback in visually presented homophones for instance.

## Feedback ambiguity at the scale of whole words

Consider the homophone phonology /braik/ and the corresponding spellings *break* and *brake*. Just as the homograph *wind* supports two pronunciations, the homophone /braik/ supports two spellings. Homophone words produce slower visual lexical decision times than control words that are not homophones (Ferrand & Grainger, 2003; Pexman, Lupker, & Jared, 2001; Pexman, Lupker, & Reggin, 2002). Homophones have slower lexical decision times even when contrasted with precisely constructed controls equated for rime-body ambiguity – feedback effects accrue across scales (Holden, 2002).

Notice that homophone effects in visual lexical decision are unintuitive. From the traditional view, activation should always flow forward from a cause to an effect, as from spelling to phonology in a visual lexical decision task. It should not matter for visual lexical decisions that *break*'s pronunciation /braik/ may have more than one spelling, unless there exists feedback from phonology to spelling. Consequently, slower visual lexical decision times to homophone words imply feedback from phonology to spelling.

## Feedback ambiguity at the scale of spelling-bodies and pronunciation-rimes

A feedback ambiguity effect at the scale of pronunciation-rimes and spelling-bodies is found in visual lexical decision. For instance, the English word *hurt* has an ambiguous rime (/ûrt/) that is linked to more than one spelling body (-urt, -ert, -irt). As one might expect, by now, words like *hurt* with ambiguous rimes yield slower visual lexical decision times and more errors than words with unambiguous rimes (Stone, Vanhoy, & Van Orden, 1997; Ziegler, Montant, & Jacobs, 1997; see also Seidenberg & Tannenhaus, 1979).

The rime ambiguity effect in visual lexical decision has yielded controversy, including claims that the original studies did not truly produce ambiguous rime effects (e.g., Peereman, Content, & Bonin, 1998). One can understand why feedback effects stir up the nest. Nevertheless, new studies with increasingly precise control continue to find reliable feedback ambiguity effects (Holden, 2002). Also, once feedback ambiguity is taken into account, reliable feedforward ambiguity effects emerge in both visual and auditory lexical decision performance, effects previously thought to be unreliable (Stone et al., 1997).

Another feedback effect at the same scale is found in auditory lexical decision. The word *pint* in an auditory lexical decision is spoken, but ambiguity in how *pint's* spelling might be pronounced slows down the lexical decision time – even though no spellings ever appear in the experiment! What is feedforward for a visually presented word is feedback for an auditory presentation of the same word. The feedback relation for an auditory presentation runs from the spelling body to the pronunciation rime. Thus the fact that auditory lexical decisions are slower to words such as *pint*, with ambiguous body spellings, is a fact that corroborates feedback (Ziegler & Ferrand, 1998; Ziegler, Muneaux, & Grainger, 2003).

The feedback effect of *pint's* ambiguous spelling body in auditory lexical decision is extremely counterintuitive from a traditional perspective. According to that perspective, spoken word recognition should be independent of the spelling of a word. Yet printed language interacts with spoken language in situations where it could just as well leave spoken language alone, as the feedback effect demonstrates (see also chapters by Lupker and Morais, current volume).

*Feedback ambiguity at the scale of phonemes*

Damian and Bowers (2003) examined phoneme ambiguity as a feedback phenomenon in a speech production task. The words *coffee* and *cushion* share the same initial phoneme and grapheme. If *coffee* is a cue to, say, *cushion*, then *cushion's* voice onset will be faster than to control items. The sequencing of words that share initial phoneme and grapheme creates a benefit for saying *cushion* aloud.

Contrast *camel* and *kidney* with the pair *coffee* and *cushion*. *Camel* and *kidney* share an ambiguous phoneme spelled *c-* in *camel* and *k-* in *kidney*. If *camel* is the cue to say *kidney*, then *kidney's* voice onset is slower than *cushion's* and no faster than to control items. The repeated phoneme with different graphemes erases the previous benefit of sequencing the same phoneme with identical graphemes.

The feedback effect of the phoneme's two different spellings is found when the cues are printed words and when they are spoken words. When the cues are spoken words no spellings appear in the experiment. Why should it matter for spoken word production that a repeated phoneme has a different spelling in each repetition? It only matters because spoken word production includes a feedforward and feedback interaction between phonology and spelling (Dijkstra, Roelofs, & Fieuws, 1995).

## Remainders

The previous sections reviewed ambiguity findings, findings that corroborate a complex interaction among spelling and phonology in visual and spoken language. Several other effects lend themselves to this framework, but do not fit so neatly into the previous story about scales of ambiguity. These additional findings concern interactions between semantics and surface forms, letter perception, and the possibility that relations are the source of perceived lexicality. These findings will be reviewed next. Also, there are theoretical and methodological loose ends that have not been discussed previously. One loose end concerns languages other than English, another concerns whether dual-process theory has been falsified, and a final point, for future reference, concerns how response times from reading tasks should be viewed.

## Ambiguity between semantics and surface forms

The relations among words' spellings, phonology, and their semantics all matter for sorting out ambiguity effects. For instance, ambiguous feedback from semantics can affect lexical decision and naming performance. More ambiguous semantic features are associated with more spellings and pronunciations and words can be more or less ambiguous in this relation between semantics and surface forms. More ambiguous words produce slower lexical decision and naming times (Pecher, 2001; Pexman, Lupker, & Hino, 2002). The effect is a striking parallel to ambiguity effects in the relations between spelling and phonology. Semantic ambiguity effects may prove to be the most important effects mentioned so far. After all they concern relations with words' meanings and it is the pursuit of meaning that drives word comprehension in reading.

## Letter perception

A briefly presented pseudohomophone such as *brane* can induce the false impression that a pre-designated letter *i* was seen (Ziegler, Van Orden, & Jacobs, 1997). Participants report that an *i* appeared in the presented spelling *brane*, but only if the letter is contained in *brane*'s sound-alike base-word *brain*. The flip side of this effect is also observed. Pseudohomophones such as *taip* may induce the false impression that a pre-designated letter *i* did not appear, but only if the letter is missing from *taip*'s sound-alike base-word *tape*. These phenomena were first demonstrated in German (Ziegler & Jacobs, 1995), then later in English (Ziegler et al., 1997) and French (Lange, 2002). Such phenomena appear quirky within a conventional framework where they may suggest postlexical inferences about which letters were seen. They are expected, however, if feedback from base-word phonology activates *brain*'s letters or inhibits letters that are not present in the base-word *tape*.

## Perceived lexicality

Relations between spelling and phonology are sources of perceived lexical structure (Vanhoy & Van Orden, 2001). Wordlike body-rimes actually add "word-ness" to letter strings that are not words. For example, it is widely reported that lexical decisions to pseudohomophones such as *jale* are slower and more likely to end in a false 'word' response than are control items. Also, correct 'word' responses to actual words are slower when pseudohomophones appear as foils.

It is not simply that pseudohomophones mimic word phonology; it also matters that they are composed of body-rime relations like those found in actual words. *Jale* is constructed on an extant body-rime that appears in the words *bale*, *sale*, and *tale*. The pseudohomophone *stahp*, which sounds like *stop* in American English, is constructed on a novel body-rime that does not appear in an actual word. In lexical decision, pseudohomophones like *jale* produce reliable pseudohomophone effects; pseudohomophones like *stahp* do not.

## Natural variation across languages

Each language presents a unique compilation of ambiguity that will be uniquely sampled by each reader. Hebrew includes mostly homographs, and Chinese includes very many homophones. Dutch, Spanish, German, and Italian minimize or eliminate ambiguity between phonology and spelling by staying closer to a system of grapheme–phoneme rules. French is more like English. French has ambiguities at multiple scales of correspondence between phonology and spelling. Serbo-Croatian has two alphabets that sometimes contradict each other in their relation to phonology, and other times not. Clearly, the consequences of ambiguity for complex interactions must be worked out carefully one language at a time (e.g., Frost, this volume; Colombo et al., 2003; Frost, Katz, & Bentin, 1987; Goswami, Ziegler, Dalton, & Schneider, 2003; Lukatela & Turvey, 1998; Ziegler, Perry, Jacobs, & Braun, 2001; Ziegler et al., 2000; and many other publications not cited here). Different languages exaggerate or reduce different sources of ambiguity and all sources interact in performance (Bosman & Van Orden, 1997; Lukatela & Turvey, 1998; Van Orden & Goldinger, 1994).

## Is dual-process theory false?

The spectrum of ambiguity effects and feedback effects that experiments demonstrate would not likely have been anticipated with dual-process theory as the guide. However, this does not mean that dual-process theory is false. Findings that contradict dual-process theory simply reveal that grapheme–phoneme rules were not the best compass to discover salient structure between phonology and spelling (Paap et al., 1992). The theory itself can be reconstituted indefinitely to absorb new contradictory findings (e.g., Coltheart, Curtis, Atkins, & Haller, 1993; Norris, 1994; Zorzi et al., 1998). Ad hoc changes create alternative ways to see the contradictory data and can be useful for that fact (Feyerabend, 1993). Nonetheless, it is a bit hard to imagine how scientists in the exclusive pursuit of mechanistic causal chains would have stumbled on these effects. The discovery of feedback effects as predicted by feedback models is a remarkable discovery of basic reading science with profound implications for all cognitive science.

*What is the nature of response time?*

The last point is a caveat that concerns how one should look at the data from all these experiments. The previous discussion has emphasized mean effects, differences between average response times or accuracy, as did almost all of the cited authors. This will prove in time to have been misleading. Ambiguity effects are not so simply expressed; they do not simply reflect shifts in average response times. Rather, they largely reflect increases in the proportion of very slow responses. They reflect redistribution of response times and changes in the shapes of response time distributions (Holden, 2002). This general observation about effects and response times is not new to reading science (Andrews & Heathcote, 2001; Balota & Spieler, 1999), but its implications have not been widely acknowledged.

Redistributions of response times often appear as changes in so-called power laws – equations in which the probability of a particular response-time is a function of the response-time itself (Holden, 2002; Van Orden, Moreno, & Holden, 2003). Power laws may suggest a complex interdependence in which the processes that compose a system change each other as they interact (Jensen, 1998). Consequently, co-instantiated relations between phonology and spelling, for example, become causally entwined and interdependent (Van Orden & Holden, 2002; Van Orden et al., 2003). It is the nature of living systems that they comprise entwined processes and do not reduce to causal elements (e.g., Rosen, 2000; Wilson, 2003).

Power law behavior could imply a radical suggestion that separate representations of phonemes and letters, for example, need not be posited. Relations between a word's spelling and its phonology, its body and rime, and its graphemes and phonemes become mutually reinforcing relations with neither being causally prior to the other. Yet there remains a useful way to think about cause in the sense of a basis or foundation for reading. Unless a child becomes attuned to the alphabetic principle in relations between spelling and phonology, learning to read does not occur or occurs with great difficulty (Rayner, Foorman, Perfetti, Pesetsky, & Seidenberg, 2001). In this sense of cause, the alphabetic principle has a causal priority in the development of skilled readers.

## Summary and Conclusions

The first half of this chapter ended on the horns of the dilemma concerning phonology and skilled reading. Over 100 years of reading research failed to decide whether skilled reading involves mediating phonology, or whether it does not. The question of mediating phonology hinges on the discovery of a task independent phonology effect for skilled readers reading familiar words. This discovery could possibly situate phonology in the architecture of word comprehension, part of cognition's larger absolute frame of reference. However, despite the plausibility that such a phonology effect could exist, all phonology factors, like all other word factors, change the pattern of their effects across the variety of task conditions.

The second half of this chapter reviewed ambiguity effects at multiple scales of relations between spelling and phonology. The reviewed findings present snapshots of a complex structure that relates phonology and spelling. In the contemporary picture of English, this relation appears as a context sensitive, bidirectional, statistical structure that changes on multiple scales and in each instance of reading – a statistical structure in perpetual motion, one might say. The complex structure of ambiguity effects intertwines written and spoken English in feedback. Some prominent intertwined relations are readily discernible, relations like those between bodies and rimes, or graphemes and phonemes. Nonetheless, the intention is not to propose a pretty hierarchy, and it would soon sprout weeds in any case. Letters and groups of letters change their relation to phonemes and groups of phonemes according to the contexts in which they appear.

Feedback models of interacting processes predict ambiguity and feedback effects. Context sensitivity within these models is useful to explain the context sensitivity of relations between spelling and phonology. It is a natural extension of this view to expect context sensitivity at all levels of a system, including sensitivity to the laboratory contexts of task demands. Until now context sensitivity has been a reason not to take some other scientist's data as conclusive. Now context sensitivity is the likely key to understand reading, the paradigmatic cognitive performance.

## Note

We acknowledge support from the National Science Foundation. The views expressed in this chapter are the authors' and do not necessarily represent those of the National Science Foundation.

# 5

# Eye Movements During Reading

## Keith Rayner, Barbara J. Juhasz, and Alexander Pollatsek

The study of eye movements has a long and rich history in reading research. Indeed, some of the earliest experimental studies of skilled reading involved measuring eye movements (see Huey, 1908). Since 1975, there has been an increasing awareness that eye movements provide very important information about the moment to moment processing that occurs during reading (Rayner, 1978, 1998). In this chapter, we first provide background information about the basic characteristics of eye movements during reading and how they are affected by reading skill. Then we review research on (1) the perceptual span during reading, (2) how much readers benefit from a preview of words to the right of the fixated word during reading (*preview benefit*), and (3) the control of eye movements during reading. Much of the research on eye movements during reading has focused on these issues. Following our discussion of these important issues, we discuss recent trends regarding eye movements and reading. We conclude with a discussion of models of eye movement control in reading.

We will begin by making two important points with respect to eye movement research. First, there are two types of research with respect to eye movements and reading (see Rayner, 1995; Rayner & Liversedge, 2004, for discussion). Some researchers are primarily interested in eye movements per se and use the task of reading as a way to study the oculomotor system. At the other extreme are researchers who use eye movements as a tool to study some aspect of language processing. This group tends not to be interested in the details of eye movements per se. From our perspective, it is important to have some understanding of research from both approaches because low-level oculomotor variables impinge on higher-order processing and vice versa (Rayner & Liversedge, 2004). Second, although a great deal of data have been collected regarding eye movements in reading, perhaps the most important recent trend is the development of sophisticated models of eye movement control that simulate reading performance. We will discuss this trend later.

## The Basic Characteristics of Eye Movements During Reading

We often have the impression that our eyes glide smoothly across the page as we read. However, this impression is not quite accurate: the eyes alternate between periods when they are relatively stable (called *fixations*, which typically last about 200–250 ms) and when they are moving (called *saccades*, which typically last only 20–40 ms). Vision is suppressed during the saccades, so visual information that is acquired from the text is obtained only during the fixations (Wolverton & Zola, 1983). Most of the time when reading English, the eyes move forward through the text from left to right across the line. At the end of the line, readers move their eyes to the beginning of the next line (via a *return sweep*). The return sweep is often inaccurate and results in an undershoot of the beginning of the line followed by a rapid (backward) corrective saccade. Even with this corrective saccade, the location of the left-most fixation on a line is typically 5–7 letter spaces from the first letter on the line. Likewise, the last fixation on a line is typically approximately 5–7 letters from the end of the line. Thus, about 80% of the letters on a line fall between the two extreme fixations.

Another important fact about eye movements is that skilled readers move their eyes backward in the text to look at previously processed words. These *regressions*, as they are called, make up about 10–15% of the fixations that skilled readers make. Regressions are not particularly well understood, but it is generally assumed that they reflect comprehension difficulties. However, most of the regressions that readers make are actually quite short (often going back only a word or two in the text) and probably reflect oculomotor variability (i.e., overshooting the target word) or word recognition problems. Rayner, Juhasz, Ashby, and Clifton (2003) recently demonstrated that there is an *inhibition of return* effect in reading wherein fixations preceding regressions back to a previously fixated word are longer than when the reader makes a regression the same distance back to a previously unfixated word. Interestingly, on the relatively few occasions when readers make longer regressions (presumably due to comprehension difficulty), they are quite accurate in going back directly to that place in the text where comprehension broke down (Frazier & Rayner, 1982; Kennedy, Brooks, Flynn, & Prophet, 2003; Meseguer, Carreiras, & Clifton, 2002).

The average saccade size in reading is about 7–8 letter spaces. For most normal sized text at a normal viewing distance, this equates to roughly 2 to 3 degrees of visual angle. In reading, the number of letter spaces is a more important index than the visual angle. If text size is held constant, but the viewing distance is altered (so more letters fall into a degree of visual angle when the text is held far from the eyes), the number of letters rather than the visual angle determines how far the eyes move (Morrison & Rayner, 1981; O'Regan, Lévy-Schoen, & Jacobs, 1983).

While the average fixation duration is about 200–250 ms and the average saccade size is 7–8 letter spaces, there is considerable variability in both measures. Figures 5.1 and 5.2 show frequency distributions for fixation durations and saccade lengths. Here it can be seen that fixations can be as short as 50 ms and as long as 500 ms. Likewise, some saccades are only 1 letter space, while others are as long as 20–25 letter spaces. In reality, these long saccades typically occur after a reader has made a regression, with the long

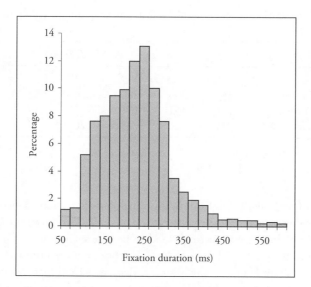

**Figure 5.1** Fixation duration distribution (adapted from Rayner, 1998).

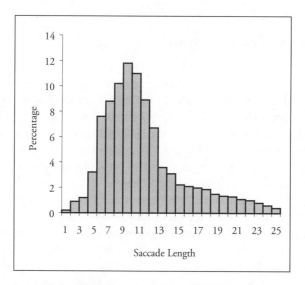

**Figure 5.2** Forward saccade length distribution (adapted from Rayner, 1998).

saccade taking the reader a bit beyond where he or she was prior to launching the regression. Some movements of the eyes are even smaller than one letter space. Reading researchers typically combine fixations separated by these very small saccades (called micro-saccades) into a single fixation.

One final point that we will make is that the nature of the writing system influences eye movements. Above, we discussed the characteristics of eye movements in alphabetic

**Table 5.1**   Developmental Characteristics of Eye Movements During Reading (Adapted from Rayner, 1998)

|  | *Grade level* | | | | | | |
|---|---|---|---|---|---|---|---|
|  | 1 | 2 | 3 | 4 | 5 | 6 | Adult |
| Fixation Duration (ms) | 355 | 306 | 286 | 266 | 255 | 249 | 233 |
| Fixations per 100 words | 191 | 151 | 131 | 121 | 117 | 106 | 94 |
| Regression Frequency (%) | 28 | 26 | 25 | 26 | 26 | 22 | 14 |

writing systems (particularly English). With nonalphabetic systems (such as Chinese or Japanese), eye movements are clearly affected. Thus, fixation durations in Chinese and Japanese tend to be longer and saccades tend to be shorter in terms of number of characters; however, a character in Chinese or Japanese conveys more information than a letter in an alphabetic system. Hebrew, which is more densely packed than English (though not as densely packed as Chinese or Japanese) because most vowels are omitted, yields shorter saccades than English.

## Reading Skill and Eye Movements

For over 80 years (Buswell, 1922), it has been known that reading skill influences eye movements. Skilled readers make shorter fixations, longer saccades, and fewer regressions than less skilled readers (Rayner, 1978, 1998). Furthermore, there are marked developmental trends in eye movements: as reading skill increases, fixation durations decrease, saccade lengths increase, and the frequency of regressions decreases. Table 5.1 shows a summary of important eye movement measures from beginning reading to sixth-grade level, with adult data for comparison. Here, it can be seen that there is a steady decrease in the average fixation duration and the number of fixations per 100 words as reading skill increases. The most marked changes occur between beginning reading and about third- or fourth-grade level. By the time children have had four years of reading experience, their eye movement behavior is not too different from adults. The exception is that the frequency of regressions is larger for a sixth-grader than an adult reader.

To date, there have been little data examining the effect of aging on eye movements. The studies that do exist (Kliegl, Grabner, Rolfs, & Engbert, 2004; Solan, Feldman, & Tujak, 1995) indicate that older readers (i.e., approximately 70 years old) have slightly longer fixations on average than younger readers, and they also make more fixations and more regressions than their younger counterparts. But Kliegl et al. (2004) concluded that the similarities that existed in the eye movement patterns of the young and older adult readers were much more impressive than the differences between them.

One area that has been highly controversial concerns the eye movements of poor readers and readers with dyslexia. Obviously, disabled readers make longer fixations, shorter saccades, more fixations, and more regressions than normal readers. Given this, it has sometimes been suggested that faulty eye movements cause poor reading and dyslexia. We will not review the research in this area (see Rayner, 1998, for a complete summary), but the best evidence indicates that eye movements rarely are the cause of reading disability. Rather, less fluent eye movements reflect the difficulties that disabled readers are having understanding the text they are reading.

There may be differences in eye movement characteristics in readers with dyslexia as a function of their writing system. Specifically, studies with Italian dyslexic readers (De Luca, Borrelli, Judica, Spinelli, & Zoccolotti, 2002; De Luca, Di Pace, Judica, Spinelli, & Zoccolotti, 1999) and German dyslexic readers (Hutzler & Wimmer, 2004) suggest some differences. Specifically, the Italian readers had moderately increased fixation durations, but not a lot of regressions. However, they made lots of fixations and short saccades. The German dyslexics, like the Italian dyslexics, made fewer regressions than are typically seen in readers of English, but had very long fixation durations. The lower incidence of regressions by the Italian and German dyslexics may be due to the fact that the orthography is more regular than English. Hutzler and Wimmer (2004) suggested that the longer fixation durations of the German dyslexics might be due to the greater syllabic complexity of German.

## Eye Movements and Measures of Processing Time in Reading

As noted above, eye movements have become recognized as one of the best ways to study moment-to-moment language processing (Rayner & Liversedge, 2004). Thus, eye movement data are widely used to study topics such as lexical ambiguity resolution (Binder, 2003; Duffy, Morris, & Rayner, 1988), phonological coding (Jared, Levy, & Rayner, 1999; Pollatsek, Lesch, Morris, & Rayner, 1992; Rayner, Pollatsek, & Binder, 1998), morphological processing (Andrews, Miller, & Rayner, 2004; Hyönä & Pollatsek, 1998; Juhasz, Starr, Inhoff, & Placke, 2003; Niswander, Pollatsek, & Rayner, 2000; Pollatsek, Hyönä, & Bertram, 2000), syntactic ambiguity and parsing (Binder, Duffy, & Rayner, 2001; Clifton et al., 2003; Frazier & Rayner, 1982), and discourse processing (Cook & Myers, 2004; Garrod & Terras, 2000; O'Brien, Shank, Myers, & Rayner, 1988). We will not attempt to review the results of these studies here. Some of these studies rely on examining the eye movement measures on a single target word, whereas others rely on examining eye movements in a larger segment of text. In this section, we will review the primary measures that eye movement recordings provide for researchers who study moment-to-moment language processing activities.

A major issue concerns how to summarize the eye movement record to obtain the best measure of processing time for a given region of text. When the unit of analysis is the word, certain measures are typically focused on, whereas when the unit of analysis is larger than a single word, other measures are employed.

With respect to the word as the unit of analysis, if readers always made only one fixation on a word there would be little difficulty choosing the most appropriate measure of processing time: the fixation duration on the word would obviously be the best measure of the time to process a word. However, many words are skipped: *content words* (nouns, verbs, adjectives, and adverbs) are fixated about 85% of the time while *function words* (prepositions, conjunctions, articles, and pronouns) are fixated about 35% of the time. One reason function words are skipped more than content words is that they tend to be short and there is clear relationship between the probability of fixating a word and its length (Rayner & McConkie, 1976). Another problem in interpreting eye movements is that many words are fixated more than once (or refixated). The problem of multiple fixations has led to alternative (highly correlated) measures. The mean fixation duration is inadequate because it underestimates the time the eyes are on a word (i.e., a 250 ms fixation and a 200 ms fixation would yield a mean of 225 ms when the eyes were actually on the word for 450 ms). The strategy of only including words that received just one fixation (*single fixation duration*) is also problematic because too many data might be eliminated. Thus, the two most frequently used measures are the *first fixation duration* and the *gaze duration* on a word. First fixation duration is the duration of the first fixation on a word regardless of whether it is the only fixation or the first of multiple fixations on a word. Gaze duration is the sum of all fixations on a word prior to an eye movement to another word. A fourth measure, the *total fixation duration* on the word reflects the sum of all fixations on the target word (including any regressions back to it). The first three measures therefore reflect the first pass processing time for a word (and are often assumed to reflect lexical access processes, as we shall discuss later in conjunction with models of eye movement control). The latter measure reflects both initial and later processing activities.

Arguments over which measure is best to use as an index of processing time partly depends on what is being examined, but the problem of assessing the average time spent processing a word is not trivial. There are three components of the problem. First, words are clearly processed when they are not fixated (Rayner, 1998). Second, readers begin processing a word before they fixate on it (which is referred to as *parafoveal preview benefit*). Third, there are *spillover effects* (Rayner & Duffy, 1986; Rayner, Sereno, Morris, Schmauder, & Clifton, 1989) as the processing of a word is not always completed by the time the eyes move; that is, processing of a word can "spill over" onto the next word and influence how long it is fixated.

Should preview benefit and spillover time be added to the time actually spent on a word? This gets complicated and can cause frustration for researchers. Given these points it is clear that any single measure of processing time for a word is a pale reflection of the reality of the true processing associated with that word. Thus, the strategy of analyzing large amounts of text with a single measure of processing time is likely to be of limited value. A strategy that most researchers have adopted is to select target words for careful analysis and then examine many different measures. By doing so, it is possible to draw reasonable inferences about the reading time for a target word.

When the unit of analysis is larger than a single word, *first pass time* is generally used as the primary measure. The first pass time is the sum of all fixations in a region prior to moving forward in the text. It is important, when analyzing larger regions to distinguish between first pass and second pass (i.e., rereading) times. There has been some controversy regarding how to best analyze a region when readers make regressions (Altmann, 1994; Rayner & Sereno, 1994a; 1994b). For example, Rayner and Sereno (1994b) noted that when readers enter a region and then quickly make a regression out of that region, the first pass time is very short in comparison to when the reader does not regress. It appears that the most appropriate way to deal with this issue is to use regression-path duration or go-past analyses (Konieczny, Hemforth, Scheepers, & Strube, 1997; Liversedge, Patterson, & Pickering, 1998; Rayner & Duffy, 1986). With this analysis, reading time is the sum of all fixations starting with the first fixation in a region and ending with the first forward saccade past the region under consideration. Liversedge et al. (1998) and Rayner & Liversedge (2004) discuss various issues related to categorizing eye movements spatially (i.e., grouping fixations that are all on the same region of text such as gaze duration or first pass) versus temporally (i.e., grouping a temporally contiguous set such as regression-path or go-past measures) and how to deal with regions that vary in length.

## Basic Issues Regarding Eye Movements in Reading

### *The perceptual span during reading*

How much information can a reader process in each fixation? Experiments that have used eye-contingent display techniques provide rather definitive answers to this question. Before discussing these results, however, we note that the main reason that readers make saccades is due to acuity limitations. While acuity in the central 2° of the visual field (the fovea) is very good, acuity drops off markedly in the parafovea, which comprises 5° on either side of the fixation, and is poor in the peripheral region, which encompasses the remaining information on a line of text. Thus, the purpose of eye movements in reading is to place the to-be-processed text in the fovea, where it can be most easily identified.

There are three main types of eye-contingent display paradigms (each has several variants), which have been useful for answering many questions (see figure 5.3). The *moving window technique*, was first used by McConkie and Rayner (1975). In this paradigm, a portion of text (defined by the experimenter) centered on a reader's fixation appears as it normally should. All of the text outside of this "window" is replaced by something meaningless (such as random letters or *x*s). This window moves as the reader's eyes move, so that each time there is a new fixation, there is a region of normal text surrounded by meaningless text (see figure 5.3). The theory behind this technique is that if the window is large enough, reading will not be affected. The second type of eye contingent display technique, called the *foveal mask technique*, is the inverse of the moving window (Rayner & Bertera, 1979). With this paradigm, letters around the fixation point are replaced by *x*s or a masking pattern. Finally, the most utilized type of eye contingent display technique is the *boundary technique* (Rayner, 1975), where there is an invisible boundary specified by the experimenter in the text. When a reader's eye crosses this boundary, the word or letter string to the right of this boundary that was originally displayed is replaced by a target word. Importantly, this change occurs during a saccade, so that it is not noticeable to the reader. Thus, all of the display change techniques affect reading because certain information is not available, not because the change itself disrupts reading (see Inhoff, Starr, Lui, & Wang, 1998).

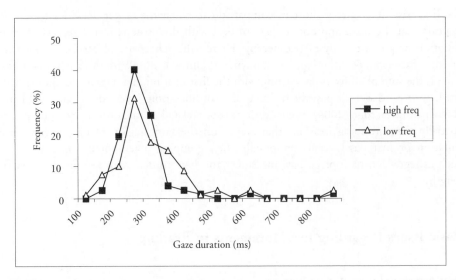

**Figure 5.3**   Examples of three eye contingent display techniques. In each panel, the asterisk indicates the eye position.

Research using these paradigms (see Rayner, 1998, for a summary) has found that the perceptual span is asymmetric. For readers of alphabetical orthographies (like English, French, and Dutch), it extends 14–15 letter spaces to the right of fixation but only 3–4 letters to the left of fixation, which usually comprises only the beginning of the fixated word. Also, readers do not obtain useful information from the line of text below the currently fixated line.

The size of the perceptual span and the nature of the asymmetry vary as a function of the writing system used. In Hebrew, where the language is written left-to-right, the opposite asymmetry in the perceptual span is observed (Pollatsek, Bolozky, Well, & Rayner, 1981). In addition, in a nonalphabetic language, such as Chinese, which is more informationally dense, the span, while still being asymmetric, is reduced. Inhoff and Liu (1998) found that the perceptual span in Chinese extended one character to the left of fixation and three characters to the right. Likewise, the span for Japanese readers is much smaller than that of English readers (Ikeda & Saida, 1978; Osaka, 1987, 1992). Finally, reading skill also affects the size of the perceptual span. Readers at the end of second grade have a smaller perceptual span than that of adults (Rayner, 1986) and readers with dyslexia have a smaller span than unimpaired readers (Rayner, Murphy, Henderson, & Pollatsek, 1989).

The fact that the perceptual span is asymmetric (depending on the direction of reading) implies that where readers are attending to is constraining the region from which information is extracted on a fixation. Similarly, differences among languages and among readers at different ability levels also are due to differences in what readers are attending to and trying to encode on a fixation. However, the limit of 14–15 characters is due to acuity. This was best demonstrated with the moving mask technique (Rayner & Bertera, 1979): when a mask covered the central 14 characters to either side of fixation (with text outside being normal), reading was virtually impossible. Thus, it is not just that readers *are not* extracting any useful information outside this region, they *cannot.*

## Preview benefit from parafoveal processing during reading

Although the perceptual span extends 14 to 15 characters to the right of fixation, only certain types of gross information are extracted from the very end of the span. Word length information is acquired further to the right of fixation than information about the letters in the word (McConkie & Rayner, 1975; Rayner, 1986). Underwood and McConkie (1985) found that incorrect letters occurring eight or more letter spaces from the point of fixation did not significantly affect fixation durations. As letter information is necessary during word recognition, this means that the word identification span (the area from which a word can be identified during a fixation) is smaller than the perceptual span. Usually, the word identification span only extends 7–8 characters to the right of fixation. However, it should be noted that both the perceptual span and the word identification span can be modulated by text properties. For example, if the next word in text is predictable from the prior context, more information is acquired from that word prior to fixation (Balota, Pollatsek, & Rayner, 1985).

Parafoveal word information can affect reading in two possible ways. One is that the word to the right of fixation (i.e., the parafoveal word) is completely identified prior to its fixation. In most cases when this occurs, the parafoveal word is skipped. Word skipping occurs more often with short words (Blanchard, Pollatsek, & Rayner, 1989; Brysbaert & Vitu, 1998) and words that are predictable (Ehrlich & Rayner, 1981; O'Regan, 1979; Rayner & Well, 1996). Skipping a word may lead to a longer fixation prior to and after the skip (Kliegl & Engbert, in press; Pollatsek, Rayner, & Balota, 1986; Rayner, Ashby, Pollatsek, & Reichle, 2004), though there is some controversy on this issue.

There is also a second way that parafoveally acquired information is used during reading: Partial information about the parafoveal word is acquired and then is used to aid processing of the word when it is fixated. The boundary technique mentioned earlier and variations of it have been very useful in revealing what types of partial parafoveal word information are obtained. Many studies have varied the properties of an initially displayed word or letter string in relation to a subsequently displayed target word (so that orthographic, phonological, and semantic similarity is varied). Preview benefit is defined as the difference between the time spent reading the target word when a helpful preview of the target word is given compared to a control preview (that does not contain the relevant information).

The results from these studies (see Rayner, 1998, for a summary) show that orthographic similarity between the preview and the target word facilitates subsequent target word reading. For example, in a boundary technique study by Balota et al. (1985), prior to crossing the boundary readers had a parafoveal preview of a nonword that was either visually similar or dissimilar to a target word. Fixation durations on the target word were shorter if a visually similar parafoveal preview was given. Importantly, facilitation does not appear to be strictly due to visual overlap, since changing the case of the letters from fixation to fixation (so OvErLaP becomes oVeRlAp) does not significantly disrupt reading

(McConkie & Zola, 1979). Therefore, abstract letter codes must be causing the facilitation. Most of the preview benefit has been shown to come from the first few letters of the parafoveal word.

Pollatsek et al. (1992) presented sentences that contained a homophone target word (e.g., *beach*). When readers were fixating the word to the left of the target word, they received a preview of the target word in their parafovea. The two critical conditions were when the preview was the target word's homophone (*beech*) or a visually similar word to the target (*bench*). Reading times on the target word were shorter when the preview was the target word's homophone than when the preview was simply visually similar. This study (see also Henderson, Dixon, Peterson, Twilley, & Ferreira, 1995; Miellet & Sparrow, 2004) indicates that phonological processing begins even before a word is fixated.

There is no evidence to suggest that semantic preprocessing of a word occurs prior to it being fixated (unless the word is fully identified and thus skipped on the ensuing saccade). Rayner, Balota, and Pollatsek (1986) found no parafoveal preview benefit on a target word (*song*) during sentence reading when a semantically related preview was given (*tune*) compared to a semantically unrelated preview (*door*). Critically, these same words did result in significant semantic priming in a standard naming task, where semantic priming is usually observed. More recently, Altarriba, Kambe, Pollatsek, and Rayner (2001) also failed to find semantic priming effects from parafoveal previews. In their experiments, Spanish–English bilingual subjects were given previews that were identical to the target word, translations (such as *strong–fuerte*), cognates (such as *cream–crema*), orthographic controls for the cognates (*grass–grasa*), or unrelated to the target word. There was no preview benefit for the translations, and the amount of preview benefit was the same for the cognates and their orthographic controls.

It is also interesting to note that for readers of English, morphological information (such as information about prefixes) does not appear to be a cause of preview benefit (Inhoff, 1989; Kambe, 2004; Lima, 1987; Lima & Inhoff, 1985). In these studies, target words were either prefixed words (as in *revive*) or pseudo-prefixed words (*rescue*). Readers were given a preview (such as *rexxxx*) and then fixation time on the target word was examined. These studies found that there was no extra benefit from having a true prefix over a pseudoprefix. The rationale for these studies was that readers might strip off the prefix parafoveally and then focus attention on the stem of the word following the saccade. But, the general pattern of results from these studies has been that morphological information is not processed in the parafovea when reading English. On the other hand, a series of studies with Hebrew readers (Deutsch, Frost, Pollatsek, & Rayner, 2000; Deutsch, Frost, Peleg, Pollatsek, & Rayner, 2003) has demonstrated that morphological information is beneficial in that when the root morpheme is provided as a preview, readers process a target word faster than when the preview is not the root morpheme. One interesting aspect of this finding is that the root morpheme is not located at the beginning of the word, but rather is spread throughout the word.

## The control of eye movements during reading

There are two important decisions that readers make (unconsciously) when moving their eyes in reading: when to move the eyes and where to move the eyes. A considerable amount of evidence suggests that these two decisions are made somewhat independently of each other (Rayner, 1998; Rayner, Kambe, & Duffy, 2000). The current models of eye movement control in reading, which we will discuss later in this chapter, tend to blur the distinction between these two decisions. But, here we will review research on the two decisions separately.

*The where decision.* Word length is a very important factor affecting the decision about where to move the eyes in reading. Research using the moving window technique has shown that saccade lengths are significantly decreased when information about word boundaries is withheld (see Rayner, 1998). Although there is some variability in where the eyes land in a word, readers usually fixate between the beginning and center of the word. This location was termed the *preferred viewing location* by Rayner (1979). This can be compared to what O'Regan and Lévy-Schoen (1987) called the *optimal viewing location*, which is slightly to the right of the preferred viewing location and is the location at which the time to recognize a word is minimized. Where a reader fixates in a word is also related to where the saccade was launched. Although the majority of saccades land towards the center of a word, this is modulated by how distant or near the previous fixation was (McConkie, Kerr, Reddix, & Zola, 1988; Rayner, Sereno, & Raney, 1996). It is also interesting that the preferred viewing location in Hebrew (Deutsch & Rayner, 1999), like English, falls between the beginning and the middle of the word.

Several researchers have found that the orthographic regularity of the initial letters of a word can influence where the eyes land in a word (e.g. Beauvillain, Dore, & Baudouin, 1996; Hyönä, 1995; Radach, Inhoff, & Heller, 2004; White & Liversedge, 2004). These landing position effects are usually very small (a fraction of a letter) but are reliable. Some earlier research suggested that the semantic content of a to-be-processed word can influence the landing position in words (Everatt & Underwood, 1992; Hyönä, Niemi, & Underwood, 1989; Underwood, Bloomfield, & Clews, 1988). However, more recent investigations (Rayner & Morris, 1992; Hyönä, 1995; White & Liversedge, 2004) failed to replicate these effects and so they must be regarded cautiously.

*The when decision.* Whereas the decision about where to move the eyes seems to be primarily modulated by low-level word length and orthographic properties, the decision about when to move the eyes is strongly related to the properties of the text that is being processed. The amount of time spent reading a word is closely related to lexical, syntactic, and discourse variables. The frequency with which a word occurs in language reliably affects the fixation durations on words (Inhoff & Rayner, 1986; Juhasz & Rayner, 2003; Rayner & Duffy, 1986; Schilling, Rayner, & Chumbley, 1998). Recent investigations have also shown that the rated familiarity of a word affects fixation times on words even when frequency is statistically or experimentally controlled (Juhasz & Rayner, 2003; Williams & Morris, 2004). Other lexical variables that have recently been found to affect fixation durations are the age at which words are acquired and the concreteness of a word's referent (Juhasz & Rayner, 2003, in press). It should be noted that word length also influences the *when* decisions. However, these effects of word length are usually not seen (or are rather small) in first fixation duration and single fixation duration, but are quite robust in gaze duration, where time spent refixating the word is taken into account. As noted earlier, there is also evidence that the properties of a previously fixated word (such as its frequency) can affect the processing of the currently fixated word. These spillover effects are usually smaller than the effects related to the properties of the currently fixated word.

Properties of the sentence and the discourse have also been found to affect *when* decisions. As noted above, words are fixated for less time when they are constrained by the context (i.e., predictable) than when they are in a neutral context (Ehrlich & Rayner, 1981; Rayner & Well, 1996). Very recently, McDonald and Shillcock (2003a, 2003b) demonstrated that the transitional probability that two words will occur together in text influences how long readers look at the second word. That is, the word *defeat* is more likely to occur following *accept* than is *losses*. McDonald and Shillcock found that fixations are shorter on *defeat* than *losses* following *accept*. In addition, it has also been found that anaphora and coreference (linking two words in the discourse, such as identifying a referent for a pronoun) can affect fixation durations, as can syntactic disambiguation (see Rayner, 1998).

Finally, it is important to note that the information that is needed for reading gets into the processing system very quickly. If readers are given 50–60 ms on each fixation before a masking pattern obscures the text, reading proceeds quite normally (Ishida & Ikeda, 1989; Rayner, Inhoff, Morrison, Slowiaczek, & Bertera, 1981). Vergilino-Perez (Rayner, Liversedge, White, & Vergilino-Perez 2003; see also Liversedge et al., 2004) recently demonstrated that if the text disappears after 60 ms (or is masked after 60 ms), readers still look longer at low-frequency than at high-frequency words (see figure 5.4). That is, even though the word is no longer there, readers leave their eyes in place longer when a low frequency word disappears than when a high frequency word disappears. This finding provides further evidence that the cognitive processes associated with processing the fixated word largely determines when the eyes move.

## Recent Trends and Current Issues

In this section we will focus on some recent trends and current controversies related to eye movements (Radach & Kennedy, 2004; Rayner & Juhasz, 2004; Starr & Rayner, 2001).

### Recent trends

Perhaps the most obvious recent trend has been the implementation of sophisticated models that simulate eye movements in reading. That is, for some time, models of eye movements in reading were largely verbal descriptions. The Strategy-Tactics model (O'Regan, 1990, 1992) was such a model that had some influence in stimulating research (see Rayner et al., 1996). However, these verbal models were not as precise as the more quantitative computer simulations that represent the more recent trend in the field. The E-Z Reader model (Reichle, Pollatsek, Fisher, & Rayner, 1998; Reichle, Rayner, & Pollatsek, 2003) was the first such model, and a number of other models have appeared since. These models will be discussed in the next section.

*Normal text:*

Fixation 1: Mary took a new shortcut to the grocery store.
                 *

Fixation 2: Mary took a new shortcut to the grocery store.
                          *

-----------------------------------------------------------------------------------

*Moving window technique*

Fixation 1 :xxxx xxxx x new xxxxxxxx xx xxx xxxxxxx xxxxx.
                 *

Fixation 2: xxxx xxxx x xxx shortcut xx xxx xxxxxxx xxxxx.
                         *

-----------------------------------------------------------------------------------

*Foveal mask technique*

Fixation 1: Mary took a xxx shortcut to the grocery store.
                 *

Fixation 2: Mary took a new xxxxxxxx to the grocery store.
                         *

-----------------------------------------------------------------------------------

*Boundary technique*

Fixation 1: Mary took a new ctiuhvsf to the grocery store.
                 *

Fixation 2: Mary took a new shortcut to the grocery store.
                         *

-----------------------------------------------------------------------------------

**Figure 5.4**   Gaze duration frequency distribution in the disappearing text condition for both low- and high-frequency words (adapted from Rayner et al., 2003).

Another trend is that eye movement data are being used increasingly to understand various aspects of how words are processed during reading. In particular, it has become apparent that eye movement data are particularly useful in studying the processing of complex, longer words (Andrews et al., 2004; Bertram & Hyönä, 2003; Hyönä & Pollatsek, 1998; Juhasz et al., 2003; Niswander et al., 2000; Pollatsek et al., 2000). There is a vast literature on word recognition in which words are presented in isolation using a naming, lexical decision, or perceptual identification tasks (see the chapters by Lupker, and by Van Orden and Kloos, in this volume for reviews). Most of these experiments typically involve short monomorphemic words, and for these shorter words, naming and lexical decisions yield significant correlations with different eye movement measures (Schilling et al., 1998). However, with longer complex words, where readers typically have to make more than a single fixation on the word to process it, it is clear that eye movement data are more informative, since more than a single response time measure is obtained. Moreover, neither naming nor lexical decisions seem like good measures of word processing – naming because the initiation of the vocal response isn't capturing all the processing and lexical decisions because the decision (rather than encoding) processes are adding noise to the response time.

A final trend is that the divide between those using eye movements to study language processing and those interested in the oculomotor characteristics per se seems to be widening (Rayner & Liversedge, 2004). In many ways this is lamentable, as it is undoubtedly a two-way street: one needs to know about the details of eye movements when using them to study language processing, yet at the same time it is clear that linguistic properties influence eye movements.

## Current controversies

Like any research area, research on eye movements in reading has generated a number of controversial findings/issues. The details of these issues have varied somewhat, though there has often been some kind of tension between researchers advocating that low-level oculomotor variables play the major role in influencing eye movements and those which advocate that cognitive/linguistic variables exert the most influence. In this section, we will briefly consider four current controversies: (1) parafoveal-on-foveal effects, (2) serial versus parallel allocation of attention, (3) word skipping, and (4) cognitive influences on fixation time.

There has recently been considerable interest in the extent to which the word to the right of fixation can influence processing of the currently fixated word (*parafoveal-on-foveal* effects). Parafoveal-on-foveal effects differ from the preview benefit effects we discussed earlier because those effects referred to how a preview of a word in parafoveal vision affected the processing of that same word when it was subsequently fixated. If parafoveal-on-foveal effects exist, then it should be the case that the frequency of the word to the right of fixation should influence the duration of the current fixation. However, a number of studies have failed to find such an effect (Carpenter & Just, 1983; Henderson & Ferreira, 1993; Rayner, Fischer, & Pollatsek, 1998). On the other hand, a number of studies (Inhoff, Starr, & Shindler, 2000; Kennedy, 2000; Kennedy, Murray, & Boissiere, 2004; Kennedy, Pynte, & Ducrot, 2002; Murray, 1998; Starr & Inhoff, 2004) have manipulated various properties of the word to the right of fixation and some effect of the manipulation has emerged. Some of these studies have obtained effects due to the meaning of the word to the right of fixation, whereas others have obtained effects related to the orthographic properties of the word to the right of fixation. However, it is far from clear that these effects, particularly if they involve meaning, are reliable (see Rayner & Juhasz, 2004; Rayner, Pollatsek, & Reichle, 2003). For example, White and Liversedge (2004) found no such semantic effects. Furthermore, Hyönä and Bertram (2004) reported five different experiments in which they looked for such effects and found very inconsistent results.

Much of the evidence for parafoveal-on-foveal effects comes from tasks that approximate reading, but are not reading. Instead, participants engage in what are closer to visual search or pattern matching tasks than reading. Given that frequency effects disappear when the task changes from reading to search (Rayner & Fischer, 1996; Rayner & Raney, 1996), one has to be concerned about whether these results generalize from searchlike tasks to reading.

The second, related, controversy has to do with serial versus parallel allocation of attention during reading. As we document in the next section, the most influential model of eye movement control in reading operates via a serial attention mechanism, whereby processing of word n + 1 does not begin until processing of word n is either completed or close to completion. However, given the existence of possible parafoveal-on-foveal effects and in reaction to the serial attention models, models such as SWIFT (Engbert, Longtin, & Kliegl, 2002) and GLENMORE (Reilly & Radach, 2003) incorporate the notion of an attentional gradient in which more than one word can be processed at a time (with the currently fixated word receiving more processing resources than other words). We say more about the E-Z Reader model in the next section. Here, let us simply point out that from a modeling standpoint, it would be easier to adopt the parallel view of attention as in the SWIFT model. In this model, attention is a gradient that is allocated in parallel to several words. In essence, the assumption that words are processed in parallel allows many more degrees of freedom in modeling the data.

The third controversy, which is also related to the prior two, deals with word skipping. There has been considerable discussion (see Brysbaert & Vitu, 1998; Rayner, 1998) over exactly what causes skipping. It is clear that word length and predictability are both factors, and there is some evidence that word frequency has an effect (Rayner et al., 1996). But, the main controversy seems to now revolve around whether or not fixations preceding (and to some extent following) a skip are inflated. Pollatsek et al. (1986) first reported that fixations prior to skips were inflated and there are other reports of such an effect (Rayner et al., 2004; Reichle et al., 1998; Pynte, Kennedy, & Ducrot, 2004). However, based on analyses using a large corpus of eye movement data, Radach and Heller (2000) and Kliegl et al. (2004) failed to find such an effect. A problem with analyzing this effect is that it is correlational. That is, the experimenter does not control exactly when the reader does or does not skip. Thus, better readers will tend to skip more and have shorter fixations, so this will work against finding a negative relation between the two factors. Moreover, even within a single reader, there can be similar variations over time, where when the reader is energized (or finds an easy passage of text), their fixations will get shorter and they will tend to skip more. Thus, the above studies finding a negative relation between skipping and fixation durations (i.e., longer fixations before and after skipping) are doing so in spite of this likely artifact. It is interesting to note that Kliegl and Engbert (in press) recently reported such an inflation effect with fixations prior to skips of low-frequency words being longer than fixations prior to skips of high-frequency words.

The final controversy we will discuss has to do with the extent to which cognitive processes influence eye movements in reading. Do cognitive processes drive the eyes in reading? At some level, we would have thought that the answer to this question has already been conclusively answered in the affirmative. Rayner (1998) identified well over 100 published articles showing some influence of cognitive processing on eye fixations and eye movements. Yet, somewhat amazingly, some researchers (see McConkie & Yang, 2003; Vitu, 2003; Yang & McConkie, 2001, 2004) continue to question this basic assumption. They do not deny that cognitive processes have effects; they just think that the effects are rather late in a fixation (too late, in general, to influence the decision of when to move the eyes). We will not discuss this issue in much detail (see Rayner, Pollatsek, & Reichle, 2003 for a more in-depth discussion) because it seems all too clear to us that effects of various lexical properties of a word do influence the time it is fixated.

Another result that has generated some recent interest has to do with the counterintuitive finding that in cases where readers make only one fixation on a word, fixations are apparently longer when the eyes land on the middle of the word than on the beginning or end of the word (Vitu, McConkie, Kerr, & O'Regan, 2001). This finding is curious since the middle of the word is where readers should get the best view of the word. This may appear problematic for models of eye movements in which cognitive processing drive the eyes through the text, because it would seem that a good view of the word should lead to shorter fixations. However, Vitu et al. did find a frequency effect independent of where the fixation was located (see also Rayner et al., 1996). This frequency effect independent of fixation location, even in this experiment, again appears to argue strongly for cognitive control of eye movements, though this strange landing position effect is far from understood. In addition, as we argued above, the fact that frequency has an effect even in the disappearing text experiments (Liversedge et al., 2004; Rayner et al., 2003) strongly supports the idea that cognitive events drive eye movements in reading.

## Models of Eye Movement Control in Reading

Perhaps the most impressive advance in the study of eye movements during reading is the emergence of detailed quantitative models of eye movement control in reading which account for a lot of data. We will focus on our E-Z Reader model (Pollatsek, Reichle, & Rayner, 2003; Rayner, Reichle, & Pollatsek, 1998; Reichle et al., 1998, 2003), partly due to limited space, and partly because it is the simplest and arguably the most parsimonious account of the data. The E-Z Reader model is an elaboration of an earlier, non-quantitative model of Morrison (1984).[1]

The essence of Morrison's conception of reading was that word identification is the engine that drives the eyes forward. More specifically, he posited that the goal on each fixation is to identify the word immediately after the last word that has been identified fully (this is usually the word that is currently fixated). Morrison posited that when the word is identified, two things happen simultaneously: (a) a command (a *program*) goes to the eye movement system to execute a saccade to the next word; (b) attention shifts from the word currently attended to to the next word as well. Although this seems like the type of mechanism that anyone would think of, it is not obvious it would work. That is, how can fixation time on a word be influenced by word encoding when: (a) fixation times on words are about 250 ms; (b) the time to access a word is about 150–200 ms; and (c) simple eye movement reaction time is 175 ms? It does not seem like there is enough processing time to encode a word on a fixation and then execute an eye movement. The answer is that the processing of words starts before they are fixated (as indicated by parafoveal preview benefit). In Morrison's model, attention shifts to the next word (and parafoveal processing of it begins) about 175 ms before the eyes move to it.

The other part of Morrison's model is that a later eye movement program can cancel an earlier one if it comes soon after the first. Morrison was inspired by Becker and Jürgens (1979), who showed that cancellation of earlier eye movements could occur. This assumption, in a qualitative way, captures the facts in reading nicely. Let us consider when a later eye movement program would be programmed soon after an earlier one. This would happen when the word to the right of fixation was easy to process – that is, if it was short, very frequent, and/or predictable from the prior text. Thus, in outline, these assumptions provide a good account of eye movements in reading.

The E-Z Reader model differs from Morrison's model in two key ways. First, the shift of attention is decoupled from the programming of the eye movement. This was done for several reasons. First, readers appear to get more preview benefit when the fixated word is easier to process. This cannot be accounted for by a model that yokes the two processes. Second, a model that yokes the two processes also cannot account for the spillover effects discussed earlier. Third, in general, it is hard to give a good quantitative fit of the data using a model where the two processes are yoked. Thus, in the E-Z Reader model, it is assumed that the eye movement is triggered by a process that is prior to fully encoding the word (a *familiarity check*), whereas the attention shift only occurs after the word is fully encoded. Moreover, the difference in time between these two events is assumed to be a function of the difficulty of processing the word. With those assumptions, the modulation of parafoveal preview benefit and spillover effects can easily be accounted for.

The second way E-Z Reader differs from Morrison's model is that it attempts to explain how there can be more than one fixation on a word. To give a flavor of how one might account for refixations, one version of the model posits that each time a fixation begins, a program is automatically initiated to refixate the word; however, this program can be canceled by a later program, which is the identical cancelation mechanism that produces skipping of words. This mechanism predicts that words which are harder to identify are more likely to be refixated, as the program initiated by the familiarity check is less likely to cancel this automatic program. As seen in table 5.2, even this early version of the model gives a good account of eye movement behavior. We should also add that assumptions have been added to E-Z Reader, inspired by McConkie's experiments on landing positions, to explain where in words readers fixate.

We have given a brief outline of E-Z Reader, and what must be dealt with to explain eye movements in reading and the reading process. Let us now indicate the major failings of the model (largely aspects that are left incomplete). One major failing is that the E-Z Reader posits that readers identify words and move inexorably forward in the text. Yet, as indicated above, regressions back to previous words are reasonably common. A major cause for regressions is that people misparse sentences and have other failures of higher-order comprehension processes. Explaining these at this stage of research is difficult, as there is much uncertainty as to how people parse sentences and construct the meaning of discourse. Yet, in reality most regressions are very short (typically to the prior word). Thus, we think it is a reasonable possibility that the E-Z Reader is the "normal" mode of reading. That is, we suspect that skilled reading is largely driven by encoding words, with higher-order language processes going on in the background and not directly controlling eye movements, and instead only intervening occasionally, when there is a comprehension failure.

A second way that the E-Z Reader is incomplete is that we now posit that the speed of word encoding is only affected by two factors: the frequency of the word and how predictable it is from the prior text. However, a large amount of research has emerged in

**Table 5.2**   Observed and Predicted Values of Gaze Durations, and First Fixation Duration, Probability of Skipping, Making a Single Fixation, and Making Two Fixations for a Version of the E-Z Reader Model (E-Z Reader 5) for Five Frequency Classes of Words in a Passage of Text (Frequencies Are out of 1,000,000 Words) (Adapted from Reichle et al., 1998)

| Freq. class | Mean freq. | Gaze duration (ms) | | First fixation duration (ms) | |
|---|---|---|---|---|---|
| | | Observed | Predicted | Observed | Predicted |
| 1 | 3 | 293 | 291 | 248 | 251 |
| 2 | 45 | 272 | 271 | 234 | 253 |
| 3 | 347 | 256 | 257 | 228 | 246 |
| 4 | 4889 | 234 | 226 | 223 | 223 |
| 5 | 40700 | 214 | 211 | 208 | 210 |

| Freq. class | Probability of skipping | | Probability of making a single fixation | | Probability of making two fixations | |
|---|---|---|---|---|---|
| | Observed | Predicted | Observed | Predicted | Observed | Predicted |
| 1 | 0.10 | 0.09 | 0.68 | 0.73 | 0.20 | 0.17 |
| 2 | 0.13 | 0.16 | 0.70 | 0.76 | 0.16 | 0.07 |
| 3 | 0.22 | 0.27 | 0.68 | 0.68 | 0.10 | 0.04 |
| 4 | 0.55 | 0.49 | 0.44 | 0.50 | 0.02 | 0.01 |
| 5 | 0.67 | 0.68 | 0.32 | 0.32 | 0.01 | 0.00 |

recent years indicating that components of words, such as morphemes, also influence the time to encode a word and may also influence where refixations occur. We have made one attempt to model this (with long Finnish compound words), but admittedly this attempt was not completely successful.

What are the competing models like? (See Reichle et al., 2003, for a comprehensive comparison of the different models.) Some attempt to model eye movements simply using low-level aspects of the stimulus, such as word length (Clark & O'Regan, 1999). Given the large amount of data indicating that all sorts of linguistic variables influence eye movements (such as the frequency and predictability of words and their component morphemes), such models are incomplete at best. Two other models, SWIFT (Engbert et al., 2002; Kliegl & Engbert, 2003) and GLENMORE (Reilly & Radach, 2003), are similar in general conception to E-Z Reader, but more complex. For example, GLENMORE attempts to derive word-frequency effects from activations in a connectionist network. However, it has not been fit to a corpus of data and it may well have difficulty explaining how linguistic variables influence fixation times. Both GLENMORE and SWIFT assume a window of attention that shifts over time, but this window is more flexible than a single word. SWIFT also makes more complex assumptions than E-Z Reader about the relation between cognitive processing and eye movement control (although roughly similar in outline to those given above in our description of E-Z Reader). Perhaps because of this flexibility, these models are able to account for eye movements in reading quite well, including some regressions. We have mixed feelings about adding this complexity to a model at this stage of research. Although this complexity allows one to account for data well, it causes some problems. The first is that these models tend to be harder to diagnose than E-Z Reader. That is, when there is a discrepancy between the data and the simulation it is harder to know what the problem is. A second problem, related to the first, is that such models tend not to be very good heuristic devices. That is, they are complex enough that it isn't intuitively clear what qualitative aspects of reading they do and do not predict. We think that this contrasts with E-Z Reader, which has generated testable predictions, such as those confirmed by the Rayner et al. (2003) and Liversedge et al. (2004) experiments cited above. In addition, most of these more complex models assume that words to the right of fixation influence fixation time on a word. However, the data on this phenomenon are, at best, mixed as we noted earlier, and we think that this parafoveal-on-foveal phenomenon is likely to be a minor effect. In fact, Hyönä, Bertram, and Pollatsek (2004) showed that parafoveal processing of the second half of a compound word has little effect on how long the first half is fixated.

## Summary

We have reviewed the basic facts about eye movements in reading, and discussed some current trends and controversies related to eye movement research. We also discussed recent models of eye movement control in reading. With respect to the latter topic, we devoted more attention to the E-Z Reader model than other models. We think this is justified, since E-Z Reader was the first such computational model and because it is the best specified of all the models. Rayner (1998) argued that research on eye movements is now into a fourth era in which computational models would be increasingly important in guiding new research questions. It is also obvious to us that more research needs to be done to determine what variables besides frequency and predictability might serve as useful inputs to the models to determine fixation duration times.

Finally, it is quite surprising that there is so little research on children's eye movements (see Feng, Miller, Shu, & Zhang, 2004; McConkie et al., 1991; Rayner, 1986, for such studies) and on eye movements during oral reading. Part of the problem with beginning readers is undoubtedly due to the fact that most eyetracking systems until recently have not been particularly child friendly.

To conclude, eye movements have been a major source of information since 1975 about the process of reading. There is every reason to believe that this trend will continue as eye movements provide an excellent window for examining the cognitive processes that readers engage in the process of comprehending text.[2]

## Notes

1. Morrison's model and E-Z Reader do not account for many phenomena beyond the comprehension of individual words, including why readers regress back to earlier words in the text.
2. Preparation of this chapter was supported by Grants HD17246 and HD26765 from the National Institutes of Health. Barbara Juhasz was also supported by a Pre-doctoral Traineeship on Grant MH016745 from the National Institute of Mental Health.

# PART II

*Learning to Read and Spell*

# Editorial Part II

Most children are already competent users of their native language by the time they go to school, and reading develops from this foundation. Indeed as Mattingly (1972) proposed more than 30 years ago, "reading is parasitic on speech." However, learning to read is not a straightforward matter because, at a minimum, it involves breaking a code that maps spoken on to written language. How difficult it is to break the code, and how much else there is to learn before reaching an adult level of proficiency will depend upon a wide range of factors, some intrinsic and others extrinsic the child. These are themes that recur in different chapters in Part III.

Byrne makes clear that reading is the product of the learner and the environment, so in this view what needs to be taught is what the child does not bring to the learning situation. He proposes that one of the reasons that learning to read is difficult is that children start out with incorrect hypotheses about what print represents; in short they think that the symbols map to morphemes rather than to phonemes and, for children learning to read in an alphabetic language, this can lead them astray. Failures of learning are discouraging, and a failure to understand the alphabetic principle (that graphemes map onto phonemes) represents just one point at which children can become discouraged about the reading enterprise. Even with alphabetic insight the child must acquire knowledge of all of the letter sounds, must understand that not all features of the sound stream are represented in the orthography and must also learn that there are one-to-many and many-to-one correspondences.

Treiman and Kessler's consideration of the process of learning to spell and their review of writing systems raises some very similar issues to those discussed by Byrne. In all writing systems, a key issue for children is to work out what the system they are learning represents and, on the other side of the coin, what it ignores. In general, writing systems ignore suprasegmental (e.g., intonation and stress) features of speech, and they do not convey information about regional dialect. What they represent depends on the system in question. Beginning with Chinese logograms, moving through syllabic writing systems (such as Cherokee), to transparent alphabets (such as Finnish), and opaque writing systems (such as English), Treiman and Kessler outline the principles children need to understand. There is a trade-off across these systems such that, as the number of symbols to be learned decreases (hence lightening the memory load), so the abstractness of mappings increases along with questions regarding the proper classification of speech sounds for writing purposes. Given the difficulty of segmenting the speech stream, alphabets are hard to learn; children with better phoneme awareness do better in this regard and letter knowledge can bootstrap the process.

Ehri reviews theories that have conceptualized the development of reading as a "stage-like" process, with a focus on English. As she points out, the term "stage" is a misnomer; in almost all of these theories there is overlap between the stages, and the term "phase" has come to be preferred to convey this notion. There are important similarities between the different phase theories. For instance, all posit an early phase of development in which reading is visually based (and the wrong hypotheses are entertained), followed by a stage of early reading when children are beginning to use the alphabetic principle but with limited success, through to adult competence where word recognition is fluent and seemingly effortless. Ehri uses her own phase theory as an exemplar, providing a detailed account of the development of "sight word reading" (the fluent recognition of printed words). Within this model, development is a process of bonding spellings to word pronunciations in memory. Ehri reviews evidence showing that, at first, the mappings are arbitrary until children acquire letter knowledge and phoneme awareness and begin to create partial mappings between the letters and sounds in the words. These partial mappings are gradually fleshed out as the child progresses to the full alphabetic phase. The consolidated alphabetic phase signals the point at which word recognition skills have become automatized. At each phase in the model, children abstract and use the mappings they possess to read words they have not seen before so that the proficiency of novel word reading increases in tandem with sight word learning. Rather than arguing that children use one process for reading words by "sight" and another for words they must decode, there are mappings between orthographic and phonological word forms in a single memory system in her model. Ehri acknowledges that there are similarities with connectionist models of reading development. A point of contrast is that Ehri's model has word-specific information embodied in the connections between printed and spoken word forms.

Bowey's chapter addresses the question of individual differences in learning to read and picks up the theme of what skills and knowledge are necessary. Beginning with a discussion of the methodological issues surrounding longitudinal studies of reading development, Bowey reviews a huge body of empirical work on the predictors of reading skills. Key amongst these are letter knowledge and phoneme sensitivity, two skills that she, like Byrne, believes co-determine early reading development (in reciprocal relationship with each other). But much else is important as well: general cognitive ability, particularly verbal ability, is important and vocabulary and grammatical skills play increasingly important roles as reading development progresses (particularly in determining reading comprehension outcomes). Bowey reminds us that identifying the predictors of individual differences in reading (in the normal range) is not the same thing as predicting who will become a poor reader (at the bottom of the range). Nonetheless, as her discussion makes clear, there are a number of phonological skills that appear to be critical to learning to read, and if in short supply presage reading failure. These skills might be considered indices of the integrity of underlying phonological representations of speech, though measurement of them is complicated by tasks demands. Indeed, one of the main tenets of Bowey's argument is that there is a complex interrelationship between the different skills that contribute to reading. It follows that learning to read effectively requires reaching at least threshold levels in each of a number of domains. Arguably, it is sometimes the case that a proficient process can bootstrap a faulty one and this may be one reason why it is hard to predict who will become a poor reader.

Mindful of what we have learnt from research on the cognitive predictors of reading skill, Phillips and Lonigan move on to focus on factors extrinsic to the child that affect the learning process. In a wide-ranging review that discusses the contribution of social factors to emergent literacy, this chapter reinforces Byrne's view that learning to read is the result of children's interactions with the environment. Of course, as we will see in a later section, teachers and schools are crucial, but before school begins a whole range of home variables are important in fostering the child's interest in, motivation for, and ability for, learning to read. In these terms, on average, children from lower-income homes are disadvantaged. It is important, however, to emphasize the "on average"; there is no single marker of socio-economic status (SES) and there are a large number of variables that can modify the relationship between SES and reading achievement. In particular, parents' beliefs are important and may override other factors.

Two key predictors of emergent literacy are responsive parenting and home literacy (and doubtless they are related). Parents who are responsive to their child's emergent language skills use scaffolding techniques to bring on vocabulary; in turn, good vocabulary is an important foundation for acquiring literacy skills in school. Home literacy has a number of meanings. Children from literate homes tend to have good language as well as good print knowledge, and this is an important predictor of their reading comprehension. In some literate homes, parents teach their children, and children who have experienced such environments come to school with better developed phonological awareness and letter knowledge, and hence are better prepared to learn to read.

The final chapter of this section is a reflection, not on the process of learning to read and spell, but on the cognitive consequences of such learning. Morais and Kolinsky gather together a body of research on the effects of literacy that compares illiterate and ex-illiterate people. Distinguishing between the effects of literacy and the effects of schooling, they show that literacy has no discernible effect on executive processes and a relatively small effect on visual cognition (although experience with graphic representation appears to promote aspects of analytic visual processing). However, becoming literate has a major impact on metalinguistic skills. In particular, alphabetic literacy fosters the development of phoneme awareness. It also facilitates the development of short-term memory and nonword repetition, perhaps because it encourages attention to the phonemic structure of speech. These findings remind us that development is essentially an interactive process; the development of orthographic skills depends upon the interplay of a number of subskills that themselves develop in synergy. Together the chapters in this section demonstrate that learning to read is a complex business and we have come a long way in our scientific understanding of it.

# 6

# *Theories of Learning to Read*

## Brian Byrne

My aim in this chapter is to outline an agenda for theories of learning to read rather than to present one of my own or review existing ones. I hope to do so in a way that identifies empirical questions on which data are sparse and that also makes clear how to identify the necessary components in an optimal instruction program. Something of a case study will be made of a particular aspect of learning to read: how children take their first steps in mastering decoding. This question furnishes a useful ground for most of the conceptual and methodological points I wish to make. In addition, the level of success that children have very early in reading development continues to characterize their later progress (Byrne, Fielding-Barnsley, & Ashley, 2000; Juel, 1988). First steps matter, apparently.

## Two Background Issues

Before turning to the main subject matter of the chapter, there are two background issues I wish to discuss: the prospect of a broadly applicable theory of learning, and the matter of motivation.

### *A theory of learning everything?*

We could hope that there exists *the* theory of learning, and reading would merely be another instance. We could then benefit from over a hundred years of scientific research into the learning process. Chomsky (1976) neatly captured the improbability of an acceptable single learning theory by pointing out that if such a theory existed humans should be as superior to rats in learning mazes as they are in learning language, but clearly they are not. He also pointed out that diverse activities such as nest building, orientation in space, and conspecific identification, all in the repertoire of a species, appear unlikely to have much in common in the way they are learned.

Judging from recent accounts of the process of learning to read, scholars for the most part share Chomsky's view, implicitly anyway, that there is little to be gleaned from how one cognitive process is acquired to assist understanding how another is. For instance, in the well-known models of literacy acquisition proposed by Ehri (2002), Frith (1985), Share (1995), and Seymour (1986), there is little reference to anything other than elements and principles of print and closely related aspects of speech such as phonology, morphology, and aspects of phonologically based processing such as verbal working memory. Learning procedures for components of spoken language such as vocabulary are not exploited, and nor are procedures for, say, the acquisition of other symbol systems such as musical notation or number. My own attempt to sketch how children learn about the alphabetic nature of English orthography (Byrne, 1998) makes scant reference to other cognitive accomplishments. So rightly or wrongly, most of us do our work as if learning to read is a unique enough process not to bother with other processes for insights.

There are exceptions. Some, for instance, have invoked more general aspects of cognitive development in domains other than literacy (e.g., Tunmer & Hoover, 1992), and others have drawn certain parallels with the child's dawning grasp of representational systems such as those for quantity and objects (e.g., Bialystok, 2000). But the most ambitious attempt to employ a single approach for a variety of learning accomplishments is embodied in connectionist models. Using computational procedures based on distributed processing, connectionist models learn using a limited number of procedures across a wide variety of processing domains – language, perception, memory, for instance. But even here, though the learning process may be (relatively) uniform, the choice of structures that are the input and output of the association procedure is relatively open. Within the restricted domain of learning to pronounce printed words, for instance, decisions about phonological units need to be made – phonemes, phones, phonetic features? – and likewise about graphemic units – letters, lines and arcs? No general-purpose theory can select forms of representation algorithmically, and the virtues of particular choices need to be tested empirically. On top of this, there remains vigorous debate about the explanatory power of connectionist approaches in general (e.g., Bowers, 2002; Marcus, 1998; McClelland & Seidenberg, 2000; Pinker, 1999), and with specific reference to printed word identification (e.g., Coltheart, Rastle, Perry, Langdon, & Ziegler, 2001; Harm & Seidenberg, 1999; Seidenberg & Plaut, 1998).

All in all, therefore, we would be unwise to take too much for granted in developing a theory of learning to read. Any claim that such-and-such a learning procedure over such-and-such a set of representations is available in the service of literacy development should be considered to be an empirical claim, not one to be accepted a priori merely because the procedure is demonstrated in some other domain.

## Motivation

The other background matter stems from the recognition that learning to read (English at least) is a prolonged affair, and a learner's motivation needs to be factored in. No theory of successful reading development gets by without postulating a substantial amount of exposure to printed language. Children require many encounters with print in order to fix in memory the patterns that correspond to linguistic structures of phoneme, syllable, morpheme, and word, all required for achieving reading rates that support comprehension close to that achieved in listening to speech (Carver, 1997; Ehri, 2002). Substantial exposure comes from reading a lot, and an unmotivated child is unlikely to do that (Stanovich, 1986). Motivational and self-concept differences among children that are contingent on their progress in reading are real, they can emerge surprisingly early in a child's schooling (Chapman, Tunmer, & Prochnow, 2000; Spear-Swerling & Sternberg, 1994, 1996), and they can continue into adulthood (Johnston, 1985).

I speculate that there are potential *points of discouragement* that can derail a child's determination to read, points that correspond to a child's first encounter with a new process that needs to be put in place for continued reading growth. I suggest that there are many potential sites for these points on the road to full reading mastery, and that we know little about how children negotiate their way through them, or fail to. The direct evidence for these points is sparse, but the fact that motivation to read has the effects that it does provides indirect evidence for their existence. Additionally, self-reports collected by Johnston (1985) from adults burdened with lifetime histories of reading failure suggest that the first of these may be a failure of insights about the nature of print, initial conceptual confusions such as believing that reading is remembering whole words. There then follow consequent affective responses, such as anxiety, and the adoption of self-defeating strategies, such as becoming the class clown to avoid exposing an inability to read. I will return to the initial failures later.

## Frameworks for Identifying the Work of Theories of Learning to Read

In recent publications I have adopted separate frameworks for considering the work that a theory of learning to read must do (Byrne, 1998, 2002). Here I will outline them and exploit aspects of both in a single scheme. They are the *division of labor* idea and an informal version of *Learnability Theory*.

### Classifying learning as division of labor

The first framework, the division of labor (not to be confused with the division of labor between the semantic and phonological pathways proposed in Plaut, McClelland, Seidenberg, & Patterson, 1996), is from Byrne (2002), and it is tuned in particular to addressing the practical goal of identifying elements of an optimal instructional program. It takes as its starting point the obvious fact that any act of learning is the joint product of the learner and the environment. It is possible to think of different acts of learning as occupying different points on a continuum representing the division of labor between the learner and the environment. At one end, the learner contributes most, with only meagre and fragmentary input required for learning to occur. At the other, the input must be rich and highly structured. In an earlier analysis (Byrne, Fielding-Barnsley, Ashley, & Larsen, 1997), we positioned learning to talk near the end where the learner contributes a great deal and learning mathematics at the end where the input needs to be substantial. Children can hardly be prevented from learning language; and in contrast many can hardly be made to learn mathematics.

A goal of theory therefore is to analyse reading into components and determine the relative contributions of learner and environment for each component. The application to instruction then emerges as a kind of subtraction: Once we know how much the child contributes to acquiring a component of reading and the nature of that contribution, we will know what is left over to teach. From this perspective, *the work that a theory of learning to read must do is to identify and describe reading's component processes and the learner's own contribution to the acquisition of each of these processes.*

*An example.* A case has been made that a necessary component process in learning to read productively in an alphabetic script is usable knowledge of the phonemic organization of speech, or *phonemic awareness* (see Byrne, 1998; Hulme et al., 2002; Lundberg, Frost, & Petersen, 1988; Share, 1995). In our group's work, this knowledge has mostly been operationalized by determining if a child can reliably affirm that words like *sun* and *sail* begin identically, that *sun* and *fish* do not, that *pot* and *hat* end identically, and so on (Byrne & Fielding-Barnsley, 1989, 1990, 1991). We have used the term *phoneme identity* to refer to this aspect of phonological awareness. Like all empirically based claims, this one is open to challenge, and challenged it has been by studies of children suffering from Down syndrome who have apparently learned to read in the absence of appropriate levels of phonemic awareness (Cossu, Rossini, & Marshall, 1993; but see Byrne, 1993; Cupples & Iacono, 2000). An extended case study of a highly precocious reader who apparently learned to pronounce words and nonwords from an early age in the absence of detectable levels of phonemic awareness also challenges the claim (see Fletcher-Finn & Thompson, 2000, 2004), as do some cases of hyperlexia for the same reason (Sparks, 1995, 2001). Whether the claim needs to be modified to take account of these apparent exceptions, or the exceptions are more apparent than real, or indeed the claim is just false, remain subjects of continuing research (see also Castles & Coltheart, 2003).

For purposes of illustration, however, let us assume that phonemic awareness is a necessary step on the way to mastering the decoding process. The next question becomes the contribution stemming from children themselves in achieving this usable knowledge of phoneme identity. At one extreme, we can hypothesize that they are born with it. Thus, as soon as they can negotiate the test's vocabulary (*starts the same*, for example), we expect that they can reliably tell us that *sun* and *sail* begin identically. If true, there is no need to teach this insight. At the other extreme, phoneme identity by hypothesis requires extensive and well-targeted instruction.

Innate phonemic awareness is untenable because it is well known that young children do not reliably succeed on tests of the process (for examples using phoneme identity, see Byrne, 1998; Byrne & Fielding-Barnsley, 1993; for a classic study using another measure of phonemic awareness, see Liberman, Shankweiler, Fischer, & Carter, 1974). They are going to need environmental input to help them achieve phonemic awareness. But how much will they need, and of what kind?

This is the hard part. There is an uncountable number of questions that can be asked about the child's contribution if it falls short of the process in its entirety. Here is one: If in Johnny's first month of school his teacher, attuned to the latest reading research, tells him that *sun* and *sail* and *snake* begin identically and he understands and believes her, will he continue to believe this to be the case if he gets a new teacher in Month 2? Does the source of the insight matter? This, like all such questions, is an empirical matter, and in this case experience tells us that acquired cognitive structures are not so fickle; they show *independence from source*. Less fanciful is the question of whether Johnny knows that *spider* also begins the same. On that point, experience is not much of a guide and an experiment is called for. Likewise, if he gains the insight that many words can begin with the phoneme /s/, will he, without needing to be told, also understand that this is just an example of a general principle of speech? Will he be able to reliably affirm, say, that *ball, bike*, and *bus* all begin the same?

To continue with this example, it turns out that the answer to both of those questions, whether generalization occurs both within phonetic classes and across them, seems to be *yes*. In an intervention study, preschool children being taught about the identity of words' beginnings and endings using a restricted number of exemplar phonemes showed a high degree of generalization not only to other words beginning with those phonemes but to untaught phonemes as well (Byrne & Fielding-Barnsley, 1991). Part of the child's contribution to this foundation for reading appears to be a helpful generalization process, and teachers do not need to work through all the 40-plus phonemes of English.

Or might they sometimes for some children? More generally, can we assume that all children make the same contribution to an act of learning? It would be surprising if we could, and it turns out that with respect to at least one aspect of transfer of training our doubts are justified. We showed that only some children trained to recognize the identity of words' beginnings transferred their insight to words' endings; for the others, phonemic awareness was position-specific (Byrne & Fielding-Barnsley, 1990). Thus, complicating the task of identifying what it is that children contribute to learning any reading-relevant process is the fact that this will not be identical for all children. There will be no single theory of learning to read.

Part of what makes children different in what they bring to learning to read is under the influence of their genes (Fisher & DeFries, 2002; see also Pennington & Olson, this volume), and it is now known that genetic effects on literacy-related processes, including a composite of phonological awareness tasks and several measures of memory and learning, can already be detected in preschool-aged children (Byrne et al., 2002). It would be unsound, however, to suggest that the tasks used for these measurements represent truly basic processes, or *endophenotypes*. As Plomin and Crabbe (2000) point out, "the key to understanding . . . when attempting to detect a genetic influence on a trait . . . will be careful and reliable ascertainment and description of the phenotype" (p. 822). Thus it is incumbent on reading researchers to properly identify the fundamental processes involved in reading acquisition if progress is to be made in tracing how genes affect them. Put another way, theories of reading development need to be both detailed and complete if they are to reveal how variations of genetic origin generate different trajectories taken by different children.

This discussion of genes raises another complication with the division of labor idea. I have been implying that a given child either does or does not contribute a particular process to literacy growth, but this might be seen as a rather static view that does not take account of the fact that experience itself can influence the course of development, including via effects on gene expression (see Johnston & Edwards, 2002, for a review). The Piagetian notion of accommodation (Piaget, 1952) describes how experience can alter cognitive structures when those structures are challenged by input that they cannot assimilate, and the increasing demands of the literary landscape that children encounter as they proceed through schooling may constitute challenging input of this kind. I will return to the Piagetian framework later, but for the moment we can acknowledge this more dynamic view of development while still admitting that in particular cases it remains an empirical matter as to whether and how experience influences conceptual structures and learning processes.

Despite these qualifications, the division of labor idea serves the purpose of motivating the kinds of empirical investigations just mentioned, and it also provides a convenient way to draw out educational implications of theory and research. I will return, too, to the question of educational implications later.

*To summarize.* A theory of learning to read needs to (1) describe the component processes of skilled reading and thus the processes that must be acquired, (2) identify the nature of the learner's contribution to acquiring each of these components, and (3), if the theory is to be practically useful, calculate by subtraction from the results of (1) and (2) what it is that the environment must supply. Many of the chapters in this book address (1), and show the considerable progress that has been made in specifying the nature of skilled reading. With respect to (2), it is important to remember that the extent of learners' contributions is virtually immeasurable. Some, such as independence from information source, might be in place in all learners and as such remain largely unobserved (and without implication for instruction). Other theoretically possible contributions, such as inborn phonemic awareness, might not be part of any learner's resources (with the implication that it needs to be taught for all children). Yet others, such as transfer of training, might be supplied by some learners and not others (with the implication that teaching practices need to compensate in certain cases and in others take account of the fact that no environmental input is needed). In total, the challenges are substantial.

## Learnability Theory

The framework just outlined asks us as a first step to identify component processes in learning to read but it gives no guidance about how to do that. Here I will summarize a second framework: one that does provide some structure.

Although on the skeptical position concerning learning theory there may be little in common across different domains in *how* learners achieve what they do, there exist conceptual and formal analyses of *what* is achieved during learning that may be relatively domain free. A well-known version is due to Gold (1967) (see also Pinker, 1979), and Byrne (1998) adapted Gold's formulation in the service of understanding the acquisition of the alphabetic principle. Here I will broaden that application to consider wider aspects of learning to read.

Learning is partitioned into subproblems:

1.  What is learned.
2.  The nature of the learner.
3.  A procedure for selecting the hypotheses that the learner adopts during learning.
4.  A learning environment.
5.  A criterion of success.

For present purposes, we can fold 1 and 5, what is learned and a success criterion, into a sketch of the final state attained by someone who learns to read. Problem 3, hypotheses entertained by the learner, can be considered as part of the learner's initial state, relevant cognitive structures available to the child prior to exposure to reading and reading instruction. The learning environment, Problem 4, constitutes the information made available to the child. The nature of the learner, Problem 2, will determine the learning mechanisms available to be brought to bear on the task.

*The final state attained by the learner.* The criterion by which we can judge that readers have become skilled is that they can understand a stretch of written text as well as they can understand the same text in spoken form. This is Hoover and Gough's (1990) "Simple View" of reading, and can be summarized as $R = D \times L$, Reading (comprehension) equals Decoding multiplied by Language (comprehension). For R to equal L, D must equal 1; the word identification process must be accurate and, although not directly captured in the Simple View, it must be reasonably rapid (Carver, 1997). Thus, in creating a theory of learning to read we need to understand how children learn to identify words accurately and in a timely fashion. This enterprise, in turn, requires a clear picture of what is involved in identifying words, and to this I now turn.

*How well do we understand the acquisition of word identification?* Let us first consider what word identification is in the context of reading. Why does a competent reader say "dog" when confronted with *dog*? Why not "dot," or "fish," or, for that matter, "uncle?" The answer is that the print sequence *constrains* the response, but as I will argue it constitutes only one constraint out of several. The question of how well we understand word identification can then be settled by asking how completely we have characterized the constraints that operate to produce accurate word identification, how they are employed, and, importantly in the present context, how they are learned, if learning they require.

*We need a definition of word identification.* I define it as *locating the lexical object intended by the writer that corresponds to the printed word.* A lexical object has at least a phonological form, a syntactic class, and a semantic interpretation. Print specifies the phonemes and their sequence. For English, this code is not a simple one, but despite the complications caused by the "quasiregularity" of the orthography (Plaut et al., 1996), there has nevertheless been impressive progress towards describing the process, with several (albeit competing) computational models in existence and under continuous development (e.g., Ans, Carbonnel, & Valdois, 1998; Coltheart, Rastle, Perry, Langdon, & Ziegler, 2001; Plaut et al., 1996; Plaut, this volume; Seidenberg & McClelland, 1989). Alongside these highly specified computer-based models sit more informal ones, also directed at describing how the phonemic sequence specified by a printed word is identified (e.g., Ehri, 2002; this volume). Although it cannot be said that we fully understand the operation of this constraint (phoneme sequence specification), it is the one on which most progress has been made because it is the one that has been the subject of most research.

However, lexical objects are richer phonological forms than just a sequence of phonemes. Multisyllable words have intonational contour, for example, and in English the print sequence underdetermines the full phonological form because it does not specify prosody. The word "banana" differs from the word "Canada" not only in its consonantal phonemes but also in its stress pattern and consequently in vowel color. In contrast to the amount of work done on identification of single syllable words in English, there is very little on how children read multisyllable ones (see Duncan & Seymour, 2003, for a recent exception), and even less on how they *learn* to do so. Informal observation indicates that failures of lexical identification can occur because of failures to assign correct stress (as in a child reading *banana* with the prosody of *Canada* and not recognizing the spoken form). It is also known that young children are less accurate in their spelling of consonants and vowels in unstressed than stressed syllables, indicating that stress patterns play a role in orthographic processing in general (Treiman, 1993; Treiman, Berch, & Weatherston, 1993).

Lexical objects are underdetermined by print sequences in other ways. Their accurate identification often depends on the linguistic context. This manifests itself in a variety of ways. Apart from frank ambiguity (e.g., *bug, bank, ball, can*), words like *tear* and *lead* each represent two distinct phoneme sequences and two or more lexical objects, and in all of these cases the appropriate word can only be determined from context. Words like *use, conflict* and *record* have different phoneme sequences or stress patterns according to syntactic class, noun or verb, and that can only be determined in a sentential context. Others, like *entrance* and *converse*, also have two stress patterns requiring contextual resolution, though the two underlying lexical objects are unrelated. A skilled reader performs the necessary computations on line, and of course sentence processing is a lively research enterprise with a host of studies on ambiguity resolution, garden pathing, and so on, mostly conducted using print rather than speech. But as *acquisition problems*, these processes are poorly understood, as is their potential to behave as points of discouragement, singly or cumulatively. Much research on word identification as a problem in learning to read is directed to single (often single syllable) words as the target behavior, and this ties the theories to learning something that falls very far short of skilled word identification in text. This, then, is one area where data are sparse and therefore needed.

*The learner's initial state: hypotheses that might be entertained.* Moving now from final to initial state, Learnability Theory directs us to consider what the child might hypothesize about print. The *division of labor* framework encourages us to ask what a child might think print is about on first contact, prior to environmental (e.g., teacher) input to act as a guide. Knowing this will help us decide what children need to be told, if they need to be told anything at all.

I have argued (Byrne, 1996, 1998) that the candidate hypotheses can be identified from extant writing systems of the world, which has graphemes representing, roughly, phoneme, syllable, and morpheme (see also Treiman & Kessler, this volume). In the case of alphabetic writing systems, each of the levels, phoneme, syllable, morpheme, as well as word, are in some sense correct, because an orthography whose elements stand in for a basic unit (phoneme) will equally stand in for, in combination, higher-level units (syllable, morpheme, word) just because phonemes combine productively to generate those higher units (see also Van Orden, Pennington, & Stone, 1990). So the hypothesis that print represents (only) the morphemes of the language, for instance, is not wrong, just incomplete.

One reason why these considerations are important is that if children do begin with, say, morphemes as the hypothesized basic currency of an alphabetic orthography, then they will either need to use their own resources to recover (to discover the phoneme as the basic unit so that they can read novel words productively) or they will need someone to tell them. Then the question shifts to whether they do indeed possess these resources. This is not an idle question, because there are indications that, for some children at least, morphemes are in fact what they first consider when attempting to map orthography onto the language they know as mature speakers of 4 years of age.

*The learner's initial state: evidence on hypotheses.*   In experiments reported in detail in Byrne (1996), preliterate children were taught small word families in which the systematic distinguishing characteristic was a letter (or letter group) that represented both a morpheme and a phoneme (or syllable). For instance, they learned to pronounce *book* and *books*, and *hat* and *hats*. They were then challenged with a forced choice between "bike" and "bikes" as the pronunciation for the written word *bikes* (*bike* in other trials), and with other pairs like this. In addition, they were asked to decide between, say, "purr' and "purse" for *purs* (or *pur*). The children performed reliably on the first type of transfer item, the one in which the *s* continued to represent both morpheme and phoneme, but not on the second type, in which the *s* represented just a phoneme (as in *purs* for "purr" versus "purse"). In another condition, a new group of preliterate children could discriminate, say, *mean* from *meaner* in a transfer trial having previously learned to read *small* and *smaller*, but could not distinguish *corn* from *corner* where the *er* has no morphemic role. The results support the contention that prior to formal reading instruction children are tuned to detect correspondences between graphemic structures and morphemic but not phonemic ones. Their initial hypothesis affords meaning a determining role in linking print to language.

There are several ways in which these results need qualification. One is that children who already knew the typical phoneme for the letter *s* performed the purely phonemic transfer task well when *s* was the critical distinguishing feature. Apparently the insight that comes with letter knowledge is sufficient to allow children to detect grapheme–phoneme links from suitably arranged whole word learning. Second, even without letter knowledge, a few children managed the phonemic transfer test, suggesting, again, individual differences in resources (or other knowledge sources present but not identified in these children).

I suspect that the self-reports offered by Johnston's (1985) informants, typically that they "learned" to read by memorizing *words*, might better be described as memorizing *morphemes*, if the results of the experiments just cited (Byrne, 1996) can be generalized. Word or morpheme, this kind of learning relies heavily on semantics, and might be captured within the triangle model of Seidenberg and McClelland (1989). In the model, one route from orthography to phonology is via semantics. Harm, McCandless, and Seidenberg (2003) suggest that such learning would be holistic because there are few systematic links between orthography and phonology through semantics other than at the morpheme level, and that this in fact mimics the character of reading in some reading-disabled children; holistic, or *noncomponential*, representations in mapping from orthography to phonology, leading to poor reading of nonwords and newly encountered real words. Typically, this kind of restricted reading is attributed to poorly developed phonological representations at the start of reading acquisition. In my view, the possibility that some cases of this deficiency result from semantically based initial hypotheses about the representational function of print is underexplored. In fact, we might capture the possibility of this occurring within Piagetian terms: Because alphabetic orthographies simultaneously represent phonemes *and* higher-levels units such as morphemes, print experience may not force a revision of the morphemic hypothesis on a learner (accommodation is not required). All new words can be assimilated into the existing conceptual structure that the orthography is based on morphemic units.

A modified position on the relation of initial hypotheses and subsequent reading growth may be that only those children with *deficits* in phonemic representation will not recover from the incomplete hypothesis of morphological representation. Thus, the empirical issue is whether there are children with normal phonological resources who are nevertheless hampered in their reading by the persistence of the morphological hypothesis. This is an important area for research.

*The nature of the learner.* Skilled reading entails being able to recognize the lexical identities of many thousands of words, even ones not previously encountered. An important part of this process is the derivation of each word's pronunciation(s), and, adopting the division of labor framework, we can ask what the learner contributes and what the environment must supply as this process is mastered. One answer attributes much to the learner: The child learns to pronounce a number of words in a paired-associate fashion, that is, without any recognition of the systematic mapping of orthography onto phonology, and then, by some kind of process of induction, derives those systematic mappings, freeing him or her to generate the pronunciation of newly encountered words. All that teaching need do is furnish the initial set of words and, in recognition that paired associate learning is not usually flawless and thus that the learner's contribution to this stage is limited, supply enough support (feedback, repeated exposure, etc.) to fix the word set in memory. A scenario like this is at the heart of connectionist theories of reading acquisition (see Plaut, this volume), and figures as a process in noncomputational ones, such as Fletcher-Finn and Thompson's *induced sublexical relations, ISRs* (e.g., Fletcher-Finn &

Thompson, 2000, 2004; Thompson, Fletcher-Finn, & Cottrell, 1999). The essential feature is that induction is available right from the beginning, requiring no environmental input (teaching) to get the process started other than facilities to teach the pronunciation of whole words.

*Evidence on induction: triggering decoding.* Paired associate learning is a clearly attested resource of humans, including children. There is much evidence that it also operates in the domain of early word learning (e.g., Byrne, 1992; Gough, Juel, & Griffith, 1992). Implicit induction of structure is also attested in humans (e.g, the classic studies of synthetic grammar learning by Reber, 1967). Is induction available at the beginning of reading acquisition?

This question motivated some early studies from my group about induction of print–speech regularities in mature language users, as a kind of analogue to the situation facing the child confronted with print–speech pairs (Byrne, 1984; Byrne & Carroll, 1989). Adults were asked to learn an artificial orthography that systematically represented the subphonemic features of voicing and place. In several studies, including one in which the participants were exposed to 2,400 exemplars of the system, there emerged no evidence that the subjects by themselves induced the representations embodied in the orthography. For instance, even though the participants readily learned symbols for phonemes designed to map onto the subphonemic features, they could not transfer successfully to partially new symbols on the basis of those features. Their learning remained holistic. So even though humans can induce patterns, they failed to do so in this particular domain.

On the basis of an extensive set of experiments (Byrne, 1992; Byrne & Fielding-Barnsley, 1989, 1990), we also concluded that induction of print–speech mappings was not part of the child's contribution to reading acquisition in the beginning stages. The experiments employed a transfer of training paradigm, similar to the one used in the adult experiments just described. In a typical experiment, a child who knew no (relevant) letter names was taught to read a pair of words such as *fat* and *bat* and challenged with a transfer task in which he or she was asked, for instance, to decide if *fun* said "fun" or "bun." In the experimental series, in which the number of learned items, the phonetics of the critical phonemes, and the position of the critical phonemes were varied, and in which over 80 preschool children participated, there were virtually no individual instances of a child succeeding at the transfer task. When forced to rely on their own resources, children showed no evidence of inducing sublexical relations.

Pursuing the question of what the child does (and does not) contribute, we can ask what precisely it is that the child is failing to deliver in this experimental situation. One possibility is that children of this age lack inductive powers in general, or inductive powers specifically when it comes to a symbol system for elements of language. However, neither the more general nor the more (language-) specific possibility turned out to be true. We conducted control experiments with larger segments of language as the target, using the same transfer of training paradigm, and children were generally successful at transfer. For instance, taught symbols for the compound nouns "bus-stop" and "doorstop," children were able to show transfer when challenged with a choice between "busman" and "doorman" with partially new symbols (Byrne & Fielding-Barnsley, 1989). Some of these experiments were particularly telling because they were within-subject; the same children who succeeded on compound nouns failed to exhibit transfer with phonemes as the object of interest (that is, they succeeded with the *bus-stop doorstop* → *busman* item type but not with *fat bat* → *fun*). Phonemes remained invisible to the otherwise available induction process, a representational rather than a process deficiency.

We need to recognize that a learning theory for the early stages of reading that excluded a triggering effect of induction of orthographic patterns over phonemes might be correct for some children and incorrect for others. That this is a possibility is suggested by the studies of Fletcher-Finn and Thompson (2000, 2004) with the precocious reader Maxine, who had advanced reading skills at 28 months in the face of very low levels of phonological awareness. Maxine *had* been taught letter sounds and names from an early age, and this may have been the source of her initial insights into the alphabetic principle (see Byrne, 1992, Experiment 4, for relevant evidence), but even without the evidence from precocious readers like Maxine, the very next child studied in an experiment of the sort I have described may succeed where many have failed.

*The theory so far.* Children's initial hypotheses about the nature of print are semantically rather than phonologically oriented. *Left to their own resources,* they will build links between print and language via morphological structures, links that are at the same time both accurate and incomplete. Further, they will not, *from their own resources,* detect the mapping of graphemes onto phonemes even after learning to read suitably arranged word families that could reveal these mappings to a mind suitably tuned to detect them. (The reason *why* this all might hold, if hold it does, may lie in the very nature of the phonetic code, in the possibility that its constituents are beyond the reach of normal consciousness – see Byrne & Liberman, 1999, and Liberman, 1999, for a defense of this position.) Available evidence also suggests that children may not require much in the way of environmental input to begin to build the appropriate links between print and speech via phonology, perhaps some letter-sound knowledge along with, one presumes, the idea that the sounds have something to do with word structure. Complicating the picture are differences among children that could come into play anywhere in this hypothesized set of processes, for good (if a child's contribution exceeds what is suggested here) or ill (if it falls short). Complications aside, the critical development is the establishment of a set of mappings between graphemes and phonemes, and (at least some) children will not develop these from internal resources even in the presence of potentially enabling input such as whole words arranged in helpful families.

*Beyond the triggering phase.* The frameworks for theory that I have presented, the division of labor idea and the Learnability idea with its subproblems, can still guide research as children grow in reading skill. We can ask, as we did for earlier phases, how much the learner contributes to acquiring the word-specific and generalized representations of print that underpin fast, accurate identification of words. This is tantamount to asking one question of the many possible about the nature of the learner.

There are some things that appear uncontroversial. One is that there are too many "rules" of English orthography to support the idea that explicit instruction is needed, or even helpful, in the acquisition of sublexical regularities (Adams, 1990; Venezky, 1967). Rules like "when two vowels go walking, the first one does the talking" may capture a truism about English orthography but is rarely taught and may be redundant if it is. So the learner is contributing *something*.

What that something is, of course, is the subject of intense research (at least for monosyllabic words up to the level of pronunciation – see earlier discussion). Models are, as they ought to be, constrained by and tested against observations of reading, including those of reading-disabled children and their responses to intervention (e.g., Harm et al., 2003), the phases children go through on the way to becoming skilled readers (see Seidenberg, 2002, and Stuart, 2002, for reviews from two different perspectives), and skilled reading (e.g., Coltheart et al., 2001; Seidenberg & McClelland, 1989). With continued research, including extensions to multisyllable words (Ans et al., 1998), it is likely that the rigorous approach entailed in computational modeling will yield a rich array of information about learning mechanisms as well as about the representation and use of print knowledge. To exploit the advantages of modeling fully it will be important to keep in firm view the complete range of processes represented by the final state, such as the computation of prosody, ambiguity resolution, and syntactic class identification.

## Learning Revisited

Learning to read is exactly that, *learning*. This rather obvious observation comes into particular focus when considering one aspect of the division of labor idea, that different children make contributions of different kinds or degrees, because whatever the proper learning theory for an organism in a domain, there will always be some differences in the rate or trajectory with which individuals achieve the final state. In a considerable amount of recent and current research, particularly into reading difficulties, the focus has been on *failures of insight* (particularly phonemic awareness) rather than on *failures of learning* (in terms of association processes such as fixing print patterns in memory). The contrast can be seen in some of my group's recent findings. In a preschool intervention study targeting phonemic awareness, we showed that the *level* of phonemic awareness achieved as a result of the training had measurable predictive value for reading up to six years later, but the *rate* at which children achieved the levels that they did was an even stronger predictor of later reading performance (Byrne et al., 2000). We interpreted this finding as indicating that a "learning rate parameter" needed to be taken into account in explaining differences among children in reading growth (the quotation marks are there in acknowledgment that this is a mere description). The basic observation, that the rate of response to intervention better predicts later reading than the outcome level itself, has been replicated in another intervention study with preschoolers burdened with a family risk factor for dyslexia (Hindson, 2001). Others have drawn attention to the *learning* in *learning disability* (e.g., Vellutino et al., 1996), and recently Snowling, Gallagher, and Frith (2003) have concluded, in another study of children at family risk, that a marker of dyslexia in such cases is a deficit in verbal association learning (see also Mayringer & Wimmer, 2000, and Windfuhr & Snowling, 2001).

In the longitudinal twin study reported in Byrne et al. (2002), learning measures have shown up as heritable, including a measure of responsiveness to preschool training in phoneme identity. We do not yet know how these preschool measures will play out phenotypically and genotypically as this sample of children matures in reading, but the hope is that we are one step closer to an aspect of the biology of reading development with the identification of a genetically influenced process. There are studies of the genetics of learning that offer tempting prospects for linking individual differences to brain processes. For instance, Tang et al. (1999) have shown that over-expression of a receptor for NMDA, a synaptic coincidence detector of the kind required by Hebbian cell assemblies (Hebb, 1949), leads to enhanced synaptic potentiation and superior learning and memory at the behavioral level in mice. Hebbian learning, based as it is on modifications among neurons that are simultaneously active, looks like the kind of device required to fix patterns of co-occurrence that must form the basis for orthographic patterns. This is all in the further reaches of speculation, of course, but it offers a hint of one direction that future theories of reading might take. That is, it shows that the prospect of a biologically grounded theory of reading development is realizable, and that behavior-genetic studies in which the phenotype is appropriately described will be one way in which behavior and biology might be mapped into each other (see also Price & McCrory, this volume).

## Applications of Theory

I stated earlier that the division of labor idea is helpful in considering the educational implications of theories of learning to read. It does so by identifying what the child contributes and, by subtraction, what must be taught. In cases where the research is as yet indeterminate on whether the child's contribution includes a particular process, there exists an evaluation procedure for competing research-based conclusions, one that has educational consequences (see Byrne, 2002, for a fuller account). The procedure and its implications are in three parts:

1. Count the number of processes contributed by the child assumed by each set of conclusions.
2. Value more highly the set with the fewest processes assumed.
3. Implement practices that follow from the more highly valued set of conclusions.

If teaching is informed in this way, more rather than less will be included in the curriculum because less rather than more is assumed on behalf of the child. The worst that can happen if the procedure is in error, and children actually do make more contributions than assumed, is that things that do not need to be taught are taught. If practices that follow from assuming more on behalf of the child are implemented and it turns out that one or more of those assumptions are flawed, then teaching will have omitted things that really needed to be taught. That strikes me as a more grievous mistake than overteaching.

To take the example of phonemic awareness, a process on whose necessity the jury may still be out: If educational practice follows the evaluation procedure, it will include phonemic awareness instruction for young readers because doing so attributes fewer capacities to the child. If it turns out not to have been needed, resources have been squandered, but that is to be preferred to omitting it and finding out it was needed. Then children have been harmed.

In some cases, the research evidence will tell us that some children make a particular contribution and some do not. Under those circumstances, unless individual children who do present with that process in place can be identified, it is better to assume that *no* children make that contribution and include it in the curriculum. Then none risk being left out. Such might apply to the generalization of phonemic awareness from sites used to teach it to other sites (say, words' beginnings to words' endings). It is better to include both positions, and others if necessary, in the instructional material.

Many of these practical points are underlined by a recent study by Hatcher, Hulme, and Snowling (2004). They demonstrated that providing extra tuition in phonological awareness to normally developing children already being taught with a strong phonics component did not enhance subsequent reading skills, but doing so did assist children identified as being at risk of reading failure. In a typical classroom, with its mixture of abilities and potentials, additional phonological work will thus be "wasted" on some pupils but be of benefit to others, an overall cost-benefit gain, one would presume.

## Concluding Remarks

I have presented an agenda for theorizing about learning to read. I suggested, first, that we are unlikely at this stage to benefit from a general theory of learning. I also suggested that we need to be mindful that motivational decline can have disastrous effects on reading growth, and that appropriate identification of the points in reading development where decline could set in should be high on the agenda (*points of discouragement*). I presented two frameworks for thinking about theories. One encourages us to address the relative contributions of the learner and the environment. The other complements the first by signposting what it is that the relative contributions are about – the subproblems of Learnability Theory. I pointed to two places where research has been sparse, on processes contributing to the full range of lexical identification problems, and on children's earliest hypotheses about the nature of print and how those hypotheses may project into later development. I then considered further questions about the nature of the learner, one of the subproblems of Learnability Theory, particularly what the child can contribute to initial insights about the nature of alphabetic script. For instance, I expressed my doubts about implicit induction of letter-phoneme mappings as being part of the child's earliest contributions to reading development. I also expressed my confidence that current computer-based modeling of later reading processes and their development offers high promise for gaining a detailed understanding of many issues, something that will be needed if we are to achieve an integration of biology and psychology in the context of reading development.

Studying reading has an obvious practical payoff in terms of education. It is also a good place to be doing psychological science. Reading is a well-delineated behavior, at least by comparison with many other domains, and hence it offers prospects for real progress. Thus, we are more likely to find out what makes a skilled reader than what makes a skilled salesperson or politician (or psychological researcher, for that matter). The hope, then, is that the lessons we learn from this endeavor will inform how we should tackle less tractable domains. The other hope, of course, is that what we learn affords a platform for offering clear and credible guidance to educators charged with teaching children to become skilled readers and with rescuing children who falter on the way.

## Note

The Australian Research Council has supported most of my research cited in this chapter, with further support from the National Institute of Child Health and Human Development, Washington. Besides the people mentioned as authors or co-authors in papers from my group cited in the reference list, I would like to thank the following for skilful and dedicated contributions to the group's research: Frances Attard, Fiona Black, Marnie Church, Nicole Church, Marreta Coleman, Cara Delaland, Carol Mackay, and Annette Stevenson.

# 7

# *Writing Systems and Spelling Development*

## Rebecca Treiman and Brett Kessler

This chapter differs from most of its companions in addressing literacy from the standpoint of the writer rather than the reader. Literacy research has concentrated on reading, but without the ability to write a person could scarcely be called literate. A full understanding of literacy development requires us to consider the development of writing skill as well as the development of reading skill. In this chapter, we focus on one important aspect of writing, the production of individual words. Good writing demands higher-level skills, of course, but the ability to spell words easily and automatically provides an important foundation for those skills.

Most of the research that has been carried out on spelling and its development has examined English. English is but one of the world's many languages, and it is a writing system with its own unique history and properties. Doubts have been expressed about the extent to which findings with English will generalize to other writing systems (e.g., Harris & Hatano, 1999). For this and other reasons, psycholinguistic studies of writing development can benefit from a broad examination of the world's writing systems. We begin the chapter, therefore, by considering the principles that characterize writing systems, especially those that are likely to affect the process of learning to write. We then turn to the learning of these principles, discussing research on the development of spelling in English and in other languages. The cross-linguistic perspective allows us to appreciate the challenges that children face in learning to spell across a variety of systems. It further shows that the stumbling blocks encountered by English-speaking children are not all that different from those encountered by children learning to write in other languages.

# Principles of Writing Systems

## Basic units of symbolization

The primary goal of writing is to record or communicate concepts in a visual medium. We are most familiar with using human language in that connection, but that is not a necessary entailment. Since at least the seventeenth century, philosophers have advocated systems by which concepts could be recorded directly, unencumbered by illogical human language. These systems have been called *semasiography*, or concept writing (Sampson, 1987). An example is the following illustration of Blissymbolics (Bliss, 1949) from Weber (1997):

凵 Λ̂ ›ı ꝍↂ⌇𖤍

This proposition can be interpreted as "The family goes to the zoo" or "There's a family walking to the zoological garden" or "Die Familie geht zum Zoo." Any reading that captures the basic meaning is equally correct.

Although we encounter specialized semasiographies every day, ranging from musical notation to numerals, general writing is always based on natural human language: It is *glottographic* (Sampson, 1987). Glottography involves far more – or less – than writing the sounds of language. Indeed, a general-purpose notation for writing sounds would be remarkably space-intensive and difficult to use.

The solution to the problem of writing language comes from the observation that humans confront the same problem when speaking. We cannot hope to speak by associating some arbitrary noise for every idea we want to express. Instead, language is organized as two parallel constituent hierarchies. One hierarchy, the morphosyntactic, structures sentences to be composed of phrases, phrases of words, and words of morphemes, the smallest meaning-bearing unit of the language. There are an infinite number of possible sentences, but they are built up from a manageable number of morphemes. The other hierarchy, the phonological, structures the sounds of languages without regard to meaning. Phonological phrases are composed of metrical feet, feet are composed of stressed syllables and their unstressed neighbors, and syllables are composed ultimately of segments, the smallest manipulable chunk of sound. We can generate an infinite number of phrases, but most languages have perhaps hundreds of different syllable types and only dozens of different segment types. Crucially, a given syllable or word can be pronounced in an uncountable number of different ways (different speakers with different timbres at different tempos, etc.), but language treats them as the same at some abstract level, and so can writing.

Writing of the normal, glottographic, variety proceeds by assigning symbols to linguistic units, and then presenting those symbols in some conventional arrangement. In principle, a writing system could map language using either of the two hierarchies at any of the finite levels. We will discuss several examples of writing systems that work with different units on the morphosyntactic and phonological hierarchies.

Writing systems that have different symbols for different units on the morphosyntactic hierarchy are called *logographic*. In practice, the only units so represented are words and morphemes. Chinese is such a system (see Hanley, this volume). In traditional Chinese, the sentence that in pinyin romanization appears *Jiārén dào dòngwùyuán qù* 'The family goes to the zoo' may be written 家人到動物園去. Note that some of the words in the Chinese sentence are spelled with more than one symbol. This is because these words consist of more than one meaning-bearing unit. The word *jiārén* 'family' is made up of morphemes meaning 'home' 家 and 'person' 人; the word *dòngwùyuán* 'zoo' is composed of morphemes meaning 'move' 動, 'thing' 物, and 'garden' 園. It is these morphemic elements that are actually written out in Chinese. The crucial details that define Chinese as logographic are first, that the individual symbols can only be used for the specific morphemes – 家 cannot be used for just any morpheme or word meaning 'home' or pronounced *jiā* – and, second, that the actual symbols are not predictable by any other rules. To be sure, most of the symbols have some motivation. For example, this symbol for 'home' is composed of symbols for 'dwelling' (*mián* 宀) and 'pig' (*shǐ* 豕). Such motivations help writers remember symbols they have already learned, but the logic is almost never sufficiently transparent to allow one to accurately write a morpheme unless one has already encountered its symbol.

Chinese is the only purely logographic writing system in current use. The great majority of the world's writing systems represent units of the phonological hierarchy and are thus called *phonographic*. The highest level of the phonological hierarchy that has few enough types to be manageable is the syllable. Modern Yi, used in some parts of China, is an example of a true *syllabary*. It contains hundreds of different symbols for different syllables, with no predictable relationships between most of them: The symbol for *dit* (the final *t* is a tone marker), ꁹ, has no connection with the symbol for *dat*, ꁖ, the symbol for *ddit*, ꀿ, or even the symbol for *di*, ꀿ, which differs only in tone.

Yi is unusual in its exhaustive coverage of all syllable types. More typically, so-called syllabaries have different values only for distinct CV (one consonant, one vowel) combinations. For example, the syllabary that was invented in the 1800s to represent the Cherokee language has 85 symbols for CV sequences. This is so even though the language actually has hundreds of different syllable types, including those with consonant clusters and codas (postvocalic consonants). Cherokee and other such *CV syllabaries* frequently have devices for indicating otherwise unrepresented elements such as codas. For example, Cherokee writes a CV symbol that matches the consonant, and leaves it to the reader to understand that the vowel should be discarded. These CV syllabaries may reflect the view, on the part of their inventors, that CV syllables are close enough to true syllables for their symbolization to enable communication.

Some other scripts do bear the hallmark of conscious decomposition of syllables into smaller units. In bopomofo, a supplementary phonographic script used in Taiwan, syllables are written analytically as onset (prevocalic) consonants, then the entire rime (vowel plus any following consonants), then the tone. There is a different symbol for each rime: The symbol for *ang* is ㄤ, which is distinct from the symbol for *eng*, ㄥ, and also from the symbol for *an*, ㄢ. The Pahawh script for Hmong is another example of a script that writes onsets and rimes.

Most phonographic scripts operate on smaller units than syllables or even rimes: They have a separate symbol for each sound segment, or phoneme. The concept of writing segment by segment will be familiar to readers of this chapter. The syllable /kæt/ has three segments, /k/, /æ/, and /t/, and so one writes three letters, *cat*. Such writing systems are called *alphabets*. (Characters placed between / / or [ ] symbols follow the conventions of the International Phonetic Association, 1996, 1999.)

A *featural* system would, in theory, go beyond even the segmental level, taking apart segments to separately represent their components. The hangeul script used for Korean is often described as a featural system, and arguably it was one when first designed in the 1400s. However, it is fairer to say that the basic unit is the segment. Like Chinese logographic symbols, hangeul letters have motivated structure, but symbols for segments cannot be reliably composed just by assembling featural symbols by rote. For example, the feature aspiration is in principle formed by adding a horizontal stroke to the symbol for the unaspirated letter, but it is not obvious a priori where to put the stroke or what other changes need to be made: ㄱ *g* becomes ㅋ, ㄷ *d* becomes ㅌ, ㅂ *b* becomes ㅍ, ㅈ *j* becomes ㅊ. The current state of affairs is mostly due to graphic changes in the letters since they were first invented. The fact that letters were changed to the obfuscation of featural symbols suggests that writers think of letters as the more basic symbols.

Each type of system we have examined requires in turn fewer symbols than the one before. Some counts of Chinese logograms used throughout history approach 90,000, of which writers of present-day Chinese might master approximately 3,000, or 2,000 if they have a good dictionary. If Chinese were written syllabically, it might require about 1200 different symbols, depending on the dialect. In contrast, the alphabetic pinyin system for Chinese has about 34 symbols. Most languages would show similar drops, although their magnitude would vary depending on the structure of the language.

The decrease in symbol set size has advantages for writers. Fewer symbols are generally easier to learn and remember. Against the benefit in memorability, though, are at least two trade-offs. The first involves segmentation: Writers may find it differentially difficult to isolate various types of units from the language stream. As our discussion proceeded, the writing types became increasingly more abstract. Logographic symbols marry meaning, syntactic function, and sound; phonographic symbols deal with sound alone. Syllables, at least, arguably have an objective phonetic correlate having to do with sonority pulses. But segments are highly abstract, and difficult to isolate in the acoustic stream.

A second trade-off is perhaps less well recognized. This is that, as the unit of symbolization gets smaller and smaller, it becomes more and more difficult to apply the basic idea of glottography – that one assigns the same symbol to units that have the same functionality, even though they may sound somewhat different. In a syllabary, it is straightforward to decide that the syllables [ɪtʃ] (as in *itch*) and [ĩntʃ] (as in *inch*) require separate symbols. In an alphabet, the task of assigning segments to phonemes is much more difficult. Do we say that the nasality on the vowel in *inch* is an insignificant side effect of the nasality of the following [n], so that the vowel is the same [ɪ] as in *itch*? If so, this would lead us to write the vowels alike, as in English. Or do we say that the two vowels are distinct, and the optional [n] is a side effect of the nasality of the vowel? This would lead us to write the vowels differently, as when Navajo writes nasal vowels with a diacritic mark under the letter and nonnasal vowels without (e.g., *į* vs *i*). In like vein we can go on to ponder whether [tʃ] comprises one segment or two. Even linguists have difficulty making decisions about the proper classification of certain sounds. As we will see, the classification problem is no easier for young learners.

*Mixtures*

Rarely is a writing system a pure logography, a pure syllabary, or a pure alphabet. More typically, scripts represent multiple types of units in language. Japanese is perhaps the best known example of such a mixture. To a first approximation, Japanese spells noun, adjective, and verb stems with logographic symbols, and it spells affixes (mostly endings) as well as other parts of speech with a CV syllabary. Other languages highlight units at different levels by the way in which they lay out their symbols. For example, Korean arranges its letters in units that correspond, more or less, to syllables. In Korean hangeul, the letters in a syllable are packed into square-shaped areas, which themselves are arranged linearly. As another example, English and many other alphabetic languages insert breaks between words, adding a morphosyntactic flavor to the script.

The sound-to-symbol correspondences in alphabetic systems are often adjusted in such a way as to make morphology more salient in the written form. In German, /d/ cannot exist in the coda of a syllable. Where it might be expected, /t/ is found instead. Thus the noun corresponding to *baden* /baːdən/ 'bathe' is /baːt/ 'bath'. One obvious approach would be to spell this latter word with *t*, which is the normal spelling of /t/ in the onset. Instead, German spells this word *Bad*, with a *d*. The general rule is that /t/ in codas is spelled *d* or *t* depending on how the consonant is pronounced when it occurs in onset position in related words, and in fact this rule applies to all obstruents. For the reader, this approach has the big advantage of morphemic constancy. The spelling *Bad* reminds the reader of words like *baden*, which share the same morpheme. It also directs the reader away from words with different morphemes, such as *bat* /baːt/ 'requested'. Nor is a native German reader likely to be tempted to read words like *Bad* as having /d/, because coda /d/ is forbidden by the language. But this spelling rule is a complication for the writer, who cannot spell purely on a phonological basis but must instead pay attention to the morphology. As we discuss later, such morphological adjustments can cause difficulties for children learning to spell.

*Underrepresentation*

As we mentioned earlier, writing systems do not usually represent all of the distinctions that are significant in the language. For example, CV syllabaries tend to seriously underrepresent the range of syllable types that are distinctive in the respective languages. Cherokee is not atypical in failing to distinguish long from short vowels, distinctive tones (pitches), most aspirated consonants from plain consonants, and syllables that have no codas from those that end in glottal segments. One symbol can ambiguously stand for quite a large number of different distinct syllables.

What writing represents, and what it ignores, have some commonalities across languages, even unrelated languages. Distinctions of length, tone, and pitch are often ignored; stress (distinguishing the most prominent syllable in the word) almost always is ignored; and we know of no full-fledged popular systems for indicating intonation at all. This is not just a matter of relative utility: Such features are often unmarked in languages where the lack leads to rather high ambiguity. For example, Vai, a syllabic script of Africa, normally does not mark tone, even though there are a number of word pairs that differ in tone alone.

Why do writing systems tend to ignore certain features? One possibility is that features such as stress, pitch, tone, and length are psycholinguistically special. Linguists call them suprasegmental, implying they are not properly segments but belong to some other class entirely. Because of the special status of these features, it may be easy for people to factor them out and then, for simplicity, discard them. A second possibility is that the tendency to ignore stress, pitch, tone, and length is less a consequence of psycholinguistic factors than of practical ones. Writers, especially beginners, tend to pronounce words slowly as they spell them. Under those conditions, suprasegmental features tend to be lost, but the word is usually still recognizable, and its other features can be easily perceived and written down.

## Graphics

The discussion so far has been rather abstract in that it has considered only in passing questions about the physical appearance of the symbols. Although a full treatment of this topic is beyond the scope of this chapter, we mention several aspects that are particularly relevant for child learners.

Symbols are easier to learn and remember if they are patterned after symbols with which the writer is already familiar. The gold standard of such iconicity is Egyptian hieroglyphics, in which most symbols were recognizable and attractive pictures of real objects. Because such symbols represented either the name of the object represented or all or part of the sound of that name, it was presumably fairly easy to learn to associate symbols with referents, though no doubt hard to draw them. Even a few of the Roman letters retain some of their original iconicity: O was originally an eye, and A was an ox's head (best seen upside down: ∀).

In addition to such external (iconic) patterning, symbols may be patterned internally, with reference to other symbols. We asserted above that Chinese logograms cannot be fully predicted by considering the meaning or the sound of the word. But if one has to learn several thousand characters, it must help if they have some internal patterning. Most characters in fact do: They are composed of other symbols, and the component symbols usually suggest some aspect of the meaning, or pronunciation, or both, of the whole.

Although it is important for the learner to be able to recognize symbols of writing as a class – and therefore they should have graphic properties in common – it is also important to be able to distinguish symbols from each other. Some scripts have such unity of style that the letters are very similar to each other: for example, the four Hebrew letters ז ר ו י. In other scripts, such as Roman lower-case letters, certain symbols differ only in their orientation, a situation that is especially likely to cause confusion for children.

Many scripts include disjoint symbols where one of the parts is otherwise a symbol in its own right, and the other part is an operator that modifies its pronunciation. Often the operator is a diacritic mark, as in French where *e* in contexts where it might otherwise be pronounced [ə] or silent can be modified by diacritics to yield such forms as *é* [e] or *è* [ɛ]. Even adults may find it difficult to decide whether such complexes are best thought of as a letter that has been modified by an operator, or whether the two symbols should be treated as one inseparable (but physically disjoint) whole.

A further complication is that a symbol that sometimes stands on its own can at other times act as an operator, such as English *h* in *hip* as compared to its function in *ship*. Literacy researchers often call sequences such as *sh* a *grapheme*, which terminology suggests that *sh* is processed as an unanalyzable unit. In some languages, though, digraphs tend to have a function that can, at least in part, be predicted from the functions of their parts. For example, Hungarian *g* is a voiced velar stop, and *gy* is a voiced palatal stop; *n* is an alveolar nasal, and *ny* is a palatal nasal. The fact that *y* gives a letter a palatal sound may be a generalization that even a youngster can appreciate and use; *gy* and *ny* may not in fact be processed as unanalyzable wholes.

## Dialect and language contact

Up to now we have written about language as a single, ideal entity, as if writers only have to access their own internalized knowledge of language and write what they find. However, that is rarely the case. Not only are writing systems standardized, but the language one chooses to write is standardized as well. Consider Finnish, which is widely recognized as having one of the world's most consistent writing systems. In colloquial speech, a Finn would normally pronounce the word for 'in the house' as /talos/. However, a Finn would normally write *talossa*. The spelling corresponds to a pronunciation that is typically heard in rather formal styles of speech. The spelling is perfectly regular, but it is only regular if the child already knows the more formal pronunciations and knows to use them when writing.

Dialect and local accents are a closely related issue. For most speakers of English, *tin* and *ten* are among the easiest words to write. But in the southern United States, they are usually pronounced alike, which makes the spelling of at least one of those two words fairly unpredictable. In English, it is hard to say which dialect's speakers would have the greatest advantage in spelling; the spelling of the language is reasonably dialect neutral. For many other languages, the writing standard has crystallized around the speech of a certain area, often the capital city. No matter how easy the writing system may be per se, writing well may be quite complicated if one first has to master another dialect.

In some cases, in fact, writing well is easy only if one has mastered a completely different language. It is quite common for languages to write borrowed words in the original spelling system, especially if the loan is recent, and especially if the lending language has the same script. For example, English has borrowed many words from Latin and Greek, while retaining the original spelling (the Greek words as they might appear in Latin texts). As a result, English now has a clearly stratified vocabulary: a native (or thoroughly nativized) layer and a Latinate level. Each level of the vocabulary has its own morpheme inventory and morphological rules and substantially different phonologies and spelling rules. For example, /f/ tends to be spelled as *f* in native words and as *ph* in Latinate words of Greek origin.

This influx of Latin vocabulary has contributed to the morphological constancy that we now see in English. Oddly enough, Latin itself did not have a principle of morphological constancy: If a morpheme was pronounced differently in different words, it was spelled differently. But when classical words were borrowed into English, a morpheme that in Latin might be pronounced the same in two different words, and hence spelled the same, might be pronounced differently in those two words when spoken with an English accent. By the rules of borrowing, it would retain the same constant Latin spelling, even though that might now correspond to two different English pronunciations. For example, the difference in pronunciation of the root vowel in *impede* and *impediment* is due entirely to English pronunciation patterns; the Latin vowel was [ɛ] in both words, and so the spelling has the same Latin *e* in both words. Such alternations are very common. So it came about that even though neither English nor Latin earlier had a principle of morphological constancy, English now seems to have one after the heavy admixture of Latin words.

Another type of language contact is the implicit dialog with the past that we see in most writing systems. Writing standards tend to reflect the structure of a somewhat earlier stage of the language. Some archaisms, the ones that are relatively recent, serve a useful purpose because they bridge divides between dialects and accents. For example, writers in England still spell *which* differently from *witch*, even though they now pronounce them the same; this is advantageous, because spelling them the same would drive an orthographic wedge between England and areas such as Ireland where the distinction is still alive. Other archaisms, however, such as spelling a /w/ in *wrist* and a /k/ and /x/ (*gh*) in *knight*, are not retained by any speakers of English, and constitute a dialog only with the past.

The conservatism of spelling, in English and other languages, has major implications. Because sound change is often conditioned by other sounds in a word, a sound often changes to another sound in one word but not another. If the spelling does not change, the end result is that multiple sounds may have the same spelling. Similar to the case with Latin borrowings, that can contribute to the impression that English spelling seeks to insure morphemic constancy. For example, *breath* and *breathe* now appear to be spelled with the same vowel, even though the sound is different, out of respect for the fact that both words have the same root morpheme. More fundamentally, however, the conservative spellings reflect the fact that the vowels in the two words were pronounced, and therefore spelled, the same a few hundred years ago.

In addition to morphemic constancy, such conditioned changes can result in what is ultimately interpretable as conditioned spellings. In English, the vowel /u/ regularly changed to /ʊ/ before /k/, without any change in spelling. Consequently, we now have pairs like *look* /lʊk/ vs. *loom* /lum/. In essence, *look* is still spelling the earlier pronunciation. But from the point of view of a writer who does not know the history of English, this conditioned change appears as a conditional spelling rule: /ʊ/ is spelled *oo* before *k*.

Conversely, distinct sounds can merge into one sound, often without any conditioning environment. A sound change currently spreading through North America merges /ɔ/ (as in *lawn*) with North American /ɑ/ (as in *lot*). In dialects where that merger is complete, it now looks like there is a single vowel with multiple spellings. Given a word like /lɑt/, it is not obvious on first principles whether it should be spelled *lot* or rather something like *laut* (cf. *taut*) or *lought* (cf. *bought*). The impact of such mergers can be great. The sound /ɑ/ will have gone from being an easy vowel to spell to a fairly inconsistent one. It does not take many such mergers, unaccompanied by changes to the spelling, to foster the perception that spelling is chaotic, and that the only way to learn to spell is to memorize whole words.

## Complexity of writing

Discussions of the relative complexity of writing systems, which have usually been framed from the point of view of the reader rather than the writer, have often characterized systems as *transparent* or *opaque*. *Transparent* means that the relationship between sound and symbol is obvious, and *opaque* means that it is not. The terms *shallow* and *deep* are often used the same way, but the distinctive idea is that in a deep orthography, morphology plays an important role, somehow. The term implies an acknowledgment of morphological constancy, but in principle that could range from the incidental constancy of an alphabetic language like English to a wholesale commitment to morpheme-by-morpheme representation as found in a true logography. The occasional acknowledgment that there may be a continuum between *transparent* and *opaque* writing systems does not completely clarify matters.

Our discussion of writing systems suggests that it may be too simple to assume that a writing system is difficult to learn to the extent to which the same phoneme may map to different symbols in different words. There can be many more inputs to spelling and reading which could make a spelling more "transparent" or "regular" than normally thought. For example, the spelling *phonics* would be unexpected if one knew that /f/ is typically spelled as *f* and that final /ks/ is often spelled as *x*; why not spell the word as *fonnix*? The conventional spelling becomes less irregular if one sees the connection to *telephone* and knows that phonics is a formal system of practice, like physics, and not a pest control company, like Terminix. In discussing how children learn to spell, the topic to which we now turn, it is important to consider what children know about spoken language that can help them make sense of the apparent irregularities that exist in the writing system they are learning.

## Learning to Spell

A first step in learning any writing system is understanding that writing is not a semasiography – a system that records concepts directly – but a glottography. Although this is something that children typically learn quite early, studies of their early writings suggest that it does need to be learned. In one study (Levin & Tolchinsky Landsmann, 1989), Hebrew-speaking preschool and kindergarten children were asked to write pairs of words whose referents contrasted in such features as size (e.g., פיל *pil* 'elephant' vs. נמלה *nemala* 'ant') or color (עגבניה *agvaniya* 'tomato' vs. מלפפון *melafefon* 'cucumber'). Children sometimes represented these semantic features in their writing, for example using more letters to spell *pil* 'elephant' than *nemala* 'ant', even though the former word is shorter than the latter in Hebrew. In Chan's study of Chinese children (cited in Tolchinsky, 2003), even those 5-year-olds who produced accurate characters tended to form them so as to empha-size the figurative link to the concept. For example, children writing a logographic symbol for 'elephant' overemphasized a long stroke to represent the elephant's trunk. A hypoth-esis like the one that bigger objects are written with more letters quickly becomes unten-able as children see that the physical appearance of a written symbol does not typically correspond to that of its referent. Children come to understand that writing symbolizes units of the language rather than directly symbolizing concepts. The challenge is then to learn which units of the language are indicated in the writing system, and how.

As mentioned earlier, one difficulty that learners of alphabetic writing systems face is that the unit of language that is represented, the phoneme, is abstract. We know from many studies that children find it more difficult to segment speech into phonemes than into syllables or onsets and rimes (e.g., Liberman, Shankweiler, Fischer, & Carter, 1974; Treiman & Zukowski, 1991). The segmentation problem can lead to spelling errors in learners of alphabetic writing systems. For example, children who have difficulty analyz-ing syllable-initial cluster onsets into segments may spell a cluster with a single letter, as in *sak* for *snake*, rather than with a two-letter sequence. Such errors have been docu-mented in learners of different languages, such as English and Czech (e.g., Caravolas & Bruck, 1993; Treiman, 1993). The errors occur even when the correct spelling is highly predictable. For example, all initial /sn/ sequences in English are spelled as *sn*, so chil-dren's misspellings of this cluster cannot be attributed to any inconsistency in the mapping of sound to spelling.

The segmentation problem is less severe for learners of syllabic and onset-rime writing systems than it is for learners of alphabetic systems, and this would be expected to give the former children an advantage in learning to write. Unfortunately, little research has examined writing development in children learning syllabic and onset-rime systems. It has been suggested that learners of alphabetic systems may, at an early age, treat the systems as if they represented the more accessible level of the syllable (Ferreiro & Teberosky, 1982). Supporters of this view cite as evidence the observation that the number of symbols in some children's spellings tends to agree with the number of syllables in the corresponding spoken words. However, researchers have rarely examined whether the agreement between the number of symbols and the number of syllables is greater than would be predicted by chance. In Spanish and other languages that have been studied by advocates of the syllabic hypothesis, many of the spellings that have been taken to support the syllabic hypothesis have an alternative explanation. A Spanish-speaking child who writes, for example, *Coca-Cola* as *oaoa* may be spelling on the basis of letter names rather than on the basis of syllables. The segments /o/ and /a/ are the names of the Spanish letters *o* and *a*, whereas the other sounds in the word are not letter names (except for /ka/, the name of the rare letter *k*). Children may proceed through the word writing letters when they hear the corresponding letter names in the word.

Whether or not learners of alphabetic systems go through a period of syllabic spelling en route to the level of the phoneme, it is clear that the segmentation of speech into phonemes is a stumbling block in learning to spell. All learners of alphabetic writing systems must cross this hurdle, regardless of the transparency of the system. The seg-mentation problem has been recognized at least since the 1970s, although its implica-tions for spelling have not been as widely discussed as its implications for reading. The classification problem, that of deciding which segments are similar enough that they should be represented with the same symbol, is less widely recognized. As we discussed earlier, classification can be a substantial problem for learners of alphabetic systems, and it can lead to systematic spelling errors. For example, some English-speaking children consider the first segment of a word like *truck* to be more similar to /tʃ/ than to /t/. Consequently, they may spell such words with an initial *ch* (or just *c*) rather than the conventional *t* (e.g., Read, 1975; Treiman, 1993). As another example, children who speak dialects of English in which the middle sounds of words like *ladder* and *latter* are pronounced alike, as flaps, may classify these segments differently than assumed by the writing system. As a result, they may make errors such as *latr* for *ladder* or *budrfi* for *butterfly* (e.g., Read, 1975; Treiman, 1993). One expects *tr* in *truck*, *d* in *ladder*, and *t* in *butterfly* if one classifies these segments in the same way that the English writing system does. However, these spellings may seem unexpected to a child whose classifications of sounds have not yet been molded by the writing system.

No writing system represents all the details of a spoken language. Underrepresentation, particularly of suprasegmental features such as stress, length, and tone, is common across the world's languages. We suggested earlier that such underrepresentation may arise, in part, because writers tend to pronounce words slowly as they spell them. Suprasegmental features are often lost when speakers do this. Supporting this idea, children may have difficulty when certain suprasegmental features *are* represented in a particular writing system. An example comes from Finnish, which distinguishes in its phonology between long and short phonemes. The long consonants and vowels are spelled with double letters, as in *kk* and *aa*, and the short phonemes are spelled with single letters. Although Finnish is widely hailed as one of the world's most regular writing systems, young Finnish children do make spelling errors. Their most common error involves writing long phonemes with a single letter rather than a double letter (Lyytinen, Leinonen, Nikula, Aro, & Leiwo, 1995). These errors may occur because children find length distinctions difficult to perceive when they say words slowly for purposes of spelling.

If a child can segment speech at the level represented by the language, and if the child classifies the segments the same way that the writing system does, the burden on memory is much smaller than it would be otherwise. A child who can subdivide speech only into syllables would need to memorize the spelling of each syllable of the language. This would be quite a burden in English, with its several thousand syllables, although it is less of a burden in Yi, the language with the syllabic writing system mentioned earlier, where the number of syllables is an order of magnitude less. A child who can segment speech into phonemes need not memorize the spelling of each syllable, if the writing system is alphabetic. The child can build the spellings of syllables and words as needed from the spellings of individual segments, reducing the burden on memory.

Learning to spell requires visual skills as well as phonological skills. Children must learn about the symbols that are used to represent the linguistic units. One of the earliest steps in this process involves distinguishing the symbols that are used for writing from the symbols that are used in other domains, such as drawing and numbers. As we mentioned earlier, the symbols of a script are often similar to one another in style and shape. Quite early, children pick up on the graphic features of the script to which they are exposed and reproduce these features in their attempts to write. For example, Chinese-speaking children as young as 3, when asked to write, tend to use the horizontal and vertical lines and dots that characterize Chinese characters (Chan & Louie, 1992). They are less likely to use circular forms, which are not typical of Chinese characters, although they do use such forms when drawing. Children exposed to Chinese may arrange the marks that they make for writing in a square pattern, as with Chinese characters, rather than along a line, as with English (Chi, 1988).

The similarity among symbols that helps children identify them as a class becomes a disadvantage when the symbols are so similar as to be easily confused. Readers of this chapter will be familiar with children's difficulties in distinguishing letters such as lower-case *b*, *p*, and *d* in Roman script. Children learning Hebrew may confuse visually similar letters such as ו and ר (Levin & Freedman, 2003).

Learning the shapes and the referents of letters places a large burden on memory. This is especially true if letters have variant forms, as with the upper-case and lower-case versions of Roman letters. To ease the demands on memory, we would expect children to take advantage of any patterning that exists in the system and that is accessible to them. In the Roman alphabet, the relationship between a letter's shape and its name is largely arbitrary, as is the relationship between a letter's shape and its sound value. However, children can benefit when letter shapes are treated as motivated, even if this is not historically accurate. For example, children can be taught *S* as a snake, and this association can help them learn the symbol's sound value as well as its shape. Other associations between letter shapes and letter sounds, although motivated, are probably less accessible to children. Consider Korean, where letters representing aspirated consonants contain a horizontal line that letters representing the corresponding unaspirated consonants lack. Given children's difficulties in accessing even the level of the segment, and given adults' (at least English-speaking adults') failure to benefit from phonetic features when learning a novel writing system (Byrne, 1984), there is reason to question whether Korean children can take advantage of the feature-level patterning in their system. We know of no research with Korean children that has addressed this question.

The burden on memory in the learning of letters increases when children need to learn about disjoint symbols, such as French *é* and *ê*, and groups of letters that can function as single units, such as English *sh*. Indeed, children learning both English and French have been found to have difficulty spelling words with digraphs (Sprenger-Charolles, Siegel, & Béchennec, 1997; Treiman, 1993). A frequent error is to omit one letter of the digraph and include the other, as in *sip* for *ship*. Even when the relationship between a phoneme and its spelling is fairly consistent, as is the relationship between /ʃ/ and *sh* in English, memory demands and hence spelling errors increase when the children cannot straightforwardly predict the identity of a two-letter sequence from the functions of the individual letters.

Although the relationships between letters' shapes and sound values are arbitrary in many languages, as are the relationships between letters' shapes and names, letters' names are related to their sounds in all writing systems that we know of (Treiman & Kessler, 2003). For example, the English name of *l*, /ɛl/, contains the phoneme that the letter represents; the same is true for Hebrew ל /lamed/, which spells /l/. Learning the names of letters can thus help children master their sounds. This helps children spell words correctly, in many cases, but it can lead to errors in other cases. For example, children may symbolize just the segments in a word that are letter names, as with the Spanish-speaking child who writes *Coca-Cola* as *oaoa*. Children may use the (relatively few) mis-leading letter names that exist in certain languages to suggest the wrong spellings for segments, as with the English-speaking beginners who symbolize /w/ as *y* (/w/ being the initial segment in *y*'s name, /waɪ/).

So far, we have discussed several challenges that children face in learning to write words. They must understand that writing represents spoken language, they must segment spoken language into units at the level assumed by the writing system, and they must classify those units in the same way that the writing system does. In addition, children must learn the shapes and referents of the visual symbols. A further challenge arises when the language that is represented by the writing system does not match the language that the children speak. For example, the Swahili-speaking children studied by Alcock and Ngorosho (2003) spoke a dialect in which initial /h/ tended to be dropped. Swahili writing represents a dialect that has initial /h/. Lacking full knowledge of that dialect, the children sometimes omitted initial *h* when it was required and sometimes added it when it was not present in the conventional spelling.

Most of the challenges that we have discussed so far are not necessarily greater in so-called transparent writing systems than in less transparent systems. For example, even children learning a transparent alphabet may misspell certain words because they classify a particular segment differently than assumed by the writing system. The challenge that we consider next – dealing with variability in sound-to-spelling mappings – is one that does not arise in fully transparent systems. In systems where the same linguistic unit may be represented in more than one way, however, children must learn which symbols are possible and, more importantly, when to use each one. If the choice is arbitrary, children must rely on rote memorization to spell the unit in question. However, as our discussion of writing systems has shown, the choice is not arbitrary in many cases. This lessens the burden on memory, allowing children to predict which spellings are used in which situations.

In some cases, consideration of the context in which a unit occurs can help children spell it correctly. For example, English /ɛ/ is more likely to be spelled as *ea* before *d* (e.g., *head*, *instead*) than before other consonants (e.g., *set*, *west*). By no means is every /ɛ/ before *d* spelled with *ea* – *bed* and *wed* do not use this spelling – but a child who knew the asso-ciation would be a better speller than a child who did not. Such context effects exist in the English vocabulary to which children are exposed (Kessler & Treiman, 2001), but we know little as yet about how and when children learn these patterns.

In other cases, morphological information can help in the choice among alternative spellings. In French, for example, the segment /o/ has numerous possible spellings, includ-ing *au*, *o*, and *eau*. When it is a diminutive suffix, as in *éléphanteau* 'elephant calf', it is systematically spelled as *eau*. Pacton, Fayol, and Perruchet (2002) found that third and fifth graders (but not second graders) were significantly more likely to transcribe /o/ as *eau* when it occurred in a pseudoword that was used as a diminutive (e.g., "A little /vitar/ is a /vitaro/") than when it occurred in the same pseudoword used in isolation. A sensi-tivity to morphological patterning has also been found in elementary-school children in the United States, who derive some benefit from their knowledge of *dirt*, which does not contain a flap, when spelling *dirty*, which does (Treiman, Cassar, & Zukowski, 1994).

This can help children avoid errors like *drdy* and *dirdy* for *dirty*, which would otherwise occur.

Context-conditioned associations are harder to learn than simple one-to-one associations: Children must be exposed to enough words to realize that a unit may be spelled in more than one way, and they must identify the factors that encourage one versus the other spelling. Even if this learning takes some time, the important point is that there are often ways to cope with the variability in sound-to-spelling associations other than rote memorization. Rather than measuring spelling difficulty solely in terms of the number of spelling options for a given unit, one must consider the extent to which the choice is eased by consideration of context, morphology, and other factors. In English, as in other writing systems that have been labeled opaque or deep, such factors do exist.

Children differ in the ease or difficulty with which they learn to spell and in their ultimate levels of attainment. Given the framework we have presented, it is not surprising that children's ability to segment spoken words into smaller units, knowledge about letters, and morphological skill all contribute to individual differences in spelling performance in English (e.g., Caravolas, Hulme, & Snowling, 2001; Nunes, Bryant, & Bindman, 1997). Linguistic skills such as these are more important determinants of spelling ability than is visual memorization skill (Caravolas et al., 2001; Giles & Terrell, 1997). Also important are children's attitudes about spelling. Teachers who consider English a chaotic and unprincipled writing system likely foster a similar view among their students. Such pupils may not look for patterns in the system because they believe that few exist to be discovered. Teachers who appreciate the writing system can help students find its patterns, fostering a positive attitude about spelling.

We end our survey of writing systems and learning to spell by considering what learning to spell does for children. Of course, learning to write words is important in itself and because it provides a foundation for higher-level writing skills. This learning also gives children insights into the structure of their language, shaping and standardizing their perceptions so that they come to see the language in terms of the same units that the writing system does. With some writing systems, notably alphabetic ones, the insights into segmental structure that children gain as a result of learning to spell are probably not ones that they would gain otherwise. Some writing systems also encourage insights into the structure and history of words, as when English speakers come to appreciate similarities among telephones, phonics, and physics as a result of learning the words' spellings. We think of winners of spelling bees, contests popular in the United States, as excellent memorizers and hard workers. They are, but these children have also learned a good deal about their own language.

Our crosslinguistic survey suggests that the hurdles that children must cross in learning to spell, although different in height for learners of different writing systems, are not substantially different in kind (see chapters by Seymour and Caravolas, this volume). We can get a better understanding of the learning process by studying a variety of languages, and so it is valuable and important that researchers have moved beyond English in studying the development of spelling. Indeed, one of our goals in writing this chapter has been to highlight the interesting work that is now being carried out in a variety of languages and to suggest areas for future investigation. The good news is that English is not so dramatically different from other writing systems. So what we learn from studies of English is still relevant for the study of other languages.

## Note

Preparation of this chapter was supported, in part, by NSF grant BCS-0130763. Thanks to Lee Collins for his comments on a draft of the chapter.

# 8

# Development of Sight Word Reading: Phases and Findings

## Linnea C. Ehri

The hallmark of skilled reading is the ability to read individual words accurately and quickly in isolation as well as in text, referred to as "context free" word reading skill (Stanovich, 1980). For a skilled reader, even a quick glance at a word activates its pronunciation and meaning. Being able to read words from memory by sight is valuable because it allows readers to focus their attention on constructing the meaning of the text while their eyes recognize individual words automatically. If readers have to stop and decode words, their reading is slowed down and their train of thought disrupted. This chapter examines theories and findings on the development of sight word reading.

Sight word reading is not limited to high-frequency or irregularly spelled words, contrary to the beliefs of some, but includes all words that readers can read from memory. Also sight word reading is not a strategy for reading words, contrary to some views. Being strategic involves choosing procedures to optimize outcomes, such as figuring out unfamiliar words by decoding (Gough, 1972) or analogizing (Goswami, 1986, 1988) or prediction (Goodman, 1970; Tunmer & Chapman, 1998). By contrast, sight word reading happens automatically without the influence of intention or choice. Reading words from memory by sight is especially important in English because the alphabetic system is variable and open to decoding errors.

## Ways to Assess Sight Word Reading

There are various ways of assessing sight word reading. One approach is to test readers' ability to read irregularly spelled words under the assumption that, if these are not known, they will be decoded phonically, resulting in errors. A second approach is to give students a sight word learning task in which they practice reading a set of unfamiliar words. Their performance over trials is tracked as well as their memory for words at the end of learning. This approach has been used to study whether readers retain specific words in memory. Readers are taught one of two phonetically equivalent spellings (e.g., cake vs. caik) and then their memory for the particular form taught is tested. Readers might be asked to recall the spelling or to choose among alternative spellings. Although the test is of spelling rather than reading, the correlation between the two skills is very high, supporting the validity of spelling as an indicator. Finally, another approach is to assess word reading speed. This works because readers take less time to read words by sight than to decode them or read them by analogy. Reading words within one second of seeing them is taken to indicate sight word reading.

Automatic word recognition has been assessed with interference tasks. Written words and pseudowords are each imposed on drawings of objects; for example, *cow* or *cos* written on a picture of a horse. Students are told to name the pictures and *ignore* the print. If the words are read automatically, readers will name pictures labeled with words more *slowly* than those with pseudowords (Rosinski, Golinkoff, & Kukish, 1975). This happens because the familiar sight words are activated in memory and readers trip over these competing words as they access the names of the pictures. Tasks involving color words have shown the same effects (e.g., word *red* written in blue ink). Researchers infer that words are known automatically if they create interference.

## Memory Processes That Enable Sight Word Reading

Growth of reading skill requires the accumulation of a huge vocabulary of sight words in memory. The magnitude of the task in English is suggested by Harris and Jacobson (1982) who tallied words that were common to at least half of eight basal series. This yielded a core list of basic words that did not count inflected forms such as *stop* and *stopped* separately. The list included 94 words from preprimers, with 175 from primer, 246 from first grade, and 908 from second-grade books. Thereafter, the numbers added at each grade level through eighth grade varied from 1,395 to 1,661 words, for a sum total of 10,240 basic words. Thus, sight word learning makes a big demand on memory.

Research findings reveal that sight words are established quickly in memory and are lasting. Reitsma (1983) gave Dutch first graders practice reading a set of words and then three days later measured their speed to read the original words as well as alternative spellings that were pronounced the same but never read (e.g., plezier vs. plesier). A minimum of four trials reading the original words was sufficient to enable students to read the familiar forms faster than the unfamiliar forms. More recently, Share (2004) found that even one exposure to words enabled Israeli third graders to retain specific information about their spellings in memory, and this memory persisted a month later. To learn sight words this rapidly requires a powerful mnemonic system.

When a reader's eyes land on a familiar written word, its pronunciation, meaning, and syntactic role are all activated in memory. Theories to explain how such memories are built involve specifying the nature of the *connections* that are formed in memory to link visual properties of the word to its other identities. Two types of connections have been proposed.

According to one approach, connections are established between visual features of words and their *meanings*. These grapho-semantic connections are arbitrary rather than systematic. They are learned by rote. They do not involve letter-sound relations, so substantial practice is required to remember the words. The visuospatial features stored in memory might be letters, letter patterns, word configurations, or length. However, no phonological information contributes to the associations. Rather pronunciations of words are activated only after the meanings of words have been retrieved. This explanation is advanced by dual-route models of word reading with decoding as the other route (Baron, 1979; Barron, 1986).

According to another approach, spellings of specific words are connected to their *pronunciations* in memory. Readers use their knowledge of the alphabetic system to create these connections. They know how to distinguish separate phonemes in pronunciations and separate graphemes in spellings. They know grapheme–phoneme correspondences. More advanced readers know larger graphosyllabic units as well (e.g., *-ing*). When readers encounter a new written word and recognize its pronunciation and meaning, they use their alphabetic knowledge to compute connections between graphemes and phonemes. Reading the word just once or a few times serves to bond the spelling to its pronunciation along with its other identities in memory. This is Ehri's (1992) theory of sight word reading. Others too have proposed visuophonological connectionist theories of word reading (Harm & Seidenberg, 1999; Perfetti, 1992; Rack, Hulme, Snowling, & Wightman, 1994; Share, 1995).

Visuophonological connections constitute a more powerful mnemonic system that better explains the rapid learning of sight words than visuosemantic connections. However, both types appear in developmental theories. Grapho-semantic connections explain the earliest forms of sight word reading. Once beginners acquire knowledge of the alphabetic system, graphophonemic connections take over.

## Developmental Theories

The development of word reading skill is portrayed as a succession of qualitatively distinct stages or phases in several theories. Use of the term "stage" denotes a strict view of development in which one type of word reading occurs at each stage, and mastery is a prerequisite for movement to the next stage. However, none of the theories is this rigid. Some theories refer to "phases" rather than "stages" of development to be explicit about relaxing these constraints. Earlier phases may occur by default because more advanced processes have not yet been acquired, so mastery is not necessarily a prerequisite for later phases.

These theories portray the succession of key processes and skills that emerge, change, and develop. Labels characterize the types of processes or skills that are acquired and predominate at each stage or phase. Theories may identify the causes producing movement from one phase to the next. Two types of causes can be distinguished, internal and external. Internal causes operate when specific cognitive or linguistic capabilities facilitate or place constraints on the acquisition of other capabilities. Internal causes include capabilities specific to reading; for example, the facilitation produced by acquiring letter knowledge. Internal causes also include general capabilities that serve purposes other than reading as well; for example, mechanisms involving vision, language, and memory (Rack,

Hulme, & Snowling, 1993). External causes include informal teaching, formal instructional programs, and reading practice. Theories provide a basis for assessing developmental levels, for predicting what students can be expected to learn at each level, for differentiating the types of instruction and feedback that are most effective at each level, and for explaining why some students do not make adequate progress.

## Synopsis of the Theories

The different stage and phase theories vary in scope and in the attention paid to sight word reading but there are also many similarities between them. There is not space in this chapter to go into the different theories in detail. Table 8.1 represents an attempt to highlight the synergies between the models as a backdrop to the discussion of sight word reading.

One of the first stage models was proposed by Philip Gough (Gough & Hillinger, 1980; Gough, Juel, & Griffith, 1992) who distinguishes two ways to read words. Cue reading is an immature form of sight word reading. Students read words by selecting a salient visual cue in or around the word and associating it with the word in memory. Cipher reading replaces cue reading when students acquire decoding skill.

Jana Mason (1980) divides Gough's cue reading period into two stages labeled to portray the written cues that beginners use to identify written words: (1) contextual dependency, (2) visual recognition, and (3) letter-sound analysis. Context dependent learners use the same learning process to recognize words as to identify pictures, by treating the words as unique visual patterns. Learners at the visual recognition stage use letters to read words but they lack decoding skill. Learners at the letter-sound analysis stage have mastered letter-sound correspondences and can use them to decode unfamiliar words.

Marsh, Friedman, Welch, and Desberg (1981) distinguish four stages characterized by changes in the strategies to read words. During the earliest stage, known words are read by rote association between unanalyzed visual forms and their pronunciations. Unknown words are read by linguistic guessing. During Stage 2, graphemic features, particularly initial letters, influence the reading of words. In learning to read words, readers remember the minimum graphemic cues necessary to distinguish among words. Stage 3 involves sequential decoding between letters and sounds. Stage 4 involves hierarchical decoding based on more complex context-dependent rules. In addition, analogizing is considered as a strategy for reading unknown words.

Jeanne Chall (1983) differentiates the process of reading acquisition into five stages from birth (Stage 0) through adulthood. Most relevant here are Stage 1 Decoding, and Stage 2 Fluency. Stage 1 is further analyzed into phases. Initially children rely on memory or contextual guessing to read. To make progress, they need to abandon these habits and become "glued to print" by processing letters and sounds. According to Chall this is facilitated by systematic phonics instruction.

Uta Frith (1985) also noted that the transition between a visual and an alphabetic stage depends on awareness of relationships between sounds and letters. Her proposal is a three-phase theory characterized by different word reading strategies: (1) a logographic phase

**Table 8.1** A Schematic Summary of the Approximate Relationships between Different Stage/Phase Theories of Learning to Read

| Proponents | Gough & Hillinger (1980) | Mason (1980) | Marsh et al. (1981) | Chall (1983) | Frith (1985) | Ehri (1998, 1999, 2002) | Stuart & Coltheart (1988) | Seymour & Duncan (2001) |
|---|---|---|---|---|---|---|---|---|
| Number of Developmental Periods | 2 | 3 | 4 | 5 | 3 | 4 | 2 | 4 |
| 1. Pre-reading | | Contextual dependency | Rote, linguistic guessing | Stage 0: Letters/Book exposure | | Pre-alphabetic | | Pre-literacy |
| 2. Early reading | Cue reading ↕ | Visual recognition | Discrimination net guessing | Memory and contextual guessing | Logographic | Partial alphabetic | Partial orthographic ↕ | Logographic / Dual Foundation |
| 3. Decoding | Cipher reading ↕ | Letter-sound analysis | Sequential decoding | Stage 1: Decoding, attending to letters/sounds | Alphabetic | Full alphabetic | Complete orthographic ↕ | Alphabetic |
| 4. Fluent reading | | | Hierarchical decoding | Stage 2: Fluency, Consolidation | Orthographic | Consolidated alphabetic, Automaticity | | Orthographic / Morphographic |

when readers recognize words on the basis of distinctive visual or contextual features; (2) an alphabetic phase when readers use spelling-sound rules to read words; (3) an orthographic phase when words are recognized by larger spelling patterns, especially morphemic units.

Building on Frith's model, Philip Seymour (Seymour & Duncan, 2001) proposes the dual-foundation model consisting of several phases of literacy development: pre-literacy, foundation, orthographic, and morphographic. In the foundation phase, two processes are acquired. The logographic process entails the accumulation of sight words in memory. In contrast to Frith's (1985) nonalphabetic logographic phase, grapheme–phoneme units are used to connect words in memory. The alphabetic process refers to decoding skill. Later phases involve the use of larger spelling units, including onsets and rimes, whole syllables, and morphemes to read words (Seymour, Aro, & Erskine, 2003).

In a rather different formulation, Morag Stuart (Stuart & Coltheart, 1988) rejects the idea of an initial logographic or visual cue stage, arguing that neither visual nor contextual cues enable children to read. When children read successfully, they use phonological processes. Her developmental theory distinguishes two important changes in the representations of sight words in memory: an early point when children acquire phonemic segmentation and letter-sound knowledge sufficient to form partial representations consisting of beginning and ending letters, and a later point when knowledge of vowel spellings provides the basis for forming more complete representations of sight words in memory. During the latter period, children also acquire decoding skill that supports the reading of new words.

In general, there is substantial agreement among theories in the periods that are distinguished to portray the development of word reading. With a few exceptions, they are consistent with my four-phase theory of sight word reading. In this view (Ehri, 1998, 1999, 2002), each phase of reading development is characterized by the predominant type of connection that bonds written words to their other identities in memory: (1) pre-alphabetic, involving visual and contextual connections, (2) partial alphabetic, involving connections between more salient letters and sounds, (3) full alphabetic, involving complete connections between all the graphemes in spellings and phonemes in pronunciations, and (4) consolidated alphabetic, involving connections formed out of syllabic and morphemic units. Whereas connections during Phase 1 are linked to the meanings of words, connections in subsequent phases are grounded in pronunciations. Decoding skill emerges in Phase 3 and enhances the quality of memory for sight words. This phase theory will be used as a framework in the remainder of the chapter to explain how word reading changes during development to become fluent and automatic.

## Phase Theory of Sight Word Reading

### Pre-alphabetic phase

During the pre-alphabetic phase, children read words by remembering visual or contextual cues. Gough et al. (1992) taught preschoolers to read four words, one accompanied by a thumbprint. Children mastered this word first. When the thumbprint was removed, fewer than half could identify the word. When the thumbprint was shown alone, nearly all pronounced the word. When the thumbprint appeared next to another word, nearly all gave the "thumbprint" word. Gough et al. also covered up parts of the words. They reasoned that if students were selecting cues rather than remembering whole words, they should not recognize the words when critical parts were covered. This is what they found. If children could not read the word when the first half was covered, then they were twice as likely to read it when the second half was covered. Gough's findings indicate that the earliest form of sight word reading consists of children selecting a salient visual cue around or in part of a word to remember how to read it.

Studies have examined the cues used by pre-alphabetic readers to read words appearing in their everyday environments, such as the names of restaurants, brands of candy, their own or friends' names printed on cubbies at school. Results showed they used salient visual features in or around the written words rather than alphabet letters. For example, Masonheimer, Drum, and Ehri (1984) studied preschoolers who read few if any common words but could read several common signs and labels in the environment, for example, *McDonalds*. The children were asked to read the same signs but with one letter altered; for example, *Pepsi* changed to *Xepsi*. Most children failed to detect the changes, even when they were prompted to look for mistakes. Although they knew about 60% of the letter names, these results showed they did not use them to read environmental print.

One criticism of the use of environmental print to study each forms of sight word reading is that signs and labels are rich in other visual cues that are more salient than letters. This reduces any need to notice letters. A form of print more likely to elicit letter processing is that of personal names. Bloodgood (1999) studied 3–5-year-olds. Although the youngest children knew only a few letters and could read few if any preprimer words, they could recognize their own names in isolation and sometimes names of their classmates. Children's comments suggested that initial letters were the salient cues remembered. Also, knowledge of the letters in their own names accounted for most of the letters they could identify. This was confirmed by Treiman and Broderick (1998). Some children could write their own names yet could not name the letters they wrote, showing that letters were remembered as visual shapes rather than as symbols for sounds. This was evident in the comments of one child, Robert, who referred to 't' as "the cross thing."

Share and Gur (1999) studied personal name recognition in pre-alphabetic children. They distinguished two types of connections to read personal names during this period: contextual and visuographic. Contextual cues are those lying outside the printed word, such as stickers on personal lockers next to personal names. Visuographic cues are non-phonetic graphic features in the printed word itself, such as the two sticks in *William* or the shape of K in *Jack*. These pre-alphabetic, Hebrew-speaking 4–5-year-olds knew few letters, had poor phonemic awareness, and could not read any common words. Their ability to read personal names declined when the names were removed from personal lockers and shown in isolation, with contextual readers losing all ability. Visuographic readers were able to read two or three names in isolation, but they recognized the names regardless of whether first or final letters were covered, indicating they did not select limited visual cues as Gough and Hillinger (1980) would expect, but rather they had memory for the whole name. Full names may have been remembered because they were overlearned visual forms, or because Hebrew names do not have distinctive initial and final letters attracting attention to this part of the name.

Studies reveal that children's memory for words is very limited during this early phase. Mason (1980) used a sight word learning task that provided several practice trials to examine how easily children at different phases of development learned to identify printed words. The least mature readers who only knew some alphabet letters learned a few of the words, but could not recognize them if the letters were changed from upper to lower case, and they forgot most of the words after 15 minutes. Other studies show that at this stage, children's learning of new words depends on how meaningful they are (Ehri & Wilce, 1987b) rather than their orthographic features. As a result, they frequently make semantic errors when reading familiar words (Goodman & Altwerger, 1981; Harste, Burke, & Woodward, 1982; Seymour & Elder, 1986).

Consistent with this finding, Byrne (1992) showed that pre-alphabetic children attend to print–meaning correspondences but not to print–sound correspondences. He gave preschoolers two word learning tasks followed by a transfer task. In his print–meaning task, children learned to say "little boy" when they saw a triangle and square and "big boy" when they saw a circle and square. Then they were shown the triangle combined with a new symbol, a cross, and were asked, "Does this say 'little fish' or 'big fish?'" In his print–sound task, the same symbols and procedures were used, but children learned to say "fat" to the triangle-square and "bat" to the circle-square. When shown the triangle-cross, they were asked, "Does this say 'fun' or 'bun?'" Byrne found that children succeeded on transfer items like "little fish," indicating that they had learned the semantic connections between the triangle and "little," but not on items like "fun," indicating they had not formed connections at a phonemic level between the triangle and /f/.

In summary, pre-alphabetic readers adopt a visual cue approach by default because they lack the knowledge or ability to use letter names or sounds to form alphabetic connections; hence the name pre-alphabetic. The lack of an alphabetic mnemonic system makes it difficult for children to learn to read words by memory.

### Transition from the pre-alphabetic to partial alphabetic phase

The partial alphabetic phase emerges when beginners acquire letter knowledge and can use it to remember how to read words by forming partial connections in memory. In a longitudinal study, letter knowledge and phonemic segmentation measured at entry to kindergarten were found to be the strongest predictors of reading one and two years later (Share, Jorm, Maclean, & Matthews, 1984), so learning letters is critical. Also personal name writing, which may provide a special incentive for children to learn the shapes and names of alphabet letters, but not personal name reading, was a strong predictor of future reading. This observation supports a proposal made by Frith (1985) that writing rather than reading may be the entrée into the partial alphabetic phase.

Gough and Hillinger (1980) claim that children use cue reading to learn their first 40 or so words, but the approach breaks down because there are not enough visual cues to distinguish among all the words they encounter. At this point, Gough and Hillinger argued, readers move into the cipher stage and use letter-sound relations to decode words.

However, Ehri and Wilce (1985) present evidence for an intermediate type of word reading between the cue and cipher stage. They showed that beginners shift from visual cue reading to a rudimentary form of alphabetic reading as soon as they can read even a few words. Stuart and Coltheart (1988) propose that the acquisition of phonic skills, rather than problems of memory load cause children to shift from cue to cipher reading and that thereafter they show rapid growth in sight vocabulary.

According to Frith (1985), the shift from pre-alphabetic to alphabetic strategies may be promoted by writing, not by reading. Whereas pre-alphabetic reading is not analytic and does not involve letters, writing by inventing spellings draws attention to the sequence of sounds in words and their connection to letters. Findings of several experiments provide some support. In these studies, novice beginners who were taught to invent phonetic spellings of words exhibited superior ability to read words by sight or by decoding compared to novices receiving other forms of instruction (Clarke, 1988; Ehri & Wilce, 1987b; Uhry & Shepard, 1993).

Frith (1985) draws attention to the dissociation between the processes used to read and to write during this early period. Bradley and Bryant (1979) observed that children were able to invent semiphonetic spellings of words, but they were unable to read back their own spellings, indicating that they did not use the same cues for writing as for reading words. Cardoso-Martins, Rodriguez, and Ehri (2003) also observed a dissociation between spelling and reading in illiterate adults who knew some letter names and sounds and produced partially phonetic spellings of words. However, they did not use letters when reading labels and signs in their environment. This was evident when they failed to notice errors, for example, *LOCA-COLA* for *COCA-COLA*, even when prompted to check for mistakes. These findings support the idea that writing may become alphabetic before reading does.

## Partial alphabetic phase

Mason's (1980) study of preschoolers at Stage 2 of her theory reveals characteristics of partial alphabetic readers. These students knew most letter names and could read a few words out of context. They used letters in reading words, as evidenced by their misreadings, which often preserved the initial consonant (e.g., misreading *kit* as *key*). After learning to read 10 words in a sight word learning task, they could recognize some of the words when the case of the letters was changed, and they could remember some of the words after 15 minutes.

According to Ehri (1998), the partial alphabetic phase emerges when children can use the sound values of some letters to form connections between spellings and pronunciations to remember how to read words. This requires not only knowing the names or sounds of letters but also being able to detect some constituent sounds in the pronunciations of words (phonemic awareness). For example, children might remember how to read *jail* by connecting the first and final letters *J* and *L* to their letter names heard in the word "jay" and "el." Because the middle letters are ignored, the connections formed are only partial; hence the name of the phase. When different words share boundary letters, children may mix them up. Children lack decoding skill at this phase. To read new words, they may guess the words using partial phonetic cues plus contextual cues, or they may mistake the words for known sight words sharing similar letters.

Ehri and Wilce (1985) proposed the partial alphabetic phase to challenge Gough and Hillinger's (1980) claim that visual cue reading provides a full account of sight word reading before beginners acquire decoding ability. Ehri and Wilce suggest that a rudimentary alphabetic form of word reading, called phonetic cue reading, precedes decoding. In their study, beginners were given several trials to learn to read two sets of words. One set was composed of visually salient spellings, such as *wBc* taught as the spelling of "giraffe." In this case the spelling had a unique shape and unique letters not occurring in other words that were taught, but none of the letters corresponded to any sound in the word. The other set of words was spelled with phonetically salient letters, such as *JRF* for "giraffe." In this case the spellings displayed letters whose names contained sounds found in the pronunciations of the words. It was predicted that pre-alphabetic readers would learn to read the visually salient spellings more easily than the phonetic spellings, whereas partial alphabetic readers would learn to read the phonetic spellings more easily than the visual spellings. This is what was found. These results have been replicated by others and show that phonetic cue reading replaces visual cue reading when alphabetic knowledge is acquired (Bowman & Treiman, 2002; De Abreu & Cardoso-Martins, 1998; Roberts, 2003; Scott & Ehri, 1989; Treiman & Rodriguez, 1999).

Even children who have not yet become readers are capable of using phonetic cues to learn to read words if they possess some knowledge of the alphabet. Scott and Ehri (1989) selected preschoolers who read few if any words out of context but knew most letter names. In a sight word learning task, these children learned to read phonetic spellings more readily than nonphonetic visual spellings. Interestingly, their learning of phonetic spellings was not influenced by whether they named or simply counted letters as they practiced reading the words, very likely because letter name knowledge was activated spontaneously during the sight word learning task.

Sight word learning is easiest when entire letter names are heard in the words. Treiman, Sotak, and Bowman (2001) used a word learning task to compare words containing letter names (e.g., TM to spell *team*) to words containing only letter-sound relations (such as TM for *time*). Preschool nonreaders learned letter-name words faster than letter-sound words. Bowman and Treiman (2002) studied whether the two positions of the letter name, at the beginning or end of words (e.g., ND for *end* vs. DN for *den*) were equally useful for forming connections. Among nonreaders who knew letters, only the initial position improved word learning compared to a visual control condition, whereas among novice beginners who knew letters and could read a few simple words, letter names in final position improved word learning over a visual control condition. These findings reveal that when children first become able to use letter names as phonetic cues in reading words from memory, before they have begun building a sight vocabulary, only letter name cues at the beginnings of words provide effective connections. However, once children begin reading simple words by sight, letter name cues in both positions can be used.

Roberts (2003) provides experimental evidence that teaching children letter names facilitates sight word learning. She selected preschoolers who knew few if any letters and could not read. She taught letter names to one group and she read stories to the control group. In a sight word learning task given at the end of training, she found that the letter group learned to read simplified phonetic spellings more readily than visual spellings, whereas the control group showed the opposite pattern. Most of the phonetic spellings contained sounds from the letter names (i.e., LN for *lunch*) rather than full letter names. This study confirms that the relationship between letter name knowledge and sight word learning is causal.

The claim that phonetic cues provide the connections that facilitate sight word learning was pursued by Rack et al. (1994). They selected partial alphabetic phase readers, those who knew letter-sound correspondences and could read some words but had little decoding skill. Children learned to read simplified spellings that contained two phonetically plausible letters combined with one target letter that was not as phonetic. In half of the words, these target letters were articulated in the same place in the mouth and hence were close phonetic neighbors of the correct letter; for example, Z in ZMR to spell *summer*, or V in RVL to spell *rifle*. In the other half of the words, the target letters were more distant phonetically, for example, V in VMR to spell *summer*, or Z in RZL to spell *rifle*. Children learned to read phonetically close spellings such as ZMR more easily than phonetically distant spellings such as VMR. Thus, even though the target letters in both spellings were off the mark, the letter that provided a phonetic connection to the word's pronunciation was the one that facilitated sight word learning. Rack et al. interpret their findings to support the direct mapping hypothesis, that spellings are linked to phonological forms of words when they are stored in memory. This is also evidence for Ehri and Wilce's (1985) concept of phonetic cue reading.

In sum, these findings indicate that as soon as children learn to name letters, they become capable of remembering how to read words by forming phonetic connections in memory. Alphabetically based sight word learning processes are thus available to learners sooner than Gough and Hillinger (1980) proposed, before children have learned to decode novel words. Phonetic cue reading identifies a way of reading sight words that is more advanced than visual cue or context dependent reading but less advanced than cipher reading.

Although the capability for sight word reading is present once children have mastered letters, this still may not be sufficient to build a sight vocabulary. In some of the experiments above, preschoolers benefited from phonetic cues in learning sight words yet they had not learned to read any words in isolation outside of the laboratory. In another study (Cardoso-Martins et al., 2003), illiterate Brazilian adults displayed characteristics of partial alphabetic phase readers. They knew the names of some alphabet letters, they invented partial phonetic spellings of words, and they learned to read phonetic spellings more readily than visual spellings in a sight word learning task. However, they were unable to read any common words, indicating they had not yet moved into reading. The lack of formal instruction and practice using alphabetic knowledge to read may explain the halt in their development as readers.

It is important to note that sight word reading during the partial alphabetic phase is an imperfect process that occurs among beginners who lack full knowledge of the alphabetic system and phonemic segmentation skill. There are no expectations about how long this phase will last. If beginners quickly acquire the skills necessary for the next phase, they may not exhibit phonetic cue reading. This issue was raised by Wimmer and Hummer (1990) who found that German-speaking Austrian children showed little evidence of using visual or partial alphabetic cues to read words. This may have occurred because German is a transparent writing system, so decoding is relatively easy to learn. In addition, from Day 1 in school, Austrian children receive systematic phonics instruction that teaches them the alphabetic system.

Wimmer and Hummer (1990) suggest that the partial alphabetic phase may not apply to children who are learning to read in transparent writing systems. However, Cardoso-Martins (2001) studied beginners reading in Portuguese, a relatively transparent system. She found that those taught with a whole-word method did exhibit phonetic cue reading and did not start out decoding words, in contrast to those taught with a phonics method. Her findings indicate that the instructional method influences how long beginners show evidence of the partial alphabetic phase and how quickly they acquire use of full graphophonemic connections.

## Transition from the Partial Alphabetic to Full Alphabetic Phase

The full alphabetic phase emerges when beginners acquire decoding skill and graphophonemic knowledge that is used to bond spellings fully to their pronunciations in memory. In a longitudinal study following students from first to second grades, Juel, Griffith, and Gough (1986) showed the importance of several capabilities for this transition (with tasks in parentheses): phonemic awareness (segmentation, blending, substitution), exposure to print (level of texts being read in classrooms), cipher knowledge (nonword decoding), and sight word knowledge (recognition of misspellings). A path analysis suggested that phonemic awareness and exposure to print helped children acquire the cipher. Cipher reading when combined with sight word knowledge was found to improve word reading, which in turn influenced text comprehension. Interestingly, correlations between reading measures were much higher, typically above .60, than correlations involving IQ, typically below $r = .40$. These findings suggest that internal causal relations among reading capabilities promote movement from the partial to the full alphabetic phase.

Stuart and Coltheart (1988) are critical of claims that phonological awareness is *the* necessary precursor for learning to read. Rather, they propose that phonological awareness combined with letter-sound knowledge initiates reading acquisition (see Bowey, this volume). Studies show that even adults may lack much phonemic awareness unless they have learned to read an alphabetic writing system (Morais, Cary, Alegria, & Bertelson, 1979; Read, Zhang, Nie, & Ding, 1986). Also studies show that teaching beginners both phonemic awareness and letter-sound correspondences produces larger effects on word reading than teaching beginners only phonemic awareness (Bradley & Bryant, 1983; Ehri et al., 2001).

In a longitudinal study, Stuart and Coltheart (1988) had beginners read a list of common words several times during the first grade. Two types of errors were distinguished, errors that preserved beginning or beginning and ending letters (e.g., *cat–car, bird–bad*) and errors that showed less resemblance to the written words (e.g., *look–baby, milk–like*). Students were grouped by the point in time during the year when they attained phonemic segmentation and letter-sound knowledge. The proportions of different error types that they produced before and after this point in time were analyzed. Results revealed that prior to the targeted point, readers produced more errors showing less resemblance to words than errors sharing beginning and end letters. However, after the targeted point, the pattern reversed and errors sharing letters with the target words rose. Furthermore, most of the errors produced by children who had reached the targeted point early were of this type. These findings support Stuart and Coltheart's claim that acquisition of phonemic awareness and letter knowledge change the quality of word reading processes and move students to a new level of development.

In a subsequent study, Savage, Stuart, and Hill (2001) examined the predictive relationship between word reading at age 6 and 8 years. Word reading errors preserving beginning and ending letters, called scaffolding errors, were strongly correlated with reading two years later, whereas word reading errors that preserved only beginning or only ending letters showed negative correlations. Scaffolding errors are claimed to play an important role in building word reading skill. Readers who can construct scaffolds of words in memory may find it easier to remember the middles of words and to learn letter-sound consistencies that recur across words.

Chall (1967) emphasizes the contribution of instruction. In her review of studies, she found that early systematic instruction in phonics led to better achievement in reading than later less systematic phonics instruction. More recently, Ehri, Nunes, Stahl, and Willows (2001) conducted a meta-analysis of experimental studies. They found that systematic phonics instruction boosted sight word reading, decoding, and reading comprehension more than other kinds of instruction including whole-word and whole-language instruction. Effects were especially pronounced in kindergarten and first grade.

The impact of phonics and whole-word instruction on students' miscues (misreadings of words) during oral text reading has been examined (Barr, 1974–1975; Carnine, Carnine, & Gersten, 1984; Cohen, 1975). Results indicate that whole-word trained beginners are more apt to guess words based on partial letter cues or context cues or resemblance to known sight words than phonics trained students. Phonically trained students are more likely to stop reading when words are unknown and to generate a nonword when they try unsuccessfully to decode the word. Barr (1974–1975) inferred use of sight word reading if students substituted only real words drawn from their reading vocabularies. She inferred use of a decoding strategy if students produced nonwords and real words that did not come from their reading vocabularies. Midway through first grade, phonics-trained students exhibited both approaches, but by the end of the year, most had shifted to a decoding strategy. In contrast, whole-word-trained students continued to use sight word reading based on partial cues throughout the year. These findings reveal that phonics instruction promotes more rapid movement from the partial to the full phase than whole-word instruction. This is because sight word reading at the full phase benefits from decoding skill.

## Full alphabetic phase

Mason's (1980) longitudinal study reveals characteristics of children in the full alphabetic phase. These children were able to decode new words. In her sight word learning task, they had no problem learning to read all 10 words and remembering them after a delay. Also they had no problem when the letter case was shifted. Parents were unable to estimate their children's sight word vocabularies because growth was so rapid.

According to Ehri (1999) during the full alphabetic phase, beginners become able to form connections between all of the graphemes in spellings and the phonemes in pronunciations to remember how to read words. This fully secures the words in memory and gives them a unique address that eliminates confusion among similarly spelled words. To learn sight words this well, readers need more complete knowledge of grapheme–phoneme relations, most importantly vowels, and how to use these relations to decode words. They also need phonemic segmentation skill to detect the full array of grapheme–phoneme connections that secure spellings in memory. One or a few reading experiences is sufficient to convert unfamiliar words to familiar sight words.

Ehri and Wilce (1979) showed that knowledge of grapheme–phoneme correspondences provides a mnemonic system that links spellings to pronunciations and enhances memory for words. In one experiment, children practiced saying the pronunciations of four nonwords, each paired with a number; for example, 1-"jad," 2-"wek," 3-"sim," and 4-"lut." During study periods, some children were shown spellings of the words. Other children repeated the words an extra time but never saw spellings. During test periods, each number was presented without any spelling, and children recalled its nonword. Children who had seen spellings remembered the words much better than those who had not. The relationship between children's ability to benefit from spellings in remembering the words and their sight vocabularies was very high, supporting the idea that this mnemonic system provides the "glue" that secures sight words in memory.

This connection-forming process works not only to secure regularly spelled words in memory but also irregularly spelled words, most of which exhibit some regularity. Irregular words can be remembered by forming connections between those letters that correspond to sounds; for example, all but the *S* in *island.* The exceptional letters may be flagged in memory as silent, or remembered as extra letters, or given a spelling pronunciation. Stuart and Masterson (1992) found that the tasks of reading regularly spelled words and reading irregularly spelled words were highly correlated in a group of 10-year-olds ($r = .93$), suggesting use of a common connection-forming process.

Results of several studies of beginners' sight word reading reveal differences that distinguish partial from full alphabetic phase readers. Ehri and Wilce (1987a) selected partial alphabetic kindergartners and randomly assigned them, either to a group that learned to process all the letters in words to read them, the full phase group, or to a group that practiced individual letter-sound relations, the partial phase group. On a sight word learning task that followed training, full alphabetic phase readers learned to read a set of 15 similarly spelled words almost perfectly after three practice trials. In contrast, partial phase readers never learned even half of the words after seven practice trials, one reason being that they mixed up similarly spelled words. On a spelling task given afterwards, full phase readers remembered middle letters better than partial alphabetic readers. However, both groups spelled initial and final letters accurately and equally well, very likely because these were the cues that the partial readers used to remember how to read the words. These findings show that sight word learning is more rapid and accurate during the full phase, and that spellings of words are better secured in memory among full phase readers than among partial phase readers. In another study, Ehri and Saltmarsh (1995) also showed that full alphabetic phase readers retained complete spellings of sight words in memory, whereas partial alphabetic phase readers retained mainly boundary letters.

Evidence that graphemes are connected to phonemes when sight words are learned comes from two studies by Ehri and Wilce (1980, 1986). They taught children to read words and then examined whether the spellings influenced children's conception of phonemes in pronunciations of the words. For example, the medial consonant in *Gretel,* *meteor,* and *glitter* is a flap pronounced more like /d/ than /t/ in American English. Children who learned to read these words perceived this phoneme as /t/ according to its spelling, whereas children who only practiced saying the words but never read them perceived the phoneme according to its spoken form, as /d/. The explanation is that conceptions of phonemes are shaped by the graphemes connected to them.

Stuart and Coltheart (1988) explain how beginners who possess full phonics skills can retain sight words in memory with minimal experience reading the words. It is because alphabetic knowledge provides learners with a basis for *expecting* specific connections between spoken and written words. For example, students who know how to segment the word *bat* into three phonemes and how to spell each phoneme will expect to see the word written b, a, t, before they ever see it. Such expectations support very rapid acquisition because word learning simply entails confirming an expectation and assimilating its form in memory.

Share (1995, 1999) has studied the contribution of a decoding strategy to the acquisition of sight words. Decoding functions as a self-teaching mechanism. When readers decode new words as they read text, those words are retained in memory. In a study by Cunningham, Perry, Stanovich, and Share (2002), second graders read 10 novel words, each repeated 6 times in a story. One of two identically pronounced spellings of each word was read (e.g., yate vs. yait). Posttests showed that students remembered the spellings of the words they read and did not confuse them with plausible alternative spellings that were not seen. In support of the self-teaching hypothesis, there was a strong correlation between correct decodings of the words and memory for the spellings seen. The relationship was not explained by general cognitive ability. This study shows that decoding helps students build a sight vocabulary.

Although decoding facilitates memory for sight words, beginning readers of English have trouble reconciling these two processes because English includes numerous high-frequency words that are not decodable and can only be read from memory. Seymour and Duncan (2001) suggest that instruction emphasizing only one of the processes may retard the development of the other process. Seymour and Elder (1986) observed the word reading of children taught in a whole-word program. They found that when given a reading task, children produced only words they had been taught and were unable to read unfamiliar words. Typically they would refuse to read or would substitute known words for the unfamiliar words. In contrast, students who received a mixed instructional approach utilized both sight word reading and a decoding strategy. This suggests that growth during the full alphabetic phase requires instruction in both decoding and sight word learning.

*Consolidated alphabetic phase*

Constituents of the consolidated alphabetic phase begin to form during the full alphabetic phase. These consist of letter sequences that symbolize blends of graphophonemic units, including morphemes (affixes and root words), onsets, and rimes (e.g., in *string*, the onset is *STR* and the rime is *ING*), monosyllabic words that have become sight words, and more frequent spellings of syllables in polysyllabic words. As readers learn to read words that share letter patterns symbolizing the same phoneme blend in different words, for example, *king, thing, bring, sing*, a consolidated unit is formed. Knowing *-ing* as a consolidated unit means that readers can read it as a whole rather than as a sequence of grapheme–phoneme units. Knowing larger blends contributes to the learning of sight words by reducing the memory load. For example, connections to learn the word *interesting* are much easier to form if the four syllabic spellings, *IN, TER, EST, ING*, are known as units than if the word is analyzed as 10 graphophonemic units (Henry, 2003).

According to Ehri's (1998, 1999, 2002) theory, the consolidated alphabetic phase replaces the full alphabetic phase when the predominant types of connections for retaining sight words in memory are morphographic. Among the first letter sequences to consolidate during the full alphabetic phase are common morphemic suffixes, *-ED, -ING, -ER, -EST*. Also monosyllabic words that have become sight words provide consolidated units available for forming connections. The most common word constituents of multisyllabic words are *ate, in, it, ant,* and *age*.

Relatively few studies have examined the facilitative effects of consolidated units on sight word learning. Ehri and Robbins (1992) conducted a study with first graders who displayed some decoding skill. In a sight word learning task, children practiced reading one set of words and then were given a second set to learn. The second set consisted of spellings that contained either the same rime endings as first set (e.g., *feed – seed*) or the same letter-sound correspondences but not the same rime patterns. Children learned the words faster when the second set shared rimes with the first set than when the second set shared letter-sounds, indicating that common letter patterns provided the connections facilitating learning.

The value of having students analyze the syllable constituents of words in a sight word learning task was studied by Bhattacharya and Ehri (2004) who worked with adolescent struggling readers reading at a third grade level. Students practiced reading and analyzing four sets of 25 multisyllabic words for 4 trials, each set learned on a different day. Words were pronounced and divided into spoken syllables that matched written syllables. Control groups received either whole-word practice on the same words or no special treatment. Performance on posttests indicated that students who received syllable training retained the spellings of sight words in memory more completely than students who practiced reading the words as wholes. Moreover, syllable students outperformed whole-word students in decoding new words and pseudowords. These findings suggest the value of practice in the consolidation of syllabic units for sight word learning and decoding skill.

Juel (1983) studied the influence of letter patterns on fifth graders' reaction times to read 64 familiar words. She found that they read words faster when they contained more common two-letter patterns occurring in the same positions in many different words than when they read words containing patterns occurring in fewer words. This shows that spelling patterns facilitate sight word reading. Juel also examined the impact of the frequency of spelling patterns occurring in running text (i.e., *th* occurs very often when counted in running text because of the frequency of *the*, but *th* occurs less often when counted in different words). This way of counting spellings patterns did not influence sight word reading, suggesting that acquisition of consolidated units is governed by the number of different sight words containing them, not by their frequency in running text.

## Development of Automaticity, Speed, and Unitization

Two other dimensions of sight word reading that undergo development are automaticity and speed. In the theories presented above, these dimensions receive less attention. Chall (1983) considers word reading speed as part of building fluency during Stage 2. Ehri and McCormick (1998) suggest that automaticity may be a separate phase that follows the consolidated phase during development and characterizes mature readers who recognize most words automatically by sight and who are facile if not automatic in decoding unfamiliar words.

Automaticity is recognizing the pronunciations and meanings of written words immediately upon seeing them without expending any attention or effort decoding the words. Studies using picture-word interference tasks show that readers' minds process the words even when they try to ignore them. Words slow down picture naming more than nonwords. Words in the same semantic category as the pictures, such as names of animals or fruit, slow down picture naming the most (e.g., the word 'cow' printed on a picture of a horse). Guttentag and Haith (1978) found that normally developing readers as young as the end of first grade processed familiar words automatically.

LaBerge and Samuels (1974) propose a theory to explain the develoment of automaticity. Two stages are distinguished, involving attention (Samuels & Kamil, 1984). At the beginning stage, readers switch their attention between decoding words and comprehending text, whereas at the fluent stage, no switching is required because words are read automatically. The advantage of automaticity is that readers' attention can be devoted entirely to understanding the text rather than having it divided and distracted by decoding issues.

LaBerge and Samuels (1974) also portray the development of visual memory for words. As a result of practice reading many words, the reader processes increasingly larger units as these units recur, from features to letters to spelling patterns to whole words, referred to as unitization. Not only letters but also other visual features of words such as word length, contour, and internal patterns may be retained in memory to support sight word reading. Visual codes become connected to phonological codes, which in turn activate semantic codes in memory.

In one study, Samuels, LaBerge, and Bremer (1978) presented common words of varying length to students (grades 2 through college) who pressed a button if the word belonged to a targeted semantic category such as "animal." Second graders' latencies increased as words grew longer from 3 to 5 letters, whereas older students' latencies did not change. The explanation is that older students read the words as single units, whereas younger students processed component letters to read the words.

Further evidence regarding the development of unitization is provided by Ehri and Wilce (1983), who measured the latencies of skilled and less skilled readers (grades 1, 2, and 4) when they read common object words, number words, and CVC nonwords (e.g., *cat, six, des*) and named single numbers. Words were read faster than nonwords, indicating that words were read by sight rather than decoding. Skilled readers read words as rapidly as they named numbers, indicating that the words were read as whole units rather than sequentially by letters. In contrast, less skilled readers below fourth grade did not show unitization. According to Ehri and Wilce, unitization indicates that spellings of sight words are fully secured to their pronunciations in memory, whereas lack of unitization results from sight words that are only partially secured.

One might question whether sight word reading occurs in transparent writing systems where most words can be decoded. Defior, Cary, and Martos (2002) and Wimmer and Goswami (1994) gave German-, Spanish-, and Portuguese-reading students the task of reading the spellings of number words and pseudowords and naming single digits. First graders took longer to read number words than to name digits. However, second graders identified number words and digits at the same speed, indicating unitization. In addition, all grade levels read number words faster than pseudowords. These findings show that sight word reading does occur in more transparent writing systems, despite the fact that decoding is a viable option.

## Concluding Comments

We have seen that several theories portray how word reading develops. Although some theories relegate sight word reading to the earliest stage and view it as an immature process that is replaced by decoding, findings of studies show that this is inaccurate even in transparent languages. The types of connections that secure sight words in memory change with development, but sight word reading exists as a way of reading words from memory throughout development. Some theories include an initial pre-literacy phase to explore possible roots of later phases. Other theories ignore this phase because children make little if any progress learning to read. Theories show agreement regarding the huge advantage to word reading that results when decoding skill is acquired. Theories explain later forms of sight word reading as involving connections that are provided by the alphabetic system and that secure sight words in memory. Some of these theories distinguish a rudimentary alphabetic period before full alphabetic knowledge is acquired. Some theories add later phases that involve syllabic and morphographic spelling patterns to form connections.

There is need for further research to enrich the picture of development. Some studies provide evidence that is exploratory and suggestive rather than definitive. Causal claims may rest on correlational findings rather than controlled experiments, so research is needed to rule out competing explanations. Especially valuable are training studies to test causal claims.

Developmental theories of word reading carry implications for instruction. Teachers and curriculum designers are using these theories to guide their work (Brown, 2003). This is illustrated by F. Johnston's testimonial:

> Phases of word recognition have so many implications for developmentally appropriate instruction. Right now I am working to convince teachers that directing students to look at the printed word is so much more important than directing them to use context and picture cues. Also I tell them that the prompts they give children when they encounter words they don't know will depend upon where the children are in their word recognition development. If they are pre-alphabetic, then they will have to use pictures, but if they are moving into the full alphabetic phase, then it is perfectly appropriate to ask them to sound out the word. Teachers seem to be very familiar with prompts but only as a generic list that is not differentiated by development. (personal communication, February 26, 2002)

Research is needed to study whether taking account of developmental theories improves instruction. Ehri's phase theory was applied to modify the Benchmark word identification program (Gaskins, Ehri, Cress, O'Hara, & Donnelly, 1996). The original program involved teaching students to read new words by analogy to a set of 120 key words. The program was revised to include teaching students to analyze words into grapheme–phoneme constituents so that the key words became fully secured sight words in memory rather than just words listed on a classroom wordwall. Data analysis comparing students' performance in the original and revised programs indicates that the new program produced superior performance during the first two years of instruction but differences were minimal during years 3 and 4.

One topic slighted in the present chapter concerns the impact of building a sight vocabulary on other ways to read words. One contribution involves analogizing. As readers' sight vocabularies grow and provide the analogs, this strategy becomes more common, especially if readers are taught how to analogize. Another contribution of sight word learning is to expand readers' knowledge of spelling-sound regularities. According to Stuart, Masterson, Dixon, and Quinlan (1999), readers hold expectations from their alphabetic knowledge about the way words will be spelled when they see them in print for the first time. When parts of these words deviate from expectations, readers notice the unexpected parts. When the same parts recur in other words, they are learned as alternative spellings for the sounds represented; for example, the *-igh* representing /ay/ in *night, light, fight*. Thompson and his colleagues (Thompson, Cottrell, & Fletcher-Flinn, 1996; Thompson, Fletcher-Flinn, & Cottrell, 1999) have also studied this learning process. They use it to explain how children who do not receive explicit systematic instruction in phonics nevertheless acquire knowledge of the alphabetic system, by learning to read specific words and remembering letter-sound consistencies across the words.

Another important topic deserving more attention involves students with reading disabilities and how they fit into these developmental schemes (Ehri & Snowling, 2004). Compared to typically developing readers, poor readers have greater difficulty decoding new words, they take longer to learn words by sight, they secure partial rather than full representations of sight words in memory (see Romani et al., this volume), and they read familiar words more slowly and take longer to unitize them. In short, they look like partial alphabetic readers. Because text reading is supported by much redundancy, deficiencies in sight word reading are compensated by other sources. Word reading is propped up by the surrounding text, by readers' spoken vocabulary and world knowledge, and by the strategy of predicting words based on partial letters and context. These sources allow poor readers to read text albeit less adequately than typical readers.

# 9

# Predicting Individual Differences in Learning to Read

## Judith A. Bowey

Any complete theory of learning to read must explain individual differences in reading development. Studies of individual differences in early reading achievement point to key processes and abilities that may underpin reading success and failure that may ultimately help us to optimize instruction. Such studies have a long history and have attracted a huge amount of research. This review must of necessity be selective and will focus on key research areas in relation to the first few years of alphabetic reading.

## Methodological Issues

Assessing the predictors of individual differences in learning to read involves longitudinal studies where a predictor variable (or variables) at one point in time ($t_1$) is related to reading at a later time ($t_2$). Where reading ability is unstable, key measures assessed at school entry will predict less variance. Predictive studies from small groups, such as single classes and perhaps even single schools, may be unreliable and, at worst, biased by the effects of particular instructional contexts. Studies of single classes and of fewer than 50 children have thus generally been excluded from this review.

The ultimate goal of reading is to understand continuous text. The higher-level processing required for this is interrupted when attention is diverted to lower-level word identification processes. Indeed, even when reading is accurate, if it is effortful, the higher-order processes involved in reading comprehension will be affected. Therefore, predictive studies of children learning to read English have typically used word reading accuracy (rather than reading rate) as a criterion measure.

*Phonological recoding* refers to the ability to pronounce unfamiliar printed words. In alphabetic scripts letters symbolize phonemes, so that skilled readers can decode newly encountered regular words. About 80% of English words can be considered regular for reading purposes (Woodcock, 1987) and, apart from strange words like *aisle* and *choir*, even exception words like *prove* and *break* contain regularities. To a considerable extent, therefore, learning to read regular and exception words involves common processes, particularly given that context and vocabulary can supplement partial phonological recoding in identifying unfamiliar words. Mastery of alphabetic reading thus entails the ability to use letter-sound correspondences to pronounce unfamiliar items *de novo* and provides the learner with what has been called a "*self-teaching device*" (Share, 1995). Phonological recoding is typically studied experimentally by asking children to read aloud nonwords, which are by definition unfamiliar. Nonword reading and word reading accuracy share 66–77% of variance in beginning readers (Bowey, 2000).

The fact that word reading is the usual criterion in predictive studies is not especially problematic when studying beginning readers who typically read simple texts containing vocabulary that is easily understood. At this stage of development, word identification and reading comprehension share 61–81% of variance (Bowey, 2000). As texts become conceptually more demanding, the variance shared by word identification and reading comprehension decreases (to 45–66% from fourth grade on; Bowey, 2000) and listening comprehension accounts for increasing variance in reading comprehension (Curtis, 1980). In addition, general cognitive and language abilities may strongly predict reading comprehension in older readers (Flynn & Rahbar, 1998).

A particular methodological issue posed by predictive studies is that of autoregressive effects – the tendency of a variable measured at $t_1$ to predict itself at $t_2$. On a philosophical level, it may be argued that abilities cannot cause themselves, and thus that it makes no sense to control the effects of $t_1$ reading within predictive studies. Such a view ignores the fact that *reading as a construct changes over time* (see Cronbach & Furby, 1970). Even when measured by the same test (e.g., word identification), reading does not necessarily represent the same cognitive process at different points in development; different processes contribute to performance as proficiency increases. Some cognitive processes drop out and are replaced by qualitatively different processes (Stuart & Coltheart, 1988). For instance, children may reconceptualize their way of thinking about spoken words once they have begun to read and they have begun to attend to phonemes (Morais & Kolinsky, this volume). When $t_1$ reading effects are ignored, abilities that are the product of early reading at $t_1$ may show inflated contributions to $t_2$ reading. Controlling $t_1$ reading effects also minimizes the possibility that predictive associations reflect the contribution of any third variable(s).

Autoregressive reading effects are far from trivial. Torgesen and Burgess (1998) found that word reading, tested early in US kindergarten, predicted 42% of variance in early first-grade word reading. This in turn predicted 58% of variance at the beginning of second grade (n = 201). Even in school entrants not yet exposed to reading instruction, early reading predicts considerable variance in later reading skill (e.g., Lundberg, Olofsson, & Wall, 1980; Wimmer, Landerl, Linortner, & Hummer, 1991).

A related issue, frequently overlooked, is that the prediction of reading from $t_1$ to $t_2$ depends on the starting level at $t_1$ even when growth from $t_1$ to $t_2$ is linear. Ideally, the prediction of reading skill should be examined by modeling both individual differences in starting levels and individual differences in growth using a number of time intervals (Rogosa & Willett, 1985). However, $t_1$–$t_2$ designs are a useful first step, provided that $t_1$

reading effects are controlled and that it is acknowledged that findings may not gene-ralize to other values of $t_1$ and $t_2$. Testing words that are common in beginning reading materials provides more sensitive measures of early reading ability (Bowey, 1994a, 1995; Ehri & Wilce, 1985; Johnston, Anderson, & Holligan, 1996) than standardized tests that sample very few items at the beginner levels and are subject to floor effects (e.g., Wagner, Torgesen, & Rashotte, 1994; Wagner et al., 1997).

In fact, few predictive studies have properly controlled $t_1$ reading effects. Studies also vary widely in their inclusion of other control variables (e.g., general cognitive ability). This chapter thus begins by examining simple correlations between key predictors, assessed in kindergarten children or school entrants, and later reading skills. Somewhat different conclusions may be reached in predictive studies that start later when children have more advanced reading skills. It should be noted that studies that do not control the effects of $t_1$ reading may overestimate the contribution to later reading of other vari-ables that correlate with early reading ability.

Findings from predictive studies that include $t_1$ control variables (e.g., general cogni-tive or verbal abilities) are often overinterpreted. Suppose a study controls the effects of $t_1$ letter knowledge when predicting $t_2$ reading from $t_1$ phonological sensitivity in school entrants with no measurable word reading ability. Assume that $t_1$ letter-name knowledge and phonological sensitivity share substantial variance and that both predict substantial variance in $t_2$ word reading (assumptions that are completely consistent with research find-ings; Naslund & Schneider, 1996). Now assume that, with $t_1$ letter-name knowledge effects controlled, $t_1$ phonological sensitivity predicts no independent variance in $t_2$ word reading. This finding only implies that the variance in $t_2$ word reading predicted by $t_1$ phonological sensitivity covaries with that explained by $t_1$ letter-name knowledge. It does *not* indicate that $t_1$ phonological sensitivity makes no contribution to $t_2$ word reading. The effects of $t_1$ phonological sensitivity on $t_2$ word reading may be mediated by $t_1$ letter-name knowledge (see Baron & Kenny, 1986). However, this conclusion is also prema-ture. Assume that further analysis suggests that the effects of $t_1$ letter-name knowledge on $t_2$ word reading may be partly or wholly mediated by $t_1$ phonological sensitivity. Because letter-name knowledge and phonological sensitivity were measured at the same time, even findings that only $t_1$ letter-name knowledge predicts unique variance in $t_2$ word reading cannot be causally interpreted. Note that the example above is hypothetical; Naslund and Schneider (1996) found that results varied in predictive analyses of this type, depending how phonological sensitivity was assessed (n = 89).

Thus, when different predictors correlate with each other, we must be wary of ever concluding that only one predictor explains independent variance when the effects of other predictors are controlled. Such conclusions may be especially unreliable in studies using single tests of each construct and with relatively small participant-to-test ratios in which outcomes may be influenced by a range of extraneous factors (including the het-erogeneity of the group tested, test sensitivity, and method variance; see also Anthony et al., 2002).

Latent variables are sometimes used to avoid the measurement error associated with the use of a single test to assess a particular construct. Latent variables comprise the common variance among measures of a particular construct, thus excluding variance that is unique to a single variable, such as measurement error, unique method variance, and the unique contributions of other abilities. However, latent variables are not free of the common contribution of general cognitive ability. Furthermore, latent variables are not necessarily pure measures of a construct. When derived from a small number of fairly similar tasks, they include method variance. For instance, Wagner et al.'s (1994) treatment of phonological analysis and blending as highly correlated but different constructs may reflect failure to consider common method variance within some of the tasks defining them (Schatschneider, Francis, Foorman, Fletcher, & Mehta, 1999). In subsequent analyses, these two latent variables were combined into a second-order phonological sensitivity latent variable, "to acknowledge that analysis and synthesis represent the same construct of phonological awareness" (Wagner et al., 1997, p. 472).

Even when latent variables are used, findings that only one $t_1$ skill uniquely predicts $t_2$ reading should be interpreted conservatively. If $t_1$ predictors assess common abilities, these findings may simply indicate that the measures explain redundant variance in reading. Furthermore, findings that any given predictor does or does not explain unique variance are *relative* to a particular analysis, and may depend on the relationships among the variables included within a given study. Uniqueness cannot be compared across studies that assess constructs differently or use different combinations of control variables. It may thus be useful to perform commonality analyses, which partition variance in $t_2$ reading that can be attributed uniquely to each $t_1$ predictor and variance that can be attributed to various combinations of $t_1$ predictors (see Pedhazur, 1982).

A common misconception is that variables that predict large amounts of variance in $t_2$ reading can accurately identify poor readers at $t_2$. However, predictors that are salient at the upper end of the reading continuum may exert little influence at the lower end. For instance, even if they explain considerable variance in $t_2$ reading, $t_1$ tasks like phoneme segmentation that are extremely difficult for substantial numbers of school entrants are not likely to identify future poor readers accurately. Often children scoring at floor on phoneme segmentation become successful readers (e.g., Perfetti, Beck, Bell, & Hughes, 1987; Wagner et al., 1994).

To determine whether $t_1$ performance accurately identifies poor readers at $t_2$ requires a quite different form of analysis (see Gredler, 1997). Torgesen and Wagner (1995, cited in Torgesen & Burgess, 1998) combined three measures taken at the beginning of kindergarten (phoneme deletion, letter-name knowledge, and continuous digit naming speed) to predict the children in the bottom 10% in word reading at the beginning of second grade. Using logistic regression techniques, 23 children of 240 children were predicted to be poor readers by second grade. Of these 23 children, 14 were indeed in the bottom 10% at the beginning of second grade. Of the 217 predicted to be reading above the bottom 10% at the beginning of second grade, 207 were. Predictive outcome analyses (Gredler, 1997) indicate that this procedure was poor at predicting poor readers.

Although rarely performed, predictive outcome analyses reveal the danger of placing high levels of confidence in screening or readiness tests. Accurate early prediction of future poor readers may be doomed to failure, as it cannot account for subsequent variance in other critical factors such as the quality of instruction that the child receives, the frequency of school changes, school attendance, and so on. It is probably more appropriate to investigate how to optimize reading instruction for all children, and for teachers to keep a firm eye on children who are falling behind so that, wherever possible, directly relevant instruction can be focused on difficulties as they occur.

## Key Predictors of Early Reading Ability

### General cognitive ability

General cognitive ability typically predicts success best early in skill acquisition, before more specific skills required for efficient processing have been learned or mastered (Sternberg, 1981). Many of the earliest attempts children make to read comprise associating distinctive graphemic cues with whole words (Seymour & Elder, 1986) and may depend on general cognitive ability (Stuart & Coltheart, 1988). In kindergarten children without even informal reading instruction, Bowey (1995) found that general cognitive ability predicted 15–22% of variance in first-grade reading (n = 116; see also de Jong & van der Leij, 1999).

As the beginner is faced with graphemically similar words, the strategy of rote memorization using distinctive graphemic cues becomes ineffective, and specific abilities and mechanisms become increasingly important. Thus, with time, abilities contributing to both phonological recoding and "back-up" strategies (e.g., the use of context) better predict word reading, although these may be mediated by general cognitive ability.

All tests of specific abilities incorporate extraneous task-specific cognitive demands. For example, phoneme reversal requires children to analyze spoken words into their constituent phonemes, hold the phonemes in phonological memory, reverse them in working memory, and then say them back in the reverse order. Phoneme reversal is not a "clean" test (Calfee, 1977); it probably taps general cognitive abilities as well as phoneme manipulation.

Controlling $t_1$ general cognitive ability allows an assessment of whether $t_1$ experimental measures predict variance in $t_2$ reading independently of extraneous task-specific requirements. Without such controls, findings are ambiguous. A $t_1$ ability may predict $t_2$ reading only by virtue of its shared variance with other cognitive abilities. Nevertheless, findings that $t_1$ general cognitive ability predicts $t_2$ word reading are not particularly informative about the underlying basis of reading achievement (see Sternberg, 1981).

### Verbal ability

Stanovich (1991) advocated the use of verbal ability, rather than general cognitive ability, to determine which abilities make specific contributions to reading. Verbal ability may control better for the particular task requirements involved in tests of phonological processing abilities that are the focus of most current research. Indeed, it is well established that preschool language development predicts *later* reading achievement within normally developing children (Bryant, Maclean, & Bradley, 1990a; Silva, McGee, & Williams, 1985), and teachers' ratings of early language development can also predict later reading achievement well (Feshbach, Adelman, & Fuller, 1974; Lundberg, 1985). However, such findings are not helpful in determining what aspects of language development contribute to reading.

Vocabulary typically predicts early reading achievement (Bowey, 1995; Bryant et al., 1990a; Caravolas, Hulme, & Snowling, 2001; Cronin & Carver, 1998; Elbro, Borstrom,

& Petersen, 1998; Hurford et al., 1993; Hurford, Schauf, Bunce, Blaich, & Moore, 1994; Naslund & Schneider, 1996; Share, Jorm, Maclean, & Matthews, 1984; Stevenson, Parker, Wilkinson, Hegion, & Fish, 1976; Stevenson & Newman, 1986; Wagner et al., 1994; Wagner et al., 1997; Wolf & Goodglass, 1986; cf. Foorman, Francis, Novy, & Liberman, 1991). Bowey (1995) found that receptive vocabulary in kindergarten children who could not yet read predicted 20–27% of variance in end-of-first-grade reading (n = 116).

Although less commonly studied, children's grammatical development also predicts early reading achievement (Bowey, 1995; Scarborough, 1990; Share et al., 1984). For instance, Share et al. (1984) found that grammatical development at the beginning of kindergarten explained 17% of variance on a composite reading achievement factor at the end of first grade (n = 479).

Bryant et al. (1990a) asked children to correct minor grammatical errors or rearrange jumbled sentences to form coherent ones. Performance on this task, at 4:7, explained 40% of variance in word identification two years later. Sentence rearrangement is not a pure test of grammatical sensitivity and also assesses children's semantic processing and verbal working memory (Bowey, 1994b; Bryant et al. 1990a); nevertheless this task clearly assesses verbal ability.

Even when assessed in kindergarten, both vocabulary and grammatical development become increasingly important predictors as reading progresses (Flynn & Rahbar, 1998). In nonreaders, phonological processing abilities like phonological sensitivity and phonological memory probably develop concomitantly with language development and may thus account for little variance in subsequent reading that is independent of the effects of language development (see Bowey & Patel, 1988). It is not clear at the present time to what extent different facets of oral language development (including vocabulary, grammatical, and phonological skills) can be meaningfully separated and how best to conceptualize the underlying causal relationships between different constructs in this domain. For example, some have argued that tests of language development may partly reflect the contribution of underlying abilities such as phonological memory (see Baddeley, Gathercole, & Papagno, 1998; Ellis & Large, 1987) or phonological processing ability (Bowey, 2001; Elbro et al., 1998).

## Phonological memory

Verbatim sentence memory reliably predicts later reading (Badian, 2000; Bruininks & Mayer, 1979; Bryant et al., 1990a; Catts, Fey, Zhang, & Tomblin, 2001; Kurdek & Sinclair, 2001; Share et al., 1984), although it may sometimes be confounded with grammatical development (but see Baddeley et al., 1998). Badian (2000) reported that verbatim sentence recall measured in kindergarten predicted 22% of variance in word reading and 25% in reading comprehension in first grade (n = 98; see also Share et al., 1984). It also predicted 40% of variance word reading and 31% in reading comprehension in fourth grade (n = 98).

Auditory word span in kindergarten children and school entrants also consistently predicts later reading (Bowey, 1995; Caravolas et al., 2001; de Jong & van der Leij, 1999;

Elbro et al., 1998; Mann & Liberman, 1984; Stevenson et al., 1976; cf. Naslund & Schneider, 1996). Nonword repetition is another measure that predicts early word and nonword reading both in children learning to read English (Baddeley & Gathercole, 1992; Bowey, 1995) and shallow orthographies (de Jong & van der Leij, 1999; Naslund & Schneider, 1996). Although nonword repetition has been proposed as a pure measure of phonological memory (Baddeley et al., 1998; Gathercole, Willis, Baddeley, & Emslie, 1994), it also incorporates substantial phonological processing (Bowey, 2001; Snowling, Chiat, & Hulme, 1991; Snowling, Goulandris, Bowlby, & Howell, 1986).

The predictive association between phonological memory and later word reading has been interpreted in several ways. Phonological memory may allow children to learn to associate letters with their names and sounds (Baddeley & Gathercole, 1992; Share et al., 1984). Alternatively, letter sounds may be held in phonological memory so that they can be blended into words. On the other hand, it could be argued that phonological memory makes no specific contribution to word reading. Rather, the predictive association between phonological memory and later reading may be mediated by verbal ability. Consistent with this view are findings that verbal span predicted later reading better than visual span (Caravolas et al., 2001; Stevenson et al., 1976) and that phonological memory predicted no variance in later word reading once earlier word reading, vocabulary, and other phonological processing abilities were controlled (n = 216; Wagner et al., 1997).

A parsimonious explanation of the predictive link between phonological memory and later word reading is the hypothesis that both skills reflect the quality of phonological representations (e.g., Brady, 1991; Wagner & Torgesen, 1987; Wagner et al., 1994; Wagner et al., 1997). Consistent with this view are findings that virtually any task that requires effortful phonological processing predicts early later word reading.

## Speech perception and production

Kindergarteners' and school entrants' ability to discriminate between spoken syllables and words differing by a minimal phonemic contrast predict later reading (Bond & Dijkstra, 1967; Bruininks & Mayer, 1979; Horn & O'Donnell, 1984; Hurford et al., 1993, 1994; Stevenson & Newman, 1986; Stevenson et al., 1976). Bond and Dijkstra (1967) reported that phoneme discrimination, tested at the beginning of first grade, predicted 20–35% of variance in end-of-year word identification and 17–32% of variance in reading comprehension (n = 488–4,266). These values were higher among methods incorporating some phonics instruction (29–35% for word identification; 25–32% for reading comprehension), relative to language experience and basal reader programs (20–23% for word identification; 17–21% for reading comprehension).

Tallal (1980) suggested that poor readers show more general auditory processing deficits and that they perform poorly on temporal order judgment tasks. However, temporal order judgment is arguably not an auditory perception task (Studdert-Kennedy & Mody, 1995). Regardless, Share et al. (1984) found kindergarten temporal order judgment to predict only 6% of variance in reading at the end of first grade (n = 479).

Articulation errors reflect speech production difficulties, although in a developmental context a child's articulation errors might be traced to faulty speech perception.

Scarborough (1990) found that consonant errors in spontaneous speech at 30 months predicted reading in grade 2, even after controlling IQ. Silva and colleagues (1985) found that 9-year-old boys with general word reading backwardness had scored lower than average on articulation when tested at age 5 (Silva et al., 1985). Elbro et al. (1998) found that the distinctness with which Danish children pronounced unstressed vowels within phonologically complex words at the beginning of kindergarten predicted variance in word reading at the end of first grade. This finding held even with the effects of letter knowledge, phonological sensitivity, digit span, receptive vocabulary, and family background factors controlled.

These findings, from studies of speech perception and production, like those from studies of phonological memory described earlier, are consistent with the proposal that early phonological processing skills predict later reading.

## Phonological sensitivity

Many studies have demonstrated that phonological sensitivity in kindergarten children and school entrants predicts later word-reading ability. Recent work has attempted to discover what *level* of phonological sensitivity (syllable, rime, phoneme) is needed to learn to read an alphabetic script.

In the absence of controls for initial reading levels, kindergarten children's and school entrants' ability to count and manipulate syllables in spoken words predicts later reading ability (Badian, 2000; Mann & Liberman, 1984). However, findings vary with task requirements (Lundberg, Frost, & Peterson, 1988; Naslund & Schneider, 1996). Onset and rime sensitivity is a better predictor of later word reading in children learning to read English than syllabic sensitivity (Bryant, Maclean, Bradley, & Crossland, 1990b; Byrne, Fielding-Barnsley, & Ashley, 2000; Cronin & Carver, 1998; Majsterek & Ellenwood, 1995; cf. Hulme et al., 2002). Indeed, onset and rime sensitivity predicted later word reading in four cohorts of children who could not identify any words on a standardized reading test at initial assessment (Bowey, 1995; Bradley & Bryant, 1983; Maclean, Bryant, & Bradley, 1987).

At a smaller unit level, phoneme manipulation consistently predicts later word reading irrespective of whether children are exposed to formal reading instruction in kindergarten (e.g., Foorman et al., 1991; Juel, Griffith, & Gough 1986; Lundberg et al., 1980; Perfetti et al., 1987; Wimmer et al., 1991, Study 1). However, such findings may be inflated by the effects of early reading skills on phoneme manipulation. For instance, Lundberg et al. (1980) found that kindergarten phoneme manipulation tasks predicted over 20% of variance in first-grade word reading rate (n = 143) and over 16% in second-grade word reading rate (n = 133). However, when kindergarten reading effects were controlled, most tasks failed to predict later reading (Wagner & Torgesen, 1987). Moreover, some have argued that phoneme manipulation cannot be a prerequisite for alphabetic reading (Morais, Cary, Alegria, & Bertelson, 1979; Stanovich, 1992). Alphabetically illiterate adults cannot perform these tasks (Morais, Bertelson, Cary, & Alegria, 1986; Morias et al., 1979), and many school entrants who score at floor on phoneme manipulation tasks become successful readers (Perfetti et al., 1987; Wagner et al., 1994; Wimmer et al., 1991).

Rather, a key prerequisite for learning to read an alphabetic script may be the facility with which children *learn* to attend to and manipulate phonemes, usually within the context of reading instruction (Morais et al., 1979; Wimmer et al., 1991). Consistent with this suggestion is the finding that preschool children's responsiveness to phoneme identity training predicted 8–19% of variance in fifth-grade reading, even with post-training phoneme identity effects controlled (n = 56; Byrne et al., 2000). So, too, is Spector's (1992) finding that a dynamic measure of phoneme segmentation given early in kindergarten predicted 36% of variance in end-of-year word identification, while a standard measure given at the same time predicted only 14% (n = 38).

The capacity to learn to manipulate phonemes may be well predicted by an earlier ability to recognize the similarity of onsets and rimes in spoken words (Bryant et al., 1990a; Bryant et al., 1990b). Byrne et al. (2000) provided indirect evidence that children who were not responsive to their preschool phoneme identity training program scored low in rime identity. Children who became poor readers in fifth grade scored lower than other children on pre-intervention rime, but not on pre-intervention vocabulary, phoneme identity, or letter knowledge or on post-intervention phoneme identity or decoding. Further work investigating this suggestion is clearly required.

There has been considerable controversy over whether onset-rime sensitivity or phoneme sensitivity better predicts later word reading (e.g., Bryant et al., 1990b; Hulme et al., 2002; Muter, Hulme, Snowling, & Taylor, 1998). The answer to this question varies with the developmental level of the child (Bowey, 2002), since the best measure of the construct of phonological sensitivity will vary with the age of the child and especially with the level of exposure to reading instruction (Anthony et al., 2002; Schatschneider, et al., 1999). When predictive studies are carried out with school entrants with some under-standing of the alphabetic principle or some reading ability, phoneme sensitivity is likely to explain more variance in later reading. The opposite may be true in younger children and in children who cannot yet read. Bowey (1995) found that, within kindergarten children who could not yet read, final phoneme identity predicted 14–19% of variance in first-grade reading but onset and rime identity predicted 24–28% (n = 116; see also Byrne et al., 2000). The strength of predictive associations between early phoneme sensitivity and later reading may also differ in children taught to read by different methods. Alegria, Pignot, and Morais (1982) found that, midway through first grade, phoneme reversal was correlated with concurrent teacher-rated reading ability in a small group of children taught to read French by phonics methods (n = 32), but not in children taught using a whole-word method (n = 32). The phonics group also scored higher on phoneme reversal, but not on syllable reversal.

Some studies have gone beyond the question of the level of phonological sensitivity that best predicts reading to examine different phonological sensitivity tasks. Sound blending is crucial to readers who are still acquiring phonological recoding skills. In children not taught to read until first grade, syllable blending at the end of kindergarten is associated with later word reading rate (Lundberg et al., 1980; Naslund & Schneider, 1996). Majsterek and Ellenwood (1995) found that a simplified sound blending task given before kindergarten predicted 15% of variance in second-grade nonword reading and 21% of variance in word identification (n = 76). Wagner et al. (1994) found that a latent sound blending variable, formed from onset-rime and phoneme blending tasks at the beginning of US kindergarten, predicted 35% of variance in word reading one year later (n = 244). At the beginning of first grade, sound blending predicted 61% of variance in word reading one year later (Wagner et al., 1994; see also the basal reading group studied by Perfetti et al., 1987). However, sound blending and reading shared considerable common variance at initial assessment (Wagner et al., 1994; see also Lundberg et al., 1980).

Although Wagner et al. (1994) reported that phonological analysis and blending comprised separate but very highly correlated factors in US kindergarten children (n = 244; see also Wagner, Torgesen, Laughon, Simmons, & Rashotte, 1993), it is highly likely that they constitute a single factor (Wagner et al., 1997). Well-designed factor-analytic studies suggest that there is a single phonological sensitivity factor (Anthony et al., 2002; Schatschneider et al., 1999; Stahl & Murray, 1994). With the effects of prior reading, verbal ability, and other phonological processing abilities controlled, phonological analysis and blending at the beginning of kindergarten or first grade, when treated as a single higher-order factor, predicted unique variance in word reading two years later (n = 216; Wagner et al., 1997). Similarly, studies teaching phonological sensitivity and phoneme manipulation in isolation from letter knowledge and reading instruction to kindergarten children with minimal knowledge of letters or reading definitively show that phonological sensitivity contributes directly to reading (Lundberg et al., 1988; Schneider, Kuspert, Roth, & Vise, 1997; see Ehri et al., 2001).

Recent research has increasingly questioned whether phonological sensitivity predicts early reading development in all alphabetic languages. Generally, findings have not been as strong in children learning to read shallow orthographies. Naslund and Schneider (1996) gave German kindergarten children tests of initial phoneme detection, rime detection, onset-rime oddity, and onset-rime blending. Only rime detection (16%) and onset-rime oddity (42%) predicted variance in a composite literacy measure administered at the end of second grade (n = 89). With early letter-sound knowledge effects controlled, rime detection explained 8% of independent variance in second-grade reading, and onset-rime oddity explained 27%. In Dutch children, de Jong and van der Leij (1999) found that rime oddity, tested at the beginning of kindergarten, predicted 13–16% of variance in second-grade reading rate. However, rime oddity did not predict variance in later reading independently of early letter knowledge and general cognitive ability (n = 82). The consistency of the orthography and the direct code methods frequently used to teach decoding skills in Dutch and German children may counteract the effects of individual differences in school entrants' letter knowledge and phonological sensitivity (de Jong & van der Leij, 1999; Wimmer, Mayringer, & Landerl, 2000).

*Letter-name knowledge*

The letter-name knowledge of school entrants strongly predicts their later reading achievement. For instance, Bond and Dijkstra (1967) reported that letter-name knowledge at the beginning of first grade predicted 26–36% of variance in end-of-year word identification and 26–35% of variance in reading comprehension (n = 488–4,266). It predicted more variance in word identification when reading instruction incorporated some phonics instruction (31–36%; n = 488–1,104), relative to language experience and basal reader programs (26–30%; n = 1431–4,266).

At its most basic level, letter knowledge implies an ability to represent in memory letters that differ from others in few distinctive ways (e.g., *n* vs. *u*, *m*, *h*, and *r*). Children who cannot discriminate and remember individual letters cannot learn to read an alphabetic script, whereas children who can effortlessly identify and name individual letters should find it easier to learn to associate sound values with them (Adams, 1990; Ehri, 1983; Share et al., 1984).

If letter-name knowledge per se makes a direct contribution to word reading, then teaching kindergarten or first-grade children letter names should enhance word reading. However, letter-name training does *not* typically transfer to early word reading (see Samuels, 1971), making it difficult to interpret at face value the predictive effects of letter-name knowledge on later reading. So, too, do suggestions that letter-name knowledge reflects other variables, such as interest in learning to read, exposure to book-reading, and informal reading instruction in the home, which may also contribute to reading success (Adams, 1990).

Some children who are surrounded by print are familiar with letters as symbols for sounds long before formal reading instruction begins (Burgess & Lonigan, 1998). For them, letter knowledge may reflect a rudimentary understanding of the alphabetic principle (Adams, 1990; Lukatela, Carello, Shankweiler, & Liberman, 1995; Morais, 1990). Ellis and Large (1988) commented that "Letter recognition is the ubiquitous entry point to the acquisition of reading, and those that have taken this step are henceforth apprentice readers" (p. 61). Bowey (1994a) found that in children not yet actually taught to read letter knowledge was associated with word reading, sharing 27% of variance, even though 79% scored at floor on the reading test (n = 96; see also Wimmer et al., 1991).

In children exposed to a range of literacy-related activities at home, letter-name knowledge may also reflect general cognitive ability, especially if letter names are not explicitly taught (Bowey, 1994a, 1995). De Jong and van der Leij (1999) found that letter knowledge and general cognitive ability, tested a year before formal reading instruction began, predicted considerable common variance in reading at the beginning of first grade (n = 166).

Given that teaching letter names does not necessarily enhance reading and the difficulties in interpreting letter-name knowledge (Adams, 1990; Calfee, 1977), letter-name knowledge is often omitted from predictive studies of early reading skill or from key analyses (e.g., Wagner et al., 1994; Wagner et al., 1997). It is not clear whether or not letter knowledge effects should be controlled within predictive studies. When they are, findings should be interpreted cautiously, as letter knowledge effects may be mediated by, or act in concert with, other variables.

## Phonological sensitivity and letter knowledge co-determine early reading ability

Phonological recoding, arguably the key skill to be acquired in early alphabetic reading, presupposes comprehension of the alphabetic principle – that letters represent sound. This understanding itself presupposes some level of phonological sensitivity; the alphabetic insight is not logically possible without *some* ability to attend to sounds within spoken words. Moreover, an understanding that the initial sounds of *mat* and *mop* are equivalent (*onset identity*) is required for children to understand why the letter *m* is used in the printed form of both words (Byrne, this volume). Without this understanding, the fact that *man*, *mop*, and *mud* all begin with the letter *m* may appear coincidental.

Even before formal reading instruction, some children discover for themselves the nonarbitrary, alphabetic, nature of the associations between letter names and the letters used to represent sounds within printed words, provided that they know letter names and have some phonological sensitivity. They first appear to notice similarities between letter names and parts of spoken words – this *is* phonological sensitivity. Treiman, Tincoff, and Richmond-Welty (1996) reported that two thirds of 5-year-old US preschoolers with no formal reading instruction said that the spoken word *beach* begins with the letter *b* (/bi/). One third said that *seem* begins with the letter *c* (/si/). Children also found it easier to say that *beach* begins with the letter *b* (/bi/), relative to *boat*. Byrne and Fielding-Barnsley (1989) found that 4-year-old nonreaders taught to read just two words (e.g., *mat* and *sat*) could not say which of the two printed words *mow* and *sow* corresponds to the spoken word /mou/ unless they were taught *both* to understand that *mat* and *mow* start with the same sound /m/ and the sounds of the letters *m* and *s*.

If some children who know letter names and who have some phonological sensitivity discover the alphabetic principle for themselves, prior to formal reading instruction, then children who can effortlessly name letters and who possess some understanding of at least onset identity should find it easier to understand the alphabetic principle when it is explicitly taught. Children familiar with both letter names and the alphabetic principle and with well-developed phonological sensitivity profit from reading and spelling instruction that teaches the sound values of letters and digraphs. In addition to meaningful and enjoyable reading activities, good early literacy instruction should teach children to attend to the sounds within spoken words to supplement the teaching of letter-sound correspondences and sound blending (Adams, 1990).

In English, letter names are often good clues to the names and sounds of letters within printed words (e.g., /bi/ within the word *beach* is identical to name of the letter *b*, and the sound for the letter *b* within the word *boat* is the onset of the letter *b*'s name). Once they have understood the alphabetic principle, phonological sensitivity and letter-name knowledge together help *some* children to derive letter sounds for themselves. For instance, beginners may spell words beginning with /w/ with the letter *y*, deriving the sound from the onset of the letter name /waɪ/ (Treiman, Weatherstone, & Berch, 1994). Furthermore, they frequently derive the letter sound /b/ from the letter name /bi/, saying that the first letter of a spoken CV nonsense syllable beginning with /b/ is the letter *b* (Treiman et al., 1994; see also Treiman et al., 1996). To do so, children must know letter names like /waɪ/ and /bi/ and be able to segment them into singleton onset and rime. Children also find it easier to derive letter sounds forming the singleton onset of letter names than the final phoneme of letter names, and hardest to learn the sounds of letters whose names do not include their sounds (Treiman, Tincoff, Rodriguez, Mouzaki, & Francis, 1998).

Even in children not yet exposed to reading instruction, letter-name knowledge is associated with phonological sensitivity (Bowey, 1994a, 1995; de Jong & van der Leij, 1999;

Johnston et al., 1996; Lonigan, Burgess, Anthony, & Barker, 1998; Mann & Wimmer, 2002; Wimmer et al., 1991). Both predict later word reading. Unpublished data from the study reported by Bowey (1995) showed that, in children who could not yet read, kindergarten letter-name knowledge predicted 34% of variance in a composite first-grade word and nonword reading measure (n = 161). Of this variance, 21% was shared with phonological sensitivity. Of this 21% of common variance, 13% was independent of general cognitive ability.

The argument that letter knowledge and phonological sensitivity *co-determine* the acquisition of the alphabetic principle and the development of reading proficiency cir-cumvents attempts to separate the effects of these variables on later reading. Such attempts are likely to be fruitless until we understand what may well be a reciprocal developmen-tal relationship between letter knowledge and phonological sensitivity. As is true for the predictive association between early phonological sensitivity and later reading, findings here are likely to depend on how phonological sensitivity is assessed.

Phonological sensitivity does predict later letter knowledge. In children who were explicitly taught letter names throughout kindergarten, Majsterek and Ellenwood (1995) found that prekindergarten phonological sensitivity predicted end-of-kindergarten letter-sound knowledge, but not letter-name knowledge (for which marked ceiling effects were observed; n = 76). Frijters, Barron, and Brunello (2000) found that in Canadian kinder-garteners with limited reading skills, phonological sensitivity and letter-name and letter-sound knowledge shared 45% of variance. They suggested that phonological sensitivity mediated the concurrent association between home literacy and letter knowledge. Home literacy explained 16% of variance in phonological sensitivity and 12% of variance in letter knowledge but, with phonological sensitivity effects controlled, home literacy no longer predicted letter knowledge (n = 94). Frijters et al. did not report contrasting analy-ses of letter knowledge as a mediator of the home literacy-phonological sensitivity association.

Burgess and Lonigan (1998) investigated the parallel development of phonological sen-sitivity and letter-name and letter-sound knowledge in 5-year-old US preschool children (n = 97), 80% of whom could not identify more than one word in a test of environ-mental print recognition when first tested. At age 5, children were given onset and rime oddity tasks, simplified sound blending and deletion tasks, and tests of letter knowledge. With the effects of initial composite phonological sensitivity, language development, and age controlled, letter-name knowledge predicted 2% of additional variance in phonolog-ical sensitivity at age 6. Letter-sound knowledge predicted none. Phonological sensitivity at age 5 was a somewhat better predictor of subsequent letter knowledge, despite ceiling effects on these measures at age 6. With the effects of initial letter-name knowledge, language development, and age controlled, phonological sensitivity predicted 6% of additional variance in letter-name knowledge, and 4% of additional variance in letter-sound knowledge at age 6.

We have seen that the effects of literacy on phoneme manipulation begin extremely early. While letter knowledge is probably the most critical factor in the acquisition of phoneme manipulation, it is difficult to disentangle its effects from the dramatic effects of acquisition of the alphabetic insight. With autoregression and vocabulary effects con-trolled, Wagner et al. (1994) found that kindergarten letter-name knowledge, but not word reading, predicted phonological sensitivity, but not verbal memory, at the beginning of first grade (n = 244). However, very marked floor effects were observed for kindergarten word reading.

The development of letter knowledge and phonological sensitivity appear to be inextricably linked, with both strongly influencing the development of early word reading and phonological recoding skills. It may be more useful to consider letter knowledge and phonological sensitivity as *co-determinants* of early reading development than to attempt to determine which of the two plays a stronger role.

## Rapid automatized naming

Rapid automatized naming (RAN) tasks have been the subject of much research on the predictors of reading skill. Rapid naming tasks assess the speed with which children name a continuous series of common items as rapidly as possible (Wolf, Bally, & Morris, 1986). The stimuli are typically letters, digits, colors, or pictures of familiar objects, and it is assumed that the naming responses are themselves overlearned (automatized).

RAN-colors and RAN-pictures in kindergarten children and school entrants consistently predict later reading (Badian, 2000; Catts et al., 2001; Cronin & Carver, 1998; de Jong & van der Leij, 1999; Share et al., 1984; Wolf et al., 1986). Wolf et al. (1986) reported that kindergarten RAN-colors predicted 20% of variance in second-grade word identification and 22% of variance in reading comprehension (n = 83). RAN-pictures at the beginning of kindergarten predicted 13% of variance in word and nonword reading rate at the end of second grade in children learning to read a shallow orthography (n = 166; de Jong & van der Leij, 1999).

RAN-letters and RAN-digits consistently predict substantial variance in later reading, particularly word identification (Badian, McAnulty, Duffy, & Als, 1990; Cronin & Carver, 1998; Wagner et al., 1994; Wolf et al., 1986). Wolf et al. (1986) reported that kindergarten RAN-letters predicted 41% of variance in second-grade word identification and 30% in reading comprehension (n = 83). Kindergarten RAN-digits predicted 44% of variance in second-grade word identification and 26% in reading comprehension. When the effects of early reading skills were not controlled, Wagner et al. (1994) found that a latent RAN variable, derived from letter and digit naming at the beginning of kindergarten, predicted 44% of variance in word reading one year later (n = 244).

The consistently stronger predictive association with reading of RAN-letters and RAN-digits, relative to RAN-colors and RAN-objects, warns us to be very careful in interpreting RAN-letters and possibly RAN-digits in beginning readers as measures of *automatized* naming. Within kindergarten children and school entrants, naming speed is confounded with knowledge of letter names (Share, 1995; Wagner & Torgesen, 1987). Letter-name knowledge predicts 26–36% of variance in early reading (Bond & Dijkstra, 1967). Several predictive studies of RAN-letters have reported in passing that not all children can name letters and digits accurately (Blachman, 1984; Catts et al., 2001; Stanovich, Feeman, & Cunningham, 1983; Walsh, Price, & Gillingham, 1988; Wagner et al., 1994). At the beginning of kindergarten, Blachman (1984) found that only 38% of inner-city children could name more than one of the five lower-case letters (*o, a, s, d, p*) used on her RAN task (n = 34). Even in US first graders showing very marked ceiling effects for letter-name knowledge, Wagner et al. (1994) found that letter-name knowledge and RAN-letters shared 16% of variance (n = 244). This figure was higher in kindergarten children (21%). Furthermore, first-grade letter-name knowledge predicted second-grade RAN for letters and digits, even with first-grade RAN and general verbal ability effects controlled. Thus, for letters and digits, RAN does not assess *automatized* naming deficits in beginners.

The gradual automatization of letter naming with exposure to reading instruction is reflected in differential growth in RAN for letters and digits, relative to other items. Cronin and Carver (1998) gave Canadian children three RAN tasks three times over the course of the year in which reading instruction commenced (n = 57). At the beginning of the year, children named digits faster than letters. Neither letters nor digits were named faster than pictures. By the end of the year, speed was similar in all three tasks. By the beginning of first grade, RAN-pictures was slowest, although RAN-letters and RAN-digits were still equivalent. Neuhaus, Foorman, Francis, and Carlson (2001) reported similar findings. They suggested that articulation duration (with pauses edited out) within continuous naming tasks assesses item familiarity. Articulation duration within RAN-letters and RAN-digits tasks, but not within RAN-pictures tasks, decreased from first to second grade, as children became more familiar with alphanumeric item names. Towards the end of first grade, articulation duration within RAN-letters explained 11–14% of variance in concurrent word identification (n = 221; Neuhaus & Swank, 2002).

RAN-letters is clearly confounded by knowledge of letter names in kindergarten children and beginning readers. For this very reason, and because letter names may need to be overlearned before this knowledge will transfer to reading (Ehri, 1983; Walsh et al., 1988), RAN could provide a useful measure of overlearned letter-name knowledge within beginners *if* it could be confidently interpreted as a pure measure of the efficiency with which letters can be identified and named. However, RAN is not so easily interpretable. There is no consensus as to what RAN measures. It reflects several distinct processing components and it is likely to reflect these components differentially at different levels of reading proficiency.

Wolf, Bowers, and Biddle (2000; Bowers & Wolf, 1993) argued that RAN should not be conceptualized as a phonological processing measure because it incorporates processes in addition to those involved in retrieving and articulating item names, including those involved in both item identification and rapid serial processing of a continuous series of items. However, apart from item identification, the processes tapped by RAN all require phonological processing of some kind. Furthermore, if it were conceded that item identification per se were a major source of variance in RAN, then RAN-letters, for example, must be interpreted as largely reflecting letter knowledge. The argument that RAN-letters and RAN-digits primarily reflect nonphonological processes thus rests on the dubious assumption that RAN does not assess item identification or name retrieval and articulation (cf. Cronin & Carver, 1998; Neuhaus et al., 2001) but, rather, other yet-to-be-understood processes that contribute to reading skill and that can be measured independently of both phonological processing skill and word reading.

It is unlikely that the rapid serial processing component of RAN reflects only non-phonological processes. Discrete-trial and continuous rapid naming do reflect somewhat different processes, in that the speech planning and articulation processes required in continuous naming are far more demanding. Furthermore, when a continuous series of items is named, minor differences in the efficiency of the first stages of letter identification and letter-name retrieval may cascade to affect those involved in programming and executing rapid sequences of articulatory gestures (see Baron & Treiman, 1980). However, even when the serial processing component of continuous naming is eliminated by using discrete-trial naming tasks, rapid naming continues to predict later reading. Although associations are typically weaker than for continuous naming, Wagner et al. (1994) found that discrete-trial naming of letters and digits at the beginning of kindergarten explained 20% of variance in word reading one year later (n = 244). When assessed at the beginning of first grade, it explained 23% of variance in word reading one year later (n = 244).

Wolf and Bowers (1999) argued that naming speed deficits are distinct from other phonological processing deficits, such as deficits in phonological sensitivity and phonological memory. However, Wagner et al. (1997) found that, with kindergarten reading, verbal ability, and other latent phonological processing abilities controlled, a latent kindergarten alphanumeric RAN variable predicted little independent variation in word reading two years later, and this was largely mediated by letter knowledge (n = 216).

Bowers and Wolf (1993) proposed that slow naming speed primarily represents a deficit in the ability to form orthographic representations of letter names, sublexical units of print, and words. More recently, they suggested that a RAN deficit is problematic only if combined with a phonological sensitivity deficit (Wolf & Bowers, 1999; Wolf et al., 2000). This *double deficit hypothesis* predicts an *interaction* between phonological sensitivity and RAN in predicting reading. The double deficit hypothesis lacks a strong theoretical motivation. Wolf et al. (2000, p. 396) conceded that "no . . . straightforward conceptualization exists to explain how the processes underlying naming speed affect word identification and word attack" and that their attempts are "highly speculative and represent work in progress."

There is no direct published test of the hypothesis that the effects of phonological sensitivity interact with RAN in predicting reading (as follows from the double deficit hypothesis). However, unpublished data from the study described in Bowey (1995) permit such a test. In kindergarten children screened for novice reading ability, and with general cognitive ability effects controlled, phonological sensitivity and RAN-colors predicted independent variance (n = 161). However, the interaction of phonological sensitivity and RAN-colors predicted no additional variance (see Baron & Kenny, 1986).

The hypothesis that RAN predicts reading only if there is also a phonological sensitivity deficit was indirectly tested by Wimmer et al. (2000), whose data did not support the double deficit account. They found no consistent differences in third- and fourth-grade reading rates between children who had entered school with either single phonological sensitivity or single RAN deficits and those with double deficits. However, in children learning to read German (a shallow orthography), phonological sensitivity appears to be a weaker predictor of reading than in children learning to read English (see above).

In summary, the predictive association between RAN and later reading is substantially greater when RAN is assessed with letters and digits, relative to colors and pictures. When RAN is assessed using letters or digits, its predictive effects appear to be largely mediated by letter knowledge (Wagner et al., 1997; see Wagner & Torgesen, 1987). Support for a role for RAN-pictures and RAN-colors in predicting later word reading that is independent of phonological sensitivity is inconsistent (de Jong & van der Leij, 1999; cf. Wimmer, et al., 2000), and may be explicable in terms of measurement error and method variance. Moreover, there is no support yet available for the interactive prediction made by the double deficit hypothesis.

In relation to letters and perhaps digits, we are left with the conclusion that RAN in kindergarten children and school entrants is best interpreted as reflecting several components, but primarily the degree of overlearning of letter and number names and the efficiency of phonological processing. The very strong associations between continuous naming speed for letters and digits and later reading where initial word reading effects are not controlled probably reflects the dual assessment of two constructs critical to alphabetic reading success.

## Conclusions

Crain-Thoreson and Dale (1992) made the interesting suggestion that "The initial stages in reading acquisition may be limited by the least advanced segment of the child's cognitive profile" (p. 427). There may be several key abilities that co-determine reading ability. Given appropriate instructional methods, children may require only threshold levels of these key abilities to find learning to read easy, but their reading progress may be held back by below-threshold levels in any of them. This plausible suggestion may partly explain why it is so hard to accurately predict future poor readers.

In the meantime, predictive studies of early reading success, when carefully considered in relation to other work on reading acquisition, are indicative of what these key abilities may be – and here overlearned letter-name knowledge and phonological sensitivity stand out. Early reading instruction should attempt to teach these skills to all children within enjoyable learning contexts. Children who are highly familiar with letter-names and easily able to detect similarities in the sounds within spoken words are likely to readily acquire the alphabetic principle and, when provided with appropriate instruction that explicitly links phonological sensitivity, letter-sound knowledge, decoding and writing, should learn phonological recoding skills with ease. It is critical that this instruction be enjoyable and be integrated with the reading of meaningful material. It should also encourage the development of a range of complementary strategies that may be helpful in decoding words in which not all letter-sound correspondences are yet known or words that contain atypical letter-sound correspondences.

This review has focused on the cognitive determinants of reading development and has examined only a limited set of predictors of early reading. It is possible that other predictors will emerge, especially in relation to subgroups of children experiencing reading difficulties. The focus on letter-name knowledge and phonological processing abilities reflects current research, but it is also motivated by consideration of the process of learning to read. Understanding the alphabetic principle and developing efficient phonological recoding skills are arguably the key competencies that the beginning reader must acquire in order for reading to become a self-teaching process, and abilities that contribute to these competencies are critical.

Nevertheless, the direct role of phonological sensitivity may be overestimated in some predictive work. Phonological sensitivity may predict reading partly because it assesses an underlying phonological processing ability that itself predicts children's ability to acquire new phonological processing skills, of which efficient phonological recoding is one par excellence, albeit one that is a component of the reading process itself. The fact that phonological sensitivity cannot be assessed without imposing some minimal extraneous task demands also means that it may partly reflect the contributions of general cognitive ability to the process of learning to read.

The current review is not exhaustive. However, it does summarize the current state of play and highlights directions for future research in this area. It is critical that researchers be aware of methodological issues and of the dangers of overinterpreting their findings. If research in this area is to be of use to practitioners, it should focus on abilities that are likely to be readily teachable and to make a direct contribution to reading development. These contributions to reading can then be assessed within studies using a training methodology. Here, too, caution must be exercised. Failure to obtain transfer effects within training studies is notoriously difficult to interpret (Schneider et al., 1997). Furthermore, it is possible that various abilities co-determine reading development. If so, then overly simple training studies may throw the baby out with the bathwater.

# 10

# Social Correlates of Emergent Literacy

**Beth M. Phillips and Christopher J. Lonigan**

To understand literacy we need to investigate the skills required to read and comprehend written text, and the sociocultural functions, values, and behaviors that are associated with being literate and teaching literacy (Baker, Fernandez-Fein, Scher, & Williams, 1998; Hart & Risley, 1992; Serpell, Sonnenschein, Baker, & Ganapathy, 2002). In recent years, attempts to improve the literacy skills of lower-income and socially disadvantaged members of society have been high on political and educational agendas. Commensurate with this public interest has been significant growth in our understanding of the predictors and causes of reading development, and an increase in research evidence about effective literacy instruction and development (see Snow & Juel, this volume). This chapter summarizes what is known about the social factors that contribute to emergent literacy in young children. Specifically, social influences are related to theories of early development and school readiness, early educational pedagogy and curricula, and parental beliefs and behaviors.

## Development of Emergent Literacy

Social influences are particularly relevant when considering school readiness, defined as the preparation of young children for success in formal schooling (Morrison, Griffith, & Alberts, 1997; Nielsen & Monson, 1996; Stipek, Milburn, Clements, & Daniels, 1992), and more specifically, the idea of "reading readiness." The general concept of readiness implies that development occurs primarily as a function of maturation (Elkind, 1987). That is, within each child the capacity to learn is innate and unfolds according to a standard timeline. Within this view, reading readiness can be assessed by a wide variety of measures purported to be predictive of children's success, many of which have been used to determine school eligibility, classroom placement, and curricular models (La Paro &

Pianta, 2000; Shepard, 1997). Proponents of "readiness" hold that children who are not "ready to learn" biologically or emotionally might actually be harmed by instruction to promote specific knowledge and skills that takes place too early. The corollary is that once children are deemed "ready," they should receive explicit instruction in the alphabet and print knowledge immediately prior to the start of formal reading instruction (Teale & Sulzby, 1986). Associated with this viewpoint are policies such as delaying school entry for children considered not mature or interested enough for school (May & Kundert, 1997; Morrison et al., 1997; Stipek, 2002).

Contradicting these maturational theories, research on school readiness practices has indicated that delayed school entry confers no significant long-term benefits to children (Morrison et al., 1997; Stipek, 2002; Stipek & Byler, 2001). Whereas some studies have found short-term advantages for children who start kindergarten or first grade several months to a year older than peers, these advantages disappear within several years. In fact, some studies indicate that there may be advantages to receiving kindergarten instruction at an earlier, rather than a later age (Crone & Whitehurst, 1999; Stipek & Byler, 2001). Moreover, research indicates that prior favorable studies failed to account for the influence of socioeconomic status (SES), preschool experiences, and children's emergent literacy skills. Other researchers have expressed concerns that delayed school entry may impede children's access to early intervention and that broad-based school readiness measures with poor predictive validity may result in inappropriate placement of some children in special "readiness" classrooms or some children having to repeat a year of preschool or kindergarten (Diamond, Reagan, & Bandyk, 2000; May et al., 1994; May & Kundert, 1997; Shepard, 1997; Stipek, 2002).

An alternative to maturational models can be seen in the constructivist perspective wherein development and learning result from children's interactions with their environment (e.g., Berk & Winsler, 1995; Bredekamp & Copple, 1997). Within this view, readiness is seen not as residing within the individual child, but rather as a product of the child's interaction opportunities, environments, and history. The constructivist model has been associated with pedagogical and societal views on "developmentally appropriate" interactions with young children as including only those that provide for learning via active exploration and engagement with environmental stimuli, and which preclude many parent- or teacher-directed interactions (Bredekamp & Copple, 1997; Neuman, Copple, & Bredekamp, 2000).

With respect to reading readiness, adoption of the constructivist perspective has been facilitated by research on reading acquisition. Rather than beginning abruptly with the onset of didactic instruction around school entry, the process of acquiring literacy skill and interest is seen as growing out of a range of early life experiences including such things as children's exposure to oral and written language, observation of others' interactions with printed material, play with written material, and shared and pretend reading (Sulzby & Teale, 1991; Teale & Sulzby, 1986; Whitehurst & Lonigan, 1998). This view of emergent literacy has been widely adopted in education, as well as by parents, who use it to frame their decisions regarding formal and informal literacy teaching interactions with children (e.g., Bredekamp & Copple, 1997; Neuman et al., 2000).

Both the maturational and constructivist perspectives on reading readiness have operated, to varying degrees, in the absence of data regarding the best predictors of successful reading acquisition. There is substantial evidence that an emergent literacy model is more accurate than one that places a discrete cutpoint between literacy and its absence (Lonigan, 2004; Lonigan, Burgess, & Anthony, 2000; Storch & Whitehurst, 2002; Whitehurst & Lonigan, 1998, 2001), and support for scaffolding and modeling as effective instructional methods. However, there is less support for many popular and commonly endorsed child behaviors as predictors or causes of literacy achievement. For example, evidence strongly supports the role of oral language abilities, phonological awareness, and print knowledge as powerful causal predictors of later decoding and comprehension skills (e.g., Lonigan et al., 2000; Sénéchal & LeFevre, 2002; Storch & Whitehurst, 2002; Whitehurst & Lonigan, 1998). Current findings suggest that whereas phonological awareness and letter knowledge are directly linked to decoding ability, oral language appears to have its primary direct influence on later comprehension abilities (Lonigan, 2004; Sénéchal & LeFevre, 2002; Storch & Whitehurst, 2002). Other predictors such as interest in, and motivation for, reading also have empirical support (Dunning, Mason, & Stewart, 1994; Scarborough & Dobrich, 1994; Tracey & Morrow, 1998; Whitehurst & Lonigan, 1998). A number of studies show that early signs of print interest and motivation are related both to precursor skills such as oral language and phonological awareness and to later reading achievement itself (e.g., Crain-Thoreson & Dale, 1992; Payne, Whitehurst, & Angell, 1994; Scarborough & Dobrich, 1994). Moreover, research suggests that motivation and coping style interact with emergent literacy skills in predicting the growth in literacy across early schooling (e.g., Lepola, Salonen, & Vauras, 2000).

## Early Childhood Education

The social influences on preschool and child care curricula include perspectives on early childhood development and school readiness as well as broader societal attitudes regarding women's participation in the workplace, the role of various governmental entities in shaping school practices, and the changing landscape of Western society bringing more English language learners and non-English speaking parents into these settings. One recent shift in public policy and perception has been from considering early childcare as serving a caretaking function, focused primarily on providing safety and nurturance, to considering these experiences educational opportunities in both cognitive and socioemotional domains. One indicator of this shift is the United States Federal Government's recent allocation of funds for Early Reading First grants to preschool settings and for sophisticated experimental evaluations of preschool curricula.

Advocates of the whole-language, entirely child-directed, approach to preschool curricula base their beliefs in part on theory, as noted above, and in part on some data suggesting that direct instruction is associated with lower quality and less positive child outcomes (e.g., Stipek et al., 1992; Stipek, Feiler, Daniels, & Milburn, 1995). More important than the methodological problems with some of this research is that it often strictly dichotomizes child-directed, socioemotionally focused classroom environments and more teacher-directed, academically focused ones. As such, entirely admirable and universally supported characteristics such as teacher warmth, attention to socioemotional development, play-based learning, and use of scaffolding, modeling, and child exploration are viewed as incompatible with use of some direct instruction targeted at critically important early reading, language, and mathematics skills. Whereas in part this dichotomizing results from findings of negative correlations between more didactic instruction and teacher warmth and responsiveness (e.g., Hauser-Cram, Sirin, & Stipek, 2003; Peisner Feinberg et al., 2001), relations that are likely driven by poor teacher training rather than by some inherent problem with intentional instruction, in part it may also result from lack of knowledge regarding the evidence of how to best promote children's emergent literacy and other educational needs.

Consistent with the idea that this dichotomy is artificial, considerable research supports the value of integrating intentional teaching methods focused on emergent literacy skills with positive classroom characteristics (e.g., Craig, et al. 2003; McGill-Franzen, Langford, & Adams, 2002; Reese, 1995; Riley, 1995). Craig et al. found that a cohort of African-American children from lower-income backgrounds who attended a preschool program focusing on literacy had second-grade reading achievement scores that surpassed those achieved by a cohort of African-American students from middle-income backgrounds who did not attend such a program. Reese (1995) found that whereas intentional instruction of preschool children predicted their later letter knowledge and decoding skill, frequency of shared reading within the classroom did not predict this or any other literacy measures. The qualitative investigation of five different preschool literacy curricula by McGill-Franzen et al. (2002) indicated that some schools explicitly banned instruction, or even display of alphabet letters, despite serving a population known to be at risk for arriving at school delayed in emergent literacy. In contrast, they profiled several classrooms where both attention to children's social and play needs and their emergent literacy needs flourished in a seamless integration. Again highlighting the benefits of a dual focus, Riley (1995) found that children who entered kindergarten with strong alphabet knowledge, print knowledge, and the ability to write their name had an 80% chance of reading at age level by the following July if they also adjusted well to school. Finally, Barnett, Young, and Schweinhart (1998) showed that the reason some early childhood interventions are successful in improving long-term outcomes is because of their impact on cognitive skill, rather than on motivation or parental beliefs.

Beyond debates over curricular content, social factors such as low pay, inadequate training for teachers, and lack of resources affect the quality of early education, particularly that which serves a predominantly lower-income population (Arnold & Doctoroff, 2003; Zigler & Styfco, 1994). Whereas recent moves in a number of US states toward providing free preschool education (as has been the case in some Western European nations for some time) suggest a shift in some of these areas, it remains to be seen whether such newer programs can have a significant positive impact on children's later academic and social achievement. Moreover, as more children attend out of home care, a figure that now exceeds 55% in the US (Federal Interagency Forum on Child and Family Statistics, FIFCS, 2003), and more of these children come from non-English-speaking homes, the societal challenge to direct attention, resources, and evidence-based practices to preschool will only increase.

## Socioeconomic Status

Whereas philosophical influences on parents and teachers are important, they do not act independently of wider social and familial circumstances such as poverty, education, and community resources. Moreover, beliefs and attitudes do not necessarily translate into behavior because of environmental constraints. It follows that no discussion of proximal social behaviors and attitudes would be complete without attention to distal variables like SES and education and to the interplay between proximal and distal influences.

A large body of research indicates that lower socioeconomic status (SES) confers great risk both for educational failure and specifically for less advanced reading skills (Arnold & Doctoroff, 2003; Bradley & Corwyn, 2002; Dubow & Ippolito, 1994; Lonigan, 2004). There is a strong relation between SES and oral language abilities, and more specifically, SES is related to children's emergent literacy skills, such as phonological awareness and letter knowledge, which likely mediate the relation between SES and reading itself (e.g., Bowey, 1995; Chaney, 1994; Hecht, Burgess, Torgesen, Wagner, & Rashotte, 2000; Lonigan, Burgess, Anthony, & Barker, 1998; Raz & Bryant, 1990). SES permeates the research on home and school predictors of emergent literacy. However, as the literature on SES has grown, it has become increasingly clear that SES is not a single factor, but rather a complex, multifaceted influence incorporating income, education, and occupational status, and also values, beliefs, cultural norms, and in some cases, ethnic perspectives on reading and education, all of which can affect a child's and family's experience with literacy. Moreover, considerable research reveals that SES groups cannot be treated as homogeneous, as there is often substantial variation within a group in behavior, values, and child outcomes (Bradley & Corwyn, 2002; Christian, Morrison, & Bryant, 1998; Fish & Pinkerman, 2003; Payne et al., 1994; Weizman & Snow, 2001).

One prominent factor to be disentangled from SES is single parenthood, especially as the number of children raised in single parent homes, and particularly in homes where the mother has never been married, has risen dramatically in recent decades (Entwisle & Alexander, 1995). This latter group is at significant risk, as these families are more likely to live in poverty than are families where a divorce has occurred. Entwisle and Alexander (1995) attempted to disentangle the effects of poverty and having only one parent in the home by analyzing early elementary math and reading achievement separately for summer and winter periods. This isolated the potential influences of number of parents, which should have an effect in summer *and* winter, from the influences of home income, which should have a more pronounced impact in the summer. Their results indicated that family economic status, and presumably the home learning environment this supported, was the key influence on summer learning in single-parent families. Ricciuti (1999) had similar findings, such that maternal education and ability, not single parent status, were the significant predictors of children's achievement.

The need to attend to complexity and the interactions among background risk factors is amplified by two further strands of research. First, a number of studies indicate that models in which multiple factors are considered, and in which risks are construed to be additive or multiplicative, are more powerful than models that use a single SES marker variable (Arnold & Doctoroff, 2003; Caughy, 1996; Bradley & Corwyn, 2002; Greenberg, Lengua, Coie, & Pinderhughes, 1999; Krishnakumar & Black, 2002). Caughy (1996) found that children's birth status (i.e., prematurity, perinatal risk) interacted with their environment, such that children at-risk had worse outcomes when born to less educated mothers who created poorer home settings. Krishnakumar and Black (2002) found that different amounts of variance in child cognitive and behavioral status were predicted by considering distal and proximal familial and child risk factors additively, exponentially, and in mediational models. Second, some evidence suggests that when investigating class and cultural differences, the best conceptualization is one of distance from the dominant culture; this variable captures the implications both of the need to adapt to the mainstream culture and of how factors, such as neighborhood and community influences, can interact in myriad ways to generate greater or lesser overall distances (Esposito, 1999; Garner & Raudenbush, 1991; Lawrence & Shipley, 1996; Leventhal & Brooks-Gunn, 2000).

## Family Beliefs and Values

Research supports the influential role of parents' beliefs about, and expectations for achievement, on their own and their children's school-related behaviors. Reynolds and Gill (1994) found that expectations predicted variations in reading, math, and social outcomes after influences of income, ethnicity, and parental education were controlled. Halle, Kurtz-Costes, and Mahoney (1997) found that parental expectations did not uniquely contribute to level of reading achievement but did contribute to change in reading scores over nine months. Luster and McAdoo's (1996) longitudinal evaluation of parental influences on educational attainment in the Perry Preschool project also showed that parental expectations contributed to adolescent attainment, as did participant identification of their parents as role models.

Studies involving younger children have been even more consistent in finding correlations between parental endorsement of a high worth for education and of high achievement expectations and child academic performance. Hess, Holloway, Dickson, and Price (1984) found, after controlling for child intelligence, that Caucasian mothers' expectations for achievement when their children were age three significantly predicted scores on the Metropolitan Readiness Test (MRT; including letter knowledge, ability to write own name, and mathematical skills) when they were age five and six. Notably, these school readiness measures were significant predictors of performance on an achievement test at age 12. Hill (2001) demonstrated that parental expectations were also predictors of achievement among African-American kindergarteners. Likewise, studies by Bennett, Weigel and Martin (2002) and DeBaryshe and Binder (1994) showed that parental beliefs about the value and purpose of shared reading and other home literacy activities were related both to the practice and frequency of home literacy activities and to measures of 3- and 4-year-old children's ability to write their names, concepts of print, and oral language skills. Whereas Bennett, et al., (2002) found these relations in a middle-income, primarily Caucasian, sample, DeBaryshe and Binder's (1994) study focused on low-income Caucasian and African-American parents. Although they found no moderation by ethnicity, both parental education and income were related to parental beliefs and to home literacy activities.

A series of studies conducted by Sonnenschein, Baker, and colleagues (e.g., Baker, Scher, & Mackler, 1997; Baker et al., 1998; Serpell et al., 2002) have investigated parental beliefs about reading and the early development of reading skills and motivation in their children. Their findings, based on work with lower- to middle-income African-American and Caucasian families, indicate that parents of preschoolers who endorse beliefs in and promote the concept of literacy as a form of entertainment, rather than a set of skills to be learned, engage in more literacy activities at home and have children who show more motivation for and interest in print. Similarly, DeBaryshe (1995) found a direct relation between parental beliefs and children's interest in reading, not one mediated by shared reading frequency or verbal interactional quality. DeBaryshe speculated that this finding might indicate that it is the affective aspect of dyadic reading that promotes child interest. Alternatively, many parents may convey their belief in the value of reading and help create good language skills through methods other than shared reading.

Typically, middle-income and Caucasian parents are more likely than minority or lower-income parents to endorse and believe in teaching children the "literacy as entertainment" theme. Some research also indicates that these parents also are less likely to endorse or enact a focus on skills teaching with children (Baker, et al. 1997; Baker et al., 1998; DeBaryshe, 1995; Stipek et al., 1992). Instead, these studies indicate that middle-income Caucasian parents are particularly likely to have adopted the constructivist philosophy on emergent literacy that suggests children's abilities are best developed through nondidactic interactions, such as shared reading, instead of more parent-directed interactions such as teaching of letter names (e.g., Bates et al., 1994; Stipek et al., 1995). Some of these studies also suggest that parents from lower-income backgrounds more readily endorse didactic teaching methods as appropriate for young children. However, the lower-income African-American sample studied by Purcell-Gates (1996) indicated that they believed that the onset of formal instruction in literacy was the appropriate time to begin or increase involvement in their children's literacy learning. Whereas these parents did not attribute their conceptualization of appropriate behaviors to a constructivist viewpoint, and this attitude actually seems more consistent with a maturational "reading readiness" model of timing, the result was less belief in formal attention toward literacy in the preschool years.

Whereas one element in middle-income family environments that promotes reading achievement may indeed be the parental endorsement of the "literacy as entertainment" theme, the correlational nature of the results raises several questions. First, although noting SES differences in beliefs and value for pleasurable uses of literacy, these researchers have not controlled for financial capital. Thus, it may be that the lesser endorsement by lower-income parents simply reflects their lack of experience with literacy as entertainment or their pragmatic recognition that their financial situations preclude spending money on enjoyable books, magazines, and the like, rather than fundamental differences in beliefs or attitudes. Second, no study has controlled for parents' impressions of, or information regarding, their child's skill level. In other words, perhaps parents in middle-income families recognize that their children's skills are adequate and therefore feel free to focus on more affective and motivation-related domains for literacy development. Alternatively, after hearing claims that intentional instruction is inappropriate for preschool children, many middle-income parents may voice beliefs consistent with this philosophy. These findings about teaching style beliefs also do not imply that no lower-income and minority parents consider emergent literacy skills and learning to read important. For example, in a study with Caucasian, Latino, and African-American families with children 4–6 years old who had not yet started kindergarten, all parents rated pre-academic skills (e.g., knowing letters and numbers) as equally important for kindergarten success as socioemotional behaviors (e.g., being able to sit and pay attention; Diamond et al., 2000).

Researchers also find differences in the meaning and value of literacy across ethnic groups (e.g. Harris, 2003; Ogbu, 1999; Okagaki & Sternberg, 1993; Purcell-Gates 1996; Qualls, 2001; Zayas & Solari, 1994). Qualls (2001) discusses the strong emphasis on oral versus written language in traditional African-American cultures, and she notes the high value placed on verbal agility, figurative language use, and the synergistic relation between verbal and nonverbal communication that is evident in commonly observed speech and conversational patterns. Harris (2003) and Qualls (2001) both remind us of the relatively short time that has elapsed since literacy was forbidden or at least strongly discouraged among African Americans, an influence current generations may not have completely disregarded, and of the more abbreviated history that African Americans have had with formal education relative to that of the majority culture. Qualls (2001) and others (e.g., Ogbu, 1990, 1999) note that within some subgroups of the African-American population there is resistance to traditional educational and literacy achievement as a means of expressing opposition to the dominant culture and of affirming their collective separate identity. This can be observed, for example, in the ambivalence some African Americans have about using standard American English rather than the dialect in which they speak at home and within their community (Ogbu, 1999).

Research suggests that parents' socialization goals may be more or less consistent with, and supportive of, the goal of academic achievement. For example, within Latino and other ethnic minority cultures (e.g., Southeast Asian), parents report that they value practical and social skills in their young children as much as or more than cognitive skills, and that obedience and conformity are taught more than independence and assertiveness (e.g., Hammer, Miccio, & Wagstaff, 2003; Okagaki & Sternberg, 1993; Zayas & Solari, 1994). This relative parental emphasis on conformity and social skills is negatively related to early achievement in reading and mathematics. These socialization practices may also influence language development because they often involve behavioral modeling and nonverbal teaching rather than verbal instruction. In contrast, the belief of Chinese-American mothers that effort and motivation are significant factors in intelligence and achievement was significantly related to their 4-year-old children's performance on basic skills tasks; these children performed better than Anglo-American children whose mothers believed that their own effort was a stronger influence (Kinlaw, Kurtz-Costes, & Goldman-Fraser, 2001).

The levels of acculturation and SES within a minority home appear to affect substantially the influence and endurance of cultural norms and behaviors. The study by Hammer et al. (2003) investigated the home literacy and language environments of Puerto Rican children living in the United States. They found that in more acculturated homes where English was more frequently spoken, and where the mothers more often were born in the United States, there were positive views about teaching early literacy skills and encouraging academic achievement. Such views were more consistent with the dominant cultural viewpoint than with the more traditional view of school as the context in which academic subjects are taught or encouraged. These authors noted, furthermore, that the relative poverty of both groups may have minimized the differences in the value and behavioral emphasis placed on literacy in the home, as the more achievement-oriented group could afford reading materials and time to read no more frequently than the more traditional group. Likewise, Gutierrez, Sameroff, and Karrer (1988) found that acculturation of ethnic minorities was more relevant to parental beliefs and values than was SES within relatively high SES groups but not in lower SES groups. In other words, lower SES overrode the influence of acculturation. One can speculate that this may be both a consequence of restricted exposure to the dominant community value systems and of the lack of resources with which to enact different behaviors and so perhaps to change beliefs.

Significant relations exist between broader parenting methods and children's school achievement (Arnold & Doctoroff, 2003; Bradley & Corwyn, 2002; Burchinal, Peisner-Feinberg, Pianta, & Howes, 2002). Differences among parenting beliefs and behaviors have also been related to SES and in some cases to ethnicity, although evidence also suggests that parenting styles may have some differential meaning and external correlates across ethnic groups (e.g., Coolahan, McWayne, Fantuzzo, & Grim, 2002). Although a detailed discussion of this literature is beyond the scope of this chapter, some findings are of particular interest. For example, Campbell, Goldstein, Schaefer, and Ramey (1991) found that among parents of kindergarten children, more traditional, authoritarian parenting beliefs were negatively related to reading achievement three years later. These beliefs were seen more often in lower-income, less educated parents, and were associated with valuing conformity, rather than self-directedness, in young children. Parental beliefs measured concurrently with reading assessments were not related, suggesting the more powerful influence of parents on younger children, before teachers and the school culture can have an effect. Notably, the subgroup of these parents who participated with their child in an early intervention program showed decreases in authoritarian beliefs across time, commensurate in some mothers with an increase in their own education. Research by Bradley, Corwyn, Burchinal, Pipes McAdoo, and Garcia Coll (2001) showed that responsive parenting was related longitudinally to receptive vocabulary, math, and reading achievement over and above the contribution of parental education, family size, and presence of the father in the home. These authors reported interactions between responsiveness and child age, ethnicity, and SES, such that the significance of parenting style altered to some degree across variations in these other dimensions. In general, responsiveness was a more uniquely relevant factor for younger children. Tiedemann and Faber (1992) found that preschool children's perceptions of maternal support for learning (i.e., positive reinforcement and sensitivity toward child) significantly predicted first- and second-grade reading and arithmetic achievement test scores and teacher ratings independent of preschool levels of early literacy and numeracy predictor skills and child intelligence.

## Home Language Stimulation

Variations in home language environments appear to be critically important in explaining some of the SES and cultural differences later seen in school achievement, particularly with respect to reading success. Influences of parental education, cultural values, and income are parlayed into the language environment parents create for their young children (Hart & Risley, 1992; Hoff, 2003; Hoff-Ginsberg, 1991; Walker, Greenwood, Hart, & Carta, 1994). In turn, evidence suggests that the home language environment is a contributing factor in children's language development (e.g., Arriaga, Fenson, Cronan, & Pethick, 1998; Hoff, 2003; Huttenlocher, Haight, Bryk, Seltzer, & Lyons, 1991; Huttenlocher, Vasilyeva, Cymerman, & Levine, 2002). Not surprisingly, home language environments differ markedly by SES. Hart and Risley's (1992) intensive observation of families from diverse SES backgrounds showed large differences in the quantity of language input to children, with children from lower SES homes receiving much less parental attention, parental language input, and parental questions to encourage verbal responses, all of which collectively were associated with lower quantities of speech production and less developed vocabularies. Similarly, Hoff (2003) and Hoff-Ginsberg (1991) reported SES differences in maternal speech overall, not just differences in child directed language, supporting the hypothesis that the language environment created for children from lower SES backgrounds is in part the product of education-, income- or culturally-related variations in the function, complexity, and reinforcement of verbal expressiveness. Effects on child outcomes even at a young age are shown by the finding of Arriaga et al. (1998) that toddlers from lower SES homes had substantially lower scores on several measures of expressive language than did children from middle SES backgrounds.

A growing body of research suggests that the language input from lower SES parents differs from that provided by middle and upper SES counterparts not only in sheer volume, but also in lexical complexity, contingent responding, and encouragement of child speech (Arriaga et al., 1998; Hoff, 2003; Hoff-Ginsberg, 1991; Weizman & Snow, 2001). For example, within the exclusively lower SES participants observed by Weizman and Snow, a very low percentage (about 1%) of maternal utterances across several routine contexts included use of infrequent vocabulary, although use of such words was likely to be associated with supportive maternal instruction and commentary about their meaning. Both scaffolding and parental word use were related to child language skill at age 5. Of great importance was the wide variation in the complexity of language used by these mothers, a finding that calls attention to the fact that, despite clear class differences, parents within SES strata vary considerably. Work by several groups also highlights the need to attend to contexts such as interaction situation, and population density within the home, when evaluating parental language and group differences (e.g., Evans, Maxwell, & Hart, 1999; Hoff-Ginsberg, 1991).

Culture- and class-related familial variations in the meaning and behaviors associated with daily routines appear to affect children's development of decontextualized language abilities. For example, several studies have shown that measures taken from prototypical family mealtime conversation predict children's language development (e.g., Beales, DeTemple, & Dickinson, 1994; Dickinson & Tabors, 1991; Serpell et al., 2002). Some research supports the idea that parents' cultural beliefs about the language itself influences their behavior and the environment they create in which to nurture child language acquisition. In the ethnographic study of Ogbu (1999), some parents' ambivalence toward standard English as contrasted with the dialect they spoke within their community led them to believe that it was the schools' responsibility to teach their children standard English.

Moreover, some parents reported discouraging their children from using standard English at home, saying that they found it off-putting and denigrating to their own way of speaking. Of even greater relevance, however, was Ogbu's finding that "[some of the African-American] parents do not and cannot teach their children standard English because they themselves do not speak it at all or do not speak it well" (1999, p. 156).

A number of studies illustrate the importance of parent interaction style in the promotion of language and general cognitive capabilities in young children and demonstrate relations between interaction style and sociocultural factors. Britto and Brooks-Gunn (2001) indicated that maternal use of decontextualized language was very rare in a sample of African-American teenage mothers, most of whom were of lower SES and had below average receptive vocabulary scores. Irrespective of their education and verbal ability, mothers' decontextualized and expressive language and warmth were significantly related to children's expressive language; child receptive language only was related to maternal education. Similarly, Smith, Landry, and Swank (2000) and Stevens, Blake, Vitale, and Macdonald (1998) found that mothers who used more explicit scaffolding of children's language, specifically by using language to describe causes, actions, concepts, and relations to 3-year-old children, and by orally narrating behaviors with 9- and 15-month-olds, had children who later had more rapid language growth and higher scores on a variety of language measures.

Related work by Landry and colleagues (e.g., Landry, Smith, Miller-Loncar, & Swank, 1997; Landry, Smith, Swank, Assel, & Vellet, 2001) has shown that consistent maternal verbal stimulation that is warm, contingently responsive, and maintains child-directed interest, provides better support for language development than interactions that are highly directive and restrictive. Both of these studies found that maternal education, social support, and SES were significantly related to such early responsive parenting. Notably, consistency of warm responsiveness across early development, coupled with flexibility that allowed for both early directiveness and later facilitation of independence, lead to children with the best language and social development. Landry et al. (2001) also showed that maternal belief in the value of low restrictiveness, child individuation, and allowing independence was related to higher consistency in responsive parenting style. Studies by Baumwell, Tamis-LeMonda, and Bornstein (1997), Hubbs-Tait et al. (2002), and Olson, Bates, and Bayles (1984) collectively reinforce the idea that contingent sensitivity is associated with cognitive stimulation, as well as indicating that maternal–child language interactions are reciprocally influenced and that early sensitivity can affect children's later language skill, particularly among children who have low skills early on. These latter two findings have implications for why children who do not receive such parenting may end up further and further behind their peers, and why some others may catch up with more precocious or advantaged children.

## Home Literacy Environment

A substantial amount of research has focused on the relationship between home literacy environment and reading achievement, particularly highlighting shared reading. Despite ongoing debate about the magnitude of the contribution of shared reading to reading and emergent literacy (Bus, van Ijzendoorn, & Pellegrini, 1995; Dunning et al., 1994; Lonigan, 1994; Payne et al., 1994; Scarborough & Dobrich, 1994) there are consistent results indicating its influence on literacy outcomes. In large measure, this is because shared reading reliably evokes effective maternal and child behaviors, such as labeling of objects, practice in speaking for infants and toddlers, and modeling and teaching of vocabulary and print knowledge (Hoff-Ginsberg, 1991; Sénéchal, Cornell, & Broda, 1995). In turn, these opportunities help build vocabulary and other oral language skills in young children (e.g., Leseman & de Jong, 1998; Sénéchal & Cornell, 1993; Sénéchal, LeFevre, Hudson, & Lawson, 1996). Data from home- and school-based intervention studies support these correlational findings (e.g., Lonigan & Whitehurst, 1998; Whitehurst et al., 1994). That is, when parents or teachers are instructed in methods of shared reading that emphasize the child's participatory role, such that the adult scaffolds and facilitates enriched speech and attention to vocabulary on the child's part (a method that in many ways mimics what many parents do naturally), effects are found on the children's oral language skills.

There are consistent findings of class differences in the frequency with which parents engage in shared reading and other literacy-related activities with their children (Burgess, Hecht, & Lonigan, 2002; Feitelson & Goldstein, 1986; McCormick & Mason, 1986). Such differences may partially mediate the relation between SES and reading-related outcomes (e.g., Baker et al., 1998; Leseman & de Jong, 1998). Baker and colleagues found that whereas over 90% of middle-income families engaged in daily book reading, only 52% of lower-income families did so. Karass, VanDeventer, and Braungart-Rieker (2003) found that even within an exclusively middle-income sample in which all parents had at least a high-school degree, income was associated with onset of maternal shared reading with infants, as was parenting stress. Although ethnicity cannot be dissociated fully from SES, recent statistics suggest that whereas 64% of Caucasian families read to their children daily, only 48% of African-American, and 42% of Hispanic parents report they do so (FIFCS, 2003). Furthermore, in the same survey, frequency of shared reading was associated positively with maternal education and negatively with poverty.

Even when engaging in shared reading with their children, evidence suggests that the interaction style and behavior exhibited by some parents from lower income backgrounds is different from that exhibited by parents from middle-income backgrounds (e.g., Hammer, 2001; Pellegrini, Perlmutter, Galda, & Brody, 1990). Moreover, it may be these very behaviors (intentional scaffolding of children's learning through nontext maternal speech and encouragement of children's speech) that are relevant for improving children's skills. For example, Pellegrini et al. (1990) found that, for familiar and some unfamiliar expository texts, the parents of children in Head Start programs used more cognitively demanding interaction strategies during shared reading; however, evidence also indicated that these were not strategies typically employed by the parents outside of the training environment. Likewise, Baker and colleagues (Munsterman & Sonnenschein, cited in Baker et al., 1998) found that with a sample of mother–child dyads of lower-income backgrounds, only 6% of spontaneous speech during an unfamiliar book reading was print related. From a broader multicultural perspective, Bus, Leseman, and Keultjes (2000) found that differences within and between Surinamese, Dutch, and Turkish ethnic groups in parents' own interest in and value for reading was significantly related to how much they would deviate from text to talk about meaning and engage in other "high demand" interactions when reading with their 4-year-old children.

As noted previously, considerable differences in home literacy environment exist within class groups, such that despite having restricted finances and limited education, many lower-SES parents do provide an enriched and supportive home literacy environment (Christian et al., 1998; Payne et al., 1994; Purcell-Gates, 1996). Christian et al. (1998) found that when they divided their lower income sample by both maternal education and home literacy environment all four groups (i.e., high education / high home literacy environment, low education / high home literacy environment, etc.) were substantially represented. Similarly, Payne et al. (1994) found considerable variation in responses to a questionnaire in an exclusively lower-income sample. However, many of the families in Purcell-Gates's study "lived busy and satisfying lives with very little mediation by print" (1996, p. 425) and thus spent little, if any, time reading with or exposing their children to print. This study also demonstrated that the most frequently found literacy materials and activities were those that required reading at the phrase or clause level (e.g., phone books, recipes, TV guide, coupons, food packaging), rather than more complex text.

On a methodological and philosophical note, a growing number of investigations have emphasized that the home literacy environment should not be identified solely with shared reading or any other single measure (e.g., Burgess et al., 2002; Frijters, Barron, & Brunello, 2000; Leseman & de Jong, 1998; Lonigan, 1994; Payne et al., 1994; Sénéchal & Lefevre, 2002; Storch & Whitehurst, 2001). Rather, these researchers suggest that the home literacy environment encompasses an array of interrelated variables including reading and factors such as literacy artifacts, functional uses of literacy, verbal references to literacy, library use, parental encouragement and value of reading, parental teaching of skills, and child interest. Burgess et al. (2002) have also drawn attention to what they label the limiting environment – such things as financial capital, SES, parental education, and parental attitudes toward education. Studies using these broader composite definitions have consistently found relations between the home literacy environment and both reading outcomes and emergent literacy skills (Burgess et al., 2002; Christian et al., 1998; Frijters et al., 2000; Griffin & Morrison, 1997; Storch & Whitehurst, 2001). While some studies of shared reading have found its primary impact to be on oral language (e.g., Lonigan, Dyer, & Anthony, 1996; Raz & Bryant, 1990), other studies using broader definitions of the home literacy environment have also found effects on phonological awareness and print knowledge (Burgess, 2002; Burgess et al., 2002; Christian et al., 1998; Evans, Shaw, & Bell, 2000; Sénéchal & LeFevre, 2002; Sénéchal, LeFevre, Thomas, & Daley, 1998). A few studies also have found predictive associations between exposure to nursery rhymes, rhyming games, and the like and later emergent literacy skills (e.g., Bryant, Maclean, Bradley, & Crossland, 1990b; Fernandez-Fein & Baker, 1997; Maclean, Bryant, & Bradley, 1987) although others have not (e.g., Chaney, 1994; Raz & Bryant, 1990).

Whereas Burgess (2002) found that all aspects of the home literacy environment contributed to the development of phonological awareness, the work by Sénéchal and colleagues (Sénéchal & LeFevre, 2002; Sénéchal et al., 1998) and Evans et al. (2000) indicated that specific parental instruction, but not shared reading, predicted phonological awareness and print knowledge. Furthermore, Frijters et al. (2000) found that the impact of home literacy environment, including shared reading and other activities but not teaching, was direct for oral language, but mediated by phonological awareness for letter knowledge. Phonological awareness was never itself included as an outcome variable; however these results do suggest the possibility that the relation between noninstructional aspects of the home literacy environment and phonological awareness was itself mediated by effects on oral language, consistent with mediational findings by Chaney (1994).

Studies consistently find no significant relations between parental reports of shared reading and of time spent intentionally teaching (Evans et al., 2000; Sénéchal et al., 1998; Sénéchal & LeFevre, 2002). Such a result is not surprising given the evidence reviewed previously that the parents most likely to engage in shared reading (i.e., those from middle-class backgrounds) are also those who are most likely to believe that direct instruction with young children is both unnecessary and even potentially harmful. For many of their children, who are from birth exposed to such rich language environments and print artifacts that their phonological awareness and print skills appear to develop without much effort, a lack of intentional instruction likely has no impact. However, for children from less language and print rich environments, the data appear to suggest that some direct instruction in both phonological awareness and print knowledge skill at home is beneficial (Baker et al., 1998; Evans et al., 2000; Lonigan, 2004). As discussed previously, there is some evidence to suggest that parents who approach shared literacy experiences with a view of "literacy as entertainment" have children who demonstrate more interest in literacy (e.g., Baker et al., 1997; Baker et al., 1998; Sonnenschein & Munsterman, 2002). However, it is difficult to determine whether these findings are the result of parents' attitudes, or a confounding of skill emphases with more authoritarian, overly directive parenting, a frequent co-occurrence in some families from lower-income, lower-education backgrounds (Baker et al., 1997; Baker et al., 1998; Stipek et al., 1992).

Data also suggest that the affective aspects of both shared reading and related experiences can have a significant impact on children's interest in, and motivation for learning to read. Bus and van Ijzendoorn (1988) reported that securely attached children benefit more from shared book reading with mothers, show more interest in these experiences, and receive less disciplinary language from mothers. Similarly, Sonnenschein and Munsterman (2002) found that the affective quality of 5-year-olds' shared reading interactions predicted their motivation for reading. In turn, as discussed previously, research supports the relationship of motivation for and interest in literacy to reading achievement (e.g., Crain-Thoreson & Dale, 1992; Dunning et al., 1994; Lonigan, 1994; Lonigan, et al., 1996; Scarborough & Dobrich, 1994). Whereas child interest and parental initiation of literacy activities are likely reciprocally related, it is probably the case that the first exposure to such experiences was created by the adults (Dunning et al., 1994; Lonigan, 1994). Thus, it is reasonable to suppose parental interest in literacy is the primary genesis of child interest.

Overall, these findings suggest that all children benefit from exposure to print-rich environments and enjoyable, supportive opportunities to engage in literacy experiences. Yet they also point to the inherent danger in assuming that all preschool children need exactly the same kinds of environmental input, as this ignores already existing skill and experiential differences. Moreover, as also noted by Baker et al. (1997), the factors that may influence motivation and those that may influence skills are not always the same. Thus, it may be erroneous to discourage parents from lower income backgrounds from focusing on intentional instruction because it contrasts with philosophical stances on "developmentally appropriate practices." Rather, in keeping with the previous discussion on preschool environments, what would be more appropriate would be an effort to imbue intentional instruction with warm responsiveness and supportive, motivating parenting styles, thus making these experiences both consistent with the evidence-based aspects of constructivist and developmental views and with the empirical research on emergent literacy skills and their relation to reading success.

## Summary and Conclusions

Children from lower-SES backgrounds are at significant risk for reading difficulties (e.g., Dubow & Ippolito, 1994; Juel, Griffith, & Gough, 1986; Smith & Dixon, 1995). This risk is indexed by slower development, prior to school entry, in the three primary domains of emergent literacy: oral language (e.g., Juel et al., 1986; Lonigan & Whitehurst, 1998; Whitehurst, 1997), letter knowledge, and phonological processing skills (Bowey, 1995; Lonigan et al., 1998; MacLean, et al., 1987; Raz & Bryant, 1990). Throughout the preschool years and beyond are substantial SES-related differences in children's experiences that might support the development of emergent literacy skills. However, the reasons for these differences are complex and varied, and may relate to the limitation of resources in poor backgrounds, differential value placed on literacy activities, or different value and belief systems associated with nonmajority cultures. Of course, cultural and value differences create variations in the emergent literacy skills of more advantaged children, but it appears that often such potentially adverse effects are mitigated by the influence of other familial, community, and cultural strengths. Moreover, there are likely a variety of more general health issues (e.g., prenatal care) and environmental factors that directly (e.g., prenatal care, nutrition, lead poisoning) or indirectly (parental stress, maternal depression) affect children's development. Emerging evidence supports the idea that intentional instruction can enhance key emergent literacy skills in preschool (Lonigan, 2004); however, there are no data supporting the idea that such interventions inoculate children against later educational difficulties (Whitehurst & Lonigan, 1998). High quality teaching in the elementary grades is needed to maintain gains from preschool and to continue to support children's literacy development to close the gap between children from disadvantaged and advantaged backgrounds.

## Note

Preparation of this work was supported, in part, by grants to the second author from the National Institute of Child Health and Human Development (HD/MH38880, HD36067, HD36509, HD30988), the National Science Foundation (REC0128970), and the Institute of Educational Science (R305J030093). Views expressed herein are solely those of the authors and have not been cleared by the grantors.

# 11

# *Literacy and Cognitive Change*

## José Morais and Régine Kolinsky

The chapters in this book are about literacy. They focus on the processes of reading and spelling, their acquisition, dissolution, and biological foundations. This chapter is different: it discusses the possible effects of becoming literate on other cognitive capacities. It focuses on the specific effects of alphabetic literacy, and tries to separate these effects from more general cognitive changes that may be the product of education or schooling. We begin by considering some conceptual and methodological issues.

## Literacy, Schooling, and Education

Literacy is the ensemble of representations and processes that an individual acquires as an obligatory and direct consequence of learning to read and write. In this view, literacy varies by degrees because reading and writing take several years to master. Literacy is usually acquired in school. The intricate relationship between literacy and schooling makes it difficult to disentangle their effects on cognitive development because many other abilities are acquired in school. While literacy is a competence that can be evaluated through the observation of performance, school is a setting where experiences take place and it is therefore less easy to specify its effects. Schooling is usually measured by the number of years completed at school or the academic level achieved. However, these measures do not take account of a potential confound between the number of years in school and the sociocultural or socioeconomic status of the individual.

Schooling must also be differentiated from education. First, there are many specialized forms of schooling (for visual arts, music, sports, etc.) that cannot be subsumed under the category of typical schooling. Second, there are a variety of personal ways of becoming educated. Theoretically, it would be more ambitious to ask about the impact of education than of schooling on cognitive development. However, education is an even more elusive variable than schooling. Schooling and education themselves must be differentiated from culture, which is not only a matter of knowledge but includes values and types of social behavior. Ishii, Reyes, and Kitayama (2003) provided an illustration of the role of culture on cognitive processing while controlling for the effects of schooling. All of the participants were undergraduates. Using emotionally relevant spoken words in a Stroop-like test, the authors found that Americans had greater difficulty ignoring verbal content, while Japanese and Tagalog-English bilinguals had greater difficulty ignoring vocal tone.

## Methodological issues

At first sight, a straightforward approach to questions concerning the effects of literacy on cognition would be to compare illiterate and literate people of the same age, sex, and country or region. However, illiterate and literate people differ from one another in very important ways. Illiterate people typically have had little or no schooling in their childhood and given that literacy is an instrument both for the acquisition of information and of social promotion, they tend to have much less sociocultural and socioeconomic status than literate people. As discussed eloquently by Coppens, Parente, and Lecours (1998, p. 184), there may be a good reason to differentiate between "*unschooled, semischooled and schooled . . .* individuals rather than to express the group differences in terms of literacy levels" (authors' italics). In short, we need to be cautious when interpreting findings concerning the cognitive effects of literacy when studies have not controlled for related factors.

A crucial research question is whether there are means of separating the cognitive effects of literacy acquisition from those of school attendance. The approach taken by Bertelson and Morais' group and by Cary (1988) and Verhaeghe (1999) is made possible by the fact that, in many countries where illiteracy and lack of schooling characterize a significant proportion of the population, there have been efforts to teach these people reading and writing in special classes. Most instructional programs are entirely or almost exclusively devoted to alphabetization, although some also include elements of arithmetic, geometry, drawing, science, and history. People who learned reading and writing in this way are here referred to as ex-illiterates. When ex-illiterates are contrasted with an illiterate group, they provide an appropriate comparison group against which to assess the impact of literacy per se on the development of cognition. In a series of studies using this paradigm, Morais and colleagues compared groups of illiterates and ex-illiterates in Portugal on tasks involving the explicit, conscious analysis of speech into phonemes (Morais, Cary, Alegria, & Bertelson, 1979; Morais, Bertelson, Cary, & Alegria, 1986) or of visual figures into segments (Kolinsky, Morais, Content, & Cary, 1987b). Neither the ex-illiterates nor the illiterates had attended school in childhood, or learned to read and write in traditional settings. Rather, the ex-illiterates had attended special classes organized by the state, the army, or the factories that employed them. These people were not fully literate: their literacy skills were usually quite rudimentary.

Although this approach controls as far as possible for differences in schooling, it does not circumvent the problem of uncontrolled differences in the knowledge acquired through reading. Most of the ex-illiterate people that were tested had learned to read and write some years before the experiments were completed and they differed from the illiterate participants not only in terms of literacy skill, but also in terms of what they had learned from being able to read. This problem is reduced in the case of ex-illiterate people who are still attending literacy classes and who have not been favored by the wider gains associated with literacy skills.

In other studies (e.g., Kolinsky, Morais, & Verhaeghe, 1994), our research strategy has been to begin by comparing illiterate unschooled participants to literate schooled ones. The observation of group differences in such a design leaves the question of the critical factors open for further investigation. But, if no difference is observed, this finding allows the researcher to proceed immediately to another capacity or issue. Moreover, the finding of a specific effect of literacy on a given skill can be corroborated by the finding that illiterates and ex-illiterates differ on that skill but not on another related skill. For example, Morais et al. (1986) reported that although illiterates were dramatically inferior to ex-illiterates in phoneme manipulation, they were only a little worse in syllable manipulation, in line with the hypothesis that phoneme but not syllable awareness depends upon alphabetic literacy.

There remains, however, a more fundamental problem. This is the possibility that illiterates differ from ex-illiterates in some characteristic other than literacy, such as motivation or engagement with the experiment. Morais et al. (1979) interpreted their finding that illiterates were unable to delete the initial phoneme of an utterance explicitly, or to add one to it, whereas ex-illiterates could do it, as evidence that phoneme awareness does not develop spontaneously. However, the observed difference, by itself, was not necessarily due to literacy. Since the ex-illiterate participants tested had attended alphabetization classes for adults, it was possible that they had just become better at paying attention to instructions. In cases such as these, where findings are equivocal, converging data can be instructive. Read, Zhang, Nie, and Ding (1986) replicated Morais et al.'s (1979) finding in a study where they compared the phoneme awareness of Chinese readers who had been taught pin-yin (an alphabetic reading system) or who had been taught only the traditional, nonalphabetic, Chinese writing system. The alphabetized readers scored at a similar level to the ex-illiterate people and the nonalphabetized readers at a similar level to the illiterate people in Morais et al.'s (1979) earlier study. Since the two groups in Read et al.'s (1986) study were comparable in terms of number of years of schooling and professional activity, differences in attention or motivation are not a plausible explanation of these findings. Thus, Read et al.'s findings, together with the earlier study by Morais et al. demonstrate that becoming literate in an alphabetic script bootstraps the development of phoneme awareness.

## The Impact of Literacy on Nonlinguistic Capacities

Does literacy affect nonlinguistic capacities such as motor behavior, music, visual cognition, mathematics, drawing, nonverbal reasoning, or executive processes? Language may intervene in many apparently nonlinguistic tasks, and the possibility that written language may affect nonverbal behaviors via inner speech must also be considered. Although writing is a representation of oral language, some of its inherent properties, such as spatial mapping and physical permanence, might allow it to distribute processing over more representations than is presumably the case for speech. For example, writing allows recovery of information from memory to be supported not only by phonological codes but also by mentally represented orthographic codes as well as by print; that is, by external memory.

## Visual cognition

A number of different aspects of visual cognition have been assessed in illiterate as compared to literate adults. Kolinsky and Morais (1999) distinguished between the early perceptual processes leading to object recognition and postperceptual processes involved in the conscious, intentional analysis of perceptual representations. A standard paradigm for examining early perceptual processes involves the observation of illusory conjunctions. These errors of recombination of correctly extracted features, which consist for example in reporting more often the presence of a red circle when green circles and red squares are presented than when green triangles and red squares are presented, indicate that the features have been unintentionally analyzed. Kolinsky et al. (1994) found no difference between illiterate and literate adults in the rate of observed illusory conjunctions for color and form, segments of geometric figures, or shape and orientation of segments. However, in a task involving intentional postperceptual processes in which the participant has to detect a part made of three segments in a figure made of six (see figure 11.1), Kolinsky et al. (1987b) found that illiterates and ex-illiterates performed at the same level and less well than children attending the second grade. Together, these findings suggest that early perceptual visual processes are universal, whereas postperceptual ones depend, not on literacy, but on schooling (or on some experience that is provided to the children usually by Grade 2 of primary school).

Brito Mendes, Kolinsky, and Morais (1988) and Brito Mendes, Morais, and Kolinsky (in press), using the same material as Kolinsky et al. (1987b), attempted to determine whether unschooled people would improve in their ability to detect highly embedded parts of a figure by providing them with analytic instructions. After each response, the subject was given feedback that consisted of placing a transparency over the figures showing the segments that should have been detected. In this way they could see whether or not each target segment was present in the figure. Correct detection of the part increased, but at the same time, the accuracy with which the participants could say when a part was not in the figure decreased. Thus, neither illiterates nor ex-illiterates benefited from the analytic feedback.

There are, however, other visual tasks in which performance does seem to be influenced by learning to read. Cooper (1976, 1980) assessed the ability of literate individuals to discriminate closed and irregular black-colored forms using a "same–different" classification paradigm designed to distinguish between holistic and analytic processing. It was argued that one group of participants used holistic matching. For them "same" responses were faster than "different" responses, and (dis)similarity did not affect the latter responses. For another group of participants who were deemed to use analytic

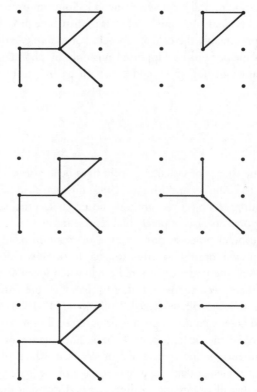

**Figure 11.1**  Example of figure-part trials used by Kolinsky et al. (1987) and by Brito Mendes, Kolinsky, and Morais (1988) and Brito Mendes, Morais, and Kolinsky (in press). In Kolinsky et al., salient parts (top line) led to good performance in all groups, whereas moderately or deeply embedded parts (second and last line) were not detected by unschooled adults.

processing, "same" responses were not faster than "different" ones, and reaction time increased as similarity decreased. According to Cooper (1980), "perceptual development proceeds from a holistic undifferentiated mode to a more analytic or differentiated one" (pp. 338–339). Following on from this, Brito Mendes et al. (in press) examined illiterate, ex-illiterate and literate people on Cooper and Podgorny's (1976) task, using the same materials as they did. Illiterates detected sameness as fast as difference and, unexpectedly, they were faster for "same" trials than ex-illiterate and literate people. Moreover, the effect of similarity was much smaller than the one displayed by the other groups. Thus, they apparently relied on holistic processing. By contrast, the ex-illiterate and the literate groups performed similarly: they were much faster on "different" trials than on "same" trials, and displayed a large effect of the degree of dissimilarity – evidence of analytic processing. In short, the acquisition of literacy seems to facilitate the development of analytic visual processing.

It is worth noting that literacy rather than schooling may also be responsible for a shift in perceptual processing of left–right mirror images. Verhaeghe and Kolinsky (1992) found that ex-illiterates displayed better mirror-image discrimination skills than illiterates. This literacy effect might be related to the fact that the alphabetic system incorporates mirror-image characters like "b" versus "d" and "p" versus "q". Indeed, readers of a writing system that does not include mirror-image signs, the Tamil syllabary, were as poor as illiterates in discriminating mirror images (Danziger & Pederson, 1999). However, other activities in addition to literacy may also encourage the development of this ability. Verhaeghe and Kolinsky (1992) found that, among illiterates, lacemakers obtained better scores than nonlacemakers. Thus, it is likely that a range of activities that draw the observer's attention to the left–right orientation of stimuli promote mirror-image discrimination. In the study described above by Brito Mendes et al. (in press), the critical factor that made the ex-illiterates behave analytically is likely to have been the training of letter discrimination associated with alphabetization.

## Reasoning and executive processes

There have been a small number of studies of the effects of literacy on reasoning processes. Scribner and Cole (1981) explored the resolution of logical problems by comparing illiterates, readers of Vai (based on syllabic writing) and readers of the Arabic alphabet. There were no group differences either in the number of problems solved, or in how the participants justified their responses. Likewise, in Brazil, Tfouni (1988) found that about one third of the illiterate participants that she interviewed could understand and explain syllogisms.

However, findings regarding reasoning skills may turn on the types of task that are used. In particular, some tasks require detailed explicit visual analysis, as for some items of the Ravens Progressive Matrices. In this case, both illiterate and ex-illiterate people performed as poorly as 7-year-old European and American children (Verhaege, 1999). Arguably, difficulties with explicit visual analysis might not be the sole factor affecting unschooled people' s performance in reasoning tasks. Another reason might be that these tasks demand a high level of executive control, for example, the inhibition of a first response, shifting between dimensions of a stimulus, or planning a response.

One task that has been used widely to assess executive processes is the classic Stroop task in which participants are required to focus on one stimulus dimension while ignoring another. In the classic paradigm, they are required to name the color of the ink (e.g., green) in which a color-word (e.g., red) is presented. In a digit Stroop test in which subjects had to count the number of presented symbols rather than to report their identity, both illiterate and ex-illiterate participants were slower overall than literate participants, even in the control, baseline condition (requiring to respond "3" to * * *), but neither the interference effect in the incongruent condition (e.g., respond "3" to 2 2 2) nor the facilitation effect in the congruent condition (requiring e.g. to respond "3" to 3 3 3) varied between the groups. Moreover, reaction time did not vary between illiterates and ex-illiterates. Thus, the presence and efficiency of the processes underlying these effects seem to be independent of both literacy and schooling (see, however, Kolinsky, 1988, and Verhaeghe, 1999, who found that both illiterate and ex-illiterate people had some difficulties on a task involving selective attention).

Shifting between alternative criteria is a basic requirement of the California Card Sorting Test. In an adaptation of this test, in which six cards could be classified according to two semantic and three perceptual criteria, Kolinsky, Penido, and Morais (in preparation) found that illiterates and ex-illiterates could shift from one dimension to another, including across domains. When compared with a literate group there was a schooling effect, with literate people finding more criteria, but there was no difference between illiterates and ex-illiterates. Finally, planning was evaluated with the Tower of London test (Shallice, 1982). The results showed no significant difference between illiterate and ex-illiterate participants in either number of movements or time needed to reach the goal configuration.

The findings on nonlinguistic capacities presented in this section can be summarized as follows. As regards visual abilities, perceptual processes are influenced neither by schooling nor by literacy, while postperceptual processes involving explicit visual segmentation are influenced by schooling but not by literacy. Nevertheless, literacy contributes both to the development of an analytic approach in same–different comparisons and to the ability to discriminate mirror images efficiently. As regards reasoning and executive processes, illiteracy per se does not seem to affect performance. Illiterates are able to reason correctly on syllogisms and other logical problems, although they do not do so spontaneously. They also use executive processes such as inhibition of irrelevant information and shifting between stimulus dimensions as well as ex-illiterates, although schooling favors these control processes.

## The Impact of Literacy on Linguistic Capacities

The impact of literacy on linguistic and, especially, on metalinguistic capacities has been examined more systematically than the impact of literacy on nonlinguistic capacities. Four domains of linguistic processing will be addressed: speech processing, verbal short-term memory, lexical and semantic knowledge, and metalinguistic abilities. Finally, we will briefly discuss the effects of orthographic skills on spoken word recognition.

### Speech processing tasks

Since learning to read in an alphabetic system involves making connections between letters and phonemes, a viable hypothesis is that acquiring literacy will affect the development of phonological representations through reciprocal interaction (e.g. Harm & Seidenberg, 1999; Snowling & Hulme, 1994a). In principle, such changes might be seen in speech recognition or speech production tasks. However, the empirical evidence shows that, at least on early processes involved in speech perception, there is no influence of literacy. The relevant studies are not considered in detail here because they have been reviewed elsewhere (Morais & Kolinsky, 2002a, 2002b). In brief, illiterate people have been found not to differ from literate people in the identification of consonants spanning an acoustic continuum from voiced to unvoiced, or from one place of articulation to another (Castro, 1993), or in the McGurk phenomenon in which visual information from the speaker's mouth movements has an effect on phonetic identification (Morais & Mousty, 1992). In a similar vein, illiterates are no less sensitive than their literate counterparts to the feature blending error (Morais, Castro, Scliar-Cabral, Kolinsky, & Content, 1987b) or to the blends of other speech units like consonantal phonemes in dichotic listening tasks. The last finding deserves special attention. The logic of such blends is the same as the logic of illusory conjunctions: if the units can be wrongly combined, they must have been separately registered at some processing stage. Testing Portuguese literate people, we found that the initial consonant of CVCV utterances is the unit that leads to the higher blending error rate, compared to the syllable and vowel (Kolinsky & Morais, 1993). Subsequent testing of Portuguese illiterate adults and preliterate children yielded the same pattern of results (Morais & Kolinsky, 1994, and Castro, Vicente, Morais, Kolinsky, & Cluytens, 1995, respectively). This demonstrates sensitivity to consonants in speech perception in a population that is unable to represent them consciously. Unconscious perceptual representations of phonemes develop prior to the onset of literacy.

Similarly no special difficulties have been reported among illiterate people at higher levels of spoken word recognition. For instance, Adrian, Alegria, and Morais (1995) found that illiterates have no difficulty in perceiving or discriminating isolated syllables or words (see also Scliar-Cabral, Morais, Nepomuceno, & Kolinsky, 1997) and they perform with a high degree of accuracy in lexical decision tasks (Morais & Kolinsky, 2002a).

The ability of illiterate and ex-illiterate people to repeat words of three, four and five syllables has been reported to be unimpaired (Morais & Kolinsky, 2002b) at least in terms of accuracy. However, there were differences between unschooled (both illiterates and ex-illiterates) and schooled people in the repetition errors they made. While 57% of the errors made by literate people were limited to a single consonant, only 24% and 26% of the errors made by illiterates and ex-illiterates, respectively, were of this type. If consonant errors reflect the possession of segmental phonological representations (as is usually assumed), then this difference suggests that, although they are sensitive to consonants in perception, unschooled people have limited access to phonemic units of speech and rely instead on representations of larger speech segments (such as syllables). If this is the case, we should predict that both illiterates and ex-illiterates may do poorly on verbal short-term memory tasks because these depend on having access to precise phonological codes.

The difference observed in global versus segmental errors in the repetition task echoes a similar difference observed in a word recognition task using dichotic presentation between highly literate people and "semiliterate" adults who were alphabetized in childhood but do not read frequently (Morais et al., 1987b). In interpreting this result, we suggested that it may reflect the availability in the highly literate people of an attentional mechanism focusing on the phonemic structure of speech. This interpretation is supported by the fact that the proportion of segmental errors can be increased in university students by asking them to pay attention to the phonemic structure of the items (Castro, 1993). A further possibility is that the phonological representations involved in speech recognition are more segmentally structured in literate people, but there is no empirical evidence supporting this view. Whatever the interpretation of the difference in segmental errors, it does not seem to depend on the mere acquisition of the alphabetic code but rather on intensive reading practice for at least some years.

## Verbal short-term memory

A number of different paradigms have been used to assess the verbal memory skills of illiterate people, with somewhat inconsistent findings. Ardila, Rosselli, and Rosas (1989) reported no effect of literacy on immediate recall of simple sentences presented sequentially, although an educational effect was observed for delayed recall of the same sentences. In a similar vein, Ostrosky-Solis, Ardila, Rosselli, Lopez-Arango, and Uriel-Mendoza (1998), using repeated presentation of six common nouns belonging to three different semantic categories, found no difference in recall between illiterates and people with 3–4 years of schooling. In contrast, Reis and Castro-Caldas (1997) used a variant of the word pair association test of the Wechsler Memory Scale (Wechsler, 1945) with illiterate adults and literate schooled adults. An important finding of this study was that when the relation between associated items was phonological, for example "lua"–"rua" (*moon–street*), the illiterates did relatively more poorly than when the relationship was semantic (e.g. *fork–spoon*). Castro-Caldas and Reis (2003, p. 84) concluded that illiterates "use preferentially semantic strategies to deal with language problems rather than strategies based on formal attributes of the words." It is important to note, however, that literacy and schooling were confounded in this study and therefore this may also be the case for unschooled people.

Moreover, although illiterate unschooled people appear to pay less attention to formal aspects of words than literate schooled people do, there is evidence that they nevertheless code nameable visual images into phonological representations spontaneously. Morais et al. (1986) presented pictures of objects successively to participants, while saying their names orally. Each picture was placed face down, and after the last one had been presented, participants were given a card displaying these together with other pictures. The task was to match the cards, without turning them up, with the pictures on the card. In this situation, performance is typically poorer in children and adults when the names of the pictures rhyme with each other (Conrad, 1971). Morais et al. observed that this rhyme effect was equivalent in illiterates and ex-illiterates. However, the overall memory performance of the participants was rather low, more so for illiterates than for ex-illiterates. A similar effect was found in a digit span task (Morais & Kolinsky, 2002a; see also Petersson, Reis, & Ingvar, 2001) and by Scribner and Cole (1981) in a comparison of illiterates and Qur'anic literate people in a task involving the ordered recall of a list of words.

In summary, there is reasonable evidence that short-term memory span is impaired in illiterate and/or unschooled populations (reduced to about three or four words or digits and certainly much inferior to that of literate adults). These findings are broadly consistent with the view that phonological representations in these people are insufficiently segmentalized to support effective maintenance of verbal information in short-term memory. However, there are other possible explanations for these findings. First, illiterate people cannot use orthographic mental representations as cues for supplementing degraded phonological information, and ex-illiterate people are unlikely to be able to activate such representations automatically. Second, unschooled participants may not use rehearsal procedures, or use them to a lesser extent than schooled ones. Consistent with this idea, the unschooled people we tested did not show any difference in span for monosyllabic and trisyllabic items, although, in the same experimental conditions, they did display the usual effect of lexicality (larger span for words than for pseudowords; Hulme, Maughan, & Brown, 1991). Third, unschooled participants, especially illiterate ones, may have difficulties attending to a sequence of unrelated phonological events to encode their order.

Taken together, findings from studies of speech processing, repetition, and verbal short-term memory (STM) in illiterate and ex-illiterate populations suggest that differences in phonological processing that would be an immediate consequence of acquisition of the alphabetic code are small and concern only verbal memory span. More importantly, there are differences between unschooled and schooled people arising at the level of segmental phonological information as well as at the level of listening strategies. These differences manifest themselves in difficult recognition tasks (e.g., under dichotic presentation) and in tasks involving memory demands (recognition of sequences, repetition, memory span).

Castro-Caldas, Petersson, Reis, Stone-Elander, and Ingvar (1998) reported a pioneering brain imaging study of illiterates while they were completing word and pseudoword repetition tasks. Using the subtraction methodology, brain activation differences between the literate (schooled) and illiterate groups were small when repeating words, but were observed for several areas when repeating pseudowords. The functional significance of these brain differences is still unclear, although Castro-Caldas and Reis (2003) suggest that they concern the phonological loop. It is possible that phonological differences between illiterates and people with relatively advanced literacy skills occur for both word and pseudoword processing, but that these differences only appear clearly, using this kind of brain imaging methodology, when there is no simultaneous activation of, or even interaction with, semantic representations, which are most probably involved in word but not pseudoword repetition.

## Lexical and semantic knowledge

It is almost a truism to state that lexical knowledge is increased by reading. Indeed, reading accounts for most of the new words that both schoolchildren and adults learn. Arguably, through reading people also become aware of associated word meanings, synonyms, and antonyms. Morais, Macedo, Grimm-Cabral, Larochelle, and Kolinsky (in preparation) used a free word association task to compare the performance of illiterates and ex-illiterates, who all attended an alphabetization class but were classified according to their word and pseudoword reading skills. Many of their responses consisted of a complete sentence or a phrase rather than a word, but such responses were considered acceptable (see Entwisle, 1966, for use of the same procedure with children). The ex-illiterates made more paradigmatic responses (including synonyms and antonyms) (51.9%) than the illiterates (36.5%). Though rare, functional responses (e.g., "to work" in response to "man") were more frequent in the illiterates (9.5%, compared with 4.9%). Many responses involved a personal reference and can be classified as syntagmatic (e.g., "I know how to clean the house" in response to "to know"); these were more frequent in the illiterate (40.4%) than in the ex-illiterate (34.9%) group.

These findings are consistent with the observation of a developmental shift from syntagmatic to paradigmatic responding in this task (Brown & Berko, 1960; Entwisle, 1966; Ervin, 1961), and with the idea that this shift is related to reading acquisition (Cronin, 2002; Cronin et al., 1986). However, given that the responses in the free word association task are strongly influenced by word association frequency, the differences observed between illiterates and literates could reflect changes in word association frequency as reading was acquired rather than a shift from syntagmatic to paradigmatic responding. To control for this possibility, Morais et al. (in preparation, b) compared knowledge of paradigmatic and syntagmatic relations in a forced-choice task. Here participants were presented with a target word and a choice of two test words: one related to the target, the other not. They considered three types of paradigmatic relation (synonymy, antonymy, and category sharing), and two types of syntagmatic relation (noun–adjective and verb–noun). Overall, after controlling for vocabulary knowledge, ex-illiterates were better at selecting the related word than the illiterates, and there was a trend for the syntagmatic relations to be more accessible (due primarily to the illiterates' problems with antonyms).

Morais, Macedo, Grimm-Cabral, and Kolinsky (in preparation, a) used the phenomenon of release from proactive interference (Wickens, Dalezman, & Eggemeier, 1976) to assess automatic access to lexical knowledge in adults varying in literacy skills and children. Proactive interference (PI) refers to the fact that, if people are asked to remember sets of items in lists, and each list consists of lists from the same semantic category, memory performance declines over trials. Release from PI occurs if the category is changed and there is a consequent upturn in memory performance. Thus, if illiterate people are sensitive to categorical relations, they should show both PI and release from PI under the appropriate conditions. In this study, names of animals were presented in all four trials of the control condition, while in the experimental condition, participants were presented with names of fruits on the first three trials and animal names in the fourth trial. Seven-to-11-year-old children outperformed unschooled adults, but both groups showed an effect of proactive interference. Importantly, there was no group difference in the release from proactive interference observed in the fourth list of the experimental condition. The analysis of intrusion errors in the different lists confirmed the idea that both proactive interference and release from it are independent of schooling and literacy. They also show that illiterates can use categorical information as a cue for retrieval, in line with the findings of Cole, Gay, Glick, and Sharp (1971) and Scribner (1974).

In a further study, Kolinsky et al. (in preparation) used a task devised by Nation and Snowling (1999) to assess implicit semantic processing skills in children with normal and poor reading comprehension. The task required children to make lexical decisions about items in a mixed list of auditorily presented words and pseudowords. While good comprehenders showed semantic priming from category-related items regardless of their degree of association with the target words, poor comprehenders only showed semantic priming between category coordinates when the words shared high association strength (e.g., doctor–nurse), not when they shared low association strength (e.g., sheep–cat). In Kolinsky et al.'s study, both illiterate and ex-illiterate adults showed a significant effect of semantic priming, and there was no convincing evidence of a literacy effect. Thus, unschooled people are sensitive to semantic relations, including abstract ones.

Turning to more explicit tasks, Luria (1976, p. 18) proposed that illiterates are "unable to group objects according to abstract semantic features." However, this idea, that categorical classification emerges with literacy and/or schooling is inconsistent with evidence that the capacity for categorization appears early in development, before the onset of literacy (e.g., Blewitt & Toppino, 1991; Mansfield, 1977; Markman, 1984; Rosch, Mervis, Gray, Johnson, & Boyes-Braem, 1976). Luria's observations on illiterate adults may reflect preference for practical schemes rather than lack of categorical organization.

Scliar-Cabral and Monteiro, Morais, and Kolinsky (2002a) asked people varying in literacy skill to complete a task that required them to match a target word, for example "duck," with either a taxonomically related word ("sparrow") or an unrelated word ("sheep"). In this task, the illiterates made as large a number of taxonomic choices as literate adults who had completed four school grades in childhood. Thus, they were able to group drawings into categories and provide justifications of a taxonomic kind for their groupings. They were also able to provide a superordinate term for sets of three items (e.g., "fruit" for apple, peach, and pineapple). However, when the proportion of justifications and responses consisting of the nearest superordinate or subordinate term was compared to those made by more highly educated people, an effect of schooling, but not of literacy, emerged. Thus, while categorical organization does not depend on either literacy or schooling, it seems, as might be expected, that education contributes to increases in the richness of the structure of an individual's semantic knowledge. Similar findings have been reported from category fluency tasks in which there is no convincing evidence of a literacy effect: illiterates use hierarchically organized categories as do more highly educated people but at the same time they produce fewer words (Ratcliff et al., 1998; Reis & Castro-Caldas, 1997).

## Metalinguistic abilities

Metalinguistic awareness refers to the ability to reflect on language at its many different levels. However, most research relevant to literacy has been directed at awareness of the sound structure of words. According to Morais, Kolinsky, Alegria, and Scliar-Cabral (1998), phonological awareness is the capacity to represent phonological information consciously. It is assessed by requiring intentional, explicit judgments or operations on phonology. Thus, it goes beyond the mere activation of phonological representations in the recognition and production of speech.

One may distinguish between word and subword awareness. Awareness of words has been examined by Cary (1988) who first asked illiterates and ex-illiterates to segment orally presented sentence into words. While ex-illiterates were able to complete this task, illiterates segmented the sentences into syntactic clauses. However, when asked to repeat the last "bit" of an interrupted sentence, a task that is less sensitive to meaning bias, the illiterates produced single words a majority of the time, suggesting that they have some conscious access to the word unit (Cary & Verhaeghe, 1991).

At the level of subword awareness, Morais et al. (1998) (Morais, 1991a) distinguished between holistic and analytic forms of phonological awareness. These forms roughly correspond to Gombert's (1992) concepts of epiphonological and metaphonological knowledge. Holistic phonological awareness is involved, for instance, in judging phonological length, and in some speech sound classification and detection tasks. To assess sensitivity to phonological length, Kolinsky, Cary, and Morais (1987a) presented participants (silently) with a series of drawings. On neutral trials, drawings represented objects of the same physical size with names varying in phonological length (e.g., "pé–peúga," meaning "foot" and "sock," respectively). The participants' task was to choose the object with the longest name. Sixty percent of the illiterates obtained scores of at least 75% correct responses, demonstrating holistic phonological awareness. However, all but one subject was better in these trials than in incongruent trials, in which the longer word denoted the smallest object (e.g., "gato–borboleta," meaning "cat" and "butterfly," respectively). Thus, most illiterates experienced an attentional conflict between semantics and phonology.

The appreciation of rhyming relationships between words may also be accomplished on the basis of holistic phonological awareness even though, from a literate point of view, it involves subsyllabic analysis. Morais et al. (1986) found that about half of the illiterate participants they tested could choose among four drawings the one whose name rhymed with a target. Similarly, Bertelson, de Gelder, Tfouni, and Morais (1989) reported that 75% of the illiterates they tested reached a criterion of six consecutive correct responses when judging whether pairs of words rhymed. Moreover, illiterate poets provide a striking illustration of the dissociation between holistic and analytic phonological awareness (Cary, Morais, & Bertelson, 1989; Morais, 1991b). The illiterate poet *FJC* performed at chance level in three out of four tests requiring the classification of either consonants or vowels; while he succeeded in classifying the vowels of triads of CV syllables, he was not able to do this with triads of VC syllables, suggesting that attention to vowels was only observed in a rhyming context (Morais et al., 1998). Although illiterate poets only display holistic phonological awareness, they have probably acquired a large rhyming lexicon that enables them, by analogy, both to identify and produce rhymes.

To assess phoneme classification, Cary (1988) used triads of CV or VC syllables in which two items had a common vowel. Illiterates were able to classify matching pairs correctly when they were perceptually close (like /pe/ and /be/ in the triad /pe, be, si/) but they had much more difficulty when within triads (e.g., /se, be, pi/) where vowel sharing (/se/ – /be/) conflicted with overall perceptual similarity (in this case, between /be/ and /pi/). The large difference in performance between the two situations suggests that illiterates rely on holistic phonological awareness or holistic acoustic similarity rather than on phonological identity. The capacity of illiterates to rely on global phonological similarity as well as their sensitivity to acoustically salient information may also explain the variability of their performance in phoneme detection tasks. As a matter of fact, Morais et al. (1986) found that the performance of illiterates in a phoneme detection task was much better when the target was an acoustically salient /R/ than when it was a stop. Phoneme detection performance was also facilitated when the detection of a target phoneme, for example /p/, remained constant throughout the testing session; this may be because from a global phonological similarity match between the target pronunciation (/pə/ and the very short stimuli (e.g., /pi/, /pa/, vs. /vi/, /va/; unpublished data by Fiadeiro, Cary, & Morais).

Intentional (explicit) segmentation of verbal items into syllables should, at first sight, be considered a simple case of analytic phonological awareness. Bertelson and de Gelder (1989) showed that ex-illiterates performed better than illiterates in syllable as well as rhyming and phoneme tasks (see also Morais et al., 1986). However, given that co-articulation effects are relatively weak between syllables, it seems more reasonable to admit that only conscious subsyllabic segmentation deserves to be called analytic phonological awareness. Indeed, both preliterate children and illiterate adults can succeed on syllable segmentation tasks (Liberman, Shankweiler, Fischer, & Carter, 1974), but they find segmenting words into phonemes very difficult (e.g., Liberman et al., 1974, and Morais et al., 1979, 1986, respectively).

Evidence from the now large body of literature on learning to read in alphabetic systems is consistent with the view that phoneme awareness is fostered by literacy instruction. We would argue that it begins to develop when one starts to learn the letters of the alphabet and to discover what they represent. Lukatela, Carello, Shankweiler, and Liberman (1995), testing adult unschooled speakers of Serbo-Croatian, found that all the participants who had poor letter recognition ability (less than 50% correct identification) scored 0% in phoneme deletion, and all the participants who identified all the letters scored between 70 and 100% correct in the same deletion test. On the other hand, given that the process of learning to read is a long one, the ability to represent phonemes mentally and to operate on them also plays a very important role in the acquisition both of the alphabetic code and of efficient grapheme–phoneme and phoneme–grapheme transcoding and assembly procedures. For this reason, it is now accepted that the relation between phoneme awareness and learning to read and write is an interactive one (Morais, Alegria, & Content, 1987a).

Whether or not the developmental course of the relations between learning to read and write and acquiring phoneme awareness is the same in children and in adults engaged in late alphabetization is an interesting question, but comparative studies are difficult to design given the multiple differences between the two populations. Using identical materials and procedure, we found a similar learning effect for phoneme segmentation through successive training blocks with preliterate children (Content, Kolinsky, Morais, & Bertelson, 1986) and illiterate adults (Morais, Content, Bertelson, Cary, & Kolinsky, 1988). On the basis of these results, it can be argued that there is no critical period for the acquisition of phoneme awareness, and furthermore, that illiterate adults can discover the alphabetic principle with the aid of instruction. But it cannot be concluded that the alphabetic principle is accessed through the same processes, and therefore that instructional methods should be the same for adults and children.

Knowledge of orthographic codes and intensive practice with them may eventually influence phonological judgments. In a classic experiment, Seidenberg and Tanenhaus (1979) found that auditory rhyme decisions were faster when words were orthographically similar (e.g., *rose–nose*) than when they were not (e.g., *rose–goes*), and the opposite effect held for nonrhyming decisions. Intentional subsyllabic segmentation is also influenced by orthographic knowledge. Testing literate people in a task requiring to blend two spoken CVC Portuguese words into a (new) CVC pseudoword, Ventura, Kolinsky, Brito-Mendes, and Morais (2001) observed a preference for CV/C blends (e.g., responding /kul/ to the word pair /kur/ – /peɪ/) for words for which the final C is followed in the orthographic representation by a mute letter ("cure," "pele"), but preference for C/VC blends (e.g., responding /beɪ/ for the word pair /bar/ /meɪ/) for words for which there is no such final mute letter ("bar," "mel"). This was observed even when instructions emphasized the importance of focusing on sound, and when possible acoustic-phonetic differences were controlled. Both Seidenberg and Tanenhaus' and Ventura et al.'s findings are instances of the impact of literacy on metaphonological representation.

Finally, before concluding it is important to note that orthographic knowledge may influence not only metaphonological judgments but also the recognition of spoken words. The evidence, by definition, comes from literate people. Thus, Ziegler and Ferrand (1998) found that French words with rimes that can be spelled in multiple ways (e.g., /ɔ̃/ as in "nom," "tronc," "long," "don," "bond," "plomb") produced longer latencies and more errors in auditory lexical decision tasks than words with rimes that are spelled only one way (e.g., /iʃ/ as in "biche," "riche"), and Ventura, Morais, Pattamadilok, and Kolinsky (2004) replicated this pattern of results in Portugese, a shallower orthographic code. Extending these findings, Ziegler, Muneaux, and Grainger (2003) found that orthographic neighborhood had a facilitatory effect in auditory lexical decision: spoken words with many orthographic neighbors yielded faster and more accurate response latencies than those with few orthographic neighbors.

## Conclusions

This chapter has reviewed evidence suggesting that learning to read and spell in alphabetic languages may bring about changes in a variety of linguistic and nonlinguistic cognitive capacities. We have focused primarily on data obtained by comparing groups of illiterates and ex-illiterates whose origin and present sociocultural status is as close as possible to each other. We are aware, however, that to distinguish the availability of literacy from the extended use of this skill is difficult. Practising any skill is likely to increase it. In the case of literacy, its use contributes both to the acquisition of knowledge and to improvements in the skill itself, leading to a "Matthew effect" (cf. Stanovich, 1986). Thus the interpretation of studies such as those described here comparing literate with ex-illiterate people, must be done cautiously.

Nevertheless the studies reviewed here suggest that learning to read an alphabetic script has only a limited impact on visual cognition. Indeed, activities other than reading and writing may also elicit change in abilities such as mirror-image discrimination. Likewise, the studies of linguistic capacities revealed relatively small or absent effects of literacy on lexical or semantic skills, though unsurprisingly, education does have an impact on accumulated lexical knowledge. In similar vein, while literacy has only a small effect on memory span, much larger effects of schooling were observed on both memory span and pseudoword repetition.

In contrast metaphonological knowledge appears to be strongly and directly influenced by learning to read an alphabetic script. We have argued that the most important effect is on the development of phoneme awareness. Phoneme awareness arises at the beginning of learning to read and write in alphabetic systems. Its analytic power allows people to deal with other phonological units or relations like syllables and rhyme, at a higher level of efficiency than that based purely on holistic phonological representations.

Phoneme awareness may also be a remote cause of the superiority of highly literate over both illiterate and ex-illiterate people in short-term memory span and in word and pseudoword repetition. Indeed, highly literate people may have capitalized on phoneme awareness to develop better specified, phonemically structured, phonological representations and/or phoneme-oriented strategies of listening, in addition to having become able to activate orthographic codes. In fact knowledge of word orthography influences phonological judgments and intuitions, and the effect of orthographic knowledge goes much farther since it extends to spoken word recognition.

# PART III

*Reading Comprehension*

# Editorial Part III

The goal of writing is to communicate, and the goal of reading is to understand. To fully understand reading comprehension would be to understand most of the fundamental problems in cognition. The challenge is daunting. A starting point for studies of reading comprehension is to assume that reading comprehension will involve many of the same processes as comprehending speech. How do we begin to grapple with how the mind represents the meanings conveyed by language, whether written or spoken?

Kintsch and Rawson lay out a highly influential theory of comprehension. The theory sees comprehension as depending upon largely automatic processes somewhat akin to the processes subserving perception. Two major levels of representation are distinguished: a textbase representation that represents the linguistic structure of the text and its meaning, and a situation model (a mental model of the situation described by the text). The textbase representation will have a number of different levels of representation, including microlevel representations (word and proposition level representations, for example) and a macrolevel representation of how ideas in a given passage relate to each other. If this were not complicated enough, for a full understanding, the textbase representation must be related to the situation model, a more abstract representation that is not exclusively verbal and includes a wide range of world knowledge that may include imagery and emotional content.

Perfetti, Landi, and Oakhill move on to consider how reading comprehension skill develops. They point to the likely critical importance of the child's ability to identify words fluently and retrieve their meanings (cf. Gough & Tunmer, 1986). In terms of Kintsch and Rawson's model, processes in accurately constructing a textbase representation are critical, and one potential set of limiting factors concerns word identification and access to adequate vocabulary knowledge. Constructing a situation model, however, will require inferences to be made and Perfetti et al. critically discuss many studies that have attempted to link inferential skills to the development of reading comprehension skill, as well as the development of comprehension monitoring strategies and syntactic skills.

A significant proportion of children have specific deficits in developing reading comprehension skills. Nation presents a review of the nature of the cognitive deficits that appear responsible for the problems displayed in these 'poor comprehenders'. Such children have adequate decoding skills for their age but they show specific deficits in understanding texts that they can read aloud accurately (so their problems cannot be explained in terms of inefficient decoding processes). Such children do, however, have weaknesses in other aspects of oral language that provide the foundations for reading comprehension, including deficits of vocabulary knowledge and higher-level language skills such as inference making. Such children therefore certainly appear to have problems in constructing an adequate textbase representation, though it is possible that they also have higher-level problems in constructing a situation model of what they have read.

The chapters in Part III converge on the view that reading comprehension builds on the foundation of spoken language skills. Arguably, this insight has important implications for educational practice that have yet to be developed.

# 12

# *Comprehension*

## Walter Kintsch and Katherine A. Rawson

"Comprehension" refers to both a set of empirical phenomena and a theoretical construct. The phenomena are ill defined, because the concept of comprehension that psychologists took over from everyday language use is fuzzy, as such concepts are. In practice, however, most psychological research on comprehension has dealt with discourse comprehension. In discourse comprehension for skilled adult readers, analytical reasoning is required only when the normal course of understanding breaks down: normal reading or listening is more akin to perception than to problem solving. As a theoretical construct, therefore, "comprehension" contrasts with conscious, deliberate problem solving. Perception and comprehension can both be described as spontaneous constraint satisfaction processes. Consider, for example, the classical sentence pair:

*The turtle sat on a log. A fish swam under the log.*

from which readers immediately conclude that

*The turtle was above the fish.*

It is possible to arrive at this conclusion through a reasoning process, using rules like

*If A is above B, and C is under B*
*then A is above C.*

Alternatively, a reader who constructs a mental image of this scene can immediately "see" that the turtle is above the fish. Most people can understand the simple sentence pair above without needing to reason it out analytically, because they know about turtles and logs and water and fish, combining these constraints into a readily comprehended scene (though, of course, analytic problem solving may be required in more complex situations). Kintsch (1998) has therefore argued that comprehension forms a contrasting paradigm for cognition, complementing but by no means supplanting problem solving as conceived in the classical monograph of Newell and Simon (1972).

## Processes Underlying Text Comprehension

Text analysis has long been the province of linguists and logicians. When psychologists became interested in text comprehension, they first followed this lead, but soon developed their own agenda: their interest was in text processing, rather than the analysis of the text per se. Below, we discuss some of the processes involved in text comprehension along with some of the major issues that have arisen in trying to understand how people understand text. We will begin by outlining the basic processes involved in text comprehension and will then illustrate them with a simple example. Subsequently, we will examine a few of these processes in greater detail.

### Levels of processing

Text comprehension is often described as involving processing at different levels (Kintsch, 1998). In keeping with this convention, we use "levels" terminology herein (e.g., "textbase," "microstructure," "macrostructure," and "situation model," described further below) to provide the reader with convenient and conventional terms used by researchers to describe the different kinds of information that may be represented by comprehension processes, although we do not claim that these kinds of information are necessarily stored in distinct or separate representations.

- *First, there is the linguistic level, or processing of the particular words and phrases contained in the text itself.* The reader must decode the graphic symbols on a page. Perceptual processes are involved, as well as word recognition and parsing (the assignment of words to their roles in sentences and phrases). Treatment of many of these processes is available in other chapters, and thus we will focus subsequent discussion on the higher-level processes involved in comprehension introduced below.
- *Semantic analysis determines the meaning of the text.* Word meanings must be combined in ways stipulated by the text, forming idea units or propositions. Propositions are interrelated in a complex network, called the *microstructure* of the text. One of the main dimensions along which propositions can be related to one another is coreference, which occurs when two or more propositions refer to the same concept (also referred to as "argument overlap"). Psychologically, the microstructure is constructed by forming propositional units according to the words of the text and their syntactic relationships and by analyzing the coherence relations among these propositions, which are often, but not always, signaled by cohesion markers at the linguistic level. Inferences, such as simple bridging inferences or pronoun identification, are often necessary to arrive at a coherent microstructure. Several models of microstructure for-

mation have been proposed, such as the construction-integration (CI) model of Kintsch (1988, 1998), the landscape model (van den Broek, Risden, Fletcher, & Thurlow, 1996) and the Langston, Trabasso, and Magliano (1998) model.

However, there is more to the meaning of a text than word meanings and the interrelationships between propositions. Whole sections of a text are also related semantically in specific ways. That is, the microstructure itself is organized into higher-order units. This global structure of a text is called the *macrostructure.* Macrostructure formation involves the recognition of global topics and their interrelationships, which are frequently conventionalized according to familiar rhetorical schemata (see Le, 2002, for demonstration that macrostructure formation can be modeled within the framework of the CI model). Microstructure and macrostructure together are called the *textbase.*

- *The textbase represents the meaning of the text, as it is actually expressed by the text.* But if a reader only comprehends what is explicitly expressed in a text, comprehension will be shallow, sufficient perhaps to reproduce the text, but not for deeper understanding. For that, the text content must be used to construct a *situation model;* that is, a mental model of the situation described by the text. Generally, this requires the integration of information provided by the text with relevant prior knowledge and the goals of the comprehender. A model in the tradition of the CI model that focuses on the situation level rather than the propositional textbase has been investigated by Louwerse (2002). Similarly, Schmalhofer, McDaniel, and Keefe (2002) have extended the CI model so that it explicitly accounts for the interaction of the propositional level and the situation model level. One important fact to note about the process of constructing situation models is that it is not restricted to the verbal domain. It frequently involves imagery, emotions, and personal experiences.

We illustrate these processes with a simple example. The text is an instructional text about the functioning of the heart, entitled "The Circulatory System." In figure 12.1, the macrostructure of the text is diagrammed: it is signaled explicitly in the text by five subheadings; the last section, which is quite long, is further subdivided into three topical subsections.

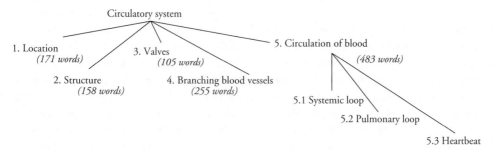

**Figure 12.1** A diagram of the macrostructure of an instructional text about the functioning of the human heart.

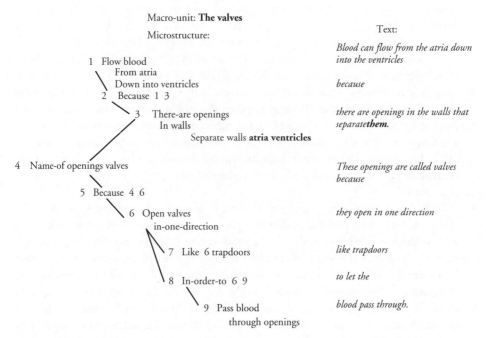

**Figure 12.2**    A sample of the microstructure based on two sentences from "The Valves" section of the instructional text on the heart.

Figure 12.2 shows an example of the microstructure of the text, specifically, the first two sentences of the macro-unit "The Valves." Note the hierarchical organization of the microstructure with the proposition introducing the concept VALVES at the top of the hierarchy. Not all relations among propositions are shown in the graph (e.g., the repetition of BLOOD in Propositions 1 and 9). The construction of the microstructure very closely follows the linguistic structure of the sentences. One relation is left implicit in the text, such that an inferential process is required to identify the referents of the pronoun "them" in the first sentence (this process is referred to as "anaphor resolution," which we will discuss further below).

The situation model constructed on the basis of these two sentences is shown in figure 12.3. This situation model is a diagrammatic representation of the human heart, showing that it is divided into two halves, and each half comprises an upper chamber (the atrium) separated by a valve from the lower chamber (the ventricle). The situation model contains much more than the information expressed in the two sentences under discussion. To understand these sentences, the reader must retrieve prior knowledge about the heart and integrate it with the new information provided by the text. The prior information (which for some readers might be prior knowledge about the heart but in this case is also information presented earlier in the text) is depicted with dotted lines: it involves the spatial layout of the chambers of the heart and their corresponding names. A reader who does not retrieve this information from his or her memory and integrate it with the new information provided by the text does not really understand the text, even if he or she formed a correct textbase. Such a reader might be able to reproduce the text by rote, or

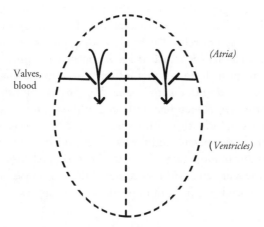

**Figure 12.3** A depiction of information that could be represented in the situation model based on the two sentences from "The Valves" section presented in figure 12.2. Information that must be drawn from prior knowledge is indicated with dotted lines or parentheses; information that is explicitly stated in the sentences is indicated with solid lines.

even make some semantic judgments: for instance, on the basis of the hierarchical textbase shown in figure 12.2, the reader could say that the sentences were about "valves." However, this reader could not make correct inferences about the functioning of the heart.

With this overview and intuitive example in hand, we now examine further some of the processes involved in construction of the textbase and the situation model. Of course, there are many more processes involved than can be discussed here, and so our discussion is limited to an illustrative sample of the many component processes that are considered fundamental to text comprehension.

Before we begin, a brief discussion of some of the performance measures used to assess comprehension processes may be helpful for some readers. In general, the various measures used are of two basic kinds, *on-line* and *off-line*. On-line measures are those that are taken while a participant is reading. One widely used on-line measure is reading time, or recording of the time spent reading a particular region of text (which may range from a word to a phrase or sentence to an entire section of text). Other on-line measures include speeded response tasks that are performed during reading, such as lexical decision (i.e., deciding as quickly as possible whether a string of letters forms an English word), naming (i.e., pronouncing a visually presented word as quickly as possible), and recognition (i.e., deciding as quickly as possible whether a word appeared earlier in the text or not). Response times from these kinds of tasks are often used to infer the relative activation of various concepts or inferences. Off-line measures are those that are taken after a participant is done reading. Off-line measures come in many forms, although they usually involve some form of test question (e.g., free recall, short answer, multiple choice, problem solving). The kinds of questions typically used vary in the extent to which they tap primarily memory for the text material, deeper understanding of the content, or both.

Both on-line and off-line measures have advantages and disadvantages. For example, because on-line measures are temporally closer to the actual processing of the text, they tend to support more fine-grained inferences about the nature of the underlying processes. However, many of the on-line measures are somewhat disruptive and may encourage task-specific strategies that may not reflect "normal" reading processes. Additionally, some of the on-line measures may reflect transient activation of conceptual information rather than the more permanent inclusion of that information into the final representation. In contrast, off-line measures do not disrupt the reading process, and they are more indicative of the more lasting representational outcome of those processes. However, off-line measures tend to be less informative with respect to specific aspects of the way in which particular reading processes operate, and they are also subject to reconstructive processes at time of test or loss due to forgetting. Ultimately, text comprehension – both the underlying processes and the representational outcomes of those processes – will best be understood with converging evidence from multiple different measures.

## Textbase Formation

As mentioned above, an important aspect of constructing the textbase involves combining word meanings to form propositions and then establishing the interrelationships between these propositions to generate the microstructure of the text. There are several different dimensions along which propositions may be related. For example, the content of two or more propositions may be related because of logical implication, because of cause and effect relationships, or because of reference to the same entity or event. This latter form of relation is referred to as *coreference* (or argument overlap), which is perhaps the most common dimension along which propositions are assumed to be related to one another. Below, we examine the factors that influence how readers establish coreference to illustrate one way in which propositions may be interrelated.

As was also mentioned previously, a textbase consists of a macrostructure as well as the microstructure formed by establishing connections between propositions. In relative terms, much less research has focused on macrostructure formation than on microstructure formation. However, one area of research relevant to understanding macrostructure formation has explored how readers identify the higher-level ideas or topics around which the microlevel units are organized and interrelated, which we discuss further below.

### *Establishing coreference: anaphor resolution*

Often, coreference is made explicit in the text, when the same words are used to refer to the same concepts (e.g., "*Dan* backed his *car* out of the garage. Unfortunately, *Dan* drove the *car* right over his brother's bike"). In many cases, however, the referential relationships are not explicit, such as when pronouns are used to refer back to a previously mentioned concept or when different terms are used to describe the same entities (e.g., "*Dan* backed his *car* out of the garage. Unfortunately, *he* drove the *old sedan* right over his brother's bike"). Any linguistic device that can be used to refer back to a previously mentioned concept is called an *anaphor*, and *anaphor resolution* is the psychological process of identifying the previously mentioned concept (or *referent*) to which an anaphor refers. To resolve an anaphor, one or more candidate referents must be activated in working memory and the appropriate referent must be selected for integration with the current content. An anaphor may go unresolved if no referent is active, or if no one referent is sufficiently salient to warrant selection when multiple candidates are active (e.g., Greene, McKoon, & Ratcliff, 1992). Thus, it is important to understand what factors can influence referent activation and referent selection.

As illustrated in the examples above, several different kinds of anaphor exist, including pronouns, synonyms, and repeated nouns. These various kinds of anaphor tend to serve different functions and thus have different distributional patterns in the language. Pronouns are typically used to refer to recently mentioned or focused concepts that have been explicitly introduced in the text and that are currently activated in working memory. Highly explicit anaphora are much less likely to refer to recent or salient entities, and in fact, repeated noun anaphora have been shown to slow down processing when they do (e.g., Gordon & Chan, 1995). For example, after the sentence "Bill bought a car," readers are slower to read, "Bill drove it home" than they are to read, "He drove it home." Instead of salient entities, explicit anaphora are much more likely to refer back to more distant or less salient concepts that are likely no longer active, and they also often refer to concepts that have not been explicitly mentioned. Thus, the form of the anaphor itself can provide some signaling information about where or what the appropriate referent may be.

Other sources of linguistic information also contribute to anaphor resolution. One factor is the morphosyntactic features of pronouns, such as gender and number (e.g., Carreiras, Garnham, & Oakhill, 1996), although the use of gender information may not be as general as intuition would suggest (for discussion, see McDonald & MacWhinney, 1995). Other linguistic sources of information that can provide information about the appropriate referents for anaphora include structural factors, including various syntactic constraints (e.g., whether a potential referent participates in the same clause as the anaphor; whether the referent is in a syntactically prominent position), order of mention within a sentence (e.g., Gernsbacher, 1990), and structural parallelism. According to the heuristic of structural parallelism, a potential referent that holds the same grammatical role as the anaphor is preferred over one that does not. As one demonstration of the operation of this heuristic in anaphor resolution, Chambers and Smyth (1998) presented readers with short texts in which a context sentence was followed by a sentence containing an ambiguous pronoun in either the subject or object position. For example, (1) was followed by either (2) or (3):

(1)  *Leonard handed Michael a sandwich.*
(2)  *Then he passed Carla an apple.*
(3)  *Then Carla passed him an apple.*

Readers were much more likely to resolve the pronoun *he* in (2) as referring to *Leonard*, whereas they were much more likely to resolve the pronoun *him* in (3) as referring to *Michael*.

In addition to linguistic factors, various semantic factors can also influence anaphor resolution. One widely researched semantic factor concerns the *implicit causality* of verbs, which refers to "a property of transitive verbs in which one or the other of the verb's arguments is implicated as the underlying cause of the action or attitude" (Long & De Ley, 2000, p. 546). For example, the verb *question* implicates the sentence's subject as the cause of the questioning, as in (4), whereas the verb *praise* implicates the sentence's object as the cause of the praising, as in (5).

(4)    *John questioned Chris because he wanted the correct answers.*
(5)    *John praised Chris because he knew the correct answers.*

The influence of implicit causality on anaphor resolution is apparent in the bias of readers to prefer the causally implicated entity as the referent of an anaphor (e.g., Stewart, Pickering, & Sanford, 2000).

In addition to the semantic information associated with particular words such as verbs or connectives, semantic information at the discourse level can also influence anaphor resolution. For example, contextual information can establish pragmatic plausibility that favors one potential referent over another. Upon reading

(6)    *Scott stood watching while Henry fell down some stairs. He ran for a doctor.*

*Scott* is a much more plausible referent for *he* than is *Henry*, given that someone who just fell down the stairs is unlikely to be able to run anywhere. Indeed, various studies have shown that pragmatic plausibility as well as other forms of discourse-level semantic information (e.g., discourse focus) can influence anaphor resolution (e.g., Gordon & Scearce, 1995; Stevenson, Knott, Oberlander, & McDonald, 2000).

The various sources of information that can be used to identify the referent for an anaphor will be more or less relevant to resolving different kinds of anaphora, because they are more or less relevant given the situations in which those different anaphora tend to be used. For instance, to the extent that more explicit anaphora are used to refer back to distant entities, structural parallelism is unlikely to exert much influence on resolution of these anaphora because surface-level information about the referent's sentence structure will have been lost during the processing of intervening sentences. In contrast, structural factors are more likely to factor in to the resolution of pronominal anaphora, as pronouns tend to occur in the same local context as their referent. Likewise, the degree of semantic overlap between the anaphor and the referent is likely to play an important role in the resolution of many noun anaphora that require the reactivation of the referent entity, to the extent that such overlap serves as a retrieval cue. However, this factor is much less relevant for resolving pronouns because they are semantically impoverished and their referent is likely to still be active upon their encounter.

Although the influence of a given factor on anaphor resolution may depend upon the form of anaphor to be resolved, one proposal is that the same basic constraint-satisfaction process underlies anaphor resolution in all cases. Current research that focuses on how these various factors interact and the time course of their respective contributions to anaphor resolution (e.g., the extent to which a factor influences activation, selection, or both) promises to shed light on this issue.

## *Macrostructure formation: topic identification*

Establishing connections between propositions that are referentially, causally, logically, or otherwise related is one important step in constructing the textbase. However, another important step is to represent the macrostructure of the text, which involves relating larger units of text into a topical structure. One key aspect of this process involves identifying the important themes or topics in a text. In some cases, a text may contain *signaling devices* that explicitly indicate topical information, such as when the theme of a text is explicitly provided by an appropriate title or when the topics of a text are explicitly indicated by outlines, summaries, or section headers (as was the case in the instructional text on the human heart described earlier). Such signaling devices have been shown to improve subsequent recall for the topics discussed within a text as well as organization of those topics (e.g., Lorch, Lorch, & Inman, 1993).

But many texts will not contain signaling devices that explicitly indicate the topical structure of the text, and research has shown that various factors will influence the content that readers identify as the important topical information in these cases. Many of these factors are surface cues, such as typeface, rhetorical cues, repetition of concept words, or structural features of the text. For example, Surber (2001) demonstrated that the degree of repetition of a concept label can influence the extent to which readers identify that concept as an important topic. Concepts that appeared frequently in the text were either referred to using the same concept label each time or were referred to using nonrepeating labels (e.g., paraphrases). Additionally, half of the target concepts were actually important topics and half were unimportant topics. After reading the text, participants were given a topic recall test in which they were asked to list the main topics and subtopics. Target concepts were listed more often in the repetition condition than in the nonrepetition condition, regardless of the actual importance of the information.

As a further example of the influence of surface cues on topic identification, Budd, Whitney, and Turley (1995) note that readers often assume that the first sentence of a text or paragraph contains important topical or thematic information. Indeed, reading times for initial sentences can be 500–1,000 ms longer than for comparable sentences. Budd et al. presented readers with short texts that began with a topic sentence followed by several sentences that provided supporting details. In one condition, the texts were presented intact. In a second condition, the topic sentence was removed such that the first sentence of the paragraph was one that provided detail information. Reading times for the detail sentence were significantly longer when it was the first sentence of the text than when it was the second sentence of the text (i.e., when the topic sentence was presented) and were just as long as reading times for the topic sentences. In a similar study, Kieras (1980) had participants read short texts that each had a target sentence expressing the intended theme of the text. The target sentence either appeared as the first sentence of the text or was embedded in the middle of the text. Immediately after reading a text, participants were asked to write a short sentence that described the main idea or theme of the text. The responses were closer to the target sentence in content when the target appeared at the beginning of the text rather than in the middle. Likewise, the responses were more similar in content to the alternate first sentence when it appeared first rather than in the middle, even though it did not express the main thematic information. Kieras found similar results in a second experiment using texts that each contained two related topics that could be discussed in either order. Participants were then given a two-alternative forced choice task for each text in which they were to decide which of two statements was a better title for the text (each title only mentioning one of the two topics in the text). Readers' choices were heavily influenced by which topic had been discussed first in the text.

Kieras also showed that for a subset of the texts in which one topic was conceptually superordinate to the other (e.g., whole–part relationship), readers' choices were also biased to favor the superordinate topic over the subordinate topic overall, although the strength of the bias was weaker when inconsistent with order of mention. Nonetheless, this superordinate bias demonstrates a role for semantic factors in addition to surface-level cues in identifying important topics or themes. Several other studies have subsequently established the role of semantic content in topic identification (e.g., Goldman, Saul, & Coté, 1995; Hyönä, 1994). For example, Hyönä (1994) showed longer reading times on sentences that introduced new topics (relative to topic continuation sentences equated along important characteristics such as length and syntactic structure), even when using a sentence-by-sentence presentation mode that did not denote paragraph boundaries.

Finally, topic identification may be influenced by a reader's prior knowledge. Relevant prior knowledge may include knowledge about the typical structure of texts within a domain or text genre, although this sort of knowledge may be more important for narratives (most of which have similar discourse structures) than for expository texts. Readers can also rely upon knowledge about content within the domain. For example, Dee-Lucas and Larkin (1988) presented beginning learners and advanced learners in physics (two to three undergraduate physics courses versus graduate-level training in physics, respectively) with instructional texts containing target sentences in one of two versions. In both versions, the substantive content of the target sentence was the same, but the content was presented either as a definition or as a fact. After reading the text, individuals were asked to rate the importance of each sentence in the text. The beginning learners rated the target sentences as more important when presented as definitions than when presented as facts, suggesting that they had developed a rudimentary understanding that definitions are generally more important than facts. In contrast, the ratings of the advanced learners did not differ with version, presumably because they could assess the importance of the information based on its content rather than having to rely on a less discriminating, category-membership heuristic.

In sum, various sources of information can influence topic identification, an important component in the process of representing the macrostructure in a textbase. Of course, topic identification is not the only macrolevel process involved in textbase construction. However, much less research has explored macrolevel processes than microlevel processes, and thus further investigating how macrostructures are represented will be an important issue for future research.

# The Situation Model

As outlined earlier, the textbase represents the meaning actually expressed by the text. But deeper comprehension also depends upon the construction of a *situation model*, or the representation of the situation described by the text. This is primarily achieved via the integration of information provided by the text with relevant prior knowledge. Thus, inferencing is critically involved in forming a situation model.

## *Inferences*

Inferences are necessary in constructing the textbase (at both the micro and macro levels), and they play a crucial role in forming a coherent situation model. Texts are almost never fully explicit, so there are always gaps left to be filled in by the reader. The gaps may be local as in

(7)    *Fred parked the car. He locked the door,*

where the reader must realize that the *door* is the

(8)    *car door.*

Or the gaps may be global, as when the theme of a story is not explicitly stated and left for the reader to construct, or when a reader must realize that a particular paragraph in an essay provides an example for a point made earlier. This gap filling has tradition- ally been labeled "inference." This is a somewhat unfortunate terminology because it lumps together processes that are quite distinct psychologically and that differ dramati- cally in the demands they make on the reader (Kintsch, 1993, 1998). First, inferences vary along a dimension from automatic to controlled. Automatic inferences are made quickly and easily, such as the bridging inference linking *car* and *door* in (7). Controlled processes, on the other hand, can be highly resource demanding, as is the case, for instance, if a text requires syllogistic reasoning. A second dimension along which infer- ences in text comprehension vary is whether they are knowledge-based or text-based. Example (7) involves a typical knowledge-based inference – the reader knows that cars have doors. In contrast, if we conclude from

(9)    *Fred is taller than Mary and Mary is taller then Tim.*

that

(10)    *Fred is taller than Tim,*

we are not using what we already knew about *Fred* and *Tim*, but must employ the infor- mation provided by the text. In the literature, all these psychologically rather distinct processes are called "inferences" – but it is crucial that we keep in mind the important differences between various types of inference in text comprehension. (And it almost goes without saying that most of these inferences have nothing to do with what logicians call inference.)

The principal question about inferences in text comprehension has been what types of inferences are made and when they are made. On the one hand, one can focus on all the inferences that can plausibly be made (e.g., Graesser, 1981). Of course, not all readers will actually generate all inferences at all times. So what do readers actually do? This simple question turns out not to have a simple answer. Whether or not a reader draws a particular inference depends on a great many factors. Under some conditions, readers are minimalists (McKoon & Ratcliff, 1992), making only those inferences that are absolutely needed to understand the text. For instance, (7) cannot be understood without making the bridging inference linking *car* and *door*; but (9) can be understood perfectly well, and many readers will not bother to figure out the relationship between Fred and Tim, unless asked to do so. On the other hand, it is easy to find conditions under which readers are far more active than minimally required (Graesser, Singer, & Trabasso, 1994). For instance, readers typically infer causal antecedents but not causal consequences (Magliano, Baggett, Johnson, & Graesser, 1993). Given

(11)    *The clouds gathered quickly and it became ominously dark.*
(12)    *The downpour lasted only 10 minutes.*

readers infer

(13)    *The clouds caused rain.*

But given only (11) readers do not necessarily jump to the conclusion (13). However, under the right conditions, it is quite possible to get readers to make predictive inferences (Klin, Guzmán, & Levine, 1999; Klin, Murray, Levine, & Guzmán, 1999).

What happens when a reader "makes the inferences" illustrated above? Is it a slow active process or a rapid, automatic one? Often, it is just that a piece of relevant knowledge is retrieved, such as that *cars* have *doors* or that *dark clouds* bring *rain*. It is not an active, controlled, effortful process, but rather happens quickly and relatively automatically. Kintsch (1998) argued that retrieval structures in long-term memory rapidly make available the relevant knowledge when the reader reads (7) or (11); similarly, Myers and O'Brien (1998) talk about a resonance process that provides the link between *car* and *door*, or *cloud* and *rain*. The fact that antecedent causal inferences are more likely than predictive inferences does not mean that the knowledge does not become available in the latter case, only that it is more likely to be used when it is linked to two items – (11) and (12) in the example above – than when it is only linked to one (Kintsch, 1998; Schmalhofer, McDaniel, & Keefe, 2002).

Many inferences in text comprehension are straightforward cases of knowledge activation. Automatic knowledge activation will work well as long as the text is in a highly familiar domain. However, the importance of active, controlled, constructive inferencing in comprehension can hardly be overestimated, especially with expository texts in less familiar topic domains. When we read a text in order to learn from it, by definition we are no longer on the kind of highly familiar ground where we can rely on retrieval structures to activate relevant knowledge. It is still necessary, however, to retrieve whatever relevant prior knowledge and experience we have, which can be a very effortful process, requiring conscious control. Without this effort, no learning is possible – the textual information will remain inert knowledge at best, not linked up with existing knowledge structures, and hence unusable.

Resource demanding, controlled inference processes in text comprehension are not restricted to knowledge retrieval. The situation model for a literary text may require construction at more than one level of analysis; to understand a story, the reader may have to infer the protagonists' motivations; to understand an argument, the exact relations between its components may have to be analyzed. Deep understanding always goes beyond the text in non-trivial ways, requiring the construction of meaning, not just passive absorption of information.

### *Knowledge representation*

Comprehension requires inferences, and inferences require knowledge. Hence to understand text comprehension we must be able to understand how knowledge is used and how it is represented. Most psychological (and linguistic and artificial intelligence) models of knowledge representation are toy models that cannot deal with the sheer amount of information in human knowledge. Recently, however, Latent Semantic Analysis (LSA) has become available, which provides psychologists at least with a tolerably good approximation to human knowledge representation (Landauer, 1998; Landauer & Dumais, 1997; see also the website at http://lsa.colorado.edu).

LSA is a machine learning method that constructs a geometric representation of meaning that resembles the structure of human knowledge about words and texts. It constructs this representation simply from observing the contexts in which words are used in a large number of texts. Formally, the problem faced by LSA might be characterized by an equation that expresses the meaning of a document as a function of its words, their order, and interrelationships, as well as the (verbal and nonverbal) context (Landauer, 2002):

(13)     *meaning(document)* = *f{word$_1$, word$_2$, word$_3$, . . . word$_n$, context}*

To solve this equation (for a large number of documents), LSA makes some simplifying assumptions:

(14)     *meaning(document$_1$)* = *meaning(word$_{11}$)* + *meaning(word$_{12}$)* + . . . *meaning(word$_{1n}$)*
*meaning(document$_2$)* = *meaning(word$_{21}$)* + *meaning(word$_{22}$)* + . . . *meaning(word$_{2m}$)*

$\cdot$
$\cdot$
$\cdot$

*meaning(document$_k$)* = *meaning(word$_{k1}$)* + *meaning(word$_{k2}$)* + . . . *meaning(word$_{1kz}$)*

In other words, we disregard word order, syntax, as well as all context, and take the meaning of a document to be just the meaning of a bag of words. These are drastic simplifications, but, as we will see, enough information is retained in this way to produce useful results.

Consider a corpus of 11 M word tokens, 90 K word types, and 40 K documents, consisting of texts a typical high-school graduate might have read. This corpus clearly underspecifies word meanings, and is furthermore inconsistent. What LSA does is to extract from such a corpus a semantic representation that does not attempt to specify "the meaning" of each word and document in absolute terms (like a dictionary or encyclopedia would), but determines only the relations among all the words and documents. That is, LSA defines meaning as the relationship of a word (or document) to all other words and documents in the corpus. LSA does this by constructing a high-dimensional semantic space, using a standard mathematical technique called singular value decomposition for optimal dimension reduction to eliminate noise in the data.

Semantic relatedness in the LSA space is measured by the cosine between vectors representing words or documents, a statistic much like the familiar correlation coefficient. The cosine between randomly chosen words is .02 +/− .04. Below are some examples that show that the similarity measure calculated by LSA yields results not unlike human intuition:

*doctor–doctors* .79
*doctor–physician* .61
*go–went* .71
*good–bad* .65
*she–her* .98
*blackbird–bird* .46
*blackbird–black* .04
*telephone– shark* .01
*telephone–justice* .01

Note that in the original corpus, co-occurrence of the words *doctor* and *doctors* (or between singular and plural, in general) is quite low, because when one talks about a singular entity one rarely also mentions the plural, and vice versa. LSA, however, has inferred that these singulars and plurals are quite similar in meaning (not identical, though), because singular and plural forms tend to occur in similar contexts.

Many words have more than one meaning, and most have several senses, depending on context. In LSA, meaning is context free, but note that in a high-dimensional space, complex relationships can be naturally represented. For instance, the homonym *mint* has (at least) three senses, as in *leaves of a plant, flavored candy,* and *coin money.* The cosines between the word *mint* and these three phrases are .20, .23, and .33, respectively. Thus, *mint* is strongly related to each of these phrases that involve different meanings, even though these three phrases are not related to each other (the average cosine between the three phrases is only .05; for a more detailed treatment of polysemy in LSA, see Kintsch, 2001).

LSA is not restricted to computing the semantic similarities among words. Sentences and whole texts can be represented in the same semantic space, and hence can be readily compared with each other. The similarity measures that LSA computes for texts correlate well with human judgments, as is most dramatically shown by the ability of LSA-based systems to grade essays as well as expert human graders do (Landauer, Laham, & Foltz, 2000). LSA is not, however, a model of human comprehension processes; it is simply a representational system that allows researchers to represent the meaning of words and texts in such a way that the relations among the words and texts represented in LSA closely resemble human semantic judgments. It thus opens up numerous exciting possibilities for research and applications, only a few of which have so far been explored.

## Situational dimensions

As discussed in the sections above, constructing a situation model involves inferences that usually depend upon general world knowledge. These inferences are often critical for representing the relationships between the entities and events described in the text. Zwaan and Radvansky (1998) have reviewed research suggesting that situation models can include representation of relationships along several different dimensions. Among other possible dimensions, research shows that situation models can include representations of the spatial locations of entities and events, the temporal relations between events, the causal relationships between actions or events, the goals and motives of protagonists, and the characteristics of protagonists and other important entities.

In much of the previous research, each of these dimensions has been examined in isolation. However, motivated by the observation that many of the situational dimensions are interrelated and that a full understanding of many texts will require representation of multiple dimensions, more recent research has begun investigating two or more dimensions at a time (e.g., Zwaan, Magliano, & Graesser, 1995). Recent theoretical work has also focused on accounting for processing along multiple dimensions. Zwaan and Radvansky (1998) propose a general framework for situation model processing in which they distinguish between the current model (i.e., the part of the model being constructed at time $T_n$) and the integrated model (i.e., the situation model that has been constructed from time $T_1$ through time $T_{n-1}$). A critical process in situation model construction involves incorporating the current model into the integrated model, which Zwaan and Radvansky refer to as *updating*. As a theoretical account of the updating process, they further describe the *event-indexing model* (Zwaan, Langston, & Graesser, 1995). A slightly more general formulation of the model can be stated as follows: consistent with previous research mentioned above, the events and entities represented in situation models can be related along several possible dimensions. Importantly, the ease of updating the integrated model – that is, the ease of incorporating the current model into the integrated model – will depend upon how many dimensions are shared between the entities and events of the current model and the integrated model. As predicted by the model, initial results show that rated coherence increases and reading times decrease additively with increases in the number of dimensions along which the content of a sentence is related to previous content.

## The role of working memory in text comprehension

As should be apparent at this point, a great deal of processing is involved in text comprehension, including linguistic-level processes, semantic processes to form the text base, and knowledge retrieval and integration to form the situation model. An assumption common to all models of comprehension is that all information processing must take place in a finite capacity working memory. For instance, if two concepts never co-occur in working memory during the processing of a text, no new associations between these concepts will be formed as a consequence of reading this text. This postulate sets severe limits on the comprehension process, especially because the capacity of short-term memory, upon which working memory must rely, at least in part, is known to be quite small, only about four chunks.

If all processing depends on working memory, and working memory is so severely limited in terms of its capacity, variations in the capacity of working memory among individual readers ought to be closely related to comprehension. Daneman and Carpenter (1980) measured working memory capacity in the context of a reading task by asking subjects to read a series of sentences and then recall the last word from each sentence. Working memory measured in this way (referred to as *reading span*) correlates quite well with reading comprehension. Reading span differs among individuals, varying between about 2 and 6, and is a reliable predictor of performance on conventional reading comprehension tests (including the SAT), as well as inferencing (Singer, Halldorson, Lear, & Andrusiak, 1992). However, while the reading span is a good predictor of individual differences in reading comprehension, it can be argued that estimates of working memory capacity arrived at in this way are too low to be able to account for everything a good reader must maintain in working memory: crucial fragments of the prior text, including its macrostructure, linguistic knowledge, relevant world knowledge, reading goals – a list much too long for even the highest reading span yet encountered. An explanation for this apparent discrepancy was provided by Ericsson and Kintsch (1995) and Kintsch, Patel, and Ericsson (1999) who introduced the concept of long-term working memory. Working memory, when we are reading a text in a familiar domain, is composed not only of a limited-capacity short-term memory but also includes a long-term component. This component contains all items in the reader's long-term memory that are linked to the current contents of short-term memory (which for this purpose can be equated with consciousness or focus of attention) via retrieval structures. Thus, retrieval structures make available information stored in long-term memory that is directly relevant to the task at hand without the need for time- and resource-consuming retrieval processes.

Retrieval structures, however, are characteristic of performance in expert domains, and, indeed, are limited to expert domains. Long-term working memory allows the chess master to "see" the next move without having to figure it out; it makes it possible for the experienced physician to integrate patient data, medical knowledge, and prior experience to arrive at an intuitive diagnosis; and it is the basis for reading comprehension, for when we are reading texts in familiar domains, we are all experts, having practiced comprehension for many years. Retrieval structures exist only in domains where people have acquired expertise, which requires a great deal of practice. Thus, the chess master and the physician are not necessarily better than anyone else outside their domain of expertise. Most people reading a paper in theoretical physics do not readily comprehend it as they comprehend the daily newspaper, or as a physicist would comprehend the physics paper. Rather than fluent reading, their reading in the latter case would be an arduous and frustrating problem-solving activity.

The concept of long-term working memory allows us to understand how readers can juggle all the things they need for comprehension in working memory. It also suggests a reinterpretation of the reading span data: it is not the capacity of working memory that varies among individuals, but the skill with which they are using this capacity. High-span readers are readers who have a high level of reading expertise: they are fluent decoders who easily organize detailed information into a hierarchical macrostructure, and who possess rich, well-elaborated knowledge of word meanings. Their efficient processing allows them to effectively employ their retrieval structures as they comprehend and enables them to recall many words. In contrast, inefficient lower-level reading processes are characteristic of readers with low reading spans.

Expert comprehension, thus, is a highly automated process, relying on readily available retrieval structures. To establish these retrieval structures, extensive practice is required. This raises a dilemma for the development of comprehension skills. Novice comprehension obviously cannot rely on automatized skills. Instead, active strategic processes must compensate for the lacking retrieval structures that make comprehension easy for the expert. The novice comprehender reading unfamiliar material must expend considerable effort, and expend it in just the right way, to achieve adequate results. A major difficulty for comprehension instruction therefore is to engage novice comprehension in the kind of active, strategic processing that is necessary to build good situation models. All too easily, novice comprehenders are satisfied with forming a reasonably accurate textbase, neglecting the more effortful construction of a situation model. But that results in shallow comprehension, which is insufficient for deep understanding and learning from texts.

## Summary

Text comprehension is a complex process, requiring the involvement of many different components, relying upon many different kinds of information, and yielding complex mental representations. No one chapter can examine every process involved at a level of detail that would do justice to their importance and complexity. Instead, we hope to have met the more modest goals of highlighting the inherent complexity of text comprehension, introducing the reader to several of the key processes thought to underlie comprehension, and pointing to relevant bodies of literature for more interested readers. Indeed, many of the processes mentioned herein enjoy substantial bodies of research that have been directed at understanding how each component process operates. Almost all of the extant research on text comprehension has focused on identifying and examining the various component processes in isolation, which has gone a long way toward furthering our understanding of how comprehension works. However, text comprehension is not simply the sum of the activity of these various processes, but *arises from their coordinated operation as a system.* Thus, an important direction for future research will be to examine the interaction of the various components to understand how they work together as a system to give rise to comprehension.

# 13

# The Acquisition of Reading Comprehension Skill

## Charles A. Perfetti, Nicole Landi, and Jane Oakhill

How do people acquire skill at comprehending what they read? That is the simple question to which we shall try to make a tentative answer. To begin, we have to acknowledge some complexities about the concept of reading comprehension and what it means to develop it.

## Introduction: Simple Ideas about Reading Comprehension

We can expect the comprehension of written language to approximate the comprehension of spoken language. When that happens, then reading comprehension has developed, for practical purposes, to its limiting or asymptotic level. (It is possible for reading comprehension skill to develop so as to exceed listening comprehension skill, but that is another matter.) All other limitations are imposed by linguistic abilities, relevant knowledge, and general intelligence. If we make things more complex than this, we push onto the concept of reading comprehension all these other important aspects of cognition, with the muddle that results from conceptual conflation.

This simple idea that the acquisition of reading comprehension is learning to understand writing as well as one understands spoken language has empirical justification. At the beginning of learning to read, the correlations between reading and spoken language comprehension are small (Curtis, 1980; Sticht & James, 1984). This is because at the beginning, children are learning to decode and identify words, so it is these word-reading processes that limit comprehension. However, as children move beyond the beginnings of learning to read, the correlations between reading comprehension and spoken language comprehension increase and then level out by high school (Sticht & James, 1984). As children learn to read words, the limiting factor in reading comprehension shifts from word recognition to spoken language comprehension. For adult college student samples, the correlation between scores on reading comprehension and listening comprehension tests reaches $r = .90$ (Gernsbacher, 1990).

If this were the end of the story, then the study of reading comprehension would fold completely into the study of language comprehension. However, there is probably more to the story. First are some methodological considerations. Studies that compare reading comprehension with listening comprehension avoid the confounding of materials, making a clean comparison between the same or equivalent passages with only the "modality" (speech or writing) different. But for most people, what they usually hear is different in content and style from what they read. These differences extend through formal, semantic, and pragmatic dimensions of language. Thus, what is necessary for experimental control is problematic for authenticity. Second, one must make a decision about the speech rate in such comparisons. What is the proper rate for a comparison with reading? The listener's preference? The speaker's preference? A rate equal to the reading rate? Finally, we take note of a more interesting possibility; namely that literacy may alter the way people process spoken language (Olson, 1977). If so, this would boost the correlation of listening and reading comprehension in adulthood.

We accept, approximately and in an idealized form, the assumption that reading comprehension is the joint product of printed word identification and listening comprehension, an idea famously asserted by Gough and Tunmer (1986) as a simple view of reading. However, we also must assume that learning to read with comprehension brings enough additional complexities to justify a chapter on how that happens.

## A Framework for Comprehension

Comprehension occurs as the reader builds a mental representation of a text message. (For a review of current ideas about reading comprehension in adults, see Kintsch & Rawson, current volume.) This situation model (Van Dijk & Kintsch, 1983) is a representation of what the text is about. The comprehension processes that bring about this representation occur at multiple levels across units of language: word level, (lexical processes), sentence level (syntactic processes), and text level. Across these levels, processes of word identification, parsing, referential mapping, and a variety of inference processes all contribute, interacting with the reader's conceptual knowledge, to produce a mental model of the text.

Questions of cognitive architecture emerge in any attempt to arrange these processes into a framework for comprehension. The various knowledge sources can interact freely, or with varying degrees of constraint. For example, computing simple syntactic representations (parsing) probably is more independent of nonlinguistic knowledge than is generating inferences. These issues of cognitive architecture are important, complex, and contentious; we will not discuss them further. Instead, we assume a general framework that exposes the processes of comprehension without making strong assumptions about constraints on their interactions. Figure 13.1 represents this framework schematically.

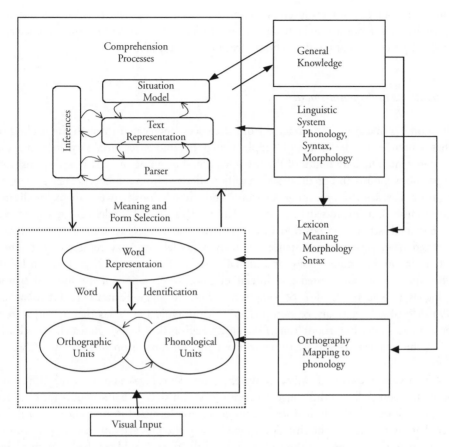

**Figure 13.1** The components of reading comprehension from identifying words to comprehending texts. Adapted from Perfetti (1999).

Within Figure 13.1 are two major classes of processing events: (1) the identification of words, and (2) the engagement of language processing mechanisms that assemble these words into messages. These processes provide contextually appropriate word meanings, parse word strings into constituents, and provide inferential integration of sentence information into more complete representations of extended text. These representations are not the result of exclusively linguistic processes, but are critically enhanced by other knowledge sources.

Within this framework, acquiring skill in reading comprehension may include developments in all these components. However, if we focus on reading, as opposed to language comprehension in general, then the unique development concerns printed words. All other processes apply to spoken as well as written language. Children must come to readily identify words and encode their relevant meaning into the mental representation that they are constructing. Although in a chapter on comprehension, we avoid dwelling on word identification, we cannot ignore it completely. Comprehension cannot be successful without the identification of words and the retrieval of their meanings. Both children and adults with low levels of comprehension may also have problems with lexical representations, a point to which we shall return later. First we address the sentence and text-level processes that are the defining features of comprehension.

## Propositions and mental models

The atoms of meaning are extracted from sentences, aggregated through the reading of other sentences of the text and supplemented by inferences necessary to make the text coherent. The bare bones of the text – its literal meaning or "text base" – consist of propositions (nouns and predicates or modifiers) derived from sentences. They are largely linguistic, based on the meanings of words and the relations between them (predicates and modifiers), as expressed in a clause. The reader's mental model can be considered an extended set of propositions that includes inferences as well as propositions extracted from actual text sentences. A mental model also may represent text information in an integrated nonpropositional format (Garnham, 1981; Johnson-Laird, 1983), preserving both stated and inferable spatial information in the form of spatial analogues (Glenberg, Kruley, & Langston, 1994; Haenggi, Kintsch, & Gernsbacher, 1995; Morrow, Greenspan, & Bower, 1987). More typical are texts that are organized, not around space, but about time (Zwaan & Radvansky, 1998). Research has clearly shown that readers are very sensitive to the temporal dimension of narratives (Zwaan, 1996).

With this framework of skilled comprehension, we can ask about the acquisition of comprehension skill and differences in comprehension skill. What accounts for comprehension failure? Are the difficulties in comprehension localized in the processes of inference that are needed for the situation model? Or in the processes of meaning extraction that are required to represent the propositions of the text? To address these questions, we examine studies that compare readers who differ in comprehension skill. In most research, the assessment of comprehension is a global one, based on readers' answers to questions following the reading (usually silent, sometimes oral) of very short texts. (For a rare example of an assessment based on the differentiation of comprehension components see Hannon and Daneman, 2001.)

We first consider those processes that go beyond understanding the literal meaning of clauses and sentences. We begin with processes commonly viewed as critical to producing higher-level comprehension.

## Higher-Level Factors in Comprehension

Among the components of the comprehension framework are three that we highlight in this section: *sensitivity to story structure, inference making,* and *comprehension monitoring.* We begin with the last two, which have been proposed as important sources of comprehension development and comprehension problems.

## Inferences

The language of any text, spoken or written, is not completely explicit. Deeper comprehension – building a situation model – requires that the reader make inferences that bridge elements in the text or otherwise support the coherence necessary for comprehension. Inferences come in a variety of forms, and various taxonomies have been proposed (e.g., Graesser, Singer, & Trabasso, 1994; Zwaan & Radvansky, 1998). Among those that appear most necessary for comprehension are inferences that are needed to make a text coherent. Additionally, skilled readers make causal inferences that make sense of otherwise unconnected actions in a story (Graesser & Kruez, 1993; Trabasso & Suh, 1993). However, readers do not routinely make predictive inferences and other elaborative inferences that are not compelled by a need for either textual or causal coherence (Graesser et al., 1994; McKoon & Ratcliff, 1992).

With the acquisition of reading skill, children come to approximate the adult model of inference making. Notice that this adult model is complex because readers make only some of the inferences that are plausible within a narrative. Two broad principles seem to be in play: (1) Inference generation is costly to processing resources. (2) The reader strives to develop some degree of coherence in the mental model. This means that inferences that can be made without much cost to resources (e.g., mapping a pronoun onto an antecedent) are more likely than inferences that are resource demanding (e.g., inferring that an action described abstractly in the text was performed in a certain way – "going to school" elaborated as taking a bus to school). And it means that inferences that support coherence are more likely to be made than inferences that merely elaborate.

What about the development of inference skills? Studies suggest that young children are able to make the same inferences as older ones, but are less likely to do so spontaneously. They may only do so when prompted or questioned (Casteel & Simpson, 1991). Because knowledge also develops with age, the availability of knowledge could be a key factor in the development of inference-making ability. However, a study by Barnes, Dennis, and Haefele-Kalvaitis (1996) suggests there may be more to the development of inference making than knowledge availability. Barnes et al. taught children (6–15 years old) a novel knowledge base to criterion, and then had the children read a multi-episode story and answer inference questions that depended on the knowledge base. Controlling for knowledge availability (by conditionalizing inferencing on the knowledge recalled), Barnes et al. found age-related differences in inference making. They also found that even the youngest children, 6–7-year-olds, were sensitive to inferences needed to maintain coherence. Furthermore, less-skilled comprehenders fail to make appropriate inferences when they read. Oakhill and colleagues (Oakhill, 1993; Oakhill & Garnham, 1988; Oakhill & Yuill, 1986; Yuill & Oakhill, 1988, 1991) have found that more skilled comprehenders make anaphoric inferences and integrate information across stories better than do less-skilled comprehenders. Skilled readers are also reported to make more causal inferences than less-skilled readers (Long, Oppy, & Seely, 1997).

What explains the variability in children's tendencies to make inferences? Satisfactory explanations for observed differences in inference making are difficult because of the dependence of inferences on lower-level comprehension processes and knowledge

(Perfetti, Marron, & Foltz, 1996). Yuill and Oakhill (1991) proposed three possibilities to explain inference-making differences between skilled and less-skilled comprehenders: (1) General knowledge deficits restrict less-skilled comprehenders' inference making. (2) Less-skilled comprehenders do not know when it is appropriate to draw inferences. (3) Less-skilled comprehenders have processing limitations, which hamper their ability to make inferences and integrate text information with prior knowledge.

*A methodological digression.* In sorting through various causal possibilities, there is a pervasive experimental design issue to consider: how to define comparison groups in relation to relative skill and age. One can sample within an age or grade level and compare the more skilled with the less skilled on measures that tap processes hypothesized to produce the differences in comprehension. But any differences in inference making, for example, between a 10-year-old highly-skilled comprehender and a 10-year-old less-skilled comprehender could have arisen because of their differences in comprehension skill or amount of reading. An alternative is to match the children not on chronological age but on "comprehension age"; that is, on their assessed level of comprehension. The comparisons then are between a group of younger children who have attained the same level of comprehension as a group of older children. The older group will be low in comprehension skill relative to their age, whereas the younger group will be average in comprehension relative to their age. These comprehension age matched (CAM) designs allow some of the causal possibilities to be ruled out. If the younger children are better at inferences than the older children, this cannot be attributed to a superior comprehension of the younger group, because the groups have the same absolute level of comprehension skill. Thus, by elimination, a causal link between inference making and comprehension skill becomes more likely. However, all comparisons, whether age- or comprehension-matched, rest on the association of differences, and thus they inherit the limitations of correlational designs for making direct causal conclusions.

## Inferences as causal in comprehension skill

In trying to determine the causal status of inference ability in comprehension development, Cain and Oakhill (1999) used the comprehension-match design described above. They compared two groups, one younger and one older, matched on comprehension (CAM) and one group of age-matched skilled comprehenders, as measured by the comprehension score of the Neale Analysis of Reading Ability (Neale, 1997). Thus, less-skilled comprehenders of age 7–8 were compared with both more skilled comprehenders of the same age and with a younger comprehension matched (CAM) group of age 6. The older two groups were matched on word reading ability according to the Neale accuracy score, whereas the younger CAM group had reading accuracy commensurate with their chronological age, about one year lower than that of the older skilled and less-skilled comprehenders.

The three groups read passages and were asked questions that required one of two types of inferences, text connecting or gap-filling. In a text-connecting inference, the reader needed to make a referential link between noun phrases in successive sentences;

for example *Michael took the drink out of his bag. The orange juice was very refreshing.* Inferring that Michael took orange juice out of his bag is a text-connecting inference. The gap-filling inferences had a more global scope; for example, they required an inference about the setting of a story. One text referred to two children playing in the sand and swimming. Inferring that the children were at the beach would be a gap-filling inference. Cain and Oakhill found that skilled readers and CAM readers were better than less-skilled readers at making text-connecting inferences. On the logic of age-match and comprehension-match comparisons, their conclusion was that comprehension skill is not a cause (it could be a consequence) of text-integration skill (as measured by the ability to make text-connecting inferences). Because skilled comprehenders were better than both the age-matched less-skilled and CAM groups at making such inferences, the causal connection between gap-filling inferences and comprehension was not clarified by the study.

If the problems in inference making arise from a poor representation of the text itself, rather than some deficit in the ability to make an inference, then attending to the text could help. When Cain and Oakhill (1999) told children exactly where to look in the text for the relevant information, their performance on the text-connecting inference questions improved, but their performance on the gap-filling inference questions remained poor. The authors concluded that less-skilled readers may have different goals when reading text, perhaps focusing on reading individual words rather than striving for coherence. This suggests that the causal relation between inference making and comprehension could be partly mediated by the reader's *standard for coherence.*

As a working hypothesis, a standard for coherence broadly determines the extent to which a reader will read for understanding, make inferences, and monitor his or her comprehension. A corollary of this hypothesis is that a low standard for text coherence is a general characteristic of low skill comprehenders. Consistent with this possibility, Cain and Oakhill (1996) found that when children were prompted to tell a story, less-skilled comprehenders told stories that had local coherence, but which lacked any overall main point.

Cain and Oakhill (1999) proposed that the less-skilled and CAM readers performed more poorly on the gap-filling questions because they failed to know when to use relevant knowledge during reading. They ruled out the availability of the knowledge because a posttest showed equivalent relevant knowledge across the groups. Cain, Oakhill, Barnes, and Bryant (2001) further examined this knowledge question by creating the relevant knowledge. Children were taught an entirely new knowledge base about an imaginary planet ("Gan"), including such facts as "The bears on Gan have blue fur" and "The ponds on Gan are filled with orange juice." Once the knowledge base had been learned to criterion (perfect recall), the children heard a multi-episode story situated on the imaginary planet, and were asked both literal and inferential questions about the story. Correct responses required children to integrate information from the knowledge base with premises from the story. Even when knowledge was controlled in this way, the skilled comprehenders were still able to correctly answer more inference questions than were the less-skilled comprehenders.

Not ruled out in either of the above studies are differences in the processing resources (i.e., working memory) that are required to juggle the demands of reading. The retrieval of relevant knowledge, the retention of text information needed for the inference, and the building of the inference itself all compete with each other and with other processes (word identification and meaning retrieval). Verbal working memory tasks in fact correlate with both inference tasks and general comprehension measures (Oakhill, Cain, & Bryant, 2003a; Oakhill & Yuill, 1986). However, when we look beyond the correlations, working memory is not the critical factor in comprehension, or at least not the only one. Oakhill et al. (2003a) showed at each of two time points in the study (when the children were age 7–8 and 8–9) that inference and text integration skills were predictive of comprehension skill over and above the contribution of working memory, verbal IQ, vocabulary, and word reading accuracy. So, although working memory is likely to contribute to comprehension-related skills like inference making, it is unlikely to be the whole story.

Finally, the Cain and Oakhill (1999) study addresses a vexing problem for conclusions about the causal status of inference making. Perfetti et al. (1996) argued that before one can conclude that inference making is a cause of poor comprehension, assurance is needed that the poor comprehender has an effective representation of the basic text meaning (i.e., its literal meaning.) An impoverished representation of the word and clause meanings will make inferences difficult. Cain and Oakhill (1999) addressed this problem by measuring responses to questions about literal content (e.g., asking for the names of the characters which were explicitly given), and found no significant differences (less-skilled readers did show nonsignificantly lower scores).

On theoretical grounds, we think the complete separation of inferences from the literal meaning of a text is difficult. In the Construction-Integration processing model of comprehension (Kintsch, 1988), the production of inferences can feed back to literal propositions and strengthen their memory representation. We ought to be surprised to find no differences at all between the literal memory of children who are making inferences and those who are not. Indeed, Cain and Oakhill (1999) showed that literal memory does predict global comprehension; however, they further found that performance on both text-connecting and gap filling inferences predicted comprehension ability even when the ability to answer literal questions (and vocabulary and word reading ability) were controlled. Notice that these results clarify the unique role of inferences in global assessments of comprehension that follow reading. However, they do not verify the assumption that literal text elements are available to the reader when the inference is to be made. As far as we know, although studies have assessed answers to literal questions *after* reading, the more direct link from a given inference to the text supporting that inference has not been established.

## Comprehension monitoring

Readers who strive for coherence in their representation of a text must be able to monitor their comprehension. Monitoring allows the reader to verify his or her understanding and to make repairs where this understanding is not sensible. Skilled readers can use the detection of a comprehension breakdown (e.g., an apparent inconsistency) as a signal for rereading and repair. Less-skilled readers may not engage this monitoring process (Baker, 1984; Garner, 1980). Again the question is why not?

This question has not been answered conclusively, but some hints are provided by the many studies on monitoring. For example, a study by Hacker (1997) examined comprehension monitoring in seventh-grade, ninth-grade, and eleventh-grade students (mean ages 12 to 16 respectively), with three levels of reading ability within each grade-level. Texts contained three types of detectable problems: contradictory sentences (semantic), various formal writing errors classified as "syntactic" errors (capitalization, verb agreement), and spelling errors. The developmental pattern was increased detection of all categories of text errors with age and, within age, with reading skill. More interesting were the results of an attention manipulation, with students asked to focus on meaning or on form (spelling and grammar). Directing attention to meaning was effective for improved monitoring of meaning errors (with no reduction in detecting form errors) but only for above-average readers. For low-skilled readers, instructional focus appeared not to matter. Thus, for a skilled reader, drawing attention to meaning improves comprehension monitoring.

Low reading comprehension appears to be associated with low monitoring performance at all age levels. In the study by Hacker (1997), eleventh-grade low-skill readers were no better than ninth-grade low-skill readers and not as good as seventh-grade skilled readers. The cause of this monitoring problem evades easy explanation. When students were given an additional chance to find the errors with an examiner pointing to the line containing an error, performance improved. However, the least skilled group of readers failed to improve as much as the more skilled groups. This certainly suggests that relevant knowledge is not always used in monitoring and that there are knowledge and basic processing differences that limit monitoring among some low-skilled readers. Thus, not all the problems can be due to a "monitoring deficit." Again, reading with a certain coherence standard is necessary for monitoring to be engaged.

It is important to note that observed differences in monitoring comprehension are not independent of the reader's ability to construct an accurate representation of the sentences in the text (Otero & Kintsch, 1992; Vosniadou, Pearson, & Rogers, 1988). Vosniadou et al. (1988) studied first-, third-, and fifth-grade readers' detection of text inconsistencies compared with their detection of false sentences that contradict facts that the child could know from memory. The familiarity of the critical information proved to be important for whether the child could detect an inconsistency, based either on memory or the text. This result, while not surprising, reinforces the important point that retrieving relevant knowledge during reading is essential for monitoring. However, when they controlled the familiarity of the critical information, Vosniadou et al. (1988) found that children were as good at detecting inconsistencies based on two contradictory text sentences as they were at detecting the contradiction of a single sentence with a familiar fact. This finding suggests that at least some problems in monitoring can be characterized as a failure to encode the meaning of a sentence in a way that promotes its comparison with other information, either in the text or in memory.

A simple explanation is difficult because comprehension monitoring, like inference making, both contributes to and results from the reader's text representation. This makes it difficult to attribute comprehension problems uniquely to a general failure to monitor comprehension. Any observed problem can result from an incomplete representation of sentence meaning, a failure to activate relevant knowledge at the critical moment, a failure to monitor the coherence of the text with respect either to its internal consistency or the readers' knowledge of the world. Finally, as in the case of inference making, the standard-of-coherence hypothesis may be relevant: Comprehension monitoring failures may result from a low standard for coherence.

## Sensitivity to story structure

The genre of texts (narrative, descriptive, etc.), their linguistic styles, and the various layouts of texts all can present novel problems that are solved only by experience in reading. Among the many text genre possibilities, the simple story of the sort encountered by children in schools has attracted the most attention, and we focus here on this specific text type.

The developmental research on this topic has focused on the understanding of story structure (e.g., Smiley, Oakley, Worthen, Campione, & Brown, 1977; Stein & Glenn, 1979). What is interesting about this development is its earliness. Stein and Albro (1997) argue that story understanding depends on knowledge about the intentions that motivate human action, and conclude that this knowledge is typically acquired by age 3. If so, although the application of narrative understanding to written texts can undergo further development with reading experience, we would not expect that story structure "deficits" would limit comprehension skill. Beyond the conceptual bases for narrative, however, is the understanding that the text itself honors the narrative structure through coherence devices. Differences in this sensitivity to text coherence could lead to differences in comprehension. Indeed, a study by Yuill and Oakhill (1991) demonstrated that, when they were required to narrate a story from a picture sequence, the less-skilled comprehenders produced fewer causal connectives and made more ambiguous use of referential ties than did skilled comprehenders. The less-skilled comprehenders also had difficulties in using linguistic elements to make their stories well structured and integrated.

Less-skilled comprehenders have been found to have weakness in other aspects of text structure understanding. Cain and Oakhill (1996) required groups of skilled and less-skilled comprehenders, together with a comprehension-age match group, to tell stories prompted by a title, such as "Pirates." The less-skilled comprehenders produced more poorly structured stories than either of the other two groups. Their poorer performance relative to the comprehension-age match group indicates that the ability to produce well-structured stories is not simply a by-product of having a certain level of comprehension skill. (Again, on the logic of comprehension match, this is because the poor comprehenders and the younger, comprehension-age match group had the same absolute level of comprehension skill.) Rather, an ability to produce a well-structured story is more likely to be associated with the causes of comprehension development. A sensitivity to story structure is one possibility for a cause of this development. A standard for coherence that extends to both production and comprehension is another possibility.

Reading comprehension skill is also related to children's knowledge about particular story features: notably titles, beginnings and endings. In one study, more than 80% of skilled comprehenders could give examples of the information contained in a story title, such as "it tells you what it's about and who's in it"; whereas, only about 25% of a same-age group of less-skilled comprehenders were able to do so (Cain, 1996). Some of the less-skilled readers claimed that the title of a story provides no useful information at all. Less-skilled comprehenders were also less aware that the beginnings of stories might provide useful information about the story setting and characters. Thus, less-skilled comprehenders appear to have less explicit awareness of the features of stories that might help scaffold their mental representation of the text. However, although less-skilled comprehenders are poor at explaining the function of a variety of text features, they must have at least some implicit awareness of the use of such features, because they benefit from integrated and goal-directed titles in both comprehension and production tasks (Cain & Oakhill, 1996; Yuill & Joscelyne, 1988).

## The Linguistic-Conceptual Machinery for Comprehension

Below the higher-level aspects of comprehension are the processes that convert sentences into basic semantic content, their propositional meaning. The derivation of propositional meaning requires knowledge about syntactic forms and the meanings of words.

### Syntactic processing

Since the defining arguments by Chomsky (1965) and early research on the development of language (e.g., McNeill, 1970), the implicit assumption seems to have been that syntax should not be an issue for the development of reading. Competence in the grammar of one's native language is acquired naturally, emerging from biological dispositions through the filters of a local linguistic environment well before entry to school. Reading would naturally use this same grammatical knowledge. However, once differences in syntax between typical spoken forms and typical written forms are acknowledged (O'Donnell, 1974), the simple story is compromised. The question becomes empirical: Are the child's syntactic abilities, cultivated in a natural social environment, enough to meet the challenges of the more formal and more complex syntax that is present in written texts? We should expect that language skill differences lead to individual differences in comprehension, and, in fact, younger less-skilled readers show a wide range of problems with syntax and morphology (Fletcher, Satz, & Scholes, 1981; Stein, Cairns, & Zurif, 1984). The question is whether such problems arise from a syntactic knowledge deficit or from some other source that affects performance on syntactic tasks (such as working memory, lack of practice, or lexical processing limitations). Research with children (Crain & Shankweiler, 1988) and adults (Carpenter, Miyake, & Just, 1994) suggests that syntactic parsing problems can arise from processing limitations rather than a lack of syntactic knowledge. Comprehension difficulties may be localized at points of high processing demands, whether from syntax or other sources.

Crain and Shankweiler (1988) concluded that even less-skilled readers have the necessary syntactic abilities to comprehend the relatively complex sentences they used in their studies. For example, children as young as three years can understand restrictive relative clauses such as "A cat is holding hands with a man that is holding hands with a woman."

Thus, difficulties with syntax, when they are observed, may be in masquerade, with the real problem lying elsewhere. The "elsewhere" has been assigned to verbal working memory ability (Crain & Shankweiler, 1988; Perfetti, 1985) or difficulty processing phonological material (Bar-Shalom, Crain, & Shankweiler, 1993).

Nevertheless, there have been few thorough studies of the broader question of the syntactic abilities of less-skilled comprehenders. Accordingly, the conclusion that all syntactic difficulties originate as working memory limitations is too strong. Differences in syntactic processing can be observed in the absence of obvious phonological problems (Stothard & Hulme, 1992).

In a study of 7–9-year-olds, Oakhill et al. (2003a) found significant relations between global comprehension skill and a measure of syntactic ability (the TROG, a picture-sentence matching test, also used by Stothard and Hulme, 1992). (Relations were also found for text integration, comprehension monitoring, and working memory.) However, with verbal ability and vocabulary controlled, syntactic ability was significant at only the second of two test points. Although a more precise role for syntactic abilities, free of other factors, remains to be worked out, its role may be genuine, reflecting variability in the development of functional language skills.

Finally, gaining experience with syntactic structures that are less common in spoken than written language, e.g., the use of nominalizations, clausal noun phrases, and other more complex structures, is something that benefits from successful reading. Experience with a variety of syntactic structures should increase functional expertise in syntax and reduce the demands of complex structures on working memory.

*Working memory systems*

Understanding a sentence involves remembering words within the sentence, retrieving information from preceding text, parsing the sentence, and other processes that require resources. Working memory – one or more systems of limited capacity that both store and manipulate information – is a bottleneck for these processes. The hypothesis that working memory factors are correlated with individual differences in comprehension has received wide support (Baddeley, Logie, & Nimmo-Smith, 1985; Crain & Shankweiler, 1988; Just & Carpenter, 1992; Perfetti & Lesgold, 1977). In addition, the evidence shows it is an active working memory system rather than a passive short-term memory store that is important in reading comprehension skill (Daneman & Carpenter, 1980; Perfetti & Goldman, 1976; Seigneuric, Ehrlich, Oakhill, & Yuill, 2000).

Different subsystems of working memory have been postulated, including one that is specialized for holding and manipulating phonological information (Baddeley, 1979). Phonological working memory has a direct link to reading through the need to keep active the contents of a sentence until the end of a clause or sentence, when integrative processes complete their work and make a verbatim memory less important. A phonological memory system directly affects the comprehension of spoken language. In fact, children who are less skilled in reading comprehension show poorer memory for words they recently heard from spoken discourse (Perfetti & Goldman, 1976). This interdependence of spoken and written language comprehension is important in the analysis of reading comprehension problems. Whether phonological memory is the critical cause of differences in both spoken and written language comprehension is another matter. As we suggest below, the basic language processing mechanisms, which include more than phonological representations, may affect performance in working memory tasks.

Phonological memory processes may affect reading comprehension by an additional pathway through the development of word identification. Dufva, Niemi, and Voeten (2001), in a longitudinal study from preschool through second grade, used assessments of phonological awareness, phonological memory, word identification, and spoken and written comprehension. Structural equation modeling showed an indirect causal link from preschool phonological memory to word recognition development between first and second grade, which was mediated by phonological awareness. Phonological memory showed a similar indirect causal link to reading comprehension, mediated by listening comprehension. The results suggest that the ability to hold and manipulate phonemes in memory may explain the relation between phonemic awareness and reading. Moreover, they suggest that phonological memory supports listening comprehension and thus, indirectly, reading comprehension.

Because word identification and listening comprehension are primary determinants of reading comprehension, phonological knowledge prior to literacy could play a role in the development of reading comprehension by either or both of two pathways. A causal path from early phonological knowledge through word identification to later reading comprehension is one possibility. Another possibility is a pathway from phonological processing to listening comprehension to reading comprehension. Of course, both causal pathways could be involved. On either description, working memory capacity is not at the heart of comprehension problems, but rather its correlations with comprehension reflect limitations in phonological processing. Indeed, Crain and Shankweiler (1988) argued that differences in working memory capacity arise from difficulties in phonological processing.

In the absence of specifically phonological problems, working memory differences are still observed and can be traced to other language processing weaknesses (Nation, Adams, Bowyer-Crane, & Snowling, 1999; Stothard & Hulme, 1992). The general conclusion appears to be that working memory differences related to reading skill are fairly specific to language processing. Indeed, the even more general conclusion is that language processing weaknesses are at the core of reading comprehension problems. These weaknesses will often be manifest specifically in phonology but they can also be reflected in other aspects of language processing.

The assumption of a limited capacity working memory system has been central in theories of cognition generally. An additional implicit assumption is that this system is more or less fixed biologically. However, alternative perspectives on working memory suppose that its limitations are not completely fixed but at least partly influenced by knowledge and experience (Chi, 1978; Ericsson & Delaney, 1999; Ericsson & Kintsch, 1995). If we see working memory as partly fixed and partly "expandable," we move toward a perspective that views the role of effective experience as critical in the development of comprehension skill. Effective experiences in a domain strengthen the functionality of memory resources in that domain. In the case of reading, the effective experience is reading itself (with a high standard for coherence) so as to support the fluent processing that effectively stretches working memory.

*Building conceptual understanding from words*

Vocabulary has been a slightly neglected partner in accounts of reading comprehension. This neglect arises not from any assumption that vocabulary is unimportant, but from theoretical interests in other aspects of the comprehension problem. The research strategies have either assumed or verified that relevant vocabulary knowledge is equal between a group of skilled and less-skilled comprehenders, so that experimental designs could focus on inferences, monitoring, working memory, or whatever component of comprehension was the target of interest. Of course, everyone accepts that knowledge of word meanings and comprehension skill are related.

The possible causal relations underlying their relationship include several plausible possibilities (Anderson & Freebody, 1981; Beck, McKeown, & Omanson, 1987; Curtis, 1987). Word meanings are instrumental in comprehension on logical as well as theoretical grounds. Nevertheless, the more one reads, the more comprehension brings along increases in the knowledge of word meanings. Sorting out causality is again difficult, and we might expect research designs to follow the lead of the comprehension-match design, making matches based on vocabulary levels.

For some purposes, it does not matter whether the causal history is from vocabulary-to-comprehension or comprehension-to-vocabulary. Indeed, the causal relationship is likely to be reciprocal. To the extent that word meanings are inferred from context, then vocabulary growth results from comprehension skill, including inference making. But at the moment a reader encounters a text, his or her ability to access the meaning of the word, as it applies in the context of this particular text, is critical.

Not knowing the meanings of words in a text is a bottleneck in comprehension. Because readers do not know the meanings of all words they encounter, they need to infer the meanings of unknown words from texts. This process, of course, requires comprehension and like other aspects of comprehension, it is correlated with working memory (Daneman & Green, 1986). This correlation might reflect working memory's role in learning the meanings of words from context (Daneman, 1988). Note also that inferring the meanings of unknown words from the text is possible only if most words are understood and if some approximation to text meaning is achieved. One estimate is that a reader must know at least 90% of the words in a text in order to comprehend it (Nagy & Scott, 2000). We know very little about the kind of text representation that results when words are not understood. The nature of this representation would depend on all sorts of other factors, from the role of an unknown word in the structure of the text message to the reader's tolerance for gaps in comprehension.

Somehow, children's knowledge of word meanings grows dramatically. Nagy and Herman (1987), based on several earlier estimates of vocabulary growth, computed the per-year growth of vocabulary at 3,000 words over grades 1–12. The gap between the number of words known by the high-knowledge and low-knowledge children is correspondingly large. According to one estimate, a first-grade reader with high vocabulary knowledge knows twice as many words as a first-grade reader with low knowledge, and this difference may actually double by the twelfth grade (Smith, 1941).

Differences in word knowledge emerge well before schooling. Large social class differences in the vocabulary heard by children at home produce corresponding differences in the vocabularies of children as they enter school (Hart & Risley, 1995a). These differences are not about only the conventional meanings of words, but the background knowledge needed to interpret messages that contain these words. Consider this example (from Hart & Risley, 1995a): *My wife and I wanted to go to Mexico, but her only vacation time was in July.* Interpreting the "but" clause, which needs to be understood as causal for an unstated action (they probably did not go to Mexico), is easier if the reader knows that Mexico is very hot in July and that some people might not want to have a vacation in high heat. Knowledge of this sort is critical in its consequences for understanding even simple texts.

Beyond the general importance of word knowledge (and associated conceptual knowledge) are specific demonstrations that children less skilled in comprehension have problems with word knowledge and semantic processing. Nation and Snowling (1998a) compared children with specific comprehension difficulties with a group of skilled comprehenders matched for decoding ability, age and nonverbal ability on semantic and phonological tasks. They found that less-skilled comprehenders scored lower on a synonym judgment task (Do BOAT and SHIP mean the same thing?), although not on a rhyme judgment task (Do ROSE and NOSE rhyme?). Less-skilled comprehenders were also slower to generate semantic category members (but not rhymes) than skilled comprehenders. This suggests that comprehension problems for some children are associated with reduced semantic knowledge (or less effective semantic processing) in the absence of obvious phonological problems. (See also Nation, this volume.)

More interesting, however, is that these same less-skilled comprehenders showed a problem in reading low-frequency and exception words. In effect, Nation and Snowling observed a link between skill in specific word identification (not decoding) and comprehension that could be mediated by knowledge of word meanings. Theoretically, such a link can reflect the role of word meanings in the identification of words that cannot be identified by reliable grapheme–phoneme correspondence rules. Children with weak decoding skills may develop a dependency on more semantically based procedures (Snowling, Hulme, & Goulandris, 1994).

Thus, knowledge of word meanings may play a role in both the identification of words (at least in an orthography that is not transparent) and in comprehension. This dual role of word meanings places lexical semantics in a pivotal position between word identification and comprehension. (Notice that figure 13.1 reflects its pivotal position.) This conclusion also accords with an observation on adult comprehenders reported in Perfetti and Hart (2002), who reported a factor analysis based on various reading component assessments. For skilled comprehenders word identification contributed to both a word form factor (phonology and spelling) and a comprehension factor, whereas for less-skilled comprehenders, word identification was associated with a phonological decoding factor but not with spelling or comprehension. This dual role of word meanings in skilled reading also may account for previous observations that less-skilled comprehenders are slower in accessing words in semantic search tasks (Perfetti, 1985).

If less-skilled readers have a weak lexical semantic system, then one might expect semantic variables that reflect the functioning of this system to make a difference. For example, concrete meanings are more readily activated than more abstract meanings.

Nation, et al. (1999) found that an advantage for concrete words was more pronounced for less-skilled readers than skilled readers who were matched for nonword reading (decoding). In a priming study, Nation and Snowling (1999) found that less-skilled comprehenders are more sensitive to associative strength among related words and less sensitive to abstract semantic relations, compared with skilled comprehenders. Research at this more specific semantic level could help clarify the nature of the semantic obstacles to comprehension.

## Word Identification, Decoding, and Phonological Awareness

If word meanings are central to comprehension and important for identification of at least some words, then we have come to an interesting conclusion: Despite trying to ignore word level processing in comprehension, we cannot. In examining the role of working memory, we were forced to conclude that a link to comprehension could go from phonological processing through word identification to comprehension. Even phonological awareness, ordinarily considered only important for decoding, has been found to predict young readers' comprehension independently of working memory (Leather & Henry, 1994).

The general association between word identification and reading comprehension skill has been well established for some time (Perfetti & Hogaboam, 1975). This association reflects the fact that word identification skill and comprehension skill develop in mutual support. The child's development of high-quality word representations is one of the main ingredients of fluent reading (Perfetti, 1985, 1991). Such representations must be acquired in large part through reading itself.

Instrumental in acquiring these word representations is a process identified by Share (Share, 1995, 1999) as self-teaching. This process allows children to move from a reading process entirely dependent on phonological coding of printed word forms to a process that accesses words quickly based on their orthography. What drives this development of orthographic access is the child's decoding attempts, which provide phonological feedback in the presence of a printed word, establishing the orthography of the word as an accessible representation. Models that simulate learning to read words can be said to implement this kind of mechanism (Plaut, McClelland, Seidenberg, & Patterson, 1996).

As children develop word-reading skills, comprehension becomes less limited by word identification and more influenced by other factors. However, even for adult skilled readers, the association between reading comprehension and word identification persists, reflecting either a lingering limitation of word identification on comprehension or a history of reading experience that has strengthened both skills. The word-level skill can be conceived as reflecting lexical quality (Perfetti & Hart, 2001), knowledge of word forms and meanings, which has its consequences in effective and efficient processing. Word level processing is never the whole story in comprehension. However, it is a baseline against which to assess the role of higher-level processes such as comprehension monitoring and inference making (Perfetti et al. 1996).

*Which components bring about growth in comprehension skill?*

To this point, we have examined the acquisition of reading skill largely through studies comparing skilled and less-skilled readers, whether matched on relevant skills or age. Longitudinal studies that track the course of changes in comprehension skill can provide additional information about the causal relations among the components of comprehension, and thus about the course of development. A few such studies have begun to appear. Muter, Hulme, Snowling, and Stevenson (2004) studied young children for two years from their entry into school, assessing a number of abilities, including phonological and grammatical abilities and vocabulary knowledge. Word identification skills, grammatical knowledge, and vocabulary assessed at age 5–6 each predicted unique variance in reading comprehension at the end of the second year of schooling. This pattern confirms the contributions to comprehension of three factors we have reviewed in previous sections.

In a longitudinal study of children in school years 3 to 6, Oakhill, Cain, and Bryant (2003b) extended the study of Oakhill et al. (2003a) by the addition of a third cohort of children and providing a longitudinal analysis of data from ages 7–8 (Year 3), 8–9 (Year 4), and 10–11 (Year 6). In each age group, there were measures of reading comprehension and reading accuracy, verbal and performance IQ (Time 1 only), working memory (both verbal and numerical span measures), phonemic awareness (phoneme deletion), vocabulary (British Picture Vocabulary Test), syntax (TROG), and measures of three comprehension related skills: inference making, comprehension monitoring and story-structure understanding (story anagram task). The results of multiple regression were applied to a causal path diagram to show the pattern and strength of relations among the various skills across time. The final causal path diagram, with only significant paths included, is shown in figure 13.2.

Initial comprehension skill was a strong predictor of later comprehension, and verbal ability (vocabulary and verbal IQ) also made significant contributions to the prediction of comprehension ability across time. Nevertheless, three distinct predictors of comprehension skill emerged, either through direct or indirect links: answering inferential questions, monitoring comprehension (by detecting inconsistencies in text), and understanding story structure (assessed by the ability to reconstruct a story from a set of jumbled sentences). These factors predicted comprehension at a later time even after the autoregressive effect of comprehension (the prediction of comprehension at later times from comprehension at earlier times) was controlled. With reading accuracy as the dependent variable, the pattern was quite different. The significant predictors were previous measures of reading accuracy and a phoneme deletion measure taken at Time 1.

From these analyses a picture of skill development emerges in which certain components of comprehension are predictive of general comprehension skill. Early abilities in inference skill, story structure understanding, and comprehension monitoring all predict a later global assessment of comprehension skill independently of the contribution of earlier comprehension skill.

Finally, to assess growth in skill, Oakhill et al. (2003b) calculated estimates of growth in reading comprehension and reading accuracy, and used these estimates as dependent variables in two further sets of regression analyses. (Verbal and performance IQ and vocabulary were entered at the first step, followed by all of the reading-related and language

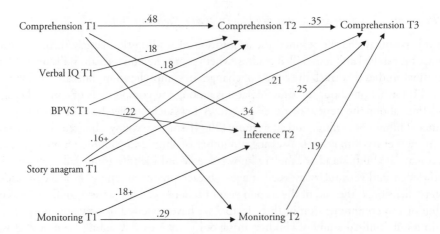

**Figure 13.2**   Path analysis based on data from longitudinal study by Oakhill, Cain, and Bryant (2003b). Variables measured at Time 1 (age 7–8) predict variables at Time 2 (age 9–10) and Time 3 (age 11–12). Variables shown were significant predictors after the effects of all other variables were removed: a global comprehension measure (COMP), a picture vocabulary test (BPVS), verbal IQ (VIQ), detection of text contradictions (MONITOR), a sensitivity to story structure (Story Anagram), and integrative inferences (INFER). Paths that linked Time 1 and Time 2 variables but not Time 3 comprehension have been excluded for clarity. Because the original data were standardized, the coefficients shown are directly comparable.

variables and working memory measures entered simultaneously.) Although vocabulary and verbal IQ predicted growth in comprehension and reading accuracy, other variables made independent predictions. Story structure understanding was the sole predictor of growth in reading comprehension. Phonemic awareness was the sole predictor of growth in reading accuracy skill.

The study confirms that a set of higher-level comprehension components, which, on theoretical grounds, ought to be instrumental in the growth of reading comprehension skill, may indeed be instrumental. Muter et al. (2004) report a slightly different pattern for their younger children. Word identification (Hatcher, Early Word Recognition Test, Hatcher, Hulme, & Ellis, 1994) was important in predicting comprehension, as one might expect for younger children, as were knowledge of word meanings and grammatical knowledge. Because Muter et al. had a comprehension assessment only at the final test point in their study, their study is not directly comparable with the study by Oakhill et al. (2003b). It is possible that all the factors identified in these two studies influence comprehension development, with the strength of their contribution depending upon the level of the child's skill. However, studies that carry out comparable assessments, including tests of comprehension at more than one time point, are needed to test this possibility.

## Comprehension Instruction

A failure to develop a high level of comprehensions skill creates a severe obstacle to educational attainment. Accordingly, there is widespread concern about how to improve children's reading comprehension. Although we cannot review the research on instruction in comprehension here, we briefly note the wide extent of such research, drawing on a comprehensive review of research on reading (National Institute of Child Health and Human Development [NICHD], 2000). The summary NICHD report refers to 453 studies between 1980 and the time of the review, augmented by a few earlier studies from the 1970s. The 205 studies that met the methodological criteria led the report to identify seven categories of comprehension instruction that appeared to have solid evidence for their effectiveness.

These seven include procedures that we characterize as drawing the reader into a deeper engagement with the text – in a phrase, active processing. They include comprehension monitoring, question answering (teacher directed questions) and question generation (student self-questioning), the use of semantic organizers (students making graphic representations of text), and student summarization of texts. Instruction in story structures was also judged to be effective. The NICHD Report concludes that these procedures are effective in isolation in improving their specific target skills (sensitivity to story structures, quality of summarization, etc.) but that improvement of scores on standardized comprehension tests may require training multiple strategies in combination.

The procedures that the NICHD Report suggests are effective are consistent with the comprehensions skills we have reviewed in this chapter. Active engagement with the meaning of text helps the reader to represent the text content in a way that fosters both learning (as opposed to superficial and incomplete understanding) and an attraction to reading. However, the NICHD report adds some cautions to its conclusions on behalf of the instruction strategies it recommends. To those, we add our own reservations. Instructional interventions may produce only short-term gains. Two years after the intervention, is the child comprehending better? Answers to this kind of question appear to be lacking. We think the complex interaction among the comprehension components and the role of motivation for reading make real gains difficult to achieve. Internalizing externally delivered procedures so that they become a habit – a basic attitude toward texts and learning – may be a long-term process. It requires both wanting to read and gaining skill in reading, which go hand in hand.

## Conclusion: A More General View of Comprehension Development

We conclude by taking a step back from the details of how skill in comprehension is acquired. With more research, the kind of developmental picture we described in the preceding sections may be confirmed or alternative pictures will emerge, based on different experimental tasks and resulting in a different arrangement of causal relations. Because a detailed model of skill acquisition seems premature, we turn to a more general, speculative account of acquisition. This general model framework, which is illustrated as a highly schematic representation in figure 3.3, can be realized by a number of specific models.

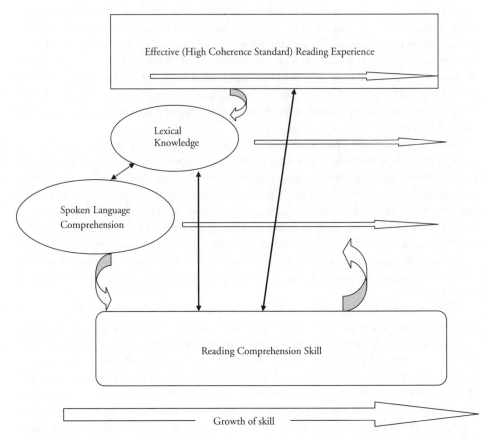

**Figure 13.3**    A schematic representation of the major components in the acquisition of reading comprehension skill. The left–right arrows represent increases in skill across with experience and gains in knowledge. Reading comprehension depends on spoken language comprehension throughout development. Early in reading, written word identification (not shown) is a limiting factor for reading comprehension. Reading comprehension has reciprocal relationships with both spoken language comprehension and lexical knowledge. Not represented: general knowledge (which, of course, also increases) and the specific processes of comprehension (e.g., syntactic processing and inference making).

We assume the following:

1.  General skill in reading comprehension and its related components increase with reading experience, and, with some component skills, with spoken language experience.
2.  Reading comprehension and listening comprehension are related throughout development. Their relation is reciprocal, with experience in each potentially affecting skill acquisition in the other. However, this does not mean that the two are "equal," and substantial asymmetries can develop.

3.  Word identification skill sets a limit on how closely reading comprehension skill can approach listening comprehension skill. It specifically limits comprehension early in reading development.
4.  Knowledge of word meanings is central to comprehension. This knowledge derives from multiple sources, including written and spoken comprehension, and grows indefinitely.
5.  Higher levels of comprehension require the reader to apply a high standard of coherence to his or her understanding of the text.

The first four assumptions comprise a basic analysis of what is necessary for comprehension. Our review of research on higher-level comprehension processes emphasizes the need for this basic analysis to be taken into account – that is, "controlled for" – in the search for higher-level comprehension factors that are strategic; for example, monitoring comprehension, making inferences. However, we conclude also that the basic analysis provides the necessary, but not sufficient, causal story.

For comprehension to develop to higher levels, the reader must adopt a high standard of coherence – to care whether the text makes sense. When coherence is a goal, inferences are made to keep things coherent. When coherence is a goal, inconsistencies between text elements or between text elements and the reader's knowledge are resolved rather than ignored or not noticed. All readers find themselves relaxing their standards for coherence occasionally. Unwanted reading and countless nontext distractions can promote this laxity. The goal, however, is adopting the high-standard criterion as the "default." We think skilled readers do this. This brings reciprocal supports into play. Adopting a high coherence standard supports interest in reading, which encourages a high standard of coherence. The result of these influences is more reading and, especially, more effective reading. This surely aids reading comprehension.

## Note

The authors are grateful to Kate Cain for providing comments on a draft of this chapter, which was prepared while the first author was a visiting research fellow at the University of Sussex. The first author's work on the chapter was supported by a Leverhulme Visiting Professorship and a comprehension research award from Institute for Educational Sciences (US Department of Education).

# 14

# Children's Reading Comprehension Difficulties

## Kate Nation

Comprehension is the ultimate goal of reading. Everyone agrees that reading comprehension is not a simple matter of recognizing individual words, or even of understanding each individual word as our eyes pass over it. All models of comprehension recognize the need for readers to build up a mental representation of text, a process that requires integration across a range of sources of information, from lexical features through to knowledge concerning events in the world (e.g., Garnham, 2001; Gernsbacher, 1990; Kintsch, 1998). Given the complex nature of reading comprehension, it is not surprising that some individuals have difficulties in this area. Individual differences in text comprehension have been observed in both developmental (e.g., Nation & Snowling, 1997; Oakhill, 1994) and college-aged populations (e.g., Gernsbacher & Faust, 1991; Long, Seely, & Oppy, 1999). Difficulty with reading comprehension has also been reported in a range of clinical disorders such as early onset hydrocephalus (Dennis & Barnes, 1993), autism (Snowling & Frith, 1986), nonverbal learning disorder (Pelletier, Ahmad, & Rourke, 2001), specific language impairment (Bishop & Adams, 1990), Turner's syndrome (Temple & Carney, 1996) and Williams syndrome (Laing, Hulme, Grant, & Karmiloff-Smith, 2001). Thus, there is no shortage of evidence pointing to the fact that some individuals experience reading comprehension difficulties.

The nature and origins of reading comprehension difficulties, however, are not so clear. The aim of this chapter is to review what is known about reading comprehension difficulties in children, with a view to addressing two major issues. First, although individuals who experience difficulty with reading comprehension can be identified, does it make sense to talk about specific reading comprehension difficulties? Second, what are the causes of reading comprehension failure? The focus of the chapter will be on children who appear to show selective impairments of reading comprehension. That is, their reading accuracy is within the normal range for their age, but their comprehension of what is read is substantially below average. Studies of such children allow us to identify cognitive systems that may be particularly crucial for the development of reading comprehension, and that are relatively independent of the processes underlying the development of word recognition skills in reading.

## "Specific" Deficits in Reading Comprehension?

Are there individuals who show specific reading comprehension deficits? The answer to this seemingly simple question is not straightforward. The starting place is to separate reading into two component parts, one concerned with recognizing printed words, and one concerned with understanding the message that the print conveys. Although the correlation between word recognition and reading comprehension is substantial (e.g., Juel, Griffith, & Gough (1986) report correlations of .74 and .69 for first- and second-grade children), it is not perfect and some individuals perform adequately on one component but poorly on the other. Oakhill and colleagues (Oakhill, 1994; Yuill & Oakhill, 1991) were the first to describe children who obtained normal-for-age text reading accuracy, but showed impaired reading comprehension. Stothard and Hulme (1992, 1995) and Nation and Snowling (1997) investigated populations of children selected in broadly similar ways. At a simple level of description, these children (who will be referred to in this chapter as "poor comprehenders") read accurately but have specific difficulty understanding what they read. Typically, poor comprehenders are rare in clinically referred samples of children with reading difficulties (e.g., Leach, Scarborough, & Rescorla, 2003; Shankweiler, Lundquist, Katz et al., 1999). However, this is probably a reflection of referral bias. Indeed, when populations of 7–10-year-old children have been screened in the UK, approximately 10% could be classified as poor comprehenders (Nation & Snowling, 1997; Stothard & Hulme, 1992; Yuill & Oakhill, 1991).

How might the "poor comprehender" profile be conceptualized? According to Hoover and Gough's (1990) "simple view" of reading, reading comprehension comprises two sets of skills, those concerned with decoding or recognizing printed words, and those involved in linguistic comprehension. The relationship between decoding and linguistic comprehension is considered to be multiplicative: there can be no reading comprehension without the ability to decipher or recognize words, and similarly, reading comprehension will fail if children lack the linguistic comprehension to understand what it is they have decoded. Put simply, both decoding and linguistic comprehension are necessary, and neither skill on its own is sufficient, if successful reading comprehension is to follow. The essence of the simple model is captured beautifully by Gough, Hoover, and Peterson's (1996) account of the elderly John Milton, who due to failing sight was unable to reread the Greek and Latin classics. His solution was to teach his daughters how to decode Greek and Latin. Having accomplished the basics of Latin and Greek letter-sound correspondences, they were able to read the texts aloud while their father listened. The product was, for Milton at least, successful reading comprehension.

Thus, according to the simple view, reading comprehension is the *product* of decoding and linguistic comprehension. It follows from this that children with poor reading comprehension must have deficits either in decoding, linguistic comprehension, or both. The logic of this view argues that reading comprehension deficits cannot be specific, but instead must be related to weaknesses in one or both of its component parts. For the children described above as having specific reading comprehension impairments, which component of reading comprehension is at fault?

## *Decoding difficulties as a source of poor reading comprehension*

According to the simple model, decoding skill can place a constraint on reading comprehension. A specific form of this hypothesis was proposed by Perfetti (1985) who claimed that when decoding is slow and effortful, resources are dedicated to word-level processing. By contrast, when decoding is automatic, resources are available for the task of comprehension. In line with Perfetti's "verbal efficiency" hypothesis, evidence demonstrates that reading comprehension is compromised when decoding is poor. Word reading speed and reading comprehension correlate in child as well as adult populations (Hess & Radtke, 1981; Jackson & McClelland, 1979), and Perfetti and Hogaboam (1975) found that children with poor reading comprehension were slower at reading words and nonwords than their classmates. Moreover, the relationship between decoding efficiency and reading comprehension is maintained over time, and measurements of nonword reading taken in early childhood predict later variations in reading comprehension measured in secondary school years and adulthood (Bruck, 1990; Perfetti, 1985).

As pointed out by Oakhill and colleagues, however, inefficient decoding is unlikely to be the only source of reading comprehension impairment. As noted above, some children have poor reading comprehension but show age-appropriate levels of text reading accuracy, leading to the conclusion that inadequate decoding cannot be the source of poor comprehenders' difficulties. However, the demonstration of adequate text reading *accuracy* does not necessarily imply efficient word-level *processing* (Perfetti 1994; Perfetti, Marron, & Foltz, 1996). Even when reading accuracy is adequate, if it is slow or inefficient, comprehension may be compromised. Thus, Perfetti argued it is necessary to show that poor comprehenders decode not just as accurately as control children, but that they do so with equivalent efficiency, if their comprehension problems are to be considered at all exceptional.

Such evidence was forthcoming from a study by Nation and Snowling (1998a) who found that poor comprehenders read nonwords as quickly as control children. This experimental finding is confirmed by observations that poor comprehenders perform at age-appropriate levels on standardized tests of nonword reading accuracy such as the *Graded Nonword Reading Test* (Snowling, Stothard, & McLean, 1996) and nonword reading efficiency such as the *Test for Word Reading Efficiency* (Torgesen, Wagner, & Rashotte, 1999; e.g., Marshall & Nation, 2003; Nation, Marshall, & Altmann, 2003). Importantly, Nation and colleagues have used the strategy of matching poor comprehenders to control children on nonword reading, thereby eliminating the possibility that group differences in reading comprehension can be accounted for by differences in decoding skill. It should be noted, however, that there are differences between poor comprehenders and typically developing children in some aspects of word reading. We will return to this point later. However, if we take the central tenet of the theory to be that inaccurate or slow decoding leads to poor reading comprehension, then the children described by Oakhill and by

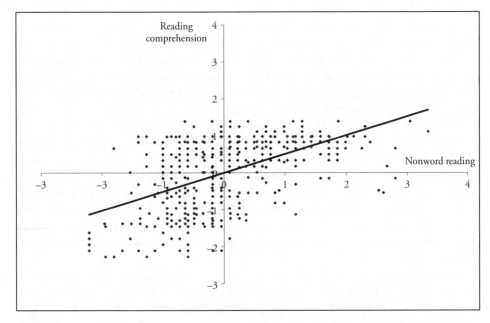

**Figure 14.1**   Scatterplot showing the relationship between reading comprehension and nonword reading in 411 7–10-year-old children (z-scores).

Nation and their colleagues (Nation & Snowling, 1997; Oakhill, 1994) are exceptions to the general pattern of association between these two factors. To illustrate this, figure 14.1 shows the relationship between nonword reading and reading comprehension in a sample of 411 7–10-year-old children; the two variables are plotted as z-scores, calculated across the whole sample of children. Children falling in the lower right quadrant show the poor comprehender profile of good nonword reading skills but poor reading comprehension.

## Linguistic comprehension as a source of poor reading comprehension

According to the logic of the simple model of reading, if poor comprehenders do not have deficits in decoding, they should show deficits in linguistic comprehension. Generally, the relationship between reading comprehension and listening comprehension is very close, especially as children get older and reading comprehension becomes more constrained by knowledge and understanding, rather than basic word-level decoding (Stanovich, Cunningham, & Freeman, 1984). In adults, listening and reading comprehension are strongly correlated ($r$'s in the region of .9; Bell & Perfetti, 1994; Gernsbacher, Varner, & Faust, 1990). Although there are important differences between spoken language and written language (e.g., in the temporal characteristics of the two modalities), evidence suggests that listening and reading comprehension depend on very similar underlying processes. As Rayner, Foorman, Perfetti, Pesetsky, and Seidenberg (2001, p. 42) put it, "It can be reasonably argued that learning to read enables a person to comprehend written language to the same level that he or she comprehends spoken language."

As would be predicted by the strong relationship between written and spoken language comprehension, children selected on the basis of their poor reading comprehension usually show poor listening comprehension. Nation and Snowling (1997) asked children to listen to stories, and at the end of each passage of text the children were asked a series of questions. Some questions tapped literal understanding of what they had heard, whereas others required inferences to be made. Poor comprehenders performed less well than control children on this listening comprehension task. Consistent with these findings, Nation, Clarke, Marshall, and Durand (2004) found that poor comprehenders also performed less well than control children (matched for age, nonverbal ability, and decoding ability) on a number of spoken language tasks, including the Comprehension subtest taken from the *Wechsler Intelligence Scale for Children* (WISC-III[uk]) (Wechsler, 1992). This test requires children to formulate a response to a variety of hypothetical situations presented orally (e.g., "what should you do if you cut your finger"?). The poor comprehenders obtained scores well below those of the control children, and as a group their performance fell more than one standard deviation below age-expected levels on this standardized test.

In summary, poor comprehenders do not have a comprehension impairment that is specific to reading. Rather, their difficulties with reading comprehension need to be seen in the context of difficulties with language comprehension more generally. Some theorists have gone further and intimated that since poor comprehenders' performance is highly consistent across both written and spoken language, they should perhaps not qualify as having a reading impairment, so much as a more general language or cognitive deficit. However, the fact that poor comprehenders' difficulties can be traced to more general difficulties with spoken language does not negate the fact that they have a reading difficulty. One can draw an analogy with developmental dyslexia. There is little doubt that dyslexic children have a reading problem. It is also the case however, that dyslexic children perform poorly on oral language tasks that involve phonological processing, such as phonological awareness, nonword repetition, rapid naming, name retrieval, and verbal short-term memory (e.g., Snowling, 2000). Some of these difficulties may be causally linked to their reading difficulties, others may be consequences, but the important point is that these difficulties do not draw attention away from the fact that children with dyslexia have "specific" difficulties with reading.

## What Causes Poor Reading Comprehension?

As Perfetti (1994, p. 885) makes clear, "there is room for lots of things to go wrong when comprehension fails." Although it is the case that reading comprehension deficits are often associated with word-level decoding difficulties (e.g., Perfetti, 1985), discussion in this chapter continues to focus on children who have "specific" reading comprehension difficulties: specific in the sense that they are able to read text, words, and nonwords at age-appropriate levels, but their reading comprehension is impaired. However, even restricting discussion in this way leaves a number of possible reasons for these children's difficulties to be considered.

Before reviewing these possible causes of reading comprehension failure, it is worth reflecting on some methodological issues surrounding the study of poor comprehenders. One issue concerns the choice of tasks used to reveal the poor comprehender profile. Oakhill and colleagues screen and select poor comprehenders from regular mainstream classrooms based on performance on the *Neale Analysis of Reading Ability* (NARA-II) (Neale, 1997). In this reading test, children read aloud short passages of text (generating a score for reading accuracy) and are then asked questions to assess their literal and inferential understanding of the text (generating a score for reading comprehension). Poor comprehenders are selected as children who show a significant discrepancy between their age-appropriate reading accuracy and their below-average reading comprehension. There are however, possible objections to this approach, not least that in this particular reading test (the NARA), reading accuracy and reading comprehension are not measured independently from one another. With this limitation in mind, Nation and colleagues have selected poor comprehenders according to performance on tasks that assess the two components of reading (accuracy and comprehension) separately. In these studies, poor comprehenders are selected and defined as those children who achieve poor reading comprehension scores on the NARA, but achieve age-appropriate scores on a standardized test of "pure" decoding (nonword reading).

A second methodological issue concerns the nature of the comparison group of control children. To ensure that any differences between poor comprehenders and control children are not a consequence of group differences in basic decoding skill, Nation and Snowling (1998a) advocated matching the two groups for nonword reading ability. Following the same logic, Nation and colleagues also match poor comprehenders and control children for nonverbal cognitive ability. This approach is not followed by other research groups (e.g., Yuill & Oakhill, 1991). However, as a minority of children selected as poor comprehenders show rather low cognitive ability (Nation, Clarke, & Snowling, 2002), failing to control for cognitive ability could result in spurious conclusions.

A final methodological note concerns the comprehension-age match design. Following the logic of the reading-age match design (e.g., Bryant & Goswami, 1986), Stothard and Hulme (1992) and Cain, Oakhill, and Bryant (2000a) reasoned that in order to identify candidate causes of poor reading comprehension, poor comprehenders should be compared with younger, normally developing children whose comprehension skills are at a similar level. If poor comprehenders show impairments in a particular cognitive or linguistic skill relative to younger control children matched for comprehension age, that skill is unlikely to be a simple consequence of comprehension level.

With these methodological issues in mind, we return to the question of what causes poor reading comprehension in children selected as poor comprehenders. Perfetti and colleagues (Perfetti, 1985, 1994; Perfetti et al., 1996) have argued that poor comprehension may be a consequence of inadequate processing, lack of knowledge, or some combination of both processing and knowledge-based weaknesses. Two sets of processes are considered essential to the comprehension process, and are described as "inevitable" sources of comprehension difficulty (Perfetti et al., 1996, p. 140); these are lexical processes and working memory resources, which together form the central elements of the verbal efficiency hypothesis. We begin by reviewing evidence concerning the performance of poor comprehenders on tasks tapping these skills.

*Lexical processes*

What is meant by lexical processes in this context? While some authors use the term to refer to the efficiency of sublexical processing, that is, the ability to make mappings between orthography and phonology, it is also used more broadly to capture, amongst other skills, phonological processing and lexical access (e.g., Perfetti, 1994). Research on poor comprehenders has revealed a systematic profile of strengths and weaknesses across different aspects of lexical processing. It is thus important to consider different aspects of lexical processing separately.

*Phonological skills.* It is well established that children's phonological skills are intimately related to the development of literacy (e.g., Goswami & Bryant, 1990) and a considerable body of evidence points to core phonological deficits characterizing individuals with poor reading (e.g., Snowling, 2000; Stanovich & Siegal, 1994). Shankweiler (1989) proposed that reading comprehension difficulties may be caused by a "phonological bottleneck." On this view, comprehension problems are a consequence of a child being unable to set up or sustain a phonological representation of verbal information when reading. Consistent with this, phonological skills do account for significant variance in reading comprehension performance (e.g., Gottardo, Stanovich, & Siegal, 1996). However, as noted by Cain, Oakhill, and Bryant (2000b), the relationship between phonology and reading comprehension may not be direct. Instead, the relationship between phonological skills and reading comprehension may be mediated by word recognition. In line with this view, a number of studies have demonstrated that phonological skills are not impaired in children with specific comprehension difficulties: across a range of different phonological processing tasks, including phoneme deletion, rhyme oddity, judgment and fluency, spoonerisms, and nonword repetition, poor comprehenders are indistinguishable from control children (e.g., Cain, et al., 2000b; Nation et al., 2004; Nation & Snowling, 1998a; Stothard & Hulme, 1995). Very clearly, a bottleneck in phonological processing cannot account for poor comprehenders' comprehension impairments.

*Semantic skills.* Despite adequate phonological skills, poor comprehenders do show weaknesses in some aspects of oral language. In a series of studies, Nation and colleagues compared poor comprehenders with skilled comprehenders matched for chronological age, decoding level, and nonverbal ability. Poor comprehenders were slower and less accurate at making semantic judgments, and they produced fewer exemplars in a semantic fluency task (Nation & Snowling, 1998a); under some conditions, differences in semantic priming (Nation & Snowling, 1999) and relative weaknesses in picture naming (Nation, Marshall, & Snowling, 2001) have also been observed. It is important to note, however, that the deficits observed in these experiments were not just symptoms of generally poor language; for instance, deficits in semantic judgment and semantic fluency were accompanied by normal levels of performance on parallel tasks tapping rhyme judgment and rhyme fluency.

What seems to unite those aspects of lexical processing that poor comprehenders find difficult is meaning. To judge whether two words mean the same, or to produce exemplars to a category label, clearly depends on an appreciation of word meaning (whereas, in contrast, commonly used measures of children's phonological skills, such as rhyme judgment, phoneme deletion, and nonword repetition are tasks that can be performed without access to semantics). Such semantic impairments are consistent with mild-to-moderate deficits in receptive and expressive vocabulary that have emerged in some, but not all, studies (e.g., Nation et al., 2004; Stothard & Hulme, 1992). Thus, in line with Perfetti's verbal efficiency hypothesis, poor comprehenders do have impairments in lexical processing, but only when semantic aspects of lexical processing are taxed.

It is important to note that although Nation and Snowling characterized poor comprehenders as having poor lexical-semantic skills, subsequent research has revealed oral language weaknesses that are not necessarily restricted to the semantic or lexical domain. For example, Nation et al. (2004) found that poor comprehenders scored lower than control children on tests tapping morphosyntax and the understanding of nonliteral aspects of language, as well as vocabulary. These findings are consistent with earlier work by Stothard and Hulme (1992) demonstrating group deficits on a test of syntactic comprehension, the *Test for the Reception of Grammar* (TROG) (Bishop, 1983). Interestingly, not all studies find TROG-deficits in children with poor text-level reading comprehension (e.g., Yuill & Oakhill, 1991); however, inconsistent findings across studies are difficult to interpret as, typically, performance levels on the TROG have been close to ceiling. A new edition of the TROG (TROG-2; Bishop, 2003) contains more items, and is standardized through to adulthood. A recent study using this more sensitive test (Cragg & Nation, in press) provides clear evidence pointing to syntactic comprehension impairments in poor comprehenders (standard scores were 80 and 94 for the poor comprehenders and control children respectively).

In summary, there is considerable evidence supporting the view that poor comprehenders have oral language weaknesses. Nation et al. (2004) concluded that low-language characterized poor comprehenders as a group, and furthermore, a substantial minority of the sample met criteria for specific language impairment (SLI; see Bishop, 1997, for a review). Importantly, however, and unlike the majority of children with SLI, poor comprehenders showed no difficulty with phonological processing. Instead, their oral language skills were characterized by relative weaknesses in dealing with the nonphonological aspects of language, ranging from lexical-level weaknesses (vocabulary) through to difficulties with interpreting nonliteral language.

*Visual word recognition.* So far discussion has focused on aspects of lexical processing captured by children's oral language skills. According to Perfetti (1985, 1994), however, the ability to make mappings between orthography and phonology is a lexical processing skill that is vital to the reading comprehension process. On this view, the ability to decode and identify words accurately and efficiently allows resources to be devoted to comprehension processes. As discussed earlier, decoding efficiency is clearly related to reading comprehension in general terms. But is there any evidence to suggest that poor comprehenders' poor comprehension is a consequence of ineffective, resource-demanding decoding or word identification processes? The answer to this question seems to be no: as reviewed above, comprehension impairments remain even when care is taken to match poor comprehenders and controls for basic decoding skill (as measured by nonword reading accuracy and efficiency). And, when groups are matched in this way, poor comprehenders show normal phonological processing skills, suggesting that their decoding is not underpinned by low-quality phonological knowledge.

Interestingly, however, even when poor comprehenders are closely matched to control children for decoding ability, subtle group differences in visual word recognition have been observed. Nation and Snowling (1998a) found that poor comprehenders were less accurate and efficient than control children at reading irregular words and low-frequency words; there were no group differences when reading regular words and high-frequency words. Drawing on Plaut, McClelland, Seidenberg, and Patterson's (1996) connectionist model of word recognition, Nation and Snowling proposed that word recognition is compromised in poor comprehenders due to weaknesses in vocabulary and semantic knowledge, as reviewed in the previous section.

To understand how these weaknesses in oral language may impact on the development of visual word recognition, we need to consider the role played by semantics in the word recognition process. According to Plaut et al.'s (1996) connectionist model of word recognition, reading development is best characterized by a division of labour between a phonological pathway (consisting of connections between phonological and orthographic representations) and a semantic pathway (connections between semantic representations, phonology and orthography). Although in the earliest stages of reading development, resources are devoted to establishing connections between orthography and phonology (akin to basic decoding or "sounding-out"), the semantic pathway becomes increasingly important later in development, especially for the efficient reading of exception or irregular words: words that are not handled so well by the phonological pathway alone.

With this framework as a backdrop, it is possible to hypothesize how children's spoken language ability influences the way in which their reading systems are established. For example, dyslexic children with impaired phonological skill are thought to come to the task of learning to read with poorly specified phonological knowledge in the spoken domain. As a result, they find it difficult to forge adequate connections between orthography and phonology and consequently find decoding (especially nonword reading) difficult (Harm & Seidenberg, 1999; Snowling, 2000). Poor comprehenders have no such difficulty: their strong phonological skills allow them to develop an efficient and well-specified phonological pathway. In contrast however, relative weaknesses in vocabulary and semantic knowledge may constrain the development of the semantic pathway. A weak semantic pathway in Plaut et al.'s simulations led to problems with irregular and low-frequency words – exactly the profile of word recognition that has been observed in poor comprehenders (Nation & Snowling, 1998a). It is important to note, however, that group differences were very subtle. The poor comprehenders were reading words and nonwords at age-appropriate levels as measured by standardized tests, and their phonological skills were well developed. It seems unlikely that such children are devoting excessive resources to word identification and decoding, or that their reading comprehension is severely compromised by inefficient word-identification processes.

In summary, a number of conclusions concerning the status of lexical processing in children selected as having "specific" reading comprehension impairments can be drawn. First, there is very little evidence to suggest that they have difficulty with phonological processing, or that their comprehension impairment is a consequence of either a phonological processing or a basic decoding bottleneck. Although central to Perfetti's verbal efficiency hypothesis, it is clear that these skills are not compromised in children selected as having a specific reading comprehension problem. However, other aspects of lexical processing are weak in poor comprehenders. Deficits in semantic processing are apparent, and these may be related to more general weaknesses with linguistic comprehension.

## *Working memory*

Language comprehension places heavy demands on working memory resources. Whether reading or listening, representations of words and sentences must be held in memory while other aspects of the text or discourse are processed and background knowledge is activated and integrated (see e.g. Kintsch & Rawson, this volume). Support for the relationship between comprehension and working memory comes from a number of sources, including observations that college students selected on the basis of low working memory span achieve lower comprehension scores than their "high span" peers, and perform less well on various components of comprehension such as pronoun resolution (Daneman & Carpenter, 1980, 1983). Most relevant for this chapter are investigations of working memory in poor comprehenders. Three studies have addressed this issue directly. Yuill, Oakhill, and Parkin (1989) asked children to read aloud triplets of numbers and then to recall the final digit in each triple. Poor comprehenders performed less well than control children, leading Yuill et al. (1989) to suggest that deficits in nonlinguistic working memory may underlie the reading comprehension problems seen in this group of children. However, as the counting span task required children to read and recall digits, the data are more suggestive of a verbal memory deficit than a nonlinguistic one. On a test of nonlinguistic spatial memory span, Nation, Adams, Bowyer-Crane, and Snowling (1999) found no differences between poor comprehenders and a control group.

To investigate verbal working memory in poor comprehenders further, Stothard and Hulme (1992) adapted Daneman and Carpenter's (1980) listening span task. They reasoned that this task would tap verbal working memory, as its task requirements (responding to short sentences and then recalling the last word of each sentence) are similar to some of the simultaneous processing and storage demands of language comprehension itself. Rather surprisingly, however, they found no group differences: poor comprehenders, age-matched controls and younger children with approximately the same level of comprehension as the poor comprehenders all performed at a similar level. From these data, Stothard and Hulme concluded that working memory deficits are unlikely to be a common cause of reading comprehension difficulties. Subsequent data, however, suggest that this conclusion was premature. The children in Stothard and Hulme's study were aged 6–7 years, and it is clear that they found the listening span task demanding because performance was close to floor. Nation et al. (1999), using the same materials as Stothard and Hulme, did observe substantial listening span deficits in 10-year-old poor comprehenders in line with the findings reported by Yuill et al. (1989). Taken together, these findings are consistent with the general relationship between verbal (but not spatial) span and reading comprehension in children (e.g., Seigneuric, Erlich, Oakhill, & Yuill, 2000).

Given the relative difficulty poor comprehenders have with the processing and storage of verbal material, it is tempting to suggest that these verbal working memory deficits may underpin their poor text comprehension. However, issues of causality are far from clear. It is generally accepted that in a complex memory span task such as listening span, individuals' storage capacity is a function of how efficient they are at the computational – or processing aspects – of the task (e.g., Daneman & Tardif, 1987). As, by definition, poor comprehenders have poor language comprehension, verbal working memory weakness may be a consequence of poor language comprehension, rather than a cause of it. For example, the listening span task used by Nation et al. (1999) required children to listen to sentences and to make a decision about their content (the processing component of the task), and then to remember the final word in each successive sentence (the storage component of the task). As poor comprehenders tend to perform less well than control children on measures of sentence comprehension (Cragg & Nation, 2006; Stothard & Hulme, 1992), differences in verbal memory are perhaps not surprising.

In summary, although further research is needed to understand issues of causality, it is clear that the relationship between language comprehension and verbal memory in poor comprehenders is an intimate one, as highlighted in a recent investigation of sentence repetition. Marshall and Nation (2003) asked poor comprehenders and controls to repeat sentences (of increasing length and complexity) verbatim. Two findings were clear. First, poor comprehenders repeated fewer sentences correctly. Thus, even though the task required only straightforward verbatim repetition (rather than a complex span procedure), verbal memory weaknesses were nevertheless evident. Second, the nature of the errors made by poor comprehenders differed from those made by control children. While both groups of children were likely to maintain the surface aspects of the sentences, poor comprehenders were less likely to maintain the meaning (or gist) of the target sentences. A possible interpretation of this finding is that the children simply did not understand the sentences as well as control children did, thus reducing the accuracy or reliability with which they were able to represent (and therefore remember) the content of sentences.

## "Higher-order" discourse-level processes

In addition to lexical processing and working memory deficits, a range of discourse-level deficits have been implicated in poor reading comprehension. Two sets of processes that have attracted considerable research will be reviewed here: inference making and comprehension monitoring processes.

*Inference making.* To understand language, it is often necessary to make inferences – to go beyond what is stated explicitly in the text or discourse to infer the intended message. Even very straightforward texts require inferences to be drawn. This point is nicely illustrated by Oakhill (1994) in her description of how the following story "can only be understood against a background knowledge about birthday parties, the convention of taking presents to them, the need for money to buy presents, and so on" (p. 822):

> *Jane was invited to Jack's birthday.*
> *She wondered if he would like a kite.*
> *She went to her room and shook her piggy bank.*
> *It made no sound.*

As this example makes clear, failure to draw inferences is likely to seriously impede comprehension. Numerous studies have demonstrated that poor comprehenders have difficulty drawing inferences when reading or listening, and it has been argued that such difficulties are causally implicated in children's poor reading comprehension (Cain & Oakhill, 1999; Oakhill, 1982, 1984; for review, see Oakhill, 1994).

Before accepting that poor comprehenders' reading difficulties are the consequence of problems with making inferences, it is important to establish that poor inference making is not an artefact of other factors. For example, to resolve an inference often requires the reader to hold information in memory across a number of sentences. Potentially, there-fore, poor comprehenders may fail to make inferences not because they are unable to do so, but simply because of failure to remember premises presented earlier in the text. To test this idea, Oakhill (1984) compared children's ability to answer comprehension ques-tions requiring an inference under two conditions. In one condition, the text remained in full view, and children were allowed to look back at the text; in a second condition, the text was removed and comprehension questions had to be answered from memory. Poor comprehenders' ability to draw inferences remained limited, even when the text was made available for the children to look back at. Following a similar procedure, Cain and Oakhill (1999) replicated these findings. They also included a condition in which poor comprehenders were encouraged (with direct prompting) to search the text in order to find the information needed from which to make an inference. Interestingly, poor com-prehenders' performance increased, leading Cain and Oakhill to suggest that it is not so much the case that poor comprehenders cannot make inferences, but rather that they fail to do so spontaneously.

The problems that poor comprehenders have making inferences raises a number of issues that have been addressed by Cain, Oakhill, and colleagues. First, linguists and psy-cholinguists distinguish between different types of inference (e.g., Singer, 1994). Do poor comprehenders have difficulty with all types of inference? Two types of inference have been studied in detail in poor comprehenders: cohesive inferences and elaborative infer-ences. Cohesive inferences are needed to establish and maintain links between premises within the text and are necessary if adequate comprehension is to follow. Elaborative infer-ences are made when information external to the text is integrated with information con-tained in the text; these inferences are not always essential, but they are thought to enrich the readers' representation of the text. Generally it appears that poor comprehenders perform less well than controls on both types of inference, although presenting the text for the children to refer back to results in greater improvement for cohesive than elabo-rative inferences (Cain & Oakhill, 1999; Cain, Oakhill, Barnes, & Bryant, 2001). A different form of inferencing was assessed by Oakhill (1983). Instantiation refers to the process whereby a specific meaning of a word is constructed, depending on context. For example, long-term recall of a sentence such as "the fish attacked the swimmer" is enhanced following a cue such as the noun *shark*, relative to the original (but less context specific) noun, *fish*. Consistent with their tendency to draw fewer elaborative inferences, poor comprehenders are also less likely to make instantiations than control children (Oakhill, 1983).

A second issue concerns whether it the *process* of inference making per se that is impaired for these children or, alternatively, is it that they lack the relevant knowledge needed to make the inference? To disentangle the effects of group differences in background knowledge from group differences in inference making skills, Cain et al. (2001) taught a novel knowledge base to groups of poor comprehenders and control children. Specifically, 12 pieces of information about the imaginary planet *Gan* were read to the children (e.g., the ponds on *Gan are filled with orange juice; bears on Gan have bright blue fur*). Cain et al. then tested acquisition of the knowledge base using a forced-choice picture recognition task, and a verbal recall task. Any items that were not recognized or recalled correctly were retaught. The children then listened to a story tapping the knowledge base and were asked questions that required either a cohesive or an elaborative inference to be made. Poor comprehenders were poor at generating both types of inference, even though they did not differ in terms of world knowledge relevant to the text. Importantly, it is interesting to note that the poor comprehenders were also poor at answering literal questions about the stories, suggesting that their lack of understanding is not just a consequence of failure to make inferences. Nevertheless, the results of this study are clear in showing that even when relevant background is familiar, poor comprehenders draw fewer inferences than do skilled comprehenders.

Arguably, a limitation of the research pointing to poor inference making as a cause of poor reading comprehension is its circularity: since children in these studies were selected as poor comprehenders precisely because they performed poorly on a standardized test of discourse comprehension containing a high proportion of inference-based questions, it might be considered unsurprising that they performed less well than control children on experimental tasks tapping inference-making ability. To address the issue of causality, Cain and Oakhill (1999) utilized the comprehension-age match design described earlier. They compared the inference-making abilities of 7–8-year-old poor comprehenders with those of normally developing children aged 6–7 years. The two groups of children did not differ in terms of comprehension scores on the test used to screen participants, the *Neale Analysis of Reading Ability*. Nevertheless, poor comprehenders made fewer inferences on the experimental tasks than the younger children, leading Cain and Oakhill to conclude that poor inference-making ability is a candidate cause of poor reading and language comprehension.

*Comprehension monitoring.* Comprehension monitoring refers to a set of metacognitive control processes that individuals can draw upon as they read or listen. In skilled reading, comprehension monitoring results in an assessment of whether comprehension has been successful, and repair strategies may be initiated if miscomprehension is detected. In short, comprehension monitoring refers to a set of strategies that indicate that a reader is engaged with the text. Oakhill and Yuill (1996) described three strands of evidence pointing to deficits in comprehension monitoring in children selected as having specific reading comprehension difficulties. First, they are less likely to resolve anomalies in text. For example, Yuill et al. (1989) presented scenarios containing an apparent anomaly (e.g., a mother is pleased that her son is not sharing sweets with his younger brother). Resolving information (that the younger son is on a diet) was presented later in the scenario. Children were then asked whether the mother had behaved appropriately, and why she took the action she did, the rationale being that these questions can only be answered correctly if the different sources of information are integrated. While poor comprehenders were able to resolve anomalies well when the two pieces of information were adjacent in the story, their performance fell dramatically when two filler sentences intervened between the two premises. These findings suggest that poor comprehenders are able to integrate information adequately, but fail to do so when the task is made more demanding by increasing its memory load.

A rather different strand of evidence pointing to comprehension monitoring deficits in poor comprehenders come from an anomaly detection task in which children are asked to underline any meaningless words or phrases (Yuill & Oakhill, 1991). Even when they were explicitly instructed that a text contained nonsense words and phrases, poor comprehenders were less likely to detect them than control children. In addition, poor comprehenders were less likely to detect inconsistencies in a text, particularly when the inconsistencies within the text were separated by a number of sentences. Taken together, these findings suggest that poor comprehenders are not engaged in constructive comprehension monitoring: they fail to notice when comprehension has gone astray and are thus not well placed to initiate repair strategies.

Observing that poor comprehenders are less likely to monitor their own comprehension does not, on its own, establish comprehension monitoring as a cause of reading comprehension failure. Instead, faulty comprehension monitoring may well be a *consequence* of faulty comprehension rather than a cause of it. Indeed, comprehension monitoring ability is not a static or fixed variable; de Sousa and Oakhill (1996) found that poor comprehenders' comprehension monitoring ability increased substantially when they engaged in a more interesting task. In contrast, comprehension monitoring levels were fairly constant for the skilled comprehenders, regardless of the task's interest level. These findings caution against the view that comprehension monitoring is a processing weakness implicated in reading comprehension failure.

In summary, studies by Oakhill and colleagues have provided numerous demonstrations of the difficulties that poor comprehenders have with discourse-level processes. Moreover, it has been proposed that poor inference skills are a likely cause of poor comprehension (e.g., Cain & Oakhill, 1999). However, on a number of counts, Perfetti has questioned the validity of the view that specific deficits in higher-level skills are *causally* implicated in reading comprehension impairments (e.g., Perfetti, 1994). His preferred account is that poor inference making or failure to detect anomalies are not examples of structural or specific deficits that cause a comprehension problem. Rather, *they are* the comprehension problem, a problem that stems from weaknesses in "the operation of basic processes that identify words, activate their meanings, configure phrases, assemble meanings and so forth" (Perfetti et al., 1996, p. 159). Before considering this perspective further, it is necessary to move away from processing factors to consider the other potential cause of comprehension failure; that is, differences in knowledge.

## Knowledge

Knowledge is essential to comprehension. Without an appreciation of the meanings of words, there can be no comprehension. Moving beyond the meaning of individual words, domain knowledge is also considered crucial for comprehension. Appreciation of the domain that is being referred to in a text allows the reader to move from a word- or propositional-level representation of the text to one which integrates this knowledge with a broader body of background knowledge, thus allowing the reader to build a potentially inference-rich mental model of the situation or event (see Kintsch & Rawson, this volume). Prior knowledge about a text predicts comprehension of it (Spilich, Vesonder, Chiesi, & Voss, 1979) and it is plain that complete lack of knowledge will result in a complete lack of comprehension (recall the example described earlier of Milton's daughters reading aloud Latin and Greek with no comprehension). But, is it the case that there are systematic deficiencies in poor comprehenders' knowledge base that can account for their faulty comprehension?

As reviewed earlier, there is evidence suggesting that poor comprehenders have relative weaknesses in expressive and receptive vocabulary (Nation et al., 2004), indicative of lack of knowledge at the word level. Although it seems likely that lack of vocabulary knowledge may contribute to impaired comprehension, it is unlikely to be the whole story: comprehension weaknesses are still apparent when care is taken to include vocabulary that is familiar, and when domain knowledge is to some extent controlled by teaching the children a novel knowledge base from which comprehension is subsequently assessed (Cain et al., 2001; although it should be noted that in this study poor comprehenders took longer to learn the knowledge base, and showed poorer retention of it over time. Although this was controlled statistically in their analyses, it cannot be ruled out that differences in knowledge base (perhaps in terms of the quality of its representation) may have existed between the two groups).

Rather than describe knowledge as being present or absent, a different approach is to ask whether individuals differ in the extent to which they activate knowledge spontaneously, or bring it to bear rapidly and efficiently at the appropriate time. For example, Nation and Snowling (1998a) reported that poor comprehenders were slower to make semantic judgments than control children. In a similar vein, Cain and Oakhill (1999) reported that poor comprehenders' ability to make inferences increased when they were assisted to find the relevant part of the text. These two observations are both examples of instances when poor comprehenders had the required knowledge, but failed to deploy it either quickly or spontaneously. Alternatively, however, these observations could be interpreted as indicative of lack of knowledge in that it is only when knowledge is thoroughly understood and properly integrated that it can be reflected on rapidly, or used to trigger inferences.

### Low-level versus high-level processing, and processing versus knowledge

As reflected in the above review, the literature on specific reading comprehension difficulties has concerned itself with dichotomies. Are poor comprehenders' difficulties best understood in terms of processing deficits or lack of knowledge? If poor comprehenders have processing weaknesses, are they "low level" or "high level"? However, it is not clear whether these dichotomies are useful or psychologically valid. Two examples will be used to illustrate what is meant here, one concerning word meaning and vocabulary and one concerning verbal memory.

There are now a number of studies demonstrating vocabulary weaknesses in children selected as having poor reading comprehension (e.g., Nation et al., 2004; Nation & Snolwing, 1998a; Stothard & Hulme, 1992). In some ways, weak vocabulary is a clear index of lack of knowledge and, as noted above, comprehension will fail if children simply do not understand the words they read or hear. However, the question then arises as to why poor comprehenders have weak vocabulary knowledge. Lack of vocabulary knowledge is associated with weaknesses in verbal IQ, and, consistent with this, poor comprehenders achieve lower verbal IQ scores than control children (Nation, et al., 2002). However, as a substantial component of verbal IQ is vocabulary knowledge, this observation does not help us understand the nature of poor comprehenders' difficulties. More interesting is the notion that an individual's ability to learn new words or acquire new information from context is a vital skill that mediates the high correlations observed between verbal ability, reading comprehension, and vocabulary knowledge (e.g., Sternberg & Powell, 1983).

Cain, Oakhill, and Elbro (2004) examined the ability of poor comprehenders to learn new words from context by presenting stories containing a novel word (whose meaning was discernible from context) and asking children to define the novel words, either before the context allowed word meaning to be inferred, or afterwards. Poor comprehenders were less likely to offer definitions for the novel words, especially when the distance between the word and the information needed to infer its meaning was lengthened by inserting filler sentences. This study is interesting, as it demonstrates how "higher-level" processes such as the ability to make inferences and integrate information within a text can influence the acquisition of basic "lower-level" knowledge such as the meaning of a new word. In turn, knowledge of word meanings and their speedy activation during reading (or listening) may well assist children's "higher-level" processing during language comprehension (Nation & Snowling, 1998b, 1999). Thus, it is perhaps not surprising to find that children who are poor at making inferences tend to have weaker vocabulary skills relative to children who are skilled at making inferences, and vice versa.

The overlap between processing and knowledge is also demonstrated when we consider the possibility that long-term memory may contribute to poor comprehenders' deficits on memory span tasks. A well-replicated finding is that poor comprehenders perform equivalently to control children on straightforward tasks of verbal short-term memory capacity (i.e., recall tasks such as forward digit span that do not require an additional processing component; e.g., Stothard & Hulme, 1992). Similarly, poor comprehenders show normal effects of word length and phonological similarity in short-term memory (Nation et al., 1999; Oakhill, Yuill, & Parkin, 1986). Taken together, these findings demonstrate that poor comprehenders do not have deficits in short-term verbal memory capacity. Importantly however, the extent to which poor comprehenders show normal short-term recall depends critically on the nature of the items to be recalled. Nation et al. (1999, Experiment 2) compared short-term serial recall for lists of concrete words (e.g., *tooth, plate, fruit*) and abstract words (e.g., *luck, pride, wise*). Although poor comprehenders and controls did not differ in memory span for concrete words, poor comprehenders recalled fewer abstract words. It is established that the availability of semantic information influences short-term recall, and that concrete words may receive more "semantic support" than abstract words during short-term recall (Walker & Hulme, 1999). Within this theoretical framework, Nation et al. (1999) suggested that as poor comprehenders have semantic weaknesses, they benefit less from semantic support, especially when the semantic contribution to recall is stressed by asking them to recall abstract rather than concrete words, and under these circumstances short-term recall – usually reported as an area of strength – is compromised.

These two examples highlight the inherent difficulty (and perhaps even futility) of distinguishing between knowledge and processing as sources of poor comprehenders' difficulties. Within an interactive (and developing) language system, it seems likely that difficulties at one level will influence performance at another; similarly, long-term knowledge will influence processing efficiency, and individual differences in processing will lead to differences in long-term knowledge. Nagy and Anderson (1984) have argued that from the beginning of third grade, the amount of free reading children engage in is the major determinant of vocabulary growth. Preliminary data (Cain, 1994, cited in Oakhill & Yuill, 1996) suggest that poor comprehenders have substantially less reading and reading-related experience than control children. Although Cain's data need to be interpreted cautiously due to the sample size being very small, they are consistent with a view that sees individual differences in reading comprehension failure becoming compounded over time. Thus, Matthew effects (see the glossary at end of this volume) are likely: poor comprehenders may read less, and learn less from their reading experiences than their peers; therefore impacting on subsequent reading and learning opportunities over time and leading to the formation of weak "intellectual habits" (Perfetti et al., 1996).

## Summary and Conclusions

Comprehension is complex and multifaceted, and it is no surprise that the population of children identified as having reading comprehension difficulties form a heterogeneous group. Even when discussion is limited to those children who have well-developed decoding ability, as in this chapter, heterogeneity is still apparent (Nation et al., 2002, 2004). However, it is possible to draw some clear conclusions. Children with "specific" comprehension problems do exist, and they are not unusual (Yuill & Oakhill, 1991), although they are rare in clinically referred populations (e.g., Leach et al., 2003; Shankweiler, et al., 1999).

While it is clear that decoding inefficiency will lead to reading comprehension difficulties (e.g., Perfetti, 1985), not all children who have comprehension difficulties have impairments in basic decoding, nor do they experience a phonological bottleneck; the children described in the studies reviewed in this chapter decode well, and they have age-appropriate phonological processing skills. Poor comprehenders do, however, have weaknesses in other aspects of language skill with deficits at both lower (e.g., vocabulary knowledge) and higher levels (e.g., inference generation, understanding figurative language) being reported (Nation et al., 2004). Although it is possible to describe different tasks according to whether they tap low-level or high-level processes, it is argued here that the distinction between different levels of processing may not be useful, at least until longer-term longitudinal data become available.

One of the difficulties facing the researcher interested in understanding the nature of poor comprehenders' difficulties is that typically, the children are selected for study on the basis of their reading profile. Consequently, we know very little about the development of language in preschool or preliterate children who go on to become poor comprehenders. Long-term longitudinal studies are needed if we are to understand better the precursors to, and consequences of, "specific" difficulties with reading comprehension.

# PART IV

*Reading in Different Languages*

# Editorial Part IV

Although there are many languages in the world, most of what we know about reading comes from studies of English. Research on reading in other writing systems started in the late 1970s and has burgeoned in recent years. There is now good evidence for the long-held belief that English, with its many irregularities, is one of the hardest orthographies to master. At the same time findings have gone a long way toward dispelling the myth that the basis of Chinese reading is visual and that, by implication, dyslexia does not "exist" in Chinese.

In the first chapter, Frost picks up the theme developed earlier by Treiman and Kessler, that orthographies have evolved to represent various sublinguistic units of spoken language including syllables, phonemes, and morphemes. However, in all natural human languages, words are phonological entities and in learning to read the task is to establish orthographic representations comprising optimal units that map to phonology. The size of these optimal units differs across languages and therefore different orthographic systems will characterize skilled reading in different languages.

Frost uses the single-route phonological theory (described by Van Orden & Kloos in Part I) as a framework for considering skilled reading in different languages. According to this theory, phonological recoding prior to lexical access is obligatory, but the efficiency of the operations involved differs between children and adults and between languages. The operations in question include the speed of assembly of the phonological form from the printed letter string, the size of the orthographic units, and the efficiency of lexical access from impoverished phonological input (a process that can be likened to completion of the word's pronunciation). An important factor determining the speed of lexical access and hence comprehension of the written word is the orthographic depth of the language: shallow orthographies (in which there are consistent relationships between letters and sounds) are read more easily than deep orthographies (in which there are inconsistencies in letter-phoneme and phoneme-letter correspondences) because they support faster assembly of phonological codes from letter strings. In turn, phoneme-level units will be optimal in shallow (but not deep) orthographies and there should be relatively little lexical influence because phonological inputs will be fully specified. Evidence from many cross-linguistic studies support the view that assembly processes are more efficient in shallow orthographies but lexical support is always necessary to a degree.

Seymour focuses on the development of early reading processes in a range of European languages and reviews data showing that both orthographic depth and syllable complexity affect the rate at which children learn to read. Learning to read is slow in English and Danish (both deep orthographies with complex syllable structures), inter-mediate in French and Portugese (shallow orthographies with complex syllable structures), and fast in a language such as Italian (shallow orthography with simple syllable struc-tures). A striking finding is that even when reading simple nonwords, readers of deep orthographies are handicapped. It follows that decoding is not an isolated linear left-to-right process but is affected by the overall complexity of the orthographic environment at the start of learning. Findings like these challenge the idea that learning to read depends upon acquiring two separate processes; there are clear lexical influences on decoding effi-ciency. These findings are in line with the single phonological route theory favoured by Frost.

For many years it was thought that learning to read Chinese was very different to learn-ing to read in an alphabetic system. Certainly there are good reasons for expecting dif-ferences, given that the mappings between print and sound are at a morphemic level in Chinese, rather than a phonemic level as in alphabetic writing systems. But, contrary to popular belief, Chinese characters do convey information about their pronunciation. The majority of Chinese characters (some 80%) are made up of a radical component (that is related to its meaning) and a phonetic component (that provides some information about its sound). However, some phonetic components have inconsistent pronunciations, intro-ducing a degree of irregularity into the orthography. Also, syllables can be pronounced using different tones that signal different morphemes, but these are not marked in the orthography.

Hanley reviews studies of Chinese children's reading. There is now a substantial body of evidence showing that children are sensitive to both the radical and the phonetic com-ponents of Chinese characters, and, interestingly, the regularity of the phonetic compo-nent (the consistency with which it is associated with the same pronunciation) affects the rate at which a character can be learned. A related finding is that readers of Chinese have better syllable and morpheme awareness than readers of English. Variations in phono-logical skills do predict learning to read in Chinese but less powerfully than in English, however the independence of phonological skills from other language skills as predictors of learning to read in Chinese has yet to be established unambiguously.

With the above findings as a backdrop, Caravolas considers the manifestations of dyslexia in different languages. Her starting point is that English-speaking children with dyslexia have phonological rather than visual processing deficits. She proceeds to ask whether the same is true for children with dyslexia learning to read in shallow orthogra-phies, such as German or Czech. Contrary to some earlier views, she concludes that phonological skills, particularly skills in dealing with phonemes, are critical to learning to read in shallow orthographies and that dyslexia, in shallow as well as deep orthogra-phies, arises from a phonological deficit.

Knowledge about dyslexia in Chinese is in a much less mature state than in alphabetic systems and as yet the symptoms of the disorder in terms of reading and spelling processes are not well documented. However, progress is being made in specifying the associated cognitive deficits. Perhaps it is unsurprising, given the nature of the orthography, that phoneme awareness deficits are experienced by a relatively low proportion of Chinese children described as having dyslexia. However, rapid naming deficits are frequent as are deficits in orthographic processing, possibly related to the visual complexity of Chinese characters. When placed together with the findings from studies of dyslexia in alphabetic systems, it seems that problems in the phonological domain will retard the development of reading in most languages. Returning to Frost, this arguably follows from the nature of all human languages in which lexical representations are, at their core, phonological. Whilst the optimal orthographic units will differ between orthographies, the essential requirement to map orthography to phonology will depend upon the efficiency of the child's phonological system in any language.

The chapters in Part IV suggest that since 1980 we have moved closer to a universal theory of reading than we ever supposed would be the case (e.g., Perfetti, Liu & Tan, in press). In essence, all writing systems map orthography to phonology although with different degrees of transparency. Phonology is important for learning to read in all languages and children with phonological difficulties will be at risk of reading failure, although the severity of their problems will vary depending on the language they learn. We still have a long way to go to understand the contribution of nonphonological (e.g., visual and semantic) skills to the development of orthographic representations and conversely to dyslexia in different languages.

# 15

# Orthographic Systems and Skilled Word Recognition Processes in Reading

## Ram Frost

The process of recognizing printed words has been studied for many years, yielding several important models of word recognition in reading. These models provide a variety of descriptions of the word recognition process, given different assumptions regarding the structure of the lexical system. Yet what all models have in common is the recognition that reading involves the processing of orthographic, phonological, semantic, and morphological information. Since this information is conveyed differently in each language, the question of how the reader's linguistic environment shapes the reading process is of primary importance. This chapter focuses on the relations between the specific characteristics of different orthographic systems and skilled reading. The starting point is an outline of the dimensions on which orthographic systems differ from each other (see also Treiman & Kessler, this volume). This discussion will be followed by a detailed description of what skilled reading entails. As such a description is necessarily model-dependent, two main approaches to skilled reading will be presented. As a final step, the discussion will outline how proficient reading is shaped by the structure of the language and its orthographic system.

## Overview of Writing Systems

In contrast to speech, which is an emerging property of human biology, orthographic systems are a human invention, just as the wheel is. All orthographies, whether alphabetic, syllabic, or logographic, were invented a few thousand years ago with the sole purpose of communicating spoken language in graphic form. How language was eventually represented graphically is of considerable interest.

One interesting solution for the graphic representation of language is the ancient Egyptian hieroglyphic script. Hieroglyphs were composed mainly of ideograms, which are pictorial signs depicting objects or actions. The hieroglyphic script is interesting because it demonstrates the futility of a representational system in which semantic concepts and words are directly represented by an analog schematic picture. The clear disadvantage of such a system is that abstract semantic concepts cannot be represented, and even for more concrete concepts, representation is not always unequivocal. This is why ideograms could not suffice as an efficient graphic communication system in written Egyptian, and consequently a large number of the old Egyptian hieroglyphic signs were alphabetic phonograms that depicted phonemes (basically consonants) and had no relations whatsoever to the concept to be represented in print. These phonograms are considered to be *the Egyptian alphabet,* and include 24 letter-signs. In addition to the 24 letter signs there were also two-phoneme and three-phoneme signs, many of which had a meaning of their own and represented individual words. In this case, however, they were completed with a stroke, the so-called *ideogram sign,* to indicate that the designated word corresponded to the pictorial value of the sign. Additionally, sometimes the two- and three-letter signs were given *phonetic complements* – one-letter signs that repeated all or some of their sound value. The purpose of these complements was to indicate that the signs were phonograms, not ideograms. Examples of Egyptian hieroglyphic signs are presented in table 15.1.

The history of the Egyptian hieroglyphic script thus provides a unique insight into the nature of this wonderful invention that we call orthography. Contrary to the layman's perception that the Egyptian script presents a viable option for representing objects and actions pictographically, it actually teaches us just the opposite lesson – namely that any human writing system cannot do without phonographic signs.

**Table 15.1**   Examples of Egyptian hieroglyphs. The First Three Hieroglyphs Represent General Concepts, Whereas the Last Three Belong to the Egyptian Alphabet

| | | |
|---|---|---|
| | | man |
| | | god, king |
| | | bird, insect |
| | *b* | foot |
| | *n* | water |
| | *m* | owl |

Orthographic systems can therefore be contrasted with pictographic systems. Pictures and many signs (e.g., a picture of a dog, an arrow sign) represent meaning directly and are characterized by nonarbitrary relations between graphic sign and transcribed meaning. The visual shape of a graphic sign per se conveys its meaning, and often this meaning can be recovered, at least to some extent, without prior explicit teaching. In contrast, for written words in any language, the relations between graphic signs and meaning are arbitrary. This arbitrariness derives precisely from the fact that the graphic signs convey only phonological units systematically, and that the mapping of phonological units into semantic meaning is indeed arbitrary.

Although in every written language the graphic signs represent phonological units, the manner in which orthographies represent their spoken language depends on the characteristics of each language. Writing systems can be distinguished by the size of the linguistic units that the orthographic units transcribe: phonemes, as in English; syllables (moras), as in Japanese Kana; or morphosyllables, as in Chinese characters. What defines the unit of representation is mainly the efficiency of the representational system in terms of memory constraints or processing limitations. For example, in the Japanese syllabic Kana orthography, the graphemes represent the 116 permissible syllables in the Japanese language. (There are several possible ways of counting the number of permissible syllables in Japanese, and the above assessment represents just one of them.) This number is fairly small, given the constraint that Japanese has 14 consonants and 5 vowels, and its syllabic structure is constrained to vowel or consonant-plus-vowel combinations. The most efficient representational system is therefore a system that provides a grapheme for each of these syllables, since learning and memorizing 116 graphic signs is not very difficult. In sharp contrast, the syllabic structure of English is far more complex (see Akmajian, Demers, Farmer, & Harnish, 2001, for a detailed description). Not only does English have 24 consonants and 15 vowels, but the permissible syllables have many possible structures (e.g., CV, VC, CVC, CCVC). This has immediate implications not only for the number of permissible syllables in the language that would require an independent symbol – about 15,000, but also, more importantly, for the ability of English native speakers to retrieve the word's syllables. The division of many English words into syllables is controversial, as syllabic boundaries are not well defined (e.g., *dagger*). These words contain ambisyllabic segments in which a clear break does not exist, and therefore different parsings into syllables can be suggested (see Kahn, 1976). For these reasons, therefore, a syllabic orthography would never work for English speakers. Learning and memorizing thousands of distinct graphic signs is an exhausting task, and matching signs to several syllabification possibilities rather than one unequivocal solution would be a very slow cognitive process. This is one reason why orthographic units in English transcribe phonemes rather than syllables.

As described above, Japanese Kana and English are alphabetic systems, which differ in the size of the sublinguistic units represented by the orthographic units. Indeed, most orthographic systems are alphabetic, and the graphic signs represent subsyllabic or syllabic linguistic units. Some orthographic systems, however, have adopted an entirely different approach for representing spoken language. Perhaps the most notable example are logographic orthographies such as Chinese in which the graphemic structure represents meaningful morphemes and not sublinguistic phonological units. But even in Chinese

90% of the characters are phonetic compounds (although not necessarily consistent) and only 10% are semantic determiners whose purpose is to differentiate between the many homophones existing in that language (DeFrancis, 1989).

Yet another transcription strategy was adopted in the logographic Japanese Kanji and Korean Hanza. As will be described in detail later on, both languages in addition to their phonographic system imported the Chinese logographs. However, the logographic symbols were meant to represent meaningful morphemes with a pronunciation differing from the one they had in their original language, since they were imported into a different spoken language, and so their phonological components were distorted. For these reasons, phonographic notations were added to the characters in both languages for the purpose of facilitating reading. In Japanese, some Kanji words are printed with a phonetic transcription next to them (Furigana), which provides the reader with the necessary cues for pronouncing the logographs. Furigana is used mainly for children and foreigners learning Kanji. In Korean, the logographic Hanza characters are mixed inconsistently with an alphabetic script, the Hangul, to facilitate reading.

To summarize, writing systems have evolved to represent various sublinguistic units of the spoken language (phoneme, syllable, morphophonemes). Although writing systems clearly are not phonographic to the same extent, they all contain at least some cues to the phonological structure of printed words. The main implication of this is that writing systems were not designed (and indeed could not have been designed) to transcribe units of meaning directly without some reference to their phonological form. This is because languages are productive by nature, new words are constantly being invented, and meanings evolve with time. The only form of orthographic system that can in principle deal with language productivity is a spelling system that transcribes subword linguistic units, thereby specifying a set of rules for representing novel words (Mattingly, 1992).

Having outlined the characteristics of the orthographic systems of natural languages, in the next section I will discuss how orthographic information is processed by proficient readers during reading.

## Models of Skilled Reading

Two major theories should be considered in the context of modeling skilled reading: the dual-route theory (e.g., Coltheart, 1980; Coltheart, Curtis, Atkins, & Haller, 1993; Coltheart, Rastle, Perry, Langdon, & Ziegler, 2001; Paap & Noel, 1991; Paap, Noel, & Johansen, 1992; Zorzi, Houghton, & Butterworth, 1998), and the single-route strong phonological theory (e.g., Frost, 1998; Lukatela & Turvey, 1994a, 1994b; Van Orden, Pennington, & Stone, 1990). The dual-route theory suggests a lexical architecture in which an orthographic input lexicon plays a major role. The dual-route theory has generated various models in the last three decades, which differ in their architectural assumptions. For example, the dual-route cascaded (DRC) model of Coltheart et al. (2001) and the model of Zorzi et al. (1998), are both dual-route models. However, the former assumes local representations, whereas the latter assumes that words are represented as distributed patterns of activation. What all these models have in common is the assumption that reading involves an interplay between prelexical phonological computation, on the one hand, and visual orthographic processing, on the other. Note, however, that dual-route models generally assume that phonological computation is relatively slow and lags behind orthographic processing. Thus, whereas beginning readers are mostly engaged in prelexical grapheme–phoneme computations, converting letters to phonemic segments to recover the printed word's phonology piece by piece, proficient readers can make use of fast, direct connections between orthographic representations and the phonological output lexicon, or between the orthographic forms and semantic meaning. Thus, skilled reading is regarded as the result of acquiring orthographic representations of printed words through repeated exposure to these words during reading acquisition. In this view, the recognition of a printed word in most cases involves fast access to well-established ortho-graphic representations, which lead to the activation of full phonological structures and/or the relevant semantic features. Generally stated, the dual-route model defines the acqui-sition of reading skills as the ability to bypass mechanisms that convert orthographic subunits into phonological subunits, thereby relying on direct connections between orthographic representations to meaning.

The main alternatives to the dual-route theory are the strong phonological models of reading (Lukatela & Turvey, 1994a, 1994b; Van Orden et al., 1990; and see Frost, 1998, for a review and a detailed description). The critical difference between the strong phono-logical view and the dual-route theory lies not in terms of architectural differences such as distributed versus localist connectionist frameworks. It lies in the relative involvement of the orthographic lexicon, on the one hand, and the nonlexical route, on the other hand, in the process of word recognition. Although the primary models that adopt a strong phonology stance are not instantiated models, they all contend that, given the phonological nature of human natural languages, the core lexical representations of words are phonologically defined. In this view, visual word recognition involves mostly the phonological, not the orthographic, lexicon. Strong phonological models regard the initial process of reading as a process of converting letters or letter clusters into phonemes or syllables (unambiguous letters first), using prelexical conversion rules (or relying on grapheme–phoneme activation in a connectionist architecture). Thus, these models suggest that phonological computation is mandatory, and lexical search consists of regis-tering and finding stored phonological units. As will be demonstrated in the following discussion, in some orthographies the computation of phonology from print is by no means simple, and often this process results in an impoverished phonological code. There-fore, strong phonological models of reading define the acquisition of reading skills along three independent dimensions: (1) the speed of the assembly process, (2) the size of the computed orthographic units, and (3) the efficiency of accessing the lexicon through impoverished phonological information.

Regarding the speed of the assembly process, the strong phonological model of reading views the acquired competence of skilled readers as their ability to complete the initial cycles of assembly in minimal time. Thus, with increased exposure to reading, the begin-ning reader's efficiency in computing a prelexical phonological representation increases, making it possible to generate a skeletal phonological structure more quickly, thus leading to fast lexical access (e.g., Berent & Perfetti, 1995; Lukatela & Turvey, 1994a, 1994b).

The second dimension involves the size of the computed units. Although in alphabetic orthographies single letters generally represent single phonemes, there are quite a few cases in which phonemes are represented by letter clusters. This necessarily introduces additional complexity into the relations between spelling and phonology, since the prelexical computation process needs to take the adjacent letters into account in order to produce the correct phoneme. The skilled reader of English needs to know, for example, that c before e is pronounced /s/, but before o it is pronounced /k/, or that *ough* could be /o/ or /off/, but is never the primary phonemic transcription of each letter. The acquisition of reading skills can therefore be characterized as an increased ability to convert larger letter clusters into phonemic clusters, rather than depending on single letter-to-phoneme conversion. Ultimately, it could be possible, in principle, to convert whole printed words into whole phonological units. This is, in fact, the notion of direct connections between orthographic representations and the phonological output lexicon that forms the conceptual basis of dual-route models (cf. also Ehri, this volume). However, strong phonological models view the process of learning to read as a fine-tuning of *optimal-sized* units (larger than the single letter but smaller than the whole word), given the specific characteristics of the reader's orthography. The proficient reader learns to parse the printed word into letter units that allow fast conversion into a preliminary phonological representation. Indeed, there is a large body of evidence suggesting that while beginning readers engage in simple grapheme–phoneme conversion strategies, skilled readers also use larger grain-sized units such as bodies and rhymes (e.g., Brown & Deavers, 1999; Goswami, Gombert, & de Barrera, 1998).

The third dimension of reading competence involves an acquired efficiency in accessing the lexicon with impoverished phonological information. What makes lexical access fast, in spite of the extreme richness of lexical information, is the ability to access an entry or activate a word node with the accumulation of phonological information that is not necessarily full or complete. However, the ability to access the lexicon with only partial phonological information is a learned process involving prolonged exposure to printed words. According to this view, beginning readers are limited to a *detailed* analysis of the printed word before lexical access is achieved, whereas skilled readers can recognize the same word *with a relatively impoverished representation* (Frost, 1995; and see Frost, 1998, for a detailed discussion). As I will discuss below, different orthographies impose different constraints on the ability to generate a detailed and accurate phonological representation.

## Orthographic Depth and How Phonology Is Represented in Different Orthographies: The Case of English, Hebrew, and Serbo-Croatian

As all orthographies represent spoken forms, one major determinant of orthographic systems concerns the specific way they represent the phonological characteristics of the language. When the writing system is alphabetic, and letters represent the phonemes of the language, some opacity may exist in the representational system. The transparency of the relation between spelling and phonology varies widely between orthographies. This variance can be attributed to phonological or morphological factors. Opacity may be present simply because the spoken language has assimilated novel phonetic variations during its history, whereas the letters in the orthographic system have remained unchanged. This will necessarily lead to some ambiguity in the relations between letters and phonemes. In addition, in some languages morphological variations are captured by phonologic variations. The orthography, however, is designed to preserve and convey the morphologic information. Consequently, in many cases, similar spellings used to denote the same morpheme will have different phonologic forms. Consider, for example, the English words "heal" and "health." These words are similarly spelled because they are morphologically related, both containing the base-morpheme *heal.* However, since the morphological derivation *health* resulted in a phonologic variation (the phoneme /i/ turning now to /e/), the orthographic cluster "ea" represents in the two words two distinct phonemes. Alphabetic orthographies thus can be classified according to the transparency of their letter to phonology correspondence. This factor is usually referred to as "orthographic depth" (Klima, 1972; Liberman, Liberman, Mattingly, & Shankweiler, 1980; Lukatela, Popadic, Ognjenovic, & Turvey, 1980; Katz & Feldman, 1981). An orthography that represents its phonology unequivocally following simple grapheme–phoneme correspondences is considered *shallow*, while an orthography in which the relation of orthography to phonology is more opaque is labeled *deep*. Orthographic depth is often regarded as a continuum, and in this view languages may be aligned one next to the other where one language would be considered deeper than another but shallower than a third one (e.g., Frost, Katz, & Bentin, 1987). In the following I will discuss a few languages with reference to their orthographic depth.

## English

English is regarded as an example of a deep orthography. The main source of complexity in English derives from its rich vowel system, about 15 vowels, which are represented by fewer graphemes. In principle, the complexity of grapheme–phoneme correspondence can generally be defined in terms of the ease of computing a phonological representation from print, given the transparent or opaque mapping of spelling patterns into phonology. The degree of transparency arises, however, from two different factors. The first factor concerns the conformity of a given letter cluster to grapheme–phoneme correspondence rules. This factor is labeled *regularity*. For example, the pronunciation of words like *yacht* or *chef* cannot be simply computed using the grapheme–phoneme conversion rules of English. Thus, *yacht* and *chef* are considered irregular. The second factor is *consistency*. Consistency involves the uniqueness of pronunciation of an orthographic body. Thus, if two words are spelled similarly but pronounced differently (such as MOTH–BOTH), the letter cluster OTH is considered inconsistent (Glushko, 1979; Patterson & Coltheart, 1987). According to this analysis, words can be regular but inconsistent, or irregular but consistent. English orthography contains many words that are either irregular or inconsistent; this is why English is called a deep orthography.

*Hebrew*

In Hebrew, letters mostly represent consonants while most of the vowels can optionally be superimposed on the consonants as diacritical marks ("points"). The diacritical marks are, however, omitted from most reading material, and can be found only in poetry, children's literature, and religious scriptures. Since different vowels may be inserted into the same string of consonants to form different words or nonwords, Hebrew unpointed print cannot specify a unique phonological unit. Therefore, a printed consonant string is always phonologically ambiguous and often represents more than one word, each with a different meaning. In this context, the depth of the Hebrew orthography is different in character from that of English orthography. Whereas in English the opaque relations of spelling to sound are related to irregularity and/or inconsistency of letter clusters, in Hebrew opaque spelling-to-sound connections arise simply from *missing* phonemic information, mainly vowel information. Note that when the diacritical marks are presented in the text, Hebrew orthography is entirely shallow, as the phonemic structure of the printed word can be easily assembled using simple grapheme–phoneme conversion rules. The Hebrew alphabet is presented in Table 15.2.

**Table 15.2**   The Hebrew Alphabet. The Hebrew Letters a and V Stand for Glottal and Pharyngeal Stops, Respectively. K, m, p, c Have Different Forms When They Appear at the End of the Word

| Hebrew print | Phonetic transcription |
| --- | --- |
| א | a |
| ב | b, v |
| ג | g |
| ד | d |
| ה | h |
| ו | o, u, v |
| ז | z |
| ח | x |
| ט | t |
| י | I, y |
| ך / כ | k, x |
| ל | l |
| ם / מ | m |
| ן / נ | n |
| ס | s |
| ע | V |
| ף / פ | p, f |
| ץ / צ | ts |
| ק | k |
| ר | r |
| ש | sh |
| ת | t |

The depth of Hebrew orthography is evident in yet another feature. Several consonants (mainly, /k/, /t/, /x/, /v/, and glottal /a/), have two letters representing them. In ancient Hebrew these letters depicted a phonetic distinction that is absent in modern Hebrew. Note, however, that the opacity between letters and phonemes is mainly relevant for correct spelling rather than for reading. This is because, although a given phoneme may be written in two different ways (as in the case of C and K in English), the reading of the printed letter is entirely consistent.

English and Hebrew are therefore considered deep orthographies, but as shown above, their depth derives from different sources. It seems clear, then, that the opacity between orthography and phonology cannot be adequately described through the one-dimensional factor of labeling languages simply as "deep" or "shallow." Rather, one should consider also the *direction* of opacity: Is it in the mapping of orthography to phonology, or is it in the mapping of phonology to orthography? Consider, for example, the French orthographic system. French has transparent relations between print and phonology. Thus, the grapheme–phoneme conversion rules in French specify the phonology of printed words almost unequivocally. There are, however, several possible spellings for a given phoneme (e.g., *o, au, eau* may represent the vowel /o/). Thus, the mapping of phonology to spelling is opaque in French. A similar problem arises in pointed Hebrew: The orthography specifies the phonology unequivocally, but since several consonants have two letters representing them, the mapping of phonology to spelling is opaque. In languages such as English, opacity exists in both directions: from print to phonology as well as from phonology to print. Some languages, such as Spanish, Italian, and Serbo-Croatian are entirely transparent in both directions. The implication of directionality of opacity for reading performance was found to affect visual word recognition (e.g., Stone, Vanhoy, & Van Orden, 1999). Stone and his colleagues labeled this factor as *feed-forward* versus *feed-backward consistency*, demonstrating that both forms of consistency affect visual word recognition in English (see also Van Orden & Kloos, this volume).

## Serbo-Croatian

In Serbo-Croatian, aside from minor changes in stress patterns, phonology almost never varies with morphologic derivations. In the nineteenth century, a new orthographic system was imposed in the former Yugoslavia, designed to represent directly the surface phonology of the language. In this system each letter denotes only one phoneme, and each phoneme is represented by only one letter. Thus, the reading of any given letter in Serbo-Croatian cannot change in different orthographic contexts. In contrast to English, Serbo-Croatian has only five vowels /a/, /e/, /i/, /o/, /u/, without any phonetic variations. Similarly, all consonants in Serbo-Croatian are read unequivocally, and adjacent letters cannot change their reading. Even imported proper nouns are printed in Serbo-Croatian so that their original orthographic structure is not preserved, and the letters employed reflect the phonemic structure of these nouns. Correct reading in Serbo-Croatian thus involves the mere application of simple grapheme–phoneme rules. Even a nonspeaker of the language can easily learn to read Serbo-Croatian after memorizing the phonemic transliteration of the 33 letters of the alphabet. Thus, Serbo-Croatian is often presented as an example of an extremely shallow orthography.

## Orthographic Depth and Visual Word Recognition

The effect of orthographic depth on reading strategies has been the focus of extensive research (e.g., Baluch & Besner, 1991; Besner & Smith, 1992; Frost et al., 1987; Katz & Feldman, 1983; Tabossi & Laghi, 1992; Ziegler, Perry, Jacobs, & Braun, 2001; see also Seymour, this volume). In general, the argument revolves around the question of whether differences in orthographic depth lead to differences in processing printed words. What is called the Orthographic Depth Hypothesis suggests that it does. The Orthographic Depth Hypothesis suggests that shallow orthographies can easily support a word-recognition process that involves the printed word's phonology. This is because the phonologic structure of the printed word can be easily recovered from the print by applying a simple process of phonological computation. The correspondence between spelling and pronunciation in these orthographies is simple and direct, so that a reader of these orthographies can easily assemble an accurate representation of the word intended by the writer. In contrast, in deep orthographies like English or Hebrew, readers are encouraged to process printed words making use of larger units.

The specific predictions from the Orthographic Depth Hypothesis refer mainly to the way a printed word's phonology is generated in the reading process. These predictions depend, however, on the specific model of skilled reading that is embraced, whether a dual-route model or a strong phonological model. Note again that each model can be described using connectionist or nonconnectionist terminology. Described from the dual-route viewpoint, since readers of shallow orthographies have simple, consistent, and fairly complete connections between graphemes and subword pronunciation, they can recover most of a word's phonological structure prelexically by assembling it directly from the printed letters. In contrast, the opaque relation of letter clusters and phonemes in deep orthographies prevents readers from using prelexical conversion rules. For these readers, a more efficient way of generating the word's phonologic structure is to rely on fast visual access of the lexicon and retrieve the word's phonology from it. Thus, according to the dual-route framework, phonology in a shallow orthography involves mostly prelexical computation, whereas in a deep orthography, phonology is retrieved from the phonological output lexicon following activation of the visual lexicon.

The strong phonological theory provides different descriptions of similar processes. The theory assumes that prelexical phonological computation is a mandatory process that is automatic and very fast. In shallow orthographies, prelexical computation produces an accurate phonological representation of the printed word. In contrast, in deep orthographies, because of the opaque relations of graphemes and phonemes, this initial phase can only provide the reader with an impoverished phonological representation. This representation, however, is shaped by lexical knowledge to produce the correct pronunciation. Thus, top-down shaping of the prelexical computation product leads to a detailed phonological representation.

From an historical perspective, two versions of the Orthographic Depth Hypothesis have been offered. What can be called the *strong* Orthographic Depth Hypothesis claimed that in shallow orthographies the complete phonological representation is derived *exclusively* through prelexical translation of letters or letter clusters into phonological units. According to this view, readers of shallow orthographies perform a phonological analysis of the word based only on knowledge of these correspondences. Rapid naming, then, is a result of this analytic process *only*, and does not involve any lexical information (see Katz & Frost, 1992, for a discussion).

It is easy to show that the strong form of the Orthographic Depth Hypothesis is untenable. It is patently insufficient to account for pronunciation, even in shallow orthographies like Spanish, Italian, or Serbo-Croatian, reverting only to the process of prelexical phonological computation. Some lexical shaping is always necessary because these orthographies do not represent syllable stress and, even though stress is often predictable, this is not always the case. For example, in Serbo-Croatian, for two-syllable words the stress is always placed on the first syllable, but this is not always true for words of more than two syllables. These words can be pronounced correctly only by reference to lexically stored information. The issue of stress assignment is even more problematic in Italian, where stress patterns are much less predictable. In Italian many pairs of words differ only in stress that provides the intended semantic meaning (Colombo & Tabossi, 1992).

In the light of these arguments, a weaker version of the Orthographic Depth Hypothesis gained increasing support. According to the weak version of the Orthographic Depth Hypothesis, the phonology needed for the pronunciation of printed words in any orthography may involve both prelexical letter-to-phonology correspondences and lexical phonology. The differences between deep and shallow orthographies are mainly quantitative, not qualitative. From the dual-route perspective, in any orthography both prelexical and lexical processes are launched. In cascaded models such as the DRC model (Coltheart et al., 2001; Coltheart this volume), the two processes also exchange information. Whether or not prelexical processes actually dominate orthographic processing for any particular orthography is a matter of probability, given the demands the two processes make on the reader's processing resources (see Seidenberg, 1992, for a discussion). These demands are affected by the depth of the orthography. Prelexical analytic processes are more useful in shallow orthographies than in deep orthographies, whereas the opposite is true for lexical processes. From the perspective of the strong phonological view, phonology is always partly prelexical and partly lexically shaped. The involvement and need for lexical shaping depends, among other things on orthographic depth. Greater lexical shaping is required in deep than in shallow orthographies, and vice versa.

## Empirical Evidence for the Orthographic Depth Hypothesis

Evidence relevant to the Orthographic Depth Hypothesis comes from experiments that investigate whether phonology is computed prelexically or whether it is lexically shaped.

Typically, latencies and error rates for naming words are monitored, to find out whether the lexical status of a printed stimulus (whether it is a word or a nonword, and whether it is a frequent or infrequent word) affects its pronunciation. If phonology is assembled from print prelexically, smaller effects of the word's frequency should be expected than if phonology is lexically mediated. A second method of investigation involves monitoring semantic priming effects in naming (see Lupker, 1984, Neely, 1991, for a review). If pronunciation involves lexical phonology, strong semantic priming effects will be revealed in naming. In contrast, if pronunciation depends mainly on prelexical phonology, naming of target words should be facilitated only weakly by semantically related primes.

Evidence supporting the weak Orthographic Depth Hypothesis is abundant. Katz and Feldman (1983) compared semantic priming effects in naming and lexical decision in both English and Serbo-Croatian, and demonstrated that while semantic facilitation was obtained in English for both lexical decision and naming, in Serbo-Croatian semantic priming facilitated only lexical decision. Similarly, a comparison of semantic priming effects for word naming in English and Italian showed greater effects in the deeper (English) than in the shallower (Italian) orthography (Tabossi & Laghi, 1992). A study by Frost et al. (1987) involved a simultaneous comparison of three languages, Hebrew, English, and Serbo-Croatian, and confirmed the hypothesis that the use of prelexical phonology in naming varies as a function of orthographic depth. Frost et al. showed that the lexical status of the stimulus (its being a high- or a low-frequency word or a nonword) affected naming latencies in Hebrew more than in English, and in English more than in Serbo-Croatian. In a second experiment, Frost et al. showed a relatively strong effect of semantic facilitation in Hebrew (21 ms), a smaller but significant effect in English (16 ms), and no facilitation (0 ms) in Serbo-Croatian.

Frost and Katz (1989) studied the effects of visual and auditory degradation on the ability of subjects to match printed to spoken words in English and Serbo-Croatian. They showed that both visual and auditory degradation had a much stronger effect in English than in Serbo-Croatian, regardless of word frequency. These results were explained by extending an interactive model that rationalized the relationship between the ortho-graphic and phonologic systems in terms of lateral connections between the systems at all of their levels. The structure of these lateral connections was determined by the rela-tionship between spelling and phonology in the language: simple isomorphic connections between graphemes and phonemes in the shallower Serbo-Croatian, but more complex, many-to-one, connections in the deeper English. Frost and Katz argued that the simple isomorphic connections between the orthographic and the phonologic systems in the shal-lower orthography enabled subjects to restore both the degraded phonemes from the print and the degraded graphemes from the phonemic information, with ease. In contrast, in the deeper orthography, because the degraded information in one system was usually con-sistent with several alternatives in the other system, the buildup of sufficient information for a unique solution to the matching judgment was delayed, so the matching between print and degraded speech, or between speech and degraded print, was slowed.

The psychological reality of orthographic depth, however, is not unanimously accepted. Although it is generally agreed that the relation between spelling and phonol-ogy in different orthographies affect reading processes (especially reading acquisition), there is some disagreement about the relative importance of this factor. What is often called "the Universal Hypothesis" argues that in all orthographic systems, print is processed essentially in the same way. The primary theoretical basis of the Universal Hypothesis is the dual-route architectural assumption that, in *any* orthography, words can easily be recognized through a fast visual-based lexical access that in most cases occurs before a phonologic representation has time to be generated prelexically from the print. In this view the primary factor determining whether or not the word's phonology is assembled prelexically or addressed from the lexicon is word frequency. The Universal Hypothesis thus suggests that the relation of spelling to phonology should not affect the recognition of frequent words. Orthographic depth exerts some influence, but only on the processing of low-frequency words and nonwords, since such verbal stimuli are less familiar and their visual lexical access is slower (Baluch & Besner, 1991; Seidenberg, 1985; Tabossi & Laghi, 1992).

A few studies involving cross-language research support the Universal Hypothesis. Seidenberg (1985) demonstrated that, in both English and Chinese, naming frequent printed words was not affected by phonologic regularity. This outcome was interpreted to mean that, in logographic as in alphabetic orthographies, the phonology of frequent words is derived after the word has been recognized on a visual basis. Similar conclusions were offered by Baluch and Besner (1991), who investigated word recognition in Persian. In this study the authors took advantage of the fact that some words in Persian are phonologically transparent whereas others are phonologically opaque. This is because, in a way that is similar to Hebrew, three of the six vowels of written Persian are represented in print as diacritics and three as letters. Because fluent readers do not use the pointed script, words that contain vowels represented by letters are phonologically transparent, whereas words that contain vowels represented by diacritics are phonologically opaque (see Frost, 1995, for an identical manipulation in Hebrew). Baluch and Besner demonstrated similar semantic priming effects in naming phonologically transparent and phonologically opaque words of Persian, provided that nonwords were omitted from the stimulus list. These results were interpreted to suggest that naming both types of words followed lexical access.

A different approach to resolving this inconsistency in results was adopted in several studies that examined the grain-size of units employed by readers of deep and shallow orthographies. Thus, rather than seeking an all-or-none answer to the question of whether phonology is lexical or not, these studies contrasted beginning or proficient readers of deep and shallow orthographies by monitoring the size of the computed units they use in reading (e.g., Frith, Wimmer, & Landerl, 1998; Goswami et al., 1998; Ziegler et al., 2001). As explained above, the strong phonological model of reading considers skilled reading as an increased ability to convert larger letter clusters into phonemic clusters, rather than depending on single letter-to-phoneme conversion. Following the same logic, the Orthographic Depth Hypothesis would suggest that while readers of shallow orthographies can effortlessly convert graphemes into phonemes, readers of deep orthographies use larger-sized letter patterns to overcome the inconsistency in the letter-to-phoneme correspondence of their writing system. Note that this theoretical approach assumes that phonological computation underlies successful reading in all orthographies (see Share, 1995, for a discussion), and that orthographic depth merely affects the nature of the computation process, mainly the size of processing units.

This hypothesis was directly tested in a recent study by Ziegler and his colleagues (Ziegler et al., 2001). Ziegler et al. examined the grain-size of units employed by skilled readers in a deep (English) and a shallow orthography (German). The authors presented German and English speakers with identical words and nonwords in their native language, and found that the naming performance of readers of German was affected by the number of letters, whereas the naming performance of readers of English was affected by the words' bodies and rhymes. These results were interpreted to suggest that skilled readers of deep orthographies like English employ large-sized units in reading aloud, whereas skilled readers of shallow orthographies like German rely on minimal-sized units, mostly letters and phonemes.

Although most studies investigating the effect of orthographic depth on skilled reading monitored reaction time or error rates to visually presented words, there is now a growing body of evidence from brain-imaging which also supports the Orthographic Depth Hypothesis. For example, Paulesu et al. (2000), in two positron emission tomography (PET) studies, examined the reading of words and nonwords in the shallow Italian and the deep English orthography. They found that the Italian readers showed greater activation in the left superior temporal regions of the brain, which are associated with phoneme processing. In contrast, English readers showed greater activation in the left posterior inferior temporal gyrus and anterior inferior frontal gyrus, which are associated with whole-word retrieval. These results were interpreted to suggest that Italian readers rely mainly on sublexical processing at the level of letters and phonemes, whereas readers of English also rely on lexical and semantic processing to generate a phonological output (see Fiez, 2000, for an extensive discussion).

The third dimension of skilled reading, according to the strong phonological theory, involves the ability to access the lexicon or activate a word node without requiring a detailed phonological representation. The relevant predictions regarding the Orthographic Depth Hypothesis are straightforward: In shallow orthographies lexical access would be based on a relatively detailed phonological representation, whereas in deep orthographies it would be based on a relatively impoverished one. This is because the opaque relations between letters and phonemes in deep orthographies create difficulties in assembling phonological representations from print by using discrete grapheme–phoneme conversion rules. Consider, for example, the English word PINT. It is labeled *irregular* because most English words ending with INT are pronounced like MINT. However, the conversion of P-N-T into their respective phonemes does not involve any substantial ambiguity. Thus, a prelexical assembly of phonology could easily produce an underspecified phonological representation consisting of a CVCC segment such as /pent/, in which the middle vowel is not clearly defined, ranging from /e/ to /I/. The Orthographic Depth Hypothesis simply suggests that skilled readers in deep orthographies are encouraged to access their lexicon with underspecified phonological representations.

Studies in Hebrew provide strong evidence that skilled readers do not rely on a detailed phonological representation, but access the lexicon via an impoverished one. As explained above, Hebrew letters represent mainly consonants, whereas the vowel marks are mostly omitted from the printed text. In Hebrew, as in other Semitic languages, all verbs and the vast majority of nouns and adjectives are composed of roots usually formed of three consonants. The three-consonant roots are embedded in preexisting morphophonological word patterns to form specific words. When the vowel marks are omitted from the consonant string, the same string of letters may sometimes denote up to seven or eight different words that share an identical orthographic structure but have different phonological forms. Bentin, Bargai, and Katz (1984) demonstrated that lexical decisions for phonologically ambiguous letter strings were as fast as for phonologically unequivocal words, whereas naming of ambiguous words was slower than naming of unambiguous ones. These results suggest that lexical decisions (in contrast to naming) are based on the recognition of the ambiguous consonantal cluster and do not require a detailed phonological analysis of the printed word. Similarly, Bentin and Frost (1987) showed that lexical decisions for ambiguous unpointed words are faster than lexical decisions for either of the disambiguated pointed alternatives. This outcome, again, suggests that lexical decisions in unpointed Hebrew are based on the early recognition of the consonantal structure shared by the phonological alternatives, and that finding a lexical entry does not necessarily entail the recovery of complete phonological information.

Support for these conclusions comes from recent studies using backward masking, which demonstrated that the phonological representation computed from print in Hebrew is indeed impoverished and underspecified (e.g., Frost & Yogev, 2001; Gronau and Frost, 1997). In the backward masking paradigm (Perfetti, Bell, & Delaney, 1988), a target word is presented for a very short duration. The target word is followed (i.e., masked) by a pseudoword that appears briefly and is then replaced by a simple pattern mask. The pseudoword that masks the target can be phonemically similar to the target, graphemically similar, or an entirely dissimilar control. The subjects' task is to report in writing what they have perceived. Typically, because of the masking effect, subjects perceive only one event, the target word, and do not have any conscious recollection of the nonword mask. The short exposure characteristic of the masking paradigm allows the on-line processing of the nonword masks to merge with the incomplete processing of the word targets. Thus, in spite of the fact that the nonword masks are not consciously perceived, they exert some influence on the detection of the target.

In general, experiments using backward masking have demonstrated that nonwords which were phonemically similar to the targets they masked produced better identification rates than graphemically similar controls (e.g., Perfetti, Bell, & Delaney, 1988; Perfetti, Zhang, & Berent, 1992). This outcome suggests that the phonologic information extracted from the masks contributed to the reinstatement of the phonological properties of the targets. However, recent investigations of phonological processing in the deep Hebrew orthography showed that the probability of obtaining phonemic effects in backward masking in Hebrew depends on the phonological contrast between phonemic and graphemic masks. If the phonemic and the control masks differ by a single consonant, a phonemic effect may not be revealed (Frost & Yogev, 2001; Gronau & Frost, 1997). This outcome was interpreted to suggest that the representations computed in brief exposures in Hebrew are indeed coarse-grained and not detailed enough to capture fine phonetic differences.

In conclusion, there is a significant body of experimental evidence which suggests that different cognitive processes are involved in skilled reading of deep and shallow orthographies. These differences concern not only the importance of prelexical phonological computation relative to lexical mediation, but also the size of the computed phonological units, as well as the ability to access the lexicon with only partial phonological information.

## Languages with Two Writing Systems: The Cases of Serbo-Croatian, Korean, and Japanese

Some languages have adopted two writing systems, in most cases under the influence of geographically adjacent cultures. Obviously, the introduction of yet another orthography to represent the same spoken forms introduces additional complexity. The implication of a redundant writing system therefore needs special elucidation. The present section reviews three such examples, Serbo-Croatian, Korean, and Japanese. The representational solutions in these three languages are quite different from one another, and therefore the implications for the reading process are different as well.

### Serbo-Croatian

In Serbo-Croatian, both the Roman and the Cyrillic alphabets are taught to all elementary school children, and are used interchangeably by the skilled reader. Most characters in the two alphabets are unique to one alphabet or the other, but there are some characters that occur in both. Of those, some receive the same phonemic interpretation regardless of the alphabet (*common* letters), but others receive a different interpretation in each alphabet (*ambiguous* letters). Letter strings that include unique letters can be pronounced in only one alphabet. Similarly, letter strings composed exclusively of common letters can be pronounced in the same manner in both alphabets. In contrast, strings that contain only *ambiguous* and *common* letters are *phonologically bivalent*. They can be pronounced in one way by treating the characters as Roman letters, and in a distinctly different way by treating them as Cyrillic letters. For example, the letter string "POTOP" can be pronounced as /potop/ if the ambiguous character *P* is interpreted according to its Roman pronunciation. By contrast, if the letter string is taken as a Cyrillic spelling, the grapheme *P* receives the pronunciation /r/ and the string must be pronounced /rotor/ (the characters O and T are common, and have the same pronunciation in both alphabets). In the case of POTOP, both pronunciations are legal Serbo-Croatian words (the former means "flood" and the latter, "rotor"). The two alphabetic systems of Serbo-Croatian are presented in figure 15.1.

When a phonologically bivalent word of Serbo-Croatian is read in isolation, the alphabet is not specified by a context and, therefore, the spelled form can be pronounced in two different ways. Two types of such bivalent strings exist. In one of these, both pronunciations are known to the reader as words (i.e., have lexical entries). Such letter strings are both phonologically *and* lexically ambiguous. In the other type, which occurs more frequently, only one of the two pronunciations is a word, while the other is a nonword.

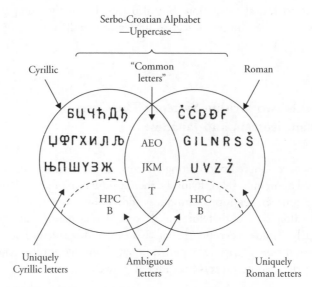

Serbo-Croatian Alphabet
—Uppercase—

Cyrillic                "Common                Roman
                        letters"

БЦЧЋДЂ            ĊĆDĐF

ЏФГХИЛЉ    AEO    GILNRSŠ

ЊПШУЗЖ    JKM    UVZŽ

            T

        HPC            HPC
        B              B

Uniquely            Ambiguous            Uniquely
Cyrillic letters      letters            Roman letters

**Figure 15.1**    The Cyrillic and Roman alphabetic systems of Serbo-Croatian.

Such strings are phonologically ambiguous, but since they are linked to only one lexical entry they are not lexically ambiguous.

*Processing implications of Serbo-Croatian orthography.* Previous studies in Serbo-Croatian investigated how fluent bi-alphabetic readers process ambiguous print. Lukatela et al. (1980) studied lexical decision performance in Serbo-Croatian, comparing phonologi- cally ambiguous and unequivocal words. They demonstrated that words that could be pronounced in two different ways were accepted more slowly as words, compared to words that could be read in only one way. Similar results were found by Feldman and Turvey (1983), who compared phonologically ambiguous and phonologically unequivocal forms of the same lexical items. This outcome was interpreted to suggest that, in contrast to English, lexical decisions in Serbo-Croatian are necessarily based on the extraction of phonology from print (Turvey, Feldman, & Lukatela, 1984).

The relative contributions of phonological and lexical factors were not directly assessed in these previous studies. Although Lukatela et al. (1980) demonstrated that phonologi- cally ambiguous letter strings incurred longer lexical decision latencies than phonologi- cally unequivocal strings, they did not find a significant difference in decision latencies between ambiguous strings with one or with two lexical entries. In fact, phonologically bivalent letter strings slowed participant's responses (although to a lesser extent), even if the two possible readings of the letter strings represented two nonwords (see also Lukatela, Savic, Gligorjevic, Ognjenovic, & Turvey, 1978). Interestingly, words composed exclu- sively of common letters that were alphabetically bivalent but *phonologically unequivocal* did not slow lexical decisions compared to their unique alphabet controls (Feldman &

Turvey, 1983). Finally, the magnitude of the difference in decision latencies for bivalent and unequivocal forms of a word varied with the number of ambiguous letters in the bivalent form of that word (Feldman, Kostic, Lukatela, & Turvey, 1983; Feldman & Turvey, 1983). In general, these results suggest that readers of Serbo-Croatian process print by a phonologically analytic strategy, which precedes lexical access. Consequently, as a rule, their performance is hindered by phonological ambiguity (see Feldman, 1987, for a review).

In another study, Lukatela, Feldman, Turvey, Carello, and Katz (1989), investigated whether the presence of semantic context can override an ambiguous alphabetic context. They showed that the correct and consistent alphabetic assignment of a letter string can indeed be offset by previously accessed lexical entries (that are activated by semantic information). Hence, in contrast to the previous conclusions of Turvey et al. (1984), who suggested that a prelexical phonological analysis of print is mandatory in Serbo-Croatian, these results demonstrate that the Serbo-Croatian reader can also be affected by the lexical characteristics of the printed stimulus, if the experimental conditions invite deeper processing.

In another study, Frost, Feldman, and Katz (1990) presented subjects with stimuli that could be pronounced differently in the Roman or the Cyrillic alphabet. Some of these strings had two different meanings, one for each pronunciation; for others, only one of the two pronunciations was meaningful. Frost et al. (1990) used a matching task in this study; participants were presented with an ambiguous printed word and, simultaneously, with a spoken word, and were required to determine if they matched. The spoken words were either presented clearly or degraded by noise. The speed of matching the spoken words to phonologically ambiguous letter strings was measured relative to their phonologically unambiguous controls. The results indicated that phonological ambiguity slowed stimulus matching. However, phonological ambiguity had a greater effect when the phonologically ambiguous form represented two meaningful words. These results again suggest that readers of Serbo-Croatian process print in a phonologically analytic manner, as they are sensitive to the ambiguity presented by the orthographic structure deriving from both phonological forms. However, readers of Serbo-Croatian are affected not only by the number of possible pronunciations of a printed word, but also by their lexical status. Thus, it seems that lexical effects can also be demonstrated in the shallow Serbo-Croatian, demonstrating the flexibility of readers in employing prelexical as well as lexical procedures for computing phonology.

## Korean

In contrast to Serbo-Croatian, which adopted two writing systems that provide different graphic signs for the same alphabet, the Korean orthography has one writing system that is alphabetic (*Hangul*) and another that is logographic (*Hanza*). In a way that is similar to English, the graphemes in Hangul represent the phonemes of spoken Korean. However, in contrast to the case of English, the representational principle in Hangul is very shallow, as graphemes represent phonemes consistently. In this context, Korean might be similar to Spanish or Italian if it did not include a second writing system that is logographic.

Because of influence from nearby China, written Korean imported a substantial number of Chinese logographs. This script, called Hanza, represents the spoken words of Korean through a logographic representation of morphemes. Thus, the printed shape of the logograph in Chinese and Korean may be the same, but its phonological reading is different. This is because the logographic symbols were meant to represent meaningful morphemes with a pronunciation differing from the original one, due to the different spoken language into which they were imported. In Korean, only 20% of printed words are written in the logographic Hanza, whereas the other 80% are written in the phonologically shallow Hangul. Also, whereas Hanza words can be printed in Hangul, the reverse is not always true and some words can be written only in Hangul. Thus, Hangul is considered to be the dominant script. The interesting aspect of printed Korean, however, is that Hanza and Hangul characters are mixed inconsistently within a given text to facilitate reading. In fact, it is not possible to find a Korean text that is printed exclusively in the logographic Hanza (see Cho & Chen, 1999, Kang & Simpson, 2001, and Simpson & Kang, 1994, for a detailed description of Korean orthography). Examples of Hangul and Hanza words are presented in table 15.3.

*Processing implications of Korean orthography.* Unsurprisingly, studies conducted in Korean revealed that Hangul and Hanza are processed differently by the Korean reader. As the Orthographic Depth Hypothesis predicts, phonological assembly is favored by Korean readers when the stimuli are printed in the shallow Hangul orthography, even when semantic processing was required by the task (Cho & Chen, 1999; Simpson & Kang, 1994). The question of interest in the case of Korean concerns, however, the *acquired flexibility* of readers to engage in entirely different modes of processing when the text includes both a shallow phonographic script and a pure logographic one. This flexibility was examined in a series of experiments by Simpson and Kang (1994). They found that when Hangul words were presented alone, there was a greatly reduced frequency effect in naming, suggesting that Hangul script is indeed processed through sublexical analytic computation. In contrast, when Hanza dominated the stimulus list, greater frequency

**Table 15.3**   Korean Words Printed in the Alphabetic Hangul and the Logographic Hanza

| Hangul | Hanza | Pronunciation | Translation |
|--------|-------|---------------|-------------|
| 남/남자 | 男 | nam/nam-dza | a man, a male |
| 인간 | 人間 | in-gan | a human being, a man, a mortal |
| 친고 | 親舊 | tchin-go | a friend |
| 항목 | 項目 | hang-mok | a head, an item |
| 우유 | 牛乳 | u-yu | cow's milk |
| 머주 | 麥酒 | mek-tsu | beer, ale |

effects were found in reading the same Hangul words, demonstrating greater lexical involvement in reading. Thus, it seems that Korean readers can control the extent of sub-lexical versus lexical computation as a function of list composition.

In a more recent study, Kang and Simpson (2001) monitored naming latencies of words printed in Hangul or Hanza, keeping track of the order of word presentation. The results showed that a single Hanza word was sufficient to initiate the lexical processing of a subsequent Hangul target. In contrast, two preceding Hangul words were required to initiate the sublexical processing of a Hangul target. This asymmetry derives from the fact that Hangul words can be named either lexically or sublexically, but Hanza words can be named only following access to the visual-input lexicon. But note that even though Hangul words can be named using the same routine as Hanza words, subjects always seem to revert to prelexical computation following the presentation of a few Hangul words, in spite of the ongoing appearance of Hanza words in the stimulus list. This outcome coincides well with the assumption that prelexical computation is the default procedure in shallow orthographies (Frost, 1998).

In yet another experiment Kang and Simpson presented subjects with Hangul and Hanza words preceded by a cue indicating which script would be seen next. Frequency effects in naming Hangul words were not found if readers were informed by the cue about the upcoming Hangul script, whereas frequency effects were clearly present when subjects were not cued. These results again suggest that subjects employ sublexical phonological computation for naming Hangul by default. Thus, the results from Korean point to two main conclusions. First, skilled readers of languages with two scripts adopt a strategic flexibility in using lexical versus sublexical routines. Second, the default routine for shallow orthographies involves mainly prelexical computation even for skilled readers.

*Japanese*

In several ways, the Japanese and Korean writing systems are similar because both were influenced by the writing system of mainland China. Thus, modern Japanese is written with a logographic script imported from China called *Kanji*, along with a phonographic system called *Kana*, which comprises two syllabaries, named *Hiragana* and *Katakana*.

Kanji are logographs representing morphemic units. Many Kanji words have two pronunciations: a Kun-reading consisting of the Japanese spoken word that conveys the meaning of the Chinese logograph, and an On-reading, which is essentially the original Chinese spoken word that was introduced and incorporated into the Japanese vocabulary. However, since Chinese is a tonal language and Japanese is not, the original Chinese pronunciation was distorted, and the On-reading does not match exactly the Chinese phonetic structure. Quite a few Kanji words have more than one On-reading reflecting different periods of borrowing from Chinese. Moreover, sometimes a given logograph stands for several morphemes with different meanings and pronunciations. Kanji characters are used mostly to represent lexical categories such as nouns, verb or adjective stems, as well as adverbs. The estimated number of Kanji characters employed in newspapers in Japan is approximately 3,200. The important feature of Kanji in the present context is that the characters cannot be decomposed into separable phonemic components. Their exact pronunciation can only be determined through context, and readers need to consider the particular set of characters that combine to form the words (most On-readings are given to Kanji words having two or more characters) to know their phonemic structure.

In addition to Kanji, Japanese has two sets of phonographic characters representing the permissible syllables in the languages: Hiragana and Katakana. The present forms of Hiragana and Katakana were fixed by the Ministry of Education of Japan in 1900. There are 46 basic hiragana syllables, to which 25 variations are added. In addition, 20 hiragana characters can be modified with diacritic marks to change their pronunciation. Hiragana is used mainly to represent the grammatical elements of a sentence, such as auxiliary verbs, particles, and inflectional affixes of nouns. It is also used to represent native Japanese words for which there are no Kanji characters. Katakana is used to write foreign names, loan-words, scientific terms, and the like. Table 15.4 presents syllabic characters in Hiragana and Katakana as well as a few examples of Kanji words.

In general, all words in Japanese can be written in Kana. Thus, it seems that there is no apparent need for Japanese to use the logographic Kanji system. However, since Japanese contains a large number of homophones, semantic disambiguation is often based on the usage of Kanji characters. Also, since Japanese is written without spaces between words, the incorporation of Kanji in the text provides important cues regarding morphological segmentation. Thus, texts printed entirely in Kana are atypical.

**Table 15.4**   Examples of Syllabic Characters Printed in Hiragana and Katakana and Examples of Words Printed in Kanji

| Hiragana | | | | | Katakana | | | | |
|---|---|---|---|---|---|---|---|---|---|
| あ<br>a | い<br>i | う<br>u | え<br>e | お<br>o | ア<br>a | イ<br>i | ウ<br>u | エ<br>e | オ<br>o |
| か<br>ka | き<br>ki | く<br>ku | け<br>ke | こ<br>ko | カ<br>ka | キ<br>ki | ク<br>ku | ケ<br>ke | ・コ<br>ko |
| さ<br>sa | し<br>shi | す<br>su | せ<br>se | そ<br>so | サ<br>sa | シ<br>shi | ス<br>su | セ<br>se | ソ<br>so |
| た<br>ta | ち<br>chi | つ<br>tsu | て<br>te | と<br>to | タ<br>ta | チ<br>chi | ツ<br>tsu | テ<br>te | ト<br>to |

| Kanji | Pronunciation | Meaning | Meaning of Each of the Characters |
|---|---|---|---|
| 日本 | Nihon or Nippon | Japan | sun/origin |
| 日本人 | Nihonjin | Japanese (people) | sun/origin/people |
| 自然 | shizen | nature | self/natural |
| 和 | wa | harmony | harmony |

*Processing implications of Japanese Orthography.* Some early research in Japanese employed the two writing systems of that language for the purpose of examining the relative superiority of visual versus phonological processing during printed word recognition. For example, Feldman and Turvey (1980) contrasted naming latencies for the same words printed in Kanji and Kana. They demonstrated that words that are usually printed in the Japanese deep logographic Kanji (e.g., color names) were named faster when printed in the shallower syllabic Kana than in their familiar Kanji form. These results were interpreted to suggest that naming in an orthography that lends itself to phonological assembly is necessarily faster than in a deep orthography that promotes visual encoding and visual access. Besner and Hildebrandt (1987), however, argued that familiarity does play a significant role in reading Japanese Kana. They showed that words regularly printed in Kana were named faster than Kanji words printed in Kana. Similar results were reported by Buchanan and Besner (1993).

There is ample evidence that the reading of Kana words involves phonological encoding. For example, Taft and Tamaoka (1994) found using the lexical decision task that the rejection of pseudohomophones printed in Katakana is affected by phonological similarity or dissimilarity to real words, at the level of single phonemes rather than full syllables. These results suggest that Japanese readers are sensitive to phonemic units when processing Kana and the smallest unit of phonological processing in Japanese is not necessarily syllabic.

The interesting question, however, concerns phonological processing during reading of Kanji. Obviously, since Kanji characters do not lend themselves to phonemic decomposition, it has been suggested that their meaning is accessed directly from the print (e.g., Shimamura, 1987). However, more recent studies using the semantic categorization task (e.g., Wydell, Butterworth, & Patterson, 1995; Wydell, Patterson, & Humphreys, 1993) have shown that the reading of Kanji characters involves access to semantics from both the orthographic input lexicon and the phonological output lexicon. Thus, it seems that phonology mediates access to meaning in reading Kanji just as it does with Kana. The suggestion that the reading of Kanji words involves direct access to phonology without semantic mediation is also supported by neurological studies. For example, Sasanuma, Sakuma, and Kitano (1992) presented several case studies of patients with severely impaired comprehension, who could nevertheless read aloud Kanji words without great difficulty. Such patterns of reading disorders suggest that the reading of Kanji characters may be independent of the retrieval of meaning.

Another study by Wydell and her colleagues (Wydell et al., 1995) investigated the grain-size of the computed phonological units of Kanji words, by monitoring print-to-sound consistency effects of characters in naming. Consistency was defined in terms of pronunciation ambiguity, reflecting whether or not the constituent Kanji characters had an alternative On-reading or Kun-reading. Clear effects of character frequency and familiarity on naming were found, but there were no effects of consistency. These results were interpreted to suggest that the phonology of Kanji words is computed at the word level rather than the character level. This conclusion coincides well with the Orthographic Depth Hypothesis prediction that readers of deep orthographies use larger-sized units than readers of shallow orthographies, while generating a phonological representation from print.

## Summary and Conclusions

This chapter has discussed how skilled word recognition processes differ in different orthographic system. In general, different models of skilled reading outline different architectures of the mental lexicon, and define different dynamic processes that operate upon these architectures. The description of what skilled reading entails is, therefore, necessarily model dependent. This chapter has focused on two main theories of visual word recognition: the dual-route theory and the strong phonological theory. From an architectural perspective, both theories postulate a nonlexical route that operates using grapheme–phoneme conversion which connects to a phonological output lexicon, and both theories recognize that an orthographic lexicon is a necessary component of a lexical system. However, in dual-route theory, skilled reading is described by an increased reliance on the orthographic input lexicon, which activates directly the phonological output lexicon as well as the semantic system. In contrast, strong phonological models regard the prelexical computation of phonology as the main engine driving the processing of printed information. Hence, the theory considers the product of this computation to be the core output of the cognitive system. Lexical influence is perceived as a subsequent top-down shaping of the prelexical product, which provides a complete and phonologically detailed representation. Given these assumptions, skilled reading in strong phonological models is seen as a convergence of three abilities: the ability to compute a phonological representation with ease using sublexical units, the ability to use larger-sized sublexical units during the computation process, and the ability to access the lexicon with relatively impoverished phonological representations.

Keeping our description of skilled reading in mind, this chapter has focused on how the linguistic environment of the native speaker shapes the structure of lexical knowledge. The phonological and morphological structure of different languages has historically determined the kind of orthography they adopted. The variety that exists in spoken languages has given rise to a variety of orthographies, reflecting a range of relationships to different languages' structural characteristics. Since orthographies differ in the relations between the spelling and phonology, as well as the size of the phonological unit transcribed by their graphemes, the cognitive processes involved in skilled reading are orthography dependent to some degree.

We have considered a variety of orthographic systems, including English, Hebrew, Serbo-Croatian, German, Korean, and Japanese. The research reviewed supports several conclusions. First, readers always display a fine-tuning to the characteristics of the presented text. Thus, if orthographies are deep or shallow, if they are phonographic or logographic, they impose different cognitive processing routines on the reader. This form of flexibility or strategic control is characteristic of our lexical processing system. Another conclusion concerns the default procedures employed during reading. The evidence described in this chapter suggests that if fast and relatively accurate sublexical computation is supported by the orthographic system, then it becomes the default procedure even for skilled readers. In this respect, deep and shallow orthographies display a clear asymmetry. Whereas lexical processing by fast access to the visual input lexicon is a viable routine in any writing system (phonographic or logographic, deep or shallow), sublexical computation requires transparent relationships between spelling and phonology. The bias for sublexical computation in shallow orthographies portrays an interesting constraint on theories of skilled reading. It suggests that the conversion of sublexical units into phonological units is not a strategy adopted only by beginning readers. Rather, it is a default operation in the reading process.

## Note

This study was supported in part by National Institute of Child Health and Human Development Grant HD-01994 to Haskins Laboratories.

# 16

# Early Reading Development in European Orthographies

## Philip H. K. Seymour

## Introduction

Despite the diversity of human languages and writing systems, most research into literacy acquisition and dyslexia has focused on English. Even where other languages are studied there is typically a reliance on theoretical concepts and methods that derive from research on written English. This bias might not be too troubling if it could be argued that a common theoretical framework is applicable to the learning of all written languages. However, there may be good reasons to question the all-inclusive role of English as the paradigm case for the study of literacy acquisition. This is especially evident when considering the contrasts between English and logographic scripts such as Chinese, syllabaries such as the Japanese Kana, consonantal scripts such as Hebrew, and highly consistent alphabetic scripts such as Finnish.

This chapter has a more restricted focus, being concerned specifically with learning to read in the European orthographies. The intention is to provide a theoretical framework for the discussion of beginning literacy acquisition in the European languages and societies. The important questions for a theory of *European literacy* are how far the differences existing between societies, educational approaches, and, especially, spoken languages and writing systems, affect the way in which literacy is acquired or dyslexia is manifest.

Theoretically, the suggestion that there may be important contrasts between societies and languages implies that an inclusive model of European literacy acquisition may need to contain free parameters and options that would allow for language or orthography-specific variations. The goal of this chapter is to give a preliminary outline of an inclusive and flexible theory of this kind. Such a theory will need to take account of commonly debated issues relating to literacy acquisition, especially:

- *Causation.* The factors that influence progress in reading acquisition and the occurrence of dyslexia.
- *Linguistic units.* The elements of language that are emphasized in the mapping between written and spoken language.
- *Sequence of orthographic development.* Whether or not there are distinct phases in reading acquisition.

## Causation

One of the most widely researched issues concerns the biological, cognitive, and experiential factors that determine success or failure in learning to read (Morton & Frith, 1995). Parenthood determines the genetic endowment. Nutritional, toxic, or pharmacological substances may affect brain development in the pre- and post-natal periods. These *biological* influences might be expected to be approximately constant across European cultures. However, there is the possibility that societies may differ in their range of genetic variation. Similarly, nutritional and toxic factors could, conceivably, differ between societies. If there were cultural differences affecting maternal diet, infant feeding practices, alcohol abuse, smoking, and so forth, these might influence reading achievement via their effects on brain development.

A theoretically more interesting proposition is that language differences may produce cognitive effects that, in their turn, are reflected in the course of brain development and organization. This possibility is suggested by brain imaging studies of adult readers of Italian and English (Paulesu et al., 2000). Italian is written in a *shallow orthography*, with very consistent correspondences between letters and sounds, whereas English is written in a *deep orthography*, with complex and inconsistent relations between letters and sounds. Italian adults named words and nonwords faster than English-speaking adults. A PET-scan investigation suggested that reading of the shallow Italian orthography activated the left planum temporale region, commonly associated with phonemic processing, while reading of the deep English orthography activated the left inferior posterior temporal gyrus and the anterior part of the left inferior frontal gyrus, regions associated with naming and lexical/semantic processing. So it appears that differences between languages may result in differences in the development of specialized brain regions underlying reading behavior.

Comparisons of the development of reading skills across different languages and cultures require assessments at the *behavioral* level. Such assessments depend upon standardized psychometric procedures that are used to assess competence in reading, memory, language, and verbal and nonverbal intelligence. These measures are determined by historical, clinical, and educational traditions that differ between cultures. Thus, in the UK, there is a collection of reading and spelling tests that can be used to define reading progress. These include graded word lists as well as text-based assessments of reading accuracy, speed, and comprehension. These scales do not exist in some other countries. Indeed, the concept of a graded word list appears incongruous in the context of a regular orthography, such as Greek, where children rapidly learn to decode novel forms. In such cases, the tendency is to define reading in terms of speed rather than accuracy, or some combination of the two measures, as in the Dutch *one-minute test* (Brus & Voeten, 1973). In other instances (Portugal, for example), there may be no formally standardized measures of reading ability at all. Similar considerations apply to assessments of intelligence, language, and memory. This lack of psychometric harmonization across Europe means that the way in which literacy (and dyslexia) are operationally defined is not equivalent in different countries.

*Socio-economic status* (SES) is known to be an important influence on reading (see Phillips & Lonigan, this volume). Duncan and Seymour (2000) investigated differences in basic literacy skills among groups differing in SES in the city of Dundee in Scotland. The study compared children in nursery and primary schools located in middle-class and disadvantaged areas. The literacy measures were letter knowledge, familiar word identification, and simple CVC nonword reading. Measures of metaphonology were included. There were large effects of SES on beginning literacy, including slower acquisition of letter-sound knowledge and delayed mastery of word and nonword identification. The gap between the middle-class and disadvantaged group was about one year of reading age. Progress in the low-SES sample was characterized by a developmental delay with performance of the two groups being identical when indexed against reading age. The same was true of metaphonological development which was poorer in the low-SES group but entirely appropriate for the reading age achieved. This study makes it clear that social disadvantage has a major delaying effect on reading acquisition in English. It is essential, therefore, to take full account of this factor when considering contrasts between European languages, as inclusion of deprived groups will depress reading scores and exaggerate the apparent difficulty of learning to read in one language relative to another.

There are also *educational differences* between countries that affect when and how literacy is taught. Formal instruction in reading usually begins at the start of primary school education. However, the age at which children start school varies between countries. In the UK, children enter primary school at about 5 years of age and embark on formal reading instruction immediately. In most European countries the starting age is 6 years but is delayed until 7 years in some, most notably Germany and Austria and some Scandinavian countries. This introduces a difference in the *maturity* of children at the time when they start to learn to read. A further complication is that literacy learning may take place outside school. Whether or not this happens depends on cultural attitudes regarding appropriate activities for preschoolers. In Denmark there is a strong social bias against informal literacy instruction and a view that preschool education should emphasize general cognitive and linguistic development (Lundberg, Frost, & Petersen, 1988). In Finland children may receive some reading instruction in the home or kindergarten and a significant proportion arrive in primary school already able to read.

Educational policy also affects the way in which literacy is taught. There may be a centralized approach, such that all schools follow the same method and materials, as in Greece, or there may be scope for individual teachers or education authorities to choose their own preferred methods and reading schemes, as in Denmark. The methods fall on a contrasting dimension which emphasizes wholistic meaningful approaches on the one hand or analytic phonic approaches on the other (see Snow & Juel, this volume, for a further discussion). The first approach treats reading as the discovery of meaning in text and emphasizes the use of context and written words as signals for concepts. The favored method is to show children words on cards and in simple texts and teach them to discriminate and recognize them on the basis of differentiating graphic features. At the opposite extreme there is the phonic method in which instruction concentrates on helping the child to identify and discriminate the letters of the alphabet, the learning of the sounds associated with each letter, and the establishment of sequential decoding and assembly procedures.

Seymour and Elder (1986) reported a study in which Scottish primary school children were taught to read using an exclusively whole-word method. There was no reference to the individual letters of the alphabet or their associated sounds and no attempt to teach decoding procedures. Under this regime of *logographic* learning many children acquired quite extensive sight vocabularies, often containing well over 100 words, but did not develop procedures for reading new words. Hence, their word recognition was restricted to words that had been taught. They were completely unable to read unfamiliar words. Errors were typically "don't know" responses or substitutions of words already established in the reading vocabularies.

This outcome contrasts with the effects of an exclusively phonic approach in which the emphasis is on *alphabetic* learning of letter-sound associations and the capacity to combine sequences of letter-sounds. A synthetic approach of this type predominates in Austria (Wimmer, 1993), Finland, and Greece. The initial product is a sequential left-to-right approach to reading in which individual letters are identified and converted to their associated sounds. The sound sequences are then combined to enable the pronunciation of written syllables. In some cases (e.g., in Finland) grouping into syllable-sized units is explicitly encouraged by printing beginning reading texts with physical demarcations between syllables as well as between words. It is apparent that, in a regular writing system, where it is approximately true that individual letters correspond reliably to individual sounds, this procedure quickly provides the learner with a method that can be used to pronounce all written words which may be encountered.

In the UK, the most commonly used method is an amalgamation of the two procedures in which children are simultaneously exposed to programmes of alphabetic and logographic learning. They are taught the letters of the alphabet and their predominant sounds and at the same time learn to recognize items from a vocabulary of 'sight words'. Seymour and Evans (1992) made a detailed analysis of learning under this dual approach. An examination of errors and reaction times in word and nonword reading during the first two years of instruction suggested that there was an initial phase during which two distinct processes developed, a logographic process of sight word recognition and an alphabetic process of letter-sound decoding. Later, as development proceeded, it appeared that these two functions converged into a single process that was capable of both word and nonword reading.

Instructional methods are likely to have large effects on comparisons between languages. The introduction of a phonic-oriented National Literacy Strategy in the UK has enhanced rates of progress and attenuated the contrast between English and German (see Landerl, 2000).

## Language Effects

*Language* is the key environmental factor that is likely to influence the development of the cognitive systems underlying reading and spelling. In particular, there are between-language differences in how the sound structure of the spoken language, the *phonology*, is represented in writing, the *orthography*. The way in which meaning is conveyed through grammar and the internal structure of words, the *morphology*, may also be important.

Traditionally, cognitive models of language processing have assigned these three aspects to distinct processing domains or modules. This is evident in the architectures developed in cognitive neuropsychological research (Seymour, 1990) and in the "triangular" format of connectionist models (Plaut, McClelland, Seidenberg, & Patterson, 1996; Seidenberg & McClelland, 1989).

At the phonological level, a key concept in developmental models of reading is the system of *phonological representations* that is postulated in the phonological deficit theory of dyslexia (Snowling, 2000). European societies have different spoken languages that contrast in their phonological structure as well as in their vocabularies, grammatical organization, and morphology. The Romance languages (Italian, Spanish, Portuguese, French) typically have a simple syllabic structure, with a majority of open CV syllables and few initial or final consonant clusters. The Germanic languages (German, English, the Scandinavian languages) have a more complex syllabic structure, with more closed CVC syllables and more numerous consonant clusters in the onset or coda positions. One possibility is that different spoken languages result in different systems of phonological representation and that these differences affect the acquisition of literacy. Similar considerations apply to the influence of grammar and morphology where different linguistic organizations – for example, the contrast between the agglutinative morphology of Finnish and the inflectional and derivational morphology of English – may affect the semantic component and the relations with phonology and orthography.

The linguistic factor most likely to influence reading acquisition is the nature of the writing system. The European orthographies are all *alphabetic* insofar as they use graphic symbols (letters) to represent small abstract segments of speech, the vocalic and consonantal *phonemes* that combine to produce the full repertoire of syllables or words in each language. The variation between European orthographies is related to the complexity and consistency of the relationship between letters (graphemes) and sounds (phonemes). A simple and consistent alphabet provides a single distinct written symbol for each phoneme and is variously referred to as "shallow" or "transparent." An approximation to such an orthography occurs in Finnish, which is written so that each phoneme is associated with a single letter. Where significant departures from this straightforward system occur, the orthography is said to be "deep" or "opaque" (see Frost, this volume, for further discussion). Complexity arises if it becomes necessary to use combinations of letters (*complex graphemes*) to represent particular phonemes. In other instances, the pronunciation of a letter may vary depending on surrounding *context*, as in the case of "c" softening (*call* vs. *cell*), or on the presence of marker letters, such as the final -e in English (*mat* vs. *mate*). Usually, the critical variation is held to relate to the *consistency* of the mapping between graphemes and phonemes (Katz & Frost, 1992). Thus, Frost, Katz, and Bentin (1987) commented:

> In a shallow orthography, the phonemic and orthographic codes are isomorphic; the phonemes of the spoken word are represented by the graphemes in a direct and unequivocal manner. In contrast, in a deep orthography, the relation of spelling to sound is more opaque. The same letter may represent different phonemes in different contexts; moreover, different letters may represent the same phoneme. (p. 104)

The concept of orthographic depth is in practice somewhat more complex than this. In a deep orthography spellings may serve to signal lexical identities, as in the contrasting orthographic forms of homophones (*choir* vs. *quire*, *weight* vs. *wait*), or morphological functions, as in the spelling of the past tense inflection as *-ed* irrespective of pronunciation (*toured, walked, sprinted*).

Thus, the European orthographies may be arranged along a complex dimension of *orthographic depth*, with languages such as Finnish located at the shallow end and a language such as English, which has numerous complexities, variations, and inconsistencies, located at the deep end. To date, there has been no comprehensive comparative computational linguistic investigation of European orthographies. Ziegler, Jacobs, and Stone (1996) quantified the consistency of pronunciation of the orthographic rime segments (feedforward consistency) and the consistency of the graphemic representation of each phonological rime segment (feedback consistency) in French and English (see also Ziegler, Stone, & Jacobs, 1997). They found that feedback inconsistency is typically more extensive than feedforward inconsistency. Shallow orthographies, such as Greek or Spanish, tend to display few or no feedforward inconsistencies but a number of feedback inconsistencies.

Recently, there has been an attempt to arrive at intuitive estimates of the relative depths of the European orthographies. This was undertaken by a European research network, the COST Action A8 (1995–1999), which involved literacy and dyslexia researchers from a range of European languages (Niessen, Frith, Reitsma, & Öhngren, 2000). The COST A8 consortium reviewed the evidence of departure from the principle of transparency (one letter/one sound) in each language and arrived at a designation of the probable variation on a shallow → deep dimension. This was cross-referenced with the phonological contrast between simple syllable structure and complex syllable structure to yield the hypothetical scheme suggested in table 16.1 (from Seymour, Aro, & Erskine, 2003).

## Linguistic Units

An important insight has been the suggestion that literacy acquisition depends on a child's capacity to develop an awareness of linguistically important segments in the stream of spoken language. This dates back to Mattingly's (1972) proposal that literacy is a secondary skill that maps onto speech and requires a *metalinguistic awareness* of the content and structure of the primary activities of speaking and listening. An implication is that

**Table 16.1**   Hypothetical Classification of European Languages Relative to the Dimensions of Syllabic Complexity (Simple, Complex) and Orthographic Depth (Shallow to Deep) (from Seymour et al., 2003)

|  |  | Orthographic depth | | | |
|---|---|---|---|---|---|
|  |  | Shallow . . . . . . . . : . . . . . . . . . . . . . . . . . : . . . . . . . . . . . . . . . . : . . . . . . Deep | | | |
| Syllabic structure | Simple | Finnish | Greek Italian Spanish | Portuguese | French |
|  | Complex |  | German Norwegian Icelandic | Dutch Swedish | Danish | English |

the structure may exist at two levels, a *primary* level that supports the natural and unconscious use of speech in communication, and a *secondary* level that is adequate to support the artificial skill of learning to read. These levels are commonly referred to as "implicit" and "explicit." Gombert (1992) used the term *epilinguistic* to refer to the first level and the term *metalinguistic* to refer to the second level. Commonly, it is a failure to develop the second level of representation that is viewed as the cause of reading disability and dyslexia.

Phonological awareness (or metaphonological skill) depends on the system of phonological representations that is postulated in the phonological deficit theory of dyslexia (Snowling, 2000). Phonological representations are assumed to contain linguistically defined sublexical segments of speech. A common view is that a hierarchical structure may be involved, either a two-level structure identifying the *syllable* and an array of *phonemes* or a multilevel structure with intervening levels corresponding to the *onset, peak,* and *coda,* or higher groupings referred to as the *rime* (peak + coda) or the head *body* (onset + peak) (Duncan, Seymour, & Hill, 1997; Treiman & Zukowski, 1991). A question in the present context is whether the development of phonological representations is likely to be approximately the same across different European languages or whether there may be differences that could affect the course of literacy acquisition.

The standard theory, termed the *progressive* model by Seymour and Evans (1994), is that there is a universal trend for development to advance down the hierarchy from representation of large segments (syllables) towards representation of small segments (phonemes). This view was supported by Liberman, Shankweiler, Fischer, and Carter's (1974) observation that the capacity to count syllables emerges before the capacity to count phonemes. Subsequent discussion suggested that development proceeded through an intermediate level of onset-rime segmentation. According to this view, phonological representations develop in a large-to-small unit sequence in response to internal pressures to store and discriminate an expanding speech vocabulary (see Metsala & Walley, 1998). Empirical support for this account has been provided by Treiman and Zukowski (1991).

Children were presented with pairs of spoken words and asked to indicate which pairs sounded similar. On positive trials, the similarity could be present at a syllabic level, or in onsets or rimes, or at the level of individual phonemes. The results clearly supported the notion of a large-to-small unit (syllable → onset-rime → phoneme) developmental sequence.

The progressive theory is widely acknowledged and claims to provide a *universal* account of metaphonological development (i.e., one that is applicable to all of the European languages). Nonetheless, there are reasons to question its general applicability:

- No account is taken of contrasting properties of languages and the possible effects on the phonological representations.
- The distinction between implicit (epilinguistic) and explicit (metalinguistic) levels of representation is not acknowledged.
- The impact of literacy acquisition on phonological representation is not considered.

Duncan, Seymour, and Hill (1997, 2000) have argued that the account of *metalinguistic development* set out by Gombert (1992) has the potential to provide a more inclusive framework that takes better account of the data and has the capability to handle differences between European languages.

Gombert's framework postulates successive levels of representation referred to as: (1) first linguistic skills, (2) epilinguistic awareness, and (3) metalinguistic awareness. One important point is that the first linguistic skills are the infant's response to the characteristics of his spoken language. These provide the basis for the subsequent levels of representation that, accordingly, might be expected to incorporate language-specific features. The second point is that achievement of the higher, metalinguistic level is not viewed as a natural development but as an optional development that occurs in response to a special "demand" imposed by communication needs (Duncan et al., 2000).

The model raises questions about the *tasks* used to assess phonological awareness. Some tasks require only global awareness of similarity or difference. Examples are the matching task used by Treiman and Zukowski (1991) or the odd-word-out task used by Bradley and Bryant (1983). Other tasks require the isolation and manipulation of specific linguistic segments, examples being the segmentation task (Seymour & Evans, 1994), the deletion task (Bruce, 1964; Morais, Cary, Alegria, & Bertelson, 1979), the inversion task (Alegria, Pignot, & Morais, 1982), and the common unit task (Duncan et al., 1997, 2000). Global tasks are capable of being performed on the basis of an implicit (epilinguistic) level of representation. Tasks demanding the isolation and manipulation of specific linguistic segments require an explicit (metalinguistic) level of representation.

Discussions about the course of metaphonological development need to take account of the tasks used to assess awareness, and, in particular, whether it is the implicit or explicit level that is being tested. Often, large units (rimes, syllables) are assessed using an epilinguistic procedure, such as matching or odd-word-out, while small units (phonemes) are assessed using a metalinguistic procedure (deletion, segmentation). This approach tends to favor the progressive, large-to-small unit account of phonological development. When explicit tasks are applied in a procedurally common way to all units (see Hulme et al., 2002), somewhat different results are found. Seymour and Evans (1994) tested preschoolers and Primary 1 and 2 English-speaking children (in Scotland) on a segmentation task with instructions to divide monosyllabic words (or nonwords) into two parts, three parts, or as many parts as possible. The task could not be performed at all by prereaders and the performance of beginning readers suggested early emergence of phonemic segmentation, no special adherence to the onset-rime division in two-part segmentation, and no evidence that segmentation developed progressively down the levels of the intrasyllabic hierarchy. Similarly, Duncan et al. (1997) presented children with pairs of monosyllabic words in a common unit task. The common unit could be a whole rime segment ("goat" – "boat" → "oat") or an initial or final phonemic segment ("bill" – "bone" → "buh"; "bake" – "dock" → "kuh"). Again, prereaders could not perform the task and the developmental trend among primary school children favored small units (phonemes) at first and rime units only at a later stage (Duncan et al., 2000).

## Cross-Language Differences in the Development of Linguistic Awareness

An important question for European literacy is how far spoken language differences affect the course of metaphonological development. As already noted, a crucial distinction relates to syllable structure and the contrast between the open CV syllables of the Romance languages and the closed CVC and more complex syllable structure of the Germanic languages. In recent studies, Lynne Duncan and Pascale Colé and colleagues have compared English- and French-speaking children at the preschool and early primary school ages on tasks assessing metaphonological awareness of syllable structures and boundaries (Duncan, Colé, Seymour, & Magnan, submitted). A common unit procedure was used in which children were presented with pairs of spoken bisyllables and asked to report the common segment. The common unit was a whole syllable in some instances but a smaller unit (a rime or initial phoneme) in others. English-speaking prereaders were unable to perform this task. By contrast, French-speaking prereaders, aged 4 or 5 years, performed the task of reporting common syllables almost perfectly. In an additional task, spoken bisyllabic words were presented under the instruction to segment the utterance into two parts. Prereaders in both languages were able to perform this task. However, while French children were entirely consistent in placing the division at a standard juncture (prior to the largest available consonantal onset group), this was not true of English-speaking children who located the boundary in many different places.

These data accord with previous studies (Bruck, Genesee, & Caravolas, 1997) in implying that there are differences in the phonological representations developed by French-speaking and English-speaking children in the period before they learn to read. For French speakers these representations include a precise segmentation into clearly defined syllabic units. This structure is absent from the representations of English-speaking children. It is important to note that this distinction refers to the explicit (metalinguistic) level of representation. In Gombert's (1992) framework, establishment of a metalinguistic representation of a unit (here, the syllable) is normally held to be a response to some kind of special "demand" imposed by language use and communication. If so, it may be that producing and listening to the French language, perhaps supported by games and songs involving syllabification, induces an explicit awareness of syllables and syllable boundaries. One possibility is that the contrast reflects the distinction between the simple syllable structure of the Romance languages as against the complex syllable structure of the Germanic languages. Alternatively, it may reflect metrical distinctions between syllable-timed languages, such as French, and stress-timed languages, such as English (Abercrombie, 1967; Ramus, Nespor, & Mehler, 1999).

As already noted, an assumption in Gombert's framework is that the establishment of the metalinguistic level of representation for a given unit is not normally the product of a simple process of maturation and experience but rather a response to a specific "demand." With regard to explicit awareness of *phonemes*, the most likely possibility is that this demand is imposed by the task of learning to read. This presumption is supported by the study by Morais et al. (1979) of Portuguese literate and illiterate adults. Morais et al. used an initial phoneme deletion task with nonword stimuli as a measure of explicit phoneme awareness. The important outcome was that literate adults could perform the task, whereas illiterate adults could not. This is consistent with numerous studies which show that capacity to perform explicit phoneme manipulation tasks, such as deletion, inversion, or common unit identification, normally emerges coincidentally with the onset of literacy (Duncan et al., 1997; Perfetti, Beck, Bell, & Hughes, 1987).

The finding that learning to read and spell promotes phonemic awareness suggests that the timing of the onset of explicit phonemic awareness will vary across European societies in line with the socioeducational variations in the *ages* at which reading is formally taught. This point can be illustrated by referring again to the work by Duncan et al. (submitted) on metaphonological development in English and French. In the UK, formal instruction in reading begins at the age of 5 years, whereas, in France, the starting age is 6 years. Metaphonemic awareness was assessed using the common unit task in which the shared segment was the initial consonant phoneme of two bisyllabic words. Capacity to isolate and report back this segment appears at 5 years in English-speaking children but not until 6 years in French-speaking children. This is not a difference in phonological capacity between the two samples (recall that the French children were much better at reporting common syllables) but seems instead to be a simple effect of the difference in the age at which reading is taught.

The emergence of phonemic awareness will also depend on the extent to which an *alphabetic* approach to teaching is adopted. Bruce (1964) long ago noted that primary school children educated in a school that favored whole-word methods were much less able to perform phoneme deletion tasks than children receiving phonic instruction. Similarly, Alegria et al. (1982) reported that Belgian French-speaking children who learned in a phonic regime were able to transpose the positions of phonemes, whereas children who learned according to a whole-word regime were not. The implication is that whole-word methods, which do not emphasize mappings between letters and subword speech segments, do not create a demand for the development of an awareness of phonemes. In the mixed method used in the UK, it appears that the alphabetic component is normally sufficient to induce metalinguistic awareness of speech segments. Duncan et al. (1997) studied the transition from nursery school into primary school in Scottish children learning by a logographic and alphabetic method and found that the teaching encouraged the formation of analytic decoding processes and the awareness of phonemic segments in speech.

## Models of Literacy Acquisition

Various models of reading acquisition have been formulated, generally with a reference to learning to read in English and without an explicit goal of encompassing learning to read in different languages (see Byrne, and Ehri, this volume, for discussions of theories of literacy acquisition). It seems important that such models should acknowledge (1) that there may be early (foundational) processes in learning to read, (2) that approaches to teaching may make a difference, (3) that there is an interactive relationship between orthography and linguistic awareness, and (4) that the eventual achievement is the fluent reading of complex (multisyllabic, multimorphemic) words. Here it is proposed that the question of literacy development across different European languages should be considered in the context of an inclusive framework deriving from previous research by Seymour and colleagues (see Seymour, 1990, 1993, 1997, 1999; Seymour & Duncan, 2001).

The framework derives from earlier analyses of reading acquisition, including stage models (Frith, 1985), decoding models (Gough & Hillinger, 1980), accounts of 'sight word' learning (Ehri, 1992, this volume), acquisition of the alphabetic principle (Byrne & Fielding-Barnsley, 1989; Byrne, this volume) as well as contemporary connectionist approaches (Plaut et al., 1996; Seidenberg & McClelland, 1989). It contends that (1) literacy acquisition involves an ongoing interaction between developing orthographic systems and phonological representations in which implicit (epilinguistic) structures become explicit (metalinguistic) in response to demands created by the structure of the orthography; (2) orthographic development may involve a series of overlapping phases in which increasingly complex structures are formed:

Phase 0:    *Letter-sound knowledge.* The essential prerequisite for all subsequent literacy development is the establishment of a knowledge base of the letters of the alphabet and their links with sounds.

Phase 1:    *Foundation literacy.* This is a preliminary phase during which the basic elements of (a) familiar sight word recognition and storage (logographic process), and (b) sequential decoding (alphabetic process), are established.

Phase 2:    *Orthographic literacy.* During this phase, a framework for definition of legitimate spellings of syllables is assembled and structured around linguistic units, especially onset-peak-coda or onset-rime elements. This is viewed as an internal reorganization that builds on structures established during the foundation phase, including stored word exemplars and letter-sound correspondences.

Phase 3:    *Morphographic literacy.* The focus of the third phase is on the formation of representations of complex words in which syllables are combined, stress is assigned, and free and bound morphemes are identified and combined.

The demand for the formation of explicit (metalinguistic) representations is expected to alter as development proceeds through these phases. In Phase 1, the introduction of the alphabetic principle and decoding procedures creates a demand for the establishment of explicit *phonemic* representations (Byrne & Fielding-Barnsley, 1989). In Phase 2, there is a requirement for an organization defined in terms of syllables and the internal structure of the syllable (i.e., metalinguistic representations of *onset* and *rime*, or *onset, peak*, and *coda*). Finally, in Phase 3, there is a requirement for the coordination of syllabic and morphological elements, or a *metamorphemic* representation. The assumption of the model is that these explicit representations build on preexisting (epilinguistic) levels of awareness and normally arise in response to demands reflecting the current emphasis in orthographic development.

## Language Effects on Orthographic Development

There is, as yet, no comprehensive study of early literacy acquisition in the European orthographies. Most existing studies involve only comparisons within subsets of languages. For example, Wimmer and Goswami (1994) compared reading of number names and nonwords by 7-, 8-, and 9-year-old children in German and English. Nonword reading was significantly slower and more error prone in English at all three age levels. Frith, Wimmer, and Landerl (1998) used structurally equivalent sets of 1-, 2-, and 3-syllable nonwords in English and German and again found consistently poorer nonword reading in English. Analogous findings are reported for comparisons of English with Spanish and French by Goswami, Gombert, and de Barrera (1998), and with Greek by Goswami, Porpodas, and Wheelwright (1997). Recently, Spencer and Hanley (2003) compared the learning of English and Welsh (which is written in a shallow orthography) and found faster development in Welsh, although this difference reduced in the later stages of development.

The COST A8 project included a wider range of languages and directly addressed the beginnings of reading (foundation literacy, phases 0 and 1). The samples consisted of first-grade primary school children who were learning under standard teaching conditions in each country. Foundation literacy was operationally defined in terms of three indicators:

- *Letter-sound knowledge.* Accuracy and speed in identifying the letters of the alphabet by giving the dominant sound (or name) and speed of labeling the letters in a list.
- *Sight word identification (logographic process).* Accuracy and speed of reading sets of very familiar words, subdivided between content words and functors, such as occur in beginning reading materials in each language.
- *Decoding unfamiliar forms (alphabetic process).* Accuracy and speed of reading simple nonwords of one syllable (VC, CV, or CVC structure) and two syllables (VCV, CVCV, VCVC structures).

The items were presented as short vertical lists for reading aloud and errors were recorded as well as the time to complete the list (time per item). The data were collected towards the latter half of the first school year.

## Phase 0: letter-sound knowledge

In the model, letter-sound knowledge is regarded as the essential basis of alphabetic literacy and the sine qua non for subsequent development (Duncan & Seymour, 2000; see also Byrne, this volume). In the study of Seymour et al. (2003), the mean accuracy for letters was over 90% in all language groups, English included (94% for the Scottish grade 1 class). Although the ages of the various groups differed, age was only very weakly related to success in letter learning. Further, there was no systematic effect of either syllabic complexity or orthographic depth on letter accuracy. Seymour et al. (2003) also measured fluency of letter identification. The rate of sounding or naming letters averaged about 1 sec/item. Speed was unrelated to age within the main group of languages (English excluded), and there were no systematic effects of orthographic depth or syllabic complexity (e.g., the rate was slower in Finnish, at 1.48 sec/item, than in most other languages). However, the Scottish children had the slowest rate overall, at 1.88 sec/item. Given that they were younger than the other children, this may suggest an effect of immaturity on fluency of letter processing.

Although children may know some letters in kindergarten, acquisition of the full alphabet normally occurs at the start of formal schooling and depends on educational factors (when letter learning starts, and at what pace and in what order the letters are introduced). Socioeconomic disadvantage may delay the achievement of full mastery of the alphabet. It is possible that there are some children, referred to as instances of *literal dyslexia* by Seymour and Evans (1999), who have difficulty in acquiring the letter sounds. This could occur in any language and would be expected to have damaging effects on subsequent development in all cases.

## Phase 1: foundation literacy

*Sight word identification (logographic process).* In the study of Seymour et al., the logographic (word identification) process was assessed by the reading of very common words such as occur in children's beginning reading materials. There are alternative models regarding the impact of language differences on this process. One possibility is that early words might be learned as patterns differentiated on the basis of visual or other features (Frith, 1985; Gough & Hillinger, 1980; Seymour & Elder, 1986). This process might be independent of effects of complexity or consistency. If so, factors such as regularity should not influence learning, and it might be expected that all children would acquire a sight vocabulary in the same way, irrespective of the depth of the orthography. The alternative view is that sight word learning is alphabetically based and exploits knowledge of letter-sound relationships (Ehri, 1992). In this account it seems reasonable to predict that sight word learning might proceed more rapidly in a simple orthographic environment than in a complex environment (cf. Rack, Hulme, Snowling, & Wightman's [1994] finding that beginners learn to read regular words more easily than irregular words).

Figure 16.1 displays accuracy levels for familiar word reading in the simple syllable and complex syllable series of languages (Seymour et al., 2003). These data are contrary

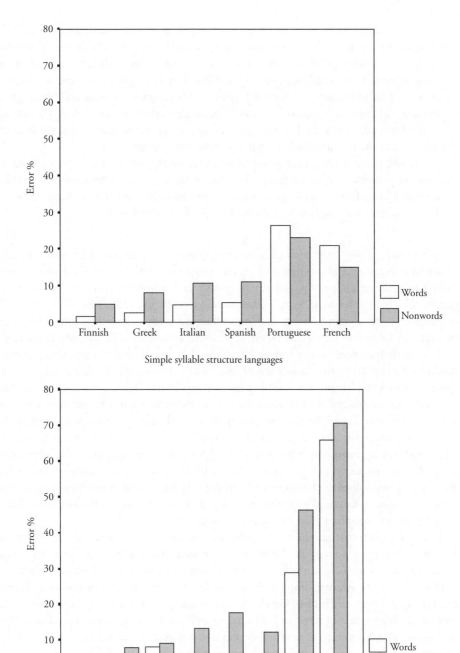

**Figure 16.1** Error rates (%) for familiar word and simple nonword reading by simple syllable language groups and complex syllable language groups (from Seymour et al., 2003).

to models in which early sight word learning is a pattern discrimination process independent of orthographic depth. In most European orthographies children read familiar words very accurately (>95% correct) and fluently (1.6 sec/item) before the end of the first school year. These levels are substantially lower in Portuguese, French, and Danish (approx 75% correct), and far lower in English (34% in grade 1, rising to 76% in grade 2). Syllable structure appeared not to have a damaging effect. Further, there was no significant relationship with age (Scottish data excluded). It seems that orthographic depth directly retards the rate at which a sight vocabulary is learned.

The results for English appear grossly different from the other European languages. In the Scottish sample, analysis suggested that two or more years of experience were needed before word identification in English matched the accuracy and fluency levels achieved in the majority of languages before the end of the first school year.

*Simple decoding (alphabetic process).* Decoding (the alphabetic process) was assessed by measures of accuracy and speed of reading very simple nonwords. The monosyllables were 2- or 3-letter items such as 'op' and 'fip' in English and equivalent forms in the other languages. The bisyllables were 3- or 4-letter items, such as 'uba' and 'afen'. The nonwords contained no consonant clusters and no orthographically complex forms. They were intended to be simple forms that could be decoded on a one-letter, one-phoneme basis.

Two theoretical possibilities can be identified. The first is that the alphabetic process might be a straightforward elaboration of letter-sound knowledge. Children might establish an isolated mechanism for scanning letter arrays left-to-right, converting graphemes to phonemes, and blending the outcome into a response. Such a mechanism could be assembled without regard to the complexity of the orthography. If so, we would expect to find that the basic decoding mechanism could be established in an approximately equivalent way by beginning readers in each of the European languages. The alternative possibility is that the development is affected by the overall complexity of the orthographic and phonological environment from the very beginning of learning. In this case, we would expect mastery of even the most simple decoding tasks to emerge more slowly in complex orthographies than in shallow orthographies.

Figure 16.1 summarizes the error scores for decoding simple nonwords by the grade 1 samples (from Seymour et al., 2003). It can be seen that, while decoding is performed accurately, at about 90% correct for monosyllables and 80% for bisyllables, there are notable exceptions. Among simple syllable languages, performance was poorer in French and Portuguese than in Finnish, Greek, Italian, or Spanish. In the complex Germanic set, there was a higher rate of error in Danish than in the other languages, and a huge effect in English. The differences were also reflected in the fluency measure. There was evidence of dysfluency in Portuguese and French and in Danish and English.

These results are contrary to the predictions of the model assuming development of an isolated decoding mechanism. From the beginnings of learning, the alphabetic decoding process develops more slowly and less efficiently in some languages than in others. The effect may be in part attributable to the phonological distinction between the simple and complex syllable languages. The inefficiency is much greater in Danish and English than in French and Portuguese, and, within the remaining languages, accuracy was marginally better for the simple syllable set (92% vs. 89%) and there was an advantage in speed (1.97 vs. 2.81 sec/item). The effect may also be a consequence of the differences in orthographic depth. French has a deeper orthography than Spanish, and, despite the equivalence of the age at which learning starts, grade 1 nonword reading is less accurate and slower (85% vs. 95% correct, 4.13 vs. 1.44 sec/item). Danish is written in a deeper orthography than German, and this again is associated with large differences in accuracy and speed (54% vs. 94% correct, 4.58 vs. 1.45 sec/item).

The most extreme disadvantage occurs in English. Although the Scottish grade 1 children were ahead of age expectation, they read only 29% of nonwords correctly and were extremely dysfluent (6.69 sec/item). Grade 2 children, aged 6.56 years, read only 64% of nonwords at a rate of 3.17 sec/item, well below all other languages tested (except for the Danish grade 1 group). Seymour et al. estimated that the reading age needed to match the level of the majority of European languages was above 7.5 years, implying that the English-speaking groups needed 2.5 years of learning, or more than twice as much time as most other languages, to establish a most minimal and basic decoding function.

These outcomes make it clear that there are very significant differences among the European orthographies in the ease with which the basic (foundational) elements of literacy are acquired. From a theoretical viewpoint, a critical question is whether the cognitive effects of linguistic complexity should be viewed as continuous or dichotomous. Orthographic depth might be described as a continuous variable (see Frost, this volume), measurable by some appropriate metric of complexity, which produces a graded delaying effect on rates of foundation literacy acquisition. Alternatively, it is possible that the cognitive effects of increasing complexity may be discontinuous, such that there is a range of low degrees of complexity, collectively classifiable as *shallow* orthographies, and then a threshold level of complexity that marks the boundary for a group of *deep* orthographies. Seymour et al. (2003) noted that their results for familiar word and simple nonword reading appeared consistent with a discontinuous account of this kind. The majority of European orthographies yielded approximately equivalent levels of good performance and a narrow range of individual variation. There then appeared to be a step change to a subset of orthographies in which acquisition was substantially more difficult and characterized by a large amount of individual variation. Seymour et al. suggested that this threshold separated English, Danish, French, and Portuguese (the *deep* European orthographies) from the remaining languages in their sample (the *shallow* European orthographies).

If this line is followed, table 16.1 can be reassembled as a 2 × 2 designation in which languages may be classified by reference to syllable structure (simple, complex) and orthographic complexity (shallow, deep). It is hypothesized that the course of early reading acquisition will vary depending on which cell is occupied by a given language. One possibility is that the deep orthographies require the development of a dual (logographic + alphabetic) foundation, while, for shallow orthographies, a unitary (alphabetic) foundation suffices. The reason for the establishment of the dual process is that too high a proportion of words encountered early in learning violate the alphabetic principle of one letter, one sound. It becomes necessary to build up a store of word forms that can be recognized and reproduced in addition to establishing a basic decoding procedure. This suggestion is consistent with the contention of Paulesu et al. (2000) that different brain functions may be developed by readers of deep and shallow orthographies. It is also consistent with the observation that contrasting reading patterns may be found in normally developing readers and readers with dyslexia in English. Seymour and Evans (1999) observed that the lexicality effect (difference between familiar words and simple nonwords) was positive in some normal readers (word reading accuracy much higher than nonword reading accuracy) and negative in others (nonwords considerably better than words). These effects were exaggerated in some dyslexic readers, suggesting contrasting patterns of *alphabetic dyslexia* and *logographic dyslexia*. Such a contrast might be expected in the deep orthographies, where a dual foundation is implemented, but not in the shallow orthographies, where a unitary (alphabetic) foundation is implemented.

The phonological contrast between the simple and complex syllable structures appears to influence the development of the alphabetic process. Seymour et al. (2003) suggested that this could be because the presence of clearly defined syllables containing few consonant clusters is optimal for the establishment of grapheme–phoneme correspondences and their merging into speech segments. In a language with complex syllables this process is more difficult because the basic correspondences are often embedded in onset and coda clusters and because the syllable boundaries are ambiguous.

An additional point is that *individual variability* is much greater in the deep orthographies than in the shallow orthographies. This effect is shown in the report by Seymour et al. (2003) that illustrates a 'normal' range for accuracy of familiar word and simple nonword reading in the main group of shallow European orthographies (defined as within ±1.75 sd of the mean). The bulk of children score above 80% for words and 70% for nonwords and the scores of the tail of outliers lie above 40% and 30% respectively. Non-readers are seldom if ever found in these orthographies. The results for the deeper orthographies contrast in showing much higher variability, with the normal range extending down to 40–50% in Portuguese and French, and the tail approaching the nonreader zone (defined as <10%). In English and Danish, the normal variation among Primary 1 children extends over almost the whole range of possible scores and includes appreciable numbers of nonreaders.

## Phase 2: orthographic level

The orthographic level is envisaged as a structure in which the legitimate orthographic forms of monosyllables are represented. This is directly comparable to the process of internalization of orthographic knowledge that has been simulated in the connectionist models (Plaut et al., 1996; Seidenberg & McClelland, 1989). This level can be tested using words of average or lower frequency (relative to primary school populations) and corresponding nonwords that reflect the range of phonological complexities (syllable structures) and orthographic complexities (multiletter graphemes, inconsistencies, irregularities) that occur in a given language. The rate of development should be influenced by phonological complexity (syllable structure) since the construction of a model of the legitimate spellings of monosyllables will depend on the size of the space required to specify all possibilities. If a syllable is defined by the presence of a peak (vowel), an (optional) onset (initial consonant group), and an (optional) coda (final consonant group), then the size of the space will reflect (a) the number of vowel forms in the phonology of the language, (b) the number of legitimate onsets, and (c) the number of legitimate codas. In the

Romance languages, the space will be relatively small because there are few possible onsets and mainly open syllables. In the Germanic languages, the space will be much larger because of the wider range of possible onset and coda clusters. In addition, the representation of monosyllables is likely to be facilitated in those languages, such as French, in which syllables are clearly and precisely defined and are objects of metalinguistic awareness for preliterate children.

It is self-evident that orthographic development will be affected by orthographic complexity. The connectionist model predicts that the rate of learning will be a continuous function of a graded index of complexity and not a dichotomous outcome of the kind proposed for the foundation level. In closed syllable languages, the rime structures will be relatively numerous and complex and a focus for variations in consistency (Treiman, Mullennix, Bijeljac-Babic, & Richmond-Welty, 1995; Ziegler et al., 1997). The prediction is that, insofar as this occurs, there will be a demand for the formation of rime units as objects of metalinguistic awareness and a move toward the capacity to perform explicit phonological tasks, such as common unit identification, in which rime units are targets (Duncan et al., 2000). The capacity to make this shift will, in turn, depend on preliterate implicit (epilinguistic) awareness of rime. Thus, Duncan et al. found that early measures of implicit riming, using the oddity task, were selectively related in fixed order multiple regression analyses to later postliterate measures of explicit rime awareness, using the common unit task. These developments appear less likely to occur in simple syllable languages and shallow orthographies (Goswami et al., 1998).

## Phase 3: morphographic level

The morphographic level is hypothesized as a structure in which syllable-sized segments may be combined to form complex multisyllabic words. A distinction may be made between monomorphemic multisyllables (such as *elephant*) and morphologically complex forms (such as *indisputable*) that can be analyzed into segments corresponding to free and bound morphemes (tense or number inflections, prefixes, derivational suffixes). The organization of the morphographic level is uncertain, but could consist of whole-word forms, or combinations of syllables, or combinations of morphemes. The way in which this level is constructed is likely to depend on the degree to which the spelling system of the language represents lexical and morphological features as distinct from phonological features. Finnish has a very complex morphology in which stems are combined with arrays of bound morphemes. However, these elements are written in a phonologically transparent manner. Consequently, a syllable-based representation would appear to be sufficient and the morphographic level might be defined simply as a mechanism for combining syllabic segments. This will not be true for deep orthographies where spelling may signal lexical identity as well as morphological structure. An additional issue is posed by the assignment of stress in multisyllables. In some languages, stress assignment may follow a regular pattern. In others (e.g., Greek or Spanish), departures from the standard pattern are marked by diacritics in the writing system. English is more complex, since stress is not marked and may vary, so that, for example, most bisyllables have first-syllable stress but some (e.g., *canoe*) have second-syllable stress. This means that the correct allocation of stress when pronouncing a multisyllable depends on lexical identification. To the extent that this is true, a morpheme- rather than syllable-based organization may be preferred.

We can speculate, therefore, that the cognitive effort required to form the Level 3 morphographic framework will depend on the degree to which lexical and morphological features are implicated in the spelling system. In shallow orthographies with a clear syllabic structure this level may be built by combining the syllabic segments that are already available. The learning time required may simply be a function of the number of possible syllables and combinations. Where syllable structure is poorly defined and where spelling is lexically or morphologically determined, then a more complex and time-consuming process may be required in which word forms internalized within the logographic process are scanned and analyzed in order to construct a new morpheme-based system.

## Conclusions

This chapter has set out a theoretical framework for the discussion of cultural and language differences that exist within the context of *European literacy*. This has been approached by outlining a developmental model in which linguistic segments are at the forefront during successive phases of development.

It is likely that phonological differences affect the content of the system of phonological representations developed during childhood. These representations may exist at (at least) two levels, an implicit (epilinguistic) level, necessary for normal language use, and an explicit (metalinguistic) level that permits the isolation and manipulation of linguistic units. Languages that have a clear and well-defined syllabic structure induce a metalinguistic representation of syllabic segments in prereaders. The metalinguistic representation of phonemes is normally facilitated by the task of learning to read in an analytic, alphabetic mode. This is a common outcome in all European languages, although the timing is contingent on the age at which reading instruction begins and the point at which alphabetic teaching is introduced.

The subset of languages discussed here may be grouped according to a $2 \times 2$ categorization of syllabic structure (simple, complex) and orthographic depth (shallow, deep). Acquisition may differ between the languages in each cell of this scheme at each of four hypothetical phases. The initial step of letter-sound acquisition (Phase 0) is common to all alphabetic orthographies. It is probably not affected by language differences but is affected by educational factors (age of starting, teaching method), social factors (SES), and, possibly, cortical maturity and dyslexia. Foundation literacy (Phase 1) differs across languages. Elementary decoding (the alphabetic process) is established more slowly in complex than in simple syllable languages and more slowly in deep than in shallow orthographies. This early stage of development depends on education (provision of alphabetic teaching at a given age). Sight word acquisition is slowed in orthographies that exceed a threshold level of depth or complexity. It is hypothesized that deep orthographies induce the formation of a dual foundation containing distinct logographic (sight word) and alphabetic (decoding) processes. This results in slowed acquisition and exaggerated individual variation among normally developing readers and readers with dyslexia.

Orthographic literacy (Phase 2) also differs between languages. The construction of an internal model of the spellings of all possible monosyllables will occur more rapidly in simple syllable than in complex syllable languages, and will be further delayed in proportion to the degree to which spelling departs from the principle of one letter/one sound. Morphographic literacy (Phase 3) is likely to be more difficult in languages having a complex and poorly defined syllable structure and in languages in which spelling signals lexical identity and morphological function.

According to this formulation, we would expect the rate and efficiency of literacy acquisition to differ between languages in the ranking (1) simple syllable shallow orthographies (Finnish, Greek, Italian, Spanish); (2) complex syllable shallow orthographies (German, Norwegian, Icelandic, Swedish, Dutch); (3) simple syllable deep orthographies (Portuguese, French); and (4) complex syllable deep orthographies (Danish, English). An unresolved issue is whether the dramatically outlying results for beginning reading in English are explicable within this scheme. It seems clear that difficulties arise for learners of English at each phase of the developmental process:

- *Phase 0*: Immaturity due to early school entry may impede the achievement of fluency in processing letter-sounds.
- *Phase 1*: A dual foundation is required, causing slower learning. Sight word acquisition is impeded by a high proportion of words that violate the one letter / one sound principle. Elementary decoding is adversely affected by complex syllabic structure.
- *Phase 2*: The number of possible syllables is very large and the language contains numerous monosyllables with inconsistent rime spellings.
- *Phase 3*: Spelling is used to signal lexical identity and to identify bound morphemes. Additional complications arise from stress assignment and a complex and ambiguous syllabic structure.

This accumulation of difficulties may be sufficient to explain the deviant results for English. If not, it may be that there are relevant contributions from social or educational factors that somehow exaggerate these difficulties.

# 17

# Learning to Read in Chinese

## J. Richard Hanley

## The Chinese Writing System

The earliest existing records of the Chinese writing system date from the Shang dynasty in 1200 BC. By that time, Chinese writing was already a highly sophisticated and fully expressive system, and modern Chinese characters are descended directly from the Shang characters (Boltz, 1996). The shape of some of the Shang characters resembles the object that they represent, either literally (pictographs) or metaphorically (ideographs). However, most of the Shang characters are compounds in which two characters are written together to form a single unit. One of the component characters provides information about the meaning of the word, and the other provides a clue to its pronunciation.

The compound characters have a complex but instructive evolutionary history. The pictographs and ideographs appear to have been the first written word forms used by the Chinese. Subsequently, some of these characters were used to represent other Chinese words that were pronounced the same way but had a different meaning. As Boltz puts it, "Hundreds of words with meanings that were not amenable to pictographic representation could now be written by the rebus principle" (1996, p. 193). Other characters were used to represent words similar in *meaning* to the words that they originally represented. The cost of the improved expressive power of the writing system was, of course, increased ambiguity of these (noncompound) characters.

Compound characters were created to solve this problem. A secondary character was placed alongside an ambiguous character in order to provide a clue as to its pronunciation (the *phonetic* component) or to its meaning (the *radical* component). So long as the phonetic and radical components were characters that were already familiar, this development immediately increased the probability that semantically related characters would be pronounced correctly, and that the correct meaning would be assigned to homophones.

For example, the compound character 伯 is pronounced "bo" and means "uncle." On the left of the compound is the radical component 亻, which means "person." On the right is the phonetic component 白, which, like the compound character itself, is pronounced "bo." The radical component therefore distinguishes this compound character from a homophone such as 舶, which contains the same phonetic component and is also pronounced "bo." In 舶, which means "ship," the radical is 舟, which means "boat."

More than 80% of modern day Chinese characters contain both a phonetic and a radical component. There are approximately 200 different radicals and 1,000 different phonetics. Chen and Allport (1995) suggest that skilled Chinese readers may identify the radical component of compound characters at a relatively early stage of visual word recognition prior to recognition of the phonetic. In most compound characters, the radical typically appears on the left and the phonetic appears on the right. In 20% of characters, however, the radical appears on the right and the phonetic appears on the left. Even more problematic is the fact that the pronunciation of some Chinese words has changed over the centuries and, as a consequence, the phonetic component does not always provide reliable information about how the character should be read. Furthermore, some radical components do not provide any useful information about the word's meaning. This issue will be discussed further in the sections below that deal with the way in which children read compound characters.

Although recent Chinese dictionaries contain as many as 60, 000 different characters, the number in use is very much lower. Mair (1996) estimated that knowledge of 2,400 characters would permit a reader to read 99% of the characters that appear in most texts. This is approximately the same number of characters as children in mainland China are expected to know by the end of elementary school.

There are 12 different strokes that Chinese characters can contain. The number of strokes in a character varies from 1 to 64, so some strokes appear more than once in many characters. Since 1956 in mainland China, approximately 2,000 characters have been simplified by reducing the number of strokes. The simplified characters contain a mean of 9.0 strokes per character (Chan, 1982). In the traditional script, the equivalent characters contain a mean of 11.2 strokes per character. The simplified characters are also used in Singapore but not in Taiwan or Hong Kong, and so different versions of the Chinese script now exist. Children are taught to write the strokes in each character in a specific order (Law, Ki, Chung, Ko, & Lam, 1998). However, because each character occupies the same amount of space on a sheet of paper, the size of the strokes will vary according to the complexity of the character. Although individual strokes of themselves do not represent units of sound or meaning, a recent model of Chinese character identification (Perfetti & Tan, 1999) claims that adult readers detect the strokes that a familiar character contains prior to recognizing the character as a whole.

## The relationship between spoken and written Chinese

In spoken Chinese, every morpheme is represented by a single syllable (see Chen, 1996, for discussion). Almost without exception, there is no equivalent in Chinese of English words that contain one morpheme and two syllables (e.g., *paper*, *tiger*). Many Chinese words are multisyllabic (80% according to Li, 1977), but a Chinese word that contains two syllables will almost always contain two morphemes.

Chinese syllables have a relatively simple form, with the majority being of consonant–vowel (CV) structure. Only five consonants ever follow the vowel in Cantonese (the first language of 90% of the population of Hong Kong), and only two of these (the nasal consonants /n/ and /ŋ/) can follow the vowel in Mandarin (the official language or "Putonghua" of mainland China and Taiwan). There are no consonant blends either before or after the vowel in Chinese. Li and Thompson (1981) estimated that there are 22 onsets and 37 rimes in Mandarin. As a consequence, there is a relatively small number of syllables in Mandarin (approximately 420), which means that in many cases different morphemes are represented by the same syllable. In spoken Chinese, a syllable can represent different morphemes when spoken in a different tone (the specific pitch pattern in which a word is spoken). There are four different tones in Mandarin (high-level, high-rising, falling-rising, high-falling) and nine different tones in Cantonese. Even taking into account tone, however, there are no more than 1,700 syllables in Mandarin. Mandarin therefore contains less than a quarter of the number of syllables that exist in English (approximately 8,000 syllables). Tones do not help distinguish morphemes in *written* Chinese, however, because there are no symbols in the Chinese writing system that convey information about tone.

Each Chinese character represents a morpheme. Because morphemes contain only one syllable, and because words that contain two morphemes contain two syllables and are written as two characters, there is a sense in which a character also represents a syllable. This raises the question of whether the Chinese writing system is a syllabary (albeit a very deep syllabary). The answer is probably "no." The presence of the semantic radical in most Chinese characters means that the character first and foremost represents the word itself rather than a phonological form. According to Boltz (1996), some characters started to appear in texts around 200 BC with their radical component missing, thereby threatening to move the system in the direction of a syllabary. He believes that influential scholars of the time may have explicitly included the radical when writing these characters in a successful bid to reverse this trend. It would of course have been possible to create a transparent syllabary for the 1,700 or so Mandarin syllables (as the Japanese successfully achieved with Kana). The price of transparency, however, would have been much greater ambiguity. The large number of homonyms that Chinese contains would have to be written as homographs, thus making them impossible to disambiguate out of context. (Exactly the same problem occurs with Pinyin and Zhu-Yin-Fu-Hua [see below], which are contemporary phonetically transparent systems that are used to write Chinese.) As was pointed out earlier, many of these homophones can be readily understood within the current Chinese writing system because the presence of the radical beside the phonetic in the compound ensures that they have a distinct orthographic representation. Such information would not be available in a syllabary, and is not available in the way that the word is written in Pinyin and Zhu-Yin-Fu-Hua.

Is the Chinese writing system therefore logographic? The answer depends on what one takes to be the defining features of a logographic writing system. Chinese characters represent lexical forms, not meanings, and so if the definition of a logographic system is that characters represent meaning rather than sound (Cheung & Ng, 2003), then Chinese is not a logographic system. If a character is a logograph only if it cannot be broken down into smaller components or if logographs "are widely characterized by a complete absence of any phonetic component" (Tzeng, Lin, Hung, & Lee, 1995), then Chinese characters are clearly not logographs. If the definition is that each word is represented by its own character, then as Shu and Anderson (1999) point out, Chinese is not a logographic system because most Chinese words contain at least two morphemes and are represented by at least two characters. If, however, its definition permits writing systems where the primary correspondences are between characters and morphemes, then Chinese is unequivocally a logographic writing system.

As the official language of China, Mandarin is spoken by approximately 70% of the population, and Chinese characters have traditionally been used as the written form of Mandarin. When children throughout mainland China and Taiwan are taught to read characters, they are taught the pronunciation of the word in Mandarin even if it is not the language that is spoken locally. In Hong Kong, even before the incorporation of Hong Kong with mainland China in July 1997, only a relatively small set of characters were taught in Cantonese at the start of elementary school. As children get older, they are taught to read in Mandarin. Contrary to what is often claimed, a Mandarin speaker would find it quite difficult to read a newspaper from Hong Kong written in Cantonese, and a monolingual Cantonese speaker would struggle to read texts written in Mandarin. This is because the syntax of the two languages is different, and because the meaning of some characters differs in Cantonese and Mandarin.

## The Teaching of Reading in China

*Learning new characters*

Formal instruction in reading starts in mainland China when children enter the first grade of elementary school between the ages of 6 and 7. It is officially forbidden to teach characters in preschools in mainland China. However, some preschools apparently turn a blind eye to this ruling (Li & Rao, 2000), and parents will often provide informal instruction to their children before they attend elementary school (Ingulsrud & Allen, 1999).

An important analysis of the characters that appear in elementary school textbooks in mainland China has recently been carried out by Shu, Chen, Anderson, Wu, and Xuan (2003). They report that children should have learnt 2,570 different characters by the end of six years of instruction. A relatively large number of new characters are introduced in the first three years at elementary school (436 in grade 1, 709 in grade 2, and 541 in grade 3). In grades 4–6, the number of new characters is smaller (358 in grade 4, 323 in grade 5, and 203 in grade 6), with greater emphasis being placed on reading comprehension. Visually less complex characters containing 6 strokes or fewer tend to be taught in grade 1. Characters containing between 7 and 12 strokes appear more frequently from grade 2 onwards, while exposure to characters containing more than 12 strokes increases gradually from grade 1 to 6. In general, more frequent characters are introduced earlier. Pictographs and ideographs are typically taught early, although compound characters predominate in all six grades. Importantly, the most frequent characters tend to be the ones with the least transparent phonetic components. Hence children are exposed to frequent characters with unpredictable pronunciations in grade 1, with a larger proportion of characters with relatively predictable pronunciations appearing as they get older.

Class teachers will routinely inform children of the meaning, the pronunciation, and the sequence of strokes when new characters are being taught. In addition, a minority of teachers will systematically decompose compound characters in class by drawing the attention of children to the phonetic and semantic components of new characters. A recent study by Cheung and Ng (2003) suggests that the number of teachers who decompose compounds for children is lowest in Singapore and highest in mainland China, with Taiwan and Hong Kong somewhere in between. In Singapore, Chinese characters are taught in preschool, and children have developed some proficiency in reading by age 4 (Li & Rao, 2000). In Hong Kong, children are taught to read and write characters during their first kindergarten year when they are as young as 3, and read much better at 4 than children of that age in Beijing (Li & Rao, 2000). By the end of second grade, children from Hong Kong should be able to read 960 different characters (Ho & Bryant, 1997a). Here children learn new characters by rote by copying them many times over.

## Pinyin and Zhu-Yin-Fu-Hao

All children in the first term at elementary school (6–7 years) in mainland China are taught to read an alphabetic script (Pinyin) before formal instruction in reading and writing Chinese characters commences in term 2. The Pinyin symbols are letters from the Roman alphabet. Pinyin is also used to teach reading of Chinese characters in Singapore, where approximately 75% of the population are native Mandarin speakers. In Hong Kong, Pinyin is sometimes used to teach children to read Mandarin, but has not been used when the children learn to read characters in Cantonese.

Taiwanese children learn a script known as Zhu-Yin-Fu-Hao during the first ten weeks of the first grade before any exposure to Chinese characters takes place. Zhu-Yin-Fu-Hao contains 37 different characters, all of which are visually different from any of the characters that comprise the Chinese writing system itself. Below are the 37 Zhu-Yin-Fu-Hao symbols as presented by Chen and Yuen (1991). To their right are the equivalent Pinyin letter or letters. Further to the right are the equivalent IPA symbols. There are symbols to represent the various single phoneme consonant onsets in Mandarin, there are symbols for vowels, and there are symbols for vowels plus endings (i.e., symbols for rimes):

| | | | | | | | | |
|---|---|---|---|---|---|---|---|---|
| ㄅ | b | p | ㄓ | zh | tʂ | ㄞ | ai | ai |
| ㄆ | p | p' | ㄔ | ch | tʂ' | ㄟ | ei | ei |
| ㄇ | m | m | ㄕ | sh | ʂ | ㄠ | ao | au |
| ㄈ | f | f | ㄖ | r | ʐ | ㄡ | ou | ou |
| ㄉ | d | t | ㄗ | z | ts | ㄢ | an | an |
| ㄊ | t | t' | ㄘ | c | ts' | ㄣ | en | ən |
| ㄋ | n | n | ㄙ | s | s | ㄤ | ang | aŋ |
| ㄌ | l | l | ㄧ | i | i | ㄥ | eng | əŋ |
| ㄍ | g | k | ㄨ | u | u | ㄦ | er | ɚ |
| ㄎ | k | k' | ㄩ | ü | y | | | |
| ㄏ | h | x | ㄚ | a | a | | | |
| ㄐ | j | tɕ | ㄛ | o | o | | | |
| ㄑ | q | tɕ' | ㄜ | ě | ə | | | |
| ㄒ | x | ɕ | ㄝ | e | ɛ | | | |

Because there are no separate Zhu-Yin-Fu-Hao symbols for the endings that can occur in Mandarin (/n/ and /ŋ/), Zhu-Yin-Fu-Hao is not, strictly speaking, an alphabetic system. Zhu-Yin-Fu-Hao and Pinyin are both transparent systems, and unlike the Chinese writing system itself, both contain symbols that indicate the tone in which a word is spoken.

Although it is learnt during the first few weeks of the first year in school, most children rapidly become competent readers of Pinyin or Zhu-Yin-Fu-Hao and continue to use it throughout their elementary school years. New characters in school textbooks are always accompanied by their representation in Pinyin or Zhu-Yin-Fu-Hao. Knowledge of these systems therefore enables children to pronounce new characters for themselves via sublexical phonology without assistance from the teacher or parent. The Zhu-Yin-Fu-Hao and Pinyin symbols continue to accompany the new character over several pages of the child's reading book until it is considered that the child should have finally learnt the character, and is capable of reading it independently. When writing an essay, a child will often write words in Pinyin or Zhu-Yin-Fu-Hao for which he or she does not know the appropriate character (Shen & Bear, 2000). Children's ability to read Chinese characters appears to be correlated with their ability to read Pinyin (Siok & Fletcher, 2001) and Zhu-Yin-Fu-Hao (Ko & Lee, 1997b).

Below are extracts from the Chinese language textbooks that are used in the first grade in mainland China and in Taiwan. In the mainland China text, the Pinyin appears immediately above the character that it represents:

qǐ    de    zǎo shàng xué xiào
起   得   早, 上 学 校,

In the Taiwanese text, the Chinese characters appear on the left with the smaller Zhu-Yin-Fu-Hao symbols to the right arranged vertically:

太 我   太 我   太 我 亮

The symbols that appear to the right of the Zhu-Yin-Fu-Hao indicate the tone in which the word is spoken.

Pinyin is also used for Chinese Braille, telegraphy, road signs, semaphore, brand names, dictionaries, and computer input (Mair, 1996). Will Pinyin ever take over from Chinese characters as the dominant written form of Mandarin? If the characters were replaced by Pinyin, then writing that is unintelligible to speakers of Mandarin might start to appear in parts of the country where other Chinese languages are in common use. For this reason, the political centre in Beijing is likely to oppose any trend towards Pinyin becoming a full-fledged script in its own right, but its increasing influence may prove difficult to resist.

## How Children Read Compound Characters

### Use of the radical component of compound characters

Shu et al. (2003) reported that 58% of the compound characters that appear in elementary textbooks in mainland China are semantically transparent in that they contain a radical whose meaning in the compound is consistent with its generic meaning. For example, the character for "mother" contains a radical that means "female." Shu et al. estimate that useful semantic information is conveyed by the radical component of a further 30% of compounds in that the radical is "indirectly related" to the meaning of the character. For example, the character for "distance" contains a radical that means "foot." Thirteen percent of characters contain no radical, or contain a radical that is unrelated to the meaning of the character.

Children appear to become sensitive to this potentially useful information as their reading skills improve (Shu, 2003; Shu & Anderson, 1997). Shu and Anderson presented children from the mainland with familiar words written in Pinyin that were known to the children in speech. The task was to select the correct character from a choice of four alternatives to replace the word that was written in Pinyin. Children performed significantly better when the correct character had a radical whose meaning was transparent than when there was no radical component or when the radical was unhelpful. The effects were stronger in the third and fifth grade than in the first grade.

Chan and Nunes (1998) showed that Hong Kong children as young as 6 were sensitive to the meaning of the radical component. The children were asked to create names for six unfamiliar objects, and were instructed to choose from six familiar radicals. The critical finding was that the radical that was typically selected by the children was the one that was semantically related to the meaning of the object concerned. They also showed evidence of creating compounds in which the phonetic was on the right and the radical on the left (as in the majority of compound characters), indicating that they had already developed sensitivity to the relative location of the phonetic and radical components of compound characters.

Ho, Wong, and Chan (1999) taught first- and third-grade children from Hong Kong the meaning of 12 new characters (clue words) and examined their ability to understand the meaning of other words that shared their radical component with one of the clue words. The ability of the children to comprehend the analogous words on a written word-picture matching task improved significantly after they had been taught the clue words. The comprehension of control words that did not share a phonetic or radical component with any of the clue words did not improve to the same extent following training. Ho et al. also found that children quite commonly made errors in which an attempt had apparently been made to use the phonetic component of a compound to infer the meaning of a character.

Tsai and Nunes (2003) investigated children's ability to learn pseudocharacters (characters consisting of unfamiliar pairings of radical and phonetic components) that contained a potentially useful radical component. They showed 7–10-year-old children from Taiwan some unusual novel objects that did not have a name in Chinese together with a pseudocharacter. Subsequently children were shown the picture and had to select from a large set the character that had appeared with the picture in the learning phase. Children from every grade performed better when the meaning of the radical component of the correct character was consistent with the meaning of the novel object.

## Use of the phonetic component of compound characters

Shu et al. (2003) categorized the phonetic components of compound characters that appear in mainland Chinese school reading books into three groups. Thirty-nine percent of compounds were designated "regular" characters because they contained phonetics that were pronounced the same way as the entire character. This category included phonetic components that were pronounced in a different tone from the character. Twenty-six percent were "semi-regular" in that the phonetic component contained the same onset or rime as the character (regardless of tone). Fifteen percent of characters were deemed "irregular" because changes in pronunciation across the centuries means that there is no longer any relationship between the pronunciation of the character and the phonetic component. A further 6% had lost their phonetics due to character simplification, while 14%

of characters were not classified because either the phonetic or character had multiple pronunciations. Overall, therefore, approximately 65% of compound characters that children learn at elementary school contain phonetic elements that provide some guide as to how they should be pronounced. As was pointed out earlier, children's attention is not typically directed towards the phonetic component by class teachers when new characters are introduced. Nevertheless, there is evidence that children soon acquire knowledge of the phonetic components of compound characters.

Chen and Yuen (1991) generated pseudocharacters in which the radical and the phonetic components from different compound characters were combined randomly. They showed that 7-year-old children from Hong Kong, Taiwan, and mainland China typically responded by pronouncing the phonetic component of the compound. The results of this study also indicated that the children from Hong Kong made the smallest number of correct responses. However, recent research by Chan and Wang (2003) involving 200 children aged between 6 and 9 failed to find any differences between children from Beijing and Hong Kong in the number of pseudowords that they read correctly.

In a similar vein, Ho and Bryant (1997a) showed that Hong Kong children were better at reading real characters when the phonetic components were identical in pronunciation to that of the character as a whole than at reading irregular characters. The effects were stronger in the grade 2 children than in the grade 1 children, suggesting that the use of the phonetic component in reading new words increases as children's reading skills develop. Shu, Anderson, and Wu (2000) reported similar findings in children from the second, fourth, and sixth grades in mainland China. Regular characters were transcribed more accurately in Pinyin than irregular characters, particularly among the fourth- and sixth-grade children. As they got older, children also made more errors in which the radical component of the character was mistakenly used as the basis for the child's response.

Consistency of the phonetic component also has effects on the rate of learning to read new words. Anderson, Li, Ku, Shu, and Wu (2003) found that characters with regular pronunciations were learnt better by children than irregular characters. Even characters that were semi-regular in that they shared the same rime and tone as their phonetic component were learnt better than irregular characters.

Tzeng et al. (1995) investigated whether the consistency of the pronunciation of a phonetic component influences children's use of the phonetic when confronted with an unfamiliar character. Children from Taiwan were quickest and most accurate (accurate in the sense of providing the usual pronunciation for the phonetic component) at reading pseudocharacters in which the phonetic component is always pronounced the same way in genuine compound characters. Performance was worst with pseudocharacters in which the phonetic component appears as part of real characters that are all pronounced differently from the phonetic itself. Where there was partial consistency in the way in which the phonetic component of the pseudocharacter was pronounced in real characters, then performance fell somewhere in between. The interesting finding with items of this type was that performance was relatively poor if the phonetic component of a pseudocharacter appears as the phonetic component of a *high-frequency* irregular real character. These results show that children are sensitive to the way in which phonetic components are pronounced in the characters in which they normally appear. The influence appears to be strongest for high-frequency characters. As Tzeng et al. point out, these results are consistent with lexical analogy models of English reading (Taraban & McClelland, 1987).

*Learning to read words of more than one syllable*

As was pointed out earlier, approximately 80% of Chinese words are multisyllabic and are written with more than one character. The majority are disyllabic words that contain two morphemes, each of which represents a monosyllabic word when presented on its own. For example, in both its written and spoken form, the Chinese word for "volcano" 火山 is a combination of the word for "fire" 火 and the word for "mountain" 山. In text, the gaps between the two characters that comprise a two-syllable word are of the same size as the gaps between characters from different words. This means that the reader must decide whether 火山 signifies "volcano" or "fire" followed by "mountain."

The way in which children read disyllabic Chinese words was examined by Chu and Leung (2005). They investigated whether children recognize the written form of multi-character words as whole units or whether they must first identify separately the individual characters that make up the disyllabic words. Their participants were grade 1, grade 3, and grade 5 children who were learning to read in Hong Kong. Chu and Leung manipulated separately the frequency of the disyllabic words and the frequency of the individual characters. Their results showed that grade 1 children made more reading errors with common two-character words when the individual characters were of low frequency than when they were of high frequency. The same finding was observed with the grade 3 and 5 children when reading disyllabic words of lower frequency. High-frequency two-character words were read equally accurately regardless of the frequency of the component characters by children in grades 3 and 5, however. This finding strongly suggests that common multicharacter words are read as whole units by these children. The results of this study show that when children first encounter two-character words, they first identify the individual component characters. Once they have encountered a two-character word in print a number of times, it becomes part of their sight vocabulary and they develop the ability to recognize it as a whole unit.

## Phonological Awareness and Learning to Read Chinese

It is well established that in English (the most studied alphabetic language) there is a close and probably causal relationship between children's phonological skills (typically assessed by measures of phonological awareness) and the rate at which they learn to read (see Bowey, current volume). It is also generally accepted, however, that learning to read in a language in which letters map onto the phonemes of spoken words may serve to facilitate the development of children's early phonemic awareness (see Morais & Kolinsky, current volume, for a review of some of the relevant evidence). As we have seen, the relationship between phonology and orthography is radically different in Chinese than in alphabetic languages. These observations lead to two obvious questions in relation to the process of learning to read in Chinese: (1) Will the relationship between underlying phonological skills and the process of learning to read be different in Chinese from that in alphabetic languages such as English? (2) Will Chinese readers, whose dominant script does not represent the phonemic structure of spoken words, show a slower and less complete development of phonological awareness?

### The relationship between reading ability and phonological awareness

Good readers of English and other European languages tend to perform well on tasks of phonological awareness such as auditory rhyme detection and counting the number of phonemes in spoken words. As a consequence, it is sometimes argued that phonological awareness is a prerequisite for successful reading of an alphabetic orthography (for discussion, see Goswami & Bryant, 1990). Given that phonemes are not directly represented in the Chinese writing system, it might be expected that the relationship between phonological skills and learning to read would be weaker in Chinese than in languages with alphabetic writing systems.

Some of the available evidence tends to support this idea. Huang and Hanley (1995) found that performance of a group of 8-year-old Taiwanese children on a test of phoneme deletion and a test of onset and rime ability correlated significantly with their character reading scores. However, the correlation was no longer significant when the effects of visual skills and vocabulary were controlled. Similar results were obtained with a group of 8-year-old children from Hong Kong. Huang and Hanley suggested that phoneme awareness is less important for learning to read Chinese than English because it is not necessary to decompose Chinese syllables into phonemes in order to read Chinese characters.

The use of both a logographic and phonetic script (Pinyin or Zhu-Yin-Fu-Hao) in many areas in China allows for highly informative comparisons to be made between the roles of phonological skills in reading the two types of script within the same language. Hu and Catts (1998) examined the relationship between phonological skills and both reading of characters and reading in Zhu-Yin-Fu-Hao in a group of Taiwanese children whose mean age was 6 years 10 months. They found strong correlations between phonological awareness (a test of onset and rime awareness) and both measures of reading. Interestingly the correlation between character reading and phonological ability remained significant even when the effects of reading in Zhu-Yin-Fu-Hao had been controlled. This suggests that the link between character reading and phonological awareness does not depend on prior learning of a transparent phonetic orthography. As a consequence, Hu and Catts suggested that there might be a universal link between phonological skills and learning to read, regardless of the nature of the orthography. However, it is difficult to establish the precise nature of this link from the results of this study in the absence of any measures of general intellectual ability or vocabulary skills.

Other studies have also revealed correlations between measures of phonological skills and individual differences in character reading in children. Ho and Bryant (1997a) reported a significant correlation between performance on a test of auditory rhyme detection and character reading in first-grade children from Hong Kong. Ho (1997) demonstrated a significant relationship between performance on a test of character reading and rime detection ability in Hong Kong second graders (aged 7–8). In both studies, the relationship between rime test scores remained significant when nonverbal ability was partialed out. However, no test of vocabulary ability was administered in either study.

So and Siegel (1997) tested elementary school children from grades 1 to 4 in Hong Kong. They found a significant correlation between character reading and performance on an auditory rime test, and between single word reading and a test in which children were asked to indicate whether words were spoken in the same tone. However, performance on all of these tasks was also correlated with scores on a test that required knowledge of word meaning.

Siok and Fletcher (2001) investigated the relationship between phonological awareness and character reading in children in grades 1–5 in an elementary school in Beijing. Once the effects of nonverbal ability had been controlled, there was no significant relationship between character reading and tests of phoneme awareness and phoneme blending. There were significant correlations between character reading and a test of onset and rime knowledge, but only in grades 2 and 5. They also found that reading of Pinyin was a good predictor of the Chinese character reading scores from grade 2 onward and suggested that the relationship between phonological awareness and character reading might be mediated by children's Pinyin ability.

Arguably, a better way of investigating the relationship between phonological skills and learning to read is to perform longitudinal studies in which children's phonological awareness before they commence formal reading instruction is compared with their reading ability at some point in the future. Huang and Hanley (1997) reported that preschool phoneme awareness scores in Taiwanese children was a significant predictor of reading ability a year later, even when the effects of vocabulary and intelligence test scores had both been controlled. However, the relationship between early phonological awareness scores and reading ability disappeared once the effects of preschool reading scores had been partialed out. Of course one cannot conclude that phonological awareness ability does not predict the ease with which children will subsequently learn to read Chinese simply because the correlation disappeared when preschool reading scores were entered into the equation. However, it becomes impossible to determine whether differences in phonological awareness produce differences in reading ability or whether differences in reading ability produce differences in phonological awareness performance.

Ho and Bryant (1997b) found significant correlations between the scores of children from Hong Kong on a rime awareness test at age 3 and their reading ability when tested two and three years later. The relationship remained significant when IQ test scores were controlled. Ho and Bryant did not enter any preschool reading test scores into the equation because they claimed that none of the children could read any words when they were given the phonological awareness tests at age 3. However, a test of vocabulary ability was not administered in this study.

Overall, therefore, there is now a large number of published studies that all show correlations, either concurrently or longitudinally, between measures of phonological skill and character reading. Nevertheless, the limitations associated with these studies means that evidence of a direct relationship between the ability of children to learn to read Chinese characters and their performance on tests of phoneme awareness remains equivocal. Because the syllable is a more important unit than the phoneme in the way that Chinese characters represent spoken language, it might be even more revealing to examine the relationship between syllable awareness and learning to read Chinese.

This issue has been investigated in a number of recent papers by McBride-Chang and her colleagues. McBride-Chang and Ho (2000) and McBride-Chang and Kail (2002) reported a significant relationship between character reading and a test of syllable dele-tion in 3-, 4-, and 5-year-old kindergarten children in Hong Kong. In this task, children were asked to delete the first, middle, or final syllable/morpheme from three-syllable words. Crucially the relationship between reading and syllable awareness remained sig-nificant even when performance on a vocabulary test had been controlled. McBride-Chang, Bialystok, Chong, and Li (in press) showed that performance on a syllable awareness test was a better predictor of performance by first-grade children in Hong Kong and mainland China on a test of character recognition than performance on a phoneme deletion test. McBride-Chang and Zhong (2003) reported a relationship between sylla-ble awareness in the 3- and 4-year-old children and their reading ability a year later even when the effects of vocabulary were controlled. Unfortunately, a causal relationship between reading and syllable awareness could not be inferred from this study because the children were already able to read some characters at age 3. When reading ability at age 3 was controlled, syllable awareness was no longer a predictor of reading a year later.

Another important issue is the relationship between reading characters and morpho-logical knowledge. Ku and Anderson (2003) asked children to perform a series of tests of morphological knowledge in which they were asked whether two words were related in meaning. Examples in English would be "book" and "bookshelf" (related) and "class-room" and "mushroom" (unrelated). Ku and Anderson found that performance on these tests was closely correlated with a measure of reading comprehension even when perfor-mance on a test of vocabulary knowledge was partialed out. However, all of the tests involved written presentation. Although children were encouraged to ask the teacher if they were unable to recognize a character, there is a danger that some of the shared vari-ance may have come about because all the tasks were sensitive to how well children could recognize characters.

This problem was overcome by McBride-Chang, Shu, Zhou, Wat, and Wagner (2003), who created two tests of morpheme awareness that did not involve any reading. In one of these tests, children were required to generate new words containing two morphemes on the basis of already known words that contained one of these morphemes. For example, children were given the two-morpheme word for "sunrise" and were asked to generate the name for "moonrise." McBride-Chang et al. argue that children could only succeed on this task if they had abstracted the meaning of the individual morphemes (e.g., "sun" and "rise") from the meaning of the two-morpheme word. Results showed that perfor-mance on these tests was significantly related to character reading scores in a sample of 100 kindergarten children from Hong Kong even when the effects of age, phonological awareness, and vocabulary had been controlled. These findings strongly suggest that morphological knowledge may play a crucial role in Chinese reading acquisition.

*The effects of learning Pinyin or Zhu-Yin-Fu-Hao on Chinese children's phonological awareness skills*

As noted earlier, it is generally accepted that there is a reciprocal relationship between the development of phonemic awareness and learning to read an alphabetic script (see Morais & Kolinsky, current volume). Some evidence that strongly supports this position comes from studies of Chinese children learning Pinyin or Zhu-Yin-Fu-Hao. The phoneme awareness skills of first-grade Taiwanese children improved substantially immediately after they had learnt Zhu-Yin-Fu-Hao (Huang & Hanley, 1997; Ko & Lee, 1997a). Huang and Hanley showed that performance on a test of phoneme deletion improved from 35% (pretest) to over 60% (posttest) immediately after children had completed a 10-week course in learning Zhu-Yin-Fu-Hao. Because there was no further improvement in performance on the phoneme deletion test when the children were retested at the end of the school year, it appears that the improvement in phoneme awareness was specific to the learning of Zhu-Yin-Fu-Hao.

There is a variety of evidence to support the idea that unless they have learnt a phonetic writing system such as Zhu-Yin-Fu-Hao or Pinyin, the development of phonological awareness is less rapid and complete in people learning to read Chinese. Read, Zhang, Nie, and Ding (1986) compared the phoneme awareness skills of two groups of adult subjects from mainland China, one of whom had learnt Pinyin while at school, and one of whom were literate only in Chinese characters. Whereas the Pinyin group found it relatively easy to add or delete phonemes from spoken Chinese words, the adults who had not learnt Pinyin found the tasks extremely difficult. Consistent with these findings, Ko and Lee (1997b) found that the phoneme deletion skills of illiterate Chinese adults improved substantially after being taught Zhu-Yin-Fu-Hao. Similarly, de Gelder, Vroomen, and Bertelsen (1993) compared the phoneme awareness performance of two groups of Chinese bilinguals, one of whom could also speak and read Dutch, and one of whom could speak but not read Dutch. De Gelder et al. reported superior phoneme awareness in the group who could read Dutch.

Children from Hong Kong who have not learnt Pinyin have been shown to perform extremely poorly on tests of phoneme deletion (Huang & Hanley, 1995) and phoneme counting (McBride-Chang et al., in press) relative to children of the same age who have been taught Zhu-Yin-Fu-Hao or Pinyin. Cheung, Chen, Lai, Wong, and Hills (2001) found no differences in phonological awareness ability between 4-year-old prereaders in Hong Kong and Guangzhou in mainland China, where children learn to read characters after first learning to read Pinyin. However, 7-year-old readers from Guangzhou performed better on a test requiring knowledge of onsets and codas than 7-year-old children from Hong Kong. This supports the view that it is the acquisition of Pinyin that produces superior phoneme awareness in children from the mainland. Consistent with this conclusion, Leong (1997) showed that university students in Hong Kong performed better on a test of phoneme addition after learning Pinyin than a control group who had not received such instruction.

The advantages of learning Pinyin or Zhu-Yin-Fu-Hao for phonological awareness of larger units such as syllables, onsets, and rhymes appear to be much smaller. Huang and

Hanley (1995) found that children from Hong Kong performed significantly worse on tests sensitive to awareness of rhyme than Taiwanese children who had learnt Zhu-Yin-Fu-Hao. However, the differences were very much smaller than the differences that they reported between the two groups on phoneme deletion. Mcbride-Chang et al. (in press) reported relatively small differences in the syllable awareness ability of Hong Kong children relative to children from the mainland despite substantial differences in phoneme awareness. In Cheung et al.'s (2001) study, the children from Hong Kong performed just as well as Guangzhou children on tests of rime and syllable awareness.

Ho and Bryant (1997c) suggested that rime awareness develops relatively slowly in children from Hong Kong because the nature of the writing system does not encourage children to pay attention to subsyllabic units such as onset and rime. In support of this claim, they reported that the ability to detect rime in spoken words was lower in children from Hong Kong compared to British children of a similar age (e.g., MacLean, Bryant, & Bradley, 1987). The children from Hong Kong, who were aged 5 years 3 months, performed at a similar level to the English children aged 4 years 7 months. However, in order to provide direct evidence to substantiate this suggestion, it would be necessary to match very carefully the rhyming stimuli across the two languages.

There is therefore clear evidence that phoneme awareness skills are very poor in Chinese readers who have not learnt to read either Pinyin or Zhu-Yin-Fu-Hao. Presumably the absence of any elements within Chinese characters that represent individual phonemes means that phoneme awareness skills do not emerge as an automatic consequence of learning to read the Chinese writing system. The evidence that phoneme awareness skills in Chinese readers increase substantially once a phonetic reading system has been learnt is overwhelming. Syllable awareness and the ability to detect rime appear to develop relatively well in Chinese readers regardless of whether they have learnt Pinyin or Zhu-Yin-Fu-Hao.

## Pinyin, phonological awareness, and learning to read and write English as a second language

Important differences in the way in which individuals from Hong Kong and the Chinese mainland read English were revealed by Holm and Dodd (1996). They compared a group of university students in Australia who were residents of mainland China (and had therefore learnt Pinyin) with students who had learnt to read in Hong Kong and had not learnt Pinyin. Although their reading and spelling of English words was matched, the students from Hong Kong were unable to read nonwords and performed extremely poorly on tests of phoneme segmentation and auditory rime judgment. They appeared to use a visual look-and-say strategy when reading English. The students from the Chinese mainland performed much better on these tasks. These findings suggest that knowledge of Pinyin can be used by Chinese readers to develop phonological reading strategies when they subsequently encounter written English.

Cheung (1999) also found poor phonological awareness of English words among 12- and 15-year-old Chinese children in Hong Kong despite several years of English reading instruction. Some of the children were then given a course of training that involved instruction in phoneme blending, phoneme counting, and rime judgment. The course appeared to produce an improvement in English reading ability. There was also a striking increase in phoneme deletion skills relative to the control group, although this improvement was only significant for the least proficient readers. Increases in phonological awareness appeared to be directly related to increases in reading ability.

Wang and Geva (2003a) studied the English writing ability of 62 Chinese children (mean age = 6 years 5 months) who were born in Canada or moved there before the age of 5. All of the children came from Cantonese families and Cantonese was their first language. They had already been taught over 100 Chinese characters by traditional Hong Kong teaching methods (rote learning and copying). Results showed that the Cantonese children were just as good as monolingual English-speaking Canadian children of the same age at spelling familiar English words, but they were much worse at spelling English pseudowords. In a further study, Wang and Geva (2003b) showed that the Cantonese children had particular problems in spelling words that contained phonemes that are present in English but not in Cantonese (e.g., /ŋ/). The children tended to spell a word such as *teeth* or *thick* by replacing *th* with a letter (e.g., *s, z, f*) that represents a phonologically similar phoneme that is found in Cantonese. These problems were observed in grade 1 when the children's mean age was 6 years 5 months, but they had decreased substantially two years later.

Another sample of Cantonese children living in Canada (mean age = 9 years 11 months) was studied by Gottardo, Yan, Siegel, and Wade-Woolley (2001). Their ability to read English was related to their ability to perform phonological awareness tasks in Cantonese (auditory rime judgment) and English (phoneme deletion). By contrast, reading of Chinese was not correlated with any of the measures of phonological awareness. It therefore appears that the Cantonese children depend on phonological reading strategies to a greater extent when reading an alphabetic script (English) than when reading Chinese characters.

McBride-Chang and Treiman (2003) created some artificial spellings in which there was either a letter-sound relationship between a pair of letters and its given name (e.g., DK = Dick), a letter-name relationship between a pair of letters and its given name (e.g., DK = Deek), or a purely visual relationship between a pair of letters and its given name (e.g., DK = Jean). Children were asked to learn these correspondences. McBride-Chang and Treiman showed that Hong Kong children aged 5 performed better in the letter-name and letter-sound conditions than in the visual condition. They argued that if a child is learning to read English via a purely logographic strategy, then poorer performance in the visual condition would not be predicted. Exactly how children from Hong Kong who can use such strategies to learn these correspondences subsequently turn out to have such low phonological awareness with English words (Cheung, 1999) and to be so poor at reading and writing English nonwords (Holm & Dodd, 1996) is an interesting issue for theorists to explain.

Differences in the phonotactic structure of Chinese and English syllables appear to produce a very distinctive pattern of performance on English phoneme awareness tasks by Chinese children from Hong Kong compared with children whose first language is English. Huang and Hanley (1995) replicated previous findings in which English children found first-sound deletion to be significantly easier in CVCC words than in CCVC words. However, children from Hong Kong (who spoke English as a second language) showed the opposite pattern; for them, first-sound deletion was significantly easier in CCVC words (on which they performed significantly better than the British children) than in CVCC words. Treiman (1985) argued that English-speaking children treat initial consonant clusters as single units, and so parse a CCVC consonant as if it were a CVC string. Because there are no consonant blends in Chinese syllables, the Chinese insert syllables between consonants in English words that contain consonant blends (Wang, 1973). The name "Clinton," for example, is written with three characters representing three syllables: [kuh]-[lin]-[ton]. If Hong Kong children are implicitly adding a vowel between consonants when they hear words with consonant clusters, then the phoneme deletion task by default becomes the equivalent of a syllable deletion task. As a consequence, this may make it relatively easy for them to parse consonant clusters into separate units. Such an account would explain a finding by Holm and Dodd (1996) that students from mainland China performed differently from native speakers on a spoonerisms test with English words. When asked to spoonerize English words that started with consonant clusters, the Chinese students were much less prone to exchanging both elements of the cluster (e.g., crowd-play > plowd-cray). than were native speakers of English, consistent with the idea that they are treating each consonant in a cluster as a separate unit.

Although the Hong Kong children performed better than the English children with consonant clusters, Huang and Hanley (1995). reported that they found it much more difficult than the British children to delete the first phoneme from an English word with a single consonant before the vowel. Huang and Hanley argued that because so many Chinese syllables have a CV structure, it would not be surprising if the Hong Kong children tended to treat a consonant followed by a vowel as a single unit. If so, this would explain why they find it so difficult to delete the consonant from CV syllables. It follows from this account that Chinese readers from Hong Kong who have been taught to read Pinyin will no longer experience such difficulties with CV syllables. Consistent with this explanation, Leong (1997) found that university students from Hong Kong who had attended a course of Pinyin instruction at university showed an advantage at segmental analysis of the initial consonant in both English and Chinese words relative to a control group, but performed no better than a control group with final consonants.

## Learning to Read Chinese As a Second Language

Relatively little research has investigated the acquisition of Chinese reading skills by second-language learners. In a well-publicized paper, Rozin, Poritsky, and Sotsky (1971) successfully taught a group of eight poor readers from the USA to read a set of 30 Chinese characters. However, the children were taught to respond to the characters with English rather than Chinese words. Wang, Perfetti, and Liu (2003) have recently investigated how 15 adults from the USA, who were already skilled readers of an alphabetic writing system (English, Spanish, French, or German), would learn to read Chinese characters. The results showed that the participants became sensitive to certain orthographic components of Chinese characters within their first year of formal instruction. They demonstrated significant frequency effects in lexical decision and in speeded naming. Most interestingly, even though they had received no specific instruction in how to decompose characters into their phonetic and radical components, they were able to reject relatively quickly nonwords that contained illegal character components, or legal components that appeared in an illegal position. This finding suggests that alphabetic readers can rapidly develop some sensitivity to the structure of Chinese character compounds at an early stage of reading development.

## Developmental Dyslexia

Despite some early claims (Rozin et al., 1971) that dyslexia may be relatively uncommon in children learning to read Chinese characters, it has been clear since the 1980s that Chinese children can suffer severe problems in learning to read (Stevenson, Stigler, Lucker, Lee, Hsu, & Kitamura, 1982). We have seen that phonological skills play a role in children learning to read Chinese but, arguably, a lesser role than they do in children learning to read in an alphabetic system. With this in mind, one question that a number of researchers have asked is whether Chinese children with dyslexia have a phonological processing impairment of the kind that is frequently observed in children with dyslexia who are attempting to learn to read English (e.g., Snowling, 2000).

There is some evidence of phonological difficulties among Chinese poor readers. For example, Huang and Zhang (1997) reported low scores on tests of phonological awareness skills in poor readers in Taiwan relative to good readers of the same age. However, differences of this kind are difficult to interpret because the problems might be as much a consequence of the children's poor reading as a cause of it. Stronger evidence would come from a comparison of children with dyslexia with young children who are reading at a similar level to themselves (reading age [RA] controls).

Lee (1997) compared poor readers in the fifth grade in Taiwan with RA controls from the third grade. Even though the ability to read characters was the same in the two groups, Lee found that the poor readers performed worse than the controls at reading words and nonwords written in Zhu-Yin-Fu-Hao. The children with dyslexia also performed worse than the RA controls on a test of phoneme deletion. Similarly, So and Siegel (1997) reported that fourth-grade poor readers in Hong Kong, whose reading performance was at a similar level to that of normal readers in the first grade, performed much worse than the younger normal readers on tests of tone and rhyme discrimination, but no worse than them on other tests of language ability that did not involve reading.

Ho, Law, and Ng (2000) examined the performance on tests of reading and phonological awareness skills of 56 children aged between 7 and 10 and of normal IQ who had been identified as dyslexic by the Hong Kong Education Department. Twenty-three of the children had been classified as having both reading and writing problems and 33 had only reading problems. The children with dyslexia performed less well than younger RA controls on phonological tasks; those with reading and writing problems had more extensive deficits affecting rime awareness and phonological memory (word and nonword repetition), whereas the reading-only group performed worse on a nonword repetition task.

Surprisingly, however, although the children with dyslexia continued to perform worse than their age-peers on visual and phonological tasks, no differences were observed between children with dyslexia and RA controls on visual, phonological awareness and memory tasks in a follow-up study (Ho, Chan, Tsang, & Lee, 2002).

A comparison of the performance of a very large sample (n = 147) of children with dyslexia from Hong Kong with average readers of the same age on a variety of cognitive measures has recently been published by Ho, Chan, Lee, Tsang, and Luan (2004). Their measures included phonological tests (onset and rime detection, word and nonword repetition), a rapid naming test (naming 40 written digits as rapidly as possible), visual skills tests (perception and memory), and orthographic tests that tested knowledge of the structure of compound characters. A deficit on a test was defined as a scaled score at least 1.5 sds below the mean of the controls. Using these criteria, 57.1% of the children with dyslexia showed a deficit on rapid naming, 42.0% showed a deficit on the orthographic tests, 29.3% showed a deficit on the phonological tests, and 27.1% showed a deficit on the visual subtests. The authors claim that the majority of Chinese readers with dyslexia suffer from either a rapid naming deficit or an orthographic deficit. However, in the absence of any reading age controls, it seems likely that these deficits are a consequence rather than a cause of their reading impairment.

If children with dyslexia have phonological processing deficits, then they might be unable to take advantage of the phonological cues provided by the phonetic component of compound characters. Contrary to this claim, however, Ho and Ma (1999) found that children as young as 8 read regular characters (in which the phonetic component has a predictable pronunciation) better than irregular characters. Indeed, they showed a stronger regularity effect for high-frequency characters than did 8-year-old normal readers. The children with dyslexia did, however, perform poorly with low-frequency regular characters. The children with dyslexia also made significantly fewer phonological errors and significantly more semantic errors than control readers of the same age. Chan and Siegel (2001) reported similar results when they looked at the performance of the worst performing 25% of Chinese readers in two primary schools in Hong Kong. The poor readers aged between 10 and 12 years made fewer phonological errors and more semantic errors than average readers of the same chronological age. However, their performance was similar to that of younger normal readers. Although they read pseudocharacters less well than 10–12-year-old normal readers, their performance was good relative to younger normal readers. Overall, there is no evidence from these studies that the reading skills of Chinese children with dyslexia are different from those of younger children who read at the same level as themselves.

In summary, the research evidence concerning the language and cognitive skills of Chinese children with dyslexia is sparse. The majority of studies that are available have examined children with dyslexia in Hong Kong; there is an almost complete absence of published research into dyslexia in mainland China. Furthermore, relatively few studies have compared the performance of readers with dyslexia with typically developing younger children of the same reading level who do not have reading problems. In those studies where such comparisons have been made (e.g., Ho et al., 2002), those with dyslexia often perform in a similar way to younger normal readers. There is some evidence (e.g., Ho et al., 2000) that poor readers of Chinese have phonological processing weaknesses but there is much more work to be done in specifying the mechanisms that account for reading failure.

## Conclusions

It is clear that there has been an enormous increase in the amount of published research that has investigated the acquisition of reading skills in children learning Chinese since the mid-1990s. There is now a much wider understanding of the nature of the Chinese writing system than was previously the case. It is now common knowledge that Chinese characters convey phonetic as well as lexical-semantic information and that the processes involved in leaning to read Chinese may not be as different from those that are involved in learning to read a script such as English as was once imagined (Tzeng, 2002).

Perhaps the most important set of findings to have emerged in recent years are those showing that Chinese children are clearly sensitive to the phonetic and semantic components that comprise compound characters in Chinese. Children learn to read characters more rapidly that contain components that provide veridical information about the meaning or the pronunciation of the characters. Furthermore, when faced with an unfamiliar character, Chinese children with good reading skills are able to use these semantic and phonetic components to make inferences about the likely meaning and/or pronunciation of the character. Another important conclusion is that the reading skills and phonological awareness skills of Chinese children are profoundly affected by those children being taught a transparent phonetic script (Pinyin in mainland China, and Zhu-Yin-Fu-Hao in Taiwan) when formal reading instruction begins in grade 1 of elementary school. The phonological awareness skills of Taiwanese children improve immediately after they have learnt Zhu-Yin-Fu-Hao. When they attempt to learn to read English, students from Hong Kong who have not learnt Pinyin seem less able to take advantage of the alphabetic nature of the English writing system and read it instead by the use of visual strategies. Whether or not phonological awareness is important for learning to read Chinese is a much more controversial issue. Many experiments show that reading Chinese is positively correlated with phonological awareness task skills (e.g., phoneme deletion). However, none of the studies allows one to conclude with confidence that phoneme awareness test scores are as good a predictor of Chinese reading ability as they are of reading success in children learning an alphabetic orthography such as English.

Finally, it is surprising to note how little we know about developmental dyslexia in Chinese. It is clear that children can suffer from severe problems in learning to read Chinese, but there are few studies in which the performance of Chinese children with dyslexia has been compared with that of a reading age matched control group. It is likely that research over the next ten years will provide us with a richer understanding of the characteristics and causes of developmental dyslexia in China than is currently the case.

# 18

# *The Nature and Causes of Dyslexia in Different Languages*

## Markéta Caravolas

Developmental dyslexia is now a recognized disorder in many literate societies. On its website, the International Dyslexia Association boasts affiliated branches on every continent and in as many as 40 countries. Yet to date, far more scientific research has been reported about dyslexia in English than in any other language. It is therefore not surprising that many misconceptions still exist about the very existence, the manifestation, and the causes of dyslexia in languages other than English. For example, a common lay belief is that dyslexia is more common among speakers/readers of English because the "chaotic" English orthography is difficult to learn; in contrast, dyslexia is thought to be virtually nonexistent in "easy phonetic" orthographies such as Finnish and Spanish. Similarly, a popular belief about Chinese is that its logographic script requires rote memorization of thousands of picture-like characters and therefore reading difficulties of the sort observed in English must not exist among Chinese readers. Fortunately, the situation is changing and dyslexia is now being studied in a large variety of languages (see Goulandris, 2003). It is becoming clear that, although many of the lay ideas about dyslexia are inaccurate, they nevertheless reflect an intuitive understanding of one important fact, namely that reading and writing skills are influenced by the characteristics of different writing systems (see chapters by Frost, Hanley, and Treiman & Kessler in this volume for further discussion of this).

This chapter considers how such influences affect the manifestation of dyslexia in different languages. More specifically, a review is presented of what is currently known about dyslexia in various non-English languages and writing systems with respect to two main issues. The first is how various characteristics of written languages influence *the types of reading and writing difficulties* experienced by children with dyslexia. The second is whether the characteristics of different languages and orthographies influence the nature of the underlying *cognitive deficits* that are associated with dyslexia. Clearly, apart from language differences, other factors also play a role in determining cross-linguistic differences in the manifestation of dyslexia, such as educational practices and social and cultural factors. However, these factors are beyond the scope of the present chapter and will only be touched on tangentially when relevant. Before examining these issues, a brief summary of the major features of different writing systems is presented.

## Characteristics of Different Writing Systems

The world's languages are represented by a large variety of writing systems, which may be broadly categorized into three main types on the basis of the units of spoken language they represent. Alphabetic orthographies such as English, Dutch, and Czech, use letters and letter clusters to represent phonemes. Syllabic orthographies, such as Japanese Kanji and Hindi use syllabographs to represent syllables. (The category of syllabic writing systems will not be discussed here, mainly because very few studies of dyslexia in these languages are currently available in English.) Logographic orthographies, such as Chinese and Japanese Kanji use characters to represent spoken words at the level of monosyllabic morphemes (see Mattingly, 1992, and also chapters by Frost, Hanley, and Treiman & Kessler, in this volume, for further discussion).

Presumably, the gross differences in the size and level of the speech units that are graphically encoded (i.e., phoneme, syllable, morpheme) are associated with differences in the processes involved in reading and writing; we will examine this issue by contrasting studies in alphabetic writing systems with those in the logographic orthography of Chinese. However, reading and writing processes may also be affected by more subtle differences between orthographies, even within the category of alphabetic systems.

### Characteristics of alphabetic writing systems

Alphabetic writing systems are based on the principle that graphemes (letters and letter strings) correspond to the phonemic units of speech. However, these systems may differ from each other in a number of ways. Several terms, such as orthographic depth, transparency, consistency, and regularity have been used to describe and compare them (see Frost, and Treiman & Kessler this volume). From the perspective of the young learner, an ideal (transparent, consistent, and regular) alphabetic orthography should contain a set of one-to-one grapheme–phoneme (or spelling–sound) and phoneme–grapheme (or sound–spelling) correspondences. Thus, there should be only one way to pronounce any given grapheme, and only one way to spell any given phoneme. A small minority of writing systems such as Finnish, Turkish, and Serbo-Croatian approach this ideal. However, the majority of alphabetic orthographies also encode information other than the phonemic content of words, such as *morphological information* (e.g., in the words "he*a*l" and "he*a*lth," two different vowel phonemes /i/ and /ɛ/ are represented by a single vowel letter string reflecting their morphological relationship); *original spellings* of words imported from other languages (e.g., the Anglicized words *château* and *connoisseur* have retained their original French spellings); and *historical spellings* that reflect archaic word pronunciations (e.g., spellings *knee* and *walk* retain graphemes that once represented articulated sounds, but as a result of phonological change have become redundant) (see Treiman & Kessler, this volume).

Alphabetic orthographies differ in the extent to which they allow these sources of variation to occur, and these differences determine the degree of spelling–sound and sound–spelling consistency and regularity. English is considered to be the most inconsistent and irregular system because (1) the relationship between graphemes and phonemes is often opaque (e.g., the letter *t* in "listen" has no corresponding phoneme), (2) the grapheme–phoneme and phoneme–grapheme correspondences are inconsistent (e.g., the grapheme *ea* has different pronunciations in "head" and "heal"; and although the words "beef," "chief," and "leaf" all contain the same vowel /i/, it is assigned a different spelling in each word), and (3) many exceptions exist to acceptable orthographic patterns (e.g., the spelling *trek* violates the rule that word-final /k/ in monosyllabic words with short vowels is spelled with the grapheme *ck*) and in sound–spelling correspondences (e.g., the grapheme *oe* in "does" and the grapheme string *cea* in "ocean" both correspond to exceptional pronunciations).

Most European orthographies are more regular and consistent than English (see Seymour this volume), although an asymmetry exists in almost every alphabetic system such that grapheme–phoneme correspondences are more consistent than phoneme–grapheme correspondences (making reading easier than spelling). For example, although written French is less complex than English in grapheme–phoneme mappings (i.e., reading), it is as inconsistent as English in phoneme–grapheme mappings (i.e., spelling) (Ziegler, Jacobs, & Stone, 1996). The relatively more shallow orthography of German has more consistent grapheme–phoneme correspondences than both English and French, however the phoneme–grapheme correspondences are considerably less consistent, still making spelling more difficult than reading (Wimmer & Mayringer, 2002). In comparison to English, French, or German, the Czech orthography is more consistent in both directions, although some inconsistencies do exist in phoneme–grapheme correspondences (Caravolas, 2005). Unfortunately, with a few exceptions, direct comparisons of orthographic consistency are currently not possible because comparable statistical estimates are still unavailable for most of the world's orthographies. Thus, at present, less formal estimates are used to rank alphabetic orthographies in terms of depth, consistency, and regularity. Figure 18.1 presents a schematic, based on published estimates and descriptions, of the relative depth of some of the alphabetic languages that are considered in the

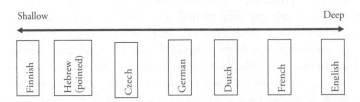

**Figure 18.1**   A schematic of the relative depth of several alphabetic writing systems.

present chapter (see e.g. Caravolas, in press; Frost, Katz, & Bentin, 1987; Seymour, Aro, & Erskine, 2003).

## *Characteristics of the logographic writing system of Chinese*

Logographic writing systems are used in Chinese and Japanese; however the focus here is primarily on the orthography used to represent various dialects of Chinese. As described by Hanley (this volume), the smallest functional units of orthographic representation in Chinese are characters that correspond to monosyllabic morphemes. A popular misconception about the Chinese logography is that its visually complex characters are pictographs or ideographs that, like icons, represent objects or concepts (e.g., the character for "rain" looks like falling rain), and, that they encode no phonological information about pronunciation.

In fact, only a small proportion of Chinese characters are strictly pictographic or ideographic (less than 18% according to Zhou [1978]). Approximately 80 to 90% of characters are semantic-phonetic compounds consisting of an element called the *semantic radical*, which gives information about the meaning, and an element called the *phonetic*, which gives information about the pronunciation of the word. Hence, it is possible to extract from most Chinese characters cues to word meaning *and* pronunciation. The ability to extract semantic information might be particularly advantageous, because Chinese has a great many homophones, and therefore semantic radicals provide a means of disambiguating the meanings of homophonic characters. Thus, the homophonic nature of the spoken language may implicitly motivate children to attend to the internal structure of characters from early stages of reading development (Shu & Anderson, 1997).

However, in contrast to alphabetic writing systems, it is more difficult for readers to make use of semantic and phonetic cues, because they are not highly reliable. For example, in Chinese children's reading materials, approximately 30% of phonetic components provide unambiguous information about the pronunciation of a character (i.e., the word is pronounced in the same way as its phonetic component), and 40% of the semantic components provide unambiguous information about its meaning. The remaining components are semitransparent or opaque offering only partial clues or no clue to pronunciation or meaning (Shu, Chen, Anderson, Wu, & Xuan, 2003). Moreover, almost one half of the phonetic components encountered by elementary school children appear in only one word; thus, they are not productive (Shu et al., 2003). Importantly, Shu et al. found that in the early grades of the Chinese reading curriculum, children learn mainly irregular characters (i.e., generally high-frequency, visually simple characters with unproductive phonetic components), while in later grades they learn increasingly more regular (productive) characters.

## Dyslexia among English Speakers: A Point of Reference

A detailed review of dyslexia research based on English-speaking populations is provided by Vellutino and Fletcher (present volume; see also Snowling, 2000a; Vellutino, Fletcher,

Snowling, & Scanlon, 2004) and only a few of the more important conclusions from this research will be highlighted here. The literacy-skills profiles of English-speakers with dyslexia typically include inaccurate and slow word recognition skills caused by difficulties with word decoding (e.g., Vellutino et al., 1996), and very poor spelling skills (e.g., Bruck & Waters, 1988). Also, a deficit during preschool and early school years is usually observed in letter knowledge, which is a foundation skill for alphabetic literacy (Snowling, Gallagher, & Frith, 2003). In addition, English-speaking readers with dyslexia have marked difficulties with grapheme–phoneme transcoding as assessed by nonword reading (Rack, Snowling, & Olson, 1992), and spelling (Caravolas, Bruck, & Genesee, 2003). A number of underlying cognitive skills that are important components of reading and spelling in English, are frequently impaired among individuals with dyslexia. The most consistently observed impairments are in phoneme awareness (e.g., Liberman & Shankweiler, 1979), verbal short-term memory (e.g., Hulme, Maughan, & Brown, 1981), slow naming speed (e.g., Bowers & Wolf, 1993), phonological learning (e.g., Vellutino, Scanlon, & Spearing, 1995), and word and nonword repetition (e.g., Brady, Shankweiler, & Mann, 1983). In contrast, visual skills such as visual memory and visuospatial skills have not generally been found to be deficient in English-speakers with dyslexia (see Vellutino & Fletcher, this volume). Also, it is important to point out that not *every* individual with dyslexia suffers impairments in *every* one of the above cognitive skills, and often one skill is more severely impaired than another.

An influential theory, referred to as the "core phonological representations hypothesis of dyslexia", proposes that all of the cognitive impairments listed above reflect an underlying deficit in phonological representation and processing (e.g., Snowling, 2000a; Stanovich, Nathan, & Zolman, 1988; Vellutino & Fletcher, this volume; Vellutino et al., 2004). According to this view, an impairment in the representation and processing of phonological information at the level of speech sounds (phonemes) disrupts the dyslexic child's ability to acquire the foundations of alphabetic literacy, namely letter knowledge (the names and sounds of the letters of the alphabet), phoneme awareness (the ability to consciously manipulate the phonemes in spoken words), and phonological recoding (knowledge and use of grapheme–phoneme and phoneme–grapheme correspondences in reading and spelling) (Byrne, 1998; Snowling & Hulme, 1989).

## Dyslexia in Non-English Languages with Alphabetic Orthographies

How might orthographic depth, as indexed by consistency and regularity, influence the manifestation of dyslexia in different languages? It is now quite well established that the *rate* at which children acquire basic reading skills varies as a function of consistency and regularity in grapheme–phoneme correspondences (e.g., Seymour et al., 2003; Seymour this volume). In every direct comparison reported to date, children learning more consistent writing systems have been found to make greater gains in the first few years of schooling than their English peers in word recognition accuracy, fluency, and conventional spelling (Caravolas et al., 2003; Geva, Wade-Wooley, & Shaney, 1993; Wimmer & Goswami, 1994). In fact, in a number of regular orthographies, such as Turkish

(Durgunoğlu, Nagy, & Hancin-Bhatt, 1993), Finnish, Greek, and German (Seymour et al., 2003), children are reported to reach ceiling levels in accuracy of word and nonword reading, by the end of grade 1. It has been proposed that the reliable correspondence between graphemes and phonemes in shallow orthographies, in combination with phonics reading instruction (which is the standard teaching method in most European countries) helps children to learn the letter-sound correspondences of their language. This in turn boosts their ability to "assemble" phonemes (e.g., when decoding) as well as to analyze words into phonemes (e.g., when spelling); thus, children acquire the skills that form the basis of alphabetic literacy *more quickly* in shallow than in deep orthographies (e.g., Caravolas & Bruck, 1993; Cossu, Shankweiler, Liberman, Katz, & Tola, 1988; Wimmer, Landerl, Linortner, & Hummer, 1991).

A further, less clearly established, claim is that in shallow orthographies the role of phonological skills, and in particular of phoneme awareness, is less important and limited to only the first year or two of literacy acquisition (de Jong & van der Leij, 1999, 2002; Landerl & Wimmer, 2000; Wimmer, 1993). That is, the effect of regular and consistent spelling–sound correspondences is thought to be sufficiently powerful to secure children's phonological recoding skills after a few months of reading experience, regardless of their prereading levels of phonological awareness. Data consistent with these hypotheses have been reported in studies of Turkish (Öney & Goldman, 1984), Dutch (Bast & Reitsma, 1998), and Hebrew (Bentin & Leshem, 1993), in which correlations between phonological awareness and reading were strong in the early stages of grade 1 but became weaker toward the end of first or second grade primarily due to ceiling effects in basic phonological recoding and word recognition. However, these ceiling effects leave open the possibility that the absence of a correlation was merely an artefact of inappropriately easy reading tasks. Instead, the best long-term predictor of reading fluency performance is reported to be rapid automatized naming of visually presented stimuli (rapid automatized naming [RAN]) (de Jong & van der Leij, 1999; Wimmer, Mayringer, & Landerl, 2000).

However, discrepant findings have also been reported. Kozminsky and Kozminsky (1995) showed that phoneme awareness in prereaders predicted literacy achievement at the end of grade 3 among learners of the regular Hebrew orthography, and concurrent correlations were obtained between these skills among children in grades 1 to 5 in studies of Finnish (Müller & Brady, 2001), Dutch (Patel, Snowling, & de Jong, in press), and Czech (Caravolas, Volín, & Hulme, 2005). These studies suggest that phoneme awareness is a relevant component skill in shallow orthographies beyond the second grade. Thus, whereas the cross-linguistic findings unequivocally demonstrate the positive effect of orthographic transparency on the rate of literacy acquisition, the importance and duration of the role, phoneme awareness is currently unresolved.

### Reading skills in children with dyslexia in languages other than English

Dyslexic children of primary school age learning consistent orthographies seem to have less serious difficulties than their English-speaking counterparts. Generally, English children with dyslexia have persistent deficits in word reading *accuracy*, and even more severe deficits in nonword reading, with error rates often ranging from 50% to 70% (see Rack et al., 1992). Their counterparts in languages such as French (Sprenger-Charolles, Siegel, Béchennec, & Serniclaes, 2003), German (Landerl, Wimmer, & Frith, 1997), Dutch (de Jong & van der Leij, in press), and Greek (Porpodas, 1999) typically attain much higher scores, with error rates in the order of 6% (Dutch) to 25% (French). Importantly, even these relatively low error rates are typically significantly higher than those of age-matched controls, and sometimes also higher than reading ability matched controls. Hence, children with dyslexia who learn relatively transparent orthographies do experience problems with word and nonword reading accuracy, but these appear to be less severe than those of their English-speaking peers.

Turning to word and nonword reading *fluency*, individuals with dyslexia seem to have more serious and pervasive difficulties across alphabetic orthographies in that they typically show a much greater reading speed deficit relative to their reading accuracy skills (e.g., de Jong & van der Leij, in press; Landerl et al., 1997; Wimmer, 1993). It is not clear, however, whether children with dyslexia learning more consistent orthographies read more quickly than their English counterparts. For example, in a direct comparison of German and English children, Landerl et al. (1997) found that the German children with dyslexia and normal readers read one-, two-, and three-syllable words more quickly than the English children. In contrast, in a recent comparison of Czech and English children with dyslexia, in which reading fluency was measured in syllables per second (as opposed to mean word-reading time), Caravolas et al. (submitted) found that, although both groups with dyslexia had a reading fluency deficit relative to younger spelling-ability-matched peers, they did not differ from each other.

However, a recent study by Ziegler, Perry, Ma-Wyatt, Ladner, and Schulte-Körne (2003) illustrated that absolute magnitude differences in cross-linguistic comparisons may be misleading due to inherent differences between the statistical properties of word lists being assessed in different languages. In a direct comparison of German- and English-speaking children with dyslexia, the authors constructed word lists that were similar in form and meaning in both languages (using cognates, such as "box" and "sport"), and similarly constructed nonword lists that were matched for number of letters, orthographic regularity, and consistency as estimated by neighborhood size (i.e., the number of other words with the same orthographic rime as the target word). Children were assessed on accuracy and speed of reading. Although the German children tended to read more quickly and accurately overall than the English, groups with dyslexia in both languages showed similar decreases in accuracy and speed when reading nonwords relative to words and when reading longer, compared to shorter, words. Both results are consistent with an impairment in phonological recoding skills. Moreover, both groups of children with dyslexia demonstrated neighborhood effects of similar magnitude as their respective reading ability controls; that is, they read words and nonwords with many neighbors more quickly than those with few neighbors, suggesting that they are sensitive to the statistical properties of orthographic patterns that extend beyond the grapheme in their language. The language groups did differ in one respect: that is, in contrast to normally developing readers, the English children with dyslexia did not seem to make use of their knowledge of larger orthographic units (e.g., orthographic rimes) to read words – they continued to read in a serial manner regardless of the length and degree of consistency of the words. This effect was much less pronounced in German, where all three groups tended to rely more strongly on a serial reading procedure. In sum, this study demonstrates that, when similar materials are used, children with dyslexia show similar *patterns and magnitudes* of reading impairment regardless of the degree of transparency of the orthography.

## Spelling skills in children with dyslexia in languages other than English

Spelling skills have been studied less than reading skills, but it is clear that individuals with dyslexia experience serious and pervasive problems in learning to spell in a variety of alphabetic orthographies (e.g., Alegria & Mousty, 1994; Bruck & Waters, 1988; Caravolas et al., 2003; Wimmer, 1996b). Direct comparisons of spelling ability between speakers of English and other languages are rare; however, a recent study of English- and French-Canadian children (Caravolas et al., 2003) demonstrated that, as in reading, English-speaking children with dyslexia tend to produce higher absolute rates of errors than their counterparts learning more transparent orthographies. In this study comparable lists of words and derived nonwords containing regular as well as irregular and inconsistent graphemes were administered to third-grade groups of poor spellers and age-matched good spellers. On both tests, the English poor spellers produced very high rates of errors (roughly 87%), and these were twice as high as those produced by the French poor spellers (roughly 43%). Despite the advantage relative to English-speaking children, these results show that even in writing systems that are more transparent than English, children with dyslexia tend to produce high error rates, particularly with irregular and inconsistent spelling patterns.

The latter was convincingly demonstrated in several French studies carried out by Alegria and Mousty (Alegria & Mousty, 1994, 1996) who found that on words containing highly consistent and context-independent phoneme–grapheme correspondences (e.g., spelling the phoneme /u/ which is always represented with the grapheme *ou*), 9- to 14-year-old children with dyslexia spelled as accurately as their normally developing, reading-matched peers. Their deficits relative to normally developing children were in learning the inconsistencies and irregularities of conventional spelling (e.g., learning that the phoneme /g/ is represented by the grapheme *g* except when followed by /i/ and /e/, in which case it is represented by the grapheme *gu*). Whereas normal readers demonstrated the ability to learn inconsistent, and context-dependent spelling rules as their reading age increased, children with dyslexia showed no such developmental pattern. Alegria & Mousty (1994) suggested that because French children with dyslexia could represent consistent graphemes quite accurately, they may not necessarily have had impairments in phonological awareness (and analysis) but rather in learning spellings for specific irregular words. They argued that this deficit arises because French readers with dyslexia probably fail to acquire fully specified orthographic representations, as they do not attend to word spellings fully in reading. However, the phonological spelling accuracy of the children with dyslexia and their normally developing peers was not compared in statistical analyses in either study; nor was phonological awareness assessed. Consequently, the status of the children's phonological skills remains unknown. Nevertheless, the main findings of Alegria and Mousty are consistent with several German studies in which children with dyslexia produced many conventional spelling errors but few phonologically implausible spelling errors (e.g., Landerl, 2001; Wimmer, 1996a), and in some cases, the children with dyslexia were as accurate in phonological spelling as their age-matched normal reader peers (Landerl & Wimmer, 2000).

Results such as these have lead to some debate regarding the basis of spelling difficulties among children learning orthographies other than English. An assumption from the phonological deficit hypothesis of dyslexia is that due to their phonological processing deficit, children with dyslexia fail to acquire basic phonological recoding skills, which are required for "assembling" the spellings of unknown words and nonwords, and in turn these weak foundation skills lead to poor reading and spelling skills (e.g., Byrne, Freebody, & Gates, 1992; Caravolas, Hulme, & Snowling, 2001). Thus, poor spelling is thought to be a consequence of poor phonological processing skills (e.g., Snowling, 2000a). A contrasting view, similar to that proposed in Bowers and Wolf's (1993) "double deficit" hypothesis, has been proposed for learners of more regular orthographies (Wimmer & Mayringer, 2002; Wimmer et al., 2000). Pointing to the relatively low phonological recoding error rates in spelling and in nonword reading that were observed in several studies (e.g., Landerl & Wimmer, 2000; Wimmer, 1993, 1996a), proponents of this view posit that although children with dyslexia may suffer phonological processing difficulties at school entry, their difficulties resolve by about the end of the second grade, due to the benefits conferred by predictable grapheme–phoneme correspondences and phonics literacy instruction. The children's persistent difficulties in spelling accuracy (and reading fluency) are attributed to a faulty "timing mechanism" that is independent from the early phonological impairment, and which impedes the formation of associations between phonemes and graphemes. This view has profound theoretical implications as it suggests that characteristics of the writing system affect the nature of the literacy and cognitive deficits in dyslexia in different languages.

However, several studies have obtained results that are more compatible with a simpler, unitary phonological deficit account. For example, children with dyslexia learning several different alphabetic orthographies have been found to experience persistent deficits not only in conventional spelling but also in phonological spelling accuracy well beyond the second grade. In the study by Caravolas et al. (2003), a qualitative analysis of the children's misspellings revealed that French third-grade poor spellers produced significantly fewer phonologically plausible spellings than good spellers, although unlike English poor spellers, they were not significantly impaired in representing the segmental structures of words (i.e., they were less likely to omit graphemes). Sprenger-Charolles, Colle, Lacert, & Serniclaes (2000) reported that fourth-grade French children with dyslexia showed a nonword spelling deficit (mean error rate of 23%) not only relative to chronological age peers (mean error rate of 4%), but also relative to younger reading-age matched children (mean error rate of 9%). It might be argued that the above results of persistent phonological recoding difficulties simply reflect the relatively low phoneme–grapheme consistency of French (Ziegler et al., 1996), and would not be observed in more consistent orthographies. However, Wimmer (1993) and Landerl (2001) found that German dyslexic children in second to fourth grade, whose overall levels of performance were admittedly high, nevertheless produced significantly fewer phonologically plausible spellings than age-matched control children, suggesting that their phonological recoding difficulties had not resolved in grade 2. Moreover, Caravolas & Volín (2001) found that dyslexic children in grades 3 to 5, learning the highly regular orthography of Czech, produced significantly fewer phonologically plausible spellings of words (19% error rate) than their age mates (4% error rate), and did not differ in this respect from spelling-matched control children who were two years younger (17% error rate). In a more recent study, Czech dyslexic children also showed a nonword spelling deficit relative to younger spelling-ability matched peers (Caravolas et al., 2005).

## Summary: reading and spelling profiles of children with dyslexia learning shallow orthographies

The results for spelling are consistent with those obtained for reading: children with dyslexia suffer milder deficits in transparent orthographies than in English. Like English children with dyslexia, children with dyslexia learning more transparent orthographies lag seriously behind normally developing readers in conventional spelling skills, and they experience persistent – if subtle – phonological spelling problems.

Further research is required to elucidate the causes of the discrepant findings in some of the studies (e.g., Landerl & Wimmer, 2000; Wimmer, 1996a) that seem more consistent with a timing mechanism impairment than with a phonological deficit. A central question is whether the reading and spelling difficulties observed in dyslexic children learning transparent orthographies, as well as English, can be reduced to a common underlying deficit in phonological skills? In this view the milder literacy difficulties found among children with dyslexia learning transparent orthographies simply reflect the lesser demands that are placed on phonological skills for all children learning such orthographies. The alternative, but less parsimonious, view is that there may be different cognitive impairments underlying the literacy difficulties of children who show dyslexic difficulties in transparent orthographies. This issue is explored further in the next section, where the main cognitive impairments that have been shown to be associated with dyslexic difficulties in transparent orthographies are presented.

## Cognitive profiles of children with dyslexia in languages other than English

In this section, we consider the findings regarding the roles of phonological awareness, verbal short-term memory, and RAN. The role of phonological awareness skills, and of phoneme awareness in particular, has received most attention in studies of developmental dyslexia in shallow orthographies. Partly, this is because it is arguably the most robust predictor of literacy achievement, at least among speakers/readers of English (Stanovich, 1992). However much of the interest in phoneme awareness has been generated by the claim that phoneme awareness is a less *important* and *time limited* component skill for normally developing learners of relatively shallow orthographies and that it does not discriminate between good and poor readers beyond the second grade (de Jong & van der Leij, 1999, 2002; Landerl & Wimmer, 2000; Wimmer, 1993).

In line with their findings regarding phonological recoding skills in nonword reading and phonological spelling, Wimmer and colleagues (Landerl & Wimmer, 2000; Wimmer, 1993; Wimmer, 1996a; Wimmer et al., 2000) report that German-speaking children with dyslexia experience significant difficulties in phoneme awareness in first grade, but that these problems resolve by about the end of the second grade and do not influence reading and spelling development thereafter. Compatible findings been reported for Dutch third-grade poor readers who had mastered phoneme blending, which did not correlate with word reading speed, although this is one of the simpler phonological awareness tasks, and, accordingly, the range of scores was restricted by ceiling effects (Wesseling & Reitsma, 2000).

This profile, however, is at odds with some findings in German as well as in other languages. For example, in a training study with German kindergarten children, Schneider, Roth, and Ennemoser (2000) demonstrated that preliterate children who had poor phonological awareness, and hence were potentially at risk of reading failure, benefited from phoneme awareness training, in combination with letter knowledge training, more than from training in either phoneme awareness or letter knowledge alone, and the benefits of the training persisted at least until the end of second grade. Similar results were obtained by Bentin and Leshem (1993) in a training study with at-risk Hebrew-speaking kindergarteners. In this study, children who underwent a 10-week phoneme awareness training programme (with or without additional training in letter knowledge) were indistinguishable at the end of first grade from same-aged peers with good initial levels of phoneme awareness on word reading accuracy and phoneme awareness tasks. Equally importantly, at-risk children who received general language (comprehension, vocabulary, syntax) training or no intervention went on to develop reading difficulties. Although neither of these studies assessed performance beyond the second grade, which according to Wimmer and colleagues is the critical point at which children with dyslexia catch up with normally developing peers in phoneme awareness and skills requiring phonological recoding, they offered no hint of relative improvement over the course of the first (Bentin & Leshem, 1993) and/or second grade (Schneider et al., 2000) for the children untrained in phoneme awareness.

In their cross-sectional study with older children with dyslexia (described earlier), Landerl et al. (1997) found that groups of German and English children aged 10 to 12 years with dyslexia, attending grades 5 and 6, both performed less well than chronological age and younger reading ability matched control children on spoonerisms, a phoneme awareness task requiring the transposition of onsets in word pairs (e.g., *boat-fish* → *foat-bish*; *blue-red* → *rue-bled*), which is thought to be conceptually appropriate for older children. Thus, these children's phoneme awareness difficulties had clearly not resolved by the second grade. Recently, however, Landerl and Wimmer (2000) reanalyzed the data from this study, arguing that the dyslexic children's difficulties may not have reflected a phoneme awareness deficit but rather a memory deficit (because the spoonerisms task places high demands on verbal short-term memory). Using a more lenient scoring scheme that reduced the effects of short-term memory on performance, they found that indeed the error rate was reduced dramatically (from 63% to 15%), and the mean of the group with dyslexia was now on par with the reading ability control group. Nevertheless, the children with dyslexia continued to perform less well than the age-matched control children.

Persistent phoneme awareness and phonological recoding difficulties among children with dyslexia have also been documented in a number of other languages with transparent orthographies. A spoonerism task was also administered in the Czech-English cross-linguistic study of Caravolas et al. (2005). Like Landerl et al. (1997) they found that both groups of children with dyslexia were significantly impaired on this task relative to chronological age peers. Moreover, controlling for verbal memory span did not alter the results. In addition, on an easier phoneme deletion task, both groups were impaired relative to age-matched peers, and, the Czech children were also impaired relative to younger spelling-ability-matched peers. In keeping with previous results on reading and spelling measures, the Czech dyslexic and younger control children obtained higher scores on both phoneme awareness tasks than their English peers, suggesting that orthographic transparency affects not only the rate of literacy development but also of phoneme awareness. Phoneme awareness deficits were also observed in recent studies with Dutch children (de Jong and van der Leij, in press; Patel et al., in press) when a sufficiently difficult phoneme deletion task was used. Similar results have been obtained among children with dyslexia from second to fifth grade in Hebrew (Ben-Dror, Bentin, & Frost, 1995; Breznitz, 1997) and French (Caravolas et al., 2003; Sprenger-Charolles et al., 2000).

To date, the results regarding the role of phoneme awareness in accounting for individual and group differences in literacy development in languages with relatively transparent writing systems are mixed. While some are consistent with the orthography-specific account of Wimmer and colleagues (1991), others suggest that phoneme awareness plays a similar role in the development of alphabetic literacy regardless of differences in orthographic transparency. Whether the discrepancies are due to differences in the types and reliability of phoneme awareness measures that have been used, or to differences in the types of literacy skills, or age groups, or the populations that have been assessed across studies, is difficult to determine. The issue clearly warrants further study, as it has serious implications for theories of the effects of orthographic consistency on cognitive processes in reading and spelling, and for our understanding of the nature of the cognitive deficits in dyslexia in different languages.

Investigations of the role of verbal short-term memory in the profile of individuals with dyslexia have produced much more unanimous results across alphabetic orthographies. On various measures, such as digit span, word span, and nonword span, school-age children with dyslexia almost invariably experience persistent impairments relative to children of the same age, and sometimes also relative to younger children with equivalent reading skills. This has been found to be the case in Dutch (de Jong, 1998), French (Sprenger-Charolles et al., 2000), German (Schneider et al., 2000), and Czech (Caravolas et al., 2005). Although verbal short-term memory deficits have sometimes been proposed to underlie the poor performance of children with dyslexia on phoneme awareness tasks (Landerl & Wimmer, 2000), this has not been borne out in analyses in which the role of both variables has been considered simultaneously, in English or in other languages. That is, group differences in phoneme awareness were not eliminated when the effect of verbal short-term memory was partialled out either for English or Czech children in Caravolas et al. (submitted) study, and, phoneme awareness contributed unique variance to reading ability over and above verbal short-term memory among English children (McDougall, Hulme, Ellis, & Monk, 1994).

The role of rapid automatized naming (RAN) has been investigated in a number of alphabetic orthographies. English-speaking individuals with dyslexia are typically slow on RAN tasks, and this is also true of their peers learning more transparent orthographies (de Jong & van der Leij, 1999, 2002; Wimmer, 1993, 1996a). However, there is considerable controversy about the nature of the cognitive mechanisms that are tapped by naming speed (see Vellutino & Fletcher, this volume). Although RAN correlates moderately with phonological awareness skills (e.g., Schatschneider, Carlson, Francis, Foorman, & Fletcher, 2002), the two abilities are separable and may be partially dissociated in some groups of individuals with dyslexia (e.g., English: Bowers & Wolf, 1993; German: Wimmer et al., 2000; Wimmer & Mayringer, 2002). Moreover, in several non-English studies, RAN has been found to be the best long-term discriminator of reading and spelling ability (e.g., de Jong & van der Leij, 1999; Wimmer, 1993; Wimmer et al., 2000), while phoneme awareness and verbal short-term memory were not. These findings have led some researchers to argue that deficits on RAN tasks indicate an impairment in the orthography–phonology timing mechanism that is independent from the phonological system per se (e.g., Bowers & Wolf, 1993; Wimmer et al., 2000). However, others have suggested that RAN tasks fall under the phonological processing skills umbrella as estimators of the efficiency in accessing phonological representations, and that deficits on RAN tasks further demonstrate a phonological processing deficit (e.g., Snowling & Hulme, 1994b; Torgesen, Wagner, Rashotte, Burgess, & Hecht, 1997). The latter claim is supported by English-language findings of Torgesen et al. (1997) that the predictive effects of RAN on later reading ability are eliminated when children's initial reading abilities are also taken into account. This suggests that differences in naming speed may be a consequence rather than a cause of differences in reading ability. Perhaps a more convincing finding, however, comes from a recent study of Dutch children with dyslexia, in which both RAN and the speed with which children performed a phoneme deletion task were simultaneously assessed as predictors of reading ability (Patel et al., in press). The results showed that although RAN was a unique predictor of reading over and above several other variables, its effect was no longer significant when phoneme deletion speed was added to the equation. This result suggests that RAN estimates some aspect of phonological processing. Nevertheless, further research is required to fully understand the RAN–literacy relationship.

Finally, it is important to note the skills that have been found to be unimpaired in children with developmental dyslexia learning to read more transparent orthographies, as well as in English. These primarily include the short-term retention of visual stimuli (e.g., Sprenger-Charolles et al., 2000) and visual processing speed tasks (e.g., de Jong, 1998; Landerl, 2001). In sum, studies in languages with alphabetic orthographies suggest that both the literacy and the cognitive profiles of individuals with dyslexia have many commonalities, and on balance these seem to outnumber the differences. Importantly, dyslexia presents as a language-based disorder, in which a critical deficit involves skills related to phonological representation and processing. The results to date indicate that the manifestation of this deficit is more pronounced in English. However, whether or not the magnitude relative to normal readers, or the duration of the phonological deficit varies as a function of orthographic transparency has yet to be determined by large-scale longitudinal studies in a variety of languages.

## Dyslexia in the Logographic Writing System of Chinese

Research examining when normally developing readers become sensitive to the components of Chinese characters is reviewed in detail by Hanley (this volume) and will not be repeated here. It is critical to understand, however, that numerous studies have now shown that children *do* become sensitive to the functions of the phonetic and semantic radicals in Chinese characters implicitly through reading experience. This suggests in turn that, as in English and other alphabetic writing systems, phonological processing skills (such as phonological awareness) as well as semantic skills may be important components in learning to read Chinese. Moreover, whereas visual processing and memory skills may be of importance in the early stages of reading (when children may place a greater reliance on rote memorization), phonological and semantic analysis skills may become increasingly important in the later years of primary school.

### Component skills of reading in Chinese

The importance of various component skills in reading has been investigated in several correlational studies. In a four-year longitudinal study, Ho and Bryant (1997b) examined the predictive relationship between phonological awareness and visual skills of Hong Kong Chinese prereaders, and their reading skills up to four years later. The authors found that children's prereading visual skills were relatively stable long-term predictors accounting for variance in reading over and above age, IQ, and maternal education, at all three subsequent time points. Prereading phonological awareness skills did not predict reading at the beginning of the first year in school, but did by the end of that year and more so in the second year. Thus, consistent with predictions based on children's reading strategies, the authors concluded that Chinese children tend to rely more strongly on visual skills in the early stages of learning to read, and they seem to rely increasingly on phonological skills as their reading skills develop. However in this study the contribution of phonological awareness skills was not assessed over and above that of visual skills, and thus it is not clear whether phonological skills accounted for unique variance when visual skills were controlled. A study of third-grade Chinese children by Huang and Hanley (1994), suggested that it does not. In their study, measures of phonological awareness and visual skills were used along with other measures as predictors of word reading, and the results showed that although both types of skills correlated significantly with reading ability, only visual skills accounted for unique variance, after accounting for IQ, vocabulary, and phonological awareness. However, the same authors (Huang & Hanley, 1997) failed to replicate this finding in a longitudinal study of Taiwanese first-grade children in which phonological awareness skills among children at the beginning of the first grade correlated much more strongly with subsequent reading than did a visual paired-associate learning task. Together these results suggest that phonological skills are associated with reading in Chinese, as are certain (but perhaps not all) types of visual processing skills. Support for the hypothesis that visual skills are more important in the earliest stages of learning to read while phonological skills increase in significance in later stages has to date been equivocal; the issue awaits further longitudinal research.

## Literacy and cognitive profiles of children with reading difficulties in Chinese

What is the nature of the literacy and cognitive difficulties of Chinese-speaking children with dyslexia, and how do they compare with those observed in English and other alphabetic orthographies? A study addressing the question of how reading difficulties manifest in Chinese was carried out by Tzeng, Zhong, Hung, and Lee (1995) who investigated the extent to which good and poor readers in third and sixth grades are sensitive to the statistical properties of the Chinese orthography. Reading ability was determined by children's grades in language arts (Chinese) class. The authors were specifically interested in whether children were influenced by characteristics such as the regularity and consistency of the phonetic components of characters in word recognition tasks. Each phonetic component has a dedicated pronunciation in isolation, though its pronunciation may differ when it forms part of a compound character. Thus, phonetics that always have the same pronunciation in characters as they do in isolation are fully regular, but many (semi-regular) phonetics have different pronunciations in some compound characters, and others (completely irregular phonetics) have different pronunciations in every character in which they appear (see also Hanley, this volume). In the Tzeng et al. (1995) study, children were asked to read lists of pseudocharacters in which the phonetic component was either completely regular, semi-regular (i.e., appeared in real characters sometimes with a regular pronunciation and sometimes with an irregular pronunciation), or completely irregular. The measures of interest were reading speed and the extent to which children regularized the pronunciations, that is, read the pseudocharacter according to the dedicated pronunciation of the phonetic element.

The analysis of reading speed revealed that all children were slowest in reading the irregular characters, regardless of grade or reading ability. However, the groups differed in the quality of their responses. Overall, the poor readers in both grades produced fewer regularized responses than the normal readers, especially to the regular items. In addition, the poor readers made more regularized responses on the irregular items than the normal readers. This suggests that poor readers are less sensitive than good readers to the internal structure of characters and to the statistical information about the phonetic component. However, no control task was administered to assess whether these children's difficulties were specific to use of the phonetic component or whether they also included the semantic component and/or the visual features of characters.

Good and poor readers' ability to use the semantic radical was examined by Shu and Anderson (1997). In this study first, third, and fifth grade children from Beijing were selected as good and poor readers on the basis of teachers' evaluations. All children were given a morphological inference task in which they were presented with a cue word in phonological form (Pinyin) and were to identify the corresponding character from a choice of four alternatives on the basis of its radical component. The degree of semantic transparency (the degree to which the radical was semantically related to the word) and character familiarity (whether children had learned the character in a previous term/year, in recent weeks, or had not yet learned it) were manipulated. The results showed that poor readers were as skilled as good readers at using the semantic component to identify words that were familiar to them; however, they were less able to use the radical to infer unfamiliar words. Moreover, when faced with unfamiliar characters, good readers were better at inferring the meaning of words with transparent radicals than opaque radicals, whereas poor readers found both types equally difficult. This study suggests that Chinese poor readers in primary grades may be aware of the components of characters they have already learned, but have difficulties in processing and using the morphological-semantic information encoded in characters productively. Unfortunately, Shu and Anderson did not include measures of phonetic inferencing, again leaving open the question of how the poor readers' difficulties in making use of the semantic radical compared with their ability to use the phonetic component. Moreover, no (nonreading) measures of vocabulary or morphological knowledge were included and so it is not clear whether the poor readers' difficulties were associated with oral language difficulties in the domain of morphology and semantics, or whether they reflected these children's low sensitivity to the morphological features of Chinese orthography.

Chan and Siegel (Chan & Siegel, 2001) investigated not only reading performance but also performance on tests of short-term memory and phonological (tone) awareness among normal and poor readers in first to sixth grades of Hong Kong primary schools. Tones play an important phonological role in Chinese as they determine the intonation of each syllable, and they often distinguish syllables that would otherwise be homophones. Importantly, tone information is not represented orthographically and therefore if tone awareness is found to be associated with reading ability, this association cannot simply arise as a consequence of learning to read. Thus, tone awareness presents an interesting measure for investigating the relationship between phonological processing and reading in Chinese. Chan and Siegel selected poor readers to be those who scored in the bottom 25% for their grade on tests of reading; the remaining children in each grade formed the normal-reader groups. On a test assessing reading performance, children read words that varied in terms of their visual complexity (defined by the number of strokes in each character) and frequency. Error analyses were carried out to determine whether children were influenced by salient visual features, phonetic information, or the semantic radicals of characters. Interestingly, poor readers were no worse than normal readers in recognizing visually complex characters relative to simple ones, suggesting that their difficulties do not arise from poor visual processing skills.

The poor readers were found to be as accurate as normal readers on high-frequency words, but they were significantly less accurate on low-frequency words, suggesting that they are sensitive to the statistical properties of printed words. The error analyses revealed that poor readers generally behaved like younger normal readers. That is, both groups made more semantic and visual errors than older, normally achieving children, who in turn made more phonologically related errors (cf. Woo and Hoosain, 1984). Poor readers showed a delay relative to normal readers on short-term verbal memory, pseudocharacter reading (a test of the ability to use the phonetic component to generate pronunciations), and tone discrimination. In sum, the poor readers of this study were not impaired in recognizing visually complex characters, or in reading high-frequency words – which they potentially learned by rote visual memorization. However, they seemed to persist in using developmentally earlier, visual word reading strategies rather than a phonetic processing strategy, suggesting that their reading difficulties may be related to weak phonological skills.

The roles of linguistic skills and working memory in Chinese reading development were further examined by So and Siegel (1997) in a study of 196 normal and poor readers in grades 1 to 4 in Hong Kong. The authors investigated whether four types of oral language skills that are important for reading development in English – phonological awareness, semantic knowledge, syntactic processing, and working memory – are also important in Chinese. Moreover, they asked whether poor readers of Chinese have specific difficulties in these skills. Children scoring in the lowest quartile on a word recognition test were identified as poor readers, and were compared to the remaining normal readers. Regression analyses showed that children's word reading skills were most strongly accounted for by tone awareness (one of the tests of phonological awareness) and syntactic processing in grades 1 to 3, and additionally by semantic skills in fourth grade. Poor readers showed a significant lag in the development of all linguistic and memory skills, although their most serious and persistent difficulties were at the levels of phonological and semantic awareness. Notably, whereas normal readers had developed tone and rime awareness to high levels by grade 1, the poor readers acquired this skill very slowly, and in fourth grade were still only half as accurate as the first-grade normal readers. Thus this study demonstrated that phonological, syntactic, and semantic skills are important to reading development in Chinese, and, in line with the study of Shu and Anderson (1997), suggest that semantic analysis skills may become important to reading somewhat later than phonetic analysis skills. Furthermore, it suggests that Chinese poor readers are particularly impaired in the two skills that may be necessary for the development of character-reading skills, namely phonological and semantic awareness.

Although suggestive, the results of the preceding studies of poor readers must be interpreted with caution in terms of what they reveal about children with dyslexia. That is, none of these studies reported any information about the cognitive or broader educational profiles of the poor readers, leaving open the possibility that many were not specifically impaired in reading but had more general learning difficulties. Moreover, with the exception of some results in the study of Chan and Siegel (2001), none of the above studies included reading ability matched control groups. Thus the results provide no indication of whether poor readers' difficulties are commensurate with or are more severe than would be expected given their reading ability. These design flaws were redressed in two studies by Ho and her colleagues.

Ho, Law, and Ng (2000) investigated whether Chinese children with dyslexia (grades 2 to 5) experience phonological processing difficulties similar to those experienced by English-speaking children. Fifty-six children diagnosed with dyslexia participated. They were categorized in two groups: a group with reading and copying delay, as well as visual spatial difficulties, and a group with specific reading difficulties (both groups had a reading lag of at least 1 year). Both groups were similar in age and had IQs in the normal range. The children with dyslexia were individually matched with chronological age and IQ controls as well as with reading ability and IQ controls. The test battery included regular and irregular character reading, pseudocharacter reading, onset and rime awareness, and "phonological memory" (i.e., word and nonword repetition) tasks. Not surprisingly, both groups with dyslexia were worse than their age peers on regular and irregular character reading, and they did not differ from the reading ability control groups on either measure. On pseudocharacter reading, the group with broader difficulties did not differ in ability from either control group, while those with a specific reading problem performed less well than the age-matched group but similarly to the reading-matched control group, suggesting that they had a more severe difficulty in "decoding" characters on the basis of the phonetic component. However, on the phonological awareness and phonological memory tasks, both dyslexic groups performed less well than the age-control groups, and no better or worse than their reading-matched counterparts on all tasks. Ho et al. concluded that a phonological deficit is a feature of dyslexia not only among readers of alphabetic orthographies but also among readers of Chinese.

More recently, Ho and her associates (Ho, Chan, Lee, Tsang, & Luan, 2004; Ho, Chan, Tsang, & Suk-Han, 2002) investigated whether different subtypes of dyslexic readers exist among Chinese children. Ho et al. (2004) examined the cognitive profiles of 147 children with developmental dyslexia on tests of visual processing, phonological processing including phonological awareness, RAN, and orthographic processing, on the assumption that each of these skills measures dissociable abilities, each related in a different way to reading ability. Specifically, they assumed that visual processing skills may be important for rote learning of whole characters; phonological processing skills may be especially important for deriving the pronunciations of words on the basis of the phonetic component. They also assumed that the RAN tests estimated the ability to rapidly make connections between orthographic patterns and their phonological representations, a skill that has been proposed to underlie the acquisition of orthographic representation (cf. Bowers, Sunseth, & Golden, 1999) and, the orthographic processing tests, which required various responses to printed characters, reflected children's ability to learn about orthographic conventions (such as the legal ordering and orientation of the components of Chinese characters).

Surprisingly, in contrast to some studies described earlier, only 29% of the children presented with a phonological awareness deficit. The deficit affecting the largest proportion of children was in RAN (57%), followed by orthographic processing (42%). Visual deficits were less common (27%), and they were most weakly associated with reading. This pattern of results was similar to that obtained in a study with a smaller sample of children (Ho et al., 2002). Moreover, RAN and orthographic processing made significant unique contributions to literacy performance, whereas phonological processing and visual skills did not. An interesting finding was that the RAN deficit never occurred in isolation; that is, when a child was deficient in RAN, she or he also had a deficit in at least one other skill, most frequently orthographic processing. The authors interpreted the results to mean that the primary cause of dyslexia in Chinese might be a problem in acquiring orthographic knowledge and representations as a consequence of RAN and orthographic processing deficits. Phonological awareness deficits, while present in a non-negligible minority of poor readers, may be of secondary importance due to the fact that Chinese has a morphosyllabic and not an alphabetic writing system.

These findings seem to contradict a number of earlier claims about the cognitive processes underlying reading in Chinese and about the causes of reading failure. A positive aspect of the study was that a variety of potentially important component skills of reading were assessed in a single cohort of children. However, Ho et al. (2004) did not report reliability coefficients for the measures used, though they did so for essentially the same battery of tests in their earlier, smaller-scale version of the above study (Ho et al., 2002). In that study, by far the least reliable measures (well below $r = .80$) were those assessing phoneme awareness, while the RAN and orthographic tests were highly reliable. It is possible, therefore, that more children with dyslexia were found to have RAN and orthographic processing deficits simply because the tests were more sensitive to individual variations in those skills than were the tests assessing phonological awareness. Also, until the cognitive processes underlying the RAN tasks are better understood, it cannot be ruled out that performance on RAN in fact estimates phonological processing (cf. Patel et al., in press). It is also difficult to interpret the finding of a prevalent orthographic processing deficit because all the tasks required judgments about the plausibility of printed characters; that is, they were types of reading tasks. Consequently, it is not clear whether these measures estimate a specific cognitive ability to set up orthographic representations or whether the tasks simply reflect children's poor character reading skills.

Clearly, further research will be necessary in order to describe and understand the causes of dyslexia in Chinese. The number of controlled studies is still small, and the studies that have been carried out with poor readers have focused on a wide variety of questions. To our knowledge, studies of writing development among Chinese children with dyslexia have not yet been published, at least in English. Studies to date suggest that phonological processing skills are associated with reading difficulties in Chinese as they are in other writing systems. In addition Chinese poor readers may also suffer impairments in semantic skills, although whether this is true to a greater extent than would be observed in other writing systems is not yet known (So & Siegel, 1997). Similarly, little is known about the timing and duration of the various impairments in the component skills of Chinese reading. However, the study of Chan and Siegel (2001) suggests that poor readers and younger normal readers rely mainly on visual skills in the early stages of learning to read, and phonological processing skills become important after the first year or two of schooling.

## Conclusions

Evidence from studies of dyslexia across different languages and writing systems suggests that, in broad terms, reading impairments present similarly in English, in other alphabetic writing systems, and in the Chinese logography. That is, across a wide variety of writing systems, poor readers may be sensitive to the statistical properties and to the internal structures of printed words that they already know, but they are not able to make use of this knowledge productively and fluently in reading unfamiliar or infrequent words or to read words more efficiently by processing larger orthographic units. Although the degree of orthographic transparency influences the rate of learning to read in both normal readers and those with dyslexia, readers with dyslexia in all languages appear to have particular difficulties in learning the inconsistencies and irregularities of writing systems.

With respect to the cognitive profiles of children with dyslexia, the impairments of those learning alphabetic systems appear more readily comparable than those of Chinese children. This is to some extent determined by the structure and nature of the spoken and written languages, as well as by differences in prevalent teaching methods. For example, due to the importance of semantic information in the Chinese writing system, Chinese individuals with dyslexia may experience semantic difficulties to a greater extent than their counterparts learning alphabetic orthographies. The converse may be true of phonological deficits in writing systems based on the alphabetic principle. Also, Chinese children who are taught new characters by rote memorization may depend more on visual strategies in word recognition than German or Czech children who are taught to read by phonics methods. However, more studies in Chinese, and comparisons with English and other alphabetic languages are required in order to answer these questions about relative differences.

Nevertheless, current evidence suggests that some of the cognitive deficits underlying dyslexia are universal. First, evidence suggests that visual processing problems are not a core cause of reading problems, and this seems to be true even in the visually complex system of Chinese. Second, two major measures of phonological processing – phonological awareness and verbal short-term memory – have been found to be deficient to lesser or greater degrees in the vast majority of populations with dyslexia. Third, a deficit in rapid naming speed (RAN) has been observed in all studies that have employed this measure. Whether the RAN deficit represents simply another aspect of a phonological processing deficit, or whether it indicates dysfunction in a separate phonology–orthography timing mechanism needs to be resolved by future research.

The study of dyslexia in languages other than English is relatively recent, and many questions remain. Some important challenges for future research are to clarify whether dyslexia may occur in the absence of phonological processing deficits in some languages, or in some subpopulations of readers with dyslexia. Similarly, it will be important to determine whether or not mild phonological deficits are functionally important in the profiles of individuals with dyslexia, or whether in the context of regular writing systems or in logographic systems for that matter, they become irrelevant to their difficulties. Future research may ultimately reveal whether specific reading and spelling difficulties can be reduced to a common set of cognitive processing difficulties in all languages. It appears at the moment that the hope of relating reading problems in all languages to a universal impairment in phonological processing is nearer than many might have dared to hope a decade ago.

# PART V

*Disorders of Reading and Spelling*

# Editorial Part V

A critical goal for theories of normal reading and reading development is to provide explanations for disorders of these processes. Conversely, theories of reading have been heavily influenced by studies of both developmental and adult (acquired) disorders. Studies of disorders of reading have a long history. Neurologists in the nineteenth century described patients who, following brain damage, lost, to varying degrees and in a variety of ways, their previously fluent reading and spelling skills (e.g., Déjerine, 1892). Developmental dyslexia (referred to as congenital word blindness) was first described by Pringle-Morgan (1896). Historically, studies of acquired and developmental disorders have often been pursued in relative isolation from each other, and the practice of trying to unite them has sometimes proved controversial (Bishop, 1997; Coltheart, Masterson, Byng, Prior, & Riddoch, 1983). In recent years there has been a coming together of research on normal and atypical reading processes, as well as greater integration of theories concerned with developmental and adult reading: both of these trends are reflected in the chapters in Part V.

In the first chapter of Part V, Vellutino and Fletcher review research on the cognitive characteristics of dyslexia in childhood. They argue that dyslexia reflects an underlying phonological deficit. Preschool children at high risk of dyslexia show delayed language development and, at school entry, have poorer letter knowledge and phonological skills than their peers. In the school years, in addition to their well-established deficits in phoneme awareness, they show impairments of verbal memory, verbal association learning, and rapid naming. Vellutino and Fletcher go on to discuss the evidence that dyslexia is heritable and has a brain basis (themes elaborated by Pennington & Olson, and Price & McCrory in Part VI) but they also emphasize the importance of "experiential" factors when considering the etiology and remediation of dyslexia. Recent research suggests that differences between children in their response to intervention may have a basis in brain circuitry (Shaywitz et al., 2003). If so, then this would have important implications for remedial practice.

Children with hearing impairments are another group who experience phonological deficits that lead to problems in learning read. The etiology of phonological difficulties in children with a hearing impairment and children with dyslexia is obviously different but there are remarkable similarities in the ways in which their reading difficulties have been conceptualized, as the chapter by Leybaert shows. One finding of great practical and theoretical importance from studies of children with hearing impairments is that the use of cued speech (a system of hand gestures that disambiguates lip-read information) appears to improve the quality of these children's phonological representations of speech and, in turn, if provided consistently from an early age, effectively protects them from reading problems.

Arguably, the reading impairments seen in children with dyslexia and children with a hearing impairment can be traced to underlying deficits in spoken language systems (specifically to impairments of phonology). In our own chapter, we look more broadly at how a variety of deficits in spoken language development affect the process of learning to read. We argue that reading development is critically dependent on a number of distinct, though interacting, language systems, of which the phonological system is but one (an idea referred to earlier in the chapter by Perfetti, Landi, & Oakhill in the context of normal reading development). It appears that different forms of language difficulty provide obstacles to mastering different aspects of reading skill, and we argue that the patterns of reading problems observed can be well accommodated by the triangle model of reading described in the chapters by Plaut and Lupker in Part I of the book.

Strikingly similar themes are developed by Lambon Ralph and Patterson in their chapter on acquired disorders of reading. They argue that the patterns of reading disorder observed following brain damage in adults can be explained in terms of damage to preexisting brain systems that support visual processing and various aspects of language processing (particularly phonological and semantic processing). There is clearly a considerable convergence between the conclusions reached in this chapter and those drawn later by Price and McCrory from brain-imaging studies (as well the conclusions from our own chapter on developmental disorders of reading).

Though reading and spelling are closely related skills, there is evidence that in some cases spelling impairments can arise that are out of line with a person's reading skills. It is not uncommon, for example, for children with dyslexia to show more severe spelling than reading difficulties. Romani, Olson, and DiBetta review studies of acquired and developmental disorders of spelling. They argue that at least two different forms of deficit can lead to problems in spelling. One source of spelling problems may be an impairment of phonological processing (as seen in developmental, and some forms of acquired, dyslexia). A second form of spelling difficulty seems related to problems in retaining information about the orthographic forms of words and is associated with an impairment of lexical learning.

It is interesting to note that Romani et al. favour a dual-route approach for explaining spelling disorders, which parallels the dual-route model of reading described by Coltheart in Part I. In both cases the highly selective deficits seen in some cases following brain damage have been particularly influential in the development of modular cognitive models (models with a number of separate processing mechanisms with localist representations [one unit standing for each item represented]). This approach, contrasts with the less modular, connectionist models, advocated by others including, Plaut, Lambon Ralph and Patterson, and ourselves. A major issue will be the extent to which connectionist models are capable of providing detailed accounts of the pattern of highly selective (modular) deficits that can be observed following brain damage.

It appears that disorders of reading and spelling may be related in a number of interesting and subtle ways to disorders in underlying spoken language systems. Studies in this area have been extremely influential in promoting a view of the mind as a "modular" system, a theoretical viewpoint central to modern cognitive psychology. In addition to their great theoretical importance, studies of reading and spelling disorders clearly have very important practical implications for how best to assess, treat, and prevent such disorders. These are issues that will be taken up again in Part VII of the volume.

# 19

# Developmental Dyslexia

## Frank R. Vellutino and Jack M. Fletcher

Most children learn to read and spell with ease while others have extraordinary difficulty. The possible causes and correlates of such difficulty have been the focus of a great deal of theorizing since before the turn of the twentieth century, when W. Pringle Morgan (1896) described a 14-year-old boy named Percy who suffered from pronounced difficulty learning to read and spell, despite normal achievement in other academic areas. Because he could find no evidence of definitive brain injury that might have caused the boy's reading and spelling problems, Morgan theorized that these problems were caused by a congenital defect that resulted in difficulty in storing visual impressions of words. James Hinshelwood (1900, 1917) held a similar view and provided the field with the first extensive description of reading impairment in otherwise normal children, which he characterized as "congenital word blindness."

The writings of Morgan and Hinshelwood called initial attention to the possibility that reading difficulties in some children may represent a neurodevelopmental disorder affecting cognitive abilities underlying the ability to learn to read, rather than frank brain injury or environmental causes such as a limited home background or inadequate instruction. Serious consideration was given to this possibility in Samuel T. Orton's seminal monograph in 1925 describing reading difficulties and correlated symptom patterns in poor readers judged to be afflicted by what he called strephosymbolia ("twisted symbols"). Orton believed strephosymbolia to be a perceptual disorder manifested in an aberrant tendency to perceive visual symbols as reversed images ("seeing" b as d or was as saw) and suggested that such difficulties are caused by a developmental delay in the establishment of hemispheric dominance. Delay in establishing hemispheric dominance was said to disrupt development of the child's ability to suppress mirror image counterparts of letters and words and this was presumed to cause optical reversibility in visual perception along with letter orientation and letter sequencing errors in oral reading and writing (Vellutino, 1979).

Orton's theory was widely accepted, especially among practitioners, and dominated the field for well over five decades. Moreover, it motivated the emergence of other visual deficit theories (e.g., Hermann's [1959] spatial confusion theory). More recently, cognitive scientists studying reading processes have turned their attention to severely impaired readers who have at least average intelligence, who do not have general learning problems, and whose reading difficulties are not associated with extraneous factors such as uncorrected sensory deficits, socioeconomic disadvantage, emotional problems, or frequent absences from school. "Dyslexia" and "specific reading disability" are contemporary terms commonly used by reading researchers to refer to this symptom pattern in such children. The disorder has been estimated to occur in 10% to 15% of the population of school children (Lyon, Fletcher, & Barnes, 2002; Shaywitz, Escobar, Shaywitz, Fletcher, & Makuch, 1992).

In the present chapter, we provide a selective review of research conducted over the past two to three decades evaluating influential theories of the basic cause(s) of developmental dyslexia. Research in this area of inquiry has pursued causal explanations at the biological, cognitive, behavioral, and environmental levels of analysis (Vellutino, Fletcher, Snowling, & Scanlon, 2004). Our primary concern in this chapter is to distinguish between manifest causes of early reading difficulties and underlying causes of such difficulties. We define manifest causes in terms of observed deficiencies in the knowledge and component skills the child must acquire in order to become a proficient reader and underlying causes in terms of biologically based cognitive deficits or environmental deficits that might impair the acquisition of those skills. Thus, we first define dyslexia and provide documentation of its primary behavioral manifestations. We proceed to discuss theories of dyslexia, specifying cognitive deficits presumed to underlie this disorder, and then go on to address the question of whether there are subtypes of dyslexia. We close with a brief discussion of research documenting the importance of distinguishing between reading problems caused primarily by biologically based cognitive deficits and reading problems caused primarily by experiential and instructional deficits.

Due to space limitations, our review cannot be exhaustive (see Vellutino et al., 2004, for a more detailed review). For example, we do not discuss acquired dyslexia nor do we discuss important areas of inquiry in the study of dyslexia that are treated more extensively in this volume, such as the neurobiological and genetic foundations of dyslexia, and its cross-linguistic manifestations (see Price & McCrory, Pennington & Olson, and Caravolas, this volume).

## Manifest Causes of Dyslexia: Deficiencies in Reading Subskills

The study of specific reading disability has made clear that developmental reading difficulties in children with dyslexia are manifested in basic and pervasive deficiencies in word identification, phonological (letter-sound) decoding, and spelling. Deficiencies in these word-level skills may be accompanied by deficiencies in language comprehension and related skills such as vocabulary knowledge and syntactic competence, but this is not necessarily the case. Thus, dyslexia is generally defined at the behavioral level as a developmental disorder characterized by significant difficulties in learning to decode print. The evidence for this generalization is straightforward.

First, there is a great deal of evidence that most children who have difficulties comprehending written text also have basic deficiencies and dysfluencies in word identification, relative to normally developing readers (e.g., Leach, Scarborough, & Rescorla, 2003; Shankweiler et al., 1999). Conversely, children who have basic deficiencies and dysfluencies in word identification are invariably found to have poor reading comprehension (Gough & Tunmer, 1986; Hoover & Gough, 1990; Snowling, 2000a; Vellutino, Scanlon, & Tanzman, 1994; Vellutino et al., 1996).

Second, studies have shown that there is a developmental asymmetry in the acquisition of skill in reading. Whereas word identification skills tend to be more important determinants of reading comprehension in beginning readers than they are in skilled readers, language comprehension skills are more important determinants of reading comprehension in skilled readers than they are in beginning readers. These studies document that adequate facility in word identification is a necessary (though not a sufficient) condition for adequate reading comprehension (Catts, Hogan, & Fey, 2003; Foorman, Francis, Shaywitz, Shaywitz, & Fletcher, 1997; Hoover & Gough, 1990; Vellutino et al., 1994).

Third, there is convergent evidence that most children with dyslexia have significant difficulty learning to map alphabetic symbols to sound and acquiring facility in phonological (letter-sound) decoding (Fletcher et al., 1994; Liberman & Shankweiler, 1979, 1991; Snowling, 1980, 2000a; Stanovich & Siegel, 1994; Torgesen, Rose, Lindamood, Conway, & Garvan, 1999; Torgesen et al., 2001a; Vellutino, 1979; Vellutino et al., 1994, 1996; Vellutino, Scanlon, & Spearing, 1995; Wagner & Torgesen, 1987; Wagner, Torgesen, & Rashotte, 1994). Such difficulties, in turn, appear to be related to limitations in their ability to acquire phonological awareness – that is, conceptual understanding of the idea that spoken words consist of individual speech sounds (phonemes) or combinations of speech sounds (syllables, onsets, and rimes).

The problems experienced by impaired readers in acquiring phonological awareness is confirmed by robust differences between these children and their normally developing peers on measures evaluating sensitivity to rhyme, phoneme segmentation, sound blending, and like measures of phonological awareness. Importantly, there is evidence for a causal relationship between deficiencies in phonological awareness and alphabetic mapping on the one hand and difficulties in acquiring facility in word identification and spelling on the other. Direct evidence for this causal relationship comes from studies finding that training designed to help children acquire phonological awareness and alphabetic mapping skills has a beneficial effect on word identification, spelling, and reading ability in general (Blachman, 2000; Bradley & Bryant, 1983; Foorman, Francis, Fletcher, Schatschneider, & Mehta, 1998; Hatcher, Hulme, & Ellis, 1994; Olson, Wise, & Ring, 1999; Scanlon & Vellutino, 1996; Scanlon, Vellutino, Small, & Fanuele, 2000; Snowling, 2000a; Torgesen et al., 1999, 2001a; Vellutino & Scanlon, 1987; Vellutino et al., 1996).

Deficiencies in phonological awareness and alphabetic mapping also tend to be accompanied by deficiencies in orthographic awareness – that is, sensitivity to the constraints on how the letters in printed words are organized (sud-legal; yxl-illegal). Phonological and orthographic awareness work in concert to facilitate the acquisition of general ortho-graphic knowledge. General orthographic knowledge is reflected in the child's growing sensitivity to the regularities and redundancies in the writing system (e.g., at in cat, fat, rat). This knowledge is critically important for acquiring reading strategies that help beginning readers reduce the load on visual memory imposed by an alphabetic system, and, thereby, promote automatic word identification (Ehri, 1999). Thus, it should not be surprising to find that dyslexic children are deficient in acquiring general orthographic knowledge (Bruck, 1990; Vellutino et al., 1994).

Finally, deficiencies in lexical skills such as word identification and spelling, along with deficiencies in related skills such as phonological awareness, that are observed in dyslexic children early in their reading development, continue to be evident in the same individ-uals well into adulthood (Bruck, 1990, 1992; Hatcher, Snowling, & Griffiths, 2002; Pennington, Van Orden, Smith, Green, & Haith, 1990; Satz, Buka, Lipsitt, & Seidman, 1998; Shaywitz et al., 1999). Such deficiencies are apparent in individuals with dyslexia across levels of intelligence outside the mentally deficient range and are indexed either by discrepancies with IQ or simply by low reading scores, independent of discrepancies with IQ (Steubing et al., 2002). Thus, in terms of manifest reading behaviors, dyslexia is most accurately defined as a basic and pervasive disorder affecting the child's ability to learn to decode print.

## Underlying Causes of Dyslexia: Cognitive Deficit Theories

### *Visual perceptual and visual memory deficits*

For many years, a dominant view was that developmental reading difficulties are caused by dysfunction in the visual system. During the 1970s and 1980s, a series of related studies were conducted that systematically evaluated these theories using a wide variety of visual processing paradigms that were designed to minimize the influence of linguis-tic coding processes (Fletcher, Foorman, Shaywitz, & Shaywitz, 1999; Snowling, 2000a; Vellutino, 1979). These studies were motivated by the observation that research sup-porting theories of dyslexia, which implicated dysfunction in visual processes as basic causes of the disorder, typically did not control for confounding by verbal mediation. Thus, in several studies comparing dyslexic and normal readers on tasks evaluating visual memory, spatial orientation, and visual sequencing in the processing of letters and words (e.g., b, d, was, saw, loin, lion), it was found that performance on such tasks was equiv-alent in these groups when the task required a written rather than a naming response (Vellutino, 1979). More impressive were findings from studies showing that performance in dyslexic and normal readers was equivalent on tasks evaluating the same processes when the letters and words were taken from a novel orthography (written Hebrew).

If visual abilities do not distinguish reliably between dyslexic and normal readers, then it might be expected that such abilities would not strongly predict performance on mea-sures of reading ability. In fact measures of visual abilities have been found to be rela-tively poor predictors of performance on measures of word identification, spelling, pseudoword decoding, and reading comprehension (Vellutino et al., 1994). Taken together, these findings suggest that difficulties in learning to read are not caused by impairments in visual processing of the types implicated in visual deficit theories of dyslexia that dominated the early literature.

## Low-level visual deficits

Difficulties in learning to read have also been attributed to low-level visual deficits, in particular, visual tracking problems caused by oculomotor deficiencies (Getman, 1985); visual masking effects caused by a hypothesized deficit in the "transient visual system" (Badcock & Lovegrove, 1981; Breitmeyer, 1989; Lovegrove, Martin, & Slaghuis, 1986; Stein, 2001); and abnormalities in visual motion perception (Eden et al., 1996). Moreover, transient system and motion perception deficits have both been linked to dysfunction in the magnocellular visual subsystem. The magnocellular subsystem is one of two parallel components of the visual system, the other being the parvocellular system. The magnocellular system consists of large neurons that are sensitive to movement and rapid changes in the visual field. It is often called the "transient system," insofar as it is presumed to be responsible for suppressing the visual trace that normally persists for a short duration (250 milliseconds) after a visual stimulus has disappeared. The parvocellular system consists of densely packed, small neurons that are sensitive to color and fine spatial details. In reading, the parvocellular system is believed to be operative during eye fixations and the magnocellular (transient) system is believed to be operative during saccadic movements of the eyes.

The visual tracking theory of dyslexia has been discredited by well-controlled eye movement studies finding no differences between dyslexic and normal readers on visual tracking of nonverbal stimuli (Olson, Kliegl, & Davidson, 1983; Stanley, Smith, & Howell, 1983). As regards magnocellular dysfunction, it has been suggested that dyslexics suffer from a deficit in the inhibitory function of the transient system. This deficit is said to produce a visual trace of abnormal duration that creates masking effects and consequent visual acuity problems when these children are reading connected text. Indirect evidence for this suggestion has been provided by studies demonstrating that poor and normal readers have different contrast sensitivity functions, such that poor readers require greater luminosity than normal readers when processing low spatial frequency grids (Badcock & Lovegrove, 1981; Lovegrove et al., 1986; Martin & Lovegrove, 1984). Observations of abnormal motion perception in individuals with dyslexia are offered as confirmatory evidence of magnocellular dysfunction in this population (Eden & Zeffiro, 1998). Additional support for this possibility is provided by anatomical and electrophysiological studies demonstrating structural and functional anomalies in the magnocellular pathways of a small number of dyslexic individuals (Lehmkuhle, Garzia, Turner, Hash, & Baro, 1993; Livingstone, Rosen, Drislane, & Galaburda, 1991).

However, no causal relationship has been established between transient system dysfunction and early reading difficulties. Moreover, there is no evidence that dyslexic readers experience visual acuity and visual masking problems under normal reading conditions. Indeed, the performance patterns prompting inferences of transient system deficits in poor readers have also been observed in some normal readers. As pointed out by Hulme

(1988), the trace persistence theory of reading disability predicts that dyslexic children should be impaired only when they are reading connected text and not when they are reading printed words one at a time under foveal vision conditions. This, of course, is counter to the common observation that poor readers have difficulty in word identification under both conditions. Additionally, Eden, Stein, Wood, and Wood (1995) found that while low-level visual processes contributed unique variance in predicting reading skills in poor readers, the amount of variance was quite small compared to the variance contributed by phonological skills.

Finally, interventions based on visual deficit hypotheses do not appear to improve the word recognition difficulties that reflect the core difficulty in children with dyslexia (Iovino, Fletcher, Breitmeyer, & Foorman, 1999). Thus, we doubt that anomalies in low-level visual processes associated with magnocellular dysfunction are causally related to difficulties in learning to read, though such anomalies may well serve as biological markers signifying deficits in other systems that may be impaired in dyslexia (Eden & Zeffiro, 1998; Fletcher et al., 1999).

## Language-based deficits

*Phonological coding deficits.* There is now strong evidence that reading difficulties in dyslexia can be traced to language-based deficits. Indeed, there is especially strong evidence that such difficulties, in most cases, can be traced to weak phonological coding – a deficient ability to use speech codes to represent information in the form of words and word parts. Thus, children with dyslexia are believed to be encumbered by poorly specified phonological representations that make it difficult for them to acquire phonological skills such as phonological awareness, alphabetic mapping, and phonological (letter-sound) decoding, along with related skills such as orthographic awareness (Elbro, 1997; Liberman & Shankweiler, 1979, 1991; Snowling, 2000a; Stanovich, 1988; Vellutino, 1979). It has also been suggested that weak phonological coding may be the cause of other problems that contribute to difficulties in learning to read, especially difficulties in storing and retrieving words in spoken language (Elbro, 1997; Fletcher et al., 1999; Gathercole & Baddeley, 1990; Snowling, 2000a; Torgesen, Wagner, Rashotte, Burgess, & Hecht, 1997; Vellutino, 1979; Vellutino et al., 1994, 1996; Wagner et al., 1994). Difficulties in word storage and retrieval could impair the child's ability to establish strong connective bonds between the visual and verbal counterparts of printed words. This, in turn, could impair his or her ability to store quality representations of word spellings, thus impeding the acquisition of fluency in word identification. Finally, weak phonological coding could also impair reading comprehension by virtue of the deleterious effect it has on working memory (Daneman & Carpenter, 1980).

Support for weak phonological coding as a basic cause of reading disability comes from studies showing that poor readers tend to perform below the level of normal readers on tests evaluating phonological skills such as phonological awareness, letter-sound decoding, visual-verbal learning, and verbal memory. These studies also show that such measures predict reading performance quite reliably (Blachman, 2000; Fletcher et al., 1994;

Stanovich & Siegel, 1994; Vellutino et al., 1994, 1995, 1996; Wagner et al., 1994). Finally, several studies have documented that poor readers tend to perform below normal readers on both speech (categorical) perception and production tasks, thereby providing additional (though somewhat inconsistent) evidence that dyslexic readers are encumbered by weak phonology (Godfrey, Syral-Lasky, Millay, & Knox, 1981; Griffiths & Snowling, 2001; Manis et al., 1997; Mody, Studdert-Kennedy, & Brady, 1997).

*Semantic and syntactic deficits.* Although existing evidence indicates that reading problems in most children are caused by deficient phonological skills, deficiencies in semantic and syntactic skills may also play a role (Dickinson & Tabors, 2001; Snow & Tabors, 1993; Vellutino, 1979; Vellutino & Scanlon, 1982). Given the likelihood that children will have less difficulty in learning to read words that are in their speaking vocabularies than in learning to read words that are not, it seems reasonable to consider the possibility that deficient vocabulary knowledge is a cause of reading problems in at least some children. Support for this possibility comes from studies finding that impaired reading development was associated with vocabulary deficits in both disadvantaged children and children with limited proficiency in English (Dickinson & Tabors, 2001; Snow Barnes, Chandler, Goodman, & Hemphill, 1991; Tabors & Snow, 2001). Furthermore, vocabulary knowledge acquired before first grade has been found to be a good predictor of later word-level reading skills as well as reading comprehension (Catts, Fey, Zhang, & Tomblin, 1999; Dickinson & Tabors, 2001; Scarborough, 1990; Snow et al., 1991; Snowling, Gallagher, & Frith, 2003; but see Schatschneider, Fletcher, Francis, Carlson, & Foorman, 2004; Storch & Whitehurst, 2002).

Additional support comes from studies using experimental tasks simulating beginning reading (Vellutino & Scanlon, 1987; Vellutino, Scanlon, & Spearing, 1995). In such tasks, children find it easier to learn to "read" high meaning (concrete) words than to learn to read low meaning (abstract) words or nonsense words. Thus, we suggest that semantic deficiencies could be a factor contributing to reading difficulties in some children, especially second-language learners or those who come from impoverished backgrounds (see also Goswami, 2001, and Metsala & Walley, 1998, for interesting discussions on the role of vocabulary development in the acquisition of phonological skills). However, such deficiencies tend to be more closely linked to comprehension processes than to word recognition processes (Storch & Whitehurst, 2002).

Finally, given the demonstrated importance of linguistic context in facilitating and monitoring word identification, especially in poor readers (Perfetti & Roth, 1981; Stanovich, 1980; Tunmer, 1989; Tunmer & Chapman, 1998), it is possible that syntactic deficits that impede a child's ability to use linguistic context to facilitate word identification and reading for meaning could contribute to difficulties in learning to read. We doubt, however, that such deficits would be a primary cause of such difficulties. Indeed, syntactic knowledge does not often distinguish between dyslexic and normally achieving readers, as these populations have typically been defined. A possible exception occurs in cases where children with long-standing reading disorders have been compared with controls (e.g., Stanovich, 1986; Vellutino, Scanlon, & Tanzman, 1988; Vellutino et al., 1995). In such cases, vocabulary and syntactic deficits may be a consequence of prolonged reading difficulties, rather than their cause.

*Low-level auditory deficits.* Another theory of dyslexia that has attracted widespread attention in recent years is Tallal's (1980) temporal order perception theory (see Farmer & Klein, 1995, and Tallal, 2003, for recent reviews). In a study motivated by previous research with language-impaired children (Tallal & Percy, 1973), Tallal (1980) found that poor readers (selected from a sample of children with significant oral language disorders) performed below normal readers in making temporal order judgments (TOJ). These temporal order judgments involved detecting the order of pairs of high and low tones presented either at short (e.g., 50 ms) or long (e.g., 400 ms) interstimulus intervals (ISIs); the poor readers performed as well as the normal readers on the TOJ task at long ISIs, but were impaired when the interstimulus intervals were short. Because of a high correlation between performance on the TOJ task and performance on a nonsense word decoding task (rho = .81), Tallal inferred that children with dyslexia suffer from a basic, nonlinguistic deficit in temporal resolution of rapidly changing auditory stimuli. In turn, this basic deficit was said to impair speech perception, and, thereby, the acquisition of skills such as phonological awareness and phonological decoding. A later study by Reed (1989) replicated Tallal's findings with TOJ tasks involving stop consonants and brief tones, but not when they involved steady-state vowels.

Although these results would appear to offer support for Tallal's theory of dyslexia, they are inconclusive, because it is not clear that the poor readers' difficulties on both the verbal and nonverbal TOJ tasks arise from the same underlying perceptual mechanism. Thus, in a series of experiments that varied discriminability of speech stimuli, Mody, Studdert-Kennedy, and Brady (1997) found that poor readers had more difficulty than normal readers making temporal order judgments at short ISIs only when the stimuli were acoustically similar consonant-vowel (CV) syllables (e.g., /ba/-da/), but not when they involved CV syllables that were acoustically very different (e.g., /ba/-/sa/, Experiments 1a and 1b). Moreover, when these two groups were given TOJ tasks using nonspeech stimuli that were acoustically matched to the onset transitions of the speech stimuli (Experiment 2), no statistically significant differences between dyslexic and normal readers emerged at any of the ISIs used in the experiment.

Support for Tallal's TOJ theory of dyslexia is also undermined by results from two recent studies evaluating the theory with well-defined samples of dyslexic readers that controlled for the presence of attention-deficit hyperactivity disorder (ADHD) (Breier, Fletcher, Foorman, & Gray, 2002; Waber et al., 2001). In both of these studies, the dyslexic readers performed below the level of normal readers on TOJ tasks involving speech stimuli, and only one of these studies reported differences on the nonverbal TOJ tasks (Waber et al., 2001). However, there were no differential effects attributable to variations in ISIs observed in either study, suggesting that previous studies may not have used adequately defined samples of poor readers free from other problems such as ADHD or pervasive oral language difficulties (Fletcher et al., 1999). Thus, although there is strong support for the possibility that children with dyslexia have difficulties with speech perception that produce deficits on temporal processing tasks, there is, at best, weak and equivocal support for the contention that they have a pervasive deficit in auditory temporal processing that is causally related to the reading problem (see also Best & Avery, 1999; Bishop, Carlyon, Deeks, & Bishop, 1999; Nittrouer, 1999, for similar conclusions).

## Subtypes of dyslexia

In attempting to account for the diverse range of cognitive deficits associated with dyslexia, some researchers have suggested that the population of dyslexic children is heterogeneous (Ellis, 1984; Lyon et al., 2002; Rourke, 1975). Further, such heterogeneity may be at least partially explained by the existence of distinct subtypes. The literature on subtypes is voluminous, representing hundreds of published studies since 1978. This research is generated by approaches to subtyping based either on rational division of poor readers into subtypes in accord with clinical experience and visual inspection of patterns of performance, or the application of multivariate classification methods (e.g., cluster analysis) to batteries of cognitive, reading, or neuropsychological tests. Many of these studies have not yielded results that have been replicated or shown to be useful beyond the partitioning of individuals into groups (Hooper & Willis, 1989; Lyon et al., 2002). In the next section, we review the evidence for four subtyping hypotheses that have been more persistent and have maintained some focus of interest in the field, largely because they do appear to have a theoretical basis.

## Double deficit subtypes

*Accuracy versus rate subtypes.* Lovett (1984) (Lovett, Steinbach, & Frijters, 2000) proposed two subtypes of reading disability based on a distinction between accuracy of word identification and fluency in word identification in reading connected text. In a series of studies involving the two dyslexic subtypes (accuracy vs. rate disabled) and a normal reader sample, the accuracy-disabled readers performed poorly on a range of oral and written language measures. In contrast, the rate-disabled readers displayed deficiencies that were more apparent in difficulties in reading connected text and spelling. Reading comprehension was highly correlated with word recognition skill in the accuracy-disabled group and this group was therefore found to be deficient on all measures of reading achievement. The rate-disabled group, however, was impaired only on reading comprehension measures related to fluency. Moreover, in intervention studies (Lovett, Ransby, & Barron, 1988; Lovett et al., 2000), differences between the accuracy-disabled and rate-disabled groups, in the efficacy of different treatments, were apparent in that training in word recognition skills improved reading outcomes in both groups, whereas training in contextual reading improved reading outcomes only in the rate-disabled group. However, the evidence for subtype by treatment interactions was weak and reading gains on standardized measures observed in these studies did not move many children into the average range, in spite of statistically significant results (Lyon et al., 2002).

*Phonological awareness versus rapid naming subtypes.* Wolf, Bowers, and their colleagues (Bowers, Golden, Kennedy, & Young, 1994; Bowers & Wolf, 1993; Wolf, Bowers, & Biddle, 2000; Wolf, Pfeil, Lotz, & Biddle, 1994) have suggested that there are three subtypes of reading disability defined by (1) deficiencies in phonological awareness that disrupt word recognition; (2) slow naming speed that disrupts orthographic processing; and (3) "double deficits" in both phonological awareness and rapid naming. They also suggest that naming speed deficits are caused by disruption in a "precise timing mechanism" that influences speed of processing and, thereby, temporal integration of the letters in printed words (Bowers & Wolf, 1993; Bowers et al., 1994; Wolf et al., 1994, 2000). Within this view it is assumed that if a word's letters cannot be identified with sufficient ease and rapidity, they will not be processed close enough in time to detect orthographic patterns (e.g., at in cat, rat, fat). In turn, this problem will impair the child's ability to store distinct and unitized representations of word specific spellings.

Three types of research provide support for Wolf and Bower's version of the double deficit theory. First, studies finding that naming speed tasks (e.g., rapid naming of letters or digits) contribute variance to performance on tests evaluating reading achievement beyond that contributed by tests evaluating phonological skills (e.g., Manis, Doi, & Bhadha, 2000; Wolf et al., 2000). Second, studies finding that the double deficit subtype generally performs below the single deficit subtypes on tests evaluating reading achievement (Wolf et al., 2000). Third, studies finding that phonological skills are more highly correlated with accuracy in word identification than is rapid naming ability, whereas rapid naming ability is more highly correlated with fluency in word identification than are phonological skills (Manis et al., 2000; Wolf et al., 2000).

Although these findings are suggestive, the double deficit theory can be questioned on several grounds. First, the type of serial letter processing said to be impaired in children manifesting naming speed deficits has long since been discredited as a component process in word recognition (Gough, 1984). Second, recent research suggests that observed relationships between rapid naming and measures of reading ability may be an artifact of the failure to control for prior reading ability, and, thereby, for the variance phonological skills and rapid naming ability share with reading ability. Thus, Torgesen et al. (1997) found that phonological awareness but not rapid naming accounted for unique variance on reading and orthographic coding tasks administered at later points in time when initial reading performance was controlled. Finally, the larger differences observed between children in double and single deficit subgroups have been found to be due primarily to deficiencies in phonological awareness and related phonological skills, rather than to the combined effects of phonological and naming speed deficits (Compton, DeFries, & Olson, 2001; Schatschneider, Carlson, Francis, Foorman, & Fletcher, 2002). These latter findings compromise a basic assumption of the double deficit theory of reading disability, while favoring phonological deficit explanations of this disorder.

*Phonological versus orthographic subtypes.* An influential approach to subtyping has been cast within the dual-route framework of reading (Coltheart, this volume). According to this model, the reading system comprises two subsystems – a sublexical system ("route") mediated by phonological rules that relate graphemes to phonemes, and a visual-orthographic lexical system that by-passes the phonologically mediated system. Some children, described as having "phonological dyslexia," have problems with the operation of the phonological route, whereas others, described as having "surface dyslexia," have difficulties with the visual-orthographic route (Castles & Coltheart, 1993). Thus, whereas "phonological dyslexics" show poorer reading of pseudowords than exception words, "surface dyslexics" show better pseudoword than exception word reading.

Although there is little doubt that phonological dyslexia is a valid subtype, whether surface dyslexia can be reliably defined is arguable (Stanovich, Siegel, & Gottardo, 1997).

Murphy and Pollatsek (1994) did not obtain evidence supporting the surface dyslexia subtype. In contrast, Manis, Seidenberg, Doi, McBride-Chang, & Peterson (1996) and Stanovich et al. (1997) did obtain evidence that supported this subtype, but the evidence was observed primarily in children younger than those used in Murphy and Pollatsek (1994) (see also Coltheart, this volume).

Stanovich et al. (1997) obtained additional evidence suggesting that most children with dyslexia have difficulties at both the phonological and orthographic level of the word recognition process. Children who were identified as showing surface dyslexia, based on comparisons with age-matched normal readers, did not show this reading profile when the comparison group was younger reading-age matched children. At the same time, Stanovich (2000) suggested that surface dyslexia appeared to represent a subtype that was not stable across definition or age, and may represent a transient delay in the development of word recognition skills. This finding was recently supported by Zabell and Everatt (2002), who found that adults with orthographic and phonological dyslexia did not differ on measures of phonological processing.

*Phonological core-variable differences classification.* In all the subtyping schemes discussed, the largest group remains one with a basic impairment in phonological processing. To account for the primacy of phonological deficits, and variation in other cognitive skills characteristic of dyslexia, Stanovich (1988) formulated the phonological core-variable differences model. This model suggests that phonological processing is at the core of all word recognition disabilities. However, children may have difficulties outside the phonological domain that do not directly contribute to the word recognition difficulties. For example, impairments in vocabulary could interfere with comprehension, leading to more pervasive disturbances of language that would result in a "garden variety" form of reading disability. Others could show fine motor and visual perceptual problems that are unrelated to word recognition or other domains of reading.

In a large-scale study of the performance of normally developing and reading disabled children on a range of cognitive measures, Morris et al. (1998) provided support for this model. The study relied on a number of theories to select potential variables to be used in subtyping, including measures of phonological skills, rapid naming, short-term memory, vocabulary, and visual perceptual skills.

Nine subtypes emerged from Morris's analyses, including five subtypes with specific reading disability, two subtypes with pervasive impairments in language and reading, and two representing normally achieving groups of children. Importantly, six of the seven reading disability subtypes shared impairment in phonological awareness skills; the largest specific subtype had impairments in phonological awareness, rapid naming, and verbal short-term memory. The other reading disability subtypes varied in rapid automatized naming and verbal short-term memory abilities. The two subtypes with pervasive impairments in language were clearly indexed by impairments in these areas and in vocabulary knowledge.

Figure 19.1 presents a schematic that summarizes the major finding of this study. It shows that the subtypes essentially varied in impairment in phonological processing, rapid naming, and lexical skills: one group of subtypes impaired in phonological awareness and/or verbal short-term memory, a subtype impaired in these two skills as well as rapid

**Subtypes of Reading Disabilities**

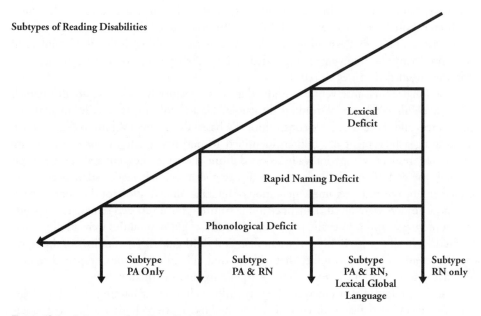

**Figure 19.1**   Subtypes of reading disabilities.

naming, and a subtype that adds lexical deficits representing children with more pervasive language impairments. Finally, one subtype in figure 19.1 was not impaired in phonological awareness, but had difficulties in rate of processing, as manifested in performance on rapid naming tests and other measures evaluating speed of processing. This rate-based subtype was not impaired in word recognition accuracy, but had difficulties on measures of reading fluency and comprehension, consistent with more recent formulations of the double deficit model and the accuracy-rate subtypes.

Altogether, these results highlight the prominent role of phonological processing as a causal deficit in dyslexia, as well as the need for more research to better understand the relationship between reading disability and other related cognitive deficits.

## *Experiential and instructional factors*

Although there is evidence that some poor readers have structurally and functionally different architectures for processing spoken and written language compared with normal readers (Grigorenko, 2001; Lyon et al., 2002; Vellutino et al., 2004), it is also apparent that early reading difficulties in some poor readers may be caused primarily by adverse environmental conditions for language and literacy development or by poor teaching. Indeed, the adverse effects of inadequate prereading experience and/or inadequate instruction may lead to reading skill deficiencies that mimic the effects of those seen in children with dyslexia who do not meet the traditional exclusionary criteria. Because the acquisition of important reading subskills, such as phonological awareness and letter-sound decoding, can be adversely influenced by the type of reading instruction to which a child has been exposed (Foorman et al., 1998), it is important to establish the presence of adequate instruction before assuming that the cause of early reading difficulties is biological in origin. Many children who are identified as dyslexic may not have received the instruction they needed (Lyon et al., 2001).

In a longitudinal-intervention study that was specifically designed to distinguish between children who have reading difficulties because of adverse environmental circumstances and those who have constitutionally based difficulties (Vellutino et al., 1996), the reading achievement of children identified in mid-first grade as poor or normally developing readers was periodically assessed from the time they entered kindergarten through the end of fourth grade, that is before and after their reader status was determined and before and after implementation of remedial intervention for the poor readers. The poor readers were given daily one-to-one tutoring for up to two semesters (depending on progress), and tests evaluating reading-related cognitive abilities were administered to children in all groups in kindergarten, first, and third grades. The findings of the study are consistent with the possibility that early reading difficulties in most impaired readers are related to limitations in early literacy experience and instruction.

First, it was found that emergent literacy skills such as letter naming and phonological awareness were deficient in virtually all of the kindergarten children who were subsequently identified as poor readers in first grade. Second, almost 70% of the tutored children were brought to within an average range of reading achievement after only one semester, and most maintained this level of functioning through the end of fourth grade (see figures 19.2 and 19.3). Because the intervention program was comprehensive, highly individualized, and reasonably well balanced, in terms of the emphasis placed on both word-level and text processing skills, it is fair to assume that it helped compensate for core reading instructional approaches that often did not differentiate instruction for children struggling to learn to read and who often received little explicit instruction in the alphabetic principle.

Third, the poor readers who were found to be the most difficult to remediate performed well below the normal readers, and quite often below the poor readers who were readily remediated, on kindergarten, first, and third grade tests evaluating phonological abilities such as phonological awareness, verbal memory, confrontational naming, and rapid serial naming. Furthermore, although there were no statistically significant differences among the groups on semantic, syntactic, and visual measures, the tutored groups tended to perform below the normal readers on these measures as well as on most of the phonological measures.

Vellutino et al. (1996) interpreted this pattern of results as evidence that experiential and instructional deficits are often the primary cause of early reading difficulties. And, given that the normal readers in this study generally scored above national norms on the measures of reading achievement, the poor scores of the tutored children on the semantic, syntactic, and visual measures were thought to imply that they were less well prepared to learn to read than the normal readers, rather than implying that the cognitive abilities evaluated by these measures were seriously deficient in these children. This interpretation is more in keeping with "gradation of risk," rather than categorical conceptualizations of dyslexia (Ellis, 1984; Olson & Gayan, 2001; Pennington & Lefly, 2001; Snowling et al., 2003; Scarborough, 1990; Stanovich, 1988).

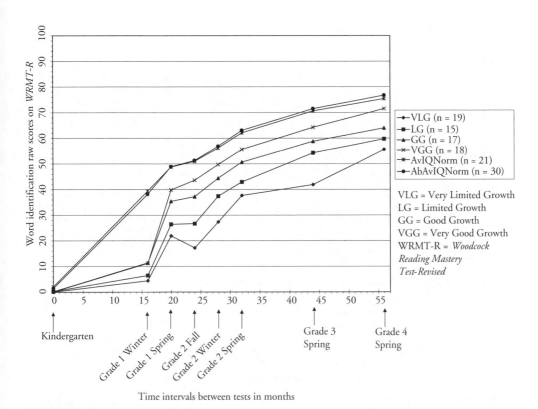

**Figure 19.2**   Growth curves for mean raw scores on the Woodock Reading Mastery Tests-Revised (WRMT-R) word identification subtest for normal and tutored poor readers.

It is interesting to note, in connection with this latter point, that in this study, the performance decrements of the children who were found to be difficult to remediate on the various measures of reading-related cognitive abilities, administered in kindergarten, first, and third grade, were generally greater than those among children who were more readily remediated. This finding is consistent with results from recent longitudinal studies of children at family-risk for dyslexia because they have a first-degree affected relative. In these studies, at-risk children tended to perform below preschool children from nondyslexic families, not only on measures of reading achievement administered at later points in their development, but also on measures of reading-related cognitive abilities, such as phonological awareness, speech perception, rapid naming, verbal memory, and oral language abilities. This was found to be true, even in high-risk children who went on to be normal readers (Pennington & Lefly, 2001; Scarborough, 1990). Note, however, that children not only inherit genes that may make them at risk for dyslexia, but also share environments that result in greater or lesser access to reading materials, parents who read to them, and schools with effective instructional programs (Olson & Gayan, 2001).

Additional support for the possibility that early reading difficulties in many impaired readers are caused primarily by experiential and instructional deficits comes from other intervention studies which have shown that most impaired readers can acquire at least average-level reading skills if they are identified early and are provided with comprehen-

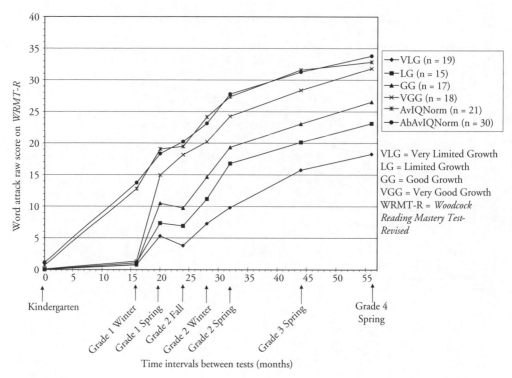

**Figure 19.3**   Growth curves for mean raw scores on the WRMT-R word attack subtest for normal and tutored poor readers

sive and well-integrated reading instruction tailored to their individual needs (Clay, 1985; Iversen & Tunmer, 1993; Pinnell, 1989; Scanlon et al., 2000; Torgesen et al., 1999, 2001a). Moreover, evidence from classroom-based studies suggests that comprehensive, well-balanced reading instruction can prevent long-term reading difficulties in children who would otherwise qualify for a diagnosis of dyslexia (Foorman et al., 1998; Scanlon & Vellutino, 1996).

One other finding from the Vellutino et al. (1996) study is worth noting. The widespread use of IQ scores to classify children as disabled readers or to predict reading achievement was questioned by the finding that the tutored groups did not differ on tests of intelligence, nor did they differ from an average IQ normal reader group on these tests. At the same time, the average IQ normal reader group did not differ from an above-average IQ normal reader group on tests of basic word level skills (e.g., word identification, phonological decoding) administered from kindergarten through the end of fourth grade. In addition, IQ-achievement discrepancy scores were not significantly correlated with initial growth in the reading performance of the tutored children following one semester of one-to-one daily tutoring. These findings are consistent with a large body of research showing that poor readers with IQ discrepant and IQ nondiscrepant reading scores cannot be adequately differentiated, vis-à-vis response to remediation or prognosis (Fletcher et al., 2002; Lyon et al., 2001, 2002; Vellutino, Scanlon, & Lyon, 2000). Moreover, they are consistent with the results of two recent meta-analyses showing null to small differences between the cognitive skills of these two populations (Hoskyn & Swanson, 2000; Steubing et al., 2002). The combined results have led many to conclude that IQ is irrelevant to reading disability.

In summary, the research to date suggests that individual differences in reading ability result from complex interactions between naturally endowed cognitive abilities underlying the ability to learn to read on the one hand, and literacy experiences and instruction on the other. While some children will have little difficulty learning to read, despite less than optimal literacy experiences and instruction, others will have a great deal of difficulty learning to read, even when literacy experiences and instruction are optimal (Lyon et al., 2001, 2002). Future research on biological factors would do well to focus on children who demonstrate an inability to respond to instruction that appears effective for most of their peers.

## Conclusions

Much has been learned about the causes and correlates of early reading difficulties in children with dyslexia. There is strong evidence that problems in acquiring adequate word identification skills constitute the basic difficulty for most of these children. Word identification problems, in turn, appear to result from underlying deficiencies in phonological skills, such as phonological awareness, alphabetic mapping, and phonological decoding, that lead to difficulties in establishing associative bonds between a word's spoken and printed counterparts. Because of the unique structural properties of an alphabetic system, it is clear that these and other phonological skills carry greater weight as determinants of reading ability in novice readers than do semantic and syntactic skills, whereas semantic and syntactic skills carry greater weight as determinants of reading ability, especially comprehension, in more advanced readers.

As regards underlying causes in children who might qualify for a diagnosis of dyslexia, the relevant research suggests that reading difficulties in most such children are caused by basic deficits in phonological coding. Phonological coding deficits tend to be manifested in reliable and robust differences between dyslexic and normal readers, not only on measures evaluating phonologically based reading subskills such as alphabetic mapping and phonological decoding, but also on measures evaluating phonological skills such as phonological awareness, verbal memory, and name encoding and retrieval. Semantic and syntactic deficits do not appear to be a primary cause of reading difficulties in most dyslexic children. Where they occur, they are quite likely a consequence of long-standing reading difficulties or of a comorbid oral language disorder. Yet, semantic and syntactic deficits may be a primary cause of reading difficulties in some children, in particular those from disadvantaged or bilingual populations. They could certainly exacerbate and complicate reading difficulties caused primarily by other factors.

Reading disability research has also established that reading difficulties are not caused by visual deficits of the types proposed in seminal theories of dyslexia, such as Orton's

(1925) optical reversibility theory and other visual deficit theories that subsequently appeared in the reading disability literature. And, although more recent research provides suggestive evidence that some poor readers may suffer from low-level sensory deficits in both the visual and auditory spheres, the evidence is inconclusive, and, in some instances, equivocal and controversial.

Nevertheless, because of the heterogeneity in cognitive functioning often observed in impaired readers, there have been significant disagreements about the primacy of phonological deficits as the central cause of dyslexia, along with a concomitant increase in attempts to identify "subtypes" of dyslexia. We have reviewed four hypotheses regarding subtypes of dyslexia: two variants of the double deficit subtype hypothesis, Lovett's accuracy and rate subtypes (Lovett, 1984), and Wolf and Bowers's phonological and naming speed deficit subtypes (Wolf et al., 2000); Castles & Coltheart's (1993) distinction between (1993) phonological dyslexia and surface dyslexia; and subtypes predicted by Stanovich's (1988) phonological core-variable differences model of dyslexia. We concluded that the extant evidence is most compatible with Stanovich's phonological core-variable differences model, although we underscored the need to better understand the relationship between specific reading disability and other cognitive deficits that may be reliably observed in children who qualify for a diagnosis of dyslexia.

Finally, there is now considerable evidence, from recent intervention studies, that reading difficulties in most beginning readers may not be directly caused by biologically based cognitive deficits intrinsic to the child, but may in fact be related to the opportunities provided for children to learn to read. As such, current estimates of the incidence of reading disabilities as an intrinsic biological disorder may be greatly inflated. However, these same studies, along with recent family-risk and life-span dyslexia studies, provide strong reason to believe that a small but significant percentage of impaired readers may well be afflicted by basic cognitive deficits of biological origin, especially phonological deficits, that make it difficult for them to acquire basic word level skills, despite instruction to which most children respond. Among children of this description, the most severely impaired are difficult to remediate, and we suggest that a diagnosis of dyslexia can be more confidently applied to such children than to impaired readers who are readily remediated. Future research targeting children with dyslexia should focus on those who are demonstrably nonresponders to instruction. Such studies may help establish not only the nature of the specific cognitive difficulties associated with dyslexia, but also may help establish its neurobiological basis.

## Note

Much of the work discussed in this chapter was supported by grants from the National Institute of Child Health and Human Development to the co-authors. The data for the intervention study reported in Vellutino et al. (1996) were collected as part of a project conducted under the auspices of a special Center grant (P50HD25806) awarded to the Kennedy Krieger Institute by NICHD. Other grants involving Vellutino supported this review, specifically RO1 HD34598 and RO1 HD42350. Several grants involving Fletcher also supported this review, including P50 HD21888, R01 HD35938, and NSF 9979968.

# 20

# Learning to Read with a Hearing Impairment

## Jacqueline Leybaert

What does it mean to be hearing impaired? The number of people counted as hearing impaired or deaf depends on how those terms are defined. If hearing impairment is used to refer to the spectrum of hearing losses from mild to profound, then 6.6% of the population may be considered to have some degree of hearing impairment in the United States (Rodda & Grove, 1987). The term "deaf" refers to a more restricted group: "those in whom the sense of hearing is non-functional for the ordinary purposes of life" (Myklebust, 1960).

Among people classified as having a hearing impairment there are wide variations in the severity of hearing loss. In the terminology used by the American Speech Language Hearing Association (http://www.asha.org/public/hearing/disorders/types.htm), there are seven categories that are typically used. The numerical values are based on the average hearing loss at three frequencies 500 Hz, 1000 Hz, and 2000 Hz in the better ear, without amplification. A very similar terminology (with fewer categories) is commonly used in several countries of Europe, based on the classification of the Bureau International d'Audiophonologie (BIAP, www.biap.org).

- Normal range or no impairment: 10 to 15 dB.
- Slight loss/minimal loss: 16 to 25 dB. This degree of hearing loss is considered to be without social effects.
- Mild loss: 26 to 30 dB.
- Moderate loss: 31 to 50 dB. Speech is perceived for normal voices, but is difficult to perceive when the voice is low or far away; most familiar noises are perceived.
- Moderate/severe hearing loss: 51 to 70 dB. Speech is perceived if the voice is raised; the person understands better if he or she can see the speaker.
- Severe hearing loss: 71 to 90 dB; loud noises can be perceived. Language acquisition occurs, but with phonological deficiencies.

- Profound hearing: 91 dB or more. No speech is perceived. Only very loud noises are perceived. Language acquisition is severely impaired. The child relies mainly on speech-reading.

The risk of having a profound hearing loss at birth is 1 per 2,500 births for healthy, full-term newborns; for premature newborns it is 1 per 1,000 births; for newborns with neonatal pathology, the incidence rises to 1 per 100 births (Périer, 1987).

In sensorineural hearing loss, the transformation of the acoustic stimulus into nerve impulses is impaired. This kind of hearing impairment may result from damage to the hair cells of the cochlea or damage to the auditory nerve. Conductive hearing loss results from a blockage of the ear canal or a mechanical impairment of the inner ear. Sensorineural hearing loss generally entails more serious impairments than conductive hearing loss. A study of 3,535 patients (with severe and profound hearing loss) recruited in British schools for children with hearing impairment (Fraser, 1974) indicated that 49.6% of the children had a hearing loss of genetic origin, 49.2% had an acquired hearing loss, and 1.1% had complex malformations. Infectious diseases (such as maternal rubella or meningitis) trauma, prematurity, and neonatal anoxia are associated with sensorineural acquired hearing losses. Hearing losses of genetic origin are due to a large variety of chromosomal aberrations and genetic mutations, most of them due to recessive autosomic transmission (60 to 70%) (Périer, 1987). Given the high incidence of hearing losses due to recessive genetic or nongenetic factors, 90 to 95% of children with hearing impairment are born to parents with normal hearing.

A variety of methods are used to communicate with children with a hearing impairment: sign languages, signed English (or French), finger-spelling, Cued Speech, and speech-reading. Sign languages are natural languages that have evolved over time in deaf communities in most countries of the world. They are articulated in the visuospatial modality. The articulators are the two hands, the expression of the face, and the body. These characteristics of sign languages entail a specific phonology (sometimes called cherology), lexicon, grammar, and discourse structure, which are distinct from those of oral languages like English or French (Stokoe, 1978). This is why it is impossible to translate literally a sign language into an oral language.

Signed English (or French) is a combination of oral language and sign language. It consists, for an English speaker, of producing a sentence in oral English, together with signs borrowed from sign language. Consequently, it is the grammar (the word order) of the oral language that is respected, and not the grammar of the sign language.

Finger-spelling is a manual alphabet. Each letter of the alphabet has a corresponding hand shape. Signers execute in rapid sequence hand shapes that correspond to each letter in the word. Finger-spelling is mainly used for proper nouns and nouns borrowed from oral language (such as CIA, Afghanistan, George W. Bush) (Padden & Le Master, 1985).

Speech-reading consists of understanding speech by using visual information from the lips and other buccofacial movements of the speaker. Because of numerous ambiguities, and the fact that syllables are articulated at the back of the mouth, only a part of the message (perhaps 30%) can be conveyed by speech-reading alone. The effective use of speech-reading requires a good knowledge of oral language (Bernstein, Demorest, & Tucker, 1998).

Cued Speech (Cornett, 1967) is a system of eight hand shapes and four placements (five in the French system, called Langage Parlé Complété) that are designed to disambiguate, or fully specify, the phonology of spoken languages. A cue consists of two parameters: (1) a hand shape, and (2) a hand placement near the mouth (see figure 20.1). Hand shapes disambiguate the consonants, and hand placements disambiguate the vowels. Consonants assigned to the same hand shape are easily discriminated by mouth shapes, while those difficult to discriminate from the information on the lips alone are assigned to different hand shapes. Similarly, vowels assigned to the same hand placement are easily discriminated by mouth shapes, while those difficult to discriminate by lips alone are assigned to different placements. Production of a single cue indicates a consonant-vowel (CV) syllable (i.e., a particular hand shape at a particular hand placement) that carries simultaneous information about both the consonant and the vowel. The goal of Cued Speech is to convey explicit phonemic information in the visual modality to people with a hearing impairment.

Treatments for hearing loss entail two major options: conventional prostheses (hearing aids) and cochlear implants. Hearing aids amplify sounds and can only be used if there is adequate residual hearing. By contrast, cochlear implants by-pass the hair cells of the cochlear and directly stimulate the neurons of the auditory nerve. These electrical signals are then transmitted to the auditory cortex and provide auditory sensations. Although today most very young children with a hearing impairment are fitted with a cochlear implant, the participants in the studies described in this chapter are typically users of conventional hearing aids. Most of the studies described in this chapter are concerned with children with congenital hearing impairments in the severe to profound range.

Since the beginning of the twentieth century, research on the reading and spelling of children with hearing impairments has been concerned with the question of how it is possible for them to develop skilled reading. Given that phonological skills are among the best predictors of reading acquisition in hearing children, an obvious question is whether there is a ceiling on the levels of reading achievement that can be reached by those who grow up with a hearing impairment. The findings of a landmark study undertaken in the United Kingdom during the 1970s suggested this might be the case. Conrad (1979) reported that the median reading level of 300 deaf school leavers aged from 15.5 to 16.5 years was equivalent to that of 9-year-old hearing children. More recently, this observation was confirmed: on average, deaf students' reading achievement levels are roughly six grade levels behind those of hearing students by age 15 (Allen, 1986; Chamberlain & Mayberry, 2000; Traxler, 2000).

However, such data should not obscure the fact that some people with profound hearing impairments do become skillful readers, demonstrating age appropriate reading skills. In Conrad's (1979) study, 5 out of the 205 teenagers with profound hearing loss were reading at the level expected for their age. These individuals were interesting because, in spite of their hearing loss, they were able to code information phonologically in a task requiring the serial recall of printed words. The memory task consisted of two types of lists; lists containing rhyming words that were orthographically and visually dissimilar (*do, who, zoo, true, screw, blue, through, few, etc.*) and nonrhyming words that were visually similar in their shape (*lane, farm, bare, bean, door, furs, have, home, etc.*). Within this paradigm it was possible to distinguish "phonological coders," who made more errors in

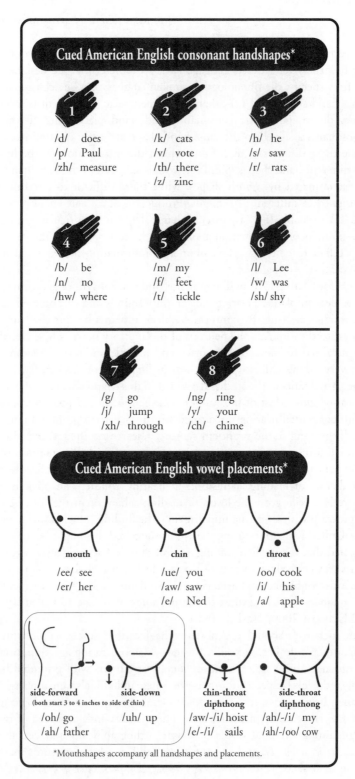

**Figure 20.1** Cued American English consonant handshapes and vowel placements. (Metzger & Fleetwood, 1991). Used by permission from Language Matters, Inc.

the rhyming list than in the visually similar list, from "visual coders," who made more errors on the visually similar lists than on the rhyming lists. Comparison of these two groups (who were matched for intelligence and degree of hearing impairment) revealed that the phonological coders had a two-year advantage in reading comprehension compared to the visual coders. From these data, Conrad concluded that a phonological code is essential for the development of reading, even in youngsters with a hearing impairment. His work brought to prominence an issue that has generated much subsequent research: the impact of deafness on internal speech (or phonological coding) and its use during written language processing.

## Do People with a Hearing Impairment Use Phonological Coding in Reading and Spelling?

Research on reading and spelling in the hearing impaired has considered whether the reading mechanisms employed by this group are similar to those used of children with normal hearing, and whether the use of a phonological code is as optimal for them as it appears to be for readers with normal hearing. Before discussing these issues, it is important to make clear that a child with a hearing impairment can develop phonological representations of speech despite a hearing deficit.

According to Hanson (Hanson, 1989) phonological representations represent the contrasts of oral language in their linguistic dimension, and not in their phonetic dimension (the surface features of speech). Put another way, phonology is abstracted from the segments that compose language, and phonological representations capture the "meaningless primitives out of which meaningful units are formed" (p. 154). One important source of information that supports the development of phonological representations in children with hearing impairments is speech-reading (lip-reading) (Dodd, 1976). Nevertheless, phonological information from lip-reading is poorer, scarcer, and less precise than information based on auditory inputs for people with normal hearing because many phonemes look the same on the lips or do not have labial (lip position) correlates. For example, the bilabial consonants /p/, /b/, and /m/ have almost the same labial images, and the velar consonants /k/ and /g/ are not readily visible.

Speech articulation may also play a role in the development of phonological representations. As first noted by Conrad (1979), people with a hearing impairment with good speech intelligibility show stronger evidence of the use of phonological coding in short-term memory for printed words than those whose speech is less intelligible. However, good speech production skills are often associated with good residual hearing, and it is possible that it is the processing of the input (rather than speech-output processes) that determines the adequacy of these children's phonology. A third factor that might play a role in the structuring of phonological representations is experience with alphabetic orthography or with finger-spelling, which represents alphabetic information visually (Padden & Hanson, 1999). Interestingly, a tendency to pronounce all the letters of an irregular word is sometimes observed in deaf speech; for example, in French, to pronounce "tabac," saying /tabak/ instead of the correct /taba/ pronunciation (Leybaert, 1993).

## Reading Processes

Several studies have investigated whether phonological information is activated during word recognition in readers with a hearing impairment. Hanson and Fowler (1987) asked participants with and without a hearing impairment to decide whether pairs of letter strings were words or nonwords. Two experimental conditions were of interest: (1) rhyming words that were spelled alike (e.g., *bribe–tribe*); and (2) nonrhyming words that were spelled alike (e.g., *have–cave*). The time to respond to these pairs was compared to the times to respond to matched pairs of control words with dissimilar sound and spelling. College students with hearing impairments, who were among the best readers in the population, demonstrated evidence of phonological processing in this task: like the participants with normal hearing, they responded fastest to the rhyming pairs, more slowly to the control pairs, and slowest to the nonrhyming pairs. Overall, however, the facilitation effect for the rhyming pairs was smaller for the participants with a hearing loss than for the participants with normal hearing. Moreover, scrutiny of the data revealed individual differences in response profile among both groups of participants. Some of the students in both groups did not show the rhyming facilitation effect, though this nonphonological pattern of responding was more common among participants with a hearing impairment (Hanson & Fowler, 1987). This study shows that some students with a hearing impairment access phonological information during reading, while others may place a heavier reliance on orthographic codes (see also Lichtenstein, 1985, 1998).

Phonological coding during sentence reading has also been investigated. McCutchen and Perfetti (1982) reported that skilled adult readers show longer reaction times and more errors when reading "tongue twisters" in silent reading tasks. With this finding as a backdrop, Hanson, Goodell, and Perfetti (1991) asked students with and without hearing impairments to evaluate the semantic acceptability of sentences containing tongue twisters (e.g., *The talented teenager took the trophy in the tournament*), comparing performance on these sentences with control sentences. The experiment included a memory load manipulation: prior to reading each sentence, participants had to read a string of digits for later recall. When the names of the digits began with the same consonants as the words in the tongue-twister sentences (e.g., /t/: *12, 20, 10*, etc.), both groups of participants were more likely to make acceptability errors on the tongue-twister sentences than when the names of the digits to be remembered were phonetically different from the words in the sentences. Thus, Hanson and her colleagues suggested that skilled child and adult readers with hearing impairments are able to use phonological information in processing text when short-term memory is involved (see Padden & Hanson, 1999).

If people with a hearing impairment are able to use phonological codes in reading, an important question is whether the phonology they use is derived prelexically or postlexically. Put another way, do people with a hearing impairment "sound out" words before they recognize them or do they retrieve phonological information after they have recognized the word. One way of assessing this issue is to investigate the use of spelling-to-sound regularity in reading words. Waters and Doehring (1990) found no effect of spelling-to-sound regularity in a lexical decision task given to a group of orally trained youngsters aged 7 to 20 years with a hearing impairment (see also Burden & Campbell,

1994; Merrills, Underwood, & Wood, 1994). However, Leybaert (1993) reported that children with hearing impairments read aloud regular words more rapidly and more accurately than irregular ones, and Leybaert and Alegria, (1993) found that they also show evidence for automatic activation of prelexical phonology in a Stroop task. In this experiment, participants were asked to name aloud the color of the ink in which a sequence of letters was printed. When the sequence was a pseudohomophone of a color word (e.g., in French, *vaire*, homophone of the color word *vert*; in English, *grean*, homophone of *green*), children with and without hearing impairments displayed longer reaction times and more errors than when the sequence was a nonhomophonic pseudoword matched for orthographic similarity with the color word (e.g., *voure*). Interestingly, when the response was given manually, only the children without hearing impairments showed the significant interference effect from the homophonic pseudowords. The results suggest that readers with hearing impairments access phonology automatically in tasks even when such processing is detrimental. They also indicate that people with hearing impairments show less automatic activation of phonological codes in reading. One possibility is that automatic activation of prelexical phonology is slower in the hearing-impaired group. Another possibility is that involuntary access to grapheme–phoneme conversion is primed in this group by the need to give an oral response.

## Individual Differences in the Use of Phonological Codes by People with a Hearing Impairment

Speech intelligibility seems a critical factor determining whether readers with a hearing impairment use phonology during written word processing. One explanation for this is that feedback from articulation allows children with a hearing impairment to represent phonology as a speech–motor pattern. Hanson (1986) found that the effect of orthographic regularity on reading performance in people with hearing impairments was modulated by the quality of participants' speech. Her deaf participants with 'good-speech' could detect letters better in orthographically regular sequences of letters (e.g., REMOND, SIFLET) than in irregular sequences (e.g. RMNOED, TLFIES), as did the hearing participants. By contrast, deaf participants with 'poor-speech' showed a reduced effect of regularity. In the Stroop task, we found that people with hearing impairments with good speech skills displayed larger interference effects from color words (green printed in red ink) in the vocal response task than in a manual response task, while those with poor speech skills displayed the same amount of interference in the two tasks (Leybaert & Alegria, 1993). This indicates that automatic availability of the name of the printed color word is related to the quality of speech in the hearing-impaired population. In a lexical decision task with no time limit, children with severe to profound prelingual hearing impairments found it more difficult to reject pseudohomophones of frequent words (e.g., the pseudoword *werd* that sounds like the word *word*) than control pseudowords matched in letter length and in similarity to source words (Beech & Harris, 1997). Transler, Gombert, and Leybaert (2001) used a similarity judgment paradigm in which children with and without hearing impairments, matched for reading level, had to circle the pseudoword of a pair that they considered "best went with the stimulus pseudoword." For the model "kise" /kiz/, the test homophone was "kyse" /kiz/ and the distractor was "kyne" /kin/. Children with a hearing impairment with good speech skills, as well as children with normal hearing, chose the pseudohomophone more often than chance level, while the scores of the hearing impaired with poor speech skills did not differ from chance.

Taken together, the evidence suggests that children with hearing impairments, especially those with good speech skills, can make use of sublexical (grapheme–phoneme) decoding processes. However, the basis of the relationship between speech intelligibility and phonological knowledge is not entirely clear. Conrad proposed a causal model in which intelligibility of speech and nonverbal intelligence governed the development of internal speech in children with hearing impairments independently of speech perception skills (as indexed by the degree of hearing loss). An alternative view is that the quality of speech output in people with hearing impairments is commensurate with the mental model of speech they have derived from speech input. Thus, people with a hearing impairment with good speech intelligibility may have derived from speech input more accurate representations of phonology that render phonological coding easier and more optimal (Leybaert, 1993; see also Gathercole & Martin, 1996). This position is supported by our work on the effect of exposure to Cued Speech on the development of phonological representations (see below).

## Spelling Processes

Although it seems clear that people with a hearing impairment can use phonological codes, it is reasonable to argue that the use of a phonological code is less optimal for them than for readers with normal hearing. Indeed, the phonological representations of people with severe and profound hearing impairments are poorer and less precise than those of people with normal hearing because of the impoverished input they are derived from. Spelling is a process that draws heavily upon the integrity of underlying phonological representations. It follows that children with hearing impairments might be expected to show impaired spelling processes. Hanson, Shankweiler, and Fischer (1983) compared the spelling of three types of words: regular words (e.g., explode) that can be spelled on the basis of highly consistent sound–letter mappings; morphological words (e.g., beginner) requiring knowledge of how to form suffixes; and opaque words (e.g., Fahrenheit) that could not be spelled on the basis of sound–letter correspondences. College students with and without hearing impairments found the regular words easiest and the opaque words hardest to spell (with the morphological words at an intermediate level). This suggests that people with hearing impairments had developed a sensitivity to the phonological and morphological constraints of an alphabetic orthography.

Leybaert and Alegria (1995) replicated this experiment in French with younger deaf and hearing children. Two groups of hearing-impaired and normally hearing children (from second and fourth grades) were tested. All groups of children with hearing impairments spelled regular words more accurately than opaque words, indicating reliance on phoneme–grapheme correspondences. However, the advantage for regular words over opaque words was smaller for second graders with hearing impairments than for the second graders with normal hearing, indicating that children with hearing impairments benefit less from the predictability of spellings from phonology.

Consistent with this view, fewer of the misspellings produced by children with hearing impairments can be considered as phonologically equivalent to the target word (Leybaert & Alegria, 1995; see also Aaron, Keetay, Boyd, Palmatier, & Wacks, 1998; Burden & Campbell, 1994; Dodd, 1980; Hanson, Shankweiler, & Fischer, 1983; Hoemann, Andrews, Florian, Hoeman, & Jensema, 1976; Sutcliffe, Dowker, & Campbell, 1999). However, some of their misspellings seem to be related to the way in which the word would appear in 'speech-reading' (e.g., in English SPONCH for *sponge*; in French OUFERT for *ouvert*). Arguably, therefore, these nonphonetic misspellings arise not because children with hearing impairments are unable to appreciate the mappings between written and spoken language, but rather because of their difficulty in establishing an accurate phonological representation of specific words.

## Phonological Awareness

Poor reading and spelling among children with hearing impairments might be mediated by poor metaphonological skills that are the direct result of the poor quality of their representations of speech. A number of studies have reported that literate youngsters with hearing impairments and adults from oral as well as from signing backgrounds can perform adequately on rhyming tasks (Campbell & Wright, 1988; Charlier & Leybaert, 2000; Dodd & Hermelin, 1977; Hanson & Fowler, 1987; Hanson & McGarr, 1989; Sterne, 1996; Sterne & Goswami, 2000). In these studies, however, the rhyming abilities of people with a hearing impairment was strongly influenced by spelling similarity as well as by speech-read/articulatory similarity, indicating that they are using different kinds of information than people with normal hearing to make these rhyme judgments. Interestingly, rhyme ability among people with a hearing impairment and, more precisely, their ability to judge that two words with different spellings rhyme, is strongly related to reading ability.

Dyer, MacSweeney, Szczerbinski, Green, and Campbell (2003) investigated the contribution of phonological awareness (a picture rhyme matching task and a pseudohomophone picture matching task) and rapid automatized naming (in speech or in sign) to reading development in 49 students with hearing impairment (mean age 13 years, mean reading age about 7 years). The performance of the students with hearing impairments on the rhyme and the pseudohomophone matching tasks was poorer than that of normally hearing controls matched for reading age. Nevertheless, performance correlated with reading age. In contrast, rapid automatized naming was faster in the hearing-impaired group than in the controls, but did not correlate with reading in the hearing-impaired group. These findings raise the issue of whether "phonological awareness precedes or follows excellence in reading in profoundly deaf individuals. That is, do profoundly deaf individuals become excellent readers because they know something about the sound system of English? Or did they learn something about the sound system of English after having become excellent readers of English orthography?" (Goldin-Meadow & Mayberry, 2001). Longitudinal studies in which the rhyming ability of children with a hearing impairment is measured before learning to read, and related to their subsequent development of reading, are the only way to address this question.

Harris and Beech (1998) administered a pictorial version of the sound oddity task (Bradley & Bryant, 1983) to children with hearing impairments and normally hearing controls who had a very small sight vocabulary and limited alphabet knowledge. The hearing-impaired children were from oral and signing backgrounds. In the oddity task, children were shown a picture of an object, which the experimenter named. They were then shown two other pictures, again named by the experimenter, and had to indicate which of the two pictures had a name like the first one. The trials involved objects with names that either shared the same initial sound (*doll*, cot, *dog*), the same middle sound (*frog*, *dog*, pig) or the same final sound (*bed*, *red*, pen). For both groups, performance on the oddity task was correlated with reading progress during the first school year. However, the performance of the children with hearing impairments in the oddity task was considerably poorer (60.5%) than that of the hearing children (81.1%) and they made considerably less reading progress over the first year of schooling (mean reading score after 1 year: 60.7% for the hearing children, 28.6% for the severely deaf, and 31.4% for the profoundly deaf).

Two important points emerged from this study. First, children with hearing impairments seem able to develop phonological awareness before learning to read, although not as precisely as hearing children do. Second, variations in phonological awareness predict early reading acquisition in deaf as well as in hearing children. For the hearing children, the correlation between reading gain during the first year and early sound categorization was .57 and for the deaf .43. In a recent longitudinal study, Colin, Magnan, Ecalle and Leybaert (in revision) investigated metaphonological skills of children with hearing impairments and normally hearing children before they started learning to read, and at the end of the first grade, together with their word recognition ability. The metaphonological tasks were adapted to children's level of development. In kindergarten, children had to judge whether two pictures' names rhymed and were also asked to generate rhymes in response to pictures' names. In the first grade, they had to judge whether two pictures' names share a common syllable or a common phoneme in one set of "epiphonological" tasks and to produce the common unit in another set of "metaphonological tasks." The metaphonological skills measured in kindergarten predicted the word recognition abilities measured one year later, for the hearing impaired (23.7% of explained variance) as well as for control children (32.6% of explained variance). The measures of epiphonological and metaphonological skills taken in first grade added a significant contribution to the variance in word recognition skills for hearing-impaired subjects only (increase of 30.3%, but only a nonsignificant increase of 14.0% in the hearing).

This suggest that knowledge of the sound system of French before learning to read favors the development of word recognition in children with a hearing impairment (as it does in the hearing), but, at the same time, that the development of this phonological knowledge is boosted more strongly by learning to read in children with hearing impairments than in normally hearing children.

## The Role of Visible Language in Reading Development of the Hearing Impaired

We have seen that it is possible for readers with a hearing impairment to use phonological coding strategies. An obvious question is whether phonological coding is the only pathway to successful reading for this group. Two areas of investigation bear significantly on this question. First, what is the effect of using Cued Speech as a strategy for presenting the phonology of spoken language to children with moderate to profound hearing impairment through the visual modality? Second, do children with hearing impairments born to hearing-impaired parents accrue linguistic advantages relevant to reading and spelling compared to peers who are born to hearing parents?

## Cued Speech

Children exposed to any language of the world can normally be expected to acquire the vocabulary and deduce the phonemic, morphological, semantic, syntactic, and pragmatic rules of their native language without explicit instruction. Indeed, language acquisition is effortless regardless of the modality of input (e.g., spoken or signed). Furthermore, children who have deduced the rules of spoken language typically do not have difficulty learning to read and write. This is not the case for children with profound, prelingual, hearing impairments who do not have early, clear, and complete access to the continuous speech stream of spoken language if their parents do not use oral–aural methods, finger-spelling, or manual systems that combine speech information with signs borrowed from signed languages (LaSasso & Metzger, 1998). It is thus not surprising that these children typically do not acquire the vocabulary, or deduce the grammar of their language, at a similar rate or in a similar manner to their peers with normal hearing.

One group of children with profound, prelingual hearing impairments who do have access to the continuous speech stream of traditionally spoken home language are those whose parents use Cued Speech to communicate with them. Research with French-speaking children who have been exposed to Cued Speech at home and school from an early age demonstrate phonological abilities and written language abilities that are comparable to hearing peers (Alegria., Leybaert, Charlier, & Hage, 1992; Charlier & Leybaert, 2000; D'Hondt & Leybaert, 2003; Leybaert, 2000; Leybaert & D'Hondt, 2003; Leybaert & Lechat, 2001a, 2001b). Children exposed to Cued Speech before the age of 3 and in their home environment (the early group) attained reading levels comparable to those of hearing children of the same age, but children exposed only late to Cued Speech and children educated with sign language showed impairments of reading development. Thus, it becomes relevant to ask whether children who are early Cued Speech users use similar processes in reading and spelling to hearing children.

Recent research has focused on the ability of children exposed to Cued Speech to use phonology–orthography mappings in spelling, as revealed by a tendency to make phonologically accurate spelling errors, such as brain → BRANE. Phonologically accurate errors demonstrate the ability to access precise phonological representations, prior to the application of phoneme–grapheme translation rules. Leybaert (2000) reported that children exposed early to Cued Speech, like their peers with normal hearing, made spelling errors that were primarily phonologically correct. In contrast, children exposed to Cued Speech late made more phonologically inaccurate spellings (e.g., brain → DRANE), a likely reflection of poorly specified (inaccurate) phonological representations. The late Cued Speech group also made more transposition errors (e.g., sport → SORPT) that did not preserve the phonetic representation of the target word. However, in this study, intensive exposure to Cued Speech was confounded with total language exposure. It could be argued, therefore, that it was early exposure to a fully accessible language, rather than exposure to Cued Speech per se, that was the critical factor in determining spelling proficiency. In a second study, Leybaert and Lechat (2001b) compared the spelling of the early Cued Speech users with that of children with hearing impairment exposed early in life to a different visual language, namely, sign language. The results were clear: it was only the hearing children and the early Cued Speech users who primarily used phoneme–grapheme correspondences when they did not know how to spell a word.

The ability to use phoneme–grapheme correspondences during spelling depends on accurate phonological awareness. Recent studies have demonstrated the superior phonological awareness (rhyme judgments about pictures, and written rhyme generation in response to pictures and written words) abilities of children who are exposed to Cued Speech consistently at home and at school, compared to children who are exposed to Cued Speech only at school or inconsistently at home (Charlier & Leybaert, 2000). Similarly, adults with hearing impairment who are Cued Speech users in American English have demonstrated phonological awareness abilities (generation of written rhymes) commensurate with hearing peers, and superior to age-matched adults with hearing impairment from none-cued-speech backgrounds (Crain, 2003; LaSasso, Crain, & Leybaert, 2003). Finally, early Cued Speech users, like normally hearing children but not other children with a hearing impairment, have been found to be able to judge the rhyming relationships between pictures before learning to read (Charlier & Leybaert, 2000; Colin et al., submitted).

The study of the phonological and written language abilities of children exposed early and intensively to Cued Speech demonstrate that hearing impairment per se does not preclude the development of phonological, metaphonological, and alphabetic recoding skills. It also highlights the importance of clear, complete access to the continuous speech stream. Without such access, there is a greatly reduced chance of developing a well-specified phonological system. The impact of exposure to Cued Speech also underlines the amodal nature of phonological knowledge. It appears that the phonological system develops on the basis of linguistically relevant contrasts presented in the visual modality (via Cued Speech) as well as from those presented in the auditory modality.

## The Linguistic Advantages for Hearing-impaired Children Born to Hearing-impaired Parents

Children raised precociously with Cued Speech can achieve reading comprehension levels comparable to those of hearing children of the same age, but other children with hearing impairment fare less well: their reading comprehension is limited by their knowledge of the vocabulary and grammar of the language they are reading. Findings such as these have led people to advocate that children with hearing impairments should be exposed to sign language as a precursor to subsequent reading development.

Since American Sign Language (ASL) and English do not share phonology, nor grammar, learning to read likely goes through a different path for these children than for children exposed to Cued Speech. Indeed, sign language does not offer the possibility of deriving the meaning of words encountered in print for the first time, because of the lack of association between graphemes and the phonological primitives of the signs (hand shape, hand movement, place of signing, hand orientation). Moreover, the storage of the written words in working memory likely entails a recoding into sign language, because the order of the words is different in the two languages.

Early studies concluded that children with a hearing impairment born to deaf parents who used ASL read better and achieved higher academic levels than those born to hearing parents who did not know ASL. However, adequate explanations for this advantage have not been forthcoming (Chamberlain & Mayberry, 2000; Marschark, 1993; Strong & Prinz, 1997, 2000; Stuckless & Birch, 1966a, 1966b). Not surprisingly, the hearing status of the parents is intricately related to several other factors. Parents with hearing impairment are better at communicating with their child with a hearing impairment in sign language; they are also able to adjust their expectations of their child, possibly leading to better mother–child interaction during reading activities. The better reading comprehension of children with a hearing impairment born to parents with a hearing impairment may therefore be the consequence of greater knowledge of the world or more advanced linguistic development in vocabulary, or morphosyntax. Put simply, early experience with sign language may have a positive effect on linguistic and intellectual development, which, in turn, promote reading comprehension (Conrad, 1979).

Recent research has attempted to disentangle the effects of having parents with a hearing impairment from having skill in ASL. Strong and Prinz (1997, 2000) examined global ASL and English literacy skill in children from parents with a hearing impairment and children from normally hearing parents. They tested 160 students between the ages of 8 and 15 from a residential school where ASL was the language of instruction and communication, classifying them according to ASL proficiency (high, medium, and low). Students with higher ASL skills also had higher English literacy skills. This was true for students of all ages, independently of whether they had a hearing-impaired or normally hearing mother. Thus, it was the level of ASL skill, and not just having a hearing-impaired parent, that was related to level of literacy. Unfortunately, the authors did not report the grade level achieved by each of the subgroups. It is therefore not possible to assess whether the high ASL/high literate group performed within the normal range for normally hearing subjects.

Since ASL and English do not share phonological features, or grammar, it is not clear why a relation should exist between signing and reading skills. According to Chamberlain and Mayberry (2000), the relationship between ASL skill and reading is largely due to the early acquisition of a natural language, which in turn, allows the development of other cognitive skills, such as memory for verbal and nonverbal material. The early language exposure account is, however, not sufficient. Indeed, while many native signers develop good reading ability, some skilled native signers experience difficulty in learning to read.

An interesting hypothesis is that specific aspects of ASL could be related to reading skills. Padden and colleagues (Padden & Hanson, 1999; Padden & Ramsey, 2000) moving beyond the notion that early experience with ASL provides a linguistic and cognitive advantage favoring the acquisition of reading, hypothesized that knowledge of specific ASL structures (e.g., finger-spelling, initialized signs) correlates with reading achievement. In finger-spelling, signers execute in rapid sequence hand shapes that correspond to each letter in the word. Initialized signs involve replacing the hand shape of an ASL sign by the hand shape corresponding to the first letter of the English (or French) translation of the sign. Initialized signs and finger-spelling are used conjointly in the classroom, when teachers are emphasizing a word's spelling. For example, one teacher used an initialized sign (e.g., VOLCANO, with the hand shape corresponding to the letter V), and then immediately finger-spelled the word. In addition to tests measuring general ASL competence, Padden and Ramsey developed tests using initialized signs and finger-spelled words. They found that young children with hearing impairment who were better able to write down words that were finger-spelled to them, and were able to translate initialized signs, also did better on reading tests. These skills were more likely to be found among children with hearing impairment who had grown up with ASL, such as those who had hearing-impaired parents, but they were also used by other children who performed well on tests of ASL ability. Padden and Ramsey interpreted their results as showing that hearing-impaired signing readers may take advantage of the explicit links between ASL and written English, such as finger-spelled or initialized signs.

In order to account for the relationship between finger-spelling abilities and reading ability Padden and Ramsey (2000) proposed that finger-spelling is a mediating tool providing a "platform" from which rudimentary phonological coding and reading development can be launched. Skilled finger-spelling involves an awareness that words in print are made up of segments. When skilled finger-spelling is achieved, signers may also develop a "speech surrogate" that maps onto finger-spelled forms. Finger-spelling may possibly interact with lip-reading and mouthing in the development of awareness about sound segments.

Taken together, these findings suggest that there are individual differences in the type of phonological coding strategy that people with a hearing impairment use. For some, this is based on visible phonology, such as the lip shapes of spoken words, or mouthing that is extensively emphasized in sign languages (Marschark, Lepoutre, & Bement, 1998). For others, finger-spelling may map onto written words.

## The Use of Orthographic Coding by Children with Hearing Impairment

Although as we have seen, children with a hearing impairment encounter difficulties in the development of phonological coding abilities, they seem as able as normally hearing children to learn about the orthographic regularities embodied in print. Sensitivity to orthotactic properties of written language emerges early among young normally hearing readers, as revealed by their performance in 'word-likeness' tasks (Cassar & Treiman, 1997; Pacton, Perruchet, Cleeremans, & Fayol, 2001). In a word-likeness task, children have to choose the more wordlike of two pronounceable nonwords. Orthographic sensitivity, such as the fact that a double consonant never occurs at the beginning of a word in French or in English, is demonstrated when children select the item from the pair that is more plausible orthographically. Such sensitivity to the statistical properties of the orthography may develop without awareness or explicit teaching, just as it occurs in implicit learning of letter sequences in an artificial grammar.

A small number of studies have investigated sensitivity to orthotactic regularities in children with hearing impairment. For instance, it has been shown that people with a hearing impairment show better recognition and recall of legal than illegal nonwords in reading tasks (Aaron et al., 1998; Gibson, Shurcliff, & Yonas, 1970; Hanson, 1982; Hanson, 1986). However, orthographic legality was confounded with pronounceability in these studies: items with legal orthographic patterns were pronounceable, whereas items with illegal patterns were not pronounceable. In a more recent study in which pronounceability was controlled, Transler and Reitsma (submitted) found that Dutch hearing-impaired and normally hearing groups more often chose items respecting orthotactic rules in a word-likeness task (e.g., they chose SCHAM rather than SGAM; SG is illegal at the beginning of a written Dutch word). Thus, children with profound hearing impairments of elementary school age demonstrate orthotactic sensitivity, despite deficits in oral language and phonological development.

Further evidence for proficiency with orthographic aspects of print comes from studies of spelling. Although children with a hearing impairment typically make a lower proportion of phonologically accurate spellings than normally hearing controls (except when they have been exposed early to Cued Speech), they make similar proportions of orthographic errors (Hanson et al., 1983; Leybaert & Lechat, 2001b; Sutcliffe et al., 1999; Transler & Reitsma, submitted). Olson and Caramazza (in press) reported that this was also the case among hearing-impaired students with good language. They theorized that the orthographic legality of the majority of these students' errors indicates that their spelling is constrained by abstract syllabic principles. They acknowledged that these student's errors do imply there were problems at the level of phonology: for example, "detective" was spelled "dectentive, dectictive, decetive, dective, delivatine, detecive, detervice, decetives." Their argument is in two steps: these errors could not be ascribed to impoverished phonological representations, because of their *diversity*; therefore, the orthographic legality of the second and third syllables cannot be driven by phonological information, and could be ascribed to abstract syllabic structure that can be relatively independent of the peripheral systems devoted to speech (Olson & Caramazza, in press; Olson & Nickerson, 2001). However, the question of how this abstract syllable structure could be acquired remains to be clarified.

## Neural Systems Underlying Reading in People with Hearing Impairment

To date, most of the evidence regarding the neural substrate of reading in people with a hearing impairment has come from the investigation of hemispheric specialization. It is known that the left hemisphere is usually specialized for the processing of written language in normally hearing children and adults. Perhaps not surprisingly, people with a hearing impairment who have abnormal early linguistic experience (and poor knowledge of grammar or phonology) generally display an abnormal pattern of hemispheric specialization. Neville and her collaborators (Neville, 1991; Neville & Bavelier, 2001; Neville & Mills, 1997; Neville, Mills, & Lawson, 1992), on the basis of a number of findings, proposed that a left-hemisphere specialization for the processing of language among the hearing impaired is determined by grammatical competence. First, normally hearing subjects showed behavioral and electrophysiological left-hemisphere asymmetry in a hemifield study requiring the identification of written words, while participants with a hearing impairment who had acquired ASL as a first language (and did not show full grammatical competence in English) did not.

More direct evidence was obtained in a study of event-related brain potentials (ERPs) during sentence reading. Closed class words (e.g., pronouns, adverbs, prepositions) elicited ERPs that were most evident over the left hemisphere (Broca's region), considered to be an index of grammatical processing. This specific response to closed class words was absent from ERPs of hearing-impaired subjects who scored more poorly on tests of English grammar, but was present in hearing-impaired subjects who scored at the higher levels on these tests. In contrast, the responses of the hearing impaired to lexical/semantic processing, elicited by content words, were indistinguishable from those of normally hearing participants. Moreover, when the same hearing-impaired subjects viewed sentences in their native language, ASL, the same region of the left hemisphere (Broca's area) was active as when native speakers of English processed written English sentences. These data suggest that the acquisition of grammatical competence in a language is a necessary condition for the development of left-hemisphere specialization for that language. Importantly, if the language is not acquired within a critical time window, as is the case for people with a hearing impairment learning English, the predisposition for left hemisphere language specialization may not be expressed. It should be noted, however, that findings from children with a hearing impairment are inconsistent. While some studies report a left hemispheric advantage for reading, others report a right hemispheric advantage, and others no hemispheric advantage at all (Conrad, 1979; D'Hondt, 2001; Gibson, 1988).

Hage, Alegria, and Périer (1991) proposed that exposure to Cued Speech could provide the conditions for the development of grammatical competence in oral language. If grammatical competence determines the development of left-hemisphere specialization, Cued Speech users should display clear evidence for left hemisphere specialization for the processing of written and Cued Speech languages. D'Hondt and Leybaert (2003) compared the lateralization pattern of Cued Speech users for the processing of written stimuli with that of normally hearing subjects matched for gender, reading level, and linguistic competence. In this study, participants had to compare a stimulus presented at the center of the screen (hereafter: central) to a stimulus presented next for 250 milliseconds in the left or right visual hemifield (hereafter: lateral), together with a digit presented centrally in order to fixate subjects' attention. Three tasks were used: two linguistic and one nonlinguistic. The nonlinguistic task involved a visual judgment: for example, are "EeeE" (central stimulus) and "Eeee" (lateral stimulus) the same or not? Performance on this task did not differ between left and right hemispheres, either in the hearing-impaired or the normally hearing participants.

The first linguistic task involved semantic judgments: for example, do CAT (central stimulus) and RABBIT belong to the same semantic category? A right visual field (left hemisphere) advantage was observed for this semantic decision task in hearing-impaired as well as in normally hearing subjects. The second linguistic task involved judging whether two orthographically dissimilar words rhymed: for example, do FEU and NOEUD rhyme (equivalent in English to: do BLUE and FEW rhyme)? In line with previous findings (Grossi, Coch, Coffey-Corina, Holcomb, & Neville, 2001; Rayman & Zaidel, 1991), normally hearing subjects showed a right visual field advantage (left hemisphere). However, a surprising finding was that no hemifield advantage was observed in Cued Speech users who were good at rhyming in a paper-and-pencil control task.

It seems possible, therefore, that the neural substrate activated during rhyme judgment is different in deaf Cued Speech users from that activated by normally hearing subjects. This would be consistent with the fact that the areas activated during speech-reading are not as left-lateralized in people with a hearing impairment as they are in hearing people. People with a congenital hearing impairment whose first language was spoken English showed significantly less left temporal activation than normally hearing subjects when performing a simple speech-reading number task (MacSweeney et al., 2001), suggesting that "hearing speech helps to develop the coherent adult speech perception system within the lateral areas of the left temporal lobe" (p. 437).

The rapid advance of brain imaging techniques means that soon it will be possible to determine the cortical organization of areas active during reading in people with a hearing impairment, and to study the effects of early modes of communication (Cued Speech, oral, sign language) on the neural systems involved in reading. As yet, no neuroimaging data are available from people with a hearing impairment during reading. The behavioral data strongly suggest that phonological codes are used less extensively by hearing-impaired than by normally hearing individuals. It therefore seems appropriate to ask the following questions: Which are the neural structures that underlie phonological representations and reading in the hearing impaired? Are these structures different in individuals who have underspecified representations than for those, like early Cued Speech users, who have well-specified representations? Are these structures related more to motor structures in the hearing impaired because of the role of speech articulation or finger-spelling in their development? Does over-reliance on orthographic coding in reading and spelling in some hearing-impaired participants have a neural signature? Are there different cortical areas activated in ASL signers and English Cued Speech users?

## Conclusions

Following three decades of reading research with hearing-impaired populations, there has been a perceptible shift in the types of questions that are being asked. The issue is no longer whether phonology is used by people with a hearing impairment during reading and spelling. There is no reason to doubt that children and adults with a hearing impairment develop phonological representations and access these representations during reading and spelling. The current view is that the phonological representations of hearing-impaired people are mainly based on *visual phonology* (lip-reading, Cued Speech, finger-spelling, and even alphabetic script). These observations extend the importance of phonology in reading by showing that phonological processing is involved in printed word recognition even in readers who are born with a profound hearing impairment. In the future, the increasing use of cochlear implants from early in life means that children with hearing impairment will rely more on auditory information to develop their language with consequent implications for the development of phonological representations, and reading acquisition by use of phoneme–grapheme correspondences.

Do studies of children with a hearing impairment show that reading development can follow alternative pathways, and can these pathways be modified (see Marschark & Harris, 1996, Perfetti & Sandak, 2000, for more detailed discussions)? Aghababian, Nazir, Lançon, & Tardy (2001) recorded the eye fixations within a word of a girl with a hearing impairment who was a beginning reader and demonstrated that she was using a logographic reading strategy, relying on salient visual features. This diagnosis led to a special training program being set up to enhance the child's understanding of grapheme–phoneme relations. The improvement of the child's reading skill was shown by a change in her fixation pattern, which became closer to that of the normally hearing readers. The general impression from the research literature is that hearing-impaired people who are good readers do get access to phonological information during reading, even if they are signers.

What emerges most impressively from this research area is the ability of the brain to reorganize to compensate for the sensory handicap imposed by a hearing impairment. The child's brain seems to be ready to process communicative gestures, whether these gestures are conveyed by the auditory or visual modality. The child's brain also seems ready to extract phonological primitives (auditory or visual) from these signals, provided there is an early and intensive experience with well-specified language.

Questions for the future concern the identification of the cortical areas involved in reading in people with a hearing impairment, and how activation of these is related to the modality through which language is perceived (auditory, visual), and to the precision of the linguistic information to which they are exposed. Identification of children with a hearing impairment who have specific written language deficits (dyslexia) is also on the research agenda.

# 21

# *Learning to Read with a Language Impairment*

## Margaret J. Snowling and Charles Hulme

Mattingly (1972) famously proposed that "reading is parasitic on speech." Mattingly was more or less right. In this chapter we propose a broader view: Reading is parasitic on language.

It is common to distinguish between four domains of spoken language: phonology, grammar, semantics, and pragmatics. For reading it is important to make a distinction between recoding (usually assessed by the accuracy of reading aloud) and comprehension (the adequacy of understanding text, usually assessed by questions about the meaning of a passage). In this chapter we will argue that *recoding* is parasitic on phonology and that *comprehension* is parasitic on grammar, semantics, and pragmatics as well as phonology (because phonology is essential for recoding, without which there can be no comprehension, Gough & Tunmer, 1986). So reading, in the sense of reading for meaning, depends on all four domains of oral language. We will develop this idea by considering the different patterns of reading impairment that can be observed in children who have a variety of different forms of language impairment.

## Models of Reading Development

To understand a disorder of development depends on having a model of normal development. To understand how different types of language impairment impact on the process of learning to read we need a model of how language processes operate to determine the course of normal reading development. We therefore need a model of reading that is explicitly concerned with learning and how this learning depends upon the integrity of underlying language skills. For this purpose the most useful theoretical framework is the "triangle" model that has guided the development of a variety of connectionist models of reading development (Harm & Seidenberg, 1999; Plaut, McClelland, Seidenberg, &

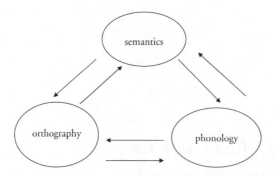

**Figure 21.1**   The triangle framework of reading development (after Seidenberg & McClelland, 1989).

Patterson, 1996; Seidenberg & McClelland, 1989; see Plaut, this volume). According to the triangle model, adult reading skills, and the development of these skills, depend upon interactions between three classes of representations in the brain. These three classes of representation deal with the sounds of words (phonology), the meaning of words (semantics), and the written form of words (orthography). As a result of training (learning to read) the model develops two interacting "pathways" that work together to read individual words. The "phonological pathway" maps orthography onto phonology: that is, given a written word as input it can be translated into its corresponding spoken form. The "semantic pathway" maps orthography onto phonology via semantics: a written word as input produces direct activation of the word's meaning, which in turn activates pronunciation (see figure 21.1).

An assumption of one variant of the triangle model (Plaut et al., 1996) is that at the beginning of reading development, the child's cognitive resources are devoted to establishing the "phonological pathway" (the system for mapping letters on to sounds) but that later, reading comes to rely increasingly on the "semantic pathway". The use of the semantic pathway is particularly important for the reading of exception words that the phonological pathway does not handle efficiently. Indeed, as training of the model proceeds there is a "division of labor" such that the semantic pathway begins to favor exception word reading, while the phonological pathway becomes specialized for reading novel words that the system has not encountered before. An important aspect of the model for present purposes is that activation from different pathways is pooled in deriving the pronunciation of a word; it is possible therefore to conceive of children with language difficulties that affect one set of representations, drawing on other representations and resources in order to learn to read.

A limitation of the triangle model is that it focuses exclusively on single word reading (though a pathway from context to semantics is envisaged; Seidenberg & McClelland, 1989). Bishop and Snowling (2004) have proposed that it is useful, particularly when considering the reading development of children with oral language difficulties, to expand the model to incorporate interactions between semantic representations and other sources of linguistic knowledge, namely grammar and discourse level processing (see figure 21.2).

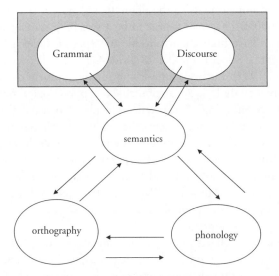

**Figure 21.2**   An extended version of the Seidenberg and McClelland triangle framework (after Bishop & Snowling, 2004).

As Share (1995, 1999) has emphasized, children make use of sentence contexts in combination with decoding rules to read new words and to establish new orthographic representations. He referred to this strategy as a "self-teaching device". Clearly the operation of such a device depends not only upon the availability of a phonological strategy (the phonological pathway in the triangle model) and on knowledge of existing orthographic representations, but also on the child's ability to activate semantic and phonological representations through sensitivity to the grammar of the language and the contexts in which specific sentences occur. It follows that an impairment of these "higher-level" language resources might impede reading development in some children with language impairments. As noted earlier it is important to distinguish between recoding and comprehension in reading. Reading disorders can affect word-level recoding skills (reading accuracy) or reading comprehension or both sets of skills. The model predicts that, while children with pervasive language impairments will experience problems of reading accuracy and comprehension, selective deficits are possible in children whose component language skills (i.e., phonological or semantic representations) are selectively impaired.

## Developmental Disorders of Reading

As other chapters in this volume have made clear, there are two different forms of developmental reading problems that are both common, and now relatively well understood: dyslexia (a specific impairment in recoding) and reading comprehension impairment (see chapters by Nation, Perfetti, Landi & Oakhill, and Vellutino & Fletcher). Dyslexia appears to arise from impairments to the phonological system (see Stanovich & Siegel, 1994; Snowling, 2000a). This may appear to be a sweeping statement given the extensive discussions there have been about possible subtypes of dyslexia (see e.g. Castles & Coltheart, 1993; Manis, Seidenberg, Doi, McBride-Chang, & Petersen, 1996, Stanovich, Siegel, & Gottardo, 1997), but we simply claim for the moment that the vast majority of cases of developmental dyslexia are attributable to a phonological deficit that may vary in severity (Griffiths & Snowling, 2002). Where the phonological deficit is circumscribed and does not affect other language systems the reading deficit typically is characterized by severe problems with nonword reading in the face of better developed word reading skills (Rack, Snowling, & Olson, 1992). In contrast, the majority of studies that have examined regular and exception word reading in dyslexia have revealed a pattern of performance that is normal for reading level (Metsala, Stanovich, & Brown, 1998). Together these findings suggest that the phonological pathway is impaired in dyslexia but the semantic pathway operates normally.

Children who decode well yet have specific difficulties with reading comprehension show a very different language profile from that of dyslexic children (see Nation, this volume, for a review). Although poor comprehenders' phonological skills are normal (Stothard & Hulme, 1995), they show deficits in a wide range of language skills outside of the phonological domain that are not simply a facet of low IQ. In particular, their vocabulary knowledge is impoverished and they have especially poor understanding of the meanings of abstract and low-frequency words. The assets and deficits of poor comprehenders point to a likely problem at the level of semantic representation, in contrast to the problems of phonological representation characteristic of dyslexic children.

Within the triangle model, children who have weak semantic skills should have particular difficulty in the later stages of learning to read when the use of the semantic pathway increases in importance. In English, this would translate to a problem in exception word reading and in the development of automatic word recognition skills. Nation and Snowling (1998a) gave poor comprehenders and reading-age matched controls sets of words to read that varied in frequency and regularity. Although the two groups read high-frequency words equally well, the poor comprehenders made more errors when reading words of low-frequency. There was also a trend for the poor comprehenders to read exception words less well and more slowly than controls. These findings are striking given that the two groups were similar in their decoding ability, as measured by a nonword reading test, and they did not differ in phonological skills. They are consistent with the hypothesis that poor comprehenders have a subtle impairment of the semantic pathway.

Differences between children with dyslexia and poor comprehenders are much more marked when reading in context (Nation & Snowling, 1998b). Although children with dyslexia are not fluent readers, they often show extensive use of comprehension monitoring strategies and self-correction to ensure they understand what they read (Frith & Snowling, 1983). In contrast, the primary impairment for poor comprehenders is in reading comprehension processes. They show a range of deficits encompassing difficulties with text integration and inference processing and they frequently fail to monitor their comprehension adequately (Yuill & Oakhill, 1991; Perfetti et al., this volume).

The finding that children with dyslexia have a selective deficit of the phonological pathway and poor comprehenders a selective deficit of the semantic pathway provides

strong evidence for the psychological reality of the two systems. However, pure dissociations are rare in developmental disorders (Bishop, 1997b). It is far more likely that the
phonological and semantic systems work in interaction with each other, either to facilitate performance (as in the case of semantic activation boosting decoding skills), or else
to compromise development, as in the case of "garden-variety" poor readers who might
be considered to have impairments of both systems (Gough & Tunmer, 1986; Stanovich
& Siegel, 1994).

## Reading Development in Children with Oral Language Impairments

### Children with speech difficulties

Childhood speech disorders affect articulation and to varying degrees the intelligibility of
a child's speech. Speech disorders can occur in isolation or be accompanied by impairments of language processes (e.g., vocabulary and grammar). There are a number of
different types of developmental speech disorder and the distinctions between them are
debated (Rapin & Allen, 1987). An important distinction is between speech difficulties
that arise because of problems with peripheral aspects of articulation (such as those that
accompany cleft palate or apraxia) and those that are associated with disorders of the
phonological system (that include speech sound disorders). There is good evidence that
peripheral speech difficulties carry a low risk of reading problems (e.g., Stackhouse, 1982).
However, the strong association between phonological skills and reading abilities (particularly recoding skills) suggests that children with phonological disorders of speech
should be at high risk of reading difficulties (see also Larrivee & Catts, 1999). Although
there is some evidence for this hypothesis (Bird, Bishop, & Freeman, 1995; Stackhouse
& Snowling, 1992), the literature presents a mixed picture and a reasonable summary of
the evidence is that the risk is lower than might be anticipated.

Catts (1993) reported one of the first studies to highlight a difference between impairments of phonological awareness and of speech production as risk factors for reading
impairments. This study followed children with speech-language impairments from
kindergarten through into second grade. Although children with widespread language
impairments in kindergarten developed reading difficulties in first grade, a surprising
finding was that children with pure speech difficulties did not. Similarly, the literacy outcomes for 12 children classified as having isolated expressive phonological problems at 4
years by Bishop and Edmundson (1987) were good. As a group these children did well
in reading and spelling tests at 8.5 years, and all but one had normal literacy skills (Bishop
& Adams, 1990). In a follow-up study involving 10 of these children in adolescence,
Stothard, Snowling, Bishop, Chipchase, and Kaplan (1998) found that none fulfilled
criteria for specific reading difficulties (dyslexia) and only one had a significant spelling
problem.

Nathan, Stackhouse, Goulandris, and Snowling (2004) assessed the risk of reading
impairments in relation to speech disorders in a study following the progress of children

with primary expressive speech difficulties from the age of 4 to 6;09 years. Nineteen of these children had pure speech difficulties (assessed by the accuracy of speech articulation on the Edinburgh Articulation Test) and another 19 children had speech problems accompanied by language difficulties (assessed on a battery of language measures including measures of receptive vocabulary, receptive grammar, and expressive grammar). These groups were compared to 19 typically developing controls. In line with the previous findings of Catts, Fey, Tomblin,and Zhang (2002), the risk of literacy difficulties was greater in the group with speech and language difficulties and these children displayed deficits in phoneme awareness at 6 years. In contrast, the literacy development of children with isolated speech problems was not significantly different from that of controls, as Stothard et al. (1998) had also found. An important finding of this study was that preschool language ability (rather than speech skill) was a unique predictor of phoneme awareness at 5 years 8 months. Thereafter, phoneme awareness together with early reading skill predicted literacy outcome just before the children were 7 years of age. In fact, neither speech perception nor speech production processes predicted variation in reading accuracy or spelling skills once phoneme awareness was controlled.

There is, however, an important caveat to these findings. It transpired that the speech difficulties of some of the children in both subgroups with speech impairments resolved between the ages of 4 and 7 years. The outcome for those with persisting speech problems is worthy of note because all but four had poor phoneme awareness at 6;07 years (and the four who did not had normal word-level reading skills). Hence, the results converge with those of Bird et al. (1995) who reported that the majority of 5-year-old children with primary expressive speech difficulties displayed reading problems accompanied by phonological awareness deficits at 6;07 and 7;07 years. In a similar vein, Carroll and Snowling (2004) reported that 5-year-old children with persisting speech difficulties showed impairments on tests of letter knowledge, phonological awareness, and early word recognition compared with typically developing controls.

However, in contrast to this, a recent study by Raitano, Pennington, Tunick, Boada, and Shriberg (2004) investigated the preliteracy skills of children with speech sound disorders without any significant language impairment (a group of children who were broadly similar to the speech-only impaired children studied by Nathan et al., 2004). They reported, in contrast to the findings of Nathan et al. (2004), that even children with isolated speech sound disorder whose speech problems had resolved by age 5 years 8 months had impaired phonological awareness skills, but not impaired letter knowledge, compared to age matched controls. This finding comes from a relatively large group of children (n = 49 SSD, 41 Controls), and the explanation for these discrepant findings is not clear. One obvious possibility is differences in age of assessment between the Raitano et al. and Nathan et al. studies. It will be important to see whether the phonological awareness problems among children with resolved speech difficulties reported by Raitano et al. (2004) persist as this sample gets older, and whether such problems lead to significant reading problems. Another relevant study by Leitao, Hogben, and Fletcher (1997) examined the phonological awareness skills of children with pure speech disorders and found a bimodal distribution of scores. Further examination revealed that only those with deviant speech showed poor phonological awareness (those who showed normal but delayed speech processes did not). Thus, another possible explanation for differences between studies is the proportion of children with deviant speech processes. It will be important for future research to take into account qualitative as well as quantitative aspects of speech development and disorder when assessing the risk of reading problems.

In summary, it is clear that there are still some outstanding questions relating to the risk of reading impairment in children with speech difficulties. Nonetheless, the findings to date are in line with a hypothesis proposed by Bird et al. (1995) that children who have speech difficulties *that persist to the point at which they need to use phonological skills for learning to read* are at high risk of reading problems (see also Bishop & Adams, 1990). There is however a rider to this conclusion: it appears to be critical that that these children's speech difficulties are accompanied by poor phoneme awareness; persisting speech difficulties without deficits in phoneme awareness (which only occurred in 4/19 children) do not appear to impact on reading (Nathan et al., 2004). Within the triangle model, what might be considered critical is the state of readiness of phonological representations as a resource for reading acquisition, and problems with phoneme awareness appears to be a highly diagnostic of problems in the phonological representations that are necessary for learning to read.

## Children with language impairments

The term "specific language impairment" (SLI) is used to refer to children whose language skills are significantly impaired for their age but whose nonverbal ability (nonverbal IQ) is within the normal range. The case of poor comprehenders, discussed above, suggests that children who have vocabulary impairments will have difficulties with reading comprehension. When language problems are more widespread, and encompass problems of phonology, grammar, and pragmatics, as is often the case in children with SLI, it is reasonable to expect that this will affect a broader range of reading processes and the reading profile should reflect the balance of strengths and weaknesses seen on oral language tasks. In line with this view, the literacy outcomes for children with language problems is variable and depends on a number of factors, including the persistence of the language impairment.

Bishop and Adams (1990) conducted one of the first studies to look at reading prognosis in relation to the age at which preschool language impairments resolve. This study assessed the reading skills at 8.5 years of children diagnosed as having a specific language impairment (SLI) some 4 years earlier (Bishop & Edmundson, 1987). Contrary to the prevailing view that reading difficulties are the developmental consequence of an earlier language delay, children whose language impairments had resolved by 5.5 years did not show reading difficulties. In fact, they performed as well as age-matched controls on tests of nonword reading and spelling, as well as on standardized measures of reading accuracy, spelling, and reading comprehension at 8.5 years. In contrast, children with persisting language impairments had reading problems, though, interestingly, their problems were not of reading accuracy. Rather, a relatively high proportion of children with persistent SLI had poor reading comprehension scores in relation to performance IQ and therefore fit the "poor comprehender" profile. In contrast, only 6% of the preschoolers had specific decoding deficits akin to dyslexia (see Catts et al., 2002, for similar findings).

In a longer-term follow-up of Bishop and Adams's cohort, Stothard et al. (1998) assessed language and literacy outcomes at 15 years of age. As a group, adolescents with a preschool history of SLI performed less well on tests of reading, spelling, and reading comprehension than an age-matched control sample. Of particular interest was the outcome of children who had been free of reading impairments at 8.5 years (the group who had resolved their oral language difficulties). Given the predictions of the triangle model, it was plausible that, as the range of vocabulary to be read increased and stretched their limited language resources, these children would experience late-emerging reading problems (e.g., Scarborough & Dobrich, 1990). In keeping with this prediction, although the children with resolved SLI performed as well as controls on spoken language tests, they had difficulties with reading, spelling, and reading comprehension. They also showed impairments of nonword reading and spelling (which had not been apparent at 8.5 years) and of phonological processing, as measured by tasks that tap verbal working memory, namely spoonerisms (a test of phonological awareness), and nonword and sentence repetition tasks. Furthermore, the proportion of children in the sample who now fulfilled criteria for dyslexia had increased from 6 to 24% (Snowling, Bishop, & Stothard, 2000). In short, even though these children had made a good start with literacy development, their later progress had been less good. Within the triangle model, it seems that these children had run into difficulties with the phonological and semantic language resources required as reading development progressed.

The subgroup of children who had persisting specific language impairments at 8.5 years had pervasive problems with word-level reading and reading comprehension at 15 years, and their spelling was weak. In fact, their language skills (both oral and written) were now as poor as those of children with more general learning difficulties, indexed by lower Performance IQ. One possible interpretation is that their poor language had contributed to a decline in literacy skills over the middle school years and in turn, their limited reading skills (and probable limited reading experience) had failed to promote the growth of oral vocabulary and related language skills.

## Possible relationships between phonological and semantic skills

Our discussion so far has focused on the role of phonological and broader language skills (particularly semantic skills as indexed by measures of vocabulary) in learning to read. Evidence from the study of poor comprehenders and children with decoding difficulties (dyslexia) provides good evidence for a degree of modularity in the developing language system. However, it seems plausible that developmentally there will be important interactions between the phonological and semantic systems. Before leaving the issue of literacy development in children with oral language difficulties, it is therefore appropriate to discuss the possible developmental interplay between phonological and semantic skills, since these resources are critical to the triangle model.

Consideration of the reading development of children with language difficulties brings into focus an important issue, namely, the origins of phoneme awareness. We have seen that children with expressive speech difficulties are at low risk of phoneme awareness deficits, unless they persist or occur with accompanying language impairments (Nathan et al., 2004; but see Raitano et al. [2004] for a contrasting pattern). These findings imply that it is oral language development that precipitates phoneme awareness, and children with language delay are slow to acquire phonological awareness (see also Scarborough, 1990). Similar findings emerge from a longitudinal study of children at family risk of dyslexia in which phoneme awareness skills at 6 years were predicted by a composite of vocabulary and expressive language skills measured at 4 years (Snowling, Gallagher, & Frith, 2003). Furthermore in normally developing children Carroll, Snowling, Hulme, and Stevenson (2003) showed that vocabulary knowledge had an indirect effect on the development of phoneme awareness at 4 years, mediated via rhyme and syllable awareness and articulatory proficiency (as measured by the percentage of phonemes produced correctly in a naming task).

The idea that vocabulary development fuels the development of phoneme awareness has been proposed by a number of theorists. Walley (1993), for example, proposed that vocabulary growth brings about a change in the nature of phonological representations, causing them to change from holistic to segmental in form (see also Gombert [1992] for a related but somewhat different view). According to this argument, storing the phonological forms of many thousands of vocabulary items as undifferentiated holistic patterns is inefficient. There is therefore pressure on the phonological system to develop segmental (phonemically structured) representations. Such a proposal might be true: over a fairly narrow developmental period (roughly 3 to 6 years), there is a sharp growth in the number of distinct phonological word forms that must be learned. Presumably such learning is driven primarily by a growth in semantic knowledge (i.e., the need to store the phonological forms that correspond to the semantic forms for words that are understood, in preparation for their use when speaking). In this view therefore, an impairment in learning the semantic forms of words early in development would carry with it inevitable knock-on effects on the development of phonological representations.

However, theoretically such a view might still be consistent with a highly modular view of the language system (the changes in the phonological system that bring about the development of phonemically structured representations are essentially internal to the phonological system, even though they may be driven by increasing semantic knowledge).

For present purposes, the important point is that children with poor oral language skills may not only experience problems within the semantic pathway as a direct consequence of vocabulary limitations; they may also be susceptible to deficits in the operation of the phonological pathway as an indirect consequence of these problems. One possible objection to this proposal comes from studies of poor comprehenders, who have limited vocabulary skills but normal phonological skills (e.g., Stothard & Hulme, 1995). Why do these children not have phoneme awareness deficits resulting from poor vocabulary? A possible answer is that such children might be slow to develop phonological skills, but that these problems have been overcome by the age at which these children are studied (typically in the middle-to-late primary school years, by which time their vocabulary knowledge, though limited in relation to other children of the same age, may have grown beyond the point at which phonemic restructuring of phonological representations was achieved).

To summarize, learning to read demands the interplay of different language skills that themselves may interact. Reading acquisition is a dynamic process that draws differentially on different language resources in different developmental phases. The literacy outcomes of children with oral language difficulties are not easy to predict; they will depend upon individual differences in cognitive skills, modified by how they are taught to read (Vellutino et al., 1996). However, thus far our discussion has focused on children whose language difficulties are specific in the sense that they occur in the absence of generally low cognitive abilities. In these children therefore we are essentially looking at relatively modular deficits – the typical dyslexic child provides an excellent example of a highly modular deficit in phonological skills in the absence of deficits in other language or other cognitive domains. A less extensive body of research has addressed the reading skills of children who show language impairments co-occurring with general learning difficulties (low IQ). An important question is the extent to which the triangle framework we have used so far can also provide an explanation for the patterns of reading impairment seen in these children with general learning difficulties.

## Language and Reading Impairments in Children with General Learning Difficulties

### Down syndrome

Down syndrome (trisomy 21) is the most frequent human chromosomal abnormality occurring in about 1.5 per 1,000 births. Children with Down syndrome usually have full-scale IQs in the 50–70 range and they often have difficulties with language acquisition (including phonological problems) that are more severe than predicted by their non-verbal abilities. Typically language production difficulties are more severe than language comprehension problems in people with Down syndrome (Chapman, 1995; Fowler, 1990). While their lexical knowledge is relatively strong, their language problems encompass syntactic, conversational, and narrative difficulties. Deficits in expressive grammatical skills have been reported to arise early and be particularly severe (Singer Harris, Bellugi, Bates, Jones, & Rossen, 1997). There is also good evidence that children with Down syndrome show relatively severe deficits in phonological memory skills that are highly persistent and tend to become more severe as they get older (Hulme & MacKenzie, 1992; Jarrold, Baddeley, & Hewes, 1999).

Studies of the cognitive processes underlying reading in children with Down syndrome burgeoned in the 1990s following the controversial claims of Cossu and Marshall (1990) that phonological awareness "is not a prerequisite of learning to read" (p. 21). They based this claim on the findings from a single case study of TA, an Italian boy aged 8 years 11 months, with Down syndrome. TA's mental age was 4 years 6 months and he had an IQ of 57. His memory span was poor with a digit span of 2, but he was considered to be a good reader. He attained a perfect score when reading words and nonwords that varied in word length and orthographic complexity, but his phonological awareness was poor and he was not aware of phonemes. On the face of it, TA's profile would appear to be inconsistent with the view that phonological skills are critical for learning to read (recode). In a second study, Cossu, Rossini, and Marshall (1993) bolstered their argument with data from 11 children with Down syndrome (DS) who were compared with 10 younger normal readers of similar reading skill. The children with DS did less well on tests of phoneme synthesis, oral spelling, phoneme counting, and phoneme deletion than the reading age-matched controls, even though they could read words and nonwords just as well.

Subsequent studies have not come to the same conclusions. Fowler (1995) studied English-speaking young adults with DS between the ages of 17 and 25 years, whose reading levels ranged from kindergarten to twelfth grade (Fowler, Doherty, & Boynton, 1995). Fowler classified participants into one of four groups based on their decoding skills. *Novice readers* were able to decode 2 or fewer nonwords. *Emerging readers* and *developing readers* could decode between 3 and 10 nonwords and between 11 and 29 nonwords, respectively. *Skilled readers* showed even more advanced decoding skill although there were too few cases to properly evaluate this possibility. Each of the participants in Fowler's (1995) study was given tasks tapping phoneme awareness, verbal memory, and word naming from line drawings. Although performance was at or below the 6-year level on phonological awareness tasks, there was a significant relationship between phonological skills and reading ability that remained strong when general cognitive ability was controlled. Phonemic awareness accounted for 36% of the variance in word recognition and 49% of the variance in decoding nonwords. Furthermore, there was not a single individual in the group who had the ability to read without possessing phoneme awareness. Thus, although the phonological skills of children with DS may not develop to the same degree as those of normal children, it is incorrect to suppose they do not possess these skills. Similar findings were reported by Cardoso-Martins and Frith (2001), who found that Portuguese-speaking persons with Down syndrome could detect phonemes as well as reading-age matched controls but had more difficulty in explicitly manipulating the phonological components of spoken words. Taken together these findings suggest that recoding skills in children with DS develop slowly and that the phonological impairments observed in these children are critical to explaining their problems in learning to read (recode).

Perhaps more interestingly, a number of recent studies have suggested that there may be highly specific deficits in the pattern of phonological development shown in children with Down syndrome. Cardoso-Martins, Michalik, and Pollo (2002) studied a group of Brazilian children and adults with Down syndrome (39 readers and 30 nonreaders). The readers with Down syndrome found a rime detection task significantly more difficult than two phoneme detection tasks that involved matching initial or medial phonemes of words to a standard. A similar trend was seen in the nonreaders, although the majority of them were unable to complete the phonological awareness tasks.

In a similar vein, Gombert (1992) examined the performance of French-speaking readers with Down syndrome on phonological awareness tasks requiring judgments at the levels of the rime and phoneme. The performance of the group with Down syndrome was relatively poorer on tasks requiring rime judgment, rime oddity, and phoneme synthesis than on tasks requiring more explicit phonological awareness involving phoneme counting, phoneme deletion, and phoneme spelling. Lastly, in three studies of English-speaking children with Down syndrome, Snowling, Hulme, and Mercer (2002) found that the group with Down syndrome performed only at chance level on tasks requiring rime awareness, while performance on initial phoneme detection was normal in relation to verbal mental age. Taken together, these findings suggest that there is a highly specific impairment of rime awareness in Down syndrome despite relatively well-developed phoneme skills.

It might be that the impoverished educational opportunities for children with DS account for this difference between them and normally developing children. However, it seems more likely that the rime deficit arises from the language impairment characterizing DS. One interpretation that we favor is that children with Down syndrome show severe and pervasive phonological problems, and that the rudimentary phoneme awareness skills observed in these children (the children studied by Snowling et al. [2002], could only identify word initial phonemes) develop as a consequence of learning to use letter-sound correspondences when they are taught to read and spell (cf. Morais, Cary, Alegria, & Bertelson, 1979). Longitudinal studies are needed to investigate this possibility. However, if this is the case, given their weak semantic and phonological skills, then it is unlikely that children with DS are capable of developing advanced decoding skills in reading. A deficiency in rime awareness would be expected to limit their ability to learn the spelling patterns recurring in words sharing rimes. Moreover, impairments of syntactic skills may limit their ability to use contextual cues to compensate in reading text. Thus, children with DS can develop limited recoding skills, but these are severely limited in most cases and reading comprehension is typically even more impaired (see Byrne, MacDonald, & Buckley, 2002).

## Language and reading skills in children with Williams syndrome

Williams syndrome is a very rare (approximately 1 in 20,000 births) genetic disorder caused by a deletion on chromosome 7 (7q11.2). Most children with Williams syndrome have IQs in the 50–65 range. These children show a contrasting pattern of cognitive strengths and deficits compared to those observed in children with Down syndrome. Many nonlinguistic functions, such as spatial cognition, number, planning, and problem solving are seriously impaired in children with Williams syndrome (Arnold, Yule, & Martin, 1985; Bellugi, Bihrle, Jernigan, Trauner, & Doherty, 1990), whereas language is often surprisingly good in comparison (Bellugi et al., 1990; Clahsen & Almazan, 1998). This effectively is the opposite pattern to that found in children with Down syndrome.

However, it is not true to claim that language skills are normal in children with Williams syndrome. They do appear to have relatively good phonological skills, and perform well on measures of phonological short-term memory (but very poorly on measures of visuospatial short-term memory; the opposite pattern to that found in Down syndrome, see Jarrold et al., 1999; Wang & Bellugi, 1994). However, children with Williams syndrome appear to have problems in learning vocabulary (Singer Harris et al., 1997) and weaknesses in both morphosyntax and semantics have been shown to occur (Karmiloff-Smith et al., 1997; Karmiloff-Smith et al., 1998; Mervis & Bertrand, 1997; Stevens & Karmiloff-Smith, 1997; Volterra et al., 1996).

Given their intact phonological skills, a natural prediction is that the development of recoding skills in reading should be relatively good in children with Williams syndrome. A number of studies support this prediction. Pagon, Bennett, LaVeck, Stewart, and Johnson (1987) examined the single word reading skills of 9 individuals with Williams syndrome between the ages of 10 and 20. They found that reading was the strongest area of school performance and that standard scores on the reading test exceeded full-scale IQ in all 9 cases. However, Howlin, Davies, and Udwin (1998) examined the cognitive skills of 67 adults with Williams syndrome, with IQ scores in the 50–69 range. The mean basic reading age obtained was 8 years, 8 months (range 72–216 months), the reading comprehension age equivalent was 7 years, 2 months (range 72–132 months) and the mean spelling age was 7 years, 7 months (range 75–150 months). It is clear therefore, as would be expected from the profile of language and other cognitive skills seen in people with Williams syndrome, that reading skills are generally poor in this group, but that recoding skills are in advance of reading comprehension skills.

Laing, Hulme, Grant, and Karmiloff-Smith (2001) examined the reading skills of 15 children with Williams syndrome and 15 controls matched for verbal mental age (using a test of receptive vocabulary). These groups had equivalent single word reading skills (recoding skills) (the mean chronological age of the group with Williams syndrome was around 15.5 years and their word recognition skills were on average around the 6.5 year level). In line with the findings of Howlin, et al. (1998), single word reading skills in the children with Williams syndrome were in advance of their reading comprehension skills. Variations in single word reading ability in the children with Williams syndrome were predicted by variations in general cognitive ability (verbal and nonverbal) but variations in phonological skills only appeared weakly related to reading ability in this group. Laing et al. (2001) went on to show that in a new word learning task that modeled the processes involved in learning a sight vocabulary in reading (Laing & Hulme, 1999) the children with Williams syndrome were sensitive to phonology, but their learning was little affected by a semantic variable (word imageability). These results suggest that children with Williams syndrome place heavy reliance on the phonological pathway when learning to read new words, but appear to use the semantic pathway much less than normally developing children of the same mental age and level of reading skill. This is the pattern that would be expected given their relatively weaker semantic, than phonological, skills.

In summary the pattern of severely impaired reading skills shown in children with Down and Williams syndrome appear to be broadly in the line with what would be expected given these children's underlying language weaknesses. More specifically, the severe phonological, semantic and syntactic difficulties in children with Down syndrome appear to present obstacles to learning to read. In contrast, children with Williams syndrome have less impaired phonological skills and their word recognition (recoding) skills are correspondingly better than those of children with Down syndrome. Children with Williams syndrome appear to acquire a sight vocabulary in reading with little support from the semantic pathway, however, and they show problems in reading comprehension as would be expected given their weak semantic skills.

## Autism spectrum disorders

Autism is a severe developmental disorder with a strong genetic component, affecting 6 per 1,000 children. The core features of autism comprise a deficit in reciprocal social interaction, a qualitative impairment in communication, and a markedly restricted repertoire of activities and interests (Frith, 2003). Each of the core symptoms of autism can, however, vary in severity and the term "autism spectrum disorders" has come to be used to capture this variability. Autism spectrum disorders can occur at all levels of general cognitive ability; children with higher IQs are likely to be diagnosed with Asperger's syndrome or high-functioning autism; in contrast, classic and atypical autism more often co-occur with general learning difficulties (low IQ).

Language delays and abnormalities are common in autism, although many children with autism develop speech following an initial period of limited communication. However, even when speech is fluent, most children with autism have enduring problems with language use and are considered to have pragmatic language impairments (Bishop & Norbury, 2002). Such problems are difficult to characterize and diagnose, but they include the overliteral use and interpretation of language, poor inferencing skills, and a failure to appreciate the appropriate level of detail needed to convey a message to a listener. Since many "higher-level" aspects of reading comprehension are likely to depend on pragmatic language skills, we can predict that children with autism should have problems with reading comprehension, even if their recoding skills (built on fluent speech skills) are normal.

Some limited evidence suggests that pragmatic language deficits may indeed be related to problems with reading comprehension. Norbury and Bishop (2002) studied the story comprehension abilities of four groups of children: those with typical specific language impairment (SLI-T), children with pragmatic language impairments who were not autistic (PLI), children with high-functioning autism (HFA), and typically developing controls. The comprehension task involved both literal and inferential questions. Children with pragmatic difficulties related to autism were more likely to have specific difficulties in inference-making ability, which, in turn, appeared to compromise reading comprehension.

In a similar vein, Snowling and Frith (1986) assessed the ability of children with autism, who were fluent readers, to integrate the meanings of sentences at the text level, a skill that requires the use of cohesive inferences. In this study, children were presented with a story to read in which they had to select words to fill "gaps" in the text. In each case, the child made a choice from three words, all of the same grammatical class but varying in their appropriateness to the context. One alternative fitted both the sentence and the story context (and was designated the story-appropriate choice), the second fitted the local context but not the story as a whole (the sentence-appropriate choice), the third was semantically anomalous. Thus, a story about a beaver contained the sentence *their mother/friends/room led the young beavers to the pond*. The child had to select the story appropriate choice "mother." If they chose "friends," this was the sentence level alternative, while "room" was inappropriate.

Children with autism with IQs in the normal range performed as well as typically developing children, usually choosing the story-appropriate completion. However, children of lower IQ performed less well than younger mental age-matched controls; although they could reject the implausible alternatives, they were evidently not following the story as it developed and hence did not show a systematic tendency to choose the story-appropriate alternative in preference to the sentence-appropriate alternative. Performance on this test requires the child to go beyond the information given to make inferences across the text as a whole. The results suggest that these children have difficulty with the processes that bring about text cohesion. They also had difficulty with text monitoring processes. This was tested by asking them to read through a text, embedded in which were anomalous words, for example the *hedgehog could smell the scent of electric flowers*, where *electric* did not fit the sentence context. Compared with younger children of similar vocabulary age, they had more difficulty in detecting the text anomalies, and were just as likely to strike out a plausible as an implausible word.

Taken together, these findings suggest that children with autism take less account of context when reading than normal readers. A clear example of this tendency was demonstrated by Snowling and Frith (1986) who showed that children with autism spectrum disorders were less likely to modify the pronunciation of homographs (e.g. *tear, lead*) according to context than normal readers of the same level of reading skill. This was true even though it could be demonstrated that they knew the pronunciation of both forms of the homograph (Frith & Snowling, 1983, see also Happé, 1997). Thus, their difficulty could not be linked to an absence of semantic knowledge for the words in question; rather it seemed that their reading system was operating as though decoupled from the control processes outside of the triangle model that monitor and regulate reading through the use of context.

An intriguing possibility is that this same "decoupling" process accounts for "hyperlexia", an extreme variant of the poor comprehender profile seen in some children with autism (as well as some nonautistic children). The proper definition of hyperlexia remains the subject of debate (Grigorenko, Klin, & Volkmar, 2003). We will use the term here to refer to unexpectedly good single word reading ability (recoding) in the presence of poor comprehension. Hyperlexic children often learn to read before they receive any formal instruction, and at a rate much in excess of that to be predicted from their IQ. Hyperlexia is typically characterized by a preoccupation with reading to the exclusion of meaning (Healy, 1982). To date, however, much of the research on hyperlexia has been at the level of case-studies which, although informative about the general features of the syndrome, have not focused in any detail on the reading mechanisms involved (see Grigorenko et al., 2003; Nation, 1999, for reviews). The field is ripe for further research.

In summary some autistic children, and some nonautistic children who share the pragmatic language difficulties that are common in autism, show problems of reading comprehension that appear to be related to their weak pragmatic language skills. A small minority of these children appear to develop an obsession with reading aloud. They practice reading a great deal and develop good (often age-appropriate) recoding skills coupled with severe comprehension deficits. In terms of the triangle model such children appear to represent the unusual pattern of a highly developed phonological pathway that may be decoupled from the wider cognitive system and the effects context exerts through the semantic pathway. This pattern appears to develop from relatively good phonological skills coupled with an obsessive interest, and a great deal of practice, in reading aloud.

## Conclusions

Reading is parasitic upon language. Phonological language skills are the foundation on which recoding skills (translating orthography into phonology) are based. Although basic recoding skills may develop by an exclusive reliance on phonological processes (as in hyperlexia, and perhaps in some children in the very early stages of normal reading development), there is evidence that that the refinement of recoding skills is promoted by semantic and syntactic language skills. Recoding skills are necessary, but not sufficient, for reading comprehension (Gough & Tunmer, 1986). A critical constraint on reading comprehension is vocabulary knowledge, or, more broadly semantic skills. In addition, adequate comprehension of what is read, like adequate comprehension of spoken language, requires adequate grammatical and pragmatic language skills. We believe that the evidence reviewed here, focusing on reading development in children with various types of language impairments, provides evidence for the critical roles of phonological, semantic, grammatical, and pragmatic language skills in reading development.

## Note

This chapter was written with the support of a grant from the Health Foundation UK. We thank Julia Carroll for her comments on the chapter.

# 22

# *Acquired Disorders of Reading*

## Matthew A. Lambon Ralph and Karalyn Patterson

## Introduction

"The problem is, I don't know what some of these words mean"
Patient EK with semantic dementia

One of the many fascinations of working with neurological patients is their uncanny ability to highlight the key deficit that underpins their poor performance on a range of specific mental activities. Semantic dementia is a neurodegenerative condition of the temporal lobes bilaterally that results in a selective yet progressive loss of conceptual knowledge (Hodges, Patterson, Oxbury, & Funnell, 1992; Snowden, Goulding, & Neary, 1989). It is not uncommon for such patients to produce statements very similar to that noted for patient EK above. Although not unexpected in the context of defining a word's meaning, these frustrations are often expressed, as they were in this instance, when patients are simply asked to transform or maintain the surface form of the items; for example, in reading aloud, delayed repetition, or immediate serial recall tasks. As we will argue in this chapter, patient EK quite rightly diagnosed that her difficulties with a range of simple language activities were all due to a common underlying cause. More specifically, there is a growing body of evidence that the major types of acquired dyslexia (and other aphasic deficits) can all be described in relation to impairments of a limited set of interacting, primary brain systems (Patterson & Lambon Ralph, 1999).

An important aspect of this approach is that acquired dyslexias are considered in the context of the patients' other language and cognitive deficits with the assumption that there are important relationships between them. This represents a recent development in the methodology applied to acquired dyslexia and cognitive neuropsychology more generally. We begin with a short overview of the classic cognitive neuropsychological approach to acquired disorders of reading and proceed to discuss this more contemporary approach in which data from such patients have been reinterpreted within a highly interactive, computationally explicit model of reading.

## The classic cognitive neuropsychological approach to acquired dyslexias

The study of acquired reading disorders has played a central role in the development of cognitive neuropsychology ever since the seminal study of Marshall and Newcombe (1973). These early, insightful studies not only gave descriptions of the major acquired dyslexias but also grounded these in the context of models of normal reading. Normal and disordered processing were encapsulated in box-and-arrow type diagrams (Coltheart, Patterson, & Marshall, 1980; Ellis & Young, 1988). With the accumulation of patient data, particularly in the form of behavioral dissociations, increasingly elaborate theories have been produced. The process of reading starts in these models with an orthographic recognition system that specifies the identity and position of the letters within each word. This orthographic information is converted into the phonological form of the word via three routes or processes. A direct pathway translates letters into sounds using grapheme–phoneme conversion (GPC) rules. Although it is a serial and thus somewhat slow process, the GPC route is able to provide the correct pronunciation for familiar words that have a regular or predictable relationship between spelling and sound, and a correct pronunciation of novel orthographic strings (nonwords). For real words two other lexical pathways are available. Both are initiated by recognizing the word, which means matching the target letter string to a familiar word form in a visual input lexicon. This module passes information onto the semantic system allowing the meaning of the word to be retrieved. The semantic representation can, in turn, activate the corresponding representation in the speech output lexicon and thereby release its phonological form. The original conception of the dual-route model contained only this semantic-based lexical route in addition to the nonlexical GPC procedure (Marshall & Newcombe, 1973). Some single-case studies, however, led to the proposition that a direct pathway existed between the visual input lexicon and the speech output lexicon, allowing lexically based reading without involvement of the semantic system (see below for further discussion of patients who read despite significant semantic impairments).

Acquired dyslexias are assumed to arise from damage to one or more of the elements or pathways within this model. Peripheral dyslexias such as pure alexia, visual, attentional, and neglect dyslexia are usually explained in terms of insufficient or inaccurate visual information arriving at the orthographic recognition system. Pure alexia, for example, refers to a reading disorder in which there is a specific difficulty in recognizing printed words, without accompanying aphasia or agraphia. This combination of alexia without agraphia leads to the striking clinical observation of patients who are unable to read what they, themselves, have just written. Many of these patients try to aid their visual recognition in reading by using a letter-by-letter strategy either overtly or covertly (as indeed normal readers tend to do when reading with poor lighting or in other unfavorable conditions). This strategy produces the cardinal feature of letter-by-letter (L-by-L) reading – significant length effects on reading times that are typically absent in normal readers, at least until words get longer than about seven letters.

Surface dyslexia refers to an abnormal form of reading signaled primarily by a much exaggerated sensitivity to the joint impact of word frequency and spelling-sound consistency (Bub, Cancelliere, & Kertesz, 1985). Surface dyslexic patients are particularly prone to error in reading aloud low-frequency, inconsistent words. Their errors predominantly correspond to the more typical pronunciation for the orthographic elements within the word (e.g., reading PINT as though it rhymed with "mint": Marshall & Newcombe, 1973). In contrast, reading of regular words and nonwords is significantly better and, in the purest cases, is close to or within normal limits. In traditional dual-route accounts of reading, surface dyslexia is assumed to reflect an impairment of lexical reading; the most typical interpretation is that it results from damage to the orthographic input lexicon itself. Regular words and nonwords can be pronounced without error through the GPC route, which does not require word recognition. High-frequency irregular words are less affected than their low-frequency counterparts because, even in its normal state but particularly after damage, the efficiency of the lexical route is modulated by word frequency (Coltheart, Rastle, Perry, Langdon, & Ziegler, 2001).

Phonological dyslexia refers to a pattern in which oral reading accuracy exhibits a significant and abnormal lexicality effect; that is, very poor performance (including lexicalization errors) in response to nonwords. In traditional cognitive neuropsychological accounts, phonological dyslexia reflects damage to the GPC route. Real words, regular and irregular, are unhindered, as these can be read efficiently by the lexical routes. In contrast, nonwords cannot be read correctly, as these orthographic strings can only be transformed into phonological representations via the application of GPC rules. The fact that phonological dyslexic patients sometimes produce lexicalization errors (e.g., BEM → "Ben") is assumed to reflect the patients' attempt to read nonwords via the lexical reading routes.

The cardinal feature of deep dyslexia is the production of semantic paralexic errors (e.g., MERRY → "happy," CARNATION → "narcissus"), which makes this, perhaps, the most striking of the acquired dyslexias. In addition to the production of semantic errors, patients with deep dyslexia tend to have a range of other reading "symptoms" – that is to say, a set of co-occurring reading deficits and characteristics. These include poor phonological activation directly from print (i.e., poor or abolished nonword reading); relatively better reading of concrete than abstract words; a graded difficulty with words from different parts of speech (nouns, adjectives, verbs, function words, in descending order of accuracy – which may in fact be just another manifestation of the marked advantage for concrete over abstract words); and the production of morphologically related (e.g., WASH → "washing"; LOVELY → "love") and visually related paralexic errors (e.g., SIGNAL → "single," MOMENT → "money"). In traditional cognitive neuropsychological accounts, deep dyslexia is assumed to reflect major, widespread damage to the reading architecture. As in phonological dyslexia, poor nonword reading results from abolished grapheme–phoneme conversion. Nonsemantic lexical reading (along the direct connection between the visual input and speech output lexicons) is also assumed to be defunct, requiring patients to read solely by an impaired lexical-semantic route. The remaining efficiency of this pathway is graded by the strength or richness of the semantic representations – leading to the imageability effect on reading accuracy. Semantically related errors reflect inaccurate translation via word meaning or corruption to the semantic representations themselves.

These traditional models typically represent the cognitive architecture thought to underlie reading specifically and say little or nothing about how these modules link with the rest of linguistic and visual processing. At least two factors may have influenced the shift to a different way of considering various types of acquired dyslexia and other neuropsychological deficits. While considerable progress has been made through focused study of each individual patient's reading disorder, this approach has tended to avoid consideration of the potential relevance of the patient's other impairments. As we shall describe in some detail below, when researchers began to look across cases with certain types of acquired dyslexia, interesting associations with more general language and visual impairments were noted. Serendipitously, these evolving explanations for acquired dyslexia provide increasing synergies with the developmental dyslexia literature. The potential for linking accounts of the development and dissolution of reading is exciting and may be regarded as further motivation for pursuing this theoretical approach. A second factor relates to the rise of computational models to simulate normal and disordered performance. Rather than elaborating the cognitive architecture of the reading system as has tended to occur with box-and-arrow diagrams, computational models have typically treated reading as part of a larger language system, impairments to which would have consequences for other language tasks.

## *The triangle model: a theoretical framework*

The "triangle" model of reading (Harm & Seidenberg, 2004; Plaut, McClelland, Seidenberg, & Patterson, 1996; Seidenberg & McClelland, 1989; the descriptive term "triangle model" was first used by Patterson & Behrmann, 1997) contains three principal components: (1) a visual component that, with respect to reading, handles orthographic processing, (2) phonology, and (3) semantics (see figure 22.1). None of these components is specific to reading; all operate in and indeed evolved for use in other language and cognitive activities (Patterson & Lambon Ralph, 1999; Savin, 1972). In effect, reading is taken to be parasitic on ontogenetically older brain systems and represents the interaction between fine visual processing and language mechanisms. The semantic system deals with all forms of verbal and nonverbal comprehension as well as any production task that requires a semantic source of activation, including speech production and drawing objects in response to their names (Bozeat, Lambon Ralph, Patterson, Garrard, & Hodges, 2000; Caramazza, Hillis, Rapp, & Romani, 1990; Lambon Ralph & Howard, 2000). Likewise the phonological representations involved in reading aloud are activated for any task requiring spoken production such as naming, repetition, immediate serial recall in addition to reading aloud (Lambon Ralph, Cipolotti, & Patterson, 1999; Lambon Ralph, Moriarty, & Sage, 2002). Again, it is interesting to note that similar arguments have been made in the developmental literature (e.g., Wagner & Torgesen, 1987; Hulme & Snowling, 1991). Finally, written word processing is accomplished by the generic visual system rather than a dedicated, reading-specific process (Behrmann, Nelson, & Sekuler, 1998a; Farah & Wallace, 1991). Some researchers have argued that a section of the left inferior occipito-temporal region – a part of the visual object recognition system – becomes specialized to orthographic recognition when people learn to read (the visual

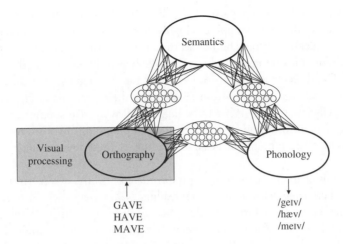

**Figure 22.1** The triangle model of reading.

word form area: McCandliss, Cohen & Dehaene, 2003). This proposal is a topic of current debate, with other researchers questioning the specificity of this region to orthographic recognition (i.e., the same region is differentially activated by other nonvisual and nonreading tasks: Price & Devlin, 2003). In any event, the points we wish to emphasize are (1) that there is no section of the brain set aside for reading before we learn to read; and, (2) that given a nonreading task that necessitated the same kind of visual processing required for reading (i.e., rapid discrimination and identification of confusable symbols at least partly in parallel), we firmly predict that this task would recruit the same neural substrates as orthographic processing.

A full description of the triangle model can be found elsewhere (Plaut, this volume); however, some of its key characteristics are reviewed here prior to a consideration of how damage to one or more of its primary systems leads to the acquired dyslexias described above. Reading aloud is accomplished in this model by the interaction of the three primary systems via sets of connections that allow activation to pass and reverberate between the three groups of units. This means that the final form of representation computed on the phonological units, for example, is influenced by both the semantic and orthographic representations. The strengths or weights of the connections between units in each set of representations change gradually as the model is trained. For learning to read English words, the direct mapping between orthography and phonology (hereinafter O→P) comes to play the dominant role (Plaut et al., 1996). This is because in alphabetic languages, such as English, graphemes and phonemes are systematically related and this tight relationship only varies a little across words. Even in a frankly irregular word like YACHT, there is a transparent pronunciation of the Y and the T, and A receives one of its common pronunciations (cf. FATHER). The O→P computation is supplemented by the interaction with word meaning, particularly through the interplay between semantics and phonology. Indeed, the S→P mapping is highly developed for speech comprehension and production considerably before children learn to read. In contrast, the efficiency of O→P develops as children learn to read and is influenced by word frequency and spelling-sound consistency. The direct mapping is least efficient for low-frequency, inconsistent words because the model has few opportunities to learn their particular, atypical mappings. Although the efficiency of S→P has to be high for all words (to support comprehension and speech production), the additional activation of phonology by word meaning is considered particularly important for accurate reading of these low-frequency inconsistent words.

Although this chapter is concerned with disordered reading, it is worth noting in this context that there is evidence that *normal* reading of low-frequency, inconsistent words is more influenced by a semantic variable – imageability – than higher-frequency or consistent words (Shibahara, Zorzi, Hill, Wydell, & Butterworth, 2003; Strain, Patterson, & Seidenberg, 1995). In addition, Rosson (1985) found that pronunciations given to nonwords such as LOUCH were influenced by a preceding word (e.g., *feel*) that semantically primed one sound-spelling pattern (*touch*) rather than another (*couch*).

In the remainder of this chapter, we will review data suggesting that each of the major acquired disorders of reading (surface dyslexia, phonological-deep dyslexia, pure alexia) is produced by impairment of a primary system (semantics, phonology, and fine visual processing, respectively).

## Semantic Memory and Surface Dyslexia

The primary systems hypothesis relates surface dyslexia to a semantic impairment or, more precisely, to a dramatic reduction in the activation of phonology by word meaning (S→P). The literature on this type of reading disorder is dominated by patients with semantic impairment and profound anomia, most commonly in the context of semantic dementia (e.g., Patterson & Hodges, 1992; Shallice, Warrington, & McCarthy, 1983; Warrington, 1975) but sometimes after acute brain damage (Bub et al., 1985). The clinically derived link between semantic impairment and surface dyslexia can be traced back at least to 1980, when Shallice and Warrington in fact referred to this reading disorder as semantic dyslexia (Shallice & Warrington, 1980).

A more formal, computational description for the link to semantic impairment is given by the triangle model (simulation 4: Plaut et al., 1996). As noted above, the direct O→P computation in the triangle model is relatively inefficient for low-frequency, inconsistent words and this is compensated for by the contribution from word meaning (S→P). Without this additional semantic input, the pronunciation of words simply corresponds to the computation along O→P. The weights learned by O→P primarily reflect the mappings in consistent words, plus word-specific mappings for frequently encountered words; accordingly, when additional input from S→P is reduced, the model then gives a more typical, consistent pronunciation for low-frequency, inconsistent words – just like patients with surface dyslexia (e.g., YACHT → "yatched," SEW → "sue").

The last decade has witnessed increasing evidence in favor of the link between semantic impairment and surface dyslexia. First, the vast majority of patients with semantic dementia (SD) have surface dyslexic reading at presentation or, if they are very mild, after there has been sufficient decline in their semantic memory (Caine, Breen, & Patterson, 2002). Only three semantic dementia patients in the literature run counter to this prediction; these are discussed in more detail below. In addition, the onset of semantic impairment in Alzheimer's disease is associated with the emergence of surface dyslexia (Strain, Patterson, Graham, & Hodges, 1998), though again there are a few exceptions to this pattern (Lambon Ralph, Ellis, & Franklin, 1995; Raymer & Berndt, 1994, 1996).

In addition to the link between semantic impairment and surface dyslexia at the level of associated deficits, an item-specific relationship has also been demonstrated. Irregular words that individual semantic dementia patients still understand relatively well are read more accurately than words that have become semantically degraded (Funnell, 1996; Graham, Hodges, & Patterson, 1994). In a similar vein, there is now evidence for category specificity in surface dyslexia: semantic dementia patients comprehend number words relatively well, and their reading of number words with atypical spelling-sound correspondences (e.g., ONE, TWO, FOUR) is more accurate than for comparable non-number words (Butterworth, Cappelletti, & Kopelman, 2001).

### Evidence for the primary systems hypothesis from behaviors beyond reading

A key aspect of the primary systems hypothesis is that the three principal components are assumed to underpin a variety of mental activities. Patients with semantic impairment demonstrate consistency by frequency interactions not only in reading but also in a whole range of verbal and nonverbal activities. When given the spoken stem of a verb and asked to produce its past tense form, for example, semantic dementia patients are particularly poor with low-frequency, irregular items (e.g., grind → ground) for which they produce regularization errors, "grinded" (Patterson, Lambon Ralph, Hodges, & McClelland, 2001). This phenomenon can also be observed in receptive as well as expressive tasks. Rogers, Lambon Ralph, Hodges, and Patterson (2004) asked semantic dementia patients to make two-alternative forced-choice lexical decisions to written words, each paired with a nonword that was either more or less consistent with typical English orthography (as measured by bigram and trigram frequencies). With greater degrees of semantic impairment, patients' lexical decisions became increasingly guided by a preference for typical orthographic patterns, whether or not these actually corresponded to real words. As with reading aloud and generating past tense verbs, the semantic dementia patients were particularly inaccurate for low-frequency words with atypical letter patterns and demonstrated a strong preference for the accompanying nonword with a more typical letter sequence (e.g., preferring GOAST to GHOST).

Analogous behavior has been observed in receptive and expressive nonverbal tasks once measures of consistency (i.e., the reliability of how elements in the input map onto their corresponding output representations) have been defined for those domains. In a parallel study, Rogers, Lambon Ralph, Hodges, and Patterson (2003) found an increasing influence of consistency in object decisions as a function of degree of semantic deficit.

Item          Immediate copy          Delayed copy

Duck

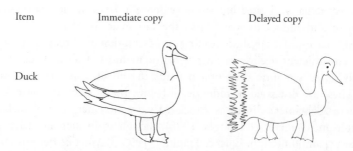

**Figure 22.2**   An example of drawing overregularization from a patient with semantic dementia.

SD patients were more likely to indicate that line drawings of animals or objects were real if their component elements were typical/consistent of those found in that domain (e.g., for animals – four legs, ears, etc.) than if the depictions contained atypical/inconsistent features (e.g., humps, stripes, antlers). Again the rate of errors was highest when the correct real object not only had atypical elements but was also of lower familiarity. This pattern can also be observed in drawing to name and delayed copying of object drawings (expressive measures of visually based knowledge). Patients are increasingly likely to omit features in their drawings that are unusual (inconsistent) for the relevant semantic domain and become more likely to include erroneous features that are typical/consistent (Bozeat et al. 2003). With sufficient semantic impairment, patients can produce striking and memorable errors such as drawing ducks with four legs (see figure 22.2 and Lambon Ralph & Howard, 2000).

A final example of semantic impairment leading to frequency by consistency effects in nonverbal tasks is that identified in object use. By using a feature-type database, Bozeat et al. (2003) were able to define not only the elements involved in object use (e.g., features of hold, manipulation, and object structure) but also co-occurring pairs of structure-hold and structure-manipulation relationships (i.e., affordances: for example, if an object has a handle it is very likely that the correct manipulation includes gripping the object in question; Bozeat, Lambon Ralph, Patterson, & Hodges, 2002). One can think of these as being analogous to typical spelling-sound correspondences in reading and thus make the prediction that afforded elements, like regular words, would be relatively impervious to the familiarity of the object or the degree of semantic impairment each patient has. Consistent with this hypothesis, Bozeat et al. (2002) found that semantic dementia patients exhibited a consistency (afforded vs. nonafforded manipulations) by familiarity interaction in their object use accuracy.

*Challenges to the primary systems hypothesis*

Given the apparent wealth of evidence for the role of conceptual knowledge in reading (Kintsch, this volume) as well as in a range of other verbal and nonverbal tasks, we would argue that the semantic corner of the triangle model is firmly established. The small number of patients described in the literature who have significant semantic impairment without the predicted surface dyslexia, however, provide a clear challenge to this approach. These include some cases with Alzheimer's disease (Lambon Ralph et al., 1995; Raymer & Berndt, 1996) as well as three with semantic dementia (Blazely, Coltheart, & Casey, in press; Cipolotti & Warrington, 1995; Schwartz, Saffran, & Marin, 1980). It can be very difficult to establish the degree of semantic impairment in Alzheimer's disease because this disorder leads to a variety of cognitive and perceptual impairments, many of which can compromise performance on tests designed to tap conceptual representations (Nebes, 1989). This is made all the more likely in Alzheimer's disease in that patients are often moderately to severely demented before clear semantic impairments emerge (Strain et al., 1998). In such circumstances, it can be easy to overestimate the true degree of semantic impairment and conclude that such patients are reading without meaning. Because of the selective nature of semantic impairment in semantic dementia, these cases provide a clearer test of the putative role of word meaning in reading aloud.

The first and, perhaps, still best known counterexample to surface dyslexia in semantic dementia is case WLP (Schwartz et al., 1980b). At one point during her decline, WLP was able to read irregular words that she failed to understand, for example correctly reading aloud the irregular word HYENA and then commenting: "hyena . . . hyena . . . what in the heck is that?" At the time, this dissociation was deemed sufficient to motivate the addition of a nonsemantic, lexical pathway to dual-route models of reading, turning them effectively into triple-route models. This conclusion is tempered though by observation that, a little later in her progression, WLP developed a surface dyslexic pattern of reading just as one would predict from the triangle model. Indeed, more recent longitudinal studies indicate that if semantic dementia patients are very mild when they first present, then the semantic impairment can be insufficient to produce surface dyslexia (Caine et al., 2002). Careful study of one relatively full computational instantiation of the triangle model (simulation 4: Plaut et al., 1996) demonstrates that the relationship between semantic impairment and reading accuracy is nonlinear. Because O→P takes the dominant role in reading, the influence of semantic representations is subtle and surface dyslexia only begins to emerge once there is considerable semantic impairment. The model is consistent, therefore, with the pattern described by Caine et al. (2002) and by Schwartz et al. (1980b) – relatively normal reading in the earliest phase of semantic dementia but emergent surface dyslexia as the inevitable semantic deterioration takes hold.

Two more recently described cases, however, do not fit with this predicted relationship. Patients DRN (Cipolotti & Warrington, 1995) and EM (Blazely et al., in press) both had semantic impairment of a degree sufficient to produce surface dyslexia in numerous other semantic dementia patients but not in these two cases. One obvious, albeit dull, explanation for the difference, that apparent variations between patients reflect differences in the test materials employed, can be immediately ruled out in these cases because DRN and EM were tested on some of the same assessments that other studies have used to demonstrate associations between semantic impairment and surface dyslexia (Graham et al., 1994; Patterson & Hodges, 1992).

This state of affairs is a challenge to the triangle model, which needs to address the atypical cases, and also to dual-route theories. The latter framework (see Coltheart, this volume) needs to explain the nearly, though not quite perfectly, predictable impact of semantic impairment on reading as well as on other verbal and nonverbal tasks. The only explanation that has been offered from this perspective is that these are accidentally asso- ciated deficits based on anatomical proximity of regions responsible for conceptual knowl- edge and reading aloud. On the basis of a steady increase in both the number of cases demonstrating the association, and the number of quite different tasks (e.g., reading, spelling, verb inflection, lexical decision, object decision, drawing, object use) demon- strating a frequency-by-typicality modulated impairment in conjunction with semantic deficits, we suggest that this "accidental association" becomes a less plausible account.

To explain such dissociations when they do (rarely) occur, Plaut (1997) demonstrated that two forms of individual difference could modulate the relationship between seman- tic impairment and reading accuracy sufficiently to account for all the patients reported in the literature, at least to that date. The efficiency of O→P can be modulated either by restricting the influence of semantic representations during learning to read or by increas- ing the computational resources of the direct O→P mapping. These individual differ- ences continua mean that the degree of surface dyslexia produced by the same semantic impairment varies and, at one end point of these continua, reading accuracy can remain intact. Demonstration that this possible explanation actually works at the computational level is a key step in producing a complete theory. Future research will have to extend this to behavioral studies of patients with semantic dementia and will need to provide methods for measuring such individual differences across patients.

## Phonology and Phonological-Deep Dyslexia

When the first case of phonological dyslexia was described, Beauvois and Dérouesné (1979) suggested that this type of disorder might represent a qualitatively different reading impairment to deep dyslexia. Although both phonological and deep dyslexic patients have problems reading nonwords, the patient they described (RG) did not make semantic errors and had little in the way of other aphasic impairments. The alternative possibility, that phonological and deep dyslexia might be more intimately related, was also noted in these early descriptions: Beauvois and Dérouesné suggested that patient RG might just have been a very pure, mild example of a deep-dyslexic-like reading disorder. Likewise in the second report of phonological dyslexia, Patterson (1982) noted that she had originally assumed patient AM to be a mild deep dyslexic rather than suffering from a different form of reading disorder.

More recently, the link between phonological and deep dyslexia has been championed by Friedman and colleagues (Friedman, 1996; Glosser & Friedman, 1990). In a review of the literature, Friedman (1996) noted a number of patients originally presenting with deep dyslexia whose reading pattern had evolved into phonological dyslexia over time. More specifically, Friedman argued that there was a succession of symptoms along a sever- ity-based continuum of phonological-to-deep dyslexia: in the mildest patients only nonword reading would be affected; then, as a function of increasing severity, morpho- logical and visual errors would appear, followed by part-of-speech effects, then image- ability effects and finally the production of semantic errors.

The appraisal of this continuum hypothesis is hindered by the fact that previous case studies have not used comparable test materials. To circumvent this difficulty, Crisp and Lambon Ralph (submitted) investigated 12 patients with phonological or deep dyslexia using the same test battery in order to facilitate direct comparisons between cases. With the exception of semantic paralexic errors, all patients including those with mild reading difficulties demonstrated most of the symptoms of deep dyslexia, including significant effects of imageability (taken by Friedman to be the penultimate symptom before semantic reading errors). Thus, the findings of this study strongly reinforced the notion of a severity-based continuum between deep and phonological dyslexia, although there was little evidence in favor of the predictable succession of symptoms suggested by Friedman (see above). In short, the phonological-deep dyslexia continuum involves a common co-occurring set of symptoms, the severity of which varies in line with the overall degree of reading impairment.

Given this fairly clear evidence favoring a phonological-deep dyslexia continuum, the most obvious next question concerns the cognitive basis of the reading disorder. The triangle model suggests that it is a general phonological impairment in which the phonological component of the language system is pathologically weak or underactivated (Patterson, Suzuki, & Wydell, 1996). Note that a significant relationship between poor phonology and impaired reading is a standard finding in the developmental literature (Harm & Seidenberg, 1999; Snowling, 2000; Vellutino & Fletcher, this volume). A generalized deficit of phonology should have an impact on reading aloud of all types of orthographic string, but there are at least two reasons why it might be expected to have disproportionate consequences for unfamiliar strings (i.e., nonwords). First, setting aside the computation from O→P, the phonological system itself develops on the basis of experience with words in the speaker's language, and it will always operate more efficiently with the familiar phonological sequences of the words that it knows than with the nonwords that it does not; this will be true even in its normal state, but the familiarity effect should be magnified by damage. The second important distinction comes from the fact that words, unlike nonwords, have meaning. As noted in the introduction at the beginning of this chapter, communication between S and P (in both directions) has to be highly efficient because it supports all forms of speech comprehension and production. Studies of phonological short-term memory in semantic dementia patients and related studies with neurologically intact participants have established that semantic representations play a role in constraining and maintaining the phonological coherence of words (e.g., Hulme, Maughan, & Brown,1991; Walker & Hulme, 1999; Jefferies, Jones, Bateman, & Lambon Ralph, in press; Patterson, Graham, & Hodges, 1994). One could easily imagine, therefore, that this interplay between semantics and phonology may assume exaggerated importance when phonology itself is compromised. Weakly activated phonological patterns can be enhanced by the interaction with intact semantic representations for words that are obviously absent for nonwords.

The interaction with meaning might also provide an explanation for some of the other symptoms found in phonological-deep dyslexia. The quality of the interplay between semantics and phonology is likely to be graded according to characteristics of the words themselves. In particular, imageability effects might reflect the relative strength of the semantic support, given that high-imageability words are thought to have relatively better specified, richer, and more context-independent semantic representations than their abstract counterparts (Jones, 1985; Plaut & Shallice, 1993). This difference might also be germane to an understanding of semantic paralexias. For patients with a very severely impaired phonological system, activation of word meaning will be computed only on the basis of the O→S pathway, the weakest link in the triangle (Harm & Seidenberg, 2004). If this results in only partial semantic activation, then the S→P computation may produce several semantically related candidates in the phonological system – those that share features with the underspecified representation activated in semantic memory (e.g., for the target HARE the group of semantically related targets might include *rabbit, squirrel, guinea pig,* etc.). For the most part, the combination of any residual O→P activation together with partial reinforcement from word meaning will favor the target word form. In very impaired cases, however, it is possible that S→P will override the target form with phonological activation of a semantically related neighbour (e.g., HARE → "rabbit"). This is particularly likely if that item is more readily activated in normal circumstances; for example, if the incorrect word has a richer semantic representation or benefits from other factors that influence the efficiency of speech production, such as imageability, age-of-acquisition, and frequency (Gerhand & Barry, 2000). It also fits with the observation that semantic errors tend to be more imageable/concrete than the target words to which they are incorrect responses (Newton & Barry, 1997; Shallice & Warrington, 1975).

Where appropriate testing has been carried out, most if not all patients with phonological and deep dyslexia have been shown to have deficits of phonology outside the domain of reading. For example, all 17 patients with phonological dyslexia reported in a special issue of *Cognitive Neuropsychology* (no. 6, 1996) performed below the normal range on nonreading phonological tasks. Impaired phonology can be revealed by poor immediate and delayed repetition of words or nonwords, though stringent assessments, such as rhyme judgment, phonological segmentation and blending tasks, or measures of verbal working memory, are more likely to highlight the phonological impairment in these patients.

As noted above, the phonological-deep dyslexic literature is dominated by single-case studies. This means that the association with poor phonology across these different cases has been the key evidence for this explanation of phonological-deep dyslexia. There are three studies, however, that greatly strengthen the case for a causal link. The first two demonstrate a tighter relationship between phonological impairment and phonological-deep dyslexia by highlighting overlapping characteristics of patients' performance in reading and nonreading tasks. If this reading deficit, characterized by such a strong lexicality effect, is underpinned by a general phonological impairment, then one might expect the lexical status of the target form to influence success in any task requiring a phonological response, whether the stimulus is orthographic or not. Patterson and Marcel (1992) found exactly this. In their study, patients were more accurate when attempting to perform phonological manipulations (segmentation or blending on the basis of auditory input) when the correct manipulation resulted in a word response ("Take the first sound off the word 'mother' and say what remains") than a nonword response ("Take the first sound off the word 'father' and say what remains").

This logic can also be extended to deep dyslexia. Beland and Mimouni's (2001) study of an Arabic–French bilingual deep dyslexic patient ZT was primarily aimed at exploring the impact of different writing systems on the symptoms of this reading disorder. In addition the authors completed a thorough investigation of the patient's nonreading language skills. Like many other patients with deep dyslexia, ZT was able to repeat single real words with very few errors. When a 5- or 10-second delay was inserted between the spoken stimulus word and ZT's repetition response, however, his repetition accuracy dropped by 30% to 40% in both languages. More interestingly, once his phonological system had been stressed in this way, the distribution of the patient's repetition errors mimicked those found in reading, including phonological, morphological, and omission errors, and perhaps most striking, semantic paraphasias too.

The case for a causal link between semantic impairment and surface dyslexia has been strengthened significantly by the demonstration that, as the degree of semantic impairment varies, so does the resultant reading accuracy (either across patients or in studies that focus on a by-items analysis). Until very recently, it has been difficult to compile parallel data for the link between phonological impairment and phonological-deep dyslexia because of the lack of comparable data across individually studied patients. This goal was tackled, however, by Crisp and Lambon Ralph's (submitted) case-series study noted above. As predicted, the patients' nonword reading accuracy was significantly correlated with their varying degrees of success on phonological manipulation tasks. In addition, the size of the patients' lexicality effect was strongly correlated with their ability to derive meaning not only from written but also spoken words (as measured by various synonym judgment tasks). This suggests that phonological-deep dyslexia reflects the interplay between the patients' general phonological impairment and the status of their semantic memory (or the efficiency of its interaction with surface word forms).

### Extension to nonreading activities

A critical aspect of the triangle framework is that any acquired reading disorder should be accompanied by a predictable range of other deficits because it arises from impairment to one of the primary systems. As noted above, semantic impairment apparently leads to consistency-by-frequency interactions not only in oral reading but in a whole set of other verbal and nonverbal tasks. There is some evidence that the same cross-task associations are true for phonological impairments. For example, in the previous section on the impact of semantic impairment, we noted that when semantic dementia patients are given the spoken stem of a verb, they demonstrate relatively poor performance for low-frequency, irregular verbs and produce regularization errors (Patterson et al., 2001). In contrast, patients with Broca-type aphasia are impaired at generating past tense forms of verbs, and particularly so for novel verb forms (i.e., they exhibit a lexicality effect). Some of these cases also demonstrate relatively lower accuracy on the past tense of regular than irregular real verbs (Ullman et al., 1997). Bird, Lambon Ralph, Seidenberg, McClelland, and Patterson (2003) argued that the Broca patients' poor verb abilities were due to their phonological deficit and, more specifically, that the difference between regular and irregular verbs reflected the variation in phonological complexity of the items (the phonological complexity of the offset or the syllable length is automatically increased when regular verbs are inflected for the past tense). Interestingly, this case-series of ten Broca aphasic patients was also impaired on a range of phonological awareness tasks and, as predicted, all had phonological-deep dyslexia.

A similar association across tasks was noted in a study designed to investigate the link between semantic/phonological impairments and word-finding difficulties in patients with aphasia following cerebral vascular accidents (stroke: Lambon Ralph et al., 2002). As noted throughout this chapter, activation from S→P is required for a variety of language activities including speech production. This predicts that the degree of word-finding difficulties found in aphasic patients should be related to the degree of their phonological and semantic deficits. Correlational analyses across the case-series of patients yielded strong support for this proposal – in fact, measures of semantic and phonological ability were as good at predicting naming scores as a separate naming test (i.e., as good a predictor as the test validity). Furthermore, phonological impairments dominated the neuropsychological profiles of this series of CVA patients, and, just as the triangle model would predict, the patients all had phonological dyslexia.

## Visual Processing and Pure Alexia (Letter-by-Letter Reading)

Although there is considerable debate about the locus of impairment that gives rise to pure alexia (Coltheart, 1998), virtually all current explanations share the notion that this reading disorder reflects a relatively early impairment in the visual-orthographic system, leading to poor whole-word recognition. Early investigations of pure alexia in the cognitive neuropsychology literature, like other studies of acquired dyslexia, used reading-specific models to interpret the patients' data. These studies suggested that pure alexic patients either had impaired letter recognition or a breakdown between letter and word representations (e.g., Patterson & Kay, 1982). As noted in the introduction above, the primary systems hypothesis views the reading process first and foremost as an interaction between visual and language processes. We have argued that surface, phonological, and deep dyslexia can all be linked to nonreading impairments within the language system. In the same way, it is also possible to consider pure alexia in terms of a more generalized visual impairment (Behrmann et al., 1998a; Farah & Wallace, 1991).

Word recognition requires the reader to discriminate amongst and identify visual symbols rapidly and, at least to some degree, in parallel. It is not hard to imagine that this places considerable demands on the visual system and, therefore, that reading might be especially vulnerable to even a mild deficit of visual processing. In support of a link between pure alexia and visual perceptual deficits, Behrmann et al. (1998b) reviewed 57 published cases of L-by-L reading and found that 50/57 showed frank deficits in single-letter identification, at least in speed/efficiency if not in accuracy; for the remaining 7, there was insufficient evidence to rule out an impairment in this rather peripheral aspect of the reading process. This rate of associated deficits is remarkably high given that most of the patients had not been assessed on tasks with nonorthographic stimuli that might tax visual discrimination/identification as heavily as word reading does. A small number of studies have carefully constructed the visual stimuli so that these nonreading, visual tasks possess some of the same processing demands as reading. When this kind of careful empirical assessment has been done, the patients were impaired on these tasks as well (Behrmann et al., 1998a; Mycroft et al., in press).

To date, there have been no case-series studies of L-by-L readers that have attempted to relate the degree of difficulty in visually demanding nonreading tasks to the severity of the patients' reading impairment (measured, perhaps, by the gradient that relates reading times to word length) as has been done for semantic impairment – surface dyslexia, and phonological impairment–phonological dyslexia. Such a study would first have to specify the nature of the critical, underlying visual deficits more precisely – a non-trivial matter. Evidence for a causal link between visual impairment and pure alexia has been provided, however, by a recent study that investigated the characteristics of reading and nonreading processing across the same set of seven patients (Mycroft et al., in press). As argued for the generalized phonological impairment underpinning phonological-deep dyslexia, the proposal for a generalized visual impairment causing L-by-L reading would be strengthened if some of the classic traits of pure alexia could be observed in nonreading tasks. Using carefully constructed visual search tasks (either for letters or symbols within a string of the same type of stimuli), Mycroft et al. demonstrated that patients' decision times were affected by the left-to-right location of the target stimulus as well as the length of the strings in the same way for both the reading and nonreading versions of the tasks. In stark contrast, normal readers showed no evidence for the influence of these factors on their decision times in either version of the task.

When considering the effects of semantic or phonological impairments, it is possible to find evidence for the impact of such deficits on a predictable set of other tasks. The same should also be true for the ramifications of a generalized visual deficit. More specifically, if pure alexia reflects the inability of the damaged visual system to support the high processing demands of word recognition, then it should also impair recognition of other classes of stimuli that share the same visual characteristics. The evidence that exists in the literature, in this regard, is mixed. At least some well-documented L-by-L readers are also significantly impaired in identifying numbers (Miozzo & Caramazza, 1998), musical notation (Horikoshi et al., 1997), and/or faces (De Renzi & di Pellegrino, 1998). There are, however, a small number of patients for whom number recognition seems significantly better than letter identification (Farah, 1999). This apparent dissociation between number and letter recognition requires further investigation and will necessitate a careful analysis of the characteristics of both types of stimuli. More generally, a major challenge for future studies of pure alexia will be to use the growing knowledge about the neural bases of visual processing to specify the elements that make up the visual corner of the triangle model. This might facilitate identification of the visual processing deficits that produce L-by-L reading behavior (which might actually vary in type across cases), and also of the basic impairments responsible for other forms of peripheral dyslexia such as attentional, neglect, and visual dyslexias (Ellis, Flude, & Young, 1987; Lambon Ralph & Ellis, 1997; Warrington, Cipolotti, & McNeil, 1993).

To finish this section on pure alexia, we will consider a further challenge to the visual impairment hypothesis – namely, the fact that some patients with severe L-by-L reading exhibit the "Saffran effect" (Lambon Ralph, Hesketh, & Sage, 2004). Although reports of implicit word recognition in pure and global alexics first appeared in the literature in the early 1960s (Kreindler & Ionasescu, 1961), the most comprehensive investigations of such patients were reported by Saffran and her colleagues (Coslett & Saffran, 1989; Coslett, Saffran, Greenbaum, & Schwartz, 1993; Saffran & Coslett, 1998). The clinical manifestation of this phenomenon is that a patient succeeds, at a rate well above chance, in categorizing the meaning of a written word (e.g., is it the name of a living or a non-living object?), or the lexical status of a letter string (is it a word or nonword?), despite being unable to identify the words themselves (i.e., to read them aloud). In the first detailed investigation of the Saffran effect (Shallice & Saffran, 1986), ML, a slow L-by-L reader, performed above chance on a series of forced-choice lexical decision and cate-gorization tasks, even when the words were presented too briefly for him to report the identity of the word or its constituent letters. Subsequent descriptions of other patients found a similar disparity between above-chance (though never perfect) performance in the context of brief presentation and little or no explicit word recognition (for an overview, see Saffran & Coslett, 1998).

It is worth noting one limiting factor on the potential significance of this contrast between word identification and word categorization: the two tasks have very unequal demands. The task at which pure alexic patients are so impaired – identification – essen-tially asks readers to decide what word they are looking at when the correct answer could be (almost) any word in the language; the task at which they are significantly better – categorization – asks them to assign the target word to one of only two classes. A fairer contrast would be to make the identification task two-choice as well: given a brief pre-sentation of the word HARE, for example, the patients could be asked in the classification task if it was a living or a nonliving thing, and in the identification task if it was the word "hare" or "hate." If they were still much more successful at the former judgment than the latter, the contrast would be more impressive. Exactly this comparison has been made in a recent study of the Saffran effect in a L-by-L reader (Lambon Ralph et al., 2004). This investigation found that the apparent difference between identification and classification was removed when a two-forced choice method was used in both tasks.

The ability to categorize words without overtly recognizing them is, perhaps, the most striking form of the Saffran effect, but a range of other results also suggests activation of higher-level, lexical-semantic representations in pure alexic patients. For instance, some L-by-L readers have exhibited a significant word superiority effect (better letter recogni-tion under masked presentation if the stimuli correspond to words, or wordlike non-words, than letter strings: Reuter-Lorenz & Brunn, 1990). In addition, pure alexics show influences of variables associated with lexical-semantic processes (frequency and image-ability: Behrmann et al., 1998b) and can also demonstrate standard Stroop interference (McKeeff & Behrmann, 2004).

At face value, explanations of pure alexia based on early visual impairment seem at odds with the Saffran effect: the early visual deficit is supposed to prevent activation of whole-word representations, thus necessitating the L-by-L strategy for word recognition; but the Saffran effect is evidence for activation of high-level representations, including word meaning. Indeed, the explanation championed by Saffran, Coslett, and their col-leagues (1998) separated the key behavioral elements observed in these patients into two groups and posited a separate, reading-specific system to account for each. They argued that a left hemisphere system supports explicit letter and word recognition and, when damaged, resorts to L-by-L reading as a compensatory strategy, whereas a second reading system in the right hemisphere reading system underpins implicit letter and word recognition. Under this proposal, when the left hemisphere system is damaged, as it is in pure alexic patients, their L-by-L behavior derives from the abnormal processing in the left hemisphere while the Saffran effect is generated by the right hemisphere.

The Saffran effect can, in fact, be explained by the generalized visual impairment hypothesis. This explanation assumes that inadequate visual input (whether in pure alexics or in normal readers operating under visually difficult conditions) drives two processes: a *single* word-processing system (i.e., the triangle model), and a separate, compensatory L-by-L strategy. Under this proposal, the Saffran effect simply reflects the partial, remaining activation of the usual (but now inadequate) word recognition system (Behrmann et al., 1998b; Feinberg, Dyches-Berke, Miner, & Roane, 1994; Lambon Ralph et al., 2004; Shallice & Saffran, 1986). This explains why performance on lexical decision and categorization tasks is significantly above chance but never perfect (indeed sometimes a long way from perfect) in these cases. The combination of early visual-orthographic impairments and partial semantic access would only be surprising if the reading system were thought to consist of discrete processes. In a cascading or interactive activation system, degraded input will still produce partial activation in subsequent parts of the processing system (Lupker, this volume; Morton & Patterson, 1980; Shallice & Saffran, 1986). In McClelland and Rumelhart's (1981) interactive activation word recognition model, reduced input to letter features still produced partial letter and word level activation. This was, of course, the basis for their explanation of the word superiority effect in normal readers under masked, brief presentation. Behrmann et al. (1998b) argued that it also explains why pure alexics can show the word superiority effect (feedback from lexical-semantic knowledge), effects of frequency and imageability (frequent and concrete words are more readily activated even under reduced visual input), and above chance performance on lexical decision and categorization tasks (partial activation of lexical and semantic representations).

## Future research directions

Up to now, the literature on acquired disorders of reading, like much of the rest of cognitive neuropsychology, has been based on the study of patients who have reached a chronic stable phase, normally several months or years after the onset of their brain injury. In contrast, studies of the decline in patients with neurodegenerative disease have provided important insights about the link between reading impairments and the underlying primary brain systems involved. This suggests that the changing brain provides useful information about the normal underlying processes that support reading as well as other aspects of cognitive performance. An area that is overlooked by most studies is the period of recovery following acute brain injury. A few notable exceptions to this "neglect" can be found in the acquired dyslexia literature and have led to important insights about the nature of the underlying systems (e.g., the recovery of deep into phonological dyslexia: Friedman, 1996). Indeed, in a recent exploration of plasticity in the context of a computational model of O→P, no clear form of acquired dyslexia emerged immediately following damage to the network (as described in earlier work: Patterson, Seidenberg, &

McClelland, 1989) but the pattern of surface dyslexia did crystallize out of the model after a period of recovery (Welbourne & Lambon Ralph, in press).

In our overview of the acquired dyslexia literature, we have attempted to summarize a growing body of evidence in favor of the idea that reading is parasitic on the pre-existing brain systems that support visual processing and language (Savin, 1972). Although there are now a considerable number of studies supporting each element of the primary systems hypothesis (Patterson & Lambon Ralph, 1999), this approach still faces a number of important challenges. Future studies of acquired disorders of reading should be able to address many of these challenges through additional neuropsychological studies and computational modeling. In addition, information from neuroimaging and transcranial magnetic stimulation studies of intact and brain damaged individuals will bring new perspectives on acquired dyslexia (Leff et al., 2001a; Leff, Scott, Rothwell, & Wise, 2001b; Price, 2000; Price & McCrory, this volume).

# 23

# *Spelling Disorders*

## Cristina Romani, Andrew Olson, and Anna Maria Di Betta

In the mind of the layperson there is still an association between intelligence and the ability to spell. Thus, spelling errors are a source of embarrassment and ridicule. Indeed, the debilitating nature of a spelling impairment is well described in the words of an adult with developmental dysgraphia:

> WF:   I hat his all was mack me ageer
>        [*I hate this. (It) always make(s) me angry.*]
>        Sum time I wot to smash thing
>        [*Some time I want to smash things.*]
>        It allwas mack me tired and furttrad
>        [*It always makes me tired and frustrated.*]
>        My hand allwas get swety
>        [*My hand always get(s) sweaty.*]
>        It is sowe frutrat this ritting,
>        [*It is so frustrating this writing.*]
>        It is like dwing a day work in one hower.
>        [*It is like doing a day's work in one hour.*]

The purpose of this chapter is to provide an overview of research on the spelling difficulties that afflict adults as well as children and patients with neurological disorders. We begin by outlining the standard model of spelling that has guided much of this research and by asking questions about the relation between reading and spelling. We will then turn to a description of acquired and developmental impairments. We will show that the study of acquired impairments has provided crucial evidence for the processes and representations involved in a mature spelling system, while the study of developmental impairments has provided crucial evidence on the relationship between cognitive skills and literacy processes.

## The Dual-Route Model of Spelling

A dual-route model of spelling has been the standard model for considering spelling disorders (dysgraphias) in both children and neurological patients (Caramazza, 1988; Ellis, 1989; Tainturier & Rapp, 2000). Variations between different types of dual-route models are not relevant for present purposes and a discussion is beyond the scope of this chapter (see Olson & Caramazza, 1994, for a critique of some aspects of these models applied to spelling). Figure 23.1 shows a simplified version of a dual-route model of spelling. A more detailed model will be presented in the section on acquired disorders.

In the case of a dictated word, it is assumed that a phonological representation will be constructed from the auditory input and kept active in a buffer component (phonological input buffer). From here, information can take one of two routes. In the *lexical route*, the phonological input accesses the corresponding word representations in the following components, one after the other: (1) the phonological lexicon, which stores the sound forms of words; (2) the semantic system, which stores the meaning of words; and (3) the orthographic lexicon, which stores word spellings in the form of series of abstract letter identities (rather than motor patterns or letter names). In the *nonlexical route*, the phonological input accesses knowledge of sublexical phoneme–grapheme correspondences. Thus, in the case of the lexical route, whole-word representations are accessed. A word will be spelled correctly provided that its corresponding orthographic representation is

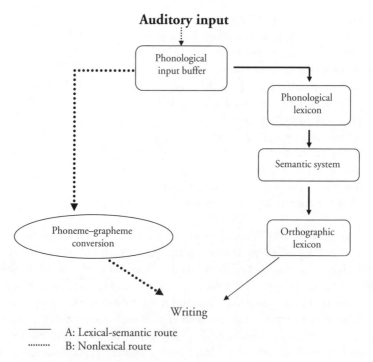

**Figure 23.1**   A schematic dual-route model of spelling.

well specified. High-frequency words will more often have complete representations than low-frequency words. In the case of the nonlexical route, the phonemes of a word will be converted into graphemes, in a piecemeal fashion, one at the time. This means that the probability of spelling a word correctly will vary depending on the word's regularity. A word that involves a highly irregular phoneme–grapheme correspondence, like *yacht*, will rarely, if ever, be spelled correctly. Words with more regular, but still inconsistent, phoneme–grapheme correspondences, like "phase", will sometimes be spelled correctly with "ph", and other times incorrectly with "f" (see Beauvois & Dérouesné, 1981; Goodman-Shulman & Caramazza, 1987).

Theoretical motivation for a dual-route model of spelling comes from the fact that many languages, including English, have many irregular words that can be spelled correctly only by rote memory of the whole word. At the same time, a nonlexical route is important to bootstrap and support lexical representations, especially during learning. In addition, the distinction between lexical and nonlexical spelling routines has been confirmed by striking dissociations between impairments in acquired cases and, to a lesser extent, in developmental cases.

The literature has described a number of people who spell nonwords and regular words well, but irregular words poorly. This pattern can be explained by hypothesizing that these individuals have poor lexical representations, but good knowledge of phoneme–grapheme correspondences. In support of this view, the errors they make are generally regularization errors that, if read aloud, will sound like the target word (phonologically plausible errors; e.g., "yacht" spelled *yot*). The profile involving better spelling of nonwords than words and especially poor spelling of irregular words is often referred to as *surface dysgraphia*. The first detailed case of this type was an acquired case described by Beauvois & Dérouesné (1981) and many more have been described since, both in the acquired literature (e.g., Behrmann & Bub, 1992; De Partz, Seron, & Van der Linden, 1992; Hatfield & Patterson, 1983; Weekes & Coltheart, 1996) and in the developmental literature (e.g., Hanley, Hastie, & Kay, 1992; Romani, Olson, & Ward, 1999).

In contrast, the term *phonological dysgraphia* is used to refer to spelling impairments that primarily affect the use of phoneme–grapheme conversion procedures. This results in the lack of a regularity effect (regular and irregular words are spelt equally well) and in an inability to spell nonwords. Errors are rarely phonologically plausible, since conversion procedures are not used. The first detailed case of phonological dysgraphia was described by Shallice (1981) and, again, many others have followed since both in the acquired literature (e.g., Bub & Kertesz, 1982; Goodman-Shulman, & Caramazza, 1987; Roeltgen, Sevush, & Heilman, 1983) and in the developmental literature (Temple & Marshall, 1983; see Temple, 1986, and Hanley & Gard, 1995, for studies describing contrasting patterns in different individuals).

## Differences between Reading and Spelling

Before describing impairments of spelling it is useful to ask whether the same structures of knowledge that support reading also support spelling. One could argue that many of the processes and representations that are involved in spelling are also involved in reading, although the process runs in reverse from sounds to letters rather than from letters to sounds. However, this is not the only possible view (see Treiman & Kessler, this volume). For example, it has been argued that an *input* orthographic lexicon is accessed for reading, and a different *output* orthographic lexicon is accessed for spelling (see Caramazza, 1988; Ellis, 1982). To anticipate our conclusions, we will suggest that the same structures of knowledge support both tasks, but we will also stress that reading and spelling make very different demands on these processes and representations and those result in different kinds of acquired and developmental impairments.

It is undisputed that selective impairments of spelling can arise from peripheral impairments. For example, impairments of motor control involving the hand or arm (apraxia) affect spelling but not reading and spelling to dictation can be selectively impaired where there are auditory problems. Peripheral aspects of the processes apart, if common mental representations are used by reading and spelling, *the same type* of impairments should be evident for both tasks. Indeed, cases have been reported where there is a correspondence between acquired deficits affecting *nonword* reading and spelling (e.g., Campbell & Butterworth, 1985; Roeltgen, 1985) or *irregular word* reading and spelling (*acquired*: De Partz et al., 1992; Kremin, 1985; Newcombe & Marshall, 1985; Parkin, 1993; Tainturier, 1996; *developmental*: Castles & Coltheart, 1996). Moreover, some acquired cases have shown remarkable similarities in reading and spelling in the words they get right or wrong (Behrmann & Bub, 1992; Coltheart & Funnel, 1987) and in the particular errors they make (Tainturier, 1996). Numerous studies, however, have also described differences between reading and spelling.

The application of conversion rules requires more blending abilities in the case of nonword reading and more parsing abilities in the case of nonword spelling. Consistent with the view that different resources are involved in applying conversion rules in reading and spelling, there are reports of acquired disorders where nonword reading is better than nonword spelling (PR, Shallice, 1981), and vice versa (RG, Beavois & Dérouesné, 1981).

More commonly, there are numerous reports where problems with word knowledge affect spelling but not reading (in the *acquired literature* see Goodman-Shulman & Caramazza, 1986; Sanders & Caramazza, 1990; Shallice, 1981; in the *developmental literature* see Castles & Coltheart, 1996; Goulandris & Snowling, 1991; Hanley et al., 1992; Romani et al., 1999). Moreover, in some of these cases, a surface pattern in spelling (better spelling of nonwords than words; poor spelling of irregular words) is accompanied by a phonological pattern in reading (better reading of words than nonwords and small regularity effects; Beavois & Dérouesné, 1981; Hanley et al., 1992; Romani et al., 1999). Most of the adults with developmental dyslexia tested in our lab, in fact, show this pattern. We would argue, however, that these differences can be explained by the different requirements of spelling and reading without invoking different representations.

First of all, spelling is a more difficult task than reading. It requires access to more detailed lexical representations, and phoneme–grapheme correspondences are more ambiguous in spelling (e.g., /f/ can be written either "f" or "ph", but "f" and "ph" are both pronounced /f/). Consistent with spelling being more difficult, cases of apparent dissociation have shown problems with reading when the task was made more difficult. An example is the aphasic patient MLB (Tainturier, 1996), who showed much better performance in reading than spelling and was only mildly impaired in a standard lexical decision task (e.g., Is *yicht* a word?). However, she was severely impaired in a harder lexical decision task that forced the use of more complete orthographic knowledge by including nonwords that sounded like real words (e.g., Is *brane* a word?). Another example is the developmental case of AW (Romani et al., 1999), a young man with severe spelling problems, but excellent reading. Even his reading, however, deteriorated dramatically when the task was made more difficult by mixing words with nonwords, and he performed poorly in tasks that required detailed discriminations between letter patterns, such as lexical decision and same–different tasks (see also Allan; Hanley et al., 1992).

Secondly, reading and spelling, by their nature, may rely differentially on a lexical and nonlexical processing strategy. Reading favors lexical processing because a match between a word on the page and a stored orthographic representation may be successful even when both are underspecified. Knowledge of existing spoken words and semantic context will restrict choices and fill in gaps. Spelling relies more on (phoneme–grapheme) conversion rules because neither semantic information nor the lexical neighborhood provide assistance in the case of underspecified representations. Only conversion rules can fill the gaps. Consistent with this interpretation, results from our laboratory show that the use of conversion rules correlates negatively with speed and accuracy in reading but positively with accuracy in spelling in both normal and developmentally impaired participants.

Given these differences, individuals who have partially specified lexical representations can show a phonological pattern in reading, because a lexical strategy will be more successful with words than nonwords (which will be mistaken for similar words). They can show a surface pattern in spelling, because here they will rely more on conversion rules which will be successful with nonwords but result in phonologically plausible errors with words. Only individuals with very severe lexical impairments will need to use conversion rules in reading as well as spelling. Consistent with this interpretation, a surface pattern has been found in both tasks only in acquired cases, which are generally more severe, and in cases of young children with developmental dyslexia (e.g., Castles & Coltheart, 1996), but not in less severe cases of adults with a developmental history of dyslexia. Finally, one can note that computerized tasks where words are mixed with nonwords generally produce an advantage for words; but an advantage for nonwords can be seen in individuals with good conversion rules when stimuli are presented in blocks and without time pressure (see Hanley et al., 1992). This, again, shows differential use of lexical and nonlexical strategies depending on task requirements.

We have argued that reading and spelling are based on the same orthographic knowledge (see also results with normal participants: Burt & Tate, 2002; Holmes & Carruthers, 1998), but that spelling requires much more detailed lexical representations than reading. For this reason, spelling often reveals an impairment that is not evident in reading and remains problematic when reading is no longer so. If representations are common, one might be tempted to conclude that research on spelling should focus on the peripheral aspects of this ability given the amount of research already focused on reading. On the contrary, we believe that research on spelling can provide a unique perspective on how orthographic knowledge is acquired, represented, and lost. In the next section, we will start to demonstrate the value of independent studies of spelling by showing how the spelling errors made by acquired cases of dysgraphia have informed models of lexical access and representation.

## Acquired Disorders of Spelling

Early studies have established the existence of lexical and nonlexical spelling procedures, mainly by considering the spelling of different kinds of stimuli (words and nonwords; regular and irregular words, high- and low-frequency words). Further studies have focused on the nature of the errors made. These studies have provided evidence consistent with a more differentiated model (figure 23.2). This model shows (1) a distinction between different lexical routes; (2) the addition of an orthographic buffer; and (3) a distinction between lexical and letter nodes in the lexicon (figure 23.3). In addition, by looking at the errors made by the patients, it has been possible to gather precious evidence on the nature of orthographic representations. For reasons of space, we focus here on impairments to the central components and will not discuss impairments that derive from damage to more peripheral spelling components (such as the allographic system, which converts abstract orthographic knowledge into motor patterns).

### *Two different lexical routes*

Theoretically, there are two different ways in which representations in the orthographic lexicon can be accessed. One way, already shown in figure 23.1, is via the semantic system.

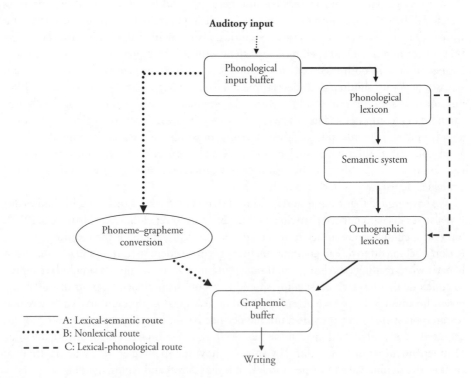

**Figure 23.2**    A more detailed model of spelling.

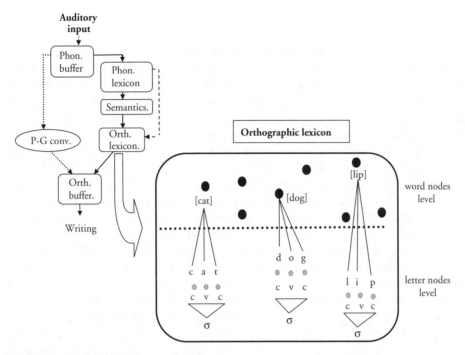

**Figure 23.3**   A model of the orthographic lexicon.

A second possible way, however, is via a direct connection from the phonological lexicon. The neuropsychological literature has provided evidence for both.

Some dysgraphic patients make semantic errors in writing (e.g., they might write "cow" as *horse*) though they do not make such errors in speech. They also show frequency effects such that high-frequency words are spelled correctly whereas low-frequency words are not (e.g., Hillis, Rapp, & Caramazza, 1999). It is possible that these patients have problems activating some (low-frequency) representations in the orthographic lexicon because of degradation or weaker connections. When this is the case, a semantically related word, which also receives some input from the semantic system, may be produced instead, resulting in a semantic error. This explanation is based on the common assumption that not only the target semantic representation, but also related representations, will pass activation to the orthographic lexicon. Independent of the particular explanation offered, however, these errors undoubtedly demonstrate that lexical access occurs via semantics.

Romani, Olson, Ward, & Ercolani (2002) described an alternative pattern where errors of lexical selection are based on phonological rather than semantic input. They described the case of DW, a global aphasic with a severe form of dysgraphia. The majority of her spelling errors involved either the mis-selection of a single related word (e.g., "fable" > *cable*) or a combination of words (e.g., "curiosity" > *suretoy*). Targets and errors were always formally related (either phonologically or visually) rather than semantically related. This pattern of impairment is evidence for a second "lexical route" to spelling (*route C* in figure 23.2) in which representations in the orthographic lexicon are activated by a phonological rather than a semantic input.

*Impairments of sustained letter activation (buffer impairments)*

Figure 23.2 shows that the lexical route and the nonlexical route come together at the level of the *orthographic buffer* (sometimes called the graphemic buffer). The function of this component is to keep an abstract orthographic representation "in mind" while it is transformed into a more peripheral representation suitable for production (e.g., allographic conversion in the case of handwriting; conversion into letter names in the case of oral spelling). Buffer errors arising from brain damage have their normal counterpart in the slips of the pen made by normal spellers. These errors consist of substitutions, deletions, insertions, and transpositions of letters that are not phonologically plausible (e.g., "table" spelled as *dable, tabe, trable, batle*). In normal spellers (e.g., Wing & Baddeley, 1980) and in some spellers with acquired dysgraphia, these errors show positional effects such that letters in the middle of words are spelled worse than letters at either end (for a symmetrical curve see Caramazza, Miceli, Villa, & Romani, 1987; Posteraro, Zinelli, & Mazzucchi, 1988; for a right-skewed curve see Jonsdottir, Shallice, & Wise, 1996).

Several patients have been interpreted as suffering from impairments to the orthographic buffer (e.g., Caramazza & Miceli, 1990; Houghton, Glasspool, & Shallice, 1994). The following characteristics motivate this interpretation. Spelling in different modalities is affected (oral spelling, handwriting, typing) as is spelling of both words and nonwords. This is predicted by the position of the buffer at the convergence of the lexical and nonlexical routes (see figures 23.1 and 23.2). Effects of lexical variables (e.g., frequency, concreteness) are absent or weak, since damage does not involve the lexicon. Equally, since the impairment does not involve knowledge of the letters in the word but a rapid loss of information while the letters are realized motorically, the same severity of impairment is seen whether or not the patient has been recently "reminded" of the spelling of the word (as in delayed copy). Finally, one should find that performance deteriorates when the capacity of the buffer is stretched as in the case of long words that both occupy more "space" and require more time to be written. The positional effect can also be interpreted as the consequence of limited capacity. Letters in the middle would be lost more easily because they are subject to more interference from flanking letters on both sides.

*Impairments retrieving letters (instead of words)*

Ward and Romani (1998) have reported the case of a patient, BA, who made the same kinds of letter transformation errors made by buffer patients, but who did not show other associated characteristics of performance. BA showed clear frequency effects and occasional semantic errors, which are generally taken to indicate lexical problems. Among her letter errors, there were more deletions and more fragments where only the beginning of the word was written ("table" > *ta . . .*) indicating, perhaps, a more complete lack of information. The length effect was not as marked. Longer words were spelled completely correctly more rarely, but error rate "per letter" remained roughly constant with short and long words. Moreover, the positional effect was different: the errors became progressively more likely from the beginning to the end of the word. Finally and most crucially, refreshing knowledge of spellings, by showing the word a few minutes before spelling was attempted (delayed copy), dramatically improved performance.

All of these characteristics of performance are more consistent with an impairment in the *knowledge* of the letter sequences associated with words than with an impairment in their *temporary* activation. According to this interpretation, BA makes a semantic error when the orthographic representation of a word is completely unavailable. She makes fragment or letter errors when only part of the orthographic representation is retrievable. She cannot fill in missing information using conversion rules since they are also damaged. The positional effects could stem from the fact that initial letters normally have more activation than subsequent letters to facilitate serial retrieval.

Other patients with characteristics similar to BA have been reported, although the interpretations have been different (patient HR, Katz, 1991; Patient TH, Schiller, Greenhall, Shelton, & Caramazza, 2001). Together with BA, these patients provide a contrast with patients who make *word errors* where the wrong word is activated from either the semantic system ('table' > *chair*) or the phonological lexicon ('table' > *cable*). This suggests a distinction between word and letter representations as shown in figure 23.3 (but see Seidenberg & McClelland, 1989, 1990, for a model *not* including this distinction). In addition, patients showing impairments in letter knowledge provide a contrast with the buffer patients, suggesting a distinction between the structure of knowledge representing letters and the mechanisms involved in their temporary activation.

## Implications for the nature of orthographic representations

Whether they result from loss of lexical knowledge or from a disruption to the memory mechanisms that keep this knowledge active in the short term, letter errors are probably the most common form of error in patients with dysgraphia. They also have been most informative about the nature of orthographic representations. They are more rarely made in reading because lexical capture will lead instead to lexical substitutions (word errors). Letter errors have demonstrated that orthographic representations are not simply linear strings of letters but, instead, are organized into larger units akin to the syllables of spoken production. Like syllables, these units have vowels at their centre and are flanked by consonants. Evidence for this organization has come mainly from three characteristics of letter errors.

First, letter errors can preserve legality in the sense that they produce possible letter sequences. For example, the word "grab" is spelled as *glab* or *gab* or *gralb*, but not *gcab* or *rgab* (Schonauer & Denes, 1994; Ward & Romani, 2000). The same preservation of legality has been found in the spelling errors of the profoundly deaf, indicating that it is the result of an orthographic organization and not a consequence of phonological input (Olson & Caramazza, 2004; Olson & Nickerson, 2001). Syllables are necessary to specify the constraints that these patients follow. Syllables, in fact, specify not only how many consonants can precede or follow a vowel, but also which consonants can occur in different positions.

Second, letter errors preserve a distinction between consonants and vowels. Consonants are substituted with consonants, and vowels with vowels (e.g., "table" > *dable* or *bable* but not *eable* or *aable*; see Caramazza & Miceli, 1990; Jonsdottir et al., 1996; Kay & Hanley, 1994; Schonauer & Denes, 1994; Ward & Romani, 2000). Keeping substitutions within CV class could be partly a consequence of the tendency to preserve legality, because errors that violate this constraint often result in illegal combinations (e.g., substituting any consonant for the "a" of *cat* will lead to an orthographically illegal sequence, but all vowel-for-vowel substitutions will be legal). There is additional evidence, however, that consonants and vowels are separate classes of units. Cubelli (1991) has reported two dysgraphic cases where *vowels* were either selectively substituted or selectively deleted (in this last case blanks were left in their places), and Kay and Hanley (1994) have reported the opposite pattern with more errors when writing consonants than vowels (see also Cotelli, Abutalebi, Zorzi, & Cappa, 2003). These dissociations indicate that the cognitive system treats consonant and vowel letters as different kinds of symbols. This, in turn, is an indication of syllabic organization. A distinction between consonant and vowel letters, in fact, does not have an independent motivation outside the syllable.

Thirdly, but more controversially, some patients with buffer deficits make more errors on words with complex syllabic structures than on words involving simple alternations of consonants and vowels (e.g., CCCVC vs. CVCVC; Caramazza & Miceli, 1990; Schonauer & Denes, 1994). This observation is consistent not only with words being organized into syllables, but also with complex syllables being more difficult to store, retrieve, and/or repair. It has been argued, however, that these effects derive from the phonology rather than being an independent property of the orthography (Jonsdottir et al., 1996). Even though the patients in question showed little evidence of spelling through sounds, they were Italian, and Italian spelling relies much more heavily on sounds than English spelling. The Italian orthography is very regular (transparent), so that words can be spelled correctly just by phoneme–grapheme conversion. The English patients with dysgraphia reported to date have not shown complexity effects (Kay & Hanley, 1994; Jonsdottir et al., 1996; Ward & Romani, 2000). It is possible that syllabic structure organizes both spoken and written words, but that effects of syllabic complexity are tied to articulatory complexity and, for this reason, are only found in spoken language (see Romani, Olson, Semenza, & Grana', 2002).

The fact that syllable structure is found in written language – as well as in spoken language – suggests that it has an additional function besides the traditional one of determining prosody (prosody characterizes only spoken language). This additional function can be described as "grammatical". Each language allows only certain segments in certain syllabic positions. For example, in English, if there are two consonants in the onset (the first part of the syllable preceding the vowel), you know that the second one must be "r" or "l". Syllables, thus, provide a convenient and economical way to represent which combinations of segments are possible and which are not. This knowledge, in turn, makes it easier to memorize new lexical items and to restore them in the case of partial degradation. This function is critical when language involves storing and retrieving hundreds of thousands of lexical items that are made up by combining a small number of symbols in different ways.

If this view of syllable structure is correct, it should have implications for developmental, as well as for acquired, disorders of spelling. In the case of individuals who fail to develop completely specified representations, one could ask whether a representation of syllable structure is intact or lacking (e.g., Caravolas, Bruck, & Genesee, 2003) and, if it is intact, whether it could be exploited in a more systematic way to facilitate learning. In more general terms, the correspondence in organizational structure between spoken and written language shown by the acquired impairments suggests that our understanding of developmental dyslexia would also benefit from considering parallel difficulties in the orthographic and spoken domain. In the following section we will suggest that a difficulty of this type could be the cause of spelling impairments that persist in adulthood.

## Developmental Spelling Disorders

Developmental spelling problems are generally associated with reading problems, even if spelling problems are sometimes the only remaining indication of dyslexia in adulthood. Developmental dyslexia, therefore, is a term that has come to cover both spelling and reading problems, and dysgraphia and dyslexia are not as clearly separated in the developmental literature as they are in the literature on acquired disorders. We will first show how different stages in learning to read and spell draw differently on lexical and sublexical processes. This different emphasis, together with the presence of impairments affecting mainly lexical or sublexical processing, suggests that a lexical/nonlexical distinction is as important to understanding developmental deficits as it is to understanding acquired deficits (even if direct analogies would be simplistic as described in the last section of the chapter).

Our contention will be that in adults with long-lasting spelling problems, poorly specified lexical representations (*surface dysgraphia*) are caused by an impairment that is different from the phonological impairment associated with poor sublexical processing, or *phonological dysgraphia*.

### Stages in literacy acquisition

In the very initial stages of literacy acquisition, it is well documented that reading skills may lag behind spelling abilities. Bryant and Bradley (1980) and Read (1980) have described cases of "preschool orthographers" who are able to spell simple words that they cannot read. Their observations are confirmed by Ottavia, the daughter of the first two authors. Ottavia is 4 years old and attends an English school. Although she is exposed to Italian at home, she is receiving no formal instruction in this language. To her delight, Ottavia has realized that she can write most short words correctly in Italian due to the transparency of the language. However, she is generally unable to read them back and her errors are often wild guesses. Taken together, this evidence suggests that in the very initial phases of literacy development, conversion rules can be applied better in writing than in reading (Cossu & Marshall, 1985).

Following this initial stage, further development of spelling depends upon children becoming sensitive to orthographic conventions. An awareness of such conventions, including spelling-sound consistencies, must develop from their experience of written words through reading (Caravolas, Hulme, & Snowling, 2001; Frith, 1985). As we have already noted, English spelling is much less consistent than is reading, and there is no analogue in spelling to guessing the identity of a word from partial orthographic knowledge. It follows that children typically become proficient readers before they master spelling and its inconsistencies. Indeed, even a moderate increase in orthographic knowledge will dramatically improve word recognition, but not necessarily spelling, due to the numerous irregular words in English that require detailed knowledge of letter identity and order.

An even stronger advantage for reading over spelling can be seen in adults with a developmental history of dyslexia (Hanley et al., 1992; Romani et al., 1999). Spelling impairments in this population have been found to involve poor lexical knowledge rather than poor knowledge of phoneme–grapheme conversion *surface* dysgraphia (e.g., Holmes & Castles, 2001; Holmes & Ng, 1993; but also see Bruck, 1993). Our hypothesis is that many children with dyslexia will be able to compensate for their phonological difficulty by using a strategy of whole-word recognition combined with increased learning efforts. Individuals who remain dyslexic, instead, suffer from a *second deficit* that affects learning of lexical representations. Because of this problem, lexical representations do not develop sufficiently to support good spelling.

## Lexical and sublexical skills in developmental dysgraphia

The fact that lexical knowledge and knowledge of conversion rules play a different role at different developmental stages is consistent with the fact that the developmental literature – like the acquired literature – has described cases where one or the other is impaired. In addition, it is possible to classify children with dyslexia according to differing profiles of reading impairment, that is, according to whether their problems focus more on phoneme–grapheme conversion or more on irregular word reading (Castles & Coltheart, 1993; Manis, Seidenberg, Doi, McBride-Chang, & Petersen, 1996; Stanovich, Siegel, & Gottardo, 1997). Although it should be noted that most children fall on a continuum, with relatively few pure cases (Griffiths & Snowling, 2002), these differences call for an explanation and this is one of the main challenges for research on developmental disorders.

The most widely researched impairments of reading and spelling in developmental disorders are those that affect phonological processing. These have been convincingly associated with problems of grapheme–phoneme translation in reading and inadequate development of phoneme–grapheme conversion rules in spelling (e.g., Campbell & Butterworth, 1985; Hulme & Snowling, 1992; Snowling & Hulme, 1989; Snowling, Stackhouse, & Rack, 1986; Temple & Marshall, 1983). It is the causes of poor lexical knowledge, and its behavioral manifestation as surface dysgraphia (with or without surface dyslexia), that is not well understood. One extreme view is that some children who show the surface dysgraphic profile are, in fact, developing along normal lines, albeit slowly ('delay dyslexia'). These children perhaps suffer from poor motivation and/or lack of learning opportunities, leading to reduced print experience (Harm & Seidenberg, 1999; Manis et al., 1996; Stanovich et al., 1997). An alternative is to attribute surface dysgraphia to a specific – albeit different – cognitive impairment. We will now turn to what this impairment might be.

*A visual processing impairment as the cause of surface dysgraphia*

Frith (1980, 1985, 1987) described the performance of individuals that she has called "unexpectedly poor spellers". In spelling, these individuals showed a pattern akin to surface dysgraphia with a large proportion of phonological plausible errors, good nonword spelling, and effects of frequency and regularity on spelling accuracy. Silent reading of text was unimpaired, but they showed a number of interesting effects indicating that they read using what Frith referred to as a "partial-cue" reading strategy. This strategy capitalizes on the redundancy present in the written language, skips details, and bases recognition on a minimal amount of information.

Frith (1980) reported a number of results in support of her theory. For example, unexpectedly poor spellers were slower than controls when asked to read a text aloud. The difference was maintained when some letters in the text were substituted, but it disappeared when the letters were obliterated. Presumably, this condition forced all participants to rely on partial cues. Poor spellers were also much slower than controls when they had to find letter "*es*" that were part of unstressed syllables in a letter cancellation task (and thus pronounced as schwas or unpronounced). However, they were equally fast when they had to find letter "*es*" that were part of stressed syllables and thus, presumably, more important for word discrimination. These results are complemented by the findings of Seymour and MacGregor (1984), who showed that some adequate readers who were poor spellers were severely disrupted by manipulations that affected word shape, such as presenting the words vertically rather than horizontally (see also Seymour, 1986). Together these results suggest that unexpectedly poor spellers read by relying on information about word shape supplemented by partial letter identification. Indeed, Frith (1980) proposed that this strategy may be fast and economical when deployed for reading but could lead to underspecified lexical representations and, thus, be an underlying cause of poor spelling.

AW (Romani et al., 1999) was a prototypical case of an "unexpectedly poor speller" in Frith's terms, and some of his characteristics of performance are clearly consistent with Frith's interpretation. He performed poorly in tasks requiring comparison of sequences of letters, but he also performed poorly in nonlinguistic tasks requiring comparison of sequences of symbols (e.g., &, %, $, etc.) or recall of sequences of abstract shapes such as Hindi and Japanese characters. Moreover, in these latter tasks, controls performed better when the characters were presented one at a time rather than all together. AW, instead, showed the opposite trend, doing better when all the characters were presented simultaneously, a mode that allowed him to combine the characters into integrated visual shapes. This pattern suggests difficulties with a sequential/analytic mode of processing and a preference for global, visuospatial processing.

It is to be noted that AW's deficit of *visuosequential* memory contrasts with the impairment shown by another case of developmental surface dyslexia reported by Goulandris and Snowling (1991). JAS suffered from a more generalized impairment, which involved not only memory for visual sequences but also memory for visuospatial patterns. Goulandris and Snowling have suggested that this more generalized impairment may also be at the root of surface dyslexia/dysgraphia.

## A lexical learning impairment as the cause of surface dysgraphia

Although a visual explanation of selective spelling problems is appealing, another explanation is also possible. It could be that poor spellers fail to develop well-specified orthographic representations for independent reasons, and these cause them to develop holistic reading strategies rather than the other way round. According to this interpretation, poor spellers read using partial orthographic cues because they have no other choice, given underspecified lexical representations. These poor representations, in turn, could be caused by a specific problem in encoding or retaining lexical representations. This could be a *linguistic* rather than a visual problem. We will refer to it as a problem of *lexical learning*. Consistent with this interpretation, AW performed very poorly in a number of tasks that required him to learn the association between a picture and a *new word* (e.g., made-up English words or Dutch words) presented either spoken or written. His poor learning was unexpected given his very high IQ, normal phonological processing, and normal performance in a number of tasks that involved learning other representations such as lists of words or visuospatial patterns.

We have assessed the generality of the pattern shown by AW in further studies of adults with dyslexia (Di Betta & Romani, submitted). These studies have confirmed that there are selective difficulties of lexical learning in such adults who are typically poor spellers, but good readers (at least in untimed conditions). As a group, these individuals performed more poorly than a control group matched for age, IQ, and education in tasks that required learning new spoken or written words, like those administered to AW. In contrast, like AW, they performed normally in tasks that required them to learn visuospatial or lexical-semantic representations.

A second study with a similar population (Romani, Di Betta, & Olson, in preparation) has shown that performance on *learning* tasks was a strong predictor of *word* reading and spelling (ahead of more traditional tasks of phonological processing and retention), while performance on sublexical *phonological* tasks was the main predictor of *nonword* reading and spelling. Furthermore, individuals with a more typical *surface* profile had milder deficits of phonological processing than the *phonological* group, but deficits of lexical learning that were as severe. A single phonological impairment would have difficulty explaining these patterns of results.

Our studies show that poorly specified lexical representations that persist into adulthood cannot be explained by poor general cognitive abilities, poor motivation, or poor learning opportunities. The people with dyslexia that we have studied have normal IQs and show normal learning ability in some domains. However, they perform poorly when required to learn new spoken and written word forms, indicative of a specific cognitive impairment that hinders lexical expansion and has particularly negative consequences for spelling. The exact nature of this impairment is still uncertain. However, our results suggest that it is different from the impairments of phonological short-term memory and phonological awareness that are traditionally identified. In our group, written learning predicted the severity of the spelling impairment independent of sublexical skills. Moreover, the impairment in lexical learning remains a significant predictor of spelling performance even when individual differences in phonological skills were controlled.

It is possible that humans are specially endowed with the ability to create an unlimited set of representations from a limited set of symbols, an ability that is fundamental to human language. Speculatively, people with dyslexia have a reduction in this ability that impacts both spoken and written language learning. However, its impact is stronger on written language, which is less practiced than spoken language. In line with Frith's theory (e.g., Frith, 1985), it is possible that while sublexical phonology plays a more important role in initial stages of literacy acquisition (for a metastudy see Ehri et al., 2001), the ability that we have called *lexical learning* plays a more crucial role later on in adults who remain poor spellers.

## Differences between Acquired and Developmental Disorders

The preceding discussion makes it clear that the distinction between lexical and sublexical processes is important in both the developmental and the acquired literature. Furthermore, many studies have assumed that the same principles of analysis apply to developmental and acquired disorders of reading and writing (e.g., Baddeley, Ellis, Miles, & Lewis, 1982; Castles & Coltheart, 1993; but see Snowling, 1983; Snowling, Bryant, & Hulme, 1996, for contrasting views). However, it seems clear that the developmental literature does not present the same range of impairments as the acquired literature and this difference is not likely to be a simple consequence of the different interests of researchers working in the two fields.

### Strength of dissociations

In an established orthographic system, processes and representations may be substantially localized and brain damage can affect specific parts of the system while leaving other functionally independent components intact. The effect of a delay or a disruption on a developing system is quite different. At the risk of stating the obvious, the impact would unfold over time in a system that must seek to function despite the lack of some resources, or with an abnormal balance of resources. As a result, developmental disorders are not likely to be as sharply defined as acquired disorders (for a more extended discussion see Bishop, 1997a). A clear example is provided by a consideration of lexical and nonlexical processes is spelling. As we have seen, these processes can be selectively impaired in developmental and acquired dysgraphia. However, in the case of a developmental impairment, a weakness in one ability will have consequences for the other. Thus, lexical impairments will affect the efficacy with which conversion rules are applied because sound-spelling conversion rules are derived from examples. With more examples and the acquisition of more detailed lexical specifications, the contexts in which different rules apply become clearer. By the same token, good conversion rules will facilitate lexical expansion since new words can be decoded and understood. The interdependence of conversion rules and lexical representations during learning explains why less complete dissociations are described in developmental than in acquired cases.

## Double dissociations

In adults, brain damage may affect not only very specific representations, leaving others unaffected, but may selectively *affect* representations in some individuals and selectively *spare* the same representations in others. We have presented the example of double dissociations between impaired/spared spelling of consonants and vowels. In developmental impairments, however, we have to consider not how a set of representations can be selectively impaired or spared, but the reasons why certain representations have failed to be acquired. The example of spelling highlights how the impairment must involve *more general resources* that, in evolutionary terms, have been developed for a different purpose.

Given these considerations, we suggest that double dissociations between classes of closely related representations will *not* be found in developmental impairments. The representation that is computationally more demanding will always be the one affected in all individuals with no reversal of pattern. To continue with the example of consonants and vowels, in English spelling, vowels are generally more error-prone across populations and spelling abilities. This is because the correspondences between letters and sounds are more complicated for vowels. The opposite dissociation does occur, but not in writing. Consonants are acquired later than vowels in *spoken* production, probably because they involve finer motor control (see also Karmiloff-Smith, Scerif, & Ansari, 2003).

## Different types of impairment

Finally, the acquired literature has argued, in different ways, that brain damage may make representations harder to access or retrieve rather than destroying representations (Rapp & Caramazza, 1993; Warrington & Shallice, 1979). It is less plausible to imagine developmental cases where knowledge is acquired but then becomes difficult to retrieve. In fact, no "access" impairments are described in the developmental literature.

## Conclusions

The study of acquired and developmental impairments has provided us with complementary information. Acquired disorders occur in a variety of forms that reveal how orthographic information is represented by the mature system. There are fewer variants of developmental disorder but these provide important information concerning the cognitive resources that underpin the mature system.

In our review of acquired disorders we have noted that there is a fundamental distinction between the knowledge structures representing information at the word level (the lexical system) and the sublexical level (in terms of correspondences between sounds and letters). Orthographic lexical representations can be accessed from either a semantic or a phonological input. They consist of word units linked to the corresponding letter units. Letters are not simply organized in a linear string, but include more complex structures that distinguish among consonants and vowels, and group them into syllabic units. Finally, there is a distinction between structures of knowledge and the mechanisms that keep them active in the short-term during production.

In our review of developmental disorders we have highlighted the importance of disorders that persist into adulthood in providing evidence for the cognitive resources underlying literacy acquisition. We have suggested that at least two impairments can contribute to problems in learning to spell (and read). One is a problem of phonological processing, which has its clearest effects on conversion rules. The second involves storing inadequate orthographic lexical representations and has its clearest effect on spelling of irregular words. Whether this second impairment is due to (1) a problem of analytic visual processing or (2) a linguistic problem in creating new lexical representations (specifically orthographic or phonological representations or both) remains for future research.

Findings from the study of acquired and developmental disorders support and inform one another. Understanding the format normally taken by orthographic representations, as revealed by acquired disorders, informs our search for factors that could be involved in lexical storage (e.g., CV or syllabic structure). Studying adults with a childhood history of dyslexia and selective spelling difficulties provides additional evidence that independent resources underpin lexical acquisition and acquisition of correspondence rules, and supports the dissociations between lexical and sublexical impairments found in the acquired literature. These examples show that studies of spelling provide a view of the capacities underlying literacy that is valuable and complementary to work on reading.

## Note

This study has been supported by Wellcome Trust Graut NO55629 to the first author.

# PART VI

*The Biological Bases of Reading*

# Editorial Part VI

Parts I to V of the book have dealt with cognitive explanations of reading and reading problems. The two chapters in Part VI move on to consider the biological substrates of reading. Reading depends upon brain mechanisms and the development of these in turn is influenced by genetic mechanisms.

Reading in evolutionary terms is a very recent development in the human species, too recent, presumably, for any specific mechanisms to have evolved to allow us to learn to read. In contrast, language is a quintessential human skill that does appear to be a unique evolutionary adaptation of the human species. Pennington and Olson review the massive body of evidence for genetic differences contributing to the development of reading skill, and more specifically genetic influences on the development of dyslexia. It appears that genetic differences among people contribute powerfully to the development of language skills, which in turn are the foundation for learning to read (see chapters in Part II and Part V for elaborations on this point). As Pennington and Olson describe, it is now well established that there is a strong tendency for dyslexia to be inherited, and using molecular genetic methods it has been possible to identify the approximate locations on different chromosomes of a number of risk loci that contribute to the inheritance of dyslexia. It appears that a number of genes contribute to the risk of becoming dyslexic, and that these genes may also contribute to continuous variations among people in the language skills (particularly phonological skills) that contribute to the development of dyslexia. These are exciting times: it may be that dyslexia is the developmental disorder whose genetic aetiology is closest to being understood.

The genetic effects described by Pennington and Olson presumably contribute, along with environmental influences, to variations in the pattern of brain development. Recent advances in functional brain imaging have allowed us to identify the areas that subserve reading in the intact human brain: Price and McCrory provide an overview of our current knowledge in this area. A circuit of areas in the left parietal, temporal and frontal lobes have been identified that are involved in reading. These areas, not surprisingly, show substantial overlap with areas known to be involved in visual recognition, speech processing, and semantic processing. A major challenge is to try to map cognitive models of word recognition in reading (see Part I of the book) on to the brain areas activated when words are read. Price and McCrory provide some suggestions about how this may be done.

Price and McCrory also review brain-imaging studies of reading in people with dyslexia. It appears that reading in the dyslexic brain engages similar areas to those activated in normal readers when reading, but there may be decreased activation in dyslexic brains, particularly in some left temporal/frontal lobe regions. Once again a major challenge is to relate such differences in patterns of brain activation to the cognitive models of reading and dyslexia described elsewhere in this volume.

There can be little doubt that in the next decade major strides will be made in understanding the way in which genetic factors influence the development of brain mechanisms underlying language and reading. The operation of these brain mechanisms can now, in turn, be observed using brain imaging techniques, and this raises the possibility of relating neural processes to cognitive mechanisms. Ultimately, it may be possible to relate genetic differences to variations in brain function, and in turn to cognitive explanations of how we read and what goes wrong in reading disorders such as dyslexia.

# 24

# Genetics of Dyslexia

## Bruce F. Pennington and Richard K. Olson

Dyslexia is an interesting example of the intersection between an evolved behavior (language) and a cultural invention (literacy). While there cannot be genes for reading or other relatively recent cultural inventions (consider agriculture, banking, and football), there can be genetic influences on evolved cognitive and behavioral traits necessary for proficiency in such cultural inventions. Because there is now extensive evidence of genetic influences on individual differences on most domains of cognition and behavior, it is not surprising that there are genetic influences on reading and spelling skills.

Dyslexia can be defined as a relatively severe difficulty in learning to recognize printed words, which is not explicable in terms of obvious intellectual or sensory impairments (for more discussion of detailed issues to do with the definition see Snowling, 2000b, and Vellutino & Fletcher, this volume). In what follows, we will first provide a *brief history* of the genetics of dyslexia, and then discuss the dramatic advances that have occurred in the last two decades using both *behavioral* and *molecular approaches*, and close with a discussion of how these approaches are being used to analyze the *comorbidities of dyslexia*. The goal is to provide an overview of this rapidly evolving field and to direct the reader to more detailed reviews of the findings, methods, and issues covered here. Earlier reviews of the genetics of dyslexia include Finucci (1978), Pennington and Smith (1983), DeFries and Gillis (1993), and Schulte-Körne (2001).

## Brief History

Clinicians have known for a long time that dyslexia runs in families. Soon after developmental dyslexia was first described by Pringle-Morgan (1896) and Kerr (1897), several reports of familial aggregation appeared (Fisher, 1905; Hinshelwood, 1907, 1911; Stephenson, 1907; Thomas, 1905).

Evidence for recurrence in families was repeatedly documented in case reports, leading Hallgren (1950) to undertake a more formal genetic epidemiological study of a large sample of families. Hallgren (1950) conducted the first test of the mode of transmission of dyslexia, and found that it fit an autosomal dominant pattern; that is, the pattern of inheritance was consistent with the possibility of a dominant gene on the nonsex chromosomes. His comprehensive monograph also documented several characteristics of dyslexia that have recently been rediscovered: (1) the widely cited male predominance (3–4 M:F) is mostly a selection artifact, since the sex ratio in relatives of probands (i.e., individuals selected for having a reading disorder from whom one identifies other family members for study) is nearly equal, about 1.5 M:F, and (2) again contrary to popular belief, there is not a significant association between dyslexia and nonright handedness. Hallgren also documented that dyslexia co-occurs with other speech/language and behavior disorders. At the end of this chapter we will review what has been learned about the genetic basis of the co-occurrence of dyslexia with some of these disorders: speech disorder, also called speech sound disorder (SSD), and attention deficit hyperactivity disorder (ADHD).

Although Hallgren and his predecessors provided considerable evidence that dyslexia ran in families, all of these data came from referred samples, leaving it unclear whether the familiality of dyslexia was widespread in the population. In addition, Hallgren (1950) mainly relied on interviews to diagnose adults and he considered family history data in making diagnoses. Such a practice could introduce a confirmatory bias and lead to over-selection of "loaded" pedigrees. Even in his sample, both parents were unaffected in 17% of his families; hence simple autosomal dominant transmission could not be the only genetic mechanism involved.

Hallgren's (1950) sample included six pairs of twins. These and other case studies of twins were reviewed by Zerbin-Rudin (1967). In twin studies of categorical disorders it is common to measure similarity between twin pairs in terms of concordance rates – the rate at which both members of a given type of twin pair share the same diagnosis. If genetic influences are important, we expect higher concordance rates for monozygotic or identical twins who share all their genes than for dizygotic or nonidentical twins who on average share just 50% of their segregating genes. Zerbin-Rudin found concordance rates of 100% vs. 52% in 17 MZ and 34 DZ pairs, respectively, providing evidence for the heritability of dyslexia (i.e., showing that genetic differences between people are important for whether or not they become dyslexic). A similar result was found by Bakwin (1973) in a same-sex twin sample in which diagnoses were based on history information provided by parents. Like the early family studies, these early twin studies had methodological limitations, including a lack of rigorous, test-based diagnostic criteria and potential recruitment biases. The limitations of these early family and twin studies prompted more methodologically adequate studies that are reviewed in the next section.

The third strand in this early history involves the application of direct genotypic measures to the task of understanding the etiology of dyslexia and other learning disabilities. Pennington and colleagues (Pennington, Bender, Puck, Salbenblatt, & Robinson, 1982; Pennington, Puck, & Robinson, 1980) found a higher rate of language and reading problems in both boys (47, XXY) and girls (47, XXX) with an extra X chromosome. Smith, Kimberling, Pennington, and Lubs (1983) used the few genetic markers then available to conduct a linkage study of dyslexia and found linkage to a centromeric marker on chromosome 15. As we will see in the later section on *molecular approaches* this kind of work has become increasingly sophisticated, and recently there has been rapid progress in identifying risk loci for dyslexia and related disorders.

## Behavioral Genetic Approaches

Family behavioral studies can provide a first step in exploring the possibility of genetic influences on a disorder. If a disorder does not run in families, there is no reason to look further for evidence of heritable genetic influence. The early family studies all reported significant familial transmission, but there were often limitations in sample selection and assessment of reading and related skills. To address these limitations in the earlier studies, John DeFries and colleagues at the University of Colorado initiated the largest family study of dyslexia to date (DeFries, Singer, Foch, & Lewitter, 1978). They recruited a sample of 133 children who were identified by teachers as having significant reading difficulty and then tested them in the laboratory with an extensive battery to confirm that they had significant reading and possibly related cognitive disabilities. An age and gender matched sample of 125 children with no reading problems was also identified by teachers and tested in the laboratory. The parents and siblings of the children with dyslexia and of the normal children were tested on the same measures.

The main result of the DeFries et al. (1978) family study was clear: There was strong evidence for the familial transmission of dyslexia. The relatives of the children ascertained with dyslexia were significantly more likely to also have reading problems, compared to the relatives of children with normal-range reading abilities. These results were consistent with those from other smaller, methodologically adequate family studies (Finucci, Guthrie, Childs, Abbey, & Childs, 1976; Owen, Adams, Forrest, Stoltz, & Fisher, 1971). However, there is an inherent limitation on the conclusions that can be drawn from family studies about genetic and environmental influences. Families share both their genes and their environment. Therefore, evidence for familial transmission provides necessary but not sufficient evidence for heritable genetic influence in dyslexia. It is possible that some or all of the observed familial transmission could be due to shared family environment.

Identical or monozygotic (MZ) and fraternal or dizygotic (DZ) same-sex twin pairs provide an ideal natural experiment that can provide direct evidence for genetic influence while the effects of shared family environment are controlled. As discussed earlier, this is because MZ twins share all their genes, while DZ twins share on average half their segregating genes (those genes related to individual differences). In 1982, John DeFries and colleagues initiated a large behavioral genetic twin study of dyslexia and potentially related disorders. As we write this chapter, the ongoing study in the Colorado Learning Disabilities Research Center (CLDRC) has collected extensive data on 622 MZ, 779 DZ same-sex, and 361 DZ opposite-sex twin pairs. The current co-investigators on the project include John DeFries and the authors of this chapter, Brian Byrne, Jan Keenan, Shelley Smith, Sally Wadsworth, and Erik Willcutt. In the remainder of this section, we will focus primarily on the behavioral genetic methods and results of this highly collaborative study (see DeFries et al., 1997, for an earlier summary).

In addition to the large sample size mentioned above, the CLDRC twin study of dyslexia has three main strengths. First, the affected members of twin pairs (probands) with dyslexia are initially ascertained from school records of third- to twelfth-grade twins with at least one twin showing a school history of reading difficulty, rather than from clinic samples or self-referral. A normal control sample of twins is also ascertained through school records for comparison. Second, a broad range of reading and potentially related cognitive skills are assessed in extensive laboratory testing. Third, rather than considering dyslexia as a categorical disorder, we acknowledge the reality that reading skill is normally distributed in the population (Rodgers, 1983; Shaywitz, Escobar, Shaywitz, Fletcher, & Makuch, 1992). Later we will describe new methods of analysis that have been developed to assess genetic and environmental influences on probands' membership in the low tail of the normal distribution for our measures of reading and related skills. These new methods also allow us to assess the degree to which genetic and environmental influences are shared across the different measures, including comorbidities with ADHD and other disorders discussed in the last section of the chapter. In what follows, we will describe (1) the sample and measures in the CLDRC twin study, (2) new methods for analyzing twin data, (3) how the heritability of dyslexia relates to IQ and other individual differences, (4) genetic and environmental influences on component reading and language skills, (5) genetic and environmental influences on normal variation in reading, and (6) genetic and environmental influences on early reading development.

## Sample and measures in the CLDRC twin study

The selection of participants with dyslexia (probands) in the CLDRC study is subject to the usual diagnostic criteria. Thus, the affected twin proband and their cotwin must have normal sensory acuity and no neurological signs such as seizures, they should have experienced no serious perinatal complications, and should have a record of normal school attendance. Children who are learning English as a second language are excluded, since this is a common and obvious cultural and environmental constraint on English reading development in Colorado. The probands are not constrained to have normal IQs or a reading discrepancy with IQ, as assessed by a standardized IQ test (the *WISC-R* or *WAIS* tests). Only a low cut-off score of at least 85 on the verbal or performance scales is used for most analyses. Full-scale IQ scores for probands with dyslexia range from 75 to 133 with a mean of 98. Inclusion of this natural variance in IQ allows us to assess the relation between IQ and the etiology of dyslexia.

The selection of reading and reading-related measures for the CLDRC twin study was based on theory, prior published studies, and substantial pilot research. Our focus is primarily on word reading because this skill is uniquely deficient in children with dyslexia and it places a major constraint on their reading comprehension (Stanovich, 2000). Several measures of reading and listening comprehension have been added to the CLDRC test battery in recent years to explore genetic influences on these skills that may be partly independent of genetic influences on word reading. Our sample of twins with these comprehension measures is currently too limited for most genetic analyses, but preliminary analyses suggest high heritability for individual differences in both reading and listening comprehension (Betjemann, Keenan, & Olson, 2003).

In addition to the inclusion of standardized measures of word reading, spelling recognition, and reading comprehension from the *Peabody Individual Achievement Test* (PIAT) (Dunn & Markwardt, 1970), we developed computer-based measures of rapid word reading, speed, and accuracy in phonological decoding (oral and silent nonword reading), and orthographic coding (which is a word, *rain* vs. *rane*? or which is a fruit, *pear* vs. *pair*?), a particularly important skill in English for correctly interpreting homophones. Previous studies by Snowling (1981) and others (see Rack, Snowling, & Olson, 1992, for a review) had identified phonological decoding as a skill that was even lower than expected given word-reading ability among readers of English with dyslexia, and thus a likely obstacle to their development of word-level reading skills. This unique deficit in phonological decoding has been confirmed in our initial studies with nontwins (Olson, 1985) and in twins (Olson, Wise, Conners, Rack, & Fulker, 1989) with reading disability.

In the oral language domain, in addition to verbal measures from the Wechsler Intelligence Scale for Children-Revised (*WISC-R*) or Wechsler Adult Intelligence Scale (*WAIS*) IQ tests, we included measures of phonological memory (nonword repetition), rapid automatic naming (RAN), rhyme generation, and, most importantly, multiple measures of the ability to isolate and manipulate phonemes in spoken language. One such measure was a task similar to the game of "Pig Latin" where the initial consonant was to be moved to the end of a word spoken by the tester, and the result spoken by the subject after adding the /ay/ sound (pig would become "igpay"). Another measure, phoneme deletion, required the subject to delete a phoneme from a spoken nonword and pronounce the word that would result from this deletion ("say prot without the /r/ sound – pot"). Prior research had identified substantial deficits in phoneme awareness in children with reading disability (cf., Rosner, 1979), and this has been confirmed in our own studies (Olson 1985; Olson, Kliegl, Davidson, & Foltz, 1985; Olson et al., 1989). We have also observed that there is a uniquely high correlation between the oral language skill of phoneme awareness and the component reading skill of phonological decoding, compared to its correlation with orthographic coding (Olson, Forsberg, & Wise, 1994).

## New methods for analyzing twin data

Our estimates of genetic influences on reading and related deficits have been based on the "DF" method for behavioral genetic analyses of group deficits on normally distributed variables (DeFries & Fulker, 1985, 1988). This technique capitalizes on the greater similarity of MZ cotwins than DZ cotwins for heritable skills. Hence, within DZ pairs, the performance of the cotwin on a measure of the skill in question should diverge further from that of the proband and be closer (regress more) to the population mean, than is the case for MZ cotwins.

In addition to estimating the proportion of genetic influence on a group deficit ($h^2_g$), the DF method can also provide estimates of the proportions of shared family environment influences ($c^2_g$), and environmental influences not shared by the twins ($e^2_g$). Shared environmental influences might include factors such as the value placed on reading in the home and the quality of schooling. Nonshared environmental influences might include biological risk events, such as illness and accidents that only happen to one member of a twin pair, different peer groups related to differences in reading practice, and any test error that would lead to differences between MZ twins. Taken together, genetic influences and the two types of environmental influences (shared and nonshared) account for all of the possible influences on probands' low-group membership.

To estimate the proportions of genetic and environmental influences with the DF method, we typically select MZ and DZ probands that are at least 1.5 SD below the normal-range control twin mean (the severity of proband selection can be varied), and then we compare the average regression to the population mean for the MZ and DZ cotwins. Each twin's score is initially divided by his or her respective MZ or DZ proband mean. Thus, the MZ and DZ probands' means equal 1, while the MZ and DZ cotwins' means fall somewhere between their proband mean and 0, the population mean. To illustrate the logic of the DF method, imagine that genetic factors were the only influence on dyslexia (i.e., heritability of the group deficit $[h^2_g] = 1$) and there was no test error. In this case MZ cotwins should show no regression to the population mean (i.e., they should show exactly the same severity of deficit as their cotwins), while DZ cotwins should regress halfway to the population mean because they share half their segregating genes, on average (see figure 24.1[a] for a graphic representation of this hypothetical result, and note that $h^2_g$ = twice the difference between MZ and DZ cotwin regression).

Of course there will always be some test error or other nonshared environmental influences on reading measures that would lead to some regression for MZ cotwins. The proportion of this MZ cotwin regression to the population mean provides a direct estimate of nonshared environment influence ($e^2_g$) on the group deficit, since MZ twins share all their genes and their family environment. For example, the MZ cotwin regression toward the population mean of 10% to .9 in figure 24.1(b) indicates that $e^2_g$ = .1. Thus, 10% of the proband group deficit is associated with nonshared environmental influence.

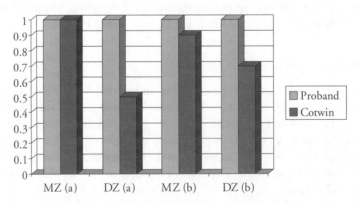

**Figure 24.1**  (a) Average MZ and DZ cotwin regression toward the population mean if a group deficit were due entirely to genetic influence. (b) Average MZ and DZ cotwin regression toward the population mean if a group deficit were due to non-shared environment (.1), genetic (.4), and shared environment influence (.5).

The proportion of the average group deficit that is due to environmental factors that are *shared* by twins within pairs ($c^2_g$) can also be estimated in DF analyses. For example, if nonshared environmental influences were small, and MZ and DZ cotwins regressed only slightly and exactly equally toward the population mean, in spite of their difference in genetic similarity, estimates of shared environment influence on the group deficit would be large and genetic influence would be zero. For many behavioral measures, there will likely be some influence from genes, nonshared environment, and shared environment. The hypothetical result for MZ and DZ cotwin regression in figure 24.1(b) shows that while the MZ cotwin mean regressed to .9, the DZ cotwin mean regressed to .7. DeFries and Fulker (1988) demonstrated that the heritability of a group deficit is equal to twice the difference between the MZ and DZ cotwin means when their scores have been divided by their respective proband means, so the example in figure 24.1(b) would indicate a heritability of $(.9 - .7) \times 2 = .4$. Since the MZ cotwin regression was to .9 indicating that $e^2_g = .1$, and $h^2_g = .4$, $c^2_g = 1 - (.1 + .4) = .5$. Thus, half of the group deficit in this example was due to shared environment influences. As with estimates for group-deficit heritability, estimates of shared-environment influences are for the group average, and the magnitude of shared-environment influence may vary among different probands with dyslexia.

## Heritability of dyslexia depending on IQ and other individual differences

DeFries, Fulker, and LaBuda (1987) first reported significant genetic influence on dyslexia based on DF analyses of the group deficit in a composite reading measure that included the PIAT word reading, spelling, and comprehension tests. Their estimate of the heritability of the dyslexic group deficit ($h^2_g$) was .29 in this initial study with a small twin sample from our first three years of testing. A more recent analysis for the composite PIAT measure in a much larger twin sample indicated that just over half the group deficit was due to heritable genetic influences ($h^2_g = .58$) (Wadsworth, Olson, Pennington, & DeFries, 2000). It is important to keep in mind that this estimate is a group average for the sample. The balance of genetic and environmental influences on dyslexia is likely to vary widely for individuals within the group.

The DF method can be extended to assess the significance of relations between genetic influence on dyslexia and other individual differences. Current evidence suggests that genetic influence may be stronger for dyslexia with high IQ compared to dyslexia with low IQ (Knopik et al., 2002; Olson, Datta, Gayan, & DeFries, 1999; Wadsworth et al., 2000). Wadsworth, Knopik, and DeFries (2000) reported no differential genetic etiology for dyslexia by gender, where the estimates of the importance of heritable effects were very similar for males and females. Castles, Datta, Gayan, and Olson (1999) found higher heritability for "phonological" than for "surface" subtypes of dyslexia. The "phonological" subtype was defined by low nonword reading relative to exception word reading, while the "surface" subtype was defined by the opposite pattern. However, it is important to keep in mind that the foregoing analyses of the variation in heritability for dyslexia related to other behavioral dimensions or categories only assess *average* relations between the variables and genetic influence on dyslexia. We cannot specify the genetic and environmental etiology of any individual's dyslexia through behavioral genetic methods. Molecular genetic studies described in the next main section of the chapter may ultimately bring us closer to the goal of individual diagnosis.

### Genetic and environmental influences on component reading and language skills

A number of our DF analyses have focused on component skills in reading and potentially related language skills. Language deficits are commonly found among children with dyslexia, so the balance of genetic and environmental influences on these skills and their shared genetic and environmental etiology with reading are of considerable interest. Gayan and Olson (2001) conducted analyses on groups selected separately for deficits in experimental measures of word reading ($h^2_g = .55$, $c^2_g = .39$, $e^2_g = .06$), oral phonological decoding ($h^2_g = .70$, $c^2_g = .18$, $e^2_g = .12$), orthographic coding accuracy ($h^2_g = .67$, $c^2_g = .17$, $e^2_g = .16$), and phoneme deletion ($h^2_g = .73$, $c^2_g = .14$, $e^2_g = .13$). (See figure 24.2(a) and (b) for the patterns of MZ and DZ cotwin regression for word reading and phoneme deletion respectively.) The heritability estimates for group deficits in all of these measures were highly significant. In contrast, only the word reading measure had substantial and statistically significant shared environment influence ($c^2_g$). The lack of strong shared environment influences on group deficits in phonological decoding, orthographic coding, and phoneme awareness in the present twin sample should *not* be taken as evidence that the environment can have little influence on these skills. For example, Wise, Ring, and Olson (2000) reported substantial gains in phonological decoding and phoneme awareness when these skills were emphasized in a remedial reading program for children in grades 2–5 (see also Torgesen, this volume).

   The high genetic contributions to group deficits in word reading, phonological decoding, orthographic coding, and phoneme awareness are of interest, but an equally impor-

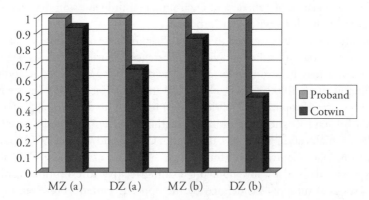

**Figure 24.2**   (a) Average MZ and DZ cotwin regression toward the population mean for word reading. (b) Average MZ and DZ cotwin regression toward the population mean for phoneme deletion.

tant question is the degree of shared genetic influence for the different pairings of skills (as this would indicate that common genetic influences were operating on a given pair of skills). Therefore, Gayan and Olson (2001) employed bivariate DF analyses to assess the genetic correlations between pairings of the variables by selecting probands on one variable and assessing cotwin regression to the mean on the second variable. The highest genetic correlation of $r_g = .99$ was found for group deficits in phonological decoding and word reading. Substantial genetic correlations were also found for group deficits in orthographic coding and word reading ($r_g = .81$), for orthographic coding and phonological decoding ($r_g = .73$), and for phoneme awareness with word reading ($r_g = .67$) and phonological decoding ($r_g = .64$). The most theoretically interesting and statistically significant contrast was between the correlations for phoneme awareness and orthographic coding ($r_g = .28$) versus phonological decoding ($r_g = .64$). It seems that the genetic link between word reading and phoneme awareness is primarily through its genetic correlation with phonological decoding. In contrast, the low genetic correlation between deficits in phoneme awareness and orthographic coding, in spite of their high individual heritabilities, suggests that there may be other genetically influenced deficits in basic processes that are associated with deficits in orthographic coding. At present it is not clear exactly what those basic processing deficits might be, though we have found that highly heritable ADHD symptoms are more strongly related to deficits in orthographic coding than to phonological decoding (Willcutt et al., 2002).

In addition to phonological awareness, rapid naming skill (RAN) has been proposed as a second important correlate and potentially independent causal factor in dyslexia (Wolf, 1991). RAN is commonly measured by having subjects name a series of pictures, color patches, letters, or numbers as rapidly as possible. Davis et al. (2001) conducted both univariate DF analyses on RAN and bivariate analyses of the shared genetic influence on RAN and reading skills, including the PIAT composite, phonological decoding, and orthographic coding. The heritabilities for the RAN group deficits were significant for both a RAN objects-and-colors composite, and a RAN numbers-and-letters composite. However, the bivariate analyses with reading measures were significant only for the RAN numbers and letters composite.

There has been much interest in whether relations between RAN and reading deficits are independent from the contributions of phonological awareness. DF methods of analysis for group deficits are not optimal for addressing the question of independent contributions when variables are correlated, as RAN and phoneme awareness are. To answer the question at another level, we must turn to behavioral genetic models of normal individual differences.

*Genetic and environmental influences on normal individual differences in reading*

Using a strategy that complements exploration of the genetic and environmental etiology of dyslexia and group deficits in related skills, we have also assessed the balance of genetic and environmental influences on individual differences in reading and related skills across the normal range. In principle, estimates of genetic influence on individual differences in a given skill could differ from the estimates for group deficits. Twin analyses focusing on individual differences derive estimates of heritability ($h^2$), shared environment ($c^2$), and nonshared environment ($e^2$) through structural equation modeling of the MZ and DZ twin correlation or variance-covariance matrices (Neale & Cardon, 1992). An advantage of this method of modeling is that it makes it possible to use multiple measures of a given skill to estimate a "latent" trait that theoretically provides error-free estimates of that trait, as well as its genetic and environmental correlations with other latent traits in the model. The models described below assume that the various genetic influences on individual differences are additive, meaning that within an individual, the effect of a reading-related gene is not dependent on its interaction with other reading-related genes. Any violation of this additivity assumption could lead to an overestimation of genetic influence (Plomin, DeFries, Craig, & McGuffin, 2003).

Gayan and Olson (2003) used individual-differences models to explore some of the same basic questions addressed in their earlier analyses of group deficits (Gayan & Olson, 2001). A detailed discussion of the methods and results of the individual differences analyses is beyond the scope of this chapter with its focus on dyslexia, so only a few main results will be mentioned here. First, estimates of the heritability for the latent traits of word reading ($h^2$ = .85), phonological decoding ($h^2$ = .80), and orthographic coding ($h^2$ = .87) were all large and highly significant. There was some indication that nonadditive genetic influences may have led to an overestimation of $h^2$ for these variables from MZ correlations more than twice the size of DZ correlations. Another factor that may have appropriately increased the heritability estimates for individual differences over those observed for group deficits was the use of latent traits. This resulted in lower estimates of nonshared environment ($e^2$) and a corresponding increase in heritability ($h^2$). With these points in mind, the present evidence suggests that the magnitude of genetic influence on individual differences in reading and related skills may be similar to that for group deficits. (A similar result has been found in a study by Harlaar, Spinath, Dale, and Plomin [in press] that will be discussed in the next subsection.) However, the similarity in magnitude for estimates of the heritability of the group reading deficit in dyslexia and of individual differences in reading more generally (denoted by $h^2_g$ and $h^2$ respectively) does not mean that the genetic mechanisms for group deficits and individual differences in reading are necessarily the same, as will be discussed in the next section on molecular genetics.

Although the levels of heritable individual differences in reading ability may have been slightly overestimated by Gayan and Olson (2003) because of nonadditive genetic factors, their tests of genetic correlations and independence among the variables should still be valid and of theoretical interest. A few of the most theoretically interesting results will be mentioned here. First, a significantly higher genetic correlation between phoneme awareness and phonological decoding ($r_g$ = .79) versus orthographic coding ($r_g$ = .55) was observed that mirrored the pattern observed for the group-deficit genetic correlations. Second, IQ was included in the hierarchical models as a first step to show that although there was shared genetic influence between IQ and reading skills, there was substantial genetic variance in the reading skills and phoneme awareness that was independent from IQ. Interestingly, when phoneme awareness was entered first, it completely accounted for the genetic correlation between the reading skills and IQ. We emphasized that this may not be the case for reading comprehension, since it depends more on higher-level language skills similar to those assessed in the verbal IQ scales. Third, although the genetic correlation between phonological decoding and orthographic coding was high ($r_g = .82$), there was also significant independent genetic variance for these component reading skills. This result raises the possibility that there may be at least partly different molecular genetic contributions to these skills (see our discussion in the Molecular Genetic Approaches section below).

In the previous subsection, we raised the question of the degree of independence for genetic influences on RAN and phoneme awareness in relation to reading. Modeling procedures for individual differences similar to those used by Gayan and Olson (2003) were used by Compton, Davis, DeFries, Gayan, and Olson (2001) to address this question. The result was that although there were significant genetic correlations between RAN, phoneme awareness, and reading measures, there was also a significant genetic correlation between RAN and the reading measures after controlling for the genetic influence of phoneme awareness. This partly independent genetic influence contributing to the relation between RAN and reading suggests the possibility of partly different molecular genetic mechanisms for RAN and phoneme-awareness relations with reading. Next we turn to an application of twin methods to understanding early reading development.

## *Genetic and environmental influences on early reading development*

The family and twin studies described so far have all been with probands who have been reading with various levels of competence for at least two years (third graders were the youngest participants). We will now discuss two ongoing studies with younger children that are being followed in preschool through second grade. One study is being conducted with unselected samples of twins in Australia, Colorado, and Norway, beginning in preschool around age 4, prior to formal reading instruction (Byrne et al., 2002). This study is also discussed by Byrne (this volume), so only a few results will be mentioned here. One interesting result from the preschool data is that there are significant genetic influences on individual differences in children's learning to identify phonemes within spoken words during our training sessions. Byrne, Fielding-Barnsley, and Ashley (2000) had previously noted that preschoolers' rate of response to training was a much stronger predictor of later reading success than their final level of phoneme awareness. Thus, it seems that early genetic constraints on learning rates for reading-related skills like phoneme awareness may be linked to the genetic correlations between phoneme awareness and reading seen in later development. This question will be formally tested in developmental genetic models when our sample with longitudinal data is of sufficient size. A second interesting result from this ongoing study is that while our first-grade sample size is still modest for behavioral genetic analyses of individual differences in reading, we already have significant evidence for apparently strong genetic influence on both kindergarten and first graders' performance on tests of nonword and word-reading speed (TOWRE) (Torgesen, Wagner, & Rashotte, 1999), though the standard errors for our estimates of heritable effects are largely due to small sample size.

Small sample size is not a problem in a remarkable ongoing longitudinal study of young twins in the UK known as the Twins Early Development Study (TEDS). As part of this larger study, Harlaar et al. (in press) tested the reading skills of a representative sample of 3,909 7-year-old twin pairs born in England and Wales, with an average of 1 year of formal reading instruction (i.e., end of first grade). The twins were tested by phone with the TOWRE word and nonword reading efficiency measure (the same measure used in the longitudinal study by Byrne et al., 2002). About two thirds of the individual differences across the whole sample were related to genetic factors while one fifth were related to environmental factors shared within families. This result is very similar to that found by Hohnen and Stevenson (1999) in a much smaller sample of first-grade UK twins.

The large twin sample from the TEDS study afforded an ideal comparison of the magnitude of genetic influence for individual differences in the whole sample versus genetic influences on the group deficit below the tenth or fifth percentile of that sample. In general, Harlaar et al. (in press) reported results for their 7-year-olds' group deficit that were remarkably similar to those found in the CLDRC study for third–twelfth graders. One difference was that the estimate of the heritability of the group deficit on the TOWRE word and nonword reading efficiency measure was lower for females than for males in the TEDS sample (10% cut, M = .68, F = .50; 5% cut, M = .60, F = .40), whereas there was virtually no difference in a composite word reading, spelling, and reading comprehension measure for males and females in the Wadsworth, Knopik, and DeFries (2000) study. It is unclear if this difference between the CLDRC and TEDS gender contrasts is due to their difference in measures, age range or other sample differences.

While the TEDS and CLDRC estimates of genetic and environmental influences on group deficits in reading are in general agreement, an earlier UK study based on a sample of 285 13-year-old twin pairs found little evidence for the heritability of group deficits in several reading measures, except for a measure of homophone recognition (Stevenson, 1991). Limited power due to the small number of twins in the low-reading tail of Stevenson's sample may have been the reason, but there is at least one other possibility that raises an important caveat for the interpretation of heritability estimates for individual differences and group deficits. These estimates will be directly influenced by the environmental range that is relevant to the target skill in the twin sample. Stevenson's sample, collected in the early 1980s in the city of London, may have had a broader range of socioeconomic and educational background, thus increasing the influence of shared family environment and reciprocally decreasing the influence of genes. The TEDS sample was fairly broad in socioeconomic status (SES), but Harlaar et al. note that their data were collected while the children were learning to read under a highly structured national curriculum. If there were less environmental variance in that curriculum, the estimates of genetic influence might have been higher and shared environment lower than in the earlier study by Stevenson, that was carried out before recent moves to standardize the teaching of reading across schools in England.

The CLDRC sample has relatively few twins from the low socioeconomic neighborhoods of the Denver metropolitan area. Most twins were from suburban schools with average or above average academic ratings. Thus, the heritability estimates for group deficits in the CLDRC sample might have been lower if more of the sample had been drawn from less advantaged areas of Denver. (There is no deliberate exclusion of twins from poor Denver schools, but few of these schools are willing to cooperate with the study, and in cooperative schools, few families respond to a letter requesting their participation.) The overriding message here is that the substantial genetic influences reported by the TEDS and CLDRC studies should not be generalized to samples with different degrees of variation in education or socioeconomic level, and we should not conclude that relatively poor reading performance in areas of poverty and poor education has any relation to genetic factors (see also Turkheimer, Haley, Waldron, D'Onofrio, & Gottesman, 2003).

One further caveat about genetic influence is equally important. Genes express themselves through their interaction with the environment throughout development. This interaction may be particularly important during reading development because genes can influence children's reading environment: Genes that influence moderate differences in learning rate for reading and related skills may lead to large differences in children's reading practice. In a competitive classroom environment, the faster reading-related learners may identify themselves as the good readers and read more, while the slow reading-related learners may tend to abandon their more difficult reading practice and opt for other activities, including looking out the window and daydreaming during the reading hour now instituted in many American classrooms. There is one bit of evidence from the CLDRC study that is consistent with this view. Measures of book-title and author recognition developed by Stanovich and West (1989) and by Cunningham and Stanovich (1997) were included in the test battery to estimate participants' print exposure. The MZ correlation for print exposure was .55 while the DZ correlation was .24, providing evidence for significant genetic influences on print exposure. The message should be clear: If we can find ways to increase the accurate reading practice of poor readers, ideally even beyond the levels experienced by their normal reading peers, the negative effects of any genetic liability for reading failure may be substantially reduced. Computer programs that support and reward accurate reading practice may be one way to realize this goal (Wise et al., 2000).

## Molecular Genetic Approaches

So behavioral genetic methods have revealed that both normal and extreme variations in reading skill (e.g., dyslexia) are heritable in part. The logical next question is where the particular genes that cause the heritability of dyslexia are.

We next consider how one finds gene variants that contribute to complex behavioral traits, like dyslexia. More detailed treatments of this topic can be found in Faraone, Tsuang, and Tsuang (1999), Fisher and DeFries (2002), and Plomin et al. (2003). First, one must identify an appropriate sample, usually of families, and one must have appropriate measures of the behavioral phenotype in question. Cognitive, developmental, and behavioral genetic analyses of the complex behavioral trait of the sort just discussed are an invaluable precursor (and concomitant) of molecular studies. Our success in finding genetic risk factors for dyslexia and related disorders is in part a direct consequence of our mature *psychological* understanding of this complex trait, which is arguably more sophisticated than our psychological understanding of many other complex behavioral disorders, like bipolar disorder, schizophrenia, and autism. Second, one must collect a source of DNA from the individuals in the sample, whether peripheral blood or (less invasively) cheek cells in the mouth. Third, the DNA is extracted from these cells and frequently amplified using a process called polymerase chain reaction (PCR). Fourth, the sample of each individual's DNA is genotyped in particular regions of interest using DNA markers. Markers are segments of DNA from highly variable portions of the genome and are therefore useful in distinguishing individuals genetically. For instance, there are repetitive base pair sequences in the genome, usually in noncoding regions, that vary considerably in the number of repeats across individuals. These variable numbers of tandem repeats (VNTR) markers are frequently used in linkage analyses. After completing these four steps, one ends up with data on genotypic and phenotypic differences in the same individuals. The next step is to test whether there is a systematic relation between the two.

Simply put, there are two broad approaches, linkage and association, for testing for such relations. Both methods exploit the fact that recombination shuffles the genetic "deck," so that most genes (and nongenes; i.e., noncoding DNA sequences) are transmitted independently across generations, which is the basis of Mendel's second law of independent assortment. Because this shuffling is not perfect, genes (and noncoding DNA sequences) that are close together on the same chromosome tend to "travel" together across generations (linkage). So an unknown variant form of a gene that increases risk for a disorder (a risk allele) and a variant form of a nearby marker (a marker allele) will be linked, whereas markers distant from the risk allele will not be linked to it. One can measure the degree of linkage (approximate physical proximity on a chromosome) between a risk allele and a marker allele by how frequently they recombine in offspring. If they recombine half the time (random assortment), then they are not linked. But if they recombine less than half the time (a deviation from random assortment), they are linked, with their proximity increasing as the rate of recombination *decreases*. So in linkage analysis, we hypothesize that at least one unknown risk allele contributes to the heritability of a trait like dyslexia, and we use marker alleles to try to find the approximate location of a risk allele. In a genome screen, we use marker alleles evenly spaced throughout the genome to try to find the approximate location of the multiple risk alleles that likely contribute to complex behavioral traits.

To understand how linkage differs from association, one needs to understand that random recombination events will usually change linkage relations across families. Usually, the exact alleles that are linked are the same within a given family but often differ between families because recombination has sorted them differently in different families. But at closer genetic distances, two linked alleles will very rarely be separated by recombination (a phenomenon called linkage disequilibrium) and thus the association between a risk allele and a marker allele will be the same both within *and* across families. In the candidate gene approach to association analysis, a putative risk allele for the disorder has already been identified and is tested to see whether it is more prevalent in individuals with the disorder. A finding of association between a marker allele and a disorder has three possible interpretations: (1) the marker allele *is* the risk allele; (2) the marker allele is very close to the risk allele (linkage disequilibrium); or (3) the finding is an artifact (e.g., of population stratification). Within-family tests of association, such as the transmission disequilibrium test (TDT), eliminate the population stratification artifact that may bias results in case-control association designs.

So linkage and association approaches have complementary strengths and weaknesses. Linkage is good at identifying broad genetic neighborhoods where risk alleles may reside, but is not useful for fine mapping. Because it operates over much smaller genetic distances, association is not useful for identifying genetic neighborhoods, but is helpful for fine mapping a risk locus and testing candidate genes. For a trait like dyslexia, where we lack neurobiological hypotheses that point to candidate genes, it is useful to start with linkage and follow up with association methods.

What method of genetic linkage analysis one uses with a phenotype like dyslexia depends on how that phenotype is transmitted in families. Transmission can be either Mendelian (e.g., a dominant, recessive, or additive single major locus) or complex (i.e., non-Mendelian). In the first case, classical parametric linkage is appropriate; in the latter case, nonparametric linkage methods are appropriate.

Parametric linkage analysis requires that we specify the parameters of the mode of transmission, such as dominance, penetrance (the probability of having the disorder if one has the risk allele), and degree of sex influence on transmission. In nonparametric linkage, specification of these parameters is not required.

## How is dyslexia transmitted?

Segregation and other analyses of both abnormal and normal reading (Finucci et al., 1976; Gilger, Borecki, DeFries, & Pennington, 1994; Lewitter, DeFries, & Elston, 1980; Pennington et al., 1991) have lead to several conclusions about the transmission of dyslexia: (1) Dyslexia is not an X-linked disorder (i.e., the genes responsible are not located on the X chromosome), and there is little evidence of parental sex effects on transmission. There is converging evidence for sex differences in penetrance, which would produce the slight preponderance of males (1.5 M:F) that is observed, and (2) Simple polygenic/multifactorial transmission appears less likely because there is a major locus effect in several samples. But this work places several important constraints on Hallgren's Mendelian hypothesis of a single autosomal dominant gene influencing dyslexia.

First, it is very unlikely to be one gene, because of the evidence for multiple risk loci (Fisher & DeFries, 2002). Second, it may not be a gene influencing dyslexia per se, since the familiality, heritability, and transmission results for normal variations in reading skill are not clearly different from those for dyslexia (Gilger et al., 1994). Hence, the same loci may be involved in the transmission of both normal reading skill and dyslexia. If this is true, then dyslexics would have just more of the unfavorable alleles at these loci and/or more environmental risk factors, so that their reading scores are pushed beyond the cutoff for dyslexia. In this case, none of these loci are necessary "disease" loci. Instead, they are better conceptualized as susceptibility loci. A susceptibility locus, unlike a disease locus, is neither necessary nor sufficient to produce the disorder in question. If a susceptibility locus influences a continuous (as opposed to categorical) trait, then it is called a quantitative trait locus (QTL). QTLs influencing dyslexia can be thought of as gene loci that confer a susceptibility to develop poor reading skills, but only in a probabilistic fashion.

It is becoming increasingly clear that complex behavioral traits, like dyslexia, are typically influenced by several QTLs rather than by a single Mendelian locus.

So instead of a classic, autosomal dominant "disease" gene, which is rare in the population and which is by itself necessary and sufficient to produce the disorder of dyslexia, we are likely dealing with several QTLs, each of which may be quite common in the population. Such a constellation of genes, each possibly having quite small and subtle effects on brain development may be involved in the transmission of both dyslexia and normal variations in reading skill. No one QTL is likely to be necessary to produce dyslexia. Whether any single QTL has a large enough effect to produce dyslexia by itself is an empirical question that only linkage methods can answer.

## Where are the QTLs for dyslexia?

By selecting sibling pairs in which at least one sibling has an extreme score, one can perform linkage analyses that screen for genetic loci influencing extreme scores on a continuous measure (QTLs). One method for doing this is with an extension of the DF method described earlier (Fulker, Cherny, & Cardon, 1995). In this method, one relates genotypic similarity at a marker locus within a sibling pair to phenotypic similarity (i.e., degree to which the co-sibling's phenotype score has regressed to the population mean). If the marker locus is close to a risk allele for having an extreme score (being dyslexic in this case), then sib pairs who share marker alleles should show less regression than sib pairs who do not share marker alleles. On the other hand, if the marker locus is not close to the risk allele (not linked), there should be no relation between allele sharing at the marker locus and phenotypic similarity for extreme scores.

Using this method, we found evidence for a QTL on the short arm of chromosome 6 across two independent samples of sib pairs and across two sets of genetic markers (Cardon et al., 1994). There have now been three replications of this finding (Gayan et al., 1999; Grigorenko et al., 1997; Fisher et al., 1999). So a QTL influencing dyslexia on chromosome 6p21.3 has now been found in five different samples by three independent laboratories. Grigorenko, Wood, Meyer, & Pauls (2000) expanded their sample and continued to find linkage to this region. However, two studies have failed to find linkage in this region, one in Canada (Field & Kaplan, 1998; Petryshen, Kaplan, Liu, & Field, 2000) and one in Germany (Nöthan et al., 1999). The reasons for these discrepant findings are unclear.

In sum, the linkage between dyslexia and the 6p21.3 region is one of the best replicated results in the genetics of complex behavioral disorders. Hence, it is quite likely that there is actually a gene in this region that influences reading skill. Work is proceeding to identify the gene. Two candidate genes in that region, a gene for GABA receptor (GABBR1) and a gene for myelin oligodendrocyte glycoprotein (MOG), both of which play a role in brain development, have now been excluded as the dyslexia locus (reviewed in Smith, Gilger, & Pennington, 2001). A recent study (Deffenbacher et al., 2003) used linkage followed by association in a larger sample of 861 sib pairs (n = 1,559 individuals from 349 nuclear families) from the CLDRC to fine map the dyslexia locus at 6p21.3. They narrowed the list of candidate genes to four, of which two appear most promising.

Interestingly, these candidate genes appear to be more important for extreme deficits in reading, suggesting that somewhat different genes may affect reading ability across the distribution.

Other replicated linkage regions for dyslexia include 1p36, 2p12–16, 3p-q, and 15q21 (reviewed in Fisher & DeFries, 2002). In addition, a whole genome screen of two separate samples identified the location of a novel QTL influencing dyslexia on chromosome 18p (Fisher et al., 2002). Hence, at this point, it appears there are at least six QTLs that influence reading disability (RD): on chromosomes 1, 2, 3, 6, 15, and 18.

Fine mapping is also being applied to these other risk loci. For instance, Francks et al. (2002) rejected two candidate genes, SEMA4F and OTX1, in the chromosome 2p12–16 region. Just recently, the gene responsible for the dyslexia linkage on chromosome 15q21 has been identified (Taipale et al., 2003). It is a novel gene expressed in the brain. This important discovery makes it possible to begin to trace the dynamic, developmental pathways that run from a risk allele to brain development to the behavior that defines dyslexia.

If there are multiple QTLs influencing dyslexia, do different QTLs influence different cognitive components of dyslexia (Pennington, 1997)? An earlier study (Grigorenko et al., 1997) found that cognitively dissociable components of the reading process are linked to separate genes and that the mapping from genes to aspects of cognition may be quite close indeed. But, the two replications of the chromosome 6 results (Fisher et al., 1999; Gayan et al., 1999) and the genome screen (Fisher et al., 2002) do not support this hypothesis. In these studies, deficits in both phonological and orthographic coding were linked to markers in the same region of chromosome 6 and the new locus on 18p. Work is underway to test more broadly for such differential effects, using all likely QTLs and all the main cognitive components of dyslexia. The behavioral genetic findings of partially independent genetic contributions to components like orthographic coding and RAN suggest that QTLs with differential effects are likely. This approach may help to clarify the cognitive processes that are directly involved in learning to read; such an approach is also highly relevant for the genetic dissection of the other complex behavioral phenotypes.

Apart from the outcome of this issue, these exciting molecular findings for dyslexia may eventually allow us to address how much variance in reading scores these genetic loci account for, and eventually address how frequently unaffected siblings have some unfavorable alleles at these loci, thus permitting the identification of protective factors, including environmental factors that protect a child from developing dyslexia. If a similar, sib-pair linkage study were conducted using probands selected for extremely *high* reading scores, we could determine whether different alleles at these same loci influence exceptionally good reading. We have already found that $h^2g$ for extreme high scores in reading is of similar magnitude ($h^2g = 0.55 \pm 0.22$) to that for extreme low scores (Boada et al., 2002). But as discussed earlier, this similarity in heritabilities does not necessarily mean the same genes are involved. If the same genes are involved, we could conclude that the same QTLs are likely affecting reading scores across the whole distribution. If not, then we would have direct evidence that dyslexia is etiologically distinct.

## Using genetics to analyze comorbidities

A pervasive characteristic of complex behavioral disorders like dyslexia is that they co-occur with other complex behavioral disorders. This co-occurrence is called "comorbidity." If comorbidity merely occurred by chance, it would not be of any scientific interest. But the comorbidities of dyslexia and other complex behavioral disorders are nonrandom; they are found much more frequently in population-based samples than chance would predict. Nonrandom comorbidity requires an explanation. This explanation will likely help us understand the developmental mechanisms operating in *both* comorbid disorders. A full treatment of explanations for comorbidity can be found in Neale & Kendler (1995). Here we focus on what we have learned about the comorbidities of dyslexia, mainly from genetic methods.

Several studies have tested the basis of the comorbidities of dyslexia, which include externalizing disorders (attention deficit hyperactivity disorder – ADHD, conduct disorder – CD, and oppositional defiant disorder – ODD), internalizing disorders (mild depression, called dysthymia, and anxiety), speech sound disorder (SSD, which is defined below), and specific language impairment (SLI). Once comorbidity with ADHD is controlled for, the association between dyslexia and ODD and CD becomes nonsignificant (Willcutt & Pennington, 2000). A longitudinal study in our lab (Boetsch, 1996, unpublished) found that future dyslexic children did not differ from controls on measures of dysthymia before kindergarten, but did after reading instruction commenced, suggesting that dysthymia is secondary to dyslexia. In contrast, in that same study, the future dyslexics did have higher rates of ADHD symptoms before kindergarten, consistent with our other results indicating a shared genetic etiology between dyslexia and ADHD (Willcutt, Pennington, & DeFries, 2000; Willcutt et al., 2002).

So some of the comorbidities of dyslexia (i.e., dysthymia, ODD, and CD) are secondary to dyslexia itself or to comorbid ADHD, whereas others (e.g., ADHD), appear to be due to a shared genetic etiology. We recently conducted one of the first molecular tests of the basis of a psychiatric comorbidity, that between dyslexia and ADHD (Willcutt et al., 2002). We found that the dyslexia QTL on chromosome 6p also influences ADHD, which means that the comorbidity is caused in part by this shared genetic risk factor, a result that is consistent with our earlier findings of bivariate heritability between dyslexia and ADHD (Light & DeFries,1995; Stevenson, Pennington, Gilger, DeFries, & Gillis, 1993; Willcutt, Pennington, & DeFries, 2000).

There is also evidence for a shared genetic etiology among SSD, SLI, and RD, but not all the findings are in agreement. Idiopathic SSD is defined by developmentally inappropriate errors in the production of spoken phonemes that affect intelligibility and are not caused peripherally (e.g., by a hearing deficit or a cleft palate) or associated with a known etiology (e.g., a genetic syndrome or a neurological insult). SSD has also been called speech disorder, phonological disorder, and is referred to colloquially as "articulation problems." An infrequent subtype of SSD is speech dyspraxia. SSD is distinct from fluency disorders, such as stuttering. Support for a shared familial etiology for SSD and dyslexia has been provided by Lewis and colleagues (Lewis, 1990, 1992; Lewis, Ekelman, & Aram, 1989), who found that SSD and dyslexia run in the same families. Other twin studies have found that SSD and SLI are moderately heritable (Bishop, North, & Donlan, 1995; Lewis & Thompson, 1992), and that SLI and dyslexia are coheritable (Bishop, 2001). We have recently found that SSD and dyslexia are coheritable as well (Tunick & Pennington, 2002).

Except for a rare autosomal dominant form of speech dyspraxia, which has been linked to a mutation in the FOXP2 gene (Fisher, Vargha-Khadem, Watkins, Monaco, & Pembrey, 1998; Lai, Fisher, Hurst, Vargha-Khadem, & Monaco, 2001), there are no previous genetic linkage results for SSD per se. There have been two genome scans of SLI, which is comorbid with both SSD and RD (reading disorders). The first (SLI Consortium, 2002) found risk loci on 16q and 19q, but, surprisingly, did not find any of the QTLs already identified for RD. This result does not support a genetic overlap between SLI and RD. A second genome scan of five extended families with SLI (Bartlett et al., 2002) found different risk loci for SLI. They used both language and dyslexia phenotypes and identified three linkage peaks: one on 2p22 linked to a language phenotype (about 40 cM away from the dyslexia locus on 2p), the strongest at 13q21 linked to a dyslexia phenotype, and a third at 17q23, also linked to a dyslexia phenotype. So, despite a phenotypic overlap between SLI and RD, neither study linked SLI to any of the previously identified QTLs for RD, except possibly the locus on 2p22.

In sum, behavioral genetic studies of the relation between SSD and dyslexia support a shared etiology but there have not been molecular studies of SSD to test this genetic overlap directly. Molecular studies of SLI have so far identified QTLs different from those identified for RD. So more work is needed to clarify the genetic overlap among these three disorders, as well as their environmental overlap.

We recently completed a sib-pair linkage study of SSD (Smith et al., 2003). We found significant linkage between SSD and the risk loci for dyslexia on chromosomes 6p and 15q. So this study provides direct molecular evidence for a genetic overlap between SSD and dyslexia, consistent with the behavioral genetic results. Hence, the 6p locus appears to contribute to three comorbid disorders: dyslexia, ADHD, and SSD. Discovering the neurobiological mechanisms underlying this three-way comorbidity would be a major breakthrough, one that will likely remap our classification of complex behavioral disorders of childhood.

## Summary and Conclusions

Since about 1980, there has been considerable progress in understanding the genetics of dyslexia. Its familiality and heritability have been clearly documented, we understand better how it is transmitted in families, and the approximate locations of six risk loci on different chromosomes have been mapped using linkage methods. Progress is now being made in identifying the actual gene variants involved; the actual risk gene on chromosome 15 has been identified and the list of candidate genes for the 6p locus has been narrowed considerably. We have also discovered that some of these risk loci influence two disorders that are comorbid with dyslexia, ADHD and SSD.

So far, the genetic influences on dyslexia do not appear to be highly specific, since they appear to affect individual differences in reading across the whole distribution, operate similarly in both males and females, affect multiple cognitive components of dyslexia, and influence comorbid disorders, although these conclusions could change as we learn more about how each risk allele for dyslexia affects development. More generally, genetic methods will lead to a much more sophisticated understanding of how both risk and protective factors act across development to influence language and literacy skills.

## Note

This work was supported by NIH grants HD27802, HD38526, MH 38820, and HD04024.

# 25

## Functional Brain Imaging Studies of Skilled Reading and Developmental Dyslexia

**Cathy J. Price and Eamon McCrory**

In this chapter, we summarize the key findings that have emerged from functional neuroimaging studies of skilled readers and individuals with developmental dyslexia. Our aim is to highlight the insights that functional neuroimaging can provide for cognitive and anatomical models of reading and dyslexia. We also take a critical look at the limitations of the functional imaging approach and explain why we think that some of the current theories of dyslexia have been reached prematurely.

### Functional Imaging Techniques: How PET and fMRI Work

Positron emission tomography (PET) and functional magnetic resonance imaging (fMRI) measure brain activity on the basis of changes in, respectively, regional cerebral blood flow (rCBF) or blood oxygenation. The relationship between neural activity and these hemodynamic responses is as follows: The presentation of a stimulus, or a mental state, involves neural activation in specific brain regions. Within a few hundred milliseconds, these activity changes mediate vasodilation in the microvessels, which increases the local flow of oxygenated blood. The increased oxygen in the blood exceeds the oxygen consumption of the neural tissue so that an increase in neural activity and rCBF is accompanied by a decrease in deoxyhemoglobin, whose paramagnetic properties are measured by fMRI.

Although there are many differences in PET and fMRI scanning techniques, both are capable of localizing brain activation to within 3 mm of its source. Furthermore, both techniques rely on detecting *changes* in rCBF or oxygenation. Thus, their experimental designs always require measurements under a range of conditions. For example, the comparison of brain activity during reading aloud to that during reading silently or the correlation of brain activity with reading accuracy. In this sense, the experimental design and analysis is similar to behavioral studies that compare reaction times and errors in different conditions. As we will discuss below, however, there are many more variables in functional imaging studies, including the anatomical localization of an effect and responses to stimuli or events that do not have behavioral correlates.

## How Can Functional Imaging Inform Cognitive Models of Reading?

It is generally accepted that functional neuroimaging is a useful technique for identifying the neural systems that sustain cognitive processes such as reading but it is often less clear how anatomical data can be used to inform cognitive models. Here we will suggest four ways in which functional imaging can provide useful contributions for cognitive models of reading. The first is that it provides a measure of cognitive function that might not be detectable from behavioral tests. This is because behavioral measures require a motor response (vocal or manual), whereas functional imaging is based on components of the hemodynamic response to neural activation that occurs even when participants are not engaged in a reading task. For example, functional imaging can provide measures of subliminal reading (Dehaene et al., 2001) and detect the degree to which reading processes are engaged by stimuli other than words.

Second, functional imaging can provide a fuller description of the neural and cognitive processes that underlie behavioral effects. In the majority of behavioral studies, the data index the reaction times (RTs) and accuracy of the manual or vocal responses that occur when the task is complete. Therefore, there are a maximum of two data points per trial (accuracy and RTs). In contrast, functional imaging indexes the neural activity that occurs during all stages of the task from anticipation of the stimulus to generation of the response. This is reflected by thousands of data points per trial provided by measurements in thousands of voxels across the whole brain. Consequently, functional imaging data can categorize a behavioral effect in terms of where it is coming from at the neural level. With sufficient understanding of the function of the brain areas, it can also indicate the level of cognitive process. For example, contrasting word and pseudoword reading may elicit a variety of activation differences – in the visual, semantic, orthographic, and phonological domains. Reaction time differences can therefore be interpreted in terms of where the differential processing is occurring.

A third way in which functional imaging can inform cognitive models of reading is by providing an additional and qualitatively different source of empirical validation. Indeed, any comprehensive model of reading will require the integration of cognitive and anatomical levels of explanation. For example, there may be separate brain regions for putative components of reading, and, in addition, sets of connections between brain regions that also instantiate specific reading processes. If a given model postulates distinct lexical and sublexical processes, we can ask if there are specific regions or connections that are specific to each of these processes. Similarly, we might ask if there is a visual word form area that is distinct from earlier visual and later semantic and phonological processing. Furthermore functional imaging data can indicate activation in areas with functions not traditionally included in reading models.

Finally, investigating the pattern of brain activation in individuals with acquired and developmental dyslexia can shed light on normal models of reading and characterize how some individuals with dyslexia manage to compensate for acquired or developmental reading difficulties. For example, is the reading process in such individuals implemented by the same set of regions as in skilled readers? Are these regions – and their associated cognitive functions – differentially engaged? Or do they recruit additional processes, resulting in the activation of brain regions that are not normally observed during reading?

## The Neural Systems for Skilled Reading

The brain regions activated by functional imaging studies of reading depend on the precise nature of the task and the baseline used to measure changes in brain activation. Here we will discuss three of the paradigms that have been used to investigate reading. In the first, participants are simply presented with single unrelated words to read aloud and the activation elicited by this condition is compared to resting with eyes closed. This comparison will reveal the full set of brain regions involved in all reading processes from seeing and attending to a visual stimulus to generating and monitoring the response. The second paradigm can be regarded as a more implicit task insofar as participants are not explicitly asked to read the words. Instead, they are presented with either written words or strings of "falsefonts" (meaningless symbols matched to the letters for visual features, see figure 25.1, row 2) and engaged in a feature detection task (press a button if one of the letters has an ascending feature as in *b, d, k,* or *l* but not *a, c, e,* or *g*). Since the task remains constant, any activation differences between words and falsefonts are attributed to "implicit" reading while the participants are engaged in the "incidental" task. A third approach for segregating reading processes from sensory and motor processing is the comparison of reading aloud to viewing falsefonts and saying "okay," which controls for articulation without requiring the retrieval of phonology from orthography (Howard & Patterson, 1992; McCrory, 2001; Moore & Price, 1999; Price et al., 2003a). We start by describing all of the areas activated by each of these paradigms and then explore the possible functions of each area in turn.

The first paradigm, reading aloud relative to rest, generates the largest set of areas (see top row of figure 25.1) including extensive activation in bilateral occipito-temporal (OT in figure 25.1), posterior superior temporal (pST in figure 25.1), sensorimotor (SM in figure 25.1), and central regions of the superior temporal lobe (cST in figure 25.1). For further details, see Bookheimer et al. (1995), Price, Moore and Frackowiak (1996a), Rumsey et al. (1997a), Brunswick et al. (1999), and Turkeltaub, Eden, Jones, & Zeffiro (2002). Activation in the sensorimotor (SM) and central superior temporal (cST) areas has been associated with articulation and hearing the sound of the spoken response respectively (Price et al., 2003a; Price et al., 1996c). For instance, the central regions of the superior temporal cortex (cST) are not observed when participants move their lips during reading but do not generate any sound. The remaining areas (the occipito-temporal [OT]

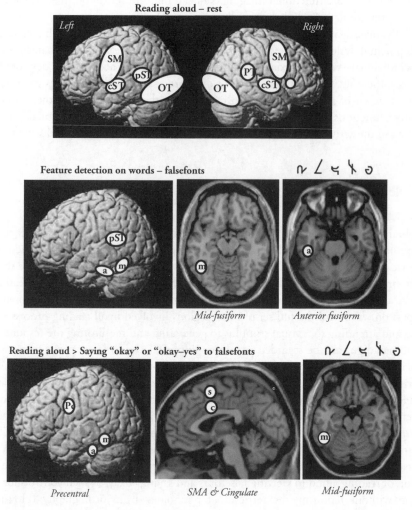

**Figure 25.1**   The neurobiology of reading single words.

and posterior superior temporal [PT] cortices) are therefore the most likely candidates for sustaining the translation of orthography to phonology in the absence of overt speech.

The second paradigm, the feature detection task on words relative to falsefonts, results in left lateralized activation in two occipito-temporal regions (mid-fusiform and anterior fusiform) and the left posterior superior temporal cortex (see second row of figure 25.1, which uses data from Brunswick et al., 1999). These results tell us that there are three left lateralized brain areas that respond differentially to words even when participants are distracted from reading. However, we do not know if activation relates to orthographic, semantic, or phonological processing, each of which might be engaged by the presence of a word. Finally, comparing reading aloud with viewing falsefonts and saying "okay" to control for articulation activates the mid- and anterior fusiform (areas m and a), left pre-central cortex (Pc), anterior cingulate (c) and the supplementary motor cortex (s), see lower row of figure 25.1 (data from 30 participants, thresholded at p < 0.05 corrected for multiple comparisons). Below, we consider the possible functions of each of these areas in turn. The mid- and anterior fusiform activations will be discussed first before we consider the left posterior superior temporal cortex, the motor areas (precentral, anterior cingulate, and SMA) and other temporal and parietal areas that have been associated with reading in other studies.

## Left mid-fusiform (area m)

The role of the left mid-fusiform during reading has received a great deal of attention. One proposal is that it houses a "Visual Word Form Area" (Cohen et al., 2000; Cohen et al., 2002; Dehaene, Le Clec'H, Poline, Bihan, & Cohen, 2002; McCandliss, Cohen, & Dehaene, 2003) because (1) this is the earliest (most posterior) point in the visual stream to be activated by words presented to either the left or right visual field, and (2) it corresponds to the site of damage in patients with pure alexia who can have more difficulty reading than naming pictures (Damasio & Damasio, 1983). However, activation in this left mid-fusiform area is not specific to reading or form processing (Price & Devlin, 2003) (see Figure 25.2). Therefore, even though this area is involved in visual word form processing, activation is not exclusively related to either orthographic processing or word identification. An alternative proposal to explain activation in the left mid-fusiform is that it reflects those processes engaged when identifying an item at a unique level (Price, Noppeney, Phillips, & Devlin, 2003b) which is required in order to integrate sensory inputs with motor outputs. Thus, the left mid-fusiform is more activated when an identification response must be made (Moore & Price, 1999) and activation increases when an object must be discriminated at a specific (e.g., is it a yacht or a ferry?) rather than a basic (e.g., is it a car or a boat?) level (Rogers, Hocking, Mechelli, Patterson, & Price, 2005). Although further experiments are required to define the function of the left mid-fusiform more precisely, we can conclude that it does not correspond neatly to any of the cognitive components of reading. Thus, it does not appear to reflect either orthographic, semantic, or phonological processing.

## Left anterior fusiform (area a)

In contrast to the posterior part of the left mid-fusiform, activation in the more anterior and ventral part of the fusiform has been associated with amodal semantic processing of words (Noppeney & Price, 2003). Therefore, we might expect increased activation in this area for reading words relative to reading pseudowords. However, only one study (Herbster, Mintun, Nebes, & Becker, 1997) has reported such an effect during reading (at $x = -36$, $y = -30$, $z = -24$, according to the brain atlas of Talairach & Tournoux, 1988). We therefore reexamined the responses in the anterior fusiform area during the word and pseudoword study reported by Brunswick et al. (1999), lowering the threshold to increase sensitivity. This revealed that left anterior fusiform activation was indeed higher for reading words than pseudowords (at $x = -32$, $y = -22$, $z = -16$; Z score = 3.3, according to the brain atlas of Talairach & Tournoux, 1988).

In summary, the left anterior fusiform area appears to be involved in semantic processing and there is some evidence that activation is greater during word reading than pseudoword reading. Figure 25.2 illustrates that activation in the anterior fusiform is also greater for picture naming than reading object names. This is consistent with cognitive models that propose that object naming is more reliant on semantic processing than reading (Glaser & Glaser, 1989).

### Left posterior superior temporal cortex (area pST)

As can be seen in figure 25.1, activation in the left posterior superior temporal cortex (pST) has been observed for reading aloud relative to rest and for viewing words relative to falsefonts during a feature detection task. However, it was not observed for reading aloud relative to saying "okay" to falsefonts (third row in figure 25.1) even when the statistical threshold is lowered. This suggests that left posterior superior temporal activation is also engaged when participants say "okay" repeatedly in the baseline condition. Indeed, we have recently demonstrated highly significant activation in this area, and its homologue in the right hemisphere, bilateral frontal operculae and the sensorimotor cortices when participants said "okay" repeatedly in response to meaningless shapes (see Price et al., 2003b). Furthermore, we found a strong effect of the number of articulated syllables on the left posterior superior temporal activation (see figure 25.3) and no other brain areas showed the same effect (McCrory, 2001). Thus, left posterior superior temporal activation was higher for words with three syllables (e.g., "onion," "okay-yes") relative to words with one syllable (e.g., "pear," "yes"). These findings indicate that left posterior superior temporal activation reflects the demands on articulation rather than phonological retrieval, although the precise nature of the articulatory role remains unclear.

### Motor areas (left precentral, anterior cingulate, and SMA)

In addition to the left fusiform areas and posterior superior temporal cortex, reading relative to saying "okay" activates a left precentral region, the anterior cingulate, and SMA. These regions are all associated with speech production. For example, they are activated during verbal fluency tasks even in the absence of written word stimuli (Petersen, Fox, Posner, Mintun, & Raichle, 1988; Warburton et al., 1996). Increased activation for reading relative to saying "okay" therefore suggests increased articulatory demands when the word produced changes with each stimulus (as in reading) relative to when the same word is produced to every stimulus (e.g. saying "okay").

### Left angular gyrus (AG)

Activation in the left angular gyrus is not usually observed for reading aloud relative to rest, fixation or viewing falsefonts (Bookheimer et al., 1995; Ingvar et al., 2002; Price,

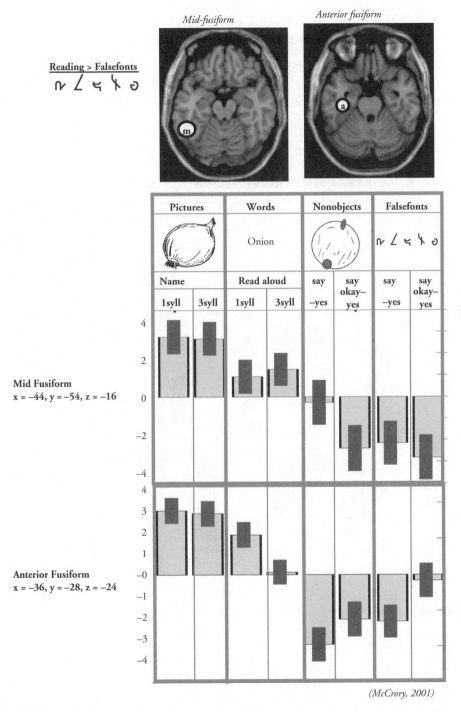

**Figure 25.2** Fusiform areas for reading and picture naming.

**Producing long vs. short speech sounds**

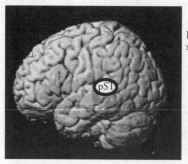

Left posterior superior temporal
x=-58, y=-34, z=+6  (p<0.03)

| Pictures | | Words | | Nonobjects | | Falsefonts | |
|---|---|---|---|---|---|---|---|
| | | Onion | | | | | |
| Name | | Read aloud | | say | say okay | say | say okay |
| 1syll | 3syll | 1syll | 3syll | –yes | –yes | –yes | –yes |

*(McCrory, 2001)*

**Figure 25.3**  The left posterior superior temporal area in speech production.

Wise, & Frackowiak, 1996b; Rumsey et al., 1997a; Turkeltaub et al., 2002). This is some-what surprising given that the left angular gyrus, a posterior parietal region (see figure 25.4), was historically designated as an important reading area. Both Déjerine (1891) and Geschwind (1965) highlighted a role for the left angular gyrus in reading on the basis of a lesion study of a patient with alexia and agraphia (difficulties reading and writing).

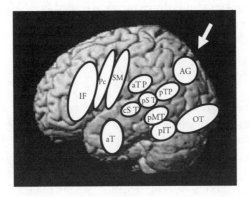

AG = Angular Gyrus
OT = Occipito-Temporal
pTP = posterior Temporo-Parietal
pST = posterior Superior Temporal
pIT = posterior Inferior Temporal
pMT = posterior Middle Temporal
aTP = anterior Temporo-Parietal
aT = anterior Temporal
cST = central Superior Temporal
IF = Inferior Frontal
Pc = Precentralgyrus
SM = Sensorimotor cortex

**Figure 25.4**   A summary of all the areas activated during reading tasks, illustrated on a standard model of the left hemisphere. The abbreviated names are defined below.

However, subsequent lesion studies have shown that alexia with agraphia is not always associated with the left angular gyrus; and conversely, lesions to the left angular gyrus do not always impair reading comprehension (Price & Friston, 2002).

Although the left angular gyrus is not activated during reading aloud relative to fixation, rest, or other baselines, it is activated when participants are instructed to focus on the semantic associations of written words (Mummery et al., 1999; Vandenberghe, Price, Wise, Josephs, & Frackowiak, 1996), auditory words (Noppeney & Price, 2003), and pictures (Mummery, Patterson, Hodges, & Price, 1998). While the left angular gyrus is frequently activated during semantic paradigms, it is not always observed in all semantic paradigms (Devlin et al., 2000; Phillips, Noppeney, Humphreys, & Price, 2002; Pilgrim, Fadili, Fletcher, & Tyler, 2002; Roskies, Fiez, Balota, Raichle, & Petersen, 2001). Indeed, it has been shown that left angular gyrus activation is greater for some semantic tasks relative to others. For example, Mummery et al. (1998) found increased left angular gyrus activation when participants selected two items within a triad of written object names on the basis of where the objects would be found (knife, saucepan, bookmark) relative to their color. Likewise, Noppeney and Price (2003) found that making decisions on verbally learnt semantics (e.g., that a banana comes from the tropics) increased left Angular Gyrus activation relative to color decisions on the same set of stimuli. The theoretical basis as to why the angular gyrus is differentially activated both within and across a range of semantic retrieval tasks is yet to be understood.

*Other areas*

In addition to the left angular gyrus (AG), several other areas participate in semantic tasks (see figure 25.4). These areas include the anterior temporal (aT) regions, the lateral posterior inferior temporal cortex (pIT), a posterior temporo-parietal region (pTP) and a lateral middle temporal area (pMT) and the left inferior frontal gyrus (iF). Remarkably, lesions to any one of these areas alone does not necessarily result in notable semantic deficits (Price & Friston, 2002). Instead, semantic deficits appear to arise only when more than one of these areas is damaged. For instance, semantic dementia (a progressive loss of semantic knowledge) impinges on semantic knowledge when the damage affects bilateral anterior temporal lobes or when the disease encompasses extensive regions of the left inferior temporal lobe (Hodges, Salmon, & Butters, 1992; Mummery et al., 2000). Likewise transcortical aphasia, which is associated with semantic loss, results from extensive damage to the temporo-parietal cortices or the underlying white matter (Alexander, Hiltbrunner, & Fischer, 1989). What these lesion data tell us is that damage to only one of the temporal or parietal areas is not sufficient to disrupt semantic retrieval. Therefore, it must be the case, that more than one temporal or parietal area is capable of retrieving semantic information (Price & Friston, 2002). This is not to say that semantic information is replicated in different brain regions, but that these regions may be involved in different strategies for retrieving semantic information. This account can also explain why activation in the temporo-parietal areas is inconsistent across different functional imaging paradigms. For instance, like the left angular gyrus, the left middle temporal area is activated during some semantic tasks (McDermott, Petersen, Watson, & Ojemann, 2003; Pilgrim et al., 2002; Roskies et al., 2001) but not others (Devlin et al., 2000; Mummery et al., 1998; Vandenberghe et al., 1996).

Although there is no clear theory at present to explain why different semantic tasks activate different temporo-parietal areas, it is becoming increasingly clear that these areas are more likely to be involved in the process of retrieving semantic associations than in the semantic associations themselves. Future studies are required to determine the precise functions of the different regions and to characterize the different strategies that can be used to retrieve semantic information. For the purposes of this chapter, which is concerned with the biological basis of reading, the discussion of semantic areas is included to provide a fuller understanding of the functional imaging literature on developmental dyslexia (see below). Likewise, it may be helpful to note that when participants are instructed to focus on the phonological aspects of words (e.g., judgments on the number of syllables or rhyming tasks), activation is observed in the precentral cortex (pC in Figures 1 and 4) and anterior parts of the temporo-parietal cortex (aTP in figure 25.4). Together, these areas have been associated with a phonological loop (Paulesu, Frith, & Frackowiak, 1993). Thus, it appears that there are distinct brain areas for retrieving semantic and phonological information (Demonet, Price, Wise, & Frackowiak, 1994; Demonet et al., 1992; Mummery et al., 1998; Roskies et al., 2001), but since the majority of these areas are not usually activated during reading aloud (compare activations in figure 25.4 with figure 25.1), they may reflect strategic retrieval processes rather than the underlying representations.

## Relating Anatomy to Current Cognitive Models of Reading

In this section we will consider whether there are any brain regions that respond specifically to written words, how reading differs from object naming, and how reading pseudowords (that must depend exclusively on mechanisms for converting orthographic codes into phonological codes) differs from reading words (that can also be read by an orthography, to semantic, to phonology route).

Cognitive models of reading have advocated two distinct, reading-specific processes (1) orthographic processing (whereby the component letters within a word are chunked into graphemes and larger sublexical letter combinations); and (2) the conversion of orthography to phonology. Neither of these processes is required for picture naming, because object names have no relation to the names of their parts. Furthermore, learning to read depends on "phonemic awareness," an appreciation of the segmental nature of speech (Hulme, 2002).

Given these constraints on reading, are there brain areas that, as a child learns to read, become specialized for segmenting orthography and assembling phonology? McCandliss et al. (2003, p. 293), for example, have recently proposed that "the unique demands on word reading and the structural constraints of the visual system lead to the emergence of the Visual Word Form Area." While this argument is theoretically plausible, the supporting evidence is slight. We will thus argue that reading may be acquired by adaptations within the object naming system.

### *Reading aloud relative to picture naming*

To our knowledge, only three studies have directly compared reading aloud with picture naming (Bookheimer et al., 1995; McCrory, 2001; Moore & Price, 1999), although several other studies have compared written word to picture processing during semantic decision tasks (Chee et al., 2000; Mummery et al., 1999; Vandenberghe et al., 1996), passive viewing (Menard, Kosslyn, Thompson, Alpert, & Rauch, 1996), and one-back tasks (Hasson, Levy, Behrman, Hendler, & Malach, 2002; Sevostianov et al., 2002). We will focus only on the studies that have required pronunciation (i.e., reading aloud object names and naming the pictures of the same objects), because other studies may be confounded by strategic effects that might be differentially engaged during complex decision tasks.

Combining the data from the studies reported by Moore and Price (1999) and McCrory (2001) shows that reading results in more activation than picture naming in the bilateral sensorimotor cortex and the left posterior superior temporal cortex (see figure 25.5 and the plot in figure 25.3). The same effects were also observed by Bookheimer

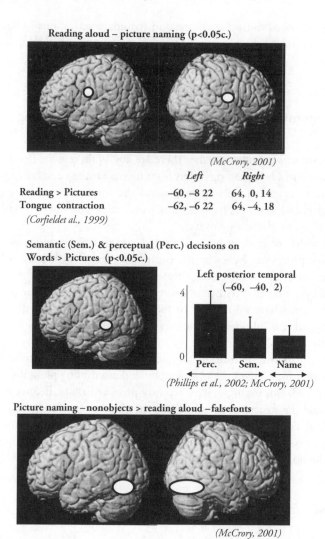

**Figure 25.5**    Reading-specific brain areas?

et al. (1995). But these effects are not specific to reading: the same areas were associated with speech production in the previous section. They are activated when participants simply say "okay" to meaningless visual stimuli without the need to retrieve phonology from the visual input (see figure 25.3); and the sensorimotor areas correspond to the areas that Corfield et al. (1999) have associated with simple nonlinguistic tongue movements. In other words, reading object names enhances activation in speech production areas relative to naming pictures of the same objects. Since speech output is identical in the two conditions, these results suggest that the generation of a phonological code from an orthographic input during reading increases the demands on speech production processes, but these speech production areas are not specific to reading, because they are also involved in picture naming.

In addition to looking for increased activation for reading, we can also look for decreased activation (i.e., increased activation for picture naming). This reveals bilateral occipito-temporal areas that include the left mid- and anterior fusiform areas that we focused on in the previous section (see Figures 1 and 2). Since activation in the fusiform areas is greater during picture naming than reading (see figure 25.2), it is difficult to support the theory that this area becomes specialized for reading (McCandliss et al., 2003). However, a study of reading acquisition in children (Shaywitz et al., 2002) indicated that as reading skill increases, activation in the left occipito-temporal cortex increases, whereas activation in the right occipito-temporal cortex decreases. If reading is more reliant than picture naming on left occipito-temporal activation, this would explain why patients with left occipito-temporal lesions can have a more profound deficit in reading compared to picture naming (Damasio & Damasio, 1983).

## Reading unfamiliar pseudowords relative to familiar words

One might argue that the reason we see the same neural system for reading object names and picture naming is because reading object names proceeds via semantics without access to sublexical orthographic and phonological processing. However, if this was the case, we would see additional reading areas when we compared pseudoword reading (that must depend on direct conversion of orthography to phonology) to reading words (that can occur by the conversion of orthography to phonology via semantics). Many studies have addressed this issue using a variety of tasks such as lexical decision (Binder et al., 2003; Fiebach, Friederici, Muller, & von Cramon, 2002) and a one-back matching task (Tagamets, Novick, Chalmers, & Friedman, 2001), as well as reading (Brunswick et al., 1999; Fiez, Balota, Raichle, & Petersen, 1999; Hagoort et al., 1999; Herbster et al., 1997; Mechelli, Gorno-Tempini, & Price, 2003). Again we will focus on the reading studies as other studies are confounded by task demands. For example, the lexical decision task requires "yes" responses to real words and "no" responses to nonwords and these decisions may impose different processing requirements that are not solely due to the word/pseudoword difference.

In most studies comparing word and pseudoword reading, effect sizes have been small (significance threshold is not corrected for the number of comparisons across the whole brain) and there are few replications across studies. The most consistent and most highly significant findings across studies are that pseudoword reading increases activation in the left frontal operculum / left insula (Brunswick et al., 1999; Hagoort et al., 1999; Fiez et al., 1999; Herbster et al., 1997; Mechelli et al. 2003; Xu et al., 2001) and the left posterior inferior temporal cortex (Brunswick et al., 1999; Fiez et al., 1999; Hagoort et al., 1999; Herbster et al., 1997; Mechelli et al., 2003; Price, Wise, & Frackowiak, 1996b; Xu et al., 2001), an area that corresponds to the left mid-fusiform area (see Mechelli et al., 2003, for a review). Again these areas are not specific to reading pseudowords, but are also observed for reading familiar words relative to nonlinguistic baselines (see Mechelli et al., 2003). Therefore, reading words modulates activation in areas involved in object naming, and pseudowords in turn enhance activation in components of the reading system.

What does this imply for cognitive models of reading? If we accept that cognitive processes are implemented by neural activity within and between brain regions, then we should use the anatomical data to constrain cognitive models. The anatomical data indicate that sublexical orthographic and phonological processing occurs within the same neural system as lexical reading and picture naming. This is more consistent with connectionist accounts of reading (Seidenberg & McClelland, 1989) than dual-route models (Coltheart, Curtis, Atkins, & Haller, 1993).

## Functional Imaging Studies of Reading in Developmental Dyslexia

Functional imaging studies of developmental dyslexia aim to identify how dyslexic reading differs from skilled reading. They may also be able to differentiate between different types of dyslexia (Castles & Coltheart, 1993; Manis, Seidenberg, Doi, McBride-Chang, & Petersen, 1996). Here we will review the current literature on studies of reading aloud (first section) or complex semantic and phonological decisions on written words (second section). Before we discuss these studies, however, we need to emphasize that the interpretation of functional imaging studies of dyslexia is extremely tenuous when the dyslexic participants do not read as accurately as the control participants. This is because if a dyslexic participant with poor reading accuracy fails to activate a region observed in the control participants, then we cannot determine whether there is abnormal processing in that region or whether the region does not activate because of deficits in another area. In other words, when activation differences co-occur with significant impairments in task performance, then it becomes impossible to distinguish the causal relationship between these factors. For example, if dyslexic participants fail to activate areas associated with semantic processing, is this because they have impaired semantic processing or is it because abnormalities at an orthographic level have prohibited activation at the semantic level? Thus, it is easier to interpret activation differences when the participants produce correct responses to show that they have accurately read the stimuli presented.

### Reading aloud in developmental dyslexia

There are five whole-brain functional imaging studies of reading in developmental dyslexia that we are aware of: (Brunswick et al., 1999; Ingvar et al., 2002; Paulesu et al., 2001; Rumsey et al., 1999; Rumsey et al., 1997b). Each of these studies acquired data using PET. We will discuss the findings in turn.

*Rumsey et al., 1997b.* This PET study compared word and nonword reading in a group of 17 adults with dyslexia and a group of 14 adult controls and found less activation for the dyslexics in a range of areas, particularly the bilateral temporal and motor regions associated respectively with articulation and hearing the sound of the spoken response (see top row of figure 25.1). Since the same differential pattern of activation was observed for both word and pseudoword conditions, the authors suggest a common underlying impairment. However, two methodological aspects of this study weaken the conclusions.

First, the activation differences reported in the dyslexic participants were accompanied by highly significant deficits in task performance (e.g., dyslexics read 39% of the pseudowords and 62% of the real words correctly, while equivalent figures for the control participants were 82% and 96%). Second, as the tasks were self-paced, the number of items viewed by each participant varied. This was reflected in a difference in the mean reaction times between the dyslexic and control participants. Less accurate and slower reading would have led to less speech production during the scanning block, which would explain the reduced activation in speech production areas. Thus, these results are more likely to be a consequence of slow and error prone reading than a reflection of the cause of dyslexia.

*Horwitz, Rumsey, & Donohue (1998).* Horwitz et al. (1998) used the same data set as Rumsey et al. (1999), but with a functional connectivity analysis that looked for areas that co-activated with the angular gyrus. The angular gyrus was the region of interest because it plays an important role in the classical neurological model of reading (Déjerine, 1891; Geshwind, 1965). However, it should be noted that the left angular gyrus was not activated during reading in either the dyslexic or control groups (or other functional imaging studies of reading aloud). Therefore, the authors selected a region of interest on the basis of previous functional imaging studies of decision-making tasks with auditory and visual words (x = −44, y = −54, z = +24, according to the atlas of Talairach & Tournoux, 1988). In fact, these coordinates do not lie in the angular gyrus; they lie in the posterior temporo-parietal cortex (pTP in figure 25.4). The authors then looked for the brain regions where activation increased or decreased with activation in the temporo-parietal cortex. For the control participants, significant positive correlations were observed in the left inferior temporal gyrus, occipital gyrus, lingual and fusiform gyri, superior temporal gyus, and left inferior frontal gyrus, but less significant effects were observed in the dyslexic participants.

Critically, since this correlational analysis was based on PET data with few data points per condition, the correlation was *across* participants. In other words, the correlation indicated that in the participants where left temporo-parietal activation was high, there was also high activation in other areas. Thus, although the authors argue that these results indicate a functional disconnection of the angular gyrus from other language areas in the dyslexic group, the results only indicate less variance within the dyslexic group. The analysis does not indicate whether activation in the angular gyrus/temporo-parietal cortex was always highly correlated with other brain regions in the dyslexic group or always weakly correlated with other brain regions. Nor does it reveal why there was more variance in the control than the dyslexic group. Was it because a few of the control participants, but none of the dyslexic participants, increased temporo-parietal activation during reading relative to baseline? Or could the differences relate to behavioral confounds in the reading performance of the two groups? These questions are yet to be answered.

*Rumsey et al., 1999.* The third paper to use the data collected by Rumsey et al. (1997b) attempts to provide further support for the role of the angular gyrus in dyslexia by establishing correlations between *blood flow* and *reading ability* as measured outside the scanner. This revealed that better reading was associated with increased temporo-parietal activation in the control group but not the dyslexic group. The interpretation of these effects is, however, not straightforward, because the correlation of temporo-parietal activation with reading ability was observed irrespective of task. In other words, even in those conditions where participants viewed a fixation cross (no reading involved), activation was correlated with reading ability in both the dyslexic and control groups. It is not possible, therefore, to infer how these effects explain reading behavior.

In summary, the findings reported by Rumsey et al. (1997b, 1999) and Horwitz et al. (1998) suggest that dyslexic and control participants have different patterns of activation in posterior temporal and parietal areas. It is, however, extremely difficult to separate the activation differences arising from gross behavioral impairments (secondary to dyslexia) from those attributable to the cause of the dyslexia. The dyslexic sample made more *errors*, which resulted in a much *slower* rate of stimulus presentation (which was self-paced). The question therefore arises whether a control group of nondyslexic poor readers, making a comparable number of errors or carrying out the task at a similarly slow pace would show a pattern of activation similar to that reported for the dyslexic group in this study.

*Brunswick et al., 1999.* Brunswick et al. (1999) attempted to control for confounds arising from differences in performance levels by selecting words (e.g., *valley, body, carrot*) or nonwords (e.g., *vassey, bofy, cassot*) that the dyslexics were able to read accurately and by using a presentation rate that was the same for the control and dyslexic samples. Six subjects read the words or the pseudowords aloud. Another six were engaged in the "incidental reading" task (see second row of figure 25.1), which required them to detect a visual feature (a letter with a feature that rises above the midline, such as *b, t, l,* versus a letter that does not rise above the midline, such as *a, c, o*) in words, pseudowords, or falsefonts. This feature detection task was included to make reading "incidental" and so reduce the possibility of differences in cognitive strategy between conditions.

The results confirmed that behavioral performance did not differ between the dyslexic and control groups in either study (although RTs were not measured in the reading aloud condition). Nevertheless, irrespective of task, the dyslexics showed less activation than the control group in the left inferior and middle temporal lobe (Talairach coordinates [x,y,z]: −42, −60, −12, and −42, −48, −6), the left frontal operculum (Talairach coordinates [x,y,z]: −40, 4, 22) and bilateral cerebellum. Increased activation was observed in a left premotor area 20 mm lateral to the area of reduced activation (BA6/44; Talairach coordinates [x,y,z]: −64, 0, 26) but only for the explicit reading condition (where participants were required to read the words aloud). No differences were reported for the dyslexic group in the region of the angular gyrus.

Brunswick et al. (1999) suggest that the reduced activation in the left posterior temporal area reflects the dyslexics' deficits in retrieving lexical phonology, while the increased left lateral premotor activation during explicit reading reflects an effortful compensatory strategy involving articulatory routines. (See figure 25.6 for further details.) Notably, the areas of differential activation identified by Brunswick et al. (1999) did not overlap with those reported by Rumsey et al. (1997b, 1999) or Horwitz et al. (1998).

*Paulesu et al., 2001.* Paulesu et al. (2001) adopted the identical explicit and incidental reading paradigms reported by Brunswick et al. (1999), using French and Italian orthogra-

**Behavior** History of delay learning to read. Impaired phonological skills.

**Question** Did learning to read engage alternative neuronal systems?

**Design** *Stimuli:* Visually presented words.
*Task:* Read words aloud or rest with eyes closed.

**Analysis** Contrast reading aloud to rest in (1) dyslexic, and (2) controls.

**Possibilities** Patient activates (1) same, (2) alternative, or (3) reduced set of areas?

**Results**

*Patient activates:*

*In normal areas*

*Less than normals* (posterior areas)

*More than normals* (anterior areas)

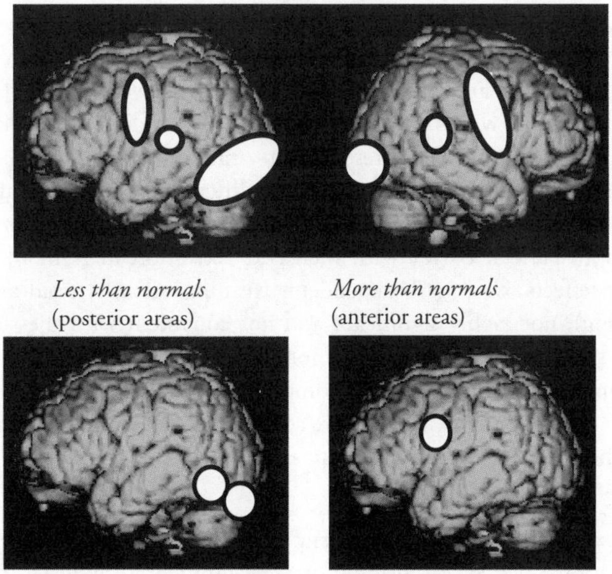

**Inference** *Dyslexic* has learnt to read with: increased reliance on anterior areas and less reliance on posterior areas.

**More questions:** Are changes due to neuronal impairment?
Or do abnormal areas respond normally during nonverbal tasks?

**Figure 25.6** Developmental dyslexia (no pathological damage observed on structural MRI).

phies. They then combined the data from the 24 English participants reported by Brunswick et al. (1999) with that obtained from 24 French participants (12 dyslexics) and 24 Italian participants (12 dyslexics). Performance of the dyslexic and control participants was matched within language. This cross-linguistic comparison not only increased the number of participants but allowed the authors to identify those regions that showed similar patterns of activation in dyslexic readers irrespective of orthography.

As in the Brunswick et al. (1999) study, significantly reduced activation in posterior inferior temporal areas is reported, with peaks in the inferior, middle, and superior temporal gyri, and the middle occipital gyrus. The authors conclude, given the cross-linguistic nature of their sample, that this pattern most likely represents the universal neurocognitive basis for dyslexia. However, it should also be noted that although the effects were consistent across dyslexic groups, the effect sizes were small and, even combined together, did not reach significance when a correction was made for multiple comparisons across the whole brain. Thus, the observed activation differences between dyslexic participants who have attained competent levels of reading and control groups are either very small or obscured by individual variation within the dyslexic group.

*Ingvar et al., 2002.* There is only one other study we are aware of that has compared the activation produced by reading aloud in developmental dyslexics to that in skilled readers. Nine dyslexics and nine control participants were scanned during four conditions. Reading aloud words, reading words silently, reading nonwords aloud, and resting with eyes open. Stimuli were presented at a rate of one per 1.6 seconds, which enabled the dyslexics to read without any notable differences in performance. The analysis revealed reduced activation for the dyslexic group in left and right frontal regions, and the right temporo-parietal cortex with increased activation in right temporal regions. However, these effects were task-dependent (reading silently, reading aloud, or pseudoword reading), not highly significant and not consistent with the studies reported above that used similar paradigms. Furthermore, although the authors report the group by task interactions, they do not report the components of the interaction. Therefore, we do not know if the effects are in areas that were activated or deactivated during reading. Further studies are therefore required to replicate and explain the findings.

*Summary of dyslexic reading.* In summary, four studies have compared whole-brain neural activation elicited by reading in developmental dyslexics and control participants. However, there are a number of problems:

1.  The study reported by Rumsey et al. (1997b, 1999) and Horwitz et al. (1998) was confounded by performance differences that can largely account for the activation differences between the dyslexic and control participants.
2.  There is very little consistency over different studies. This is likely to reflect a range of differences in task demands, selection criteria when matching with control participants, statistical methodology, and, perhaps most significantly, the degree of heterogeneity within the dyslexic participants at both the behavioral and neural levels.
3.  The activation differences between groups were not highly significant and did not survive correction for multiple comparisons. Therefore, there is likely to be a high false positive rate. If this is due to heterogeneity within a dyslexic group, it could be overcome by studying dyslexics at the individual level.

Despite our emphasis on the limitations of these studies, the results are still informative. They suggest that there are only subtle differences in the neural systems engaged by normal individuals and individuals with developmental dyslexia during reading. Indeed, dyslexic adults appear to adopt broadly the same neural system as normal adult readers, but differentially weight distinct components within this system. The consistency of these activation differences across individuals and across tasks demands, and their relation to well-established deficits in phonological processing in dyslexia (Hulme & Snowling, 1992; Snowling, 2000) remain exciting areas for future research.

## Dyslexic activation during complex semantic and phonological tasks

Several studies have examined dyslexia when participants are engaged in complex semantic and phonological tasks. In addition to evaluating reading comprehension or production, these tasks also tap the executive processes that are required to make decisions (e.g., short-term memory, lexical search, decision making). Therefore, any deficits observed in the developmental dyslexics are not necessarily directly related to reading.

*Rumsey et al., 1997b.* In the same PET study that studied word and pseudoword reading (see above), Rumsey et al. (1997b) also engaged their 17 dyslexic and 14 control male adults in two lexical decision tasks that involved viewing pairs of items on either side of a monitor. In the phonological condition, participants had to decide which of two pseudo-words sounded like a familiar word (e.g., "bape" or "baik"). In the orthographic condition, participants chose the correctly spelled word from a word and a pseudoword distractor (e.g., "hole" or "hoal"). Responses were made silently by pressing a button held in either the right or left hand. Visual fixation on a cross hair represented the baseline condition.

Behaviorally, the dyslexic participants were slower (4.4 seconds for the phonological task, and 2.1 seconds for the orthographic task, compared with 1.8 seconds and 1.1 seconds in the control participants). Since the tasks were self-paced, this would result in fewer stimuli for the dyslexics than the control participants. Therefore, the results are again complicated by differences in performance levels between groups. Furthermore, although several areas were identified in the task by group interactions, most of these effects are difficult to interpret because they were not qualified by simple main effects (i.e., activation for reading relative to fixation in either the control or dyslexic group). Nevertheless, the reduced left occipito-temporal activation for dyslexics relative to controls does correspond to the effects observed by Brunswick et al. (1999) and Paulesu et al. (2001) during simple reading tasks. Therefore, there is at least some consistency among studies.

*Shaywitz et al., 1998.* In an fMRI study, Shaywitz et al. (1998) presented a hierarchy of tasks to a group of 29 adult dyslexic readers and 32 control readers. The tasks were hypothesized to make progressively greater demands on phonological analysis. At the base of the hierarchy was a line orientation judgment task that required only visuospatial processing (e.g., Do \\V and \\V match?). The second task was letter case judgment (e.g., do bbBb and bbBb match?). The third task was a letter rhyme task (Do T and V rhyme?), the fourth a rhyme judgment of nonwords (e.g., Do "lete" and "jete" rhyme?) and the fifth a semantic categorization task (e.g., are "corn" and "rice" in the same semantic category?).

Less activation was observed for the dyslexic group than the control group in the superior temporal cortex, the angular gyrus and striate cortex (BA 17) while increased activation was observed in the left inferior frontal gyrus (as in the study by Brunswick et al., 1999). These data are taken by the authors to represent evidence of a "functional disruption in an extensive system in posterior cortex encompassing both traditional visual and traditional language regions" (Shaywitz et al., 1998, p. 2639). Like Rumsey et al. (1999) particular attention is drawn to the abnormal activation of the angular gyrus within this system, which they state "is considered pivotal in carrying out those cross-modal integrations necessary for reading" (Shaywitz et al., 1998, p. 2639). However, activation in the left angular gyrus has not been reported for reading aloud relative to rest, fixation, or falsefonts and it is not consistently activated during semantic decisions. Even in the tasks reported by Shaywitz et al. (1998), it is primarily activated during semantic decision.

Once again, there was a substantial task performance confound between the dyslexic and control groups. Reduced activation in the left angular gyrus might, therefore, simply reflect reduced semantic processing as a result of lower levels of accuracy across tasks. Furthermore, the poorer performance even on the baseline task suggests that the control and dyslexic participants differed not only in reading skill, but in cognitive abilities beyond those expected by such an impairment. Indeed, the dyslexic group were characterized by a significantly lower Full Scale IQ (FSIQ: 91) relative to their control group (FSIQ: 115). This discrepancy in overall cognitive ability renders the origin of any differences in task specific activation changes uncertain. For example, it has been shown that verbal abilities, as measured by verbal IQ, directly predict reading accuracy (Berninger, Abbott, & Thompson, 2001).

*Shaywitz et al., 2002.* In a second fMRI study, Shaywitz et al. (2002) investigated 70 dyslexic children and 74 children with no reading impairment. The children ranged in age between 7 to 18 years of age. The experimental tasks largely mirrored those employed in their previous study with adults (see above); a judgment of line orientation task, a nonword rhyme task, and a semantic category judgment task.

As in the adult study, behavioral performance of the dyslexic participants was impaired relative to that of the control participants. For the nonword rhyme and the category judgment tasks dyslexic children scored 59% and 75% correct, respectively, while the control children scored 79% and 91% correct. In addition, as in the adult study, the children constituting the dyslexic group were characterized by a significantly lower Full Scale IQ than their peers. Therefore, although the dyslexics activated a distributed set of left hemisphere regions less than the controls, it is difficult to determine the extent to which disparities in the level of behavioral performance influenced these differential patterns of brain activation.

The more interesting results of this paper come from two further analyses. In the first, a correlation analysis was carried out between individual differences in measures of reading performance obtained outside the scanner and brain activation during the experimental tasks (as in Rumsey et al., 1999). Positive correlation (increased activation with greater reading skill) was reported in the inferior aspect of the left middle temporal cortex (Talairach coordinates x: −42; y: −42; z: −5), during both the nonword rhyme and category judgment tasks and in bilateral temporo-parietal areas during the category task only. Negative correlations were reported for the right occipito-temporal region. It is of interest that the precise region that correlated with reading ability during both tasks was the same as one of the regions reported by Brunswick et al. (1999) and Paulesu et al., 2001 (Talairach coordinates x: −42; y: −48; z: −6) as showing reduced activation during implicit and explicit reading in adult dyslexics. This suggests that, even in childhood, activation in the posterior inferior temporal area accurately indexes reading ability. In addition, correlations between reading skill and activity in the region around the angular gyrus (observed during the category judgment task only) replicates the finding of Rumsey et al. (1999) that left temporo-parietal activation correlates with reading skill during reading aloud.

In the second analysis, age was correlated with degree of activation during the nonword rhyme and category judgment task. For the nonword rhyme task, dyslexic participants showed a positive correlation between age and bilateral inferior frontal activation, as well as in a number of other areas. This effect, which was not observed in the control group of children, is interpreted in terms of increased compensatory activity as the dyslexic participants become more experienced. By contrast, in the category judgment task, age of the dyslexic children tended to show a correlation in the right inferior frontal gyrus, suggesting that this region is involved in compensating for poor semantic performance or is simply a reflection of poor reading performance.

*Shaywitz et al. (2003).* In their third fMRI study, Shaywitz and colleagues distinguished between two different types of adult dyslexia (age 18–22 years): 19 compensated (accuracy improved) readers and 24 persistently poor readers. The persistently poor readers were identified as those with reading difficulties through second to tenth grade (Mean Full Scale IQ = 97), whereas the "accuracy improved readers" had reading difficulties in second or fourth grade but not in ninth or tenth grade (Mean Full Scale IQ = 108). The dyslexic participants were studied with the same nonword rhyming, semantic decision, and line judgment tasks as in the authors' first and second studies (see above), and activation was compared to that evoked by 27 control participants (Mean Full Scale IQ = 116) who had never experienced reading difficulties. Behaviorally, the "accuracy improved readers" were slower than the control group on both the nonword rhyming and semantic decision tasks and the persistently poor readers were even less accurate on the nonword rhyming task (71% relative to 88% in control participants and 81% in the "accuracy improved readers").

The interesting imaging finding is that different patterns of reading activation were observed for the "accuracy improved readers" and the persistently poor dyslexics and these effects were task-dependent. Notably, during the semantic decision task, only the "accuracy improved readers" underactivated posterior regions, whereas the poor readers showed abnormal occipito-temporal activation (correlating with right rather than left prefrontal activation). During the nonword rhyming task, by contrast, both dyslexic groups showed underactivation in the posterior temporal gyri and overactivation in the right inferior frontal gyrus, with the "accuracy improved readers" also increasing activation in the right superior frontal, right middle temporal, and the left anterior cingulate gyri. Shaywitz and colleagues tie these results together by speculating that the "accuracy improved readers" had a genetic abnormality and their normal IQs allowed them to adopt compensatory strategies to overcome their difficulties. In contrast, the persistently poor readers with significantly lower IQ represent a type of dyslexic reader whose problems may be environmentally determined and who rely more heavily on memory-based systems.

The important point about this study is that it distinguishes different patterns of activation for different types of poor readers. This may explain the inconsistencies observed in previous studies and points to the need for investigations of more specific types of dyslexics in future studies. Enhanced activation in right prefrontal regions for the dyslexic relative to control participants is also consistent with the authors' previous study with children that indicated increased activation in this area with age (see above). However, yet again, the differences between dyslexic groups were confounded by performance differences.

## Summary of functional imaging studies of developmental dyslexia

Although substantial effort has been invested in characterizing the neural bases of developmental dyslexia using brain imaging, the results are very difficult to interpret. First, there are few consistent findings across studies. Second, in the majority of studies, we cannot tease apart abnormal neuronal processing (the causal basis of dyslexia) from effects that are due to differences in performance levels that arise as a consequence of dyslexia. Nevertheless, we will discuss the most consistent effects over studies and consider what they might mean.

Reduced left posterior inferior and middle temporal activation has been observed in dyslexic participants when reading aloud and silently (Brunswick et al., 1999; Paulesu et al., 2001), and when making phonological decisions (Rumsey et al., 1997b; Shaywitz et al., 2003) and semantic decisions (Shaywitz et al., 2003). Activation in this area has also been shown to correlate positively with reading skill in children, while a negative correlation with reading skill occurs in the right occipito-temporal region. Activation in the left posterior inferior temporal lobe therefore appears to index reading ability irrespective of dyslexia. An index of reading ability, however, does not provide evidence for the cause of poor reading ability in dyslexia.

Reduced left temporo-parietal or angular gyrus activation has been observed during semantic decisions (Shaywitz et al., 2002, 2003) and letter rhyming (Temple et al., 2001). In addition, activation in these areas was found to correlate with reading skill during semantic decisions (Shaywitz et al., 2002) and reading (Rumsey et al., 1999). Since (1) studies of skilled reading have associated left temporo-parietal areas with semantic retrieval strategies, and (2) reduced left temporo-parietal activation has only been observed in the context of poor reading behavior, it may simply reflect reduced access to semantic processing as a consequence of deficits at an earlier stage in the reading system. In other words, reduced left temporo-parietal activation is likely to be a consequence, not the cause, of dyslexia.

Increased left premotor/inferior frontal activation was found during explicit but not implicit reading tasks (Brunswick et al., 1999; Shaywitz et al., 1998) and to correlate positively with age (Shaywitz et al., 2002). Support for an interpretation in terms of compensatory processing within the normal system comes from the observation that the area where activation increased during reading aloud in developmental dyslexics (Talairach coordinates [x,y,z]: −64, 0, 26) in Brunswick et al. (1999) corresponds almost exactly to the area where Price et al. (2003b) observed increased activation in a surface dyslexic patient (Talairach coordinates [x,y,z]: −56, 2, 34). Since we know that the surface dyslexic patient was relying on nonsemantic reading strategies and that in control subjects activation in this area increases during phonological relative to semantic decisions (Mummery et al., 1998), it may reflect increased reliance on phonological decoding.

Increased right inferior frontal activation was found in both accuracy improved and persistently poor dyslexics during phonological decisions (Shaywitz et al., 2003). It also correlated with age during both phonological and semantic tasks (Shaywitz et al., 2002) with abnormal correlations during semantic decisions in persistently poor dyslexics (Shaywitz et al., 2003). These effects are likely to reflect strategic processes, as this area is not involved when either dyslexic individuals or controls read aloud. More specifically, Shaywitz et al. (2003) associated the right inferior frontal effects with working memory and memory retrieval demands.

## Conclusions and Future Directions

Functional imaging studies of skilled readers are revealing the neural systems that sustain reading. The results suggest that reading emerges from adaptations within the picture naming system. Although further studies are required to understand the precise mechanisms of each region and how activation changes with different types of words, the findings are already placing constraints on cognitive models of reading. Functional imaging studies of developmental dyslexia are far more challenging because the very deficit of interest results in impaired performance, thereby confounding differences in activation levels with differences in performance levels. Even when performance is matched in the dyslexic and control samples (Brunswick et al., 1999; Ingvar et al., 2002; Paulesu et al., 2001), differential activation in the dyslexic sample may be a consequence, rather than a cause, of their slow and inefficient reading. The challenge for future studies will be to disentangle whether observed differences reflect primary cognitive deficits, secondary consequences of those deficits, compensatory processing, or differences on some other parameter such as intelligence. This could be achieved by comparing dyslexic individuals with younger controls who were carefully matched for both behavioral performance during scanning and background characteristics (such as intellectual level). Longitudinal studies of both normal and dyslexic readers will also play an important role in providing a developmental framework within which functional differences can be mapped over time.

Understanding the cognitive basis for activation differences will be further aided by the development of a more detailed model of the phonological deficit at the cognitive level. A common view is that the deficit reflects a lack of phonological specification (Hulme & Snowling, 1992; Snowling & Hulme, 1989; Swan & Goswami, 1997a; Swan & Goswami, 1997b) or a lack of segmental organization at the representational level (Fowler, 1991). One proposal to account for the phonological deficit is that dyslexic individuals have difficulty resolving the competition at the phonological level when multiple phonological codes are activated (the Phonological Competition Account, McCrory, 2001). According to this account, dyslexics should experience greater difficulty with reading than naming and greater difficulty in turn with more irregular orthographies such as English, whose orthography generates a higher level of ambiguity and elicits the activation of multiple and competing sublexical codes. Likewise, naming pictures at a rapid pace, may lead to phonological competition from preceding items. The behavioral impairments shown by dyslexic readers even when naming pictured items presented singly (Wolff, Michel, & Ovrut, 1990) might reflect a longer refractory period at the phonological level. Viewing phonological representation within a dynamic context such as this may provide a more complementary explanatory framework within which activation differences may be interpreted.

We conclude that functional neuroimaging studies to date have not yet established the components of reading that show reliable differences in dyslexic readers, or indeed determined which of these differences may be causal to the reading impairment in dyslexia. However, a pattern is beginning to emerge, with increased prefrontal activation and decreased occipito-temporal activation now observed over several studies. This pattern suggests that dyslexic readers largely activate the same neural system as skilled readers, but show subtle differences in how the components of this system are engaged. It will be important to explore how this pattern of differential activation pertains to the encoding, storage, or activation of phonological information if we are to integrate cognitive and neural accounts of developmental dyslexia. Thus, although functional imaging studies of developmental dyslexia are fraught with difficulties, there are ways to overcome the problems and so advance our understanding of the neural bases of reading in skilled readers as well as developmental dyslexic readers.

# PART VII

*Teaching Reading*

# Editorial Part VII

Undoubtedly the most important application for The Science of Reading, is to reading instruction. If we understand how people read, and how this skill develops, this will certainly have important implications for how best to teach people to read. Though it is common to talk about reading development (cf. language development, motor development, or perceptual development), it is important to remember that reading is a skill that is culturally determined, and above all else, a skill that is directly taught at school. Indeed, in much of the English-speaking world, learning to read is seen as one of the most important attainments of the first several years of formal education.

The two chapters in Part VII deal with the teaching of reading. Snow and Juel give an overview of current knowledge about how best to teach children to read. As they point out, historically the major methods for teaching reading have been around for at least a century, and disputes about how best to teach reading have focused on two issues. First, the size of unit that should be used to teach children the rules of reading (large units [words] or small units [letter-sound correspondences]). Second, the extent to which explicit instruction is needed (does reading have to be taught, or will it be caught given adequate exposure). Based on a thorough review of the evidence, Snow and Juel come down firmly in favour of the need to teach children explicitly about letter-sound correspondences in reading, but while not forgetting about the importance of reading for meaning. They also emphasize, however, the considerable evidence showing that the quality of teaching has a larger effect on children's reading skills than the nature of the curriculum that is followed. So simply prescribing an evidence-based approach to teaching reading is far from enough – how such an approach is implemented, by teachers in the classroom, is critical.

The importance of good teaching appears to be much more critical for children with dyslexia than for children whose cognitive skills make them well prepared to learn to read. Torgesen reviews studies that have attempted to remediate the reading difficulties of children with dyslexia. These children have severe and specific difficulties in learning to recognize words accurately and quickly. The studies reviewed in this chapter document that it is possible, using explicit instruction in phonemic awareness and phonemically-based decoding strategies, to bring about large improvements in reading accuracy in children with dyslexia; but intensive and highly expert teaching will be necessary. It also appears that improving reading fluency in such children may be more difficult to accomplish, and that this, in turn, may be critically dependent upon extensive practice.

In summary, the two chapters in Part VII demonstrate some of the practical fruits of The Science of Reading. We now know a great deal about how to teach reading to typically developing children, and how best to help children with dyslexia to overcome their difficulties. A major practical challenge is how to put such hard-won knowledge into practice – many policy issues, regarding how best to make these advances widely available to the children who need them, remain to be solved.

# 26

# Teaching Children to Read: What Do We Know about How to Do It?

## Catherine E. Snow and Connie Juel

Many of the chapters in this volume focus on literacy development. Typically they discuss the complexities of learning to read: the problem of the alphabetic principle, which requires learning how to segment speech into sounds represented by graphemes; the problem of English orthography, which requires going beyond simple phoneme–grapheme links to represent the morphemic, historical, and etymological information preserved in the writing system; and the problem of comprehension, which requires building a representation of textual and situational information. In contrast, this chapter considers the issue of literacy pedagogy: what constitutes good teaching and curriculum in the domain of literacy?

Of necessity our focus is limited to the English-speaking world, and within that largely to the US. Issues of reading pedagogy are delightfully minimized in many parts of the world. In Korea, for instance, educators worry little about reading pedagogy, as the Korean alphabetic system is rarely a source of learner difficulties. In Japan, where "lesson study" absorbs considerable time and energy among teachers (Stigler & Hiebert, 1999), the lessons studied are all mathematical. Literacy lessons in Japan are not seen as problematic.

In the US and the UK, on the other hand, the initial teaching of reading is a major source of worry and the focus of attention from many directions. In the US, primary grade teachers commit the bulk of their serious teaching time to reading; many of the comprehensive school reform plans prescribe a 90- to 150-minute literacy block. In the UK, each child receives one hour of literacy instruction each day through the elementary grades (Department for Education and Employment, 1998). Textbook publishers, curriculum developers, and purveyors of professional development also devote enormous amounts of time, attention, and resources to early reading, and of course reap even more enormous benefits from their investments.

In this chapter, we attempt to explain why issues around reading pedagogy have attracted so much time and attention in the English-speaking world. We offer a brief historical orientation to the teaching of reading, highlighting the nineteenth century antecedents of the various positions staked out in current controversies about teaching methods. We then summarize the curricular recommendations that have achieved consensus at the beginning of the twenty-first century, and some of the challenges to turning research directly into improved practices.

## Controversies about Teaching Reading

### History of the reading skirmishes

There has been a long history of conflict about the best way to teach English-speaking children how to read and write. In 1908, for example, E. B. Huey in his book *The psychology and pedagogy of reading* started the section on pedagogy with the following sentence: "The methods of learning to read that are in common use to-day may be classed as alphabetic, phonic, phonetic, word, sentence, and combination methods" (Huey 1908/1979, p. 265).

He went on to describe these different methods, noting that the alphabetic method (focusing on teaching letter names and letter recognition) was "now chiefly of historical interest." The various phonic and phonetic methods Huey reviewed typically addressed the issue of orthographic depth by introducing adapted alphabets in which different sounds represented by a single letter were differentiated using diacritics, invented symbols, or alternative spellings.

One of the most popular phonic series in the late 1800s was the McGuffey readers. A lesson began with a review of words that contained taught letter sounds and an introduction to new letter sounds. By the third lesson, "short a" is already being reviewed along with some previously taught consonants in common phonograms, and the letter *f* is introduced. Children see, with a diacritical mark over the *â*, indicating it is short, and a line through the *¢*, indicating it should be pronounced as /k/, the words *Nat, hat, fan,* and *can*. They then read the text:

> Ann and Nat.
> Ann has a fan.
> Nat has a hat.
> Ann can fan Nat. (McGuffey, 1879)

One method that incorporated no novel symbols was described by Huey as "purely phonic, almost arrogantly so." Pollard's *Synthetic method of reading and spelling* (n. d.) offered techniques highly reminiscent of some used today to create vivid memories of letter-sound associations; /h/, for example, is introduced as a "pant" and the child is instructed "you may think little *h* is the picture of the chair Bess sits in when she is very tired. As she sits down she breathes very hard, *h, h, h.*" Further information in Pollard's narrative introduction of letter sounds prefigures the Lindamood-Bell articulatory techniques (Lindamood & Lindamood, 1998) as well:

There are pigeons in the barn, mama. What letter stands for the sound they make?
This one: d = D. It is a sound made by young pigeons. . . .
This sound presses the tongue up, near its point, a little harder than *n*. Try the two together,
*n, d, n, d.*

Early dissenters to these popular approaches voiced concern about the potential for boredom in such texts, and the inappropriateness of turning children into "little phoneticians." The force of science was also raised in objection. Both gestalt psychology/philosophy and scientific experiments were considered to refute phonic methods. In 1842 the renowned educator Horace Mann wrote:

> When we wish to give to a child the idea of a new animal, we do not present successively the different parts of it – an eye, an ear, the nose, the mouth, the body, or a leg; but we present the whole animal as one object. And this would be still more necessary if the individual parts of the animal with which the child had labored long and hard to become acquainted, were liable to change their natures as soon as they were brought into juxtaposition, as almost all the letters do when combined in words. (Cited in Mathews, 1966, p. 80)

This holistic view foreshadows that later espoused by Frank Smith (1973), who argued that readers do not identify individual letters in words. Rather, the printed gestalt functions like a Chinese logogram. In Smith's words, "we can read as efficiently as most of us do only because we treat our written language as if it were ideographic" (p. 118). As such, of course, it would be foolish to teach children phonics. "Readers do not use (and do not need to use) the alphabetic principle of decoding to sound in order to learn or identify words" (p. 105).

The gestalt view was buttressed by the first scientific experiments on word recognition, conducted by James McKeen Cattell (1886). In Cattell's classic experiment, subjects were briefly exposed to words or letters and asked to report what they saw. Subjects were better reporting words than even single letters! Cattell concluded, "We do not therefore perceive separately the letters of which a word is composed, but [rather we perceive] the word as a whole" (Cattell, 1886, p. 74). Cattell's *word superiority effect* was ignored during the early twentieth century, but engendered renewed investigation in the 1960s and 1970s. In general the finding was replicated (Reicher, 1969). Later technical advances in eye-movement tracking and computer simulations would challenge Cattell's interpretation – that processing is too fast for readers to process every letter in a word. Today we know that readers do indeed routinely process every letter in every word, but they do so by parallel processing of letter groups. Processing of letters within words can be enhanced by knowledge of orthographic patterns; this is why pseudowords are also apprehended more readily than single letters. (See Lupker, this volume, for a review of this research.) But in the late nineteenth century, before such interpretations were available, the word superiority effect contributed to dooming the phonic readers by undermining their foundation in science.

The whole-word method, which Huey described as in general use but almost always in combination with other approaches, was clearly visible in the curricular materials of the early twentieth century. Sometimes popular texts such as nursery rhymes, poems, songs, and folktales were read. Other times texts were created that emphasized the repetition of phrases and words, as in this play designed to be read at the beginning of first grade in the Silver Burdett series:

**The Apple Man**
*The Girl*
> The Apple Man is coming
> down the street!
> The Apple Man is coming
> down the street!

*The Boy*
> The Apple Man is coming
> down the street!
> The Apple Man is coming
> down the street!
> The Apple Man is coming!
> The Apple Man is coming! (Coleman, Uhl, & Hosic, 1925)

Phrase and sentence repetition were sometimes reduced to an emphasis on repetition of what were thought to be high-frequency words. The whole-word method reached its zenith with texts like those in the Scott Foresman series:

> Oh, Father.
> See Spot.
> Look, Father, look.
> See Spot play.
> Oh, oh, oh. (Robinson, Monroe, & Artley, 1946).

The Scott Foresman series dominated the reading field for decades, just as the McGuffey readers had a half-century before.

The sentence method relied on child-generated sentences about a topic or a picture, transcribed by the teacher on the board, and used as the text in teaching reading. Cited advantages of this method were the interest and motivation it generated, and its use of natural, childlike language structures, in sharp contrast, in Huey's view, to the unnatural, boring, and meaningless sentences found in phonics primers, which he decried as "sentence-hash." The sentence method shares much with initial literacy methods still in use, for example, the Language Experience approach in which teachers transcribe child utterances, typically recording a shared experience or the outcome of a group discussion. The text, made up of accumulated child sentences, transcribed by the teacher, then becomes the source of lessons about letter-sound correspondence.

From Huey we learn that all the various approaches to teaching reading current today had been developed by 1870, and that complaints standard today about quality of the texts used in teaching reading and about effectiveness of instruction were voiced in response to every reform of reading methods. Huey avoided endorsing specific methods by recommending as the best model for classroom reading pedagogy the activities of the literate household, in which encounters with print were frequent and always meaningful.

## *Nature of the conflict*

The conflict about how to teach reading, in its various specific forms at different historical moments, has always centered around two major issues: Using what unit of language should the rules of reading and writing be taught? And to what degree can we trust children to induce an adequate understanding of the system themselves, without explicit instruction about its character?

Although these two issues are in principle independent of one another, in fact the positions pedagogical theorists have adopted on the two questions are highly correlated. Theorists who have argued for a focus on large, meaningful units in teaching reading have also argued that children can rely on induction to a very large degree – that the processes of learning to read are, in Byrne's (this volume) terms *learner dependent.* In contrast, theorists who have argued for a focus on small, analytic, meaningless units have also in general argued that children need a fairly structured and teacher-supported introduction to reading – Byrne's *environment-dependent* process. Ironically, though, those who express the greatest faith in children's capacity to induce the rules for translating print into language relatively autonomously have also become identified with the movement to professionalize teaching and to honor practitioner knowledge (Adams and Bruck, 1993; see e.g. Goodman, 1965, 1993), whereas insistence on the need for a substantial role for the teacher in providing instruction has often been paired with techniques (e.g., scripting of lessons, prescriptiveness about sequencing of topics, and time use) that take control out of the hands of teachers.

Interestingly, the rationales offered by those taking directly opposing positions on the issue of unit size have been remarkably similar. Those who prefer direct teaching of analytic units, that is, how letters represent sounds, invoke the complexity of English orthography, and the resultant difficulty of using processes of induction to arrive at an understanding of the alphabetic principle as it applies to English. Those who, on the other hand, promote rich exposure to and involvement with literate representations of meaningful units argue that the orthographic system of English is too complicated to teach directly. It would require, it is argued, too many rules and too many exceptions, so it is better to let children just figure it out, as they do (it is claimed) for oral language. In both cases, orthographic depth is the villain of the piece.

In the 1800s, and continuing well into the twentieth century, adapted alphabets were expected to solve the problem of orthographic depth. By rendering the orthography "regular," it was expected that children would more readily grasp the alphabetic principle. EVNING HIM, from the *Furst Fonetic Redur*, begins: *Jizos, ten'der Shep'erd* (Longley, 1852). About a hundred years later, the Initial Teaching Alphabet (Masurkiewicz & Tanyzer, 1963) included texts like the one presented in figure 26.1. These adapted alphabets, however, never gained general popularity. Their failure to survive has cast the burden back onto the shoulders of either the teaching (teacher, curriculum, method) or the child learner, depending on one's view of the basic conflict.

Phonics programs put the burden on curriculum. The active child learner was seen as central in whole-language approaches (Smith, 1973). Contextual knowledge was invoked as the key predictor of good reading, because it helped readers cope with difficult English orthography, and because reading development was seen as just like language develop-

a gæm ov baull

"Cum on, paul.
hit the baull," sed ted.
"See if you can hit it.
see if you can hit the baull
with the bat."

**Figure 26.1** A page from ⟨Early-to-read: i/t/a/program⟩, an adapted-alphabet reader by Masurkiewicz and Tanyzer (1963).

ment – a natural process. Smith (1971, 1973, 1978) and Goodman (1967, 1968) saw readers as actively predicting their way through text. The reader formed guesses about upcoming content/words based on knowledge of the meaning of a text. The reader sampled sparsely from orthographic information to confirm such predictions. "Skill in reading involves not greater precision, but more accurate first guesses based on better sampling techniques, greater control over language structure, broadened experiences and increased conceptual development" (Goodman, 1976, p. 504). Smith clearly minimized the role that orthographic information played in reading:

> The more difficulty a reader has with reading, the more he relies on the visual information; this statement applies to both the fluent reader and the beginner. In each case, the cause of the difficulty is inability to make full use of syntactic and semantic redundancy, of nonvisual sources of information. (1971, p. 221)

Two views of Goodman and Smith in particular had a tremendous influence on the teaching of reading: that readers used multiple cueing systems, and that novice and expert readers processed text similarly.

The reader was presumed to use multiple cues in normal word recognition. The cues provided by context, that is, by semantics and syntax, were considered as helpful as those provided by orthography (see Adams, 1998, for a history of the cueing notion). Generations of teachers were trained to do "miscue" analysis: a rather elaborate classification of reader's oral reading errors into syntactic, semantic, and visual/graphic-based causes. For example, reading "big" for "large" is a semantic-based miscue, indicating understanding. The extension of this notion was that teachers would encourage children to make best guesses in reading based on meaning, even covering up words with tape or their fingers to promote thinking about meaning and guessing the word. Looking at the spelling was the last resource.

Early on the multiple cueing systems approach was questioned by reading researchers, for example Charles Perfetti:

> The main failing of this approach [Goodman's 1968 "psycholinguistic guessing game"] is that it does not recognize that one of the "cueing systems" is more central than the others. A child who learns the code has knowledge that can enable him to read no matter how the semantic, syntactic, and pragmatic cues might conspire against him. No matter how helpful they are to reading, these cues are not really a substitute for the ability to identify a word. (1985, p. 239)

There is now abundant evidence that the prediction model of reading is incorrect. Eye-movement studies indicate skilled readers do not use context to reduce processing of graphic information (see Rayner, this volume). Numerous studies in the 1980s indicated use of context for word identification is both inefficient and minimally useful. At best, for example, adult readers can accurately predict one out of four words in text, and the most accurate predictions are of function words (Gough, Alford, & Holley-Wilcox, 1981). Skilled readers can only accurately predict one in ten content words, and predicting words takes longer than just looking at the word (Gough, 1983).

The second notion that took hold was that beginning readers and skilled readers used the same processes in reading (Goodman & Goodman, 1979; see discussion in Juel, 1991). That is, good readers differ from poor readers primarily in better prediction-making skills, and increased knowledge of the world and of language. All views of reading would agree this is true for comprehension; the "psycholinguistic guessing game" described it as true of word reading. The better reader used syntactic and semantic information to form hypotheses about the content of text, with minimal orthographic input. Language-rich texts promote better readers because they promote better predictions. The whole-language movement blossomed, with the emphasis on authentic children's literature and the minimizing of phonics or phonics-influenced texts.

We now have reams of studies that show that good and poor readers differ not in the use of context to make better predictions, but in the swift and efficient identification of words (see chapters by Perfetti et al., and Vellutino & Fletcher, this volume). Nonetheless, until recently, this research and its message had not reached classrooms. Rather, it was the "psycholinguistic guessing game" model that held sway. Its power among practitioners no doubt derived in part from its admirable insistence on teacher professionalism and teacher autonomy, in contrast to many phonics methods, which impose curricular control. Furthermore, there is no doubt that the rich and varied literacy materials whole-language teachers relied on were more attractive and engaging than phonics texts, with their controlled vocabulary and often-insipid language. Furthermore, whole-language practitioners would argue that they do teach letter-sound correspondence – when needed and appropriate, embedded in meaningful encounters with texts. Two questions remained: whether such unsystematic methods were adequate to ensure all children learned the alphabetic principle, and whether all teachers were well enough prepared to design their own methods for letter-sound teaching.

## The Introduction of Science and Orthodoxy into Pedagogical Decision Making

Ironies in the history of the conflicts about teaching reading abound. The irony in the US is that, in the face of unprecedented commitments to improving reading outcomes and a rich research basis for improving pedagogy, political forces are playing such a large role in determining how children are taught. The political forces involved, though no doubt well-intentioned, force oversimplifications and orthodoxies into a system that is trying to present itself as research-based.

### Key publications on reading instruction

Efforts to systematize what the research base can tell us about improving reading outcomes have occurred regularly since the mid-1960s. In 1966, Mitford Mathews published a book called *Teaching to read*, in which he took an historical perspective on the long-standing controversies about methods for teaching reading. Mathews recounted the historical alliance between the preference for using larger units and progressive education, an association rooted in the personal relationship between Colonel Francis Parker, an extremely effective proponent of the whole-word method, and John Dewey. Though his book was primarily historical, Mathews's concluding chapter reviewed the then contemporary research on the relative effectiveness of various reading methods. He concluded unequivocally that early attention to letters and sounds was much more productive than an exclusive focus on larger units in teaching children to read.

Two landmark events happened in 1967. The Cooperative Research Program in First Grade Reading Instruction published its first comprehensive report (Bond & Dijkstra, 1967) and Jeanne Chall first published a report written for the Carnegie Corporation of New York, called *Learning to read: The great debate*. The so-called First Grade Studies compared the basal programs of the era – programs all characterized by controlled vocabulary, teaching sight words first, and a relatively casual treatment of phonics – with five enhancements to basals. The Bond and Dijkstra report concluded that, in general, the basal-plus methods performed better than the basal-only programs, and that letter knowledge at first-grade entry was the best predictor of word reading outcomes. The results were complex, though, and actual outcomes varied enormously across sites and classrooms.

Chall's report comprised an interpretive review of the literature on various reading methods and their effectiveness, information collected from authors and publishers of reading curricula about their sources of information, and an analysis of the content of widely used reading programs. The debate focused on in the first edition of the report was that between whole-word and phonics methods, which was raging in those decades. In a sense, then, Chall's 1967 book was the academic version of Rudolf Flesch's enormously popular and influential 1955 treatise *Why Johnny can't read.*

By 1983, when the second and updated edition of Chall's *The great debate* appeared, whole-language methods had risen to occupy the large-unit learner-dependent pole of the debate – signaling an important change in reading methods, and the decline of word-based methods. Chall's updated introduction to the 1983 edition made clear her view that an explicit focus on the alphabetic principle early in the process of teaching reading was to be preferred over any method that endorsed meaning over code. She also challenged the proponents of the then relatively new whole-language methods to provide comparative studies showing their methods produced better reading outcomes than code-focused methods.

In 1990 Marilyn Adams wrote *Beginning to read,* a comprehensive review of cognitive and psycholinguistic, as well as instructional, research about reading. Adams's research led her to conclusions identical to Mathews's and Chall's concerning the importance of early and explicit exposure to the alphabetic code in the successful acquisition of reading. Both Chall's and Adams's volumes had considerable influence (in fact, in the 1983 edition Chall documented changes in reading curricula that she attributed to the impact of the 1967 report), but practices in the field of reading instruction continued to be influenced by eclecticism more than by science. Furthermore, since one of the consequences of strictly phonics-based programs is the wide use in early instruction of relatively boring, strictly controlled, texts, programs using more attractive and authentic texts maintained their appeal. In fact, in 1996 Chall published a third edition documenting the decline of attention to phonics in newly published reading curricula.

Thus, conflicts about the best methods for teaching reading continued to rage, but gained greater urgency as worries about standards increased worldwide towards the end of the twentieth century.

## Preventing reading difficulties

In 1995 the National Research Council (NRC) established a committee to write a report on the topic of Preventing Reading Difficulties in Young Children. It was felt that a report produced through the consensus process intrinsic to a committee-authored product, and that had gone through rigorous review overseen by the National Academies, might have more influence on practice than individually authored volumes. The charge to the Committee on Preventing Reading Difficulties went beyond answering questions about reading instruction. Reading was implicitly defined as an expectable outcome for children in a rich, highly literate, country with universal schooling. Thus, a public health, rather than a purely educational, perspective was adopted, a perspective that dictated identifying the sources of reading difficulties in order to guide the direction of resources to those placed at the highest risk of failure. Furthermore, a developmental perspective that placed the beginning of reading well before first exposure to formal instruction was endorsed, acknowledging the huge body of work showing relationships between preschool accomplishments (letter knowledge, phonological awareness, vocabulary, familiarity with the functions of written language) and later reading success (see Bowey, this volume). Research on the characteristics of skilled reading was also reviewed, as a guide to the components of effective instruction.

The NRC report (1998) included a wide array of recommendations, of which only a small subset were directed to issues of reading instruction. These instructional recommendations addressed the mechanics of reading (providing practice with letters and sounds in kindergarten, providing explicit instruction and practice with spelling-sound correspondences in first grade, teaching children strategies for focusing on print in identifying unknown words in later grades, assessing word reading accuracy and fluency regularly), comprehension (building linguistic and conceptual knowledge orally from kindergarten on, including explicit instruction on comprehension strategies either during reading aloud or student reading, and assessing both conceptual knowledge and comprehension strategy use regularly), writing (encouraging the use of invented spelling to promote both phonological awareness and writing for communication, teaching spelling explicitly and holding children accountable for correct spelling of taught words, requiring daily writing), as well as reading practices and motivation (providing daily opportunities for reading a self-selected text at an appropriate level, providing opportunities for daily assisted or supported reading, and promoting independent reading).

These instructional recommendations were endorsed by the International Reading Association, which interpreted them as consonant with their commitment to balanced reading instruction, and were simultaneously dismissed by others who characterized them as *wishy-washy.* To clarify the instructional implications, thus, the preface to the third printing of the NRC report made the following explicit statement:

> The committee's position has often been presented as one endorsing "balance" or "some phonics and some whole language." "Balance" is not the right metaphor to carry our message, and we certainly did not suggest an approach that involved "a little of this and a little of that." "Balance" could mean splitting one's time evenly across activities designed to practice the alphabetic principle and activities designed to support comprehension. "Integration" means precisely that these opportunities to learn these two aspects of skilled reading should be going on at the same time, in the context of the same activities, and that the choice of instructional activities should be part of an overall, coherent approach to supporting literacy development, not a haphazard selection from unrelated, though varied, activities. (1998, pp. vii–viii)

This kind of integration is, of course, no easy task. It is clearly much easier to select ten phonics activities followed by ten comprehension activities; and, overall, for the beginning reader, this "balance" is likely better than 0 of one and 20 of the other. But there are at least two compelling reasons brought to us by research for striving for integration: (1) much is required to "learn" a word, and (2) coherent approaches to literacy development must take into consideration a particular child's literacy skills.

## *"Learning" a word*

Most researchers would argue that the development of detailed orthographic representations is vital to the automatization of word recognition. On the road to fully specified orthographic representations, the beginner slowly "amalgamates" information (see Ehri, this volume). So, the child with limited orthographic knowledge may link letter names to their phonological cues and recall *bee* because of the letter name for *b* or *e*. The word "moon" may be recalled because it has two moons in the middle of it, or is on the page with the picture of the moon, or simply because its first letter, *m*, is recalled with the knowledge that a few letters come after it. As long as the meaning of the word is known, then what may be amalgamated at first to get meaning is something like "the letter 'm' on a certain page signals a lunar sphere." And, the child will say *moon* when approximating its location on the page. Incomplete orthographic information will likely not enable the recognition of the printed "moon" in another book and may yield the spelling of "moon" as simply *m* in a child's early writing. But with the aid of knowledge of the letter-sound connection *m* to /m/, and other connections, as well as having read enough text to see *soon* and *moo* and *boo* and *moon* several more times, a complete orthographic representation of "moon" will be established. That orthographic representation then also becomes a resource for reading other words – *noon, loon, loom, vroom*, and so on. It also becomes a resource, though perhaps not a perfect one, in reading *good, stood*, and *look*.

Many phonics programs try to help children by actually teaching the "two" sounds of *oo*. The 1963 Lippincott first-grade reader, for example, instructs children about the "long and the short *oo*," then presents a text about *Ronny Hooper's encounter with Hoot Tooter, the Oogle-Google Goblin* (McCracken & Walcutt, 1963). The lengthy and language-rich (if slightly unconvincing) story goes on to state that *Hoot* lived in *Ronny Hooper's* drain because their names shared oo's. Some children may need such explicit instruction, but many probably do not. Once children have read words like "too," "boo," and "moon" often enough, they may be operating with both complete orthographic information about specific words (like *moon*), and/or enough generalized knowledge of orthography (e.g., *oo*) to be able to apply it to novel words like *gloom*, to pseudowords like *oogle*, and to words with slightly different vowels like *shook*.

The Lippincott phonics program was distinguished from most others by its very heavy vocabulary load and use of relatively sophisticated words (Chall, 1967). In this it differed from most phonics approaches, which used simpler vocabulary on the assumption that "sounding out" would enable a child to retrieve words already in their oral vocabularies. The assumption that first graders all know a particular list of words, though, is clearly wrong. Many children come to school with limited oral vocabularies – not just non-native speakers of English entering reading instruction with only a few dozen English vocabulary words at their disposal, but also children like those in the lowest income group studied by Hart and Risley (1995b). Their "word poverty" (Moats, 2001) is precisely why an integrated approach is so needed for many children. In this respect, we concur with Gough's statement:

> I conclude that Goodman is dead wrong about what separates the skilled adult from the beginning reader, and hence about what must be accomplished in reading acquisition. The

most conspicuous difference between good and poor readers is found in the swift and accurate recognition of individual words, in decoding, and the mastery of this skill is at the heart of reading acquisition (cf. Gough & Hillinger, 1980). But it should not be inferred from this that I completely disagree with Goodman's views on reading instruction. I believe that Goodman's insistence on reading for meaning is exactly right. Our problem is to find a way to teach the child to decode while doing just that. (1981, p. 95)

## Individualizing instruction

The second argument for integration in early reading instruction is that children bring different knowledge and abilities to a classroom (Byrne, this volume). Some children may have extensive oral vocabularies and just need help with decoding, such as that provided in phonics. Some children may not have sufficiently developed phonological awareness to benefit from phonics unless that instruction includes specific attention to elongating phonemes and to blending them together. Some very unfortunate children may have such difficulty with phonemic awareness they cannot profit from phonics unless it is highly individualized or, perhaps, at all (see Torgesen, this volume). Some children may have limited ability to generalize; they may need the "oo" instruction or multiple, extensive exposures to short vowel sounds. Other children will quickly induce the orthography and their learning curve will accelerate so that each new spelling-sound pattern is learned more quickly than the last. Byrne (this volume) clearly explicates this point of view when he says there are really many theories of learning to read, not just one. Of course, these many requirements – knowing what children need to learn, assessing children's skills across those various domains, and knowing what to do for those lagging in one or more domains – all require very high levels of teacher knowledge.

## National reading panel report

Shortly before the publication of the NRC committee report in 1998, a panel of researchers, practitioners, and parents was invited by the National Institute of Child Health and Human Development to carry out a review of the literature focused specifically on the issue of effective reading pedagogy. This second group, called the National Reading Panel (NRP), reviewed experimental and quasi-experimental literature only, and conducted a quantitative meta-analysis for domains where enough studies were found. The criteria established by the NRP for its literature review emphasized domains that were easily subject to intervention studies. Random assignment studies of entire literacy programs or curricula are very difficult to carry out, so such studies have been infrequent. But it is rather easy to introduce a phonological awareness or vocabulary intervention into a classroom, or to add the teaching of comprehension strategies to ongoing literacy instruction. Thus, the literature available to the NRP for review addresses some aspects of literacy instruction more satisfactorily than others (as the lists of gaps and unaddressed research questions included in the report itself richly acknowledge).

The NRP (2000) found a basis in research findings for endorsing instruction in five areas: phonological awareness, phonics, fluency, vocabulary, and comprehension strategies. At the first level, the recommendations were simply to attend to these five areas in reading instruction. For some of the domains, though, it was possible to make somewhat more specific recommendations about the type or appropriate length of such instruction. In the domain of phonological awareness, for example, the literature reviewed suggested that instruction was most effective before second grade, that 5–20 hours total instruction had the maximum effect, that focusing on a few phonological awareness skills was better than trying to cover them all, and that linking phonological awareness instruction to letters made it more effective. The literature on early code teaching reviewed suggested that systematic instruction in phonics was more effective than allowing children to induce letter-sound relationships, but did not support the recommendation of one particular approach to teaching letter-sound relationships over any other. For example, there was no evidence that working with the smallest analytic units (phonemes) was better than working with slightly larger analytic units (onset-rime), or that synthetic approaches (focusing on blending) were better than analytic approaches (focusing on word families). In the domain of fluency, evidence was found to support the effectiveness of oral guided reading, though the research base was insufficient to draw any conclusions about the value of sustained silent reading. In support of comprehension, the recommendations included paying attention to both explicit and implicit teaching of vocabulary, using read-alouds and student independent reading to promote opportunities for vocabulary growth, and ensuring repeated exposures to target vocabulary items. In addition, specific support was found for the use of seven comprehension strategies: comprehension monitoring, cooperative learning, graphic and semantic organizers, question answering, question generation, and summarization. On the other hand, there are not recommendations for exactly when, how, or how long any of these comprehension supports should be taught.

Given these fairly nonspecific conclusions from the NRP report, it is not surprising that all the major American publishers of reading curricula found it possible within a few months of the report's appearance to advertise that their products addressed all five "research based" instructional domains. Comparison across various programs reveals considerable variety in how such components as phonics instruction, vocabulary instruction, or strategy instruction are actually implemented, but every publisher has introduced these topics as headings in student workbooks, in teacher manuals, and in their scope and sequence charts. Some of the curriculum overviews seem to suggest that these five components added together constitute their instructional program. In fact, as is well attested in the prose of the full NRP report and in the interpretations of the report provided by the Partnership for Reading, a collaboration including the US Department of Education (2001), these five instructional domains need to *be incorporated into* a reading instructional program, but they do not by themselves constitute such a program.

## Problems with Horse Race Studies

Most of the work that we have reviewed so far has focused on curriculum – the sequence and composition of activities in a reading program and the texts to be used. The studies that have compared reading programs, though, all suggest that differences across curricula explain only a small portion of the variance in reading outcomes (Bond & Dijkstra, 1967; Tivnan & Hemphill, 2004). The quality of implementation of programs turns out to be much more important in explaining outcomes than the nature of the program.

Solving reading difficulties through the curriculum is an attractive option, but there are many reasons why comparisons of programs or curricula are an inadequate basis for improved practice. These reasons include at least the following: the role of the teacher and teacher knowledge is clearly key but difficult to quantify; the level of information available to guide classroom level implementation of curriculum is typically inadequate; how the instructional experiences actually get translated into learning, and thus what aspects of them are most important, is often obscure; different instructional strategies may be optimal for different children, yet instruction is typically described at the classroom- rather than dyad- or small-group-level; and effects of site, school, and district often interact with the program.

## Role of the teacher

There are considerable data suggesting that teacher qualifications make a difference in outcomes no matter what program or curriculum is in place. Effective teacher practices reviewed and summarized by Taylor, Pearson, Clark, & Walpole (2000) include spending more time on academic tasks, making learning goals clear and providing feedback to students, maintaining a warm, cooperative atmosphere, and responding to individual differences among students with individualized amounts and kinds of instruction. Pressley and his colleagues, in a significant program of research on effective instruction (e.g., Bogner, Raphael, & Pressley, 2002; Pressley et al., 2001), have found that the students of highly effective first-grade teachers spent more time engaged in literacy activities, in part because the teachers had excellent management skills. Even in first grade, effective literacy teachers teach comprehension strategies, vocabulary, and writing as well as word reading skills. In other words, the most effective practices could occur in conjunction with a wide variety of specific programs, if teachers are ensuring that the several elements of literacy instruction all receive attention.

Tivnan and Hemphill (2004) conducted a study of early literacy instruction in a school district serving children at high risk of educational difficulties. The district had required each school to choose one of four literacy programs: *Balanced Early Literacy, Developing Literacy First, Literacy Collaborative,* or *Success for All.* At the end of first grade, there were no differences across programs in word reading, pseudoword reading, spelling, or vocabulary, though *Developing Literacy First* was significantly better than *Success for All* in comprehension, and *Literacy Collaborative* better than *Success for All* or *Balanced Early Literacy* in writing outcomes. Furthermore, the majority of children in all programs were scoring at levels below grade expectation, particularly on the comprehension assessment. Despite these circumscribed program effects, differences among teachers were enormous; in only 8 of the 36 classrooms were more than 50% of the children scoring at or above expected level, while in 4 of the classrooms fewer than 25% of the children achieved expected scores for their grades. In the other 24 classrooms 30 to 45% of the children achieved the reading comprehension levels expected of them, and prerequisite to future success. Neither the group of eight teachers with greater success nor the four with very low outcomes clustered within any of the programs. But the most successful teachers used the practices described by Taylor, Pressley, and Pearson above as characteristic of effective teachers, including responding with explicit instruction to children in need, promoting independent reading, organizing lively engaging discussions about texts being read, holding children accountable for reading with meaning, asking open-ended questions, and holding high expectations.

The NRC report on the Prevention of Reading Difficulties in Young Children (1998) devoted four recommendations to aspects of professional training and development, arguing that the complexities of preventing reading difficulties for all children dictate that teachers be both widely knowledgeable and well supported in their practice. Those recommendations were further developed in a book based on the NRC report, entitled *Preparing our teachers* (Strickland et al., 2002). The NRP also reviewed research on teacher education and concluded that, while the accumulated evidence supported the effectiveness of teacher preparation and professional development in changing teachers and in improving their students' outcomes, the research basis was insufficient to make recommendations about the specific content or organization of teacher preparation programs.

Thus, though we have little basis to make claims about the specific preparation teachers need, we have considerable basis for identifying teacher skill and the specifics of teacher practices as factors influencing students' reading outcomes.

## Describing the classroom instruction adequately

It is difficult to come to a consensus about the interpretation of classroom studies, and to elicit from these studies useful information about what teachers should be doing, at least in part because of the difficulty of capturing sufficient information about classroom instruction. Even in programmatic comparisons, methods are often confounded with factors that accompany the method. The kinds of texts read (Juel & Roper/Schneider, 1985), time spent reading, the social setting for instruction, structured versus less-structured curricula, and the patterns of teacher and student interaction are examples of such factors. As Lauren Resnick noted in 1979, the success of phonics may be attributable to factors less related to its content than to its direct instruction delivery.

Most studies have provided only relatively general descriptions of program and student characteristics. So we learn which programs affect mean classroom or school performance overall, but these average descriptors may misrepresent what instruction really looks like for specific groups of children. This is particularly the case for early elementary classes, where the most salient aspects of reading instruction likely occur in small groups. Mean values reflecting whole-class instruction may be far from what any one group or child actually experienced.

In short, very few studies have documented in sufficient detail the form of instruction, the characteristics of texts being read, amount of phonemic awareness instruction, amount of time spent on writing, or degree of fit of texts to children. The level at which instruction needs to be defined goes far beyond "phonics or not." Phonics can be done many ways, with many different kinds of materials, many different types and number of texts, and badly or well.

## Understanding how instruction functions

While research since the time of Resnick's comment has continued to point to the importance of the content itself, we are left uncertain how precisely the content functions to generate learning, and thus how much of that content actually matters. The actual spelling-sound relations used by readers may bear little or no resemblance to what is taught in phonics (Gough & Hillinger, 1980). The rules of phonics presented to children are explicit, few in number, and slow in application, whereas identification of spelling-sound patterns by skilled readers is implicit, requires considerable orthographic information, and is very fast. Phonics programs rarely provide direct instruction on more than 90 phonics rules, whereas many more than that – perhaps 500 spelling-sound relations – are needed to read (Gough & Hillinger, 1980; Juel, 1994). And, as connectionist models of reading have indicated, skilled readers may ultimately be responding to the specific orthography of individual words (see Plaut, this volume). So, phonics may be useful to children not because of the specific letter-sound relations taught, but because a phonics approach gives children the chance to discover the alphabetic principle, and provides practice looking closely at word spelling.

In other words, phonics instruction may simply point children in the direction of looking deeply into the printed form of the word as they attach sound to it, rather than looking for clues outside the printed word. Indeed, each time the child skips over scrutinizing the internal structure of a printed word in favor of using contextual cues or illustrations to identify the word, the child loses an opportunity to imprint the orthography (Harm, McCandliss, & Seidenberg, 2003). If children basically learn to read by developing some phonological awareness, learning some letter-sound patterns that help them approach print, and then phonologically recoding a specific printed word a few times, as has been suggested by the self-teaching hypothesis (Share, 1995; Share & Stanovich, 1995; Torgesen & Hecht, 1996), then phonics probably helps the child both by developing phonological awareness and by focusing the child on orthography. However, other forms of instruction, such as writing for sounds in modeled spelling or fostering invented spelling by elongating the sounds in words, might do just as well (or better) to promote phonological awareness and enough letter-sound knowledge to actualize self-teaching (Dahl, Scharer, Lawson, & Grogan,1999).

## Child-specific and developmental effects

It is crucial to consider what instruction is effective for whom. This is a widely mentioned issue, but not one that any researcher has addressed to complete satisfaction. In 1967 the First Grade Studies analyses considered the possibility of differential effects for children scoring high versus low on IQ, letter knowledge, and phonological discrimination tests, but no effects were found for groups differentiated this generally. Chall (1967) emphasized the importance of direct instruction and phonics approaches in particular for low-SES (socioeconomic status) children, those with lower vocabularies and less previous exposure to literacy. Juel and Minden-Cupp (2000) looked at the effect of different instructional emphases on children with different profiles; their findings indicated, for example, that phonics approaches were best for children entering first grade with very weak letter-sound knowledge. Torgesen (this volume) has considered appropriate instruction for children with delays or difficulties in the early grades. But most of the studies comparing programs have not carefully differentiated which instruction works best for which children.

Deciding which instruction is well adapted to which child also requires assessing how instruction changes as children learn more. Perhaps the key feature of classroom instruction ensuring that one child learns to read is systematic progress through a long list of letter-sound correspondence rules, whereas for another child the key feature is teaching just a few phonics rules but providing lots of interesting and increasingly difficult books for practice and self-teaching. How does a brief classroom-level observation capture both the differentiation and the developmental sensitivity of this teacher's approach?

## School and district effects

The Center for the Improvement of Early Reading Achievement (CIERA) carried out a "Beat the Odds" study, focused on schools doing much better than their student demographics would predict. The schools beating the odds had coherent, cross-grade instructional programs, and involved parents effectively. They had school-wide assessment systems and mechanisms to use assessment-generated data. The teachers spent more time in small-group instruction, "coached" students rather than telling them, asked more high-level questions, and had students read more independently (Pearson & Taylor, 1998) – in part because of a school-wide commitment to certain kinds of instruction. The kindergarten and first-grade teachers in these schools used rhymes, writing, and other motivating contexts to promote phonemic awareness and letter name knowledge, and carefully monitored student progress to ensure that students with more serious needs received more instructional time (Sulzby, 1998), again reflecting school-wide instructional policies and professional development opportunities.

Perhaps the best-documented example of a district-wide success at literacy reform is New York City's District 2 (Stein & D'Amico, 2002). District 2 developed its own model of Balanced Literacy, supplemented with one-on-one tutoring for students who struggled. The reforms in District 2 reflected commitment to shared understandings of how to teach reading, how to improve teachers' practice, and how to promote meaningful literacy engagement. Strengths of the District 2 approach include its coherence across the grades and the schools within the District; achieving this required considerable shared learning and collaboration across all the district teachers, but it ensured that children could move ahead relatively seamlessly even as they changed grades, teachers, or schools within the district.

## Back to the Reading Skirmishes

In our view, then, the findings from a wide array of sources – studies of reading development, studies of specific instructional practices, studies of teachers and schools found to be effective – converge on the conclusion that attention to small units in early reading instruction is helpful for all children, harmful for none, and crucial for some. This finding is richly supported in studies done both in the US (NRP, 2000) and the UK (Hatcher, Hulme, & Snowling, 2004). In light of this convergence, it is perhaps puzzling that there remains any conflict about methods for teaching initial reading. There are, in our view, four major reasons why conflicts, though somewhat less virulent than at times in the past, nonetheless persist.

### Emphasizing the differences

The first of these reasons has to do with the strong tendency of participants in discussions about reading methods to be operating defensively, taking positions that might be characterized as intellectual affirmative action. No proponent of phonics, however insistent on the need to teach children letters and sounds as the basis for reading, would deny the need to teach some sight words, or would exclude authentic children's literature from the kindergarten or first-grade classroom, or would preclude the use of clues to pronunciation or spelling from meaningful units like the names of classmates, or would prevent children from attempting to spell words using spelling patterns not yet taught. And no proponent of whole language, however insistent that reading is a naturally developing and intrinsically social activity, would deny that children benefit from having their attention brought to letter-sound correspondences, or that they need explicit instruction in spelling, or that simple, repetitive, predictable texts are a better basis for teaching initial reading than more literary texts. When engaged in face-to-face conversations, adherents of different sides in the reading wars can, in fact, be shamed into admitting that they agree on almost everything. But when not in dialogue, scholars on both sides, seemingly overcome by mistrust, overemphasize their own favorite aspects of reading instruction, in order to be sure those components are not overlooked by practitioners, curriculum publishers, and whoever is keeping score.

### Active child learners

Another source of the deep gulf between proponents of opposing views on reading instruction is the apparent link between those views and deeply held beliefs about human nature and the nature of education. As noted above, reliance on large meaningful units in early reading instruction has been linked historically and philosophically to progressive education, to notions of active child learners who can figure things out for themselves. We would argue that providing structured exposure to phonological segmentation, to the nature of the alphabetic principle, and to a variety of spelling rules in no way conflicts with belief in the autonomy of the child learner. In fact, as argued earlier in this chapter, structured phonics instruction never covers all the spelling rules of English; many children "get the point" after having had only a few spelling-sound correspondences taught explicitly, and most are reading independently well before all the rules have been taught. Nonetheless, teaching phonics is often seen as in conflict with constructivist views of learning.

## Teacher roles

Another source of ongoing conflict arises from the paradox concerning beliefs about literacy instruction and beliefs about teacher roles. The paradox here is that those whose views of literacy development define a central, crucial, instructional role for the teacher are more likely to be aligned with approaches to teaching reading that deprofessionalize teachers by dictating their moves and scripting their lines. There is no epistemological imperative for this alignment; nonetheless, those most insistent on structured phonics approaches are also most likely to despair that teachers have the knowledge base necessary to deliver instruction adequately (Moats 2001). Thus, it is not surprising that many practitioners see whole-language methods, which are explicitly associated with the values of teacher autonomy and teacher professionalism, as liberating and empowering. We argue that doing a good, responsive job of explicit phonics teaching, based in a rich understanding of children's strengths and weaknesses, and integrating teaching about the code with teaching for meaning requires very high levels of teacher skill, which will only develop with extensive pre-service and in-service support. Many of our colleagues, though, insist that scripted curricula constitute a safer approach.

## The nature of reading

Finally, apparent conflicts in approaches to teaching children to read derive from radically different views about what reading is. One view of reading is the print-driven one – a definition of reading that emphasizes the transfer to the reader's cognition of information encoded by the writer. This view of reading places accuracy of word reading, fluency, and correct analysis of syntactic and discourse structures at the center of the enterprise. Another view of reading sees it as an essentially interpretive process – one in which the reader can never exactly reproduce the cognitions of the writer, in which true comprehension is defined as establishing opinions and cognitions in reaction to what one has read. It is obvious that these two views of reading would dictate somewhat different emphases in reading instruction and very different practices in assessing reading outcomes, and thus have considerable potential to lead to conflict.

We would argue, though, that these views are not in conflict. They represent, first, approaches to different kinds of texts. When reading a recipe it is important not to misread "tablespoon" for "teaspoon," and interpretation is rarely called for (at least from the novice cook). When reading literature, on the other hand, interpretive skills are more important than memory for details. When reading political opinion, a critical or reactive stance is crucial to comprehension.

The two views of reading represent, further, perspectives that should receive different levels of emphasis at different points of reading development. Accurate and fluent reading is a challenge for young readers, and they have few cognitive resources to devote to reaction or interpretation while still struggling with the challenges of decoding. They are, of course, fully capable of reacting and interpreting – but to texts that are read aloud, not to those they are reading themselves. Furthermore, interpretation and reaction are irresponsible if applied to texts that have been only semi-accurately read, and are themselves skills that need to be nurtured and taught throughout the school years.

Thus, the issues of early reading pedagogy focused on in this chapter, although they have received much attention from researchers, practitioners, and policymakers, represent only a small portion of the challenges involved in actually teaching children to read.

# 27

# Recent Discoveries on Remedial Interventions for Children with Dyslexia

## Joseph K. Torgesen

The search for effective remedial methods for children with dyslexia has a long and productive history (Clark & Uhry, 1995). However, it is only quite recently that objective information has been available in sufficient quantities to provide reliable answers to even basic questions about remedial interventions for older children with serious reading disabilities. The primary goal of this chapter is to describe and justify a few of the most important conclusions from recent research on remedial interventions for children with dyslexia. Along the way we will also discover a number of critical areas in which there is currently a glaring lack of useful information.

## Defining the Target of Intervention

One the most obvious and yet difficult lessons to keep in mind about reading and learning disabilities is that they are heterogeneous. The fact that the broad category of "learning disabilities" encompasses a variety of different kinds of learning difficulty is widely acknowledged in definitions (Hammill, 1990), and this should be reflected in the way research is conducted in this area. Because the term "learning disabilities" is used to refer to a collection of different types of learning problems, it is not feasible to build a coherent theory or science of "learning disabilities" per se (Stanovich, 1993; Torgesen, 1993). Rather, researchers in this area must carefully specify the subtype of learning disability they are focusing on, whether a disability in reading, in mathematics, or in social/behavioral learning.

Although the field of reading disabilities is, by definition, narrower than the field of learning disabilities, the same need to specify the target population as clearly as possible seems critical in order to build a coherent scientific knowledge base about children who have different kinds of problems learning to read. For example, in the comprehensive summary of research on reading and reading instruction published by the National Research Council in the United States (Snow, Burns, & Griffin, 1998), three broad reasons for reading difficulties were identified: (1) problems in understanding and using the alphabetic principle to acquire fluent and accurate word reading skills; (2) failure to acquire the verbal knowledge and strategies that are specifically needed for comprehension of written material; and, (3) absence or loss of initial motivation to read, or failure to develop a mature appreciation of the rewards of reading. Although a simple trichotomy such as this undoubtedly oversimplifies the range of difficulties children have in learning to read, it does illustrate the need to specify the type of reading difficulty on which one's research is focused. Intervention research focusing on children whose primary difficulty is accurate and fluent word identification will certainly produce different conclusions about the essential elements of instruction than research on children who can read words accurately, but have difficulty constructing the meaning of text (see Nation, this volume, for a summary of research on such children).

The research reported in this chapter focused on children who met the recent definition of dyslexia proposed by the International Dyslexia Association: "Dyslexia is one of several distinct learning disabilities. It is a specific language-based disorder of constitutional origin characterized by difficulties in single word decoding" (Lyon, 1995, p. 7). The reference to "language based disorder" in this definition is supported by a range of converging findings indicating that the word reading difficulties of children with this type of reading disability are caused primarily by weaknesses in the ability to process the phonological features of words (Liberman, Shankweiler, & Liberman, 1989; Torgesen, 1999; Vellutino & Fletcher, this volume). The phonological processing disabilities of these children make it difficult for them to acquire skill in using the alphabetic principle to identify novel words in text (Share & Stanovich, 1995), and this, in turn, places severe constraints on the word learning process necessary for becoming a fluent reader (Ehri, 2002).

When children with dyslexia have been in school three or four years and have not had sufficiently strong preventive instruction, they will show two obvious difficulties when asked to read text at their grade level. First, they will not be able to recognize as high a proportion of the words in the text as fluently as average readers. There will be many words they stumble on, guess at, or attempt to "sound out." The second problem is that their attempts to identify words they do not immediately recognize will produce many errors. They will not be efficient in using graphophonemic clues in combination with context to identify unknown words. Because these children often have broad verbal abilities that are substantially higher than their word reading abilities, it is the word reading difficulties of these children that are thought to present the most immediate barrier to good reading comprehension.

The intervention research reviewed in this chapter focuses primarily on children with phonologically based reading disabilities that manifest themselves in problems in learning to identify words in text with fluency and accuracy. Of course, many of these children also suffer from a lack of motivation for reading, particularly after they have failed in learning to read for three or four years. Some may also have subtle oral language or verbal knowledge problems that play a role in limiting their comprehension (Snowling, 2000). Additionally, the biological or constitutional basis of these children's reading difficulties was not directly examined for any of the intervention samples to be discussed. Thus, it is clearly possible that the samples contained a mix of children whose difficulties were primarily constitutional in origin and those who may have entered school delayed in phonological development because of limitations in their preschool language experience. Conceptually, however, this chapter is focused on remedial research for children who struggle in reading because they have special difficulties mastering the process of identifying words in print.

## An Early Case Study and Other Discouraging Examples

One of the most famous and well-documented case studies describing the development of reading skill in a student with phonologically based reading disabilities is the case of JM, reported initially by Snowling and her colleagues (Snowling, Stackhouse, & Rack, 1986). JM was almost prototypical in the extent to which his characteristics matched those specified in current definitions of dyslexia. He had strong general learning abilities (Full Scale IQ = 123), coupled with inordinate difficulties in mastering the alphabetic principle and showed evidence of phonological processing disabilities (very low performance on verbal short-term memory tasks). At some point during his eighth year, JM began attending a special school for dyslexic children, which provided specialized, intensive teaching. Although the exact details of the instruction he received are not provided in the follow-up report (Snowling & Hulme, 1989), it is clear that they did involve structured reading activities and a multisensory approach to spelling. During his four years in this special school placement, JM progressed in reading by only half the average rate, and even less in spelling. His weakness with alphabetic reading skills improved very little: when he was 12, he was able to decode novel words at only the level of a 7 year old. The conclusion one might arrive at by studying JM's development is that the ultimate prognoses for intervention efforts with older dyslexic children is bleak, and particularly so for the skills required to decode unknown words. That JM's educational progress is not unique among children with phonologically based reading disabilities is attested by the expression we frequently hear in schools: "If a child hasn't acquired phonics skills by the third grade (8 years old), they are not going to learn it, and we should try something else."

This conclusion is reinforced in an excellent and widely cited study (Lovett, Bordon, Lacerenza, Benson, & Brackstone, 1994) that examined the relative effectiveness of several carefully contrasted interventions for older children with phonologically based reading disabilities. This study produced useful information about critical elements of instruction for children with reading disabilities, and it showed that their core disabilities could be improved somewhat through direct instruction. However, at the conclusion of the study (in which the children were taught in pairs for 35 one-hour sessions) their reading skills still fell in the severely disabled range. The children in the two strongest interventions began the study with an average standard score on a measure of word reading ability of 64.0 (which is below the first percentile), and at the conclusion of the study, their score was 69.5 (which is still below the second percentile), with pre- and posttest scores on a measure of reading comprehension being 66.4 and 70.8. In other words, after 35 hours of relatively intensive instruction (one teacher: two students), the children in this study still would be classified as having a very serious reading disability. Although one might argue that continued application of the successful instructional techniques from this study would eventually bring the student's reading skills into the average range, in the absence of direct evidence there is no way to know if this assumption is correct.

There is also evidence from a variety of sources that typical public school interventions for children with reading disabilities can most accurately be characterized as *stabilizing* their degree of reading failure rather than *remediating*, or normalizing, their reading skills (Kavale, 1988; Schumaker, Deshler, & Ellis, 1986). For example, in a carefully monitored longitudinal study, McKinney and his colleagues (McKinney, 1990) found that special education placements for children with reading disabilities produced no gains in word level reading skills relative to normal readers during a three-year period in elementary school. The children with reading disabilities began their instruction in special education with an average standard score of 92, and after three years of this instruction, their standard score for word level skills was 90. The children actually experienced a significant relative decline in their standing on a test of reading comprehension, falling from an average score of 94 to a standard score of 88 three years later.

Standard scores are an excellent metric for determining the "success" or "failure" of interventions for children with reading disabilities, because they describe the child's relative position within the distribution of reading skills in a large standardization sample. For most of the measures referred to in this chapter, standard scores will have a mean of 100 and a standard deviation of 15. Thus, an increase in standard score indicates that a student has "closed the gap" with average readers. By the same token, if standard scores decrease, it means the child has fallen even further behind relative to his/her same-age peers.

## A Recent Study with a Different Outcome for Children with Severe Reading Disabilities

When we began our intervention research in 1996, we were aware of previous findings about the difficulties of dramatically altering the reading skills of older children with severe phonologically based reading disabilities. We designed our initial study (Torgesen et al., 2001a) to provide extremely intensive instruction using two different phonologically based remedial strategies, and our goal was to discover the extent to which the reading difficulties of these children could be remediated if we intervened as powerfully as our resources would allow. We provided 67.5 hours of one-to-one instruction delivered in two 50-minute sessions each a day for about eight weeks. Sixty children, who had been receiving special education services for an average of 16 months at the time they were identified for participation in the study, were randomly assigned to the two intervention conditions.

Although both of the instructional programs in this study provided explicit instruction in phonemic awareness and phonemically based decoding strategies, they differed dramatically in the amount of time spent in three major instructional domains. For example, children in one condition, which was based on an earlier version of the *Lindamood Phoneme Sequencing Program for Reading, Spelling, and Speech* (Lindamood & Lindamood, 1998), spent 85% of their time learning and practicing articulatory/phonemic awareness and phonemic decoding and encoding skills in single-word activities (activities that did not involve reading meaningful text), 10% of their time learning to fluently recognize high-frequency words, and only 5% of their time reading meaningful text. Children in the other instructional condition, labeled Embedded Phonics (EP), spent 20% of their time on phonemic awareness and phonemic decoding activities involving single words, 30% of their time learning high-frequency "sight words," and 50% of their time reading meaningful text with teacher support.

The reading skills and language/cognitive characteristics of the children at the start of this study are shown in table 27.1. It is clear from the data presented in this table that children in both conditions, on average, met the definitional criteria for children with severe phonologically based reading disabilities. Children in both groups were severely impaired in their ability to use phonemic strategies to decode unknown words (Word Attack scores below the first percentile), and they also had very limited abilities to identify words, as shown by their scores on the Word Identification test. Both groups were also relatively impaired in phonemic awareness, verbal short-term memory, and rapid automatic naming (RAN) abilities, which are all characteristics of children with phonemically based reading difficulties (Snowling, 2000; Torgesen, 1999). On average, the students in

**Table 27.1**   Subject Characteristics

| *Variable Phonics* | *Instructional condition* | |
| --- | --- | --- |
|  | *Lindamood* | *Embedded* |
| N | 30 | 30 |
| Age (in months) | 117.6 (10.5) | 117.6 (12.6) |
| Full Scale IQ | 96.2 (9.9) | 95.6 (10.3) |
| Verbal IQ | 92.2 (8.5) | 93.0 (12.3) |
| Phonemic Decoding-Word Attack[a] | 67.8 (12.3) | 69.4 (8.5) |
| Word Identification[a] | 67.8 (8.6) | 66.5 (9.1) |
| Phoneme Awareness (LAC)[b] | 54.7 (15.6) | 47.6 (14.3) |
| Phonemic Awareness (Elision)[c] | 88.8 (13.10) | 84.2 (11.2) |
| Verbal Short-Term Memory[d] | 88.8 (14.6) | 88.3 (13.5) |
| RAN Digits[e] | 86.9 (10.7) | 84.2 (9.l3) |
| Spelling[f] | 75.6 (4.6) | 74.4 (4.9) |
| Sex Ratio | 22M/8F | 21M/9F |

[a] Subtests from the *Woodcock Reading Mastery Test-Revised* – standard scores with mean of 100 and Standard Deviation of 15.

[b] *Lindamood Auditory Conceptualization Test* – raw scores.

[c] Elision subtest from the *Comprehensive Test of Phonological Processes* – standard score (X = 100, SD = 15).

[d] Digit memory from the *Comprehensive Test of Phonological Processes* – standard score (X = 100, SD = 15).

[e] Rapid automatic naming of Digits from the *Comprehensive Test of Phonological Processes* – standard score (X = 100, SD = 15).

[f] Spelling subtest from *Kaufman Tests of Educational Achievement* – standard score (X = 100, SD = 15).

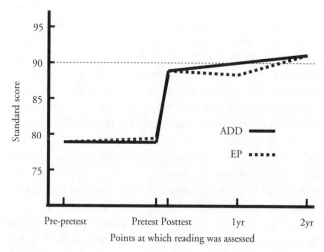

**Figure 27.1**    Standard Scores on the Broad Reading Cluster before, during, and following 67.5 hours of intensive intervention (from Torgesen et al., 2001a). ADD = Auditory Discrimination in Depth, EP = Embedded Phonics.

this sample were probably not as impaired in verbal short-term memory as JM, although this can only be estimated, since JM did not take a standardized test in this area.

Figure 27.1 provides the best overall summary of results from this study. It charts the growth of children in both instructional conditions on a broad measure of reading skill that combined scores for word reading accuracy and reading comprehension into a single standard score (on this test, a score of 100 is average). The figure shows changes in standard scores on this measure of broad reading ability over the 16-month period the children were attending special education classes, during the 8-week intervention period, and during a two-year follow-up period in which about half the children were no longer receiving special education classes at their schools.

Three aspects of this figure deserve particular mention. First, it is apparent that the instruction these children received in their special education classes was sufficient to maintain the level of their reading deficiency (they did not fall further behind, but neither did they close the gap with same-age peers). Second, the intensive intervention period produced a dramatic increment in their rate of reading growth for reading accuracy and comprehension. Third, as a whole, the children continued to make gains relative to average children during the two-year follow-up period. During the period of instruction in special education, the children's broad reading abilities remained at about the seventh percentile, and at the two-year follow-up point, they were at about the thirtieth percentile.

Although the data reported in figure 27.1 provide a useful summary of the impact of the intervention on the children's reading skills, it is equally important to understand the effects of the interventions on more differentiated components of reading skill. Figure 27.2 illustrates the immediate and long-term growth in phonemic decoding skills as measured by the Word Attack subtest of the *Woodcock Reading Mastery Test-Revised* (Woodcock, 1987) (top panel), text reading accuracy as measured by the *Gray Oral Reading Test-3rd Edition* (Wiederholt & Bryant, 1992), text reading fluency from the *Gray*, and Passage

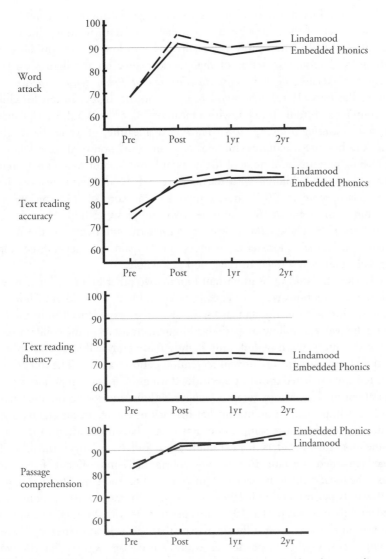

**Figure 27.2** Growth in standard scores on measures of phonemic decoding, reading accuracy, reading rate, and reading comprehension for children receiving 67.5 hours of intensive intervention.

Comprehension from the *Woodcock*. If a standard score of 90 is taken as the bottom boundary of the "average range" of reading ability, then it is apparent that, with the exception of reading fluency, children in both groups ended the follow-up period either solidly in the average range or at the low end of the average range in reading ability. The only statistically reliable difference between the groups in reading achievement occurred for phonemic decoding ability at the immediate posttest. Overall, the impact of both reading interventions was remarkably similar. The strongest impact of both interventions was on the children's ability to apply phonemic decoding strategies to unknown words.

In order to produce a group of children that might be more comparable to JM in terms of the degree of their impairment in verbal short-term memory, the 60 children who participated in the interventions were divided into low (n = 8), middle (n = 45), and high (n = 7) groups in terms of their performance on the digit span test from an experimental version of the *Comprehensive Test of Phonological Processes* (Wagner, Torgesen, & Rashotte, 1999). The standard scores on the digit span test for children in the low group ranged from 70 to 85, with a mean of 78.3. The Word Attack subtest from the *Woodcock Reading Mastery Test-Revised* is a measure of generalized phonemic decoding skills because it requires children to "sound out" nonwords that follow regular English spelling patterns, and none of the nonwords on this test were taught in either of the interventions. The children with the weakest verbal short-term memory improved from a standard score of 70.2 on the pretest to a score of 93.5 on the posttest. Corresponding improvements for the other two groups were: middle – 67.4 to 91.6, high – 74.1 to 95.6. These data indicate that even the children with the most severe impairments in verbal short-term memory made gains in generalized phonemic decoding skills that were similar to the group as a whole.

Before leaving this study, it is important to note two other findings. First, as would be expected, the interventions were not equally successful with all children. About a fourth of the children lost most of the standard score gains they experienced from the intervention during the two-year follow-up period. Although almost all of the children responded well during the intervention period, only slightly more than half were able to sustain or improve their gains once the intensive intervention period was over. The student variables that most reliably predicted growth trajectories during the follow-up period were teacher ratings of attentional behaviors, receptive language skills, and socioeconomic status.

Second, it is important to point out that the lack of change in the standard score for reading fluency for the entire sample does not mean that the children in this study did not become more fluent readers in an absolute sense. In fact, as long as the difficulty level of passages remained constant, they became substantially more fluent. For example, at the pretest, the most difficult passage the children read on the *Gray Oral Reading Test* was read at 38 words per minute with 10 errors. At the two-year follow-up point, a passage of equivalent difficulty was read at 101 words per minute with 2 errors. The same pattern was observed on the next most difficult passage that was read at pretest at 42 words per minute with 6 errors, while at posttest an equivalent passage was read at 104 words per minute with one error. Thus, the children did show marked improvement in the fluency with which they could read relatively simple passages; it was only when they were compared to their peers on passages closer to their grade level that they continued to show a striking lack of fluency while reading text.

## Reading Gains in Other Studies of Intensive Interventions

In an effort to determine whether the rates of growth in phonemic decoding skills and other reading skills obtained in our initial study are comparable to other recent reports of interventions with older children, we examined results from 13 intervention samples using a common growth metric. This metric is calculated by dividing the amount of gain in standard score units by the number of hours of instruction that are provided, so rate of growth is expressed as the number of standard score points gained per hour of instruction. Of course, this metric depends on the common use across studies of standardized measures that have the same standard deviation, but there are a number of studies that have used measures similar enough to allow rough comparisons. Table 27.2 reports these growth rates for phonemic decoding (Ph. Dec.), word reading accuracy (Acc.), and passage comprehension (Comp.), along with other characteristics of the samples and the interventions they received. Not all scores are represented for each study, because standardized measures were not provided in all three areas of reading skill for all samples.

All of the studies reported in table 27.2 provided interventions to children with severe to moderate word-level reading difficulties. In almost all the studies, the students began the interventions with scores in either phonemic decoding or word reading accuracy below the fifth percentile. In three of the samples (Rashotte, MacPhee, & Torgesen, 2001, and the small group [1:4] intervention samples in Torgesen, Rashotte, Alexander, Alexander, & MacPhee, 2003a), the students began with phonemic decoding skills around the tenth percentile. The intervention methods used in five of the studies (Torgesen et al., 2001a; Wise, Ring, & Olson, 1999; Alexander, Anderson, Heilman, Voeller, & Torgesen, 1991; Truch, 1994; the 1:1 study in Torgesen et al., 2003a) were variants of the Lindamood method (Lindamood & Lindamood, 1998), and all of the methods provided explicit instruction in phonemic awareness and phonemic decoding skills. The studies reported by Lovett et al. (2000) and by Torgesen et al. (2001a) contained two approximately equally effective interventions, and results for both interventions are reported separately.

Several aspects of the data reported in table 27.2 are worthy of specific discussion. First, there is remarkable consistency in the rates of growth for phonemic decoding skills, word reading accuracy, and passage comprehension skills reported across the studies. The consistency in rate of gain across these studies suggests that the high rates of growth obtained in the study described earlier in this section (Torgesen et al., 2001a) should be generalizable to other settings, with other teachers implementing the interventions. The similarities in growth rate between the LIPS (*The Lindamood Phoneme Sequencing Program for Reading, Spelling, and Speech*) and EP conditions in the Torgesen et al. (2001a) study, along with the consistencies across other studies that did not use the Lindamood method, suggests that, given the right level of intensity and teacher skill, it may be possible to obtain these rates of growth using a variety of approaches to direct instruction in reading. One might even suggest that these rates could serve as benchmarks for "reasonable progress" in reading for students receiving remedial instruction in both public and private settings. As such, they are clearly much higher than is typically achieved in most current special education settings.

Another point to note from table 27.2 is that growth rates for phonemic decoding skills are consistently higher than they are for word reading accuracy and passage comprehension. Not only the substantial growth rate, but also the essential "normalization" of phonemic decoding skills reported in a number of these studies indicates that even children with severe difficulties in the phonological domain can acquire productive and generative phonemic decoding skills if they are taught with intensity and skill.

**Table 27.2** Gains in Standard Score Points per Hour of Instruction for Three Measures of Reading Skill

| Authors of study | Name of intervention | Ave. age of subjects | Group size | Hours of intervention | Pretest SS | | Posttest SS | | SS Gains per hour of instruct. | | |
|---|---|---|---|---|---|---|---|---|---|---|---|
| | | | | | Ph. Dec. | Acc. | Ph. Dec. | Acc. | Ph. Dec. | Acc. | Comp. |
| Torgesen et al. (2001a) | LIPS | 9 yr, 10 mo. | 1:1 | 67.5 | 68.5 | 68.9 | 96.4 | 82.4 | .41 | .20 | .12 |
| Torgesen et al. (2001a) | EP | 9 yr, 10 mo | 1:1 | 67.5 | 70.1 | 66.4 | 90.3 | 80.5 | .30 | .21 | .15 |
| Wise et al. (1999) | | 8 yr, 9 mo | 1:4, 1:1 | 40 | 81.8 | 73.6 | 93.7 | 83.4 | .30 | .24 | .14 |
| Lovett et al. (1994) | PHAB/DI | 9 yr, 7 mo | 1:2 | 35 | – | 64.0 | – | 69.5 | – | .16 | .14 |
| Alexander et al. (1991) | ADD | 10 yr, 8 mo | 1:1 | 65 | 77.7 | 75.1 | 98.4 | 87.6 | .32 | .19 | – |
| Truch (1994) | ADD | 12 yr, 10 mo | 1:1 | 80 | – | 76.0 | – | 93.0 | – | .21 | – |
| Rashotte et al. (2001) | Spell Read | 9 yr, 8 mo | 1:4 | 35 | 82.6 | 87.4 | 98.9 | 98.1 | .47 | .31 | .32 |
| Torgesen et al. (2003a) | Spell Read | 12 yr | 1:4 | 100 | 88 | 77 | 111.0 | 96.0 | .23 | .19 | .19 |
| Torgesen et al. (2003a) | Spell Read | 12 yr | 1:4 | 51 | 87 | 82 | 102.0 | 90.0 | .29 | .16 | .24 |
| Lovett et al. (2000) | PHAB/WIST | 9 yr, 8 mo | 1:3 | 70 | 67.0 | 62 | 84.0 | 75.0 | .24 | .18 | .16 |
| Lovett et al. (2000) | WIST/PHAB | 9 yr, 8 mo | 1:3 | 70 | 59.0 | 56.0 | 80.0 | 70.0 | .30 | .20 | .18 |
| Truch (2003) | Phono-Graphix | 12 yr, 10 mo | 1:1 | 80 | – | 83.5 | – | 98.8 | – | .19 | – |
| Torgesen et al. (2003a) | LIPS +Fluency + Vis/Verb | 9 yr, 10 mo | 1:1, 1:2 | 133 | 72.0 | 76.0 | 96.0 | 85.0 | .18 | .07 | .07 |
| Hatcher, et al. (1994) | Sound Linkage | 7 yr, 6 mo | 1:1 | 20 | – | 76.8 | – | 83.0 | – | .31 | .39 |

Finally, it is important to understand a number of factors that probably influenced differences across studies in both the rate of growth and outcome status. These factors range from obvious things such as the particular measure of word reading accuracy that was used, to more subtle things such as the hours of intervention that were provided. For example, in our studies, we find that estimates of word reading accuracy are consistently higher when a measure of text reading accuracy (such as the *Gray Oral Reading Test*) is used rather than a measure of single word reading accuracy (such as the *Woodcock Reading Mastery Test*). The particular test used to assess word reading accuracy affects the estimate of final status more than it does the estimate of growth rate. For example, in the Torgesen et al. (2001a) intervention study, posttest standard scores for word reading accuracy as measured by the *Woodcock* were 82.4 and 80.5 for the LIPS and EP programs, respectively. In contrast, posttest scores for word reading accuracy from the *Gray* were 89.4 and 87.5, respectively. The higher scores for the Gray undoubtedly reflect the student's ability to use passage level context as an aid to more accurate identification of words (Stanovich & Stanovich, 1995).

Another factor that is likely to influence the estimate of growth rate obtained within any single study is the number of hours of intervention that were provided. Truch (2003) has recently documented that rate of gain may decelerate quite rapidly for intensive interventions after the first 12 hours of the intervention. In his study, 80 hours of intensive instruction using the Phono-Graphix method (McGuinness, McGuinness, & McGuinness, 1996) were provided to 202 students ranging in age from 6 to over 17. For students ranging in age from 10 to 16, the average gain per hour of instruction for single-word reading accuracy was .74 standard score points per hour of instruction for the first 12 hours of instruction. For the next 12 hours, the rate was .11, and for the final 56 hours, it was .10 standard score points per hour. Although this study did not calculate standard scores for their phonemic decoding measure, the findings were similar, but expressed in terms of grade level units per hour of instruction. For phonemic decoding, the growth rate for the first 12 hours of instruction was .25 grade level units per hour of instruction, for the next 12 hours it was .07, and for the final 56 hours, it was .04. This deceleration in growth rate across time within intensive interventions is probably part of the explanation for the particularly low growth rates observed in the 133-hour intervention study reported by Torgesen et al. (2003a). However, another factor may have also been operating in this study to moderate the growth rates that were observed.

This study was conducted in the same school district, and within many of the same schools, as a previously reported (Torgesen et al. 2001a) study of intensive interventions. In spite of the fact that children in the second study received twice as much instruction as those in the first study, they actually improved less in text reading accuracy and comprehension than the first group. Since both the first and second groups had received very similar interventions and had been selected by the same criteria, the most likely explanation for this unexpected finding is that the latter group had more severe reading disabilities than the first one. Our primary evidence for this assertion is that the special education classes from which the children were selected had improved substantially during the three years that intervened between the selections of the two samples. It was actually more difficult to find students who read poorly enough to meet our selection criteria when we selected the second sample than it was when we identified children for the first study. Teachers who had worked in both studies also noticed immediately that the second group was "much more difficult to teach" than children in the first sample.

This finding introduces an important moderating variable that must be kept in mind when looking at the results of intervention studies. The actual reading impairment a child shows at any point is always the result of an interaction between the child's degree of disability and the strength of instruction that has been provided. Children with a mild reading disability who are provided only weak instruction (in the regular classroom or in a special education setting) will show larger reading impairments when tested than will children with the same degree of reading disability who have had stronger instruction. By the same token, children who remain severely reading impaired within a strong instructional environment are likely to have a more serious reading disability than those who have remained impaired after receiving only weak instruction. Thus, if researchers select their intervention samples from among children who have already received a good dose of appropriate and reasonably intensive instruction, the children in those samples will be more difficult to teach than children who are selected by the same reading criteria from a weaker instructional environment. This moderating factor raises the clear possibility that if schools are successful in organizing instruction to provide powerful support for the initial acquisition of reading skills in young children (Foorman & Torgesen, 2001; Torgesen, 2002), growth rates for students in special education may not show the improvement one might expect, even with better models of intervention.

## What about the Remaining Problems in Fluency?

One of the consistent findings in our remedial research for children who begin the intervention with moderate or serious impairments in word reading ability is that the interventions have not been sufficient to close the gap in reading fluency. Although the gap in phonemic decoding, reading accuracy, and comprehension can be substantially or completely closed by current interventions, the gap in fluency has remained much less tractable to intervention for moderately and seriously impaired children.

When teachers or other researchers see these results, they think immediately that there must be something wrong with our interventions. Perhaps the interventions we have used emphasize "phonics" too much, perhaps they focus on accuracy too much, or perhaps they do not provide enough practice in reading fluency itself. We do not entirely discount these possibilities, but we also have considerable evidence that the problem may lie in the nature of reading fluency itself, rather than in the interventions. First, in one study with severely impaired readers (Torgesen et al., 2001a), one of the instructional interventions invested 50% of instructional time in reading connected text, while the other invested only 5%. There was no difference in fluency outcomes.

Second, we have reported a series of interventions with students who had mild (tenth percentile) or moderate (thirtieth percentile) impairments in word level reading skills, and which focused considerable instructional time in text reading activities with an emphasis on both modeling and practicing fluent reading (Torgesen et al., 2003a). Again, the students who began the intervention with moderate level (tenth percentile) word reading

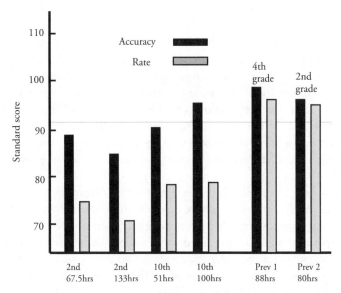

**Figure 27.3**   Outcomes for reading accuracy and reading rate from remedial and preventive studies of children with phonologically based reading disabilities.

difficulties showed only small improvement in their age-based percentile ranking for fluency, although they increased substantially in other dimensions of reading skill. Third, and probably most important, we have not obtained the same differences in outcomes between reading fluency and reading accuracy in our prevention studies as has occurred in the remedial studies. Figure 27.3 shows the standard scores (a score of 100 is average) for reading accuracy and fluency outcomes for four samples of 9–12-year-old children with severe (below second percentile) to moderate (tenth percentile) word level reading difficulties. Each sample is identified by their reading accuracy percentile at the beginning of the intervention. For reference, outcomes for these samples were also reported in table 27.2. The leftmost data is from Torgesen et al. (2001a), next is from the severely impaired sample in Torgesen et al. (2003a), next is from the moderately impaired sample that received 51 hours of intervention from Torgesen et al. (2003a), and next is the moderately impaired sample that received 100 hours of intervention.

Outcomes for text reading fluency and accuracy from two prevention studies are presented on the right side of figure 27.3. The most obvious difference between the outcomes from the prevention and remediation studies is that the gap between reading fluency and reading accuracy is not nearly as large for the prevention as for the remediation studies. The first prevention study (Prev 1) (Torgesen et al., 1999) provided 2.5 years of instruction to children in 20-minute sessions four days a week from the second semester of kindergarten through second grade. The children were identified as the 10% most at risk for reading failure because of low scores in phonemic awareness and letter knowledge in the first semester of kindergarten. The data in table 27.1 show the performance of children in the most effective instructional condition at the end of fourth grade (which was based on the LIPS program), two years after the intervention was concluded.

The children's scores for both reading accuracy and fluency are solidly in the average range.

In the second study (Prev 2) (Torgesen, Wagner, Rashotte, & Herron, 2003b), we provided preventive instruction during first grade to children identified at the beginning of first grade as the 20% most at risk for reading failure. The children were taught in small groups using a combination of teacher-led and computer-assisted instruction in 50-minute sessions, four days a week from October through May. The data in figure 27.3 show the performance of the children from the most effective condition at the end of second grade, one year after the intervention concluded. Again, both reading accuracy and fluency scores are solidly within the average range, and the gap between these scores is very small.

We have proposed elsewhere (Torgesen, Rashotte, & Alexander, 2001b) several possible explanations for the difficulty we have experienced in helping older children to "close the gap" in reading fluency after they have struggled in learning to read for several years. The most important factor appears to involve difficulties in making up for the huge deficits in reading practice the older children have accumulated by the time they reach late elementary school. These differences in reading practice emerge during the earliest stages of reading instruction (Allington, 1984; Beimiller, 1977–1978) and they become more pronounced as the children advance across the grades in elementary school. For example, Cunningham and Stanovich (1998) reported evidence suggesting enormous differences in the amount of reading done by fifth-grade good and poor readers outside of school. A child at the ninetieth percentile of reading ability may read as many words in two days as a child at the tenth percentile reads in an entire year outside the school setting. Reading practice varies directly with the severity of a child's reading disability, so that children with severe reading disabilities receive only a very small fraction of the total reading practice obtained by children with normal reading skills.

One of the major results of this lack of reading practice is a severe limitation in the number of words the children with reading disabilities can recognize automatically, or at a single glance (Ehri, 2002; Share & Stanovich, 1995), which is sometimes referred to by teachers as the child's "sight word vocabulary." This limitation of "sight word" vocabulary is a principle characteristic of most children with reading disabilities after the initial phase in learning to read (Rashotte et al., 2001; Torgesen et al., 2001a; Wise et al., 1999). The limitation arises because children must read specific words accurately a number of times before they can become part of their sight vocabulary (Reitsma, 1983). As Ehri (2002) points out, "sight words include any word that readers have practiced reading sufficiently often to be read from memory" (p. 10).

We have shown elsewhere (Torgesen, Rashotte, & Alexander, 2001b) that inefficiency in identifying single words is the most important factor in accounting for individual differences in text reading fluency in samples of children with reading disabilities. When these findings are combined with the fact that the number of less frequent words (words children are less likely to have encountered before in text) increases rapidly after about third-grade level (Adams, 1990), it is easy to see why it is so difficult for children who have failed in reading for the first three or four years of school to close the gap in reading fluency with their normally achieving peers. If successively higher-grade-level passages include increasing numbers of less-frequent words, and normal readers are continually expanding their sight vocabularies through their own reading behavior, it should be very difficult for children, once significantly behind in the growth of their sight word vocabulary, to close the gap in reading fluency. Such "catching up" would seem to require an extensive period of time in which the reading practice of the previously disabled children was actually *greater* than that of their peers. Even if word reading accuracy is dramatically increased through the more efficient use of analytic word reading processes, reliance on analytic processes will not produce the kind of fluent reading that results when most of the words in a passage can be recognized "by sight."

## Additional Areas of Knowledge from Intervention Research with Older Children

This chapter has focused rather narrowly on reporting knowledge about the extent to which the reading skills of older children with phonologically based reading disabilities can be "normalized" by current interventions. However, a complete science of intervention should include at least two other types of knowledge. Perhaps most fundamental to a science of intervention is knowledge about the specific instructional methods that are most effective for children with various kinds of disabilities. Findings from research on reading and reading growth (Ehri, 2002; Rayner, Foorman, Perfetti, Pesetsky, & Seidenberg, 2001) as well as from intervention studies (Foorman, Francis, Fletcher, Schatschneider, & Mehta, 1998; Hatcher, Hulme, & Snowling, 2004; Torgesen et al., 1999) suggest that phonemically based interventions are essential for children with phonologically based reading difficulties. The data from table 27.2 indicate that there are a number of equally effective ways to provide this instruction, although the comparisons available from table 27.2 do not involve random assignment to methods within the same population of children, so they must be interpreted with caution. It is also true that others (Lovett et al., 2000) have documented significant differences in effectiveness for methods that contain phonemically explicit instruction but vary in the range of word identification strategies that are taught. Hatcher et al. (2004) have also provided some recent evidence that, for children with more severe disabilities, it may be particularly important to provide explicit instruction at the level of the individual phoneme rather than, for example, at the level of onset/rime units. It is clearly necessary for future research to continue to refine our knowledge about the elements of instruction that can most powerfully accelerate the reading development of older children with phonologically based reading disabilities.

Research is also needed to determine whether there are interventions that may be particularly successful in addressing the reading fluency problems of children once their reading accuracy problems are remediated. There is a substantial body of evidence in support of the use of repeated reading as an intervention for children with fluency problems (Meyer & Felton, 1999), but there is no evidence available that this technique can produce "normalization" of fluency in children who have struggled in learning to read for several years. Wolf and her colleagues (Wolf, Miller, & Donnelly, 2000) are currently investigating interventions specifically targeted on fluency issues that extend considerably beyond the use of repeated reading, but as yet there are no reports of findings available from these studies.

A second area of inquiry that is part of an emerging science of intervention concerns questions about changes in the localization and timing of brain functions that occur because of effective interventions. The central question addressed in this type of research is whether the localization and timing of brain processes that support reading are "normalized" in reading disabled individuals after effective interventions (Papanicalaou et al., 2003). Initial findings suggest that powerful interventions with older and younger children do produce a relative "normalization" of localization and timing of brain functions that support phonological processes in reading, but this area of research is still in its infancy, so conclusions remain very tentative at this point.

## A Final and Significant Remaining Gap in Our Knowledge

In the United States, there is a strong national movement toward school-based accountability for the reading achievement of all children. The provisions of the No Child Left Behind Act of 2002 requires states to set reading standards by third grade that determine whether or not a child has attained adequate reading skills. Within each state, the effectiveness of both preventive and remedial programs in reading will ultimately be evaluated by examining the percentage of children who fail to meet standards for adequate reading ability by the end of third grade. Typically, the tests that states use to assess reading outcomes are group administered reading comprehension tests. The best of these tests include lengthy passages, and require both multiple choice and written answers to questions.

The new accountability standards require students in special education to be tested by the same measures that are used to evaluate reading outcomes in all children. Thus, the effectiveness of remedial instruction for students such as those reported on in this chapter will ultimately be evaluated in terms of their ability to respond adequately on these complex measures of reading comprehension. To date, none of the recent studies of intensive interventions for older students with phonologically based reading disabilities has included information about the success of students on these "high stakes," state administered reading achievement tests. Measures typically used in intervention research are administered 1:1, and may provide performance supports that are not available in group settings.

Given the remaining problems in reading fluency that remain after effective remediation, it seems doubtful that many of the students from current intervention research would be successful when faced with the challenge of responding to questions from lengthy passages in a group setting. Although these tests do not typically have a stringent time limit, they also do not provide unlimited time to respond, and thus reading fluency problems may create special difficulties for older children whose reading accuracy problems have been substantially remediated by effective interventions. It is thus a matter of some urgency to examine the conditions that need to be in place to raise the reading skills of children with reading disabilities into the acceptable range on the kinds of group administered reading comprehension tests that are becoming the "benchmark" for acceptable reading performance in public schools in the United States and many other countries.

## Conclusion

As documented in this chapter, we now have considerable evidence available concerning the effectiveness of intensive and explicit reading interventions for children who have struggled in learning to read. We know, for example, that it is possible to teach almost all children to accurately apply the alphabetic principle in decoding novel words, even if they have struggled to acquire this skill during the first 3–4 years of schooling. We also know that the text reading accuracy and reading comprehension of children with relatively severe reading disabilities can be accelerated dramatically by carefully administered interventions that are more intensive than instruction typically provided in special education settings. We have yet to discover interventions that can "normalize" the reading fluency of students who have missed out on 2–4 years of reading practice because of very poor reading skills during the early elementary school years. However, this problem may ultimately arise from the nature of reading fluency itself and the fact that fluency continues to accelerate rapidly in "average" readers during the late elementary, middle, and high school years, rather than being an inherent problem with the instructional methods available.

The most important questions that one is left with after considering the results of the effective interventions described in this chapter (other than those already described) concern the extent to which it may be possible to make these high-quality interventions available to all children who need them. What conditions of funding, procedure, training, and support are necessary to insure that all children receive the kinds of reading instruction they require to become proficient? As we learn more and more about "what works" for these children, our attention may more confidently begin to focus on the practical applications of our new knowledge. Even at first glance, it is clear that a wider range of expertise and methods may need to be applied to solving the problems of application than has thus far been required to produce the knowledge reported in this chapter.

# Glossary of Terms

*Acculturation.* The process by which an individual from a different culture or nationality has adapted his or her behavior, beliefs, and attitudes to be consistent with those of the dominant culture in which he or she is now living.

*Affordances.* Aspects of an object's structure that reliably predict how it should be held, manipulated, or used.

*Agglutinative morphology.* System of word formation in which a large array of affixes may be attached to a root morpheme to express complex meanings. As in the Finnish language.

*Agraphia.* A spelling disorder acquired following brain damage.

*Allele.* A DNA sequence that varies across individuals, either in a gene or a noncoding region.

*Alphabetic principle.* Usable knowledge of the fact that graphic forms represent phonemic segments of speech, such that whenever a particular phoneme occurs it can be represented by a particular letter.

*American sign language (ASL).* The sign language of the American deaf community.

*Anaphor.* A linguistic device that is used to refer back to a previously mentioned or implied concept.

*Anomia.* Word-finding difficulties following brain damage.

*Association analysis.* Method for testing whether a risk-allele is related to a trait.

*Attractor.* The tendency for a recurrent connectionist network to settle to a stable pattern of activity in response to a given input such that, if the pattern is perturbed (i.e., some activation values are changed), interactions among units cause the new pattern to be cleaned up into the same final pattern. Attractors are particularly useful in categorization contexts, in which a range of inputs need to be mapped to the same output.

*Autism spectrum disorder.* A group of developmental disorders, varying in severity, in which there is a deficit in reciprocal social interaction and communication, and a restricted repertoire of activities and interests. Includes classic autism and Asperger's syndrome.

*Autosomal dominant transmission.* Pattern of inheritance of a disease caused by a single major gene on a nonsex chromosome in which a single copy of the mutant allele is sufficient to produce the disease.

*Back-propagation.* A procedure for adjusting the weights between units in a connectionist network so as to reduce the discrepancy – as measured by an error function – between the output pattern produced by the network and the correct pattern for each input pattern.

*Backward masking.* A three-field masking paradigm in which a target word is presented for a very short duration, it is masked by a pseudoword that appears briefly, and is then replaced by a simple pattern mask.

*Behavior genetics.* Quantitative analyses of data from relatives to model the etiology of behavioral traits.

*Bigram frequency.* Frequency of occurrence in the language of a given two-letter sequence.

*Buffer impairment.* An impairment in the temporary activation of phonemes or letters that need to be kept in memory while other operations are carried out. In the case of an impairment to an orthographic output buffer, letters need to be kept in memory while they are converted into movements for writing.

*Cascaded processing.* Processing in a model is cascaded if, whenever any component of the model receives information about a stimulus, it immediately passes this information on to all the other components to which it is connected. Cascaded processing contrasts with thresholded processing, where a component completes its processing of a stimulus and only then passes information on to all the other components to which it is connected.

*Coda.* A syllable-final consonant or consonant cluster.

*Cohesive inference.* An inference that is made to establish and maintain premises in a text; for example, anaphora and pronoun resolution. In the passage "It was Tom's birthday. Jack gave a present to him", a cohesive inference is needed to link the pronoun "him" to the character Tom.

*Comorbidity.* Co-occurrence of two disorders.

*Complex syllables.* Syllables that often have a 'closed' consonant-vowel-consonant structure and consonant clusters in the initial (onset) and final (coda) positions. Typical of Germanic languages.

*Comprehension-age match.* Following the logic of the reading-level match design, the comprehension-age match design has been used to investigate underlying factors contributing to reading comprehension impairments. Children with poor comprehension are matched to younger children who score at the same level on a comprehension test. If poor comprehenders show an impairment in a particular cognitive or linguistic skill relative to comprehension-age controls, that skill is unlikely to be a simple consequence of comprehension level.

*Concordance.* When two family members, such as twins, share a particular condition.

*Connectionist models.* Also called neural networks or parallel distributed processing systems, connectionist models are a type of computational system intended to approximate the central characteristics of neural computation. In such a system, large numbers of neuron-like processing interact across weighted connections to produce a pattern of activity over output units in response to any given input pattern. Learning involves modifying the connection weights to improve performance.

*Connectives.* Linguistic devices that are used to explicitly indicate the relationship between two or more propositions in a text (e.g., "and," "or," "because").

*Consolidated alphabetic phase.* In Ehri's (1998) developmental theory of sight word reading, the fourth phase characterizing readers who have consolidated recurring patterns of graphemes and phonemes into larger units that are used to read sight words.

*Coreference.* One of the dimensions along which propositions can be related to one another; when two or more propositions refer to the same concept or concepts.

*Cued Speech.* Is a system of manual cues that disambiguate lip-reading and provides fully specified information about syllables and phonemes.

*Decontextualized language.* This term is used to define spoken language that refers to objects, events, or people not present in the immediate environment of the speaker. Comprehension and use of decontextualized language requires that the speaker and listener share a common understanding of the things or people to whom the words apply.

*Derivational morphology.* System of word formation in which a base word or root is modified by an attachment that signals a change of syntactic function. As in the use of – *ment* in English to signal nominalization (agree + *ment* → agreement).

*Distributed representation.* A style of encoding information as patterns of activity over a group of units in a connectionist network such that each entity in a domain (e.g., a written word) is encoded by the simultaneous activity of multiple processing units, and each unit participates in encoding multiple entities. Distributed representations contrast with localist ones, which assign individual units to specific entities (e.g., a separate unit to represent each word).

*Down syndrome.* The most frequent human chromosomal abnormality caused by trisomy of chromosome 21, occurring in about 1.5 per 1,000 births. Children with Down syndrome usually have IQs in the 50–70 range and often have difficulties with language acquisition that are more severe than predicted by their nonverbal abilities.

*Dual-route model of reading.* A model of reading that contains two different procedures for going from print to speech (dual-route model of reading aloud) or two different procedures for going from print to meaning (dual-route model of reading comprehension).

*Elaborative inference.* An inference that is not necessary to establish cohesion in a text, but serves to enrich a reader's representation of the text. Such inferences may help a reader or listener to build a full mental model of an event or situation.

*Emergent literacy.* The idea that literacy begins not with formal instruction or decoding skill, but well before that in the form of language and print-related abilities. A more specific use refers to the actual skills and behaviors that are the developmental precursors to later decoding, writing, and comprehension skills that form conventional literacy.

*Epilinguistic.* Representation of linguistic structure that is held to be implicit and inaccessible to conscious inspection or mental manipulation.

*Event related potentials (ERPs).* Refers to the recording of the electrical activity of the brain in response to stimuli by electrodes fixed on the subject's scalp.

*Expository text.* A text that primarily expresses facts or information.

*Eye-contingent displays technique.* An experimental paradigm in which changes are made in the text contingent on the reader's eye location.

*E-Z reader.* A computer simulation that does a reasonably good job of predicting where readers will fixate and how long they fixate on words.

*Familial.* When family members are more alike for a trait than unrelated people.

*Feedforward network.* A pattern of connectivity in a connectionist network in which units are organized into a series of layers, such that units in each layer receive incoming connections only from units in earlier layers.

*Fixation.* The amount of time that a reader's eyes remain relatively still on a given word.

*Full alphabetic phase.* In Ehri's (1998) developmental theory of sight word reading, the third phase characterizing beginners who possess full knowledge of the graphophonemic system and word attack skill.

*Functional magnetic resonance imaging (fMRI).* A form of functional brain imaging that depends upon the use of powerful magnetic fields to detect changes in levels of cerebral blood oxygenation.

*Functional neuroimaging.* Techniques to identify different brain areas that are activated during different cognitive tasks and the time course of this activation.

*Genetic linkage.* Physical proximity of two genes or DNA sequences on a chromosome.

*Genotype.* An individual's genome or the combination of two alleles at a particular locus.

*Germanic languages.* A subset of Indo-European languages, including German, Dutch, and some Scandinavian languages.

*Glottography.* A writing system whose symbols represent units of natural human language; cf. *semasiography.*

*Graceful degradation.* The tendency for a system, such as a connectionist network, to exhibit a gradual rather than abrupt decline in performance as a function of increasing severity of damage. Systems that exhibit graceful degradation typically use representations and processes that are somewhat distributed in nature, so that localized damage does not completely remove any particular type of information.

*Hangul.* The Korean alphabetic writing system.

*Hanza.* The Korean logographic writing system coming from mainland China.

*Head Start.* A federally funded preschool program available to three- to four-year-old children in the United States who qualify by means of family income at or near the poverty level. Head Start traditionally has been a half-day or full-day program that addresses health, nutrition, and socioemotional domains as well as academic readiness.

*Hemifield.* Refers to the presentation of a stimulus that is processed by the contralateral hemisphere.

*Hemispheric specialization.* Specialization of one cerebral hemisphere for the processing of a given type of information (e.g., linguistic).

*Heritability.* Proportion of phenotypic variance attributable to genes.

*Hidden units.* Internal units in a connectionist network that are neither input nor output units. Representations over hidden units are not specified by the training environment but are learned by the network in response to task demands.

*Hyperlexia.* Unexpectedly good single word reading ability, coupled with poor text comprehension. Children with hyperlexia often learn to read before they receive any formal instruction. Sometimes associated with childhood autism.

*Inferences, bridging / knowledge-based.* Two seemingly unrelated terms in a text are related by making implicit knowledge explicit.

*Inflectional morphology.* System of word formation in which an element is attached to a base word in order to express aspects such as tense, number, or possession without modifying the syntactic function of the base. As in the use of *-ed* to signal the past tense in English (walk + *ed* → walked).

*Input units.* The units in a connectionist network that encode the input to the system from the training environment. A network can have more than one group of input units (e.g., encoding different types of information) and receive input over different groups for different tasks. For example, a network that maps bidirectionally between phonology and semantics might receive phonological input on comprehension trials and semantic input on production trials.

*Interactive activation model.* An early connectionist model of letter and word perception, developed by McClelland and Rumelhart (1981, *Psychological Review*), in which layers of letter feature units, letter units, and word units, bidirectionally interact across weighted connections to settle on the set of units at each layer that best characterizes the input.

*Kana.* The Japanese phonographic writing system that represents the permissible syllables in the language.

*Kanji.* The Japanese logographic system coming from mainland China.

*Labial images.* The visible correlates (on the lips) of speech articulation.

*Language Experience approach.* An approach to teaching reading that uses texts generated by children themselves during teacher-guided and teacher-transcribed discussions. Generally the teacher writes down the children's words and this process creates the text children read.

*Latent semantic analysis.* A machine learning method that constructs a high-dimensional semantic space automatically from reading a large number of documents; the relations among words and documents in that semantic space mirror human semantic judgments.

*Learnability theory.* A formal representation of learning as a problem, designed to discover states of the learner and conditions of the environment that will achieve specified learning outcomes.

*Letter retrieval impairment.* Disorder in which the deficit is in the retrieval of the letters of a word in the correct sequence *after* a correct word representation has been accessed. The errors consist of letter transformations that rarely result in another word of the language.

*Letter-by-letter reading.* A strategy for recognizing written words by identifying the constituent letters in serial order (see *pure alexia*).

*Lexical decision.* Experimental paradigm that requires a participant to decide if a letter string is a word (YES) or not (NO).

*Lexical learning.* The ability to store in memory as 'unitized' representations novel combinations of linguistic units (phonemes or letters), to maintain them over time, and to retrieve them when needed.

*Listening comprehension.* A general term to refer to an individual's ability to extract meaning from spoken discourse.

*Listening span.* A test of working memory that requires the simultaneous processing and storage of verbal information. Typically, participants hear a sentence that they have to make a decision about (processing); they are then asked to remember the last word of each sentence in correct serial order (processing).

*Localist representation.* A one-to-one assignment of units in a connectionist network to entities in a domain (e.g., written words) such that each entity is encoded by the activity of its own dedicated processing unit. Localist representations contrast with distributed ones, which encode different entities as alternative patterns of activity over a common group of units.

*Logographic writing system.* A logographic system is a writing system in which individual written symbols represent whole words. Chinese characters (where the primary correspondence is between written symbols and morphemes) should probably be referred to as logographs.

*Logography.* A writing system whose symbols represent the morphemes of a language; cf. *phonography.*

*Macrostructure.* The global conceptual structure of a text; a representation of the interrelationships between the higher-order topics or units of microstructure.

*Matthew effect.* Term adopted to describe how early achievement fosters subsequent achievements. For example, the consequences of reading success or failure: children who are reading well experience more print, acquire more vocabulary, and develop even stronger reading skills; conversely, children who are poor readers read less, fail to develop knowledge and vocabulary, thus inhibiting further growth in reading.

*Microstructure.* The local conceptual structure of a text; a representation of the interrelationships between the propositions expressed in the content of the text.

*Miscue analysis.* A procedure for systematically classifying children's errors produced during oral reading, distinguishing visually induced, semantically induced, and syntactically induced errors, as a basis for identifying their strengths and weaknesses as readers.

*Modeling approaches.* This is a general term used to refer to the idea that adults can teach behaviors or attitudes to a child by demonstration. Whereas some modeling may be deliberate and include repeated demonstrations designed to improve the child's independent performance, other modeling and learning may occur more naturalistically in the course of daily interactions.

*Morphosyntactic hierarchy.* A view of language where the basic units are morphemes, which can be combined by rules of morphology to form words, which in turn are combined by rules of syntax to form phrases and sentences.

*Narrative.* A text that primarily tells a fictional or nonfictional story (e.g., fairy tales, novels).

*Neighbor (orthographic).* When a letter string is just one letter different from a real word, that word is an orthographic neighbor of the letter string. Thus *care, sore,* and *sane* are all neighbors of *sare.*

*Onset.* A syllable-initial consonant or consonant cluster.

*Orthographic Depth Hypothesis.* The hypothesis that the correspondence between spelling and phonology in different orthographies affects the processes of visual word recognition.

*Orthographic representations.* Sequences of abstract letter identities that are temporarily or permanently represented in memory. They can be either known or novel words of the language.

*Output units.* The units in a connectionist network that encode the response of the network to any given input. A network can have multiple output groups to code different types of responses for different training trials. In supervised learning, output units have "targets" that specify their correct activations for each input.

*Partial alphabetic phase.* In Ehri's (1998) developmental theory of sight word reading, the second phase characterizing beginners who know letter names or sounds and can use this knowledge to read sight words by remembering connections between some of the letters in spellings and sounds in the pronunciations of the words.

*Perceptual span in reading.* The region from which readers obtain useful information during an eye fixation in reading.

*Phase theory.* A theory that postulates two or more qualitatively distinct periods to portray the course of development of specific processes or capabilities. Although the phases emerge sequentially, mastery of each is not necessarily required for the emergence of the next phase.

*Phenotype.* A trait or traits influenced by genes and environment.

*Phonics methods.* Approaches to teaching reading that emphasize the need to provide children with explicit information about the systematic nature of sound–letter relationships.

*Phonography.* A writing system whose symbols represent phonological units of a language, such as syllables or segments (phonemes); cf. *logography.*

*Phonological dysgraphia.* An impairment of spelling where the ability to convert sounds into letters is disproportionately affected relative to the ability to recollect whole-word spellings from memory. This means that spelling of novel or unfamiliar words is particularly affected, but spelling familiar irregular words is not.

*Phonological dyslexia.* (see *phonological-deep dyslexia*).

*Phonological hierarchy.* A view of language where the basic units are phonetic features, which combine to form segments, which in turn are combined by rules of phonology to form sound-based structures such as onsets, rimes, and syllables.

*Phonological-deep dyslexia.* Phonological dyslexia is a disorder of reading acquired following brain damage. Patients with phonological dyslexia exhibit a significant lexicality effect in reading accuracy with relatively poor reading of nonwords. The cardinal feature of deep dyslexia is the production of semantic related reading errors. Traditionally deep and phonological dyslexia have been considered to be separate types of reading disorder. More recent studies have argued that phonological dyslexia is simply a milder version of deep dyslexia.

*Pinyin.* An alphabetic writing system developed in the 1950s that uses letters from the Roman alphabet to represent the phonemes in Mandarin. All children in the first term at elementary school in mainland China are taught to read Pinyin before formal instruction in reading and writing Chinese characters commences. Pinyin appears alongside new characters in reading books to indicate to children how the word should be pronounced in Mandarin. Pinyin is also used in dictionaries and in computer keyboards.

*Poor comprehenders.* Children who, despite age-appropriate reading accuracy, are poor at understanding what they read. Poor reading comprehension usually arises in the context of more general difficulties with language comprehension.

*Positron emission tomography (PET).* A form of functional brain imaging that detects changes in cerebral blow flow (CBF) by measuring changes in levels of a radioisotope circulating in the blood.

*Pragmatic language impairment.* Language impairment characterized by problems in the use rather than the form of language. Includes he overliteral use and interpretation of language, and a failure to appreciate the appropriate level of detail needed to convey a message to a listener.

*Pre-alphabetic phase.* In Ehri's (1998) developmental theory of sight word reading, the earliest phase characterizing beginners who read familiar words by memorizing contextual cues or visual cues in or around them.

*Preview benefit.* The benefit derived from having a preview of a word prior to fixating on it.

*Print knowledge.* An individual's understanding that words and letters convey meaning, that there are 26 letters in the English alphabet, and that these letters have corresponding sounds. Some researchers and educators also use the term to refer to concepts of print, a more general term for the conventions of written English, such as books having covers and authors, reading from left to write, the use and meaning of punctuation, and other written language concepts.

*Proband.* The index case with a particular condition from whom one identifies other family members (usually for genetic research).

*Proposition.* An idea unit, or a unit of meaning involving a predicate and one or more arguments. Arguments can be thought of as conceptual entities, and predicates typically either modify arguments or indicate the relations between them.

*Pseudohomophone.* A letter string that is not a word as far as its spelling is concerned but whose pronunciation is exactly like the pronunciation of a real English word; e.g., *brane* and *yot.*

*Psycholinguistic guessing game.* The term used by Kenneth Goodman to refer to the hypothesized process of reading by predicting one's way through text, rather than by attending exhaustively to print cues.

*Pure alexia.* A reading disorder acquired following brain damage in which there is a specific difficulty in recognizing printed words, without accompanying aphasia or agraphia. Many patients try to aid their visual recognition in reading by using a letter-by-letter strategy (either overtly or covertly) leading to significant length effects on reading times.

*QTL.* Quantitative trait locus, a gene that contributes to variation in a quantitative trait.

*Reading pedagogy.* The procedures and methods used for teaching reading, which are in turn closely connected to beliefs about the nature of reading and the dependence of children on explicit instruction, and which are typically guided by curricular materials such as basal reading series.

*Reading readiness.* This phrase is used to convey the idea that a child has the language- and print-related skills necessary to be successful at formal literacy instruction. Among some theorists and educators, the term is used to convey the belief that such readiness matures naturally within a child, and that reading instruction should not begin until the child displays his or her innate readiness.

*Recurrent network.* A class of connectionist network that has unrestricted connectivity. In contrast to a feedforward network in which activation flows only in one direction, units in a recurrent network can interact and mutually constrain each other. As a result, units in a recurrent network must typically be updated multiple times before they settle to their final states.

*Regressions.* An eye movement (or saccade) back in the text to look at a previously read word.

*Reinforcement learning.* A class of learning procedures in which the parameters of a system (e.g., the weights in a connectionist network) are adjusted in order to maximize a scalar reinforcement signal that depends on the success of the system's responses in achieving goals. When the external reinforcement signal is available only intermittently (e.g., when a specific goal is achieved), the approach focuses on developing an internal "critic" that provides an estimate of the expected reinforcement, over the long run, of any possible action. Reinforcement learning contrasts both with supervised learning (which assumes the training environment specifies the correct output for each input) and with unsupervised learning (which assumes no performance feedback).

*Rime.* A vowel, together with any following consonant(s) in the same syllable.

*Romance languages.* A subset of Indo-European languages of Latin origin, including Italian, Spanish, Portuguese, and French.

*Saccade.* The actual movement of the eyes.

*Scaffolding.* Adult interactions with children that aid skill or conceptual development by providing support at a level at, or just beyond, the child's current level of ability. Scaffolding allows for the adult to match the support provided to the individual needs of different children, and also allows for the gradual removal of explicit support once the child is able to independently enact the target behavior.

*Segmental representations.* Term used to refer to phonological representations of speech that are structured at a phonemic level.

*Segregation.* Separation of two alleles at a locus, one from each parent, in subsequent generations.

*Semantic dementia.* The temporal lobe variant of frontotemporal dementia that leads to a relatively selective yet progressive degradation of conceptual knowledge / semantic memory.

*Semantic paralexia.* Semantically related reading errors (e.g. reading ELF as 'fairy'; see phonological-deep dyslexia).

*Semantic priming.* The facilitatory effect in recognizing a target word if a semantically related prime appears prior to the target's presentation.

*Semasiography.* A writing system whose symbols represent concepts directly; cf. *glottography.*

*Shared Reading.* Any event during which a literate child or adult reads aloud to one or more children, who may or may not be literate themselves. Shared reading implies that the listener is passive and not contributing orally to the interaction. This contrasts with the more interactive, reciprocal reading dialogues that are thought to have a greater impact on children's language development.

*Sight word reading.* The primary means used by readers to read familiar words from memory rather than by decoding, analogizing, or predicting the words.

*Sign languages.* Natural languages that have evolved over time in deaf communities and are articulated in the visuospatial modality. The articulators are the two hands, the expression of the face, and the body. These characteristics of sign languages entail a specific phonology (sometimes called *cherology*), lexicon, grammar, and discourse structure, which are distinct from those of oral languages.

*Simple recurrent network.* A special class of recurrent network in which connectivity is restricted to flow in one direction, but in which the previous activations of some groups of units are copied onto additional "context" groups that serve as additional inputs when processing the next input. Simple recurrent networks are as computationally efficient as feedforward networks, but are capable of learning to exhibit complex temporal behavior like fully recurrent networks.

*Simple syllables.* Syllables that have a consonant–vowel structure ('open' syllables) and in which consonant clusters in the initial (onset) position are infrequent. Typical of Romance languages.

*Simple view of reading.* The hypothesis that reading comprehension ability is a product of listening comprehension ability (language) and word reading ability (decoding).

*Situation model.* A mental model of the situation described by the text, which typically involves combining information explicitly stated in the text with prior knowledge.

*Socioeconomic status (SES).* SES is traditionally defined as the joint product of an adult's income and educational status. Some definitions of SES use a rating of adult occupation. In households or families with multiple adult residents, the higher status occupation or the highest educational achievement is typically used.

*Specific language impairment.* Developmental disorder of language in which language skills are significantly below the age-appropriate level and nonverbal skills are within the normal range.

*Speech intelligibility.* Clarity of the oral production of deaf persons.

*Speech sound disorders.* An umbrella term used to refer to children who make developmentally inappropriate speech errors (their language skills may be normal or impaired).

*Speech-reading.* Understanding speech by processing information delivered by the lips and other buccofacial movements of the speaker.

*Stage theory.* A theory that postulates two or more qualitatively distinct periods to portray the course of development of specific processes or capabilities. The stages are ordered sequentially with mastery of each necessary for the development of the next stage.

*State space.* A conceptualization of patterns of activity over a group of units in a connectionist network (or over the network as a whole), in which each pattern corresponds to a particular point in a high-dimensional space with a dimension for each unit. The unit activations in the pattern specify the coordinates of the position of the corresponding point in state space, so that similar activation patterns correspond to nearby points in state space.

*Strong phonological theory.* The theory that assumes that the core lexical representations are phonologically defined, and that phonological computation is the main engine driving the processing of printed information.

*Structural parallelism.* A heuristic basis for identifying the referent of an anaphor, according to which a potential referent that holds the same grammatical role as the anaphor is preferred over one that does not.

*Supervised learning.* A class of learning procedures in which the parameters of a system (e.g., the weights in a connectionist network) are adjusted based on an explicit comparison between the output generated by the system for a given input and the correct output for that input as specified by the learning environment. A well-known supervised learning procedure is back-propagation.

*Surface dysgraphia.* An impairment of spelling that particularly affects memory for the spellings of familiar words in the face of a good ability to convert sounds into letters. This means that spelling low-frequency, irregular words that do *not* follow the most common sound-to-letter correspondences will be particularly error prone.

*Surface dyslexia.* A form of reading disorder acquired following brain damage. Patients with this type of reading disorder demonstrate a frequency by consistency interaction in reading accuracy with relatively poor reading of low-frequency words with inconsistent spelling–sound correspondences. To these words, surface dyslexics typically give a pronunciation which is more typical for that particular spelling pattern (e.g., YACHT → "yatched", SEW → "sue").

*Susceptibility locus.* A gene that confers risk for a disorder, but is not sufficient and may not be necessary to cause the disorder by itself.

*Syllabary.* A syllabary is a writing system (e.g., Kana in Japan) in which each written symbol represents a syllable. Most syllabaries are *CV syllabaries*, having distinct symbols only for combinations of one onset consonant plus vowel. Syllabaries are only practical in languages that (unlike English) contain a relatively small number of syllables.

*Syllabification.* Explicit subdivision of a multisyllabic word into component syllables.

*Textbase.* The representation of the content of a text; the microstructure and the macrostructure together.

*Tone.* Tone refers to the specific pitch pattern in which a word is spoken in Chinese. There are four different tones in Mandarin (high-level, high-rising, falling-rising, high-falling) and nine different tones in Cantonese. There are no symbols in the Chinese writing system that convey information about tone.

*Triangle model of reading.* A connectionist framework for word reading, first proposed by Seidenberg and McClelland (1989, *Psychological Review*), in which lexical processing takes the form of simultaneous, parallel, bidirectional interactions among orthographic, phonological, and semantic representations, coded as distributed patterns of activity over separate groups of units (typically depicted at each corner of a triangle). Although it structurally contains two pathways from print to sound, it contrasts with standard "dual-route" theories in that the entire system participates in processing all types of written input using the same computational mechanisms throughout.

*Trigram frequency.* Frequency of occurrence in the language of a given sequence of three letters.

*Unitization.* Applied to word recognition when a sequence of letters is so familiar that it can be read as quickly as a single unit, such as a familiar letter or digit. The letter sequence is recognized as a unitized whole, rather than as a result of analyzing the sequence of constituent letters.

*Unsupervised learning.* A class of learning procedures in which the parameters of a system (e.g., the weights in a connectionist network) are adjusted to capture the statistical structure of the training environment, without making any use of feedback concerning the system's own responses.

*Whole language.* An approach to teaching reading that emphasizes the value of authentic children's literature, of multiple forms of engagement with text, and of focusing on meaning during all instructional activities, and that proceeds from the assumption that learning to read is a 'natural' process like learning to talk. Kenneth Goodman defined whole language in the following way: "Whole language learning builds around whole learners learning whole language in whole situations" (1986, p. 40). Thus systematic instruction in phonics is not typically included.

*Williams syndrome.* A rare genetic disorder affecting 1 in 20,000 live births, caused by a deletion on chromosome 7 (7q11.2). Most children with Williams syndrome have IQs in the 50–65 range. Language skills are a relative strength for these children.

*Working memory.* A limited capacity system that supports both the maintenance and processing of information during a task.

*Zhu-Yin-Fu-Hua.* Phonetic script containing 37 different characters that children in Taiwan learn during the first ten weeks at elementary school before any exposure to Chinese characters takes place. Zhu-Yin-Fu-Hua appears alongside new characters in reading books to indicate to children how the word should be pronounced in Mandarin.

# References

Aaron, P. G., Keetay, V., Boyd, M., Palmatier, S., & Wacks, J. (1998). Spelling without phonology: A study of deaf and hearing children. *Reading and Writing, 10*, 1–22.

Abercrombie, D. (1967). *Elements of general phonetics.* Edinburgh: Edinburgh University Press.

Ackley, D. H., Hinton, G. E., & Sejnowski, T. J. (1985). A learning algorithm for Boltzmann Machines. *Cognitive Science, 9*, 147–169.

Adams, M. J. (1990). *Beginning to read: Thinking and learning about print.* Cambridge, MA: MIT Press.

Adams, M. J. (1998). The three-cueing system. In F. Lehr & J. Osborn (Eds.), *Literacy for all: Issues in teaching and learning* (pp. 73–99). New York: Guilford.

Adams, M. J., & Bruck, M. (1993). Word recognition: The interface of educational policies and scientific research. *Reading and Writing, 5*, 113–139.

Adrian, J. A., Alegria, J., & Morais, J. (1995). Metaphonological abilities of Spanish illiterate adults. *International Journal of Psychology, 30*, 329–353.

Aghababian, V., Nazir, T. A., Lançon, C., & Tardy, M. (2001). From "logographic" to normal reading: The case of a deaf beginning reader. *Brain and Language, 78*, 212–223.

Akmaijian, A., Demers, R. A., Farmer, A. K., & Harnish, R. M. (2001). *Linguistics: An introduction to language and communication* (5th ed.). Massachusetts: MIT Press.

Alcock, K. J., & Ngorosho, D. (2003). Learning to spell a regularly spelled language is not a trivial task: Patterns of errors in Kiswahili. *Reading and Writing, 16*, 635–666.

Alegria, J., Leybaert, J., Charlier, B., & Hage, C. (1992). On the origin of phonological representations in the deaf: Hearing lips and hands. In J. Alegria, D. Holender, J. J. D. Morais, & M. Radeau (Eds.), *Analytic approaches to human cognition* (pp. 107–132). Amsterdam: Elsevier.

Alegria, J., & Mousty, P. (1994). On the development of lexical and nonlexical spelling procedures of French-speaking normal and disabled children. In G. Brown & N. Ellis (Eds.), *Handbook of spelling: Theory, process and invervention* (pp. 211–226). Chichester: Wiley.

Alegria, J., & Mousty, P. (1996). The development of spelling procedures in French-speaking, normal and reading-disabled children: Effects of frequency and lexicality. *Journal of Experimental Child Psychology, 63*, 312–338.

Alegria, J., Pignot, E., & Morais, J. (1982). Phonetic analysis of speech and memory codes in beginning readers. *Memory and Cognition, 10*, 451–456.

Alexander, A., Anderson, H., Heilman, P. C., Voeller, K. S., & Torgesen, J. K. (1991). Phon-ological awareness training and remediation of analytic decoding deficits in a group of severe dyslexics. *Annals of Dyslexia, 41*, 193–206.

Alexander, M. P., Hiltbrunner, B., & Fischer, R. S. (1989). Distributed anatomy of transcortical sensory aphasia. *Archives of Neurology, 46*, 885–92.

Allen, T. E. (1986). Patterns of academic achievement among hearing impaired students: 1974 and 1973. In A. N. Schildroth & M. A. Karchmer (Eds.), *Deaf children in America* (pp. 161–206). San Diego, CA: College-Hill.

Allington, R. L. (1984). Content coverage and contextual reading in reading groups. *Journal of Reading Behavior, 16*, 85–96.

Altarriba, J., Kambe, G., Pollatsek, A., & Rayner, K. (2001). Semantic codes are not used in inte-grating information across eye fixations in reading: Evidence from fluent Spanish–English bilin-guals. *Perception and Psychophysics, 63*, 875–890.

Altmann, G. T. M. (1994). Regression-contingent analyses of eye movements during sentence processing: A reply to Rayner and Sereno. *Memory and Cognition, 22*, 286–290.

Anderson, R. C., & Freebody, P. (1981). Vocabulary knowledge. In J. T. Guthrie (Ed.), *Compre-hension and teaching: Research reviews* (pp. 77–117). Newark, DE: International Reading Association.

Anderson, R. C., Li, W. L., Ku, Y. M., Shu, H., & Wu, N. (2003). Use of partial information in learning to read Chinese characters. *Journal of Educational Psychology, 95*, 52–57.

Andrews, S. (1982). Phonological recoding: Is the regularity effect consistent? *Memory and Cognition, 10*, 565–575.

Andrews, S. (1992). Frequency and neighborhood effects on lexical access: Lexical similarity or orthographic redundancy? *Journal of Experimental Psychology: Learning, Memory, and Cognition, 18*, 234–254.

Andrews, S. (1996). Lexical retrieval and selection processes: Effects of transposed-letter confus-ability. *Journal of Memory and Language, 35*, 775–800.

Andrews, S. (1997). The effect of orthographic similarity on lexical retrieval: Resolving neighbor-hood conflicts. *Psychonomic Bulletin and Review, 4*, 439–461.

Andrews, S., & Heathcote, A. (2001). Distinguishing common and task-specific processes in word identification: A matter of some moment? *Journal of Experimental Psychology: Learning, Memory, and Cognition, 27*, 514–544.

Andrews, S., Miller, B., & Rayner, K. (2004). Eye movements and morphological segmentation of compound words: There is a mouse in mousetrap. *European Journal of Cognitive Psychology, 16*, 285–311.

Ans, B., Carbonnel, S., & Valdois, S. (1998). A connectionist multiple-trace memory model for polysyllabic word reading. *Psychological Review, 105*, 678–723.

Anthony, J. L., Lonigan, C. J., Burgess, S. R., Driscol, K., Phillips, B. M., & Cantor, B. G. (2002). Structure of preschool phonological sensitivity: Overlapping sensitivity to rhyme, words, syllables, and phonemes. *Journal of Experimental Child Psychology, 82*, 65–92.

Ardila, A., Rosselli, M., & Rosas, P. (1989). Neuropsychological assessment in illiterates: Visuospatial and memory abilities. *Brain and Cognition, 11*, 147–166.

Arnold, D. H., & Doctoroff, G. L. (2003). The early education of socioeconomically disadvan-taged children. *Annual Review of Psychology, 54*, 517–545.

Arnold, R., Yule, W., & Martin, N. (1985). The psychological characteristics of infantile hyper-calcaemia: A preliminary investigation. *Developmental Medicine and Child Neurology, 27*, 49–59.

Arriaga, R. I., Fenson, L., Cronan, T., & Pethick, S. J. (1998). Scores on the MacArthur Com-munication Developmental Inventory of children from low- and middle-income families. *Applied Psycholinguistics, 19*, 209–223.

Azuma, T., & Van Orden, G. C. (1997). Why SAFE is better than FAST: The relatedness of a word's meanings affects lexical decision times. *Journal of Memory and Language, 36,* 484–504.

Badcock, D., & Lovegrove, W. (1981). The effects of contrast stimulus, duration and spatial frequency in visual persistence in normal and specifically disabled readers. *Journal of Experimental Psychology: Human Perception and Performance, 1,* 495–505.

Baddeley, A. D. (1979). Working memory and reading. In P. A. Kolers, M. E. Wrolstad, & H. Bouma (Eds.), *Procession of visible language* (Vol. 1, pp. 355–370). New York: Plenum.

Baddeley, A. D., Ellis, N., Miles, T., & Lewis, V. (1982). Developmental and acquired dyslexia: A comparison. *Cognition, 11,* 185–197.

Baddeley, A., & Gathercole, S. (1992). Learning to read: The role of the phonological loop. In J. Alegria, D. Holender, J. J. Morais, & M. Radeau (Eds.), *Analytic approaches to human cognition* (pp. 153–167). Amsterdam: Elsevier.

Baddeley, A., Gathercole, S., & Papagno, C. (1998). The phonological loop as a language learning device. *Psychological Review, 105,* 158–173.

Baddeley, A., Logie, R., & Nimmo-Smith, I. (1985). Components of fluent reading. *Journal of Memory and Language, 24*(1), 119–131.

Badian, N. A. (2000). Do preschool orthographic skills contribute to the prediction of reading? In N. Badian (Ed.), *Prediction and prevention of reading failure* (pp. 31–56). Parkton, MD: York.

Badian, N. A., McAnulty, G. B., Duffy, F. H., & Als, H. (1990). Prediction of dyslexia in kindergarten boys. *Annals of Dyslexia, 40,* 152–169.

Baker, L. (1984). Spontaneous versus instructed use of multiple standards for evaluating comprehension: Effects of age, reading proficiency, and type of standard. *Journal of Experimental Child Psychology, 38,* 289–311.

Baker, L., Fernandez-Fein, S., Scher, D., & Williams, H. (1998). Home experiences related to the development of word recognition. In J. L. Metsala & L. C. Ehri (Eds.), *Word recognition in beginning literacy* (pp. 263–287). Mahwah, NJ: Erlbaum.

Baker, L., Scher, D., & Mackler, K. (1997). Home and family influences on motivations for reading. *Educational Psychologist, 32,* 69–82.

Bakwin, H. (1973). Reading disability in twins. *Developmental Medicine and Child Neurology, 15*(2), 184–187.

Balota, D. A., & Chumbley, J. I. (1984). Are lexical decisions a good measure of lexical access? The role of word frequency in the neglected decision stage. *Journal of Experimental Psychology: Human Perception and Performance, 10,* 340–357.

Balota, D. A., Ferraro, R. F., & Connor, L. T. (1991). On the early influence of meaning in word recognition: A review of the literature. In P. J. Schwanenflugel (Ed.), *The psychology of word meanings* (pp. 187–221). Hillsdale, NJ: Erlbaum.

Balota, D. A., Pollatsek, A., & Rayner, K. (1985). The interaction of contextual constraints and parafoveal visual information in reading. *Cognitive Psychology, 17,* 364–390.

Balota, D. A., & Spieler, D. H. (1999). Frequency, repetition, and lexicality effects in word recognition: Beyond measures of central tendency. *Journal of Experimental Psychology: General, 128,* 32–55.

Baluch, B., & Besner, D. (1991). Strategic use of lexical and nonlexical routines in visual word recognition: Evidence from oral reading in Persian. *Journal of Experimental Psychology: Learning, Memory, and Cognition, 17,* 644–652.

Baluch, B., & Besner, D. (2001). Basic processes in reading: Semantics affects speeded naming of high-frequency words in an alphabetic script. *Canadian Journal of Experimental Psychology, 55,* 63–69.

Barnes, M. A., Dennis, M., & Haefele-Kalvaitis, J. (1996). The effects of knowledge availability and knowledge accessibility on coherence and elaborative inferencing in children from six to fifteen years of age. *Journal of Experimental Child Psychology, 61*, 216–241.

Barnett, W. S., Young, J. W., & Schweinhart, L. J. (1998). How preschool education influences long-term cognitive development and school success: A causal model. In W. S. Barnett & S. S. Boocock (Eds.), *Early care and education for children in poverty: Promises, programs, and long-term results. SUNY series, youth social services, schooling, and public policy* (pp. 167–184). Albany, NY: State University of New York.

Baron, J. (1977). Mechanisms for pronouncing printed words: use and acquisition. In D. LaBerge & S. J. Samuels (Eds.), *Basic processes in reading: Perception and comprehension* (pp. 175–216). Hillsdale, NJ: Erlbaum.

Baron, J. (1979). Orthographic and word specific mechanisms in children's reading of words. *Child Development, 50*, 587–594.

Baron, J., & McKillop, B. J. (1975). Individual differences in speed of phonemic analysis, visual analysis, and reading. *Acta Psychologica, 39*, 91–96.

Baron, J., & Strawson, C. (1976). Use of orthographic and word-specific knowledge in reading words aloud. *Journal of Experimental Psychology: Human Perception and Performance, 4*, 207–214.

Baron, J., & Treiman, R. (1980). Some problems in the study of differences in cognitive processes. *Memory and Cognition, 8*, 313–321.

Baron, R. M., & Kenny, D. A. (1986). The moderator–mediator variable distinction in social psychological research: Conceptual, strategic, and statistical considerations. *Journal of Personality and Social Psychology, 51*, 1173–1182.

Barr, R. (1974–1975). The effect of instruction on pupil reading strategies. *Reading Research Quarterly, 10*, 555–582.

Barron, R. (1986). Word recognition in early reading: A review of the direct and indirect access hypotheses. *Cognition, 24*, 93–119.

Bar-Shalom, E., Crain, S., & Shankweiler, D. (1993). A comparison of comprehension and production abilities of good and poor readers. *Applied Psycholinguistics, 14*, 197–227.

Bartlett, C. W., Flax, J. F., Logue, M. W., Vieland, V. J., Bassett, A. S., Tallal, P., et al. (2002). A major susceptibility locus for specific language impairment is located on 13q21. *American Journal of Human Genetics, 71*, 45–55.

Bast, J., & Reitsma, P. (1998). Analyzing the development of individual differences in terms of Matthew effects in reading: Results from a Dutch longitudinal study. *Developmental Psychology, 34*, 1373–1399.

Bates, J. E., Marvinney, D., Kelly, T., Dodge, K. A., Bennett, D. S., & Pettit, G. S. (1994). Child-care history and kindergarten adjustment. *Developmental Psychology, 30*, 690–700.

Baumwell, L., Tamis-LeMonda, C. S., & Bornstein, M. H. (1997). Maternal verbal sensitivity and child language comprehension. *Infant Behavior and Development, 20*, 247–258.

Beals, D. E., DeTemple, J. M., & Dickinson, D. K. (1994). Talking and listening that support early literacy development of children from low-income families. In D. K. Dickinson (Ed.), *Bridges to literacy: Children, families, and schools* (pp. 19–40). Cambridge, MA: Blackwell.

Beauvillain, C., Dore K., & Baudouin, V. (1996). The "center of gravity" of words: Evidence for an effect of the word-initial letters. *Vision Research, 36*, 589–603.

Beauvois, M.-F., & Dérousné, J. (1979). Phonologia alexia: Three dissociations. *Journal of Neurology, Neurosurgery and Psychiatry, 42*, 1115–1124.

Beauvois, M. F., & Dérouesné, J. (1981). Lexical or orthographic agraphia. *Brain, 104*, 21–49.

Beck, I., McKeown, M., & Omanson, R. (1987). The effects and uses of diverse vocabulary instruction techniques. In M. McKeown & M. E. Curtis (Eds.), *The nature of vocabulary acquisition* (pp. 147–163). Hillsdale, NJ: Erlbaum.

Becker, C. A. (1976). Allocation of attention during visual word recognition. *Journal of Experimental Psychology: Human Perception and Performance, 2,* 556–566.

Becker, C. A. (1979). Semantic context and word frequency effects in visual word recognition. *Journal of Experimental Psychology: Human Perception and Performance, 5,* 252–259.

Becker, S., Moscovitch, M., Behrmann, M., & Joordens, S. (1997). Long-term semantic priming: A computational account and empirical evidence. *Journal of Experimental Psychology: Learning, Memory, and Cognition, 23,* 1059–1082.

Becker, W., & Jürgens, R. (1979). An analysis of the saccadic system by means of double step stimuli. *Vision Research, 19,* 967–983.

Beech, J. R., & Harris, M. (1997). The prelingually deaf young reader: A case of reliance on direct lexical access? *Journal of Research in Reading, 20,* 105–121.

Behrmann, M., & Bub, D. (1992). Surface dyslexia and dysgraphia: Dual routes, a single lexicon. *Cognitive Neuropsychology, 9,* 209–258.

Behrmann, M., Nelson, J., & Sekuler, E. (1998a). Visual complexity in letter-by-letter reading: "Pure" alexia is not so pure. *Neuropsychologia, 36,* 1115–1132.

Behrmann, M., Plaut, D. C., & Nelson, J. (1998b). A literature review and new data supporting an interactive account of letter-by-letter reading. *Cognitive Neuropsychology, 15,* 7–51.

Beimiller, A. (1977–1978). Relationships between oral reading rates for letters, words, and simple text in the development of reading achievement. *Reading Research Quarterly, 13,* 223–253.

Beland, R., & Mimouni, Z. (2001). Deep dyslexia in the two languages of an Arabic/French bilingual patient. *Cognition, 82,* 77–126.

Bell, L., & Perfetti, C. A. (1994). Reading skill: Some adult comparisons. *Journal of Educational Psychology, 86,* 244–255.

Bellugi, U., Bihrle, A., Jernigan, T., Trauner, D., & Doherty, S. (1990). Neuropsychological, neurological and neuroanatomical profile of Williams syndrome. *American Journal of Medical Genetics, Supplement, 6,* 115–125.

Ben-Dror, I., Bentin, S., & Frost, R. (1995). Semantic, phonological, and morphological skills in children with reading disabilities and normally achieving readers: Evidence from perception and production of spoken Hebrew words. *Reading Research Quarterly, 30,* 876–893.

Bennett, K. K., Weigel, D. J., & Martin, S. S. (2002). Children's acquisition of early literacy skills: Examining family contributions. *Early Childhood Research Quarterly, 17,* 295–317.

Bentin, S., Bargai, N., & Katz, L. (1984). Orthographic and phonemic coding for lexical access: Evidence from Hebrew. *Journal of Experimental Psychology: Learning Memory, and Cognition, 10,* 353–368.

Bentin, S., & Frost, R. (1987). Processing lexical ambiguity and visual word recognition in a deep orthography. *Memory and Cognition, 15,* 13–23.

Bentin, S., & Leshem, H. (1993). On the interaction of phonological awareness and reading acquisition: It's a two-way street. *Annals of Dyslexia, 43,* 125–148.

Berent, I. (1997). Phonological effects in the lexical decision task: Regularity effects are not necessary evidence for assembly. *Journal of Experimental Psychology: Human Perception and Performance, 23,* 1–16.

Berent, I., & Perfetti, C. (1995). A rose is a REEZ: The two cycles model of phonology assembly in reading English. *Psychological Review, 102,* 146–184.

Berent, I., & Van Orden, G. C. (2000). Homophone dominance modulates the phoneme-masking effect. *Scientific Studies of Reading, 42,* 133–167.

Berent, I., & Van Orden, G. C. (2003). Do null phonemic masking effects reflect strategic control of phonology? *Reading and Writing, 16,* 349–376.

Berk, L. E., & Winsler, A. (1995). *Scaffolding children's learning: Vygotsky and early childhood education.* Washington, DC: National Association for the Education of Young Children.

Berninger, V., Abbott, R., & Thompson, J. (2001). Language phenotype for reading and writing disabiltty: A family approach. *Scientific Studies of Reading, 5,* 59–106.

Bernstein, L. E., Demorest, M. E. & Tucker, P. E. (1998). What makes a good speechreader? First you have to find one. In R. Campbell, B. Dodd, & D. Burnham (Eds.), *Hearing by eye* (Vol. 2, pp. 211–228). Hove, UK: Psychology Press.

Bertelson, P., & de Gelder, B. (1989). Learning about reading from illiterates. In A. M. Galaburda (Ed.), *From reading to neuron* (pp. 1–23). Cambridge, MA: MIT Press.

Bertelson, P., de Gelder, B., Tfouni, L. V., & Morais, J. (1989). Metaphonological abilities of adult illiterates: New evidence on heterogeneity. *European Journal of Cognitive Psychology, 1,* 239–250.

Bertram, R., & Hyönä, J. (2003). The length of a complex word modifies the role of morphological structure: Evidence from eye movements when reading short and long Finnish compounds. *Journal of Memory and Language, 48,* 615–634.

Besner, D., & Hildebrant, N. (1987). Orthographic and phonological codes in the oral reading of Japanese Kana. *Journal of Experimental Psychology: Learning, Memory, and Cognition, 13,* 335–343.

Besner, D., & Smith, M. C. (1992). Basic processes in reading: is the orthographic depth hypothesis sinking? In R. Frost & L. Katz (Eds.), *Orthography, phonology, morphology, and meaning* (pp. 45–66). Advances in Psychology. Amsterdam: Elsevier.

Besner, D., Twilley, L., McCann, R. S., & Seergobin, K. (1990). On the connection between connectionism and data: Are a few words necessary? *Psychological Review, 97,* 432–446.

Best, C. T., & Avery, R. A. (1999). Left hemisphere advantage for click consonants is determined by linguistic significance and experience. *Psychological Science, 10,* 65–70.

Betjemann, R., Keenan, J. M., & Olson, R. K. (2003, June). Listening comprehension in children with reading disability. Presented at the Annual Meeting of the Society for the Scientific Study of Reading. Boulder, CO.

Bhattacharya, A., & Ehri, L. C. (2004). Graphosyllabic analysis helps adolescent struggling readers read and spell words. *Journal of Learning Disabilities, 37,* 331–348.

Bialystok, E. (2000). Symbolic representation across domains in preschool children. *Journal of Experimental Child Psychology, 76,* 173–189.

Binder, J. R., McKiernan, K. A., Parsons, M. E., Westbury, C. F., Possing, E. T., Kaufman, J. N., et al. (2003). Neural correlates of lexical access during visual word recognition. *Journal of Cognitive Neuroscience, 15,* 372–93.

Binder, K. S. (2003). Sentential and discourse topic effects on lexical ambiguity processing: An eye movement examination. *Memory and Cognition, 31,* 690–702.

Binder, K. S., Duffy, S. A., & Rayner, K. (2001). The effects of thematic fit and discourse context on syntactic ambiguity resolution. *Journal of Memory and Language, 44,* 297–324.

Bird, H., Lambon Ralph, M. A., Seidenberg, M. S., McClelland, J. L., & Patterson, K. (2003). Deficits in phonology and past tense morphology. *Journal of Memory and Language, 48,* 502–526.

Bird, J., Bishop, D. V. M., & Freeman, N. H. (1995). Phonological awareness and literacy development in children with expressive phonological impairments. *Journal of Speech and Hearing Research, 38,* 446–462.

Bishop, D. V. M. (1983). *Test for the Reception of Grammar.* Manchester, UK: Age and Cognitive Performance Research Centre, University of Manchester.

Bishop, D. V. M. (1997a). Cognitive neuropsychology and developmental disorders: Uncomfortable bedfellows. *Quarterly Journal of Experimental Psychology, 50A,* 899–923.

Bishop, D. V. M. (1997b). *Uncommon understanding.* Hove, UK: Psychology Press.

Bishop, D. V. M. (2001). Genetic influences on language impairment and literacy problems in children: Same or different? *Journal of Psychology and Psychiatry, 42,* 189–198.

Bishop, D. V. M. (2003). *Test for the Reception of Grammar-2*. London: Psychological Corporation.

Bishop, D. V. M., & Adams, C. (1990). A prospective study of the relationship between specific language impairment, phonological disorders and reading retardation. *Journal of Child Psychology and Psychiatry, 31*, 1027–1050.

Bishop, D. V. M., Carlyon, R. P., Deeks, J. M., & Bishop, S. J. (1999). Auditory temporal processing impairment: Neither necessary nor sufficient for causing language impairment in children. *Journal of Speech, Language, and Hearing Research, 42*, 1295–1310.

Bishop, D. V. M., & Edmundson, A. (1987). Language-impaired 4-year-olds: Distinguishing transient from persistent impairment. *Journal of Speech and Hearing Disorders, 52*, 156–173.

Bishop, D. V. M., & Norbury, C. F. (2002). Exploring the borderlands of autistic disorder and specific language impairment: A study using standardised diagnostic instruments. *Journal of Child Psychology and Psychiatry, 43*, 917–929.

Bishop, D. V. M., North, T., & Donlan, C. (1995). Genetic basis of specific language impairment: Evidence from a twin study. *Developmental Medicine and Child Neurology, 37*, 56–71.

Bishop, D. V. M., & Snowling, M. J. (2004). Developmental dyslexia and specific language impairment: Same or different? *Psychological Bulletin, 130*, 858–888.

Bisiacchi, P. S., Cipolotti, L., & Denes, G. (1989). Impairment in processing meaningless verbal material in several modalities: The relationship between short-term memory and phonological skills. *Quarterly Journal of Experimental Psychology, 41A*, 293–319.

Blachman, B. A. (1984). Relationship of rapid naming ability and language analysis skills to kindergarten and first-grade reading achievement. *Journal of Educational Psychology, 76*, 610–622.

Blachman, B. A. (2000). Phonological awareness. In M. L. Kamil, P. B. Mosenthal, P. D. Pearson, & R. Barr (Eds.), *Handbook of reading research* (Vol. 3, pp. 483–502). Mahwah, NJ: Erlbaum.

Blanchard, H. E., Pollatsek, A., & Rayner, K. (1989). The acquisition of parafoveal word information in reading. *Perception and Psychophysics, 46*, 85–94.

Blazely, A. M., Coltheart, M., & Casey, B. J. (in press). Semantic impairment with and without surface dyslexia: Implications for models of reading. *Cognitive Neuropsychology.*

Bleasdale, F. A. (1987). Concreteness-dependent associative priming: Separate lexical organization for concrete and abstract words. *Journal of Experimental Psychology: Learning, Memory, and Cognition, 13*, 582–594.

Blewitt, P., & Toppino, T. C. (1991). The development of taxonomic structure in lexical memory. *Journal of Experimental Child Psychology, 51*, 296–319.

Bliss, C. K. (1949). *International semantography*. Sydney: Semantography.

Bloodgood, J. (1999). What's in a name? Children's name writing and name acquisition. *Reading Research Quarterly, 34*, 342–367.

Boada, R., Willcutt, E. G., Tunick, R. A., Chhabildas, N. A., Olson, R. K., DeFries, J. C., et al. (2002). A twin study of the etiology of high reading ability. *Reading and Writing: An Interdisciplinary Journal, 15*, 683–707.

Boetsch, E. A. (1996). A longitudinal study of the relationship between dyslexia and socio-emotional functioning in young children. PhD dissertation, University of Denver.

Bogner, K., Raphael, L. M., & Pressley, M. (2002). How grade-1 teachers motivate literate activity by their students. *Scientific Studies of Reading, 6*, 135–165.

Boltz, W. G. (1996). Early Chinese writing. In P. T. Daniels & W. Bright (Eds.), *The world's writing systems* (pp. 191–199). Oxford: Oxford University Press.

Bond, G. L., & Dijkstra, R. (1967). The cooperative research program in first-grade reading. *Reading Research Quarterly, 2*, 5–42.

Bookheimer, S. Y., Zeffiro, T. A., Blaxton, T., Gaillard, W., & Theodore, W. (1995). Regional cerebral blood flow during object naming and word reading. *Human Brain Mapping, 3*, 93–106.

Borowsky, R., & Masson, M. E. J. (1996). Semantic ambiguity effects in word identification. *Journal of Experimental Psychology: Learning, Memory, and Cognition, 22,* 63–85.

Borowsky, R., Owen, W. J., & Fonos, N. (1999). Reading speech and hearing print: Constraining models of visual word recognition by exploring connections with speech perception. *Canadian Journal of Experimental Psychology, 53,* 294–305.

Bosman, A. M. T., & de Groot, A. M. B. (1996). Phonologic mediation is fundamental to reading: Evidence from beginning readers. *Quarterly Journal of Experimental Psychology, 49A,* 715–744.

Bosman, A. M. T., & Van Orden, G. C. (1997). Why spelling is more difficult than reading. In C. A. Perfetti, L. Rieben, & M. Fayol (Eds.), *Learning to spell* (pp. 173–194). Mahwah, NJ: Erlbaum.

Bourassa, D. C., & Besner, D. (1998). When do nonwords activate semantics? Implications for models of visual word recognition. *Memory and Cognition, 26,* 61–74.

Bowers, J. (2002). Challenging the widespread assumption that connectionism and distributed representations go hand-in-hand. *Cognitive Psychology, 45,* 413–445.

Bowers, P. B., Sunseth, K., & Golden, J. (1999). The route between rapid naming and reading progress. *Scientific Studies of Reading, 3*(1), 31–53.

Bowers, P. G., Golden, J., Kennedy, A., & Young, A. (1994). Limits upon orthographic knowledge due to processes indexed by naming speed. In V. W. Berninger (Ed.), *The varieties of orthographic knowledge* (Vol. 1, pp. 173–218). Dordrecht, the Netherlands: Kluwer Academic.

Bowers, P. G., & Wolf, M. (1993). Theoretical links among naming speed, precise timing mechanisms and orthographic skill in dyslexia. *Reading and Writing, 5,* 69–85.

Bowey, J. A. (1994a). Phonological sensitivity in novice readers and nonreaders. *Journal of Experimental Child Psychology, 57,* 134–159.

Bowey, J. A. (1994b). Grammatical awareness and learning to read: A critique. In E. M. H. Assink (Ed.), *Literacy acquisition and social context* (pp. 122–149). New York: Harvester-Wheatsheaf.

Bowey, J. A. (1995). Socioeconomic status differences in preschool phonological sensitivity and first-grade reading achievement. *Journal of Educational Psychology, 87,* 476–487.

Bowey, J. A. (2000). Recent developments in language acquisition and reading research: The phonological basis of children's reading difficulties. *Australian Educational and Developmental Psychologist, 17,* 5–31.

Bowey, J. A. (2001). Nonword repetition and young children's receptive vocabulary: A longitudinal study. *Applied Psycholinguistics, 22,* 441–469.

Bowey, J. A. (2002). Reflections on onset-rime and phoneme sensitivity as predictors of beginning word reading. *Journal of Experimental Child Psychology, 82,* 29–40.

Bowey, J. A., & Francis, J. (1991). Phonological analysis as a function of age and exposure to reading instruction. *Applied Psycholinguistics, 12,* 89–118.

Bowey, J. A., & Patel, R. K. (1988). Metalinguistic ability and early reading achievement. *Applied Psycholinguistics, 9,* 366–383.

Bowman, M., & Treiman, R. (2002). Relating print and speech: The effects of letter names and word position on reading and spelling performance. *Journal of Experimental Child Psychology, 82,* 305–340.

Bozeat, S., Lambon Ralph, M. A., Graham, K., Patterson, K., Wilkin, H., Rowland, J., et al. (2003). A duck with four legs: Investigating the structure of conceptual knowledge using picture drawing in semantic dementia. *Cognitive Neuropsychology, 20,* 27–47.

Bozeat, S., Lambon Ralph, M. A., Patterson, K., Garrard, P., & Hodges, J. R. (2000). Non-verbal semantic impairment in semantic dementia. *Neuropsychologia, 38,* 1207–1215.

Bozeat, S., Lambon Ralph, M. A., Patterson, K., & Hodges, J. R. (2002). When objects lose their meaning: What happens to their use? *Cognitive, Affective and Behavioural Neuroscience, 2,* 236–251.

Bradley, L., & Bryant, P. E. (1979). The independence of reading and spelling in backward and normal readers. *Developmental Medicine and Child Neurology, 21*, 504–514.

Bradley, L., & Bryant, P. E. (1983). Categorizing sounds and learning to read – a causal connection. *Nature, 301*, 419–421.

Bradley, R. H., & Corwyn, R. F. (2002). Socioeconomic status and child development. *Annual Review of Psychology, 53*, 371–399.

Bradley, R. H., Corwyn, R. F., Burchinal, M., Pipes McAdoo, H., & Garcia Coll, C. (2001). The home environments of children in the United States. Part 2: Relations with behavioral development through age thirteen. *Child Development, 72*, 1868–1886.

Brady, S. A. (1991). The role of working memory in reading disability. In S. A. Brady & D. Shankweiler (Eds.), *Phonological processes in literacy: A tribute to Isabelle Y. Liberman* (pp. 129–151). Hillsdale, NJ: Erlbaum.

Brady, S. A., Shankweiler, D., & Mann, V. (1983). Speech perception and memory coding in relation to reading ability. *Journal of Experimental Child Psychology, 35*, 345–367.

Bredekamp, S., & Copple, C. (1997). *Developmentally appropriate practice in early childhood programs – revised edition.* Washington, DC: National Association for the Education of Young Children.

Breier, J. I., Fletcher, J. M., Foorman, B. R., & Gray, L. C. (2002). Perception of speech and nonspeech stimuli by children with and without reading disability and attention deficit hyperactivity disorder. *Journal of Experimental Child Psychology, 82*, 226–250.

Breitmeyer, B. G. (1989). A visual based deficit in specific reading disability. *Irish Journal of Psychology, 10*, 534–541.

Breznitz, Z. (1997). Enhancing the reading of dyslexic children by reading acceleration and auditory masking. *Journal of Educational Psychology, 89*, 103–113.

Brito Mendes, C., Kolinsky, R., & Morais, J. (1988). Spécificité de l'analyse post-perceptive de figures géométriques. In P. Tap (Ed.), *Conduites et représentations* (pp. 197–199). Toulouse: Privat.

Brito Mendes, C., Morais, J., & Kolinsky, R. (2005). Analytic and holistic processing in postperceptual visual cognition. In J. Morais & P. Ventura (Eds.), *Studies in Cognitive Psychology* (pp. 177–196). Lisbon: Colibri.

Britto, P. R., & Brooks-Gunn, J. (2001). Beyond shared book reading: Dimensions of home literacy and low-income African American preschoolers' skills. In P. R. Britto & J. Brooks-Gunn (Eds.), *The role of family literacy environments in promoting young children's emerging literacy skills* (pp. 73–89). New directions for child and adolescent development. San Francisco: Jossey-Bass.

Brown, G. D. A., & Deavers, R. P. (1999). Units of analysis in nonword reading. *Journal of Experimental Child Psychology, 73*, 208–242.

Brown, K. (2003). What do I say when they get stuck on a word? Aligning teachers' prompts with students' development. *Reading Teacher, 56*, 720–733.

Brown, R. W., & Berko, J. (1960). Word association and the acquisition of grammar. *Child Development, 31*, 1–14.

Bruce, D. J. (1964). The analysis of word sounds. *British Journal of Educational Psychology, 34*, 158–170.

Bruck, M. (1990). Word recognition skills of adults with childhood diagnosis of dyslexia. *Developmental Psychology, 26*, 439–454.

Bruck, M. (1992). Persistence of dyslexics' phonological awareness deficits. *Developmental Psychology, 28*, 874–886.

Bruck, M. (1993). Component spelling skills of college students with childhood diagnosis of dyslexia. *Learning Disabilities Quarterly, 16*, 171–184.

Bruck, M., Genesee, F., & Caravolas, M. (1997). A cross-linguistic study of early literacy acquisition. In B. Blachman (Ed.), *Foundations of reading acquisition and dyslexia* (pp. 145–162). Hillsdale, NJ: Erlbaum.

Bruck, M., & Waters, G. (1988). An analysis of the spelling errors of children who differ in their reading and spelling skills. *Applied Psycholinguistics, 9*, 77–92.

Bruininks, V. L., & Mayer, J. H. (1979). Longitudinal study of cognitive abilities and academic achievement. *Perceptual and Motor Skills, 48*, 1011–1021.

Brunswick, N., McCrory, E., Price, C. J., Frith, C. D., & Frith, U. (1999). Explicit and implicit processing of words and pseudowords by adult developmental dyslexics: A search for Wernicke's Wortschatz? *Brain, 122*, 1901–1917.

Brus, B. T., & Voeten, M. J. M. (1973). One and two minute task (tests of reading automaticity). Nijmegen: Berkhout.

Bryant, P. E., & Bradley, L. (1980). Why children sometimes write words which they do not read. In U. Frith (Ed.), *Cognitive processes in spelling* (pp. 355–370). London: Academic.

Bryant, P. E., & Goswami, U. (1986). The strengths and weaknesses of the reading level design. *Psychological Bulletin, 100*, 101–103.

Bryant, P. E., MacLean, M., & Bradley, L. L. (1990a). Rhyme, language, and children's reading. *Applied Psycholinguistics, 11*, 237–252.

Bryant, P. E., MacLean, M., Bradley, L. L., & Crossland, J. (1990b). Rhyme, alliteration, phoneme detection, and learning to read. *Developmental Psychology, 26*, 429–438.

Brysbaert, M., & Praet, C. (1992). Reading isolated words: No evidence for automatic incorporation of the phonetic code. *Psychological Research, 54*, 91–102.

Brysbaert, M., & Vitu, F. (1998). Word skipping: Implications for theories of eye movement control in reading. In G. Underwood (Ed.), *Eye guidance in reading and scene perception* (pp. 125–148). Oxford: Elsevier.

Bub, D., Cancelliere, A., & Kertesz, A. (1985). Whole-word and analytic translation of spelling to sound in a non-semantic reader. In K. E. Patterson, J. C. Marshall, & M. Coltheart (Eds.), *Surface dyslexia* (pp. 15–34). London: Erlbaum.

Bub, D., & Kertesz, A. (1982). Deep agraphia. *Brain and Language, 17*, 146–165.

Buchanan, L., & Besner, D. (1993). Reading aloud: Evidence for the use of whole word non-semantic pathway. *Canadian Journal of Experimental Psychology, 47*, 133–152.

Budd, D., Whitney, P., & Turley, K. J. (1995). Individual differences in working memory strategies for reading expository text. *Memory and Cognition, 23*, 735–748.

Bullinaria, J. A. (1997). Modeling reading, spelling, and past tense learning with artificial neural networks. *Brain and Language, 59*, 236–266.

Burchinal, M. R., Peisner-Feinberg, E., Pianta, R., & Howes, C. (2002). Development of academic skills from preschool through second grade: Family and child predictors of developmental trajectories. *Journal of School Psychology, 40*, 415–436.

Burden, V., & Campbell, R. (1994). The development of word coding skills in the born deaf: An experimental study of deaf school leavers. *British Journal of Psychology, 72*, 371–376.

Burgess, S. R. (2002). The influence of speech perception, oral language ability, the home literacy environment, and pre-reading knowledge on the growth of phonological sensitivity: A one-year longitudinal investigation. *Reading and Writing, 15*, 709–737.

Burgess, S. R., Hecht, S, A., & Lonigan, C. J. (2002). Relations of home literacy environment to the development of reading-related abilities: A one-year longitudinal study. *Reading Research Quarterly, 37*, 408–426.

Burgess, S. R., & Lonigan, C. J. (1998). Bi-directional relations of phonological sensitivity and pre-reading abilities: Evidence from a preschool sample. *Journal of Experimental Child Psychology, 70*, 117–141.

Burt, J. S., & Tate, H. (2002). Does a reading lexicon provide orthographic representations for spelling? *Memory and Language, 46*, 518–543.

Bus, A. G., Leseman, P. P. M., & Keultjes, P. (2000). Joint book reading across cultures: A comparison of Surinamese–Dutch, Turkish–Dutch, and Dutch parent–child dyads. *Journal of Literacy Research, 32*(1), 53–76.

Bus, A. G., & van Ijzendoorn, M. H. (1988). Mother–child interaction, attachment, and emergent literacy: A cross-sectional study. *Child Development, 59*, 1262–1272.

Bus, A. G., van Ijzendoorn, M. H., & Pellegrini, A. D. (1995). Joint book reading makes for success in learning to read: A meta-analysis on intergenerational transmission of literacy. *Review of Educational Research, 65*, 1–21.

Buswell, G. T. (1922). *Fundamental Reading Habits: A study of their development.* Chicago: University of Chicago Press.

Butterworth, B., Cappelletti, M., & Kopelman, M. (2001). Category specificity in reading and writing: The case of number words. *Nature Neuroscience, 4*, 784–786.

Byrne, A., MacDonald, J., & Buckley, S. (2002). Reading, language and memory: A comparative study of children with Down syndrome and their mainstream peers. *British Journal of Educational Psychology, 72*, 513–529.

Byrne, B. (1984). On teaching articulatory phonetics via an orthography. *Memory and Cognition, 12*, 181–189.

Byrne, B. (1992). Studies in the acquisition procedure for reading: Rationale, hypotheses, and data. In P. B. Gough, L. C. Ehri, & R. Treiman (Eds.), *Reading acquisition* (pp. 1–34). Hillsdale, NJ: Erlbaum.

Byrne, B. (1993). Learning to read in the absence of phonemic awareness? A comment on Cossu, Rossini, and Marshall (1993). *Cognition, 48*, 285–288.

Byrne, B. (1996). The learnability of the alphabetic principle: Children's initial hypotheses about how print represents spoken language. *Applied Psycholinguistics, 17*, 401–426.

Byrne, B. (1998). *The foundation of literacy: The child's acquisition of the alphabetic principle.* Hove, UK: Psychology Press.

Byrne, B. (2002). The process of learning to read: A framework for integrating research and educational practice. In R. Stainthorpe & P. Tomlinson (Eds.), *Learning and teaching reading. British Journal of Educational Psychology Monograph Series II; Psychological Aspects of Education – Current Trends, 1*, 29–43.

Byrne, B., & Carroll, M. V. (1989). Learning artificial orthographies: Further evidence of a non-analytic acquisition procedure. *Memory and Cognition, 17*, 311–317.

Byrne, B., Delaland, C., Fielding-Barnsley, R., Quain, P., Samuelsson, S., Hoien, T., et al. (2002). Longitudinal twin study of early reading development in three countries: Preliminary results. *Annals of Dyslexia, 52*, 49–73.

Byrne, B., & Fielding-Barnsley, R. (1989). Phonemic awareness and letter knowledge in the child's acquisition of the alphabetic principle. *Journal of Educational Psychology, 81*, 313–321.

Byrne, B., & Fielding-Barnsley, R. (1990). Acquiring the alphabetic principle: A case for teaching recognition of phoneme identity. *Journal of Educational Psychology, 82*, 805–812.

Byrne, B., & Fielding-Barnsley, R. (1991). Evaluation of a program to teach phonemic awareness to young children. *Journal of Educational Psychology, 83*, 451–455.

Byrne, B., & Fielding-Barnsley, R. (1993). Recognition of phoneme invariance by beginning readers: Confounding effects of global similarity. *Reading and Writing, 6*, 315–324.

Byrne, B., Fielding-Barnsley, R., & Ashley, L. (2000). Effects of preschool phoneme identity training after six years: Outcome level distinguished from rate of response. *Journal of Educational Psychology, 92*, 659–667.

Byrne, B., Fielding-Barnsley, R., Ashley, L., & Larsen, K. (1997). Assessing the child's and the environment's contribution to reading acquisition: What we know and what we don't know. In

B. Blachman (Ed.), *Foundations of reading acquisition and dyslexia: Implications for early intervention* (pp. 265–286). Mahwah, NJ: Erlbaum.

Byrne, B., Freebody, P., & Gates, A. (1992). Longitudinal data on the relations of word-reading strategies to comprehension, reading time, and phonemic awareness. *Reading Research Quarterly, 27,* 142–151.

Byrne, B., & Liberman, A. M. (1999). Meaninglessness, productivity and reading: Some observations about the relationship between the alphabet and speech. In J. Oakhill & R. Beard (Eds.), *Reading development and the teaching of reading: A psychological perspective* (pp. 157–173). Oxford: Blackwell.

Caccappolo-van Vliet, E., Miozzo, M., & Stern Y. (2004). Phonological dyslexia without phonological impairment? *Cognitive Neuropsychology, 21,* 820–839.

Caine, D., Breen, N., & Patterson, K. (2002). Reading and writing in semantic dementia. Paper presented at the Macquarie Conference on Cognitive Neuropsychology, Sydney.

Cain, K. (1996). Story knowledge and comprehension skill. In C. Cornoldi & J. V. Oakhill (Eds.), *Reading comprehension difficulties: Processes and interventions* (pp. 167–192). Mahwah, NJ: Erlbaum.

Cain, K., & Oakhill, J. V. (1996). The nature of the relationship between comprehension skill and the ability to tell a story. *British Journal of Developmental Psychology, 14,* 187–201.

Cain, K., & Oakhill, J. V. (1999). Inference ability and its relation to comprehension failure in young children. *Reading and Writing, 11,* 489–503.

Cain, K., Oakhill, J. V., Barnes, M. A., & Bryant, P. E. (2001). Comprehension skill, inference-making ability, and the relation to knowledge. *Memory and Cognition, 29*(6), 850–859.

Cain, K., Oakhill, J. V., & Bryant, P. E. (2000a). Investigating the causes of reading comprehension failure: The comprehension-age match design. *Reading and Writing, 12,* 31–40.

Cain, K., Oakhill, J. V., & Bryant, P. E. (2000b). Phonological skills and comprehension failure: A test of the phonological processing deficit hypothesis. *Reading and Writing, 13,* 31–56.

Cain, K., Oakhill, J. V., & Elbro, C. (2004). The ability to learn new word meanings from context by school-age children with and without language comprehension difficulties. *Journal of Child Language, 30*(3), 681–694.

Calfee, R. C. (1977). Assessment of independent reading skills: Basic research and practical applications. In A. S. Reber & D. L. Scarborough (Eds.), *Toward a psychology of reading* (pp. 289–323). Hillsdale, NJ: Erlbaum.

Campbell, F. A., Goldstein, S., Schaefer, E. S., & Ramey, C. T. (1991). Parental beliefs and values related to family risk, educational intervention, and child academic competence. *Early Childhood Research Quarterly, 6,* 167–182.

Campbell, R., & Butterworth, B. (1985). Phonological dyslexia and dysgraphia in a highly literate subject: A developmental case with associated deficits of phonemic processing and awareness. *Quarterly Journal of Experimental Psychology, 37A,* 435–475.

Campbell, R., & Wright, H. (1988). Deafness, spelling and rhyme: How spelling supports written word and picture rhyming skills in deaf subjects. *Quarterly Journal of Experimental Psychology, 40A,* 771–788.

Caramazza, A. (1988). Some aspects of language processing revealed through the analysis of acquired dysgraphia: The lexical system. *Annual Review of Neuroscience, 11,* 395–421.

Caramazza, A., Hillis, A. E., Rapp, B. C., & Romani, C. (1990). Multiple semantics or multiple confusions? *Cognitive Neuropsychology, 7,* 161–168.

Caramazza, A., & Miceli, G. (1990). The structure of graphemic representations. *Cognition, 37,* 243–297.

Caramazza, A., Miceli, G., Villa, G., & Romani, C. (1987). The role of the graphemic buffer in spelling: Evidence from a case of acquired dysgraphia. *Cognition, 26,* 59–85.

Caravolas, M. (2005). Spelling development in alphabetic writing systems: How orthographic consistency may influence the acquisition of literacy skills. In M. Joshi (Ed.), *Handbook of orthography and literacy* (pp. 497–511) Lawrence Eribaum Publishers.

Caravolas, M., & Bruck, M. (1993). The effect of oral and written language input on children's phonological awareness: A cross-linguistic study. *Journal of Experimental Child Psychology, 55,* 1–30.

Caravolas, M., Bruck, M., & Genesee, F. (2003). Similarities and differences between English- and French-speaking poor spellers. In N. Goulandris (Ed.), *Dyslexia in different languages: Cross-linguistic comparisons* (pp. 157–180). London: Whurr.

Caravolas, M., Hulme, C., & Snowling, M. J. (2001). The foundations of spelling ability: Evidence from a 3-year longitudinal study. *Journal of Memory and Language, 45,* 751–774.

Caravolas, M., & Volín, J. (2001). Phonological spelling errors among dyslexic children learning a transparent orthography: The case of Czech. *Dyslexia, 7,* 229–245.

Caravolas, M., & Volín, J. (in preparation). Caveats in cross-linguistic comparisons of children with dyslexia.

Caravolas, M., Volín, J., & Hulme, C. (2005). Phoneme awareness is a key component of alphabetic literacy skills in consistent and inconsistent orthographies: Evidence from Czech and English children *Journal of Experimental Child Psychology, 92,* 107–139.

Cardon, L. R., DeFries, J. C., Fulker, D. W., Kimberling, W. J., Pennington, B. F., & Smith, S. D. (1994). Quantitative trait locus for reading disability on chromosome 6. *Science, 265,* 276–279.

Cardoso-Martins, C. (2001). The reading abilities of beginning readers of Brazilian Portuguese: Implications for a theory of reading acquisition. *Scientific Studies of Reading, 5,* 289–317.

Cardoso-Martins, C., & Frith, U. (2001). Can individuals with Down syndrome acquire alphabetic literacy skills in the absence of phoneme awareness? *Reading and Writing, 14,* 361–375.

Cardoso-Martins, C., Michalik, M. F., & Pollo, T. C. (2002). Is sensitivity to rhyme a developmental precursor to sensitivity to phoneme? Evidence from individuals with Down syndrome. *Reading and Writing, 15,* 439–454.

Cardoso-Martins, C., Rodriguez, L., & Ehri, L. C. (2003). Place of environmental print in reading development: Evidence from nonliterate adults. *Scientific Study of Reading, 7,* 335–355.

Carnine, L., Carnine, D., & Gersten, R. (1984). Analysis of oral reading errors made by economically disadvantaged students taught with a synthetic phonics approach. *Reading Research Quarterly, 19,* 343–356.

Carpenter, P. A., & Just, M. A. (1983). What your eyes do while your mind is reading. In K. Rayner (Ed.), *Eye movements in reading: Perceptual and language processes* (pp. 275–307). New York: Academic.

Carpenter, P. A., Miyake, A., & Just, M. A. (1994). Working memory constraints in comprehension: Evidence from individual differences, aphasia, and aging. In M. Gernsbacher (Ed.), *Handbook of psycholinguistics* (pp. 1075–1122). San Diego, CA: Academic.

Carr, T. H., Davidson, B. J., & Hawkins, H. L. (1978). Perceptual flexibility in word recognition: Strategies affect orthographic computation but not lexical access. *Journal of Experimental Psychology: Human Perception and Performance, 4,* 674–690.

Carr, T. H., McCauley, C., Sperber, R. D., & Parmelee, C. M. (1982). Words, pictures, and priming: On semantic activation, conscious identification, and the automaticity of information processing. *Journal of Experimental Psychology: Human Perception and Performance, 8,* 757–777.

Carreiras, M., Garnham, A., & Oakhill, J. (1996). Understanding anaphora: The role of superficial and conceptual information. In M. Carreiras, J. E. García-Albea, & N. Sebastián-Gallés (Eds.), *Language processing in Spanish* (pp. 241–274). Mahwah, NJ: Erlbaum.

Carroll, J. M., & Snowling, M. J. (2004). Language and phonological skills in children at high-risk of reading difficulties. *Journal of Child Psychology and Psychiatry, 45*, 631–640.

Carroll, J. M., Snowling, M. J., Hulme, C., & Stevenson, J. (2003). The development of phonological awareness in pre-school children. *Developmental Psychology, 39*, 913–923.

Carver, R. P. (1997). Reading for one second, one minute, or one year from the perspective of rauding theory. *Scientific Studies of Reading, 1*, 3–42.

Cary, L. (1988). *A análise explícita das unidades da fala nos adultos não alfabetizados.* PhD dissertation, University of Lisbon.

Cary, L., Morais, J., & Bertelson, P. (1989). A consciência fonológica dos poetas analfabetos: *Anais do Simpósio Latino-Americano de Psicologia do Desenvolvimento* (pp. 160–166). Recife, Brazil: Ed. Universitária da EFPE.

Cary, L., & Verhaeghe, A. (1991). Efeito da prática da linguagem ou da alfabetização no conhecimento das fronteiras formais das unidades lexicais: Comparação de dois tipos de tarefas. *Actas das 1as Jornadas de Estudo dos Processos Cognitivos da Sociedade Portuguesa de Psicologia* (pp. 33–49). Lisbon: Astoria.

Cassar, M., & Treiman, R. (1997). The beginning of orthographic knowledge: Children's knowledge of double letters in words. *Journal of Educational Psychology, 89*, 631–644.

Casteel, M. A., & Simpson, G. B. (1991). Textual coherence and the development of inferential generation skills. *Journal of Research in Reading, 14*, 116–129.

Castles, A., & Coltheart, M. (1993). Varieties of developmental dyslexia. *Cognition, 47*, 149–180.

Castles, A., & Coltheart, M. (1996). Cognitive correlates of developmental surface dyslexia: A single case study. *Cognitive Neuropsychology, 13*, 25–50.

Castles, A., & Coltheart, M. (2003). Is there a causal link from phonological awareness to success in learning to read? *Cognition, 91*, 77–111.

Castles, A., Datta, H., Gayan, J., & Olson, R. K. (1999). Varieties of developmental reading disorder: Genetic and environmental influences. *Journal of Experimental Child Psychology, 72*, 73–94.

Castro, S. L. (1993). *Alfabetização e percepção da fala.* Porto, Portugal: Instituto Nacional de Investigação Científica.

Castro, S. L., Vicente, S., Morais, J., Kolinsky, R., & Cluytens, M. (1995). Segmental representation of Portuguese in 5- and 6-year olds: Evidence from dichotic listening. In I. Hub Faria & J. Freitas (Eds.), *Studies on the acquisition of Portuguese. Proceedings of the first Lisbon meeting on child language* (pp. 1–16). Lisbon: Colibri.

Castro-Caldas, A., Petersson, K. M., Reis, A., Stone-Elander, S., & Ingvar, M. (1998). The illiterate brain. Learning to read and write during childhood influences the functional organization of the adult brain. *Brain, 121*, 1053–1063.

Castro-Caldas, A., & Reis, A. (2003). The knowledge of orthography is a revolution in the brain. *Reading and Writing, 16*, 81–97.

Cattell, J. McK. (1886). The time taken up by cerebral operations. *Mind, 11*, 220–242.

Catts, H. F., Hogan, T. P., & Fey, M. (2003). Subgrouping poor readers on the basis of individual differences in reading-related abilities. *Journal of Learning Disabilities, 36*, 151–164.

Catts, H. W. (1993). The relationship between speech-language and reading disabilities. *Journal of Speech and Hearing Research, 36*, 948–958.

Catts, H. W., Fey, M. E., Tomblin, J. B., & Zhang, X. (2002). A longitudinal investigation of reading outcomes in children with language impairments. *Journal of Speech, Hearing, and Language Research, 45*, 1142–1157.

Catts, H. W., Fey, M. E., Zhang, X., & Tomblin, J. B. (1999). Language basis of reading and reading disabilities. *Scientific Studies of Reading, 3,* 331–361.

Catts, H. W., Fey, M. E., Zhang, Z., & Tomblin, J. B. (2001). Estimating the risk of future reading failure difficulties in kindergarten children: A research-based model and its clinical implementation. *Language, Speech, and Hearing Services in Schools, 32,* 38–50.

Caughy, M. O. (1996). Health and environmental effects on the academic readiness of school-age children. *Developmental Psychology, 32,* 515–522.

Chall, J. S. (1967/1983/1996). *Learning to read: The great debate.* Fort Worth: Harcourt Brace College Publishers.

Chamberlain, C., & Mayberry, R. (2000). Theorizing about the relationship between ASL and reading. In C. Chamberlain, J. Morford, & R. Mayberry (Eds.), *Language acquisition by eye* (pp. 221–259). Mahwah, NJ: Erlbaum.

Chambers, C. G., & Smyth, R. (1998). Structural parallelism and discourse coherence: A test of centering theory. *Journal of Memory and Language, 39,* 593–608.

Chambers, S. M. (1979). Letter and order information in lexical access. *Journal of Verbal Learning and Verbal Behavior, 18,* 225–241.

Chan, C. K. K., & Siegel, L. (2001). Phonological processing in reading Chinese among normally achieving and poor readers. *Journal of Experimental Child Psychology, 80,* 23–43.

Chan, L., & Louie, L. (1992). Developmental trend of Chinese preschool children in drawing and writing. *Journal of Research in Childhood Education, 6,* 93–99.

Chan, L., & Nunes, T. (1998). Children's understanding of the formal and functional characteristics of written Chinese. *Applied Psycholinguistics, 19,* 115–131.

Chan, L., & Wang, L. (2003). Linguistic awareness in learning to read Chinese: A comparative study of Beijing and Hong Kong children. In C. McBride-Chang & H. C. Chen (Eds.), *Reading development in Chinese children* (pp. 87–102). Westport, CT: Praeger.

Chan, M. Y. (1982). Statistics on the strokes of present-day Chinese script. *Chinese Linguistics, 1,* 299–305.

Chaney, C. (1994). Language development, metalinguistic awareness, and emergent literacy skills of 3-year-old children in relation to social class. *Applied Psycholinguistics, 15,* 371–394.

Chapman, J. W., Tunmer, W. E., & Prochnow, J. E. (2000). Early reading-related skills and performance: Reading self-concept, and the development of academic self-concept: A longitudinal study. *Journal of Educational Psychology, 92,* 703–708.

Chapman, R. S. (1995). Language development in children and adolescents with Down syndrome. In P. Fletcher & B. MacWhinney (Eds.), *The handbook of child language* (pp. 641–663). Cambridge, MA: Blackwell.

Charlier, B. L., & Leybaert, J. (2000). The rhyming skills of deaf children educated with phonetically augmented speechreading. *Quarterly Journal of Experimental Psychology, 53A*(2), 349–375.

Chee, M. W. L., Weekes, B., Ming Lee, K., Siong Soon, C., Schreiber, A., J. J., Hoon, & Chee, M. (2000). Overlap and dissociation of semantic processing of Chinese characters, English words, and pictures: Evidence from fMRI. *NeuroImage, 12,* 392–403.

Chen, M. J. (1996). An overview of the characteristics of the Chinese writing system. *Asia Pacific Journal of Speech, Language and Hearing, 1,* 43–54.

Chen, M. J., & Yuen, J. C.-K. (1991). Effects of Pinyin and script type on verbal processing: Comparisons of China, Taiwan and Hong Kong experience. *International Journal of Behavioral Development, 14,* 429–484.

Chen, Y. P., & Allport, A. (1995). Attention and lexical decomposition in Chinese word recognition: Conjunctions of form and position guide selective attention. *Visual Cognition, 2,* 235–268.

Cheung, H. (1999). Improving phonological awareness and word reading in a later learned alphabetic script. *Cognition, 70,* 1–26.

Cheung, H., Chen, H. C., Lai, C. Y., Wong, O. C., & Hills, M. (2001). The development of phonological awareness: Effects of spoken language experience and orthography. *Cognition, 81,* 227–241.

Cheung, H., & Ng, L. (2003). Chinese reading development in some major Chinese societies: An introduction. In C. McBride-Chang & H. C. Chen (Eds.), *Reading development in Chinese children* (pp. 1–15). Westport, CT: Praeger.

Chi, M. M. (1988). Invented spelling/writing in Chinese-speaking children: The developmental patterns. *National Reading Conference Yearbook, 37,* 285–296.

Chi, M. T. H. (1978). Knowledge structures and memory development. In R. Siegler (Ed.), *Children's thinking: What develops?* (pp. 73–96). Hillsdale, NJ: Erlbaum.

Cho, J.-R., & Chen, H.-C. (1999). Orthographic and phonological activation in the semantic processing of the Korean Hanza and Hangul. *Language and Cognitive Processes, 14,* 481–502.

Chomsky, N. (1965). *Aspects of the theory of syntax.* Cambridge, MA: MIT Press.

Chomsky, N. (1976). *Reflections on language.* New York: Pantheon.

Christian, K., Morrison, F. J., & Bryant, F. B. (1998). Predicting kindergarten academic skills: Interactions among child care, maternal education, and family literacy environment. *Early Childhood Research Quarterly, 13,* 501–521.

Chu, K.-K. M., & Leung, M.-T. (2005). Reading strategy of Hong Kong school-aged children: The development of word level and character level processing. *Applied Psycholinguistics,* 26: 505–520.

Cipolotti, L., & Warrington, E. K. (1995). Semantic memory and reading abilities: A case report. *Journal of the International Neuropsychological Society, 1,* 104–110.

Clahsen, H., & Almazan, M. (1998). Syntax and morphology in Williams syndrome. *Cognition, 68,* 167–198.

Clark, D. B., and Uhry, J. K. (1995). *Dyslexia: Theory and practice of remedial instruction* (2nd ed.). Baltimore: York.

Clark, H. H. (1973). The language-as-fixed-effect fallacy: A critique of language statistics in psychological research. *Journal of Verbal Learning and Verbal Behavior, 12,* 335–359.

Clark, J. J., & O'Regan, J. K. (1999). Word ambiguity and the optimal viewing position in reading. *Vision Research, 39,* 843–857.

Clarke, L. (1988). Invented versus traditional spelling in first graders' writings: Effects on learning to spell and read. *Research in the Teaching of English, 22,* 281–309.

Clay, M. M. (1985). *The early detection of reading difficulties* (3rd ed.). Auckland: Heinemann.

Clifton, C., Traxler, M. J., Mohamed, M. T., Williams, R. S., Morris, R. K., & Rayner, K. (2003). The use of thematic role information in processing: Syntactic processing autonomy revisited. *Journal of Memory and Language, 49,* 317–334.

Cohen, A. (1975). Oral reading errors of first grade children taught by a code-emphasis approach. *Reading Research Quarterly, 10,* 616–650.

Cohen, L., Dehaene, S., Naccache, L., Lehericy, S., Dehaene-Lambertz, G., Henaff, M., et al. (2000). The visual word form area: Spatial and temporal characterization of an initial stage of reading in normal subjects and posterior split-brain patients. *Brain, 123,* 291–307.

Cohen, L., Lehericy, S., Chochon, F., Lemer, C., Rivard, S., & Dehaene, S. (2002). Language-specific tuning of visual cortex? Functional properties of the visual word form area. *Brain, 125,* 1054–1069.

Cole, M., Gay, J., Glick, J. A., & Sharp, D. W. (1971). The cultural context of learning and thinking. New York: Basic.

Coleman, B. B., Uhl, W. L., & Hosic, J. F. (1925). *The Pathway to Reading primer.* New York: Silver, Burdett.

Colin, S., Magnan, A., Ecalle, J., & Leybaert, J. (in revision). *Relation between early phonological skills and later reading performances in deaf children: A longitudinal study.*

Collins, A. M., & Loftus, E. F. (1975). A spreading-activation theory of semantic processing. *Psychological Review, 82,* 407–428.

Colombo, L. (1986). Activation and inhibition with orthographically similar words. *Journal of Experimental Psychology: Human Perception and Performance, 12,* 226–234.

Colombo, L., & Tabossi, P. (1992). Strategies and stress assignment: Evidence from a shallow orthography. In R. Frost & L. Katz (Eds.), *Orthography, phonology, morphology, and meaning* (pp. 319–340). Advances in Psychology. Amsterdam: Elsevier.

Colombo, L., Zorzi, M., Cubelli, R., & Brivio, C. (2003). The status of consonants and vowels in phonological assembly: Testing the two-cycles model with Italian. *European Journal of Cognitive Psychology, 15,* 405–433.

Coltheart, M. (1978). Lexical access in simple reading tasks. In G. Underwood (Ed.), *Strategies of information processing* (pp. 151–216). London: Academic.

Coltheart, M. (1980). Reading phonological recoding and deep dyslexia. In M. Coltheart, K. Patterson, & J. C. Marshall (Eds.), *Deep dyslexia* (pp. 197–226). London: Routledge & Kegan Paul.

Coltheart, M. (1998). Seven questions about pure alexia (letter-by-letter reading). *Cognitive Neuropsychology, 15,* 1–6.

Coltheart, M. (2000). Dual routes from print to speech and dual routes from print to meaning: Some theoretical issues. In A. Kennedy, R. Radach, J. Pynte, & D. Heller (Eds.), *Reading as a perceptual process* (pp. 475–490). Oxford: Elsevier.

Coltheart, M. (Ed.) (1996). *Phonological dyslexia.* Hove, UK: Erlbaum.

Coltheart, M., Curtis, B., Atkins, P., & Haller, M. (1993). Models of reading aloud: Dual-route and parallel-distributed-processing approaches. *Psychological Review, 100,* 589–608.

Coltheart, M., Davelaar, E., Jonasson, J. T., & Besner, D. (1977). Access to the internal lexicon. In S. Dornic (Ed.), *Attention and performance VI* (pp. 535–555). Hillsdale, NJ: Erlbaum.

Coltheart, M., & Funnell, E. (1987). Reading and writing: One lexicon or two? In D. A. Allport, D. McKay, W. Prinz, & E. Scheerer (Eds.), *Language perception and production: Common processes in listening, speaking, reading, and writing* (pp. 313–339). London: Academic.

Coltheart, M., Masterson, J., Byng, S., Prior, M., & Riddoch, J. (1983). Surface dyslexia. *Quarterly Journal of Experimental Psychology, 35,* 469–495.

Coltheart, M., Patterson, K., & Marshall, J. C. (Eds.) (1980). *Deep dyslexia.* London: Routledge & Kegan Paul.

Coltheart, M., Rastle, K., Perry, C., Langdon, R., & Ziegler, J. (2001). DRC: A dual-route cascaded model of visual word recognition and reading aloud. *Psychological Review, 108,* 204–256.

Compton, D. L., Davis, C. J., DeFries, J. C., Gayan, J., & Olson, R. K. (2001). Genetic and environmental influences on reading and RAN: An overview of results from the Colorado Twin Study. In M. Wolf (Ed.), *Conference proceedings of the Dyslexia Research Foundation Conference in Extraordinary Brain Series: Time, fluency, and developmental dyslexia* (pp. 277–303). Baltimore: York.

Compton, D. L., DeFries, J.C., & Olson, R. K. (2001). Are RAN and phonological awareness deficits additive in children with reading disabilities? *Dyslexia, 7,* 125–149.

Conrad, R. (1971). The chronology of the development of covert speech in children. *Developmental Psychology, 5,* 398–405.

Conrad, R. (1979). *The deaf school child.* London: Harper & Row.

Content, A., Kolinsky, R., Morais, J., & Bertelson, P. (1986). Phonetic segmentation in prereaders: Effect of corrective information. *Journal of Experimental Child Psychology, 42,* 49–72.

Cook, A., & Myers, J. L. (2004). Processing discourse roles in scripted narratives: The influence of context and world knowledge. *Journal of Memory and Language, 50*, 268–288.

Coolahan, K., McWayne, C., Fantuzzo, J., & Grim, S. (2002). Validation of a multidimensional assessment of parenting styles for low-income African American familes with preschool children. *Early Childhood Research Quarterly, 17*, 356–373.

Cooper, L. A. (1976). Individual differences in visual comparison processes. *Perception and Psychophysics, 19*, 433–444.

Cooper, L. A. (1980). Recent themes in visual information processing: A selected overview. In R. S. Nickerson (Ed.), *Attention and performance VIII* (pp. 319–345). Hillsdale, NJ: Erlbaum.

Cooper, L. A., & Podgorny, P. (1976). Mental transformation and visual comparison processes: Effects of complexity and similarity. *Journal of Experimental Psychology: Human Perception and Performance, 2*, 503–514.

Coppens, P., Parente, M. A., & Lecours, A. R. (1998). Aphasia in illiterate individuals. In P. Coppens, Y. Lebrun, & A. Basso (Eds.), *Aphasia in atypical populations* (pp. 175–202). Mahwah, NJ: Erlbaum.

Corfield, D. R., Murphy, K., Josephs, O., Fink, G. R., Frackowiak, R. S. J., Guz, A., et al. (1999). Cortical and subcortical control of tongue movement in humans: A functional neuroimaging study using fMRI. *Journal of Applied Physiology, 86*(5), 1468–1477.

Cornett, O. (1967). Cued Speech. *American Annals of the Deaf, 112*, 3–13.

Cortese, M. J., Simpson, G. B., & Woolsey, S. (1997). Effects of association and imageability on phonological mapping. *Psychonomic Bulletin and Review, 4*, 226–231.

Coslett, H. B., & Saffran, E. M. (1989). Evidence for preserved reading in pure alexia. *Brain, 112*, 327–359.

Coslett, H. B., Saffran, E. M., Greenbaum, S., & Schwartz, H. (1993). Reading in pure alexia – the effect of strategy. *Brain, 116*, 21–37.

Cossu, G., & Marshall, J. C. (1985). Dissociation between reading and written spelling in two Italian children: Dyslexia without dysgraphia? *Neuropsychologia, 23*, 697–700.

Cossu, G., & Marshall, J. C. (1990). Are cognitive skills a prerequisite for learning to read and write? *Cognitive Neuropsychology, 7*, 21–40.

Cossu, G., Rossini, F., & Marshall, J. C. (1993). When reading is acquired but phonemic awareness is not: A study of literacy in Down's syndrome. *Cognition, 46*, 129–138.

Cossu, G., Shankweiler, D., Liberman, I., Katz, L., & Tola, G. (1988). Awareness of phonological segments and reading ability in Italian children. *Applied Psycholinguistics, 9*, 1–16.

Cotelli, M., Abutalebi, J., Zorzi, M., & Cappa, S. (2003). Vowels in the buffer: A case study of acquired dysgraphia with selective vowel substitutions. *Cognitive Neuropsychology, 20*(2), 99–114.

Cragg, L., & Nation, K. (2006). Exploring written narrative in children with poor reading comprehension. *Educational Psychology, 26*, 55–72.

Craig, H. K., Connor, C. M., & Washington, J. A. (2003). Early positive predictors of later reading comprehension for African American students: A preliminary investigation. *Language, Speech, and Hearing Services in Schools, 24*, 31–43.

Crain, K. L. (2003). The development of phonological awareness in moderately-to-profoundly deaf developing readers: The effect of exposure to Cued American English. PhD dissertation, Gallaudet University, Washington, DC.

Crain, K. L., & Shankweiler, D. (1988). Syntactic complexity and reading acquisition. In A. Davison & G. M. Green (Eds.), *Linguistic complexity and text comprehension: Readability issues reconsidered* (pp. 167–192). Hillsdale, NJ: Erlbaum.

Crain-Thoreson, C., & Dale, P. S. (1992). Do early talkers become early readers? Linguistic precocity, preschool language, and emergent literacy. *Developmental Psychology, 28*, 421–429.

Cree, G. S., McRae, K., & McNorgan, C. (1999). An attractor model of lexical conceptual processing: Simulating semantic priming. *Cognitive Science, 23*, 371–414.

Crick, F. H. C. (1989). The recent excitement about neural networks. *Nature, 337*, 129–132.

Crisp, J., & Lambon Ralph, M. A. (submitted). The continuum between phonological and deep dyslexia: The keys are in phonology and semantics.

Cronbach, L. J., & Furby, L. (1970). How should we measure "change" – or should we? *Psychological Bulletin, 74*, 68–80.

Crone, D. A., & Whitehurst, G. J. (1999). Age and schooling effects on emergent literacy and early reading skills. *Journal of Educational Psychology, 91*, 604–614.

Cronin, V. (2002). The syntagmatic-paradigmatic shift and reading development. *Journal of Child Language, 29*, 189–204.

Cronin, V., & Carver, P. (1998). Phonological sensitivity, rapid naming, and beginning reading. *Applied Psycholinguistics, 19*, 447–461.

Cronin, V., Pratt, M., Abraham, J., Howell, D., Bishop, S., & Manning, A. (1986). Word association and the acquisition of reading. *Journal of Psycholinguistic Research, 15*, 1–11.

Cubelli, R. (1991). A selective deficit for writing vowels in acquired dysgraphia. *Nature, 353*, 258–260.

Cunningham, A. E., Perry, K. E., Stanovich, K., & Share, D. (2002). Orthographic learning during reading: Examining the role of self-teaching. *Journal of Experimental Child Psychology, 82*, 185–199.

Cunningham, A. E., & Stanovich, K. E. (1997). Early reading acquisition and its relation to reading experience and ability ten years later. *Developmental Psychology, 33*, 934–945.

Cunningham, A. E., & Stanovich, K. E. (1998). What reading does for the mind. *American Educator, 22*, 8–15.

Cupples, L., & Iacono, T. (2000). Phonological awareness and oral reading skill in children with Down syndrome. *Journal of Speech, Language and Hearing Research, 43*, 595–608.

Curtis, M. E. (1980). Development of components of reading skill. *Journal of Educational Psychology, 72*, 656–669.

Curtis, M. E. (1987). Vocabulary testing and vocabulary instruction. In M. McKeown & M. E. Curtis (Eds.), *The nature of vocabulary acquisition* (pp. 37–51). Hillsdale, NJ: Erlbaum.

Dahl, K., Scharer, P., Lawson, L., & Grogan, P. (1999). Phonics instruction and student achievement in whole language first-grade classrooms. *Reading Research Quarterly, 34*, 312–341.

Damasio, A., & Damasio, H. (1983). The anatomic basis of pure alexia. *Neurology, 33*, 1573–1583.

Damian, M. F., & Bowers, J. S. (2003). Effects of orthography on speech production in a form-preparation paradigm. *Journal of Memory and Language, 49*, 119–132.

Damper, R., & Marchand, Y. (2000). Pronunciation by analogy in normal and impaired readers. Fourth Conference on Computational Language Learning, Lisbon. http://cnts.uia.ac.be/conll2000/proceedings.html.

Daneman, M. (1988). Word knowledge and reading skill. In M. Daneman, G. MacKinnon, & T. G. Waller (Eds.), *Reading research: Advances in theory and practice* (Vol. 6, pp. 145–175). San Diego, CA: Academic.

Daneman, M., & Carpenter, P. A. (1980). Individual differences in working memory and reading. *Journal of Verbal Learning and Verbal Behavior, 19*, 450–466.

Daneman, M., & Carpenter, P. A. (1983). Individual differences in integrating information between and within sentences. *Journal of Experimental Psychology: Learning, Memory, and Cognition, 9*, 561–584.

Daneman, M., & Green, I. (1986). Individual differences in comprehending and producing words in context. *Journal of Memory and Language, 25*, 1–18.

Daneman, M., & Reingold, E. M. (2000). Do readers use phonological codes to activate word meanings? Evidence from eye movements. In A. Kennedy, R. Radach, J. Pynte, & D. Heller (Eds.), *Reading as a perceptual process* (pp. 447–473). Oxford: Elsevier.

Daneman, M., & Tardif, T. (1987). Working memory and reading skill re-examined. In M. Coltheart (Ed.), *Attention and performance: The psychology of reading.* (Vol. 12, pp. 491–508). Hove, UK: Erlbaum.

Danziger, E., & Pederson, E. (1999). Through the looking-glass: Literacy, writing systems and mirror-image discrimination. *Written Language and Literacy, 1,* 153–164.

Davelaar, E., Coltheart, M., Besner, D., & Jonasson, J. T. (1978). Phonological recoding and lexical access. *Memory and Cognition, 8,* 195–209.

Davis, C. J. (1999). The Self-Organising Lexical Acquisition and Recognition (SOLAR) model of visual word recognition. PhD dissertation, University of New South Wales, Sydney.

Davis, C. J., Castles, A., & Iakovidis, E. (1998). Masked homophone and pseudohomophone priming in children and adults. *Language and Cognitive Processes, 13,* 625–651.

Davis, C. J., Gayan, J., Knopik, V. S., Smith, S. D., Cardon, L. R., Pennington, B. F., et al. (2001). Etiology of reading difficulties and rapid naming: The Colorado Twin Study of Reading Disability. *Behavior Genetics, 31*(6), 625–635.

De Abreu, M., & Cardoso-Martins, C. (1998). Alphabetic access route in beginning reading acquisition in Portuguese: The role of letter-name knowledge. *Reading and Writing, 10,* 85–104.

DeBaryshe, B. D. (1995). Maternal belief system: Linchpin in the home reading process. *Journal of Applied Developmental Psychology, 16,* 1–20.

DeBaryshe, B. D., & Binder, J. C. (1994). Development of an instrument for measuring parental beliefs about reading aloud to young children. *Perceptual and Motor Skills, 78,* 1303–1311.

Dee-Lucas, D., & Larkin, J. H. (1988). Novice rules for assessing importance in scientific texts. *Journal of Memory and Language, 27,* 288–308.

Deffenbacher, K. E., Kenyon, J. B., Hoover, D. M., Olson, R. K., Pennington, B. F., DeFries, J. C., et al. (2003). Refinement of the 6p21.3 QTL influencing dyslexia: Linkage and association analyses. *Human Genetics, 115,* 128–138.

Defior, S., Cary, L., & Martos, F. (2002). Differences in reading acquisition development in two shallow orthographies: Portuguese and Spanish. *Applied Psycholinguistics, 23,* 135–148.

DeFrancis, J. (1989). Visible speech: *The diverse oneness of writing systems.* Honolulu: University of Hawaii Press.

DeFries, J. C., Filipek, P. A., Fulker, D. W., Olson, R. K., Pennington, B. F., Smith, S. D., et al. (1997). Colorado Learning Disabilities Research Center. *Learning Disabilities, 8,* 7–19.

DeFries, J. C., & Fulker, D. W. (1985). Multiple regression analysis of twin data. *Behavior Genetics, 15,* 467–473.

DeFries, J. C., & Fulker, D. W. (1988). Multiple regression analysis of twin data: Etiology of deviant scores versus individual differences. *Acta Geneticae Medicae et Gemellogiae, 37,* 205–216.

DeFries, J. C., Fulker, D. W., & LaBuda, M. C. (1987). Evidence for a genetic aetiology in reading disability of twins. *Nature, 239,* 537–539.

DeFries, J. C., & Gillis, J. J. (1993). Genetics of reading disability. In R. Plomin & G. E. McClearn (Eds.), *Nature, Nurture, and Psychology* (pp. 121–145). Washington, DC: American Psychological Association.

DeFries, J. C., Singer, S. M., Foch, T. T., & Lewitter, F. I. (1978). Familial nature of reading disability. *British Journal of Psychiatry, 132,* 361–367.

de Gelder, B., Vroomen, J., & Bertelson, P. (1993). The effects of alphabetic reading competence on language representation in bilingual Chinese subjects. *Psychological Research, 55,* 315–321.

de Groot, M. M. B. (1989). Representational aspects of word imageability and word frequency as assessed through word association. *Journal of Experperimental Psychology: Learning, Memory, and Cognition, 15*, 824–845.

Dehaene, S., Le Clec'H, G., Poline, J. B., Bihan, D. L., & Cohen, L. (2002). The visual word form area: A prelexical representation of visual words in the left fusiform gyrus. *Neuroreport, 13*(3), 321–325.

Dehaene, S., Naccache, L., Cohen, L., Bihan, D. L., Mangin, J. F., Poline, J. B., et al. (2001). Cerebral mechanisms of word masking and unconscious repetition priming. *Nature Neuroscience, 4*, 752–758.

D'Hondt, M. (2001). Spécialisation hémisphérique pour le langage chez la personne à déficience auditive: Effet de l'expérience linguistique précoce. PhD dissertation, Free University of Brussels, Brussels.

D'Hondt, M., & Leybaert, J. (2003). Lateralization effect during semantic and rhyme judgement tasks in deaf and hearing children. *Brain and Language, 87*, 227–240.

Dejerine, J. (1891). Sur un cas de cécité verbale avec agraphie, suivi d'autopsie. *Memoires Societe Biologique, 3*, 197–201.

Déjerine, J. (1892). Contribution a l'etude anatamo-pathologique et clinique des differentes varietes de cecite verbale. *Compte Rendu Hebdomadaire des Seances et Memoires de la Societe de Biologie, 4*, 61–90.

de Jong, P. (1998). Working memory deficits of reading disabled children. *Journal of Experimental Child Psychology, 70*, 75–96.

de Jong, P. F., & van der Leij, A. (1999). Specific contributions of phonological abilities to early reading acquisition: Results from a Dutch latent variable longitudinal study. *Journal of Educational Psychology, 91*, 450–476.

de Jong, P., & van der Leij, A. (2002). Effects of phonological abilities and linguistic comprehension on the development of reading. *Scientific Studies of Reading, 6*(1), 51–77.

de Jong, P., & van der Leij, A. (in press). Developmental changes in the manifestation of a phonological deficit in dyslexic children learning to read a regular orthography. *Journal of Educational Psychology.*

De Luca, M., Borrelli, M., Judica, A., Spinelli, D., & Zoccolotti, P. (2002). Reading words and psuedowords: An eye movement study of developmental dyslexia. *Brain and Language, 80*, 617–626.

De Luca, M., Di Pace, E., Judica, A., Spinelli, D., & Zoccolotti, P. (1999). Eye movement patterns in linguistic and non-linguistic tasks in developmental surface dyslexia. *Neuropsychologia, 37*, 1407–1420.

Demonet, J.-F., Chollet, F., Ramsay, S., Cardebat, D., Nespoulous, J.-L., Wise, R., et al. (1992). The anatomy of phonological and semantic processing in normal subjects. *Brain, 115*, 1753–1768.

de Moor, W., & Brysbaert, M. (2000). Neighborhood-frequency effects when primes and targets have different lengths. *Psychological Research/Psychologische Forschung, 63*, 159–162.

Dennis, I., Besner, D., & Davelaar, E. (1985). Phonology in visual word recognition: Their is more two this than meats the I. In D. Besner, T. G. Waller, & G. E. MacKinnon (Eds.), *Reading research: Advances in theory and practice* (Vol. 5, pp. 170–197). New York: Academic.

Dennis, M., & Barnes, M. A. (1993). Oral discourse after early-onset hydrocephalus: Linguistic ambiguity, figurative language, speech acts, and script-based inferences. *Journal of Pediatric Psychology, 18*, 639–652.

Department for Education and Employment (1998). *The national literacy strategy: Framework for teaching.* London: HMSO.

De Partz, M. P., Seron, X., & Van der Linden, M. (1992). Re-education of a surface dysgraphic with a visual imagery strategy. *Cognitive Neuropsychology, 9,* 369–401.

De Renzi, E., & di Pellegrino, G. (1998). Prosopagnosia and alexia without object agnosia. *Cortex, 34,* 403–415.

Dérouesné, J., & Beauvois, M.-F. (1985). The "phonemic" stage in nonlexical reading: Data from dyslexia. In K. E. Patterson, J. C. Marshall, & M. Coltheart (Eds.), *Surface dyslexia: Cognitive and neuropsychological studies of phonological reading* (pp. 399–457). Hove, UK: Erlbaum.

De Saussure, F. (1922). *Course in general linguistics.* Translated by R. Harris, 1983. London: Duckworth.

de Sousa, I., & Oakhill, J. V. (1996). Do levels of interest have an effect on children's comprehension monitoring performance? *British Journal of Educational Psychology, 66,* 471–482.

Deutsch, A., Frost, R., Pelleg, S., Pollatsek, A., & Rayner, K. (2003). Early morphological effects in reading: Evidence from parafoveal preview benefit in Hebrew. *Psychonomic Bulletin and Review, 10,* 415–422.

Deutsch, A., Frost, R., Pollatsek, A., & Rayner, K. (2000). Early morphological effects in word recognition in Hebrew: Evidence from parafoveal preview benefit. *Language and Cognitive Processes, 15,* 487–506.

Deutsch, A., & Rayner, K. (1999). Initial fixation location effects in reading Hebrew words. *Language and Cognitive Processes, 14,* 393–421.

Devlin, J. T., Russell, R. P., Davis, M. H., Price, C. J., Wilson, J., Matthews, P. M., et al. (2000). Susceptibility and semantics: Comparing PET and fMRI on a language task. *NeuroImage, 11*(5), S257.

Diamond, K. E., Reagan, A. J., & Bandyk, J. E. (2000). Parents' conceptions of kindergarten readiness: Relationships with race, ethnicity, and development. *Journal of Educational Research, 94,* 93–100.

Di Betta, A. M., & Romani, C. (submitted). Lexical learning and dysgraphia in a group of adults with developmental dyslexia.

Dickinson, D. K., & Tabors, P. O. (1991). Early literacy: Linkages between home, school, and literacy achievement at age five. *Journal of Research in Childhood Education, 6,* 30–46.

Dickinson, D. K., & Tabors, P. O. (Eds.) (2001). *Building literacy with language: Young children learning at home and school.* Baltimore: Brookes.

Dijkstra, T., Roelofs, A., & Fieuws, S. (1995). Orthographic effects on phoneme monitoring. *Canadian Journal of Experimental Psychology, 49,* 264–271.

Doctor, E. A., & Coltheart, M. (1980). Children's use of phonological encoding when reading for meaning. *Memory and Cognition, 8,* 195–209.

Dodd, B. (1976). The phonological system of deaf children. *Journal of Speech and Hearing Disorders, 41,* 185–198.

Dodd, B. (1980). The spelling abilities of profoundly, pre-linguistically deaf children. In U. Frith (Ed.), *Cognitive processes in spelling* (pp. 423–443). New York: Academic.

Dodd, B., & Hermelin, B. (1977). Phonological coding by the prelinguistically deaf. *Perception and Psychophysics, 21,* 413–417.

Donnenwerth-Nolan, S., Tanenhaus, M. K., & Seidenberg, M. S. (1981). Multiple code activation in word recognition. *Journal of Experimental Psychology: Human Learning and Memory, 7,* 170–180.

Dubow, E. F., & Ippolito, M. F. (1994). Effects of poverty and quality of the home environment on changes in the academic and behavioral adjustment of elementary school-age children. *Journal of Clinical Child Psychology, 23,* 401–412.

Duffy, S. A., Morris, R. K., & Rayner, K. (1988). Lexical ambiguity and fixation times in reading. *Journal of Memory and Language, 27,* 429–446.

Dufva, M., Niemi, P., & Voeten, M. J. M. (2001). The role of phonological memory, word recognition, and comprehension skills in reading development from preschool to grade 2. *Reading and Writing, 14*, 91–117.

Duncan, L. G., Colé, P., Seymour, P. H. K., & Magnan, A. (submitted). Differing sequences of metaphonological development in French and English.

Duncan, L. G., & Seymour, P. H. K. (2000). Socio-economic differences in foundation-level literacy. *British Journal of Psychology, 91*, 145–166.

Duncan, L. G., & Seymour, P. H. K. (2003). How do children read multisyllabic words? Some preliminary observations. *Journal of Research in Reading, 26*, 101–120.

Duncan, L. G., Seymour, P. H. K., & Hill, S. (1997). How important are rhyme and analogy in beginning reading? *Cognition, 63*, 171–208.

Duncan, L. G., Seymour, P. H. K., & Hill, S. (2000). A small to large unit progression in metaphonological awareness and reading? *Quarterly Journal of Experimental Psychology, A53*, 1081–1104.

Dunn, L. M., & Markwardt, F. C. (1970). *Examiner's manual: Peabody Individual Achievement Test.* Circle Pines, MN: American Guidance Service.

Dunning, D. B., Mason, J. M., & Stewart, J. P. (1994). Reading to preschoolers: A response to Scarborough and Dobrich (1994) and recommendations for future research. *Developmental Review, 14*, 324–339.

Durgunoğlu, A. Y., Nagy, W. E., & Hancin-Bhatt, B. J. (1993). Cross-language transfer of phonological awareness. *Journal of Educational Psychology, 85*, 453–465.

Dyer, A., MacSweeney, M., Szczerbinski, M., Green, L., & Campbell, R. (2003). Predictors of reading delay in deaf adolescents: The relative contributions of rapid automatized naming speed and phonological awareness and decoding. *Journal of Deaf Studies and Deaf Education, 8*(3), 215–230.

Eden, G. F., Stein, J. F., Wood, M. H., & Wood, F. B. (1995). Verbal and visual problems in dyslexia. *Journal of Learning Disabilities, 28*, 272–290.

Eden, G. F., Van Meter, J. W., Rumsey, J. M., Maisog, J. M., Woods, R. P., & Zeffiro, T. A. (1996). Abnormal processing of visual motion in dyslexia revealed by functional brain imaging. *Nature, 382*, 66–69.

Eden, G. F., & Zeffiro, T. A. (1998). Neural systems affected in developmental dyslexia revealed by functional neuroimaging. *Neuron, 21*, 279–282.

Ehri, L. C. (1983). A critique of five studies related to letter-name knowledge and learning to read. In L. M. Gentile, M. L. Kamil, & J. Blanchard (Eds.), *Reading research: Advances in theory and practice* (Vol. 1, pp. 63–116). New York: Academic.

Ehri, L. C. (1992). Reconceptualizing the development of sight word reading and its relationship to recoding. In P. Gough, L. C. Ehri, & R. Treiman (Eds.), *Reading acquisition* (pp. 107–143). Hillsdale, NJ: Erlbaum.

Ehri, L. C. (1998). Grapheme–phoneme knowledge is essential for learning to read words in English. In J. Metsala & L. Ehri (Eds.), *Word recognition in beginning literacy* (pp. 3–40). Mahwah, NJ: Erlbaum.

Ehri, L. C. (1999). Phases of development in learning to read words. In J. V. Oakhill & R. Beard (Eds.), *Reading development and the teaching of reading: A psychological perspective* (pp. 79–108). Oxford: Blackwell.

Ehri, L. C. (2002). Phases of acquisition in learning to read words and implications for teaching. *British Journal of Educational Psychology: Monograph Series, 1*, 7–28.

Ehri, L. C., & McCormick, S. (1998). Phases of word learning: Implications for instruction with delayed and disabled readers. *Reading and Writing Quarterly, 14*, 135–163.

Ehri, L. C., Nunes, S., Stahl, S., & Willows, D. (2001). Systematic phonics instruction helps students learn to read: Evidence from the National Reading Panel's meta-analysis. *Review of Educational Research, 71,* 393–447.

Ehri, L. C., Nunes, S. R., Willows, D. M., Schuster, B. V., Yaghoub-Zadeh, Z., & Shanahan, T. (2001). Phonemic awareness instruction helps children learn to read: Evidence from the National Reading Panel's meta-analysis. *Reading Research Quarterly, 36,* 250–287.

Ehrlich, S. F., & Rayner, K. (1981). Contextual effects on word perception and eye movements during reading. *Journal of Verbal Learning and Verbal Behavior, 20,* 641–655.

Ehri, L. C., & Robbins, C. (1992). Beginners need some decoding skill to read words by analogy. *Reading Research Quarterly, 27,* 12–26.

Ehri, L. C., & Saltmarsh, J. (1995). Beginning readers outperform older disabled readers in learning to read words by sight. *Reading and Writing:, 7,* 295–326.

Ehri, L. C., & Snowling, M. (2004). Developmental variation in word recognition. In C. A. Stone, E. R. Silliman, B. Ehren, & K. Apel (Eds.), *Handbook of language and literacy development and disorders* (pp. 433–460). New York: Guilford.

Ehri, L. C., & Wilce, L. S. (1979). The mnemonic value of orthography among beginning readers. *Journal of Educational Psychology, 71,* 26–40.

Ehri, L. C., & Wilce, L. S. (1980). The influence of orthography on readers' conceptualization of the phonemic structure of words. *Applied Psycholinguistics, 1,* 371–385.

Ehri, L. C., & Wilce, L. S. (1983). Development of word identification speed in skilled and less skilled beginning readers. *Journal of Educational Psychology, 75,* 3–18.

Ehri, L. C., & Wilce, L. S. (1985). Movement into reading: Is the first stage of printed word learning visual or phonetic? *Reading Research Quarterly, 20,* 163–179.

Ehri, L. C., & Wilce, L. S. (1986). The influence of spellings on speech: Are alveolar flaps /d/ or /t/? In D. Yaden & S. Templeton (Eds.), *Metalinguistic awareness and beginning literacy* (pp. 101–114). Portsmouth, NH: Heinemann.

Ehri, L. C., & Wilce, L. S. (1987a). Cipher versus cue reading: An experiment in decoding acquisition. *Journal of Educational Psychology, 79,* 3–13.

Ehri, L. C., & Wilce, L. S. (1987b). Does learning to spell help beginners learn to read words? *Reading Research Quarterly, 22,* 47–65.

Einstein, A., & Infeld, L. (1938). *The evolution of physics.* New York: Simon & Schuster.

Elbro, C. (1997). Early linguistic abilities and reading development: A review and a hypothesis about underlying differences in distinctiveness of phonological representations of lexical items. *Reading and Writing, 8,* 453–485.

Elbro, C., Borstrom, I., & Petersen, D. (1998). Predicting dyslexia from kindergarten: The importance of distinctness of phonological representations of lexical items. *Reading Research Quarterly, 33,* 36–60.

Elkind, D. (1987). *Miseducation: Preschoolers at risk.* New York: Knopf.

Ellis, A. W. (1982). Spelling and writing (and reading and speaking). In A. W. Ellis (Ed.), *Normality and pathology in cognitive functions* (pp. 113–146). New York: Academic.

Ellis, A. W. (1984). The cognitive neuropsychology of developmental (and acquired) dyslexia: A critical survey. *Cognitive Neuropsychology, 2,* 169–205.

Ellis, A. W. (1989). *Reading, writing and dyslexia.* Hove, UK: LEA.

Ellis, A. W., Flude, B. M., & Young, A. W. (1987). "Neglect dyslexia" and the early visual processing of letters in words and nonwords. *Cognitive Neuropsychology, 4,* 439–464.

Ellis, A. W., & Monaghan, J. (2002). Reply to Strain, Patterson, and Seidenberg (2002). *Journal of Experimental Psychology: Learning, Memory, and Cognition, 28,* 215–220.

Ellis, A. W., & Young, A. W. (1988). *Human cognitive neuropsychology.* London: Erlbaum.

Ellis, N., & Large, B. (1987). The development of reading: As you seek so you will find. *British Journal of Psychology, 78*, 1–28.

Ellis, N., & Large, B. (1988). The early stages of reading: A longitudinal study. *Applied Cognitive Psychology, 2*, 47–76.

Engbert, R., Longtin, A., & Kliegl, R. (2002). A dynamical model of saccade generation in reading based on spatially distributed lexical processing. *Vision Research, 42*, 621–636.

Entwisle, D. R. (1966). *The word association of young children.* Baltimore: Johns Hopkins University Press.

Entwisle, D. R., & Alexander, K. L. (1995). A parent's economic shadow: Family structure versus family resources as influences on early school achievement. *Journal of Marriage and the Family, 57*, 399–409.

Ericsson, K. A., & Delaney, P. F. (1999). Long-term working memory as an alternative to capacity models of working memory in everyday skilled performance. In A. Miyake & P. Shah (Eds.), *Models of working memory: Mechanisms of active maintenance and executive control* (pp. 257–297). Cambridge: Cambridge University Press.

Ericsson, K. A., & Kintsch, W. (1995). Long-term working memory. *Psychological Review, 102*(2), 211–245.

Ervin, S. M. (1961). Changes with age in the verbal determinants of word association. *American Journal of Psychology, 74*, 361–372.

Esposito, C. (1999). Learning in urban blight: School climate and its effect on the school performance of urban, minority, low-income children. *School Psychology Review, 28*, 365–377.

Evans, G. W., Maxwell, L. E., & Hart, B. (1999). Parental language and verbal responsiveness to children in crowded homes. *Developmental Psychology, 35*, 1020–1023.

Evans, M. A., Shaw, D., & Bell, M. (2000). Home literacy activities and their influence on early literacy skills. *Canadian Journal of Experimental Psychology, 54*, 65–75.

Everatt, J., & Underwood, G. (1992). Parafoveal guidance and priming effects during reading: A special case of the mind being ahead of the eyes. *Consciousness and Cognition, 1*, 186–197.

Evett, L. J., & Humphreys, G. W. (1981). The use of abstract graphemic information in lexical access. *Quarterly Journal of Experimental Psychology, 33A*, 325–350.

Farah, M. J. (1999). Are there orthography-specific brain regions? Neuropsychological and computational investigations. In R. Klein & P. A. McMullen (Eds.), *Converging methods for understanding reading and dyslexia* (pp. 221–243). Cambridge, MA: MIT Press.

Farah, M. J., & Wallace, M. (1991). Pure alexia as a visual impairment: A reconsideration. *Cognitive Neuropsychology, 8*, 313–334.

Faraone, S. V., Tsuang, M. T., & Tsuang, D. W. (1999). *Genetics of mental disorders.* New York: Guilford.

Farmer, M. E., & Klein, R. (1995). The evidence for a temporal processing deficit linked to dyslexia: A review. *Psychonomic Bulletin and Review, 2*(4), 460–493.

Farrar, W. T., & Van Orden, G. C. (2001). Errors as multistable response options. *Nonlinear dynamics, psychology, and life sciences, 5*, 223–265.

Federal Interagency Forum on Child and Family Statistics (2003). *America's children: Key national indicators of well-being.* Retrieved December 8, from http://www.childstats.gov.

Feinberg, T., Dyches-Berke, D., Miner, C. R., & Roane, D. M. (1994). Knowledge, implicit knowledge and metaknowledge in visual agnosia and pure alexia. *Brain, 118*, 789–800.

Feitelson, D., & Goldstein, Z. (1986). Patterns of book ownership and reading to young children in Israeli school-oriented and nonschool-oriented families. *Reading Teacher, 39*, 924–930.

Feldman, L. B. (1987). Phonological and morphological analysis by skilled readers of Serbo-Croatian. In A. Allport, D. MacKay, W. Prinz, & E. Scheerer (Eds.), *Language perception and production* (pp. 198–209). London: Academic.

Feldman, L. B., Kostic, A., Lukatela, G., & Turvey, M. T. (1983). An evaluation of the "Basic Orthographic Syllabic Structure" in a phonologically shallow orthography. *Psychological Research, 45*, 55–72.

Feldman, L. B., & Turvey, M. T. (1980). Words written in Kana are named faster than the same words written in Kanji. *Language and Speech, 23*, 141–147.

Feldman, L. B., & Turvey, M. T. (1983). Word recognition in Serbo-Croatian is phonologically analytic. *Journal of Experimental Psychology: Human Perception and Performance, 9*, 228–298.

Feng, G., Miller, K., Shu, H., & Zhang, H. C. (2004). Orthography and the development of reading processes: An eye-movement study of Chinese and English.

Fera, P., & Besner, D. (1992). The process of lexical decision: More words about a parallel distributed processing model. *Journal of Experimental Psychology: Learning, Memory, and Cognition, 18*, 749–764.

Fernandez-Fein, S., & Baker, L. (1997). Rhyme and alliteration sensitivity and relevant experiences in preschoolers from diverse backgrounds. *Journal of Literacy Research, 29*, 433–459.

Ferrand, L., & Grainger, J. (1992). Phonology and orthography in visual word recognition: Evidence from masked nonword priming. *Quarterly Journal of Experimental Psychology, 42A*, 353–372.

Ferrand, L., & Grainger, J. (1993). The time course of orthographic and phonological code activation in the early phases of visual word recognition. *Bulletin of the Psychonomic Society, 31*, 119–122.

Ferrand, L., & Grainger, J. (1994). Effects of orthography are independent of phonology in masked form priming. *Quarterly Journal of Experimental Psychology, 47A*, 365–382.

Ferrand, L., & Grainger, J. (2003). Homophone interference effects in visual word recognition. *Quarterly Journal of Experimental Psychology Section A: Human Experimental Psychology, 56*, 403–419.

Ferreiro, E., & Teberosky, A. (1982). *Literacy before schooling*. New York: Heinemann.

Feshbach, S., Adelman, H., & Fuller, W. W. (1974). Early identification of children with high risk of reading failure. *Journal of Learning Disabilities, 10*, 49–54.

Feyerabend, P. (1993). *Against method*. New York: Verso.

Fiebach, C. J., Friederici, A. D., Muller, K., & von Cramon, D. Y. (2002). fMRI evidence for dual routes to the mental lexicon in visual word recognition. *Journal of Cognitive Neuroscience, 1*, 11–23.

Field, L. L., & Kaplan, B. J. (1998). Absence of linkage of phonological coding dyslexia to chromosome 6p23-p21.3 in a large family data set. *American Journal of Human Genetics, 63*, 1448–1456.

Fiez, J. A. (2000). Sound and meaning: How native language affects reading strategies. *Nature Neuroscience, 3*, 3–5.

Fiez, J. A., Balota, D. A., Raichle, M. E., & Petersen, S. E. (1999). Effects of lexicality, frequency, and spelling-to-sound consistency on the functional anatomy of reading. *Neuron, 24*, 205–218.

Finucci, J. M. (1978). Genetic considerations in dyslexia. *Progress in Learning Disabilities, 4*, 41–63.

Finucci, J. M., Guthrie, J. T., Childs, A. L., Abbey, H., & Childs, B. (1976). The genetics of specific reading disability. *Annual Review of Human Genetics, 40*, 1–23.

Fischler, I., & Goodman, G. O. (1978). Latency of associative activation in memory. *Journal of Experimental Psychology: Human Perception and Performance, 4*, 455–470.

Fish, M., & Pinkerman, B. (2003). Language skills in low-SES rural Appalachian children: Normative development and individual differences, infancy to preschool. *Applied Developmental Psychology, 23*, 539–565.

Fisher, J. H. (1905). Case of congenital word-blindness. *Ophthalmic Review, 24,* 315.

Fisher, S. E., & DeFries, J. C. (2002). Developmental dyslexia: Genetic dissection of a complex cognitive trait. *Nature Reviews Neuroscience, 3,* 767–780.

Fisher, S. E., Francks, C., Marlow, A. J., MacPhie, I. L., Newbury, D. F., Cardon, L. R., et al. (2002). Independent genome-wide scans identify a chromosome 18 quantitative-trait locus influencing dyslexia. *Nature Genetics, 30,* 86–91.

Fisher, S. E., Marlow, A. J., Lamb, J., Maestrini, E., Williams, D. F., Richardson, A. J., et al. (1999). A quantitative-trait locus on chromosome 6p influences different aspects of developmental dyslexia. *American Journal of Human Genetics, 64,* 146–156.

Fisher, S. E., Vargha-Khadem, F., Watkins, K. E., Monaco, A. P., & Pembrey, M. E. (1998). Localization of a gene implicated in a severe speech and language disorder. *Nature Genetics, 18,* 168–170.

Flesch, R. (1955). *Why Johnny can't read: And what you can do about it.* New York: Harper.

Fletcher J. M., Foorman, B. R., Shaywitz, S. E., & Shaywitz, B. A. (1999). Conceptual and methodological issues in dyslexia research: A lesson for developmental disorders. In H. Tager-Flugsberg (Ed.), *Neurodevelopmental disorders* (pp. 271–306). Cambridge, MA: MIT Press.

Fletcher, J. M., Lyon, G. R., Barnes, M., Steubing, K. K., Francis, D. J., Olson, R. K., et al. (2002). Classification of learning disabilities: An evidenced-based evaluation. In R. Bradley, L. Danielson, & D. Hallahan (Eds.), *Identification of learning disabilities: Research to practice* (pp. 185–250). Mahwah, NJ: Erlbaum.

Fletcher, J. M., Satz, P., & Scholes, R. J. (1981). Developmental changes in the linguistic performance correlates of reading achievement. *Brain and Language, 13,* 78–90.

Fletcher J. M., Shaywitz, S. E., Shankweiler, D. P., Katz, L., Liberman, I. Y., Stuebing, K. K., et al. (1994). Cognitive profiles of reading disability: Comparisons of discrepancy and low achievement definitions. *Journal of Educational Psychology, 86,* 6–23.

Fletcher-Finn, C. M., & Thompson, G. B. (2000). Learning to read with underdeveloped phonemic awareness but lexicalized phonological recoding: A case study of a 3-year-old. *Cognition, 74,* 177–208.

Fletcher-Finn, C. M., & Thompson, G. B. (2004). A mechanism of implicit lexicalized phonological recoding used concurrently with underdeveloped explicit letter-sound skills in both precocious and normal reading development. *Cognition, 90,* 303–335.

Flynn, J., & Rahbar, M. H. (1998). Kindergarten screening for risk of reading failure. *Journal of Psychoeducational Assessment, 16,* 15–35.

Fodor, J. A. (1981). The mind–body problem. *Scientific American, 244,* 114–123.

Foorman, B. R., Francis, D. J., Fletcher, J. M., Schatschneider, C., & Mehta, P. (1998). The role of instruction in learning to read: Preventing reading failure in at-risk children. *Journal of Educational Psychology, 90,* 37–55.

Foorman, B. R., Francis, D. J., Novy, D. M., & Liberman, D. (1991). How letter-sound instruction mediates progress in first-grade reading and spelling. *Journal of Educational Psychology, 83,* 456–469.

Foorman, B. R., Francis, D. R., Shaywitz, S. E., Shaywitz, B. A., & Fletcher, J. M. (1997). The case for early reading intervention. In B. A. Blachman (Ed.), *Foundations of reading acquisition and dyslexia: Implications for early intervention* (pp. 243–264). Mahwah, NJ: Erlbaum.

Foorman, B., & Torgesen, J. K. (2001), Critical elements of classroom and small-group instruction to promote reading success in all children. *Learning Disabilities Research and Practice, 16,* 203–121.

Forster, K. I. (1976). Accessing the mental lexicon. In R. J. Wales & E. Walk (Eds.), *New approaches to language mechanisms* (pp. 257–287). Amsterdam: Elsevier.

Forster, K. I. (1981). Priming and the effects of sentence and lexical context on naming time: Evidence for autonomous lexical processing. *Quarterly Journal of Experimental Psychology, 33A,* 465–495.

Forster, K. I. (1989). Basic issues in lexical processing. In W. Marslen-Wilson (Ed.), *Lexical representation and processing* (pp. 75–107). Cambridge, MA: MIT Press.

Forster, K. I. (1999). Beyond lexical decision: Lexical access in categorization tasks. Paper presented at the fortieth Annual Meeting of the Psychonomic Society, Los Angeles.

Forster, K. I., & Chambers, S. M. (1973). Lexical access and naming time. *Journal of Verbal Learning and Verbal Behavior, 12,* 627–635.

Forster, K. I., & Davis, C. (1984). Repetition priming and frequency attenuation in lexical access. *Journal of Experimental Psychology: Learning, Memory, and Cognition, 10,* 680–698.

Forster, K. I., Davis, C., Schoknecht, C., & Carter, R. (1987). Masked priming with graphemically related forms: Repetition or partial activation? *Quarterly Journal of Experimental Psychology, 39A,* 211–251.

Forster, K. I., & Hector, J. (2002). Cascaded versus noncascaded models of lexical and semantic processing: The *turple* effect. *Memory and Cognition, 30,* 1106–1117.

Forster, K. I., Mohan, K., & Hector, J. (2003). The mechanics of masked priming. In S. Kinoshita & S. J. Lupker (Eds.), *Masked priming: State of the art* (pp. 3–37). Hove, UK: Psychology Press.

Forster, K. I., & Shen, D. (1996). No enemies in the neighborhood: Absence of inhibitory effects in lexical decision and semantic categorization. *Journal of Experimental Psychology: Learning, Memory, and Cognition, 22,* 696–713.

Fowler, A. (1990). Language abilities in children with Down syndrome: Evidence for a specific syntactic delay. In D. Chicchetti and M. Beeghly (Eds.), *Children with Down syndrome: A developmental perspective* (pp. 302–308). Cambridge: Cambridge University Press.

Fowler, A. (1991). How early phonological development might set the stage for phoneme awareness. In S. Brady & D. Shankweiler (Eds.), *Phonological processes in literacy: A tribute to I.Y. Liberman* (pp. 97–117). Hillsdale, NJ: Erlbaum.

Fowler, A. (1995). Linguistic variability in persons with Down syndrome. In L. Nadel & D. Rosenthal (Eds.), *Down syndrome: Living and learning* (pp. 121–131). New York: Wiley-Liss.

Fowler, A., Doherty, B., & Boynton, L. (1995). The basis of reading skill in young adults with Down syndrome. In L. Nadel & D. Rosenthal (Eds.), *Down syndrome: Living and jearning* (pp. 182–196). New York: Wiley-Liss.

Francis, W. N., & Kucera, H. (1982). *Frequency analysis of English usage.* Boston: Houghton-Mifflin.

Francks, C., Fisher, S. E., Olson, R. K., Pennington, B. F., Smith, S. D., DeFries, J. C., et al. (2002). Fine mapping of the chromosome 2p12-16 dyslexia susceptibility locus: Quantitative association analysis and positional candidate genes SEMA4F and OTX1. *Psychiatric Genetics, 12,* 35–41.

Fraser, G. R. (1974). Epidemiology of profound childhood deafness. *Audiology, 13,* 335–341.

Frawley, W. (1992). *Linguistic semantics.* Hillsdale, NJ: Erlbaum.

Frazier, L., & Rayner, K. (1982). Making and correcting errors during sentence comprehension: Eye movements in parsing lexically ambiguous sentences. *Journal of Memory and Language, 14,* 178–210.

Frederiksen, J. R., & Kroll, J. F. (1976). Spelling and sound: Approaches to the internal lexicon. *Journal of Experimental Psychology: Human Perception and Performance, 2,* 361–379.

Friedman, R. B. (1996). Recovery from deep alexia to phonological alexia: Points on a continuum. *Brain and Language, 52,* 114–128.

Frijters, J. C., Barron, R. W., & Brunello, M. (2000). Direct and mediated influences of home literacy and literacy interest on prereaders' oral vocabulary and early written language skill. *Journal of Educational Psychology, 92,* 466–477.

Frith, U. (1980). Unexpected spelling problems. In U. Frith (Ed.), *Cognitive processes in spelling* (pp. 495–515). London: Academic.

Frith, U. (1985). Beneath the surface of developmental dyslexia. In K. E. Patterson, J. C. Marshall, & M. Coltheart (Eds.), *Surface dyslexia: Neuropsychological and cognitive studies of phonological reading* (pp. 301–330). London: Erlbaum.

Frith, U. (1987). The similarities and differences between reading and spelling problems. In J. R. Beech & A. M. Colley (Eds.), *Cognitive approaches to reading* (pp. 453–472). Chichester: Wiley.

Frith, U. (2003). *Autism: Explaining the enigma* (2nd ed.). Oxford: Blackwell.

Frith, U., & Snowling, M. J. (1983). Reading for meaning and reading for sound in autistic and dyslexic children. *British Journal of Developmental Psychology, 1,* 329–342.

Frith, U., Wimmer, H., & Landerl, K. (1998). Differences in phonological recoding in German- and English-speaking children. *Journal of the Society for the Scientific Study of Reading, 2,* 31–54.

Frost, R. (1995). Phonological computation and missing vowels: Mapping lexical involvement in reading. *Journal of Experimental Psychology: Learning, Memory, and Cognition, 21,* 398–408.

Frost, R. (1998). Toward a strong phonological model of reading: True issues and false trails. *Psychological Bulletin, 123,* 71–99.

Frost, R., Ahissar, M., Gotesman, R., & Tayeb, S. (2003). Are phonological effects fragile? The effect of luminance and exposure duration on form priming and phonological priming. *Journal of Memory and Language, 48,* 346–378.

Frost, R., Feldman, L. B., & Katz, L. (1990). Phonological ambiguity and lexical ambiguity: Effects on visual and auditory word recognition. *Journal of Experimental Psychology: Learning, Memory, and Cognition, 16,* 569–580.

Frost, R., & Katz, L. (1989). Orthographic depth and the interaction of visual and auditory processing in word recognition. *Memory and Cognition, 17,* 302–311.

Frost, R., Katz, L., & Bentin, S. (1987). Strategies for visual word recognition and orthographical depth: A multilingual comparison. *Journal of Experimental Psychology: Human Perception and Performance, 13,* 104–115.

Frost, R., & Yogev, O. (2001). Orthographic and phonological computation in visual word recognition: Evidence from backward masking in Hebrew. *Psychonomic Bulletin and Review, 8,* 524–530.

Fulker, D. W., Cherny, S. S., & Cardon, L. R. (1995). Multipoint interval mapping of quantitative trait loci using sib pairs. *American Journal of Human Genetics, 56,* 1224–1233.

Funnell, E. (1996). Response biases in oral reading: An account of the co-occurrence of surface dyslexia and semantic dementia. *Quarterly Journal of Experimental Psychology, 49,* 417–446.

Funnell, E., & Davison, M. (1989). Lexical capture: A developmental disorder of reading and spelling. *Quarterly Journal of Experimental Psychology, 41A,* 471–488.

Fushimi, T., Komori, K., Ikeda, M., Patterson, K., Ijuin, M., & Tanabe, H. (2003). Surface dyslexia in a Japanese patient with semantic dementia: Evidence for similarity-based orthography-to-phonology translation. *Neuropsychologia, 41,* 1644–1658.

Garner, C. L., & Raudenbush, S. W. (1991). Neighborhood effects on educational attainment: A multilevel analysis. *Sociology of Education, 64,* 251–262.

Garner, R. (1980). Monitoring of understanding: An investigation of good and poor readers' awareness of induced miscomprehension of text. *Journal of Reading Behavior, 12,* 5–63.

Garnham, A. (1981). Mental models as representations of text. *Memory and Cognition, 9,* 560–565.

Garnham, A. (2001). *Mental models and the interpretation of anaphor.* Hove, UK: Psychology Press.

Garrod, S., & Terras, M. (2000). The contribution of lexical and situational knowledge to resolving discourse roles: Bonding and resolution. *Journal of Memory and Language, 42,* 526–544.

Gaskins, I., Ehri, L. C., Cress, C., O'Hara, C., & Donnelly, K. (1996). *Procedures for word learning: Making discoveries about words. Reading Teacher, 50,* 312–327.

Gathercole, S. E., & Baddeley, A. D. (1990). Phonological memory deficits in language disordered children: Is there a connection? *Journal of Memory and Language, 29,* 336–360.

Gathercole, S. E., & Martin, A. J. (1996). Interactive processes in phonological memory. In S. E. Gathercole (Ed.), *Models of short-term memory* (pp. 73–100). Hove, UK: Psychology Press.

Gathercole, S. E., Willis, C., Baddeley, A. D., & Emslie, H. (1994). The children's test of nonword repetition: A test of phonological working memory. *Memory, 2,* 103–127.

Gayan, J., & Olson, R. K. (2001). Genetic and environmental influences on orthographic and phonological skills in children with reading disabilities. *Developmental Neuropsychology, 20*(2), 487–511.

Gayan, J., & Olson, R. K. (2003). Genetic and environmental influences on individual differences in printed word recognition. *Journal of Experimental Child Psychology, 84,* 97–123.

Gayan, J., Smith, S. D., Cherny, S. S., Cardon, L. R., Fulker, D. W., Brower, A. M., et al. (1999). Quantitative-trait locus for specific language and reading deficits on chromosome 6p. *American Journal of Human Genetics, 64,* 157–164.

Gerhand, S. (2001). Routes to reading: a report of a non-semantic reader with equivalent performance on regular and irregular words. *Neuropsychologia, 39,* 193–208.

Gerhand, S., & Barry, C. (2000). When does a deep dyslexic make a semantic error? The roles of age-of-acquisition, concreteness, and frequency. *Brain and Language, 74,* 26–47.

Gernsbacher, M. A. (1990). *Language comprehension as structure building.* Hillsdale, NJ: Erlbaum.

Gernsbacher, M. A., & Faust, M. E. (1991). The mechanism of suppression: A component of general comprehension skill. *Journal of Experimental Psychology: Learning, Memory, and Cognition, 17,* 245–262.

Gernsbacher, M. M., Varner, K. R., & Faust, M. E. (1990). Investigating individual differences in general comprehension skill. *Journal of Experimental Psychology: Learning, Memory, and Cognition, 16,* 430–445.

Geschwind, N. (1965). Disconnection syndromes in animals and man. *Brain, 88,* 237–294.

Getman, G. N. (1985). A commentary on vision. *Journal of Learning Disabilities, 18,* 505–511.

Geva, E., Wade-Wooley, L., & Shaney, M. (1993). The concurrent development of spelling and decoding in two different orthographies. *Journal of Reading Behavior, 25,* 383–406.

Gibbs, P., & Van Orden, G. C. (1998). Pathway selection's utility for control of word recognition. *Journal of Experimental Psychology: Human Perception and Performance, 24,* 1162–1187.

Gibson, C. (1988). The impact of early developmental history on cerebral asymmetries: Implications for reading ability in deaf children. In D. L. Molfese & S. J. Sagalowitz (Eds.), *Brain lateralization in children: Developmental implications* (pp. 591–604). New York: Guilford.

Giles, D. C., & Terrell, C. D. (1997). Visual sequential memory and spelling ability. *Educational Psychology, 17,* 245–253.

Gilger, J. W., Borecki, I. B., & Pennington, B. F. (1994). Commingling and segregation analysis of reading performance in families of normal reading. *Behavior Genetics, 24,* 345–355.

Glaser, W. R., & Glaser, M. O. (1989). Context effects in stroop-like word and picture processing. *Journal of Experimental Psychology General, 118,* 13–42.

Glenberg, A. M., Kruley, P., & Langston, W. E. (1994). Analogical processes in comprehension: Simulation of a mental model. In M. A. Gernsbacher (Ed.), *Handbook of psycholinguistics* (pp. 609–640). San Diego, CA: Academic.

Glosser, G., & Friedman, R. B. (1990). The continuum of deep/phonological alexia. *Cortex, 26,* 343–359.

Glushko, R. J. (1979). The organization and activation of orthographic knowledge in reading aloud. *Journal of Experimental Psychology: Human Perception and Performance, 5,* 674–691.

Godfrey, J. J., Syral-Lasky, A. K., Millay, K., & Knox, C. M. (1981). Performance of dyslexic children on speech perception tests. *Journal of Experimental Child Psychology, 32,* 401–424.

Gold, E. M. (1967). Language identification in the limit. *Information and Control, 16,* 447–474.

Goldin-Meadow, S., & Mayberry, R. I. (2001). How do profoundly deaf children learn to read? Learning disabilities research and practice. *Emergent and Early Literacy: Current Status and Research Directions, Special Issue, 16,* 221–228.

Goldman, S. R., Saul, E. U., & Coté, N. (1995). Paragraphing, reader, and task effects on discourse comprehension. *Discourse Processes, 20,* 273–305.

Gombert, J. E. (1992). *Metalinguistic development.* London: Harvester-Wheatsheaf.

Goodman, K. S. (1965). A linguistic study of cues and miscues in reading. *Elementary English, 42,* 639–643.

Goodman, K. S. (1967). Reading: A psycholinguistic guessing game. *Journal of the Reading Specialist, 6,* 126–135.

Goodman, K. S. (1968). *The psycholinguistic nature of the reading process.* Detroit: Wayne State University Press.

Goodman, K. S. (1970). Behind the eye: What happens in reading. In K. Goodman & O. Niles (Eds.), *Reading: Process and program* (pp. 3–38). Urbana, IL: National Council of Teachers of English.

Goodman, K. S. (1976). Reading: A psycholinguistic guessing game. In H. Singer & R. Ruddell (Eds.), *Theoretical models and processes of reading* (2nd ed., pp. 497–508). Newark, DE: International Reading Association.

Goodman, K. S. (1986). *What's whole in whole language?* Portsmouth, NH: Heinemann.

Goodman, K. S. (1993). *Phonics phacts.* Portsmouth, NH: Heinemann.

Goodman, Y., & Altwerger, B. (1981). *Print awareness in preschool children: A working paper. A study of the development of literacy in preschool children.* Occasional Papers No. 4, Program in Language and Literacy, University of Arizona.

Goodman, K. S., & Goodman, Y. M. (1979). Learning to read is natural. In L. B. Resnick & P. A. Weaver (Eds.), *Theory and practice of early reading* (Vol 1., pp. 137–154). Hillsdale, NJ: Erlbaum.

Goodman-Shulman, R. A., & Caramazza, A. (1986). Aspects of the spelling process: Evidence from a case of acquired dysgraphia. *Language and Cognitive Processes, 1,* 263–296.

Goodman-Shulman, R. A., & Caramazza, A. (1987). Patterns of dysgraphia and the nonlexical spelling process. *Cortex, 123,* 143–148.

Gordon, P. C., & Chan, D. (1995). Pronouns, passives, and discourse coherence. *Journal of Memory and Language, 34,* 216–231.

Gordon, P. C., & Scearce, K. A. (1995). Pronominalization and discourse coherence, discourse structure and pronoun interpretation. *Memory and Cognition, 23,* 313–323.

Goswami, U. (1986). Children's use of analogy in learning to read: A developmental study. *Journal of Experimental Child Psychology, 42,* 73–83.

Goswami, U. (1988). Orthographic analogies and reading development. *Quarterly Journal of Experimental Psychology, 40,* 239–268.

Goswami, U. (2001). Early phonological development and the acquisition of literacy. In S. B. Neuman & D. K. Dickinson (Eds.), *Handbook of early literacy research* (pp. 111–125). New York: Guilford.

Goswami, U., & Bryant, P. E. (1990). *Phonological skills and learning to read.* Hove, UK: Psychology Press.

Goswami, U., Gombert, J. E., & de Barrera, L. F. (1998). Children's orthographic representations and linguistic transparency: Nonsense word reading in English, French and Spanish. *Applied Psycholinguistics, 19,* 19–52.

Goswami, U., Porpodas, C., & Wheelwright, S. (1997). Children's orthographic representations in English and Greek. *European Journal of Psychology of Education, 12,* 273–292.

Goswami, U., Ziegler, J. C., Dalton, L., & Schneider, W. (2003). Nonword reading across orthographies: How flexible is the choice of reading units? *Applied Psycholinguistics, 24,* 235–247.

Gottardo, A., Stanovich, K. E., & Siegal, L. S. (1996). The relationships between phonological sensitivity, syntactic processing and verbal working memory in the reading performance of third-grade children. *Journal of Educational Psychology, 63,* 563–582.

Gottardo, A., Yan, B., Siegel, L. S., & Wade-Woolley, L. (2001). Factors related to English reading performance in children with Chinese as a first language: More evidence of cross-language transfer of phonological processing. *Journal of Educational Psychology, 93,* 530–542.

Gottlob, L. R., Goldinger, S. D., Stone, G. O., & Van Orden, G. C. (1999). Reading homographs: Orthographic, phonologic, and semantic dynamics. *Journal of Experimental Psychology: Human Perception and Performance, 25,* 561–574.

Gottlob, L. R., Goldinger, S. D., Stone, G. O., & Van Orden, G. C. (1999). Reading homographs: Orthographic, phonologic, and semantic dynamics. *Journal of Experimental Psychology: Human Perception and Performance, 25,* 561–574.

Gough, P. B. (1972). One second of reading. In J. P. Kavanagh, & I. G. Mattingly (Eds.), *Language by ear and by eye* (pp. 331–358). Cambridge, MA: MIT Press.

Gough, P. B. (1981). A comment on Kenneth Goodman. In M. L. Kamil (Ed.), *Directions in reading: Research and instruction* (pp. 92–95). Washington, DC: National Reading Conference.

Gough, P. B. (1983). Context, form, and interaction. In K. Rayner (Ed.), *Eye movements in reading: Perceptual and language processes* (pp. 203–211). New York: Academic.

Gough, P. B. (1984). Word recognition. In P. D. Pearson, R. Barr, M. L. Kamil, & P. Mosenthal (Eds.), *Handbook of reading research* (pp. 225–253). New York: Longman.

Gough, P. B., Alford, J. A., Jr., & Holley-Wilcox, P. (1981). Words and contexts. In O. J. L. Tzeng & H. Singer (Eds.), *Perception of print: Reading research in experimental psychology* (pp. 85–102). Hillsdale, NJ: Erlbaum.

Gough, P. B., & Hillinger, M. L. (1980). Learning to read: An unnatural act. *Bulletin of the Orton Society, 30,* 179–196.

Gough, P. B., Hoover, W. A., & Peterson, C. L. (1996). Some observations on the simple view of reading. In C. Cornoldi and J. V. Oakhill (Eds.), *Reading comprehension difficulties* (pp. 1–13). Mahwah, NJ: Erlbaum.

Gough, P. B., Juel, C., & Griffith, P. L. (1992). Reading, spelling, and the orthographic cipher. In P. B. Gough, L. C. Ehri, & R. Treiman (Eds.), *Reading acquisition* (pp. 35–48). Hillsdale, NJ: Erlbaum.

Gough, P. B., & Tunmer, W. E. (1986). Decoding, reading and reading disability. *Remedial and Special Education, 7,* 6–10.

Goulandris, N. K. (Ed.) (2003). *Dyslexia in different languages: Cross-linguistic comparisons.* London: Whurr.

Goulandris, N. K., & Snowling, M. (1991). Visual memory deficits: A plausible cause of developmental dyslexia? Evidence from a single case study. *Cognitive Neuropsychology, 8(2),* 127–154.

Graesser, A. C. (1981). *Prose comprehension beyond the word*. New York: Springer.

Graesser, A. C., & Kreuz, R. J. (1993). A theory of inference generation during text comprehension. *Discourse Processes, 16*, 146–160.

Graesser, A. C., Singer, M., & Trabasso, T. (1994). Construction inferences during narrative comprehension. *Psychological Review, 101*, 371–395.

Graham, K. S., Hodges, J. R., & Patterson, K. E. (1994). The relationship between comprehension and oral reading in progressive fluent aphasia. *Neuropsychologia, 32*, 299–316.

Grainger, J. (1990). Word frequency and neighborhood frequency effects in lexical decision and naming. *Journal of Memory and Language, 29*, 228–244.

Grainger, J., & Jacobs, A. M. (1996). Orthographic processing in visual word recognition: A multiple read-out model. *Psychological Review, 103*, 518–565.

Grainger, J., O'Regan, J. K., Jacobs, A. M., & Segui, J. (1989). On the role of competing word units in visual word recognition: The neighborhood frequency effect. *Perception and Psychophysics, 45*, 189–195.

Gredler, G. R. (1997). Issues in early childhood screening and assessment. *Psychology in the Schools, 34*, 99–106.

Greenberg, M. T., Lengua, L. J., Coie, J. D., & Pinderhughes, E. E. (1999). Predicting developmental outcomes at school entry using a multiple-risk model: Four American communities. *Developmental Psychology, 35*, 403–417.

Greene, S. B., McKoon, G., & Ratcliff, R. (1992). Pronoun resolution and discourse models. *Journal of Experimental Psychology: Learning, Memory, and Cognition, 18*, 266–283.

Griffin, E. A., & Morrison, F. J. (1997). The unique contribution of home literacy environment to differences in early literacy skills. *Early Childhood Development and Care, 127–128*, 233–243.

Griffiths, Y. M., & Snowling, M. J. (2001). Auditory word identification and phonological skills in dyslexic and average readers. *Applied Psycholinguistics, 22*, 419–439.

Griffiths, Y. M., & Snowling, M. J. (2002). Predictors of exception word and nonword reading in dyslexic children: The severity hypothesis. *Journal of Educational Psychology, 94*(1), 34–43.

Grigorenko, E. L. (2001). Developmental dyslexia: An update on genes, brains, and environment. *Journal of Child Psychology and Psychiatry, 42*, 91–125.

Grigorenko, E. L., Klin, A., & Volkmar, F. (2003). Annotation: Hyperlexia: disability or superability? *Journal of Child Psychology and Psychiatry, 44*, 1079–1091.

Grigorenko, E. L., Wood, F. B., Meyer, M. S., Hart, L. A., Speed, W. C., Shuster, A., et al. (1997). Susceptibility loci for distinct components of developmental dyslexia on chromosome 6 and 15. *American Journal of Human Genetics, 60*, 27–39.

Grigorenko, E. L., Wood, F. B., Meyer, M. S., & Pauls, D. L. (2000). Chromosome 6p influences on different dyslexia–related cognitive processes: Further confirmation. *American Journal of Human Genetics, 66*(2), 715–723.

Gronau, N., & Frost, R. (1997). Prelexical phonologic computation in a deep orthography: Evidence from backward masking in Hebrew. *Psychonomic Bulletin and Review, 4*, 107–112.

Grossberg, S., & Stone, G. O. (1986). Neural dynamics of word recognition and recall: Priming, learning, and resonance. *Psychological Review, 93*, 46–74.

Grossi, G., Coch, D., Coffey-Corina, S., Holcomb, P. J., & Neville, H. J. (2001). Phonological processing in visual rhyming: A developmental ERP study. *Journal of Cognitive Neuroscience, 13*(5), 610–625.

Gutierrez, J., Sameroff, A. J., & Karrer, B. M. (1988). Acculturation and SES effects on Mexican-American parents' concepts of development. *Child Development, 59*, 250–255.

Guttentag, R., & Haith, M. (1978). Automatic processing as a function of age and reading ability. *Child Development, 49*, 707–716.

Hacker, D. J. (1997). Comprehension monitoring of written discourse across early-to-middle adolescence. *Reading and Writing, 9*, 207–240.

Haenggi, D., Kintsch, W., & Gernsbacher, M. A. (1995). Spatial situation models and text comprehension. *Discourse Processes, 19*, 173–199.

Hage, C., Alegria, J., & Périer, O. (1991). Cued Speech and language acquisition: The case of grammatical gender morpho-phonology. In D. S. Martin (Ed.), *Advances in cognition, education and deafness* (pp. 395–399). Washington, DC: Gallaudet University Press.

Hagoort, P., Brown, C., Indefrey, P., Herzog, H., Steinmetz, H., & Seitz, R. (1999). The neural circuitry involved in the reading of German words and pseudowords: A PET study. *Journal of Cognitive Neuroscience, 11*, 383–398.

Halle, T. G., Kurtz-Costes, B., & Mahoney, J. L. (1997). Family influences on school achievement in low-income, African American children. *Journal of Educational Psychology, 89*, 527–537.

Hallgren, B. (1950). Specific dyslexia (congenital word-blindness): A clinical and genetic study. *Acta Psychiatrica et Neurologica Supplement, 65*, 1–287.

Hammer, C. S. (2001). "Come sit down and let Mama read": Book reading interactions between African American mothers and their infants. In J. L. Harris, A. G. Kamhi, & K. E. Pollock (Eds.), *Literacy in African American communities* (pp. 21–43). Mahwah, NJ: Erlbaum.

Hammer, C. S., Miccio, A. W., & Wagstaff, D. A. (2003). Home literacy experiences and their relationship to bilingual preschoolers' developing English literacy abilities: An initial investigation. *Language, Speech, and Hearing Services in the Schools, 34*, 20–30.

Hammill, D. D. (1990). On defining learning disabilities: An emerging consensus. *Journal of Learning Disabilities, 23*, 74–84.

Hanley, J. R., & Gard, F. (1995). A dissociation between surface and phonological dyslexia in 2 undergraduate students. *Neuropsychologia, 33*(7), 909–914.

Hanley, J. R., Hastie, K., & Kay, J. (1992). Developmental surface dyslexia and dysgraphia: An orthographic processing impairment. *Quarterly Journal of Experimental Psychology, 44A*(2), 285–319.

Hanley, J. R., & Kay, J. (1992). Does letter by letter reading involve the spelling system? *Neuropsychologia, 30*, 237–256.

Hannon, B., & Daneman, M. (2001). A new tool for measuring and understanding individual differences in the component processes of reading comprehension. *Journal of Educational Psychology, 93*, 103–128.

Hanson, V. L. (1982). Use of orthographic structure by deaf adults: Recognition of fingerspelled words. *Applied PsycholinguistiCued Speech, 3*, 343–356.

Hanson, V. L. (1986). Access to spoken language and the acquisition of orthographic structure: Evidence from deaf readers. *Quarterly Journal of Experimental Psychology, 38A*, 193–212.

Hanson, V. L. (1989). Phonology and reading: Evidence from profoundly deaf readers. In D. Shankweiler & I. Liberman (Eds.), *Phonology and reading disabilities* (pp. 69–89). Ann Arbor: University of Michigan Press.

Hanson, V. L., & Fowler, C. (1987). Phonological coding in word reading: Evidence from deaf and hearing readers. *Memory and Cognition, 15*, 199–207.

Hanson, V. L., Goodell, E. W., & Perfetti, C. A. (1991). Tongue-twister effects in the silent reading of hearing and deaf college students. *Journal of Memory and Language, 30*, 319–330.

Hanson, V. L., & McGarr, N. S. (1989). Rhyme generation by deaf adults. *Journal of Speech and Hearing Research, 32*, 2–11.

Hanson, V. L., Shankweiler, D., & Fischer, F. W. (1983). Determinants of spelling ability in deaf and hearing adults: Access to linguistic structure. *Cognition, 14*, 323–344.

Happé, F. G. E. (1997). Central coherence and theory of mind in autism: Reading homographs in context. *British Journal of Developmental Psychology 15*, 1–12.

Harlaar, N., Spinath, F. M., Dale, P. S., & Plomin, R. (in press). Genetic influences on word recognition abilities and disabilities: A study of 7 year old twins. *Journal of Child Psychology and Psychiatry.*

Harm, M. W., McCandliss, B. D., & Seidenberg, M. S. (2003). Modeling the successes and failures of interventions for disabled readers. *Scientific Studies of Reading, 7*(2), 155–183.

Harm, M. W., & Seidenberg, M. S. (1999). Phonology, reading acquisition and dyslexia: Insights from connectionist models. *Psychological Review, 106,* 491–528.

Harm, M. W., & Seidenberg, M. S. (2001). Are there orthographic impairments in phonological dyslexia? *Cognitive Neuropsychology, 18,* 71–92.

Harm, M. W., & Seidenberg, M. S. (2004). Computing the meanings of words in reading: Cooperative division of labor between visual and phonological processes. *Psychological Review, 111*(3), 662–720.

Harris, A., & Jacobson, M. (1982). *Basic reading vocabularies.* New York: Macmillan.

Harris, J. L. (2003). Toward an understanding of literacy issues in multicultural school-age populations. *Language, Speech, and Hearing Services in the Schools, 34,* 17–19.

Harris, M., & Beech, J. R. (1998). Implicit phonological awareness and early reading development in prelingually deaf children. *Journal of Deaf Studies and Deaf Education, 3*(3), 205–216.

Harris, M., & Hatano, G. (1999). Introduction: A cross-linguistic perspective on learning to read and write. In M. Harris & G. Hatano (Eds.), *Learning to read and write: A cross-linguistic perspective* (pp. 1–9). Cambridge: Cambridge University Press.

Harste, J., Burke, C., & Woodward, V. (1982). Children's language and world: Initial encounters with print. In J. Langer & M. Smith-Burke (Eds.), *Bridging the gap: Reader meets author* (pp. 105–131). Newark, DE: International Reading Association.

Hart, B., & Risley, T. R. (1992). American parenting of language-learning children: Persisting differences in family–child interactions observed in natural home environments. *Developmental Psychology, 28,* 1096–1105.

Hart, B., & Risley, T. R. (1995a). *Learning to talk.* Baltimore: Brookes.

Hart, B., & Risley, T. R. (1995b). *Meaningful differences in the everyday experiences of young American children.* Baltimore: Brookes.

Hasson, U., Levy, I., Behrman, M., Hendler, T., & Malach, R. (2002). Eccentricity bias as an organizing principle for human higher-order object areas. *Neuron, 34,* 479–490.

Hatcher, P., Hulme, C. and Ellis, A. W. (1994). Ameliorating early reading failure by integrating the teaching of reading and phonological skills: The phonological linkage hypothesis. *Child Development, 65,* 41–57.

Hatcher, P. J., Hulme, C., & Snowling, M. J. (2004). Explicit phonological training combined with reading instruction helps young children at risk of reading failure. *Journal of Child Psychology and Psychiatry, 45,* 338–358.

Hatcher, J., Snowling, M. J., & Griffiths, Y. M. (2002). Cognitive assessment of dyslexic students in higher education. *British Journal of Educational Psychology, 72,* 119–133.

Hatfield, F. M., & Patterson, K. E. (1983). Phonological spelling. *Quarterly Journal of Experimental Psychology, 35A,* 451–458.

Hauser-Cram, P., Sirin, S. R., & Stipek, D. (2003). When teachers; and parents' values differ: Teachers' ratings of academic competence in children from low-income families. *Journal of Educational Psychology, 95,* 813–820.

Healy, J. M. (1982). The enigma of hyperlexia. *Reading Research Quarterly 7,* 319–338.

Hebb, D. O. (1949). *The organization of behavior: A neuropsychological theory.* New York: Wiley.

Hecht, S. A., Burgess, S. R., Torgesen, J. K., Wagner, R. K., & Rashotte, C. A. (2000). Explaining social class differences in growth of reading skills from beginning kindergarten through fourth-grade: The role of phonological awareness, rate of access, and print knowledge. *Reading and Writing, 12,* 99–127.

Henderson, J. M., Dixon, P., Peterson, A., Twilley, L. C., & Ferreira, F. (1995). Evidence for the use of phonological representations during trans saccadic word recognition. *Journal of Experimental Psychology: Human Perception and Performance, 21,* 82–97.

Henderson, J. M., & Ferreira, F. (1993). Eye movement control during reading: Fixation measures reflect foveal but not parafoveal processing difficulty. *Canadian Journal of Experimental Psychology, 47,* 201–221.

Henry M. (2003). *Unlocking literacy: Effective decoding and spelling instruction.* Baltimore: Brookes.

Herbster, A. N., Mintun, M. A., Nebes, R. D., & Becker, J. T. (1997). Regional cerebral blood flow during word and nonword reading. *Human Brain Mapping, 5*(2), 84–92.

Hermann, K. (1959). *Reading disability.* Copenhagen: Munksgaard.

Hess, R. D., Holloway, S. D., Dickson, W. P., & Price, G. P. (1984). Maternal variables as predictors of children's school readiness and later achievement in vocabulary and mathematics in sixth grade. *Child Development, 55,* 1902–1912.

Hess, T. M., & Radtke, R. C. (1981). Processing and memory factors in children's comprehension skill. *Child Development, 52,* 479–488.

Hill, N. E. (2001). Parenting and academic socialization as they relate to school readiness: The role of ethnicity and family income. *Journal of Educational Psychology, 93,* 686–697.

Hillis, A. E., & Caramazza, A. (1991). Category-specific naming and comprehension impairment: A double dissociation. *Brain, 114,* 2081–2094.

Hillis, A. E., Rapp, B., & Caramazza, A. (1999). When a rose is a rose in speech but a tulip in writing. *Cortex, 35,* 337–356.

Hindson, B. A. (2001). Linguistic and cognitive characteristics of preschoolers at risk for developmental reading disability. PhD dissertation, University of New England, Armidale, Australia.

Hines, D., Czerwinski, M., Sawyer, P. K., & Dwyer, M. (1986). Automatic semantic priming: Effect of category exemplar level and word association level. *Journal of Experimental Psychology: Human Perception and Performance, 12,* 370–379.

Hino, Y., & Lupker, S. J. (1996). Effects of polysemy in lexical decision and naming: An alternative to lexical access accounts. *Journal of Experimental Psychology: Human Perception and Performance, 22,* 1331–1356.

Hino, Y., & Lupker, S. J. (2003). Number-of-meanings and relatedness-of-meanings effects in lexical decision: Does the relatedness of the multiple meanings matter? Presented at the forty-fourth Annual Meeting of the Psychonomic Society, Vancouver, BC.

Hino, Y., Lupker, S. J., & Pexman, P. M. (2001). *Effects of polysemy and relatedness of meanings in lexical decision and semantic categorization tasks.* Presented at the forty-second Annual Meeting of the Psychonomic Society, Orlando, FL.

Hino, Y., Lupker, S. J., & Pexman, P. M. (2002). Ambiguity and synonymy effects in lexical decision, naming, and semantic categorization tasks: Interaction between orthography, phonology, and semantics. *Journal of Experimental Psychology: Learning, Memory, and Cognition, 28,* 686–713.

Hino, Y., Lupker, S. J., Sears, C. R., & Ogawa, T. (1998). The effects of polysemy for Japanese katakana words. *Reading and Writing, 10,* 395–424.

Hinshelwood, J. (1900). Congenital word blindness. *Lancet, 1,* 1506–1508.

Hinshelwood, J. (1907). Four cases of congenital word-blindness occurring in the same family. *British Medical Journal, 2,* 1229–1232.

Hinshelwood, J. (1911). Two cases of hereditary word-blindness. *British Medical Journal, 1,* 608–609.

Hinshelwood, J. (1917). *Congenital word blindness.* London: Lewis.

Hinton, G. E., McClelland, J. L., & Rumelhart, D. E. (1986). Distributed representations. In D. E. Rumelhart & J. L. McClelland (Eds.), *Parallel distributed processing: Explorations in the microstructure of cognition* (Vol. 1, pp. 282–317). Cambridge, MA: MIT Press.

Hinton, G. E., & Sejnowski, T. J. (1986). Learning and relearning in Boltzmann Machines. In D. E. Rumelhart, J. L. McClelland, & the PDP Research Group (Eds.), *Parallel distributed processing: Explorations in the microstructure of cognition.* Vol. 1: *Foundations* (pp. 282–317). Cambridge, MA: MIT Press.

Hinton, G. E., & Shallice, T. (1991). Lesioning an attractor network: Investigations of acquired dyslexia. *Psychological Review, 98*, 74–95.

Ho, C. S.-H. (1997). The importance of phonological awareness and verbal short-term memory to children's success in learning to read Chinese. *Psychologia, 40*, 211–219.

Ho, C. S. H., & Bryant, P. (1997a). Learning to read Chinese beyond the logographic phase. *Reading Research Quarterly, 32*, 276–289.

Ho, C. S.-H, & Bryant, P. (1997b). Phonological skills are important in learning to read Chinese. *Developmental Psychology, 33*(6), 946–951.

Ho, C. S.-H., & Bryant, P. (1997c). Development of phonological awareness of Chinese children in Hong Kong. *Journal of Psycholinguistic Research, 26*, 109–126.

Ho, C. S.-H., Chan, D. W.-O., Lee, S.-H., Tsang, S.-M., & Luan, V. H. (2004). Cognitive profiling and preliminary subtyping in Chinese developmental dyslexia. *Cognition, 91*, 43–75.

Ho, C. S.-H., Chan, D. W.-O., Tsang, S.-M., & Suk-Han, L. (2002). The cognitive profile and multiple-deficit hypothesis in Chinese developmental dyslexia. *Developmental Psychology, 38*, 543–553.

Ho, C. S.-H., Law, T. P.-S., & Ng, P. M. (2000). The phonological deficit hypothesis in Chinese developmental dyslexia. *Reading and Writing, 13*, 57–79.

Ho, C. S.-H., & Ma, R. N. L. (1999). Training in phonological strategies improves Chinese dyslexic children's character reading skills. *Journal of Research in Reading, 22*, 131–142.

Ho, C. S.-H., Wong, W. L., & Chan, W. S. (1999). The use of orthographic analogies in learning to read Chinese. *Journal of Child Psychology and Psychiatry, 40*, 393–403.

Hodges, J. R., Patterson, K., Oxbury, S., & Funnell, E. (1992). Semantic dementia: Progressive fluent aphasia with temporal lobe atrophy. *Brain, 115*, 1783–1806.

Hodges, J., Salmon, D., & Butters, N. (1992). Semantic memory impairment in Alzheimer's disease: Failure of access or degraded knowledge? *Neuropsychologia, 30*, 301–314.

Hoemann, H. W., Andrews, C. E., Florian, V. A., Hoeman, S. A., & Jensema, C. J. (1976). The spelling proficiency of deaf children. *American Annals of the Deaf, 121*, 489–493.

Hoff, E. (2003). Causes and consequences of SES-related differences in parent-to-child speech. In M. H. Bornstein & R. H. Bradley (Eds.), *Socioeconomic status, parenting, and child development* (pp. 147–160). Mahwah, NJ: Erlbaum.

Hoff-Ginsberg, E. (1991). Mother–child conversation in different social classes and communicative settings. *Child Development, 62*, 782–796.

Hohnen, B., & Stevenson, J. (1999). The structure of genetic influences on general cognitive, language, phonological, and reading abilities. *Developmental Psychology, 35*, 590–603.

Holden, J. (2002). Fractal characteristics of response time variability. *Ecological Psychology, 14*, 53–86.

Holm, A., & Dodd, B. (1996). The effect of first written language on the acquisition of English literacy. *Cognition, 59*, 119–147.

Holmes, V. M., & Carruthers, J. (1998). The relation between reading and spelling in skilled adult readers. *Journal of Memory and Language, 39*, 264–289.

Holmes, V. M., & Castles, A. E. (2001). Unexpectedly poor spelling in university students. *Scientific Studies of Reading, 5*(4), 319–350.

Holmes, V. M., & Ng, E. (1993). Word-specific knowledge, word-recognition strategies, and spelling ability. *Journal of Memory and Language, 32*, 230–257.

Holmes, V. M., & Standish, J. M. (1996). Skilled reading with impaired phonology: A case study. *Cognitive Neuropsychology. 13*, 1207–1222.

Hooper, D. A., & Paap, K. R. (1997). The use of assembled phonology during performance of a letter recognition task and its dependence on the presence and proportion of word stimuli. *Journal of Memory and Language, 37*, 167–189.

Hooper. S. R., & Willis, W. G. (1989). Learning disability subtyping: Neuropsychological foundations, conceptual models, and issues in clinical differentiation. New York: Springer-Verlag.

Hoover, W. A., & Gough, P. B. (1990). The simple view of reading. *Reading and Writing, 2,* 127–160.

Horikoshi, T., Asari, Y., Watanabe, A., Nagaseki, Y., Nukui, H., Sasaki, H., & Komiya, K. (1997). Music alexia in a patient with mild pure alexia: Disturbed visual perception of nonverbal meaningful figures. *Cortex, 33,* 187–194.

Horn, W. F., & O'Donnell, J. P. (1984). Early identification of learning disabilities: A comparison of two methods. *Journal of Educational Psychology, 76,* 1106–1118.

Horwitz, B., Rumsey, J. M., & Donohue, B. C. (1998). Functional connectivity of the angular gyrus in normal reading and dyslexia. *Proceedings of the National Academy of Sciences, USA, 95,* 8939–8944.

Hoskyn, M., & Swanson, H. L. (2000). Cognitive processing of low achievers and children with reading disabilities: A selective meta-analytic review of the published literature. *School Psychology Review, 29,* 102–119.

Houghton, G., Glasspool, D., & Shallice, T. (1994). Spelling and serial recall: Insights from a competitive queueing model. In G. D. A. Brown & N. C. Ellis (Eds.), *Handbook of spelling: Theory, process and intervention* (pp. 365–404). Chichester: Wiley.

Howard, D., & Best, W. (1996). Developmental phonological dyslexia: Real word reading can be completely normal. *Cognitive Neuropsychology, 13,* 887–934.

Howard, D., & Patterson, K. (1992). *Pyramids and palm trees: A test of semantic access from pictures and words.* Bury St. Edmunds, UK: Thames Valley.

Howlin, P., Davies, M., & Udwin, O. (1998). Cognitive functioning in adults with Williams syndrome. *Journal of Child Psychology and Psychiatry, 39,* 183–189.

Hu, C. F., & Catts, H. W. (1998). The role of phonological processing in early reading ability: What can we learn from Chinese? *Scientific Studies of Reading, 2,* 55–79.

Huang, H. S., & Hanley, J. R. (1994). Phonological awareness and visual skills in learning to read Chinese and English. *Cognition, 54,* 73–98.

Huang, H. S., & Hanley, J. R. (1995). Phonological awareness and visual skills in learning to read Chinese and English. *Cognition, 54,* 73–98.

Huang, H. S., & Hanley, J. R. (1997). A longitudinal study of phonological awareness, visual skills, and Chinese reading acquisition among first-graders in Taiwan. *International Journal of Behavioral Development, 20*(2), 249–268.

Huang, H. S., & Zhang, H. R. (1997). An investigation of phonemic awareness, word awareness and tone awareness among dyslexic children. *Bulletin of Special Education and Rehabilitation, 5,* 125–138.

Hubbs-Tait, L., Culp, A. M., Huey, E., Culp, R., Starost, H. J., & Hare, C. (2002). Relation of Head Start attendance to children's cognitive and social outcomes: Moderation by family risk. *Early Childhood Research Quarterly, 17,* 539–558.

Huey, E. B. (1908/1979/1968). *The psychology and pedagogy of reading* (5th ed.). Cambridge, MA: MIT Press.

Hulme, C. (1988). The implausibility of low-level visual deficits as a cause of children's reading difficulties. *Cognitive Neuropsychology, 5,* 369–374.

Hulme, C. (2002). Phonemes, rimes and the mechanisms of early reading development. *Journal of Experimental Child Psychology, 82,* 58–64.

Hulme, C., Hatcher, P. J., Nation, K., Brown, A., Adams, J., & Stuart, G. (2002). Phoneme awareness is a better predictor of early reading skill than onset-rime awareness. *Journal of Experimental Child Psychology, 82,* 2–28.

Hulme, C., Maughan, S., & Brown, G. D. A. (1991). Memory for familiar and unfamiliar words: Evidence for a long-term memory contribution to short-term memory span. *Journal of Memory and Language, 30,* 685–701.

Hulme, C., & MacKenzie, S. (1992). *Working memory and severe learning difficulties.* Hove, UK: Erlbaum.

Hulme, C., & Snowling, M. J. (1991). Deficits in output phonology cause developmental phonological dyslexia. *Mind and Language, 6,* 130–134.

Hulme, C., & Snowling, M. J. (1992). Deficits in output phonology: An explanation of reading failure. *Cognitive Neuropsychology, 9,* 47–72.

Humphreys, G. W., Evett, L. J., & Quinlan, P. T. (1990). Orthographic processing in visual word recognition. *Cognitive Psychology, 22,* 517–560.

Hurford, D. P., Darrow, L. J., Edwards, T. L., Howerton, C. J., Mote, C. R., Schauf, J. D., et al. (1993). An examination of phonemic processing abilities in children during their first-grade year. *Journal of Learning Disabilities, 26,* 167–177.

Hurford, D. P., Schauf, J. D., Bunce, L., Blaich, T., & Moore, K. (1994). Early identification of children at risk for reading disabilities. *Journal of Learning Disabilities, 27,* 371–382.

Huttenlocher, J., Haight, W., Bryk, A., Seltzer, M., & Lyons, T. (1991). Early vocabulary growth: Relation to language input and gender. *Developmental Psychology, 27,* 236–248.

Huttenlocher, J.,Vasilyeva, M., Cymerman, E., & Levine, S. (2002). Language input and child syntax. *Cognitive Psychology, 45,* 337–374.

Hutzler, F., & Wimmer, H. (2004). Eye movements of dyslexic children when reading in a regular orthography. *Brain and Language, 89,* 235–242.

Hyönä, J. (1994). Processing of topic shifts by adults and children. *Reading Research Quarterly, 29,* 76–90.

Hyönä, J. (1995). Do irregular letter combinations attract readers' attention? Evidence from fixation location in words. *Journal of Experimental Psychology: Human Perception and Performance, 21,* 68–81.

Hyönä, J., & Bertram, R. (2004). Do frequency characteristics of nonfixated words influence the processing of fixated words during reading? *European Journal of Cognitive Psychology, 16,* 104–127.

Hyönä, J., Bertram, R., & Pollatsek, A. (2004). Are long compound words identified serially via their constituents? Evidence from an eye-movement contingent display change study. *Memory and Cognition, 32,* 523–532.

Hyönä, J., Niemi, P., & Underwood, G. (1989). Reading long words embedded in sentences: Informativeness of word halves affects eye movements. *Journal of Experimental Psychology: Human Perception and Performance, 15,* 142–152.

Hyönä, J., & Pollatsek, A. (1998). The role of component morphemes on eye fixations when reading Finnish compound words. *Journal of Experimental Psychology: Human Perception and Performance, 24,* 1612–1627.

Ikeda, M., & Saida, S. (1978). Span of recognition in reading. *Vision Research, 18,* 83–88.

Ingulsrud, J. E., & Allen, K. (1999). *Learning to read Chinese: Sociolinguistic perspectives on the acquisition of literacy.* Lewiston, NY: Mellen.

Ingvar, M., Trampe, P., Greitz, T., Eriksson, L., Stone-Elander, S., & von Euler, C. (2002). Residual differences in language processing in compensated dyslexics revealed in simple word reading tasks. *Brain and Language, 83,* 249–267.

Inhoff, A. W. (1989). Lexical access during eye fixations in reading: Are word access codes used to integrate lexical information across interword fixations? *Journal of Memory and Language, 28,* 444–461.

Inhoff, A. W., & Liu, W. (1998). The perceptual span and oculomotor activity during the reading of Chinese sentences. *Journal of Experimental Psychology: Human Perception and Performance, 24,* 20–34.

Inhoff, A. W., & Rayner, K. (1986). Parafoveal word processing during eye fixations in reading: Effects of word frequency. *Perception and Psychophysics, 40,* 431–439.

Inhoff, A. W, Starr, M., Lui, W., & Wang, J. (1998). Eye-movement-contingent display changes are not compromised by flicker and phosphor persistence. *Psychonomic Bulletin and Review, 5,* 101–106.

Inhoff, A. W., Starr, M., & Shindler, K. L. (2000). Is the processing of words during eye fixations strictly serial? *Perception and Psychophysics, 62,* 1474–1484.

International Phonetic Association. (1996). *Reproduction of The International Phonetic Alphabet* [on-line]. Retrieved from http://www2.arts.gla.ac.uk/IPA/ipachart.html.

International Phonetic Association. (1999). *Handbook of the International Phonetic Association: A guide to the use of the International Phonetic Alphabet.* Cambridge: Cambridge University Press.

Iovino, I., Fletcher, J. M., Breitmeyer, B. G., & Foorman, B. R. (1999). Colored overlays for visual perceptual deficits in children with reading disability and attention deficit/hyperactivity disorder: Are they differentially effective? *Journal of Clinical and Experimental Neurospychology, 20,* 791–806.

Ishida, T., & Ikeda, M. (1989). Temporal properties of information extraction in reading studied by a text-mask replacement technique. *Journal of the Optical; Society A: Optics and Image Science, 6,* 1624–1632.

Ishii, K., Reyes, J. A., & Kitayama, S. (2003). Spontaneous attention to word content versus emotional tone. *Psychological Science, 14,* 39–46.

Iversen, S., & Tunmer, W. (1993). Phonological processing skills and the reading recovery program. *Journal of Educational Psychology, 85,* 112–126.

Jackson, M. D., & McClelland, J. L. (1979). Processing determinants of reading speed. *Journal of Experimental Psychology: General, 108,* 151–181.

Jacobs, A. M., & Grainger, J. (1994). Models of visual word recognition – Sampling the state of the art. *Journal of Experimental Psychology: Human Perception and Performance, 20,* 1311–1334.

Jacobs, A. M., Grainger, J., & Ferrand, L. (1995). The incremental priming technique: A method for determining within-condition priming effects. *Perception and Psychophysics, 57,* 1101–1110.

Jacobs, A. M., Rey, A., Ziegler, J. C., & Grainger, J. (1998). MROM-P: An interactive activation, multiple read-out model of orthographic and phonological processes in visual word recognition. In J. Grainger & A. M. Jacobs (Eds.), *Localist connectionist approaches to human cognition* (pp. 147–188). Mahwah, NJ: Erlbaum.

James, C. T. (1975). The role of semantic information in lexical decisions. *Journal of Experimental Psychology: Human Perception and Performance, 1,* 130–136.

Jared, D., Levy, B. A., & Rayner, K. (1999). The role of phonology in the activation of word meanings during reading: Evidence from proofreading and eye movements. *Journal of Experimental Psychology: General, 128,* 219–264.

Jared, D., & Seidenberg, M. S. (1991). Does word identification proceed from spelling to sound to meaning? *Journal of Experimental Psychology: General, 120,* 358–394.

Jarrold, C., Baddeley, A. D., & Hewes, A. K. (1999). Genetically dissociated components of working memory: Evidence from Down's and William's syndrome. *Neuropsychologia, 37,* 637–651.

Jastrzembski, J. E. (1981). Multiple meanings, number of related meanings, frequency of occurrence, and the lexicon. *Cognitive Psychology, 13*, 278–305.

Jastrzembski, J. E., & Stanners, R. F. (1975). Multiple word meanings and lexical search speed. *Journal of Verbal Learning and Verbal Behavior, 14*, 534–537.

Jefferies, E., Jones, R., Bateman, D., & Lambon Ralph, M. A. (in press). When does word meaning affect immediate serial recall in semantic dementia? *Cognitive and Affective Behavioural Neuroscience.*

Jensen, H. J. (1998). *Self-organized criticality.* Cambridge: Cambridge University Press.

Johnson-Laird, P. N. (1983). *Mental models.* Cambridge, MA: Harvard University Press.

Johnston, J. C., & McClelland, J. L. (1973). Visual factors in word perception. *Perception and Psychophysics, 14*, 365–370.

Johnston, P. H. (1985). Understanding reading disability. *Harvard Educational Review, 55*, 153–177.

Johnston, R. S., Anderson, M., & Holligan, C. (1996). Knowledge of the alphabetic and explicit awareness of phonemes in pre-readers. *Reading and Writing, 8*, 217–234.

Johnston, T. D., & Edwards, L. (2002). Genes, interactions, and the development of behavior. *Psychological Review, 109*, 26–34.

Jones, G. V. (1985). Deep dyslexia, imageability, and ease of predication. *Brain and Language, 24*, 1–19.

Jonsdottir, M. K., Shallice, T., & Wise, R. (1996). Phonological mediation and the graphemic buffer disorder in spelling: Cross-language differences? *Cognition, 59*, 169–197.

Joordens, S., & Besner, D. (1994). When banking on meaning is not (yet) money in the bank: Explorations in connectionist modeling. *Journal of Experimental Psychology: Learning, Memory, and Cognition, 20*, 1051–1062.

Juel, C. (1983). The development and use of mediated word identification. *Reading Research Quarterly, 18*, 306–327.

Juel, C. (1988). Learning to read and write: A longitudinal study of 54 children from first through fourth grades. *Journal of Educational Psychology, 80*, 437–447.

Juel, C. (1991). Beginning reading. In R. Barr, M. L. Kamil, P. D. Pearson, & P. Mosenthal (Eds.), *Handbook of reading research* (Vol. 2, pp. 759–788). New York: Longman.

Juel, C. (1994). *Learning to read and write in one elementary school.* New York: Springer-Verlag.

Juel, C., Griffith, P. L., & Gough, P. B. (1986). Acquisition of literacy: A longitudinal study of children in first and second grade. *Journal of Educational Psychology, 78*, 243–255.

Juel, C., & Minden-Cupp, C. (2000). Learning to read words: Linguistic units and instructional strategies. *Reading Research Quarterly, 35*, 458–492.

Juel, C., & Roper/Schneider, D. (1985). The influence of basal readers on first-grade reading. *Reading Research Quarterly, 20*, 134–152.

Juhasz, B. J., & Rayner, K. (2003). Investigating the effects of a set of intercorrelated variables on eye fixation durations in reading. *Journal of Experimental Psychology: Learning, Memory, and Cognition, 29*, 1312–1318.

Juhasz, B. J., & Rayner, K. (in press). The role of age-of-acquisition and word frequency in reading: Evidence from eye fixation durations. *Visual Cognition.*

Juhasz, B. J., Starr, M., Inhoff, A. W., & Placke, L. (2003). The effects of morphology on the processing of compound words: Evidence from naming, lexical decisions, and eye fixations. *British Journal of Psychology, 94*, 223–244.

Just, M. A., & Carpenter, P. A. (1992). A capacity theory of comprehension: Individual differences in working memory. *Psychological Review, 99*, 122–149.

Kahn, D. (1976). *Syllable-based generalizations in English phonology.* New York: Garland.

Kambe, G. (2004). Parafoveal processing of prefixed words during eye fixations in reading: Evidence against morphological influences on parafoveal preprocessing. *Perception and Psychophysics, 66,* 279–292.

Kang, H., & Simpson, G. B. (2001). Local strategic control of information in visual word recognition. *Memory and Cognition, 29,* 648–655.

Karass, J., VanDeventer, M. C., & Braungart-Rieker, J. M. (2003). Predicting shared parent–child book reading in infancy. *Journal of Family Psychology, 17,* 134–146.

Karmiloff-Smith, A., Grant, J., Berthoud, I., Davis, M., Howlin, P., & Udwin, O. (1997). Language and Williams syndrome: How intact is "intact"? *Child Development, 68,* 246–262.

Karmiloff-Smith, A., Scerif, G., & Ansari, D. (2003). Double dissociations in developmental disorders? Theoretically misconceived, empirically dubious. *Cortex, 39,* 161–163.

Karmiloff-Smith, A., Tyler, L. K., Voice, K., Sims, K., Udwin, O., Howlin, P., et al. (1998). Linguistic dissociations in Williams syndrome: Evaluating receptive syntax in on-line and off-line tasks. *Neuropsychologia, 36,* 343–351.

Katz, L., & Feldman L. B. (1981). Linguistic coding in word recognition. In A. M. Lesgold & C. A. Perfetti (Eds.), *Interactive processes in reading* (pp. 85–105). Hillsdale, NJ: Erlbaum.

Katz, L., & Feldman L. B. (1983). Relation between pronunciation and recognition of printed words in deep and shallow orthographies. *Journal of Experimental Psychology: Learning, Memory, and Cognition, 9,* 157–166.

Katz, L., & Frost, R. (1992). Reading in different orthographies: the Orthographic Depth Hypothesis. In R. Frost & L. Katz (Eds.), *Orthography, phonology, morphology, and meaning* (pp. 67–84). Advances in Psychology. Amsterdam: Elsevier.

Katz, R. (1991). Limited retention of information in the graphemic buffer. *Cortex, 27,* 111–119.

Kavale, K. A. (1988). The long-term consequences of learning disabilities. In M. C. Wang, H. J. Walburg, & M. C. Reynolds (Eds.), *The handbook of special education: Research and practice* (pp. 303–344). New York: Pergamon.

Kawamoto, A. H. (1993). Nonlinear dynamics in the resolution of lexical ambiguity: A parallel distributed processing approach. *Journal of Memory and Language, 32,* 474–516.

Kawamoto, A. H., Farrar, W. T., & Kello, C. T. (1994). When two meanings are better than one: Modeling the ambiguity advantage using a recurrent distributed network. *Journal of Experimental Psychology: Human Perception and Performance, 20,* 1233–1247.

Kawamoto, A. H., Kello, C., & Jones, R. (1994). Locus of the exception effect in naming. In *Proceedings of the 35th Annual Meeting of the Psychonomic Society* (p. 51). St. Louis, MO.

Kawamoto, A. H., & Zemblidge, J. H. (1992). Pronunciation of homographs, *Journal of Memory and Language, 31,* 349–374.

Kay, J., & Hanley, R. (1994). Peripheral disorders of spelling: The role of the graphemic buffer. In G. D. A. Brown & N. C. Ellis (Eds.), *Handbook of spelling: theory, process and intervention* (pp. 295–315). Chichester: Wiley.

Kellas, G., Ferraro, F. R., & Simpson, G. B. (1988). Lexical ambiguity and the timecourse of attentional allocation in word recognition. *Journal of Experimental Psychology: Human Perception and Performance, 14,* 601–609.

Kello, C. T., & Plaut, D. C. (2000). Strategic control in word reading: Evidence from speeded responding in the tempo-naming task. *Journal of Experimental Psychology: Learning, Memory, and Cognition, 26,* 719–750.

Kennedy, A. (2000). Parafoveal processing in word recognition. *Quarterly Journal of Experimental Psychology, 53A,* 429–456.

Kennedy, A., Brooks, R., Flynn, L., & Prophet, C. (2003). The reader's spatial code. In J. Hyönä, R. Radach, & H. Deubel (Eds.), *The mind's eye: Cognitive and applied aspects of eye movement research* (pp. 192–212). Oxford: Elsevier

Kennedy, A., Murray, W. S., & Boissiere, C. (2004). Parafoveal pragmatics revisited. *European Journal of Cognitive Psychology, 16*, 128–153.

Kennedy, A. Pynte, J., & Ducrot, S. (2002). Parafoveal-on-foveal interaction in word recognition. *Quarterly Journal of Experimental Psychology, 55A*, 1307–1337.

Kerr, J. (1897). School hygiene, in its mental, moral, and physical aspects. Howard Medical Prize Essay. *Journal of the Royal Statistical Society, 60*, 613–680.

Kessler, B., & Treiman, R. (2001). Relationships between sounds and letters in English monosyllables. *Journal of Memory and Language, 44*, 592–617.

Kieras, D. E. (1980). Initial mention as a signal to thematic content in technical passages. *Memory and Cognition, 8*, 345–353.

Kihlstrom, J. F. (1987). The cognitive unconscious. *Science, 237*, 1445–1452.

Kinlaw, C. R., Kurtz-Costes, B., & Goldman-Fraser, J. (2001). Mothers' achievement beliefs and behaviors and their children's school readiness: A cultural comparison. *Applied Developmental Psychology, 22*, 493–506.

Kintsch, W. (1988). The role of knowledge in discourse processing: A construction—integration model. *Psychological Review, 95*, 163–182.

Kintsch, W. (1993). Information accretion and reduction in text processing: Inferences. *Discourse Processes, 16*, 193–202.

Kintsch, W. A. (1998). *Comprehension: A paradigm for cognition.* Cambridge: Cambridge University Press.

Kintsch, W., Patel, V. L., & Ericsson, K. A. (1999). The role of long-term working memory in text comprehension. *Psychologia, 42*, 186–198.

Klein, D. E., & Murphy, G. L. (2001). The representation of polysemous words. *Journal of Memory and Language, 45*, 259–282.

Klein, D. E., & Murphy, G. L. (2002). Paper has been my ruin: Conceptual relations of polysemous senses. *Journal of Memory and Language, 47*, 548–570.

Kliegl, R., & Engbert, R. (2003). SWIFT explorations. In J. Hyönä, R. Radach, & H. Deubel (Eds.), *The mind's eye: Cognitive and applied aspects of eye movement research* (pp. 391–412). Oxford: Elsevier.

Kliegl, R., & Engbert, R. (in press). Fixation durations before word skippings in reading eye movements. *Psychonomic Bulletin and Review.*

Kliegl, R., Grabner, E., Rolfs, M., & Engbert, R. (2004). Length, frequency, and predictability effects of words in eye movements in reading. *European Journal of Cognitive Psychology, 16*, 262–284.

Klima, E. S. (1972). How alphabets might reflect language. In F. Kavanagh & I. G. Mattingly (Eds.), *Language by ear and by eye* (pp. 75–80). Cambridge, MA: MIT Press.

Klin, C. M., Guzmán, A. E., & Levine, W. H. (1999). Prevalence and persistence of predictive inferences. *Journal of Memory and Language, 40*, 593–604.

Klin, C. M., Murray, J. D., Levine, W. H., & Guzmán, A. E. (1999). Forward inferences: From activation to long-term memory. *Discourse Processes, 27*, 241–260.

Knopik, V. S., Smith, S. D., Cardon, L., Pennington, B., Gayan, J., Olson, R. K., et al. (2002). Differential genetic etiology of reading component processes as a function of IQ. *Behavior Genetics, 32*, 181–198.

Ko, H., & Lee, J. R. (1997a). Chinese children's phonological awareness ability and later reading ability: A longitudinal study. *Journal of the National Chung-Cheng University, 7*, 49–66.

Ko, H., & Lee, J. R. (1997b). Phonological awareness and learning to read in illiterate adults. *Journal of the National Chung-Cheng University, 7*, 29–47.

Kolinsky, R. (1988). *La séparabilité des propriétés dans la perception des formes.* PhD dissertation, Université Libre de Bruxelles, Brussels.

Kolinsky, R., Cary, L., & Morais, J. (1987a). Awareness of words as phonological entities: The role of literacy. *Applied Psycholinguistics, 8*, 223–232.

Kolinsky, R., Macedo, C., Gontijo, P., Grimm-Cabral, L., Cabral, & Morais, J. (in preparation). *Semantic priming in illiterate adults.*

Kolinsky, R., & Morais, J. (1993). Intermediate representations in spoken word recognition: A cross-linguistic study of word illusions. Proceedings of the third European conference on speech communication and technology, Eurospeech 93, Berlin, Germany (pp. 731–734).

Kolinsky, R., & Morais, J. (1999). We all are Rembrandt experts – or how task dissociations in school learning effects support the discontinuity hypothesis. *Behavioral and Brain Sciences, 22*, 381–382.

Kolinsky, R., Morais, J., Content, A., & Cary, L. (1987b). Finding parts within figures: A developmental study. *Perception, 16*, 399–407.

Kolinsky, R., Morais, J., & Verhaeghe, A. (1994). Visual separability: A study on unschooled adults. *Perception, 23*, 471–486.

Kolinsky, R., Penido, F., & Morais, J. (in preparation). Attentional and executive processes in illiterate adults.

Konieczny, L., Hemforth, B., Scheepers, C., & Strube, G. (1997). The role of lexical heads in parsing. Evidence from German. *Language and Cognitive Processes, 12*, 307–348.

Kozminsky, L., & Kozminsky, E. (1995). The effects of early phonological awareness training on reading success. *Learning and Instruction, 5*, 187–201.

Kreindler, A., & Ionasescu, V. (1961). A case of pure word blindness. *Journal of Neurology, Neurosurgery and Psychiatry, 24*, 275–280.

Kremin, H. (1985). Routes and strategies in surface dyslexia and dysgraphia. In K. E. Patterson, J. C. Marshall, & M. Coltheart (Eds.), *Surface dyslexia: Neuropsychological and cognitive studies of phonological reading* (pp. 105–137). London: LEA.

Krishnakumar, A., & Black, M. A. (2002). Longitudinal predictors of competence among African American children: The role of distal and proximal risk factors. *Applied Developmental Psychology, 23*, 237–266.

Kroll, J. F., & Merves, J. S. (1986). Lexical access for concrete and abstract words. *Journal of Experimental Psychology: Learning, Memory, and Cognition, 12*, 92–107.

Ku, Y. M., & Anderson, R. C. (2003). Development of morphological awareness in Chinese and English. *Reading and Writing, 16*, 399–422.

Kucera, H., & Francis, W. N. (1967). *Computational analysis of present-day American English.* Providence, RI: Brown University Press.

Kurdek, L. A., & Sinclair, R. J. (2001). Predicting reading and mathematics achievement in fourth-grade children from kindergarten readiness scores. *Journal of Educational Psychology, 93*, 451–455.

LaBerge, D., & Samuels, J. (1974). Toward a theory of automatic information processing in reading. *Cognitive Psychology, 6*, 293–323.

Lai, C. S., Fisher, S. E., Hurst, J. A., Vargha-Khadem, F., & Monaco, A. P. (2001). A forkhead-domain gene is mutated in a severe speech and language disorder. *Nature, 413*, 519–523.

Laing, E., & Hulme, C. (1999). Phonological and semantic processes influence beginning readers' ability to learn to read words. *Journal of Experimental Child Psychology, 73*, 183–207.

Laing, E., Hulme, C., Grant, J., & Karmiloff-Smith, A. (2001). Learning to read in Williams syndrome: Looking beneath the surface of atypical development. *Journal of Child Psychology and Psychiatry, 42*, 729–739.

Lambon Ralph, M. A., Cipolotti, L., & Patterson, K. (1999). Oral naming and oral reading: Do they speak the same language? *Cognitive Neuropsychology, 16*, 157–169.

Lambon Ralph, M. A., & Ellis, A. W. (1997). 'Patterns of Paralexia' revisited: Report of a case of visual dyslexia. *Cognitive Neuropsychology, 7*, 953–974.

Lambon Ralph, M. A, Ellis, A. W, & Franklin, S. (1995). Semantic loss without surface dyslexia. *Neurocase, 1*, 363–369.

Lambon Ralph, M. A., Hesketh, A., & Sage, K. (2004). Implicit recognition in pure alexia: The Saffran effect – a tale of two systems or two procedures? *Cognitive Neuropsychology, 21*, 401–421.

Lambon Ralph, M. A., & Howard, D. (2000). Gogi aphasia or semantic dementia? Simulating and assessing poor verbal comprehension in a case of progressive fluent aphasia. *Cognitive Neuropsychology, 17*, 437–466.

Lambon Ralph, M. A., Moriarty, L., & Sage, K. (2002). Anomia is simply a reflection of semantic and phonological impairments: Evidence from a case-series study. *Aphasiology, 16*, 56–82.

Landauer, T. K. (1998). Learning and representing verbal meaning: The Latent Semantic Analysis theory. *Current Directions in Psychological Science, 7*, 161–164.

Landauer, T. K. (2001). Single representations of multiple meanings in Latent Semantic Analysis. In D. S. Gorfein (Ed.), *On the consequences of meaning selection* (pp. 217–232). Washington, DC: American Psychological Association.

Landauer, T. K., & Dumais, S. T. (1997). A solution to Plato's problem: The Latent Semantic Analysis theory of acquisition, induction and representation of knowledge. *Psychological Review, 104*, 211–240.

Landauer, T. K., Laham, D., & Foltz, P. W. (2000). The Intelligent Essay Assessor. *IEEE Intelligent Systems*, 27–31.

Landerl, K. (2000). Influences of orthographic consistency and reading instruction on the development of nonword reading skills. *European Journal of Psychology of Education, 15*, 239–257.

Landerl, K. (2001). Word recognition deficits in German: More evidence from a representative sample. *Dyslexia, 7*, 183–196.

Landerl, K., & Wimmer, H. (2000). Deficits in phoneme segmentation are not the core problem of dyslexia: Evidence from German and English children. *Applied Psycholinguistics, 21*, 243–262.

Landerl, K., Wimmer, H., & Frith, U. (1997). The impact of orthographic consistency on dyslexia: A German—English comparison. *Cognition, 63*, 315–334.

Landry, S. H., Smith, K. E., Miller-Loncar, C. L., & Swank, P. R. (1997). Predicting cognitive-language and social growth curves from early maternal behaviors in children at varying degrees of biological risk *Developmental Psychology, 33*, 1040–1053.

Landry, S. H., Smith, K. E., Swank, P. R., Assel, M. A., & Vellet, S. (2001). Does early responsive parenting have a special importance for children's development or is consistency across early childhood necessary? *Developmental Psychology, 37*, 387–403.

Lange, M. (2002). Activation of multiple phoneme associates of graphemes in visual word recognition. *Brain and Language, 80*, 610–620.

Langston, M. C., Trabasso, T. et al. (1998). Modeling on-line comprehension. In A. Ram & K. Moorman (Eds.), *Computational models of reading and understanding* (pp. 181–226). Cambridge, MA: MIT Press.

La Paro, K. M., & Pianta, R. C. (2000). Predicting children's competence in the early school years: A meta-analytic review. *Review of Educational Research, 70*, 443–484.

Larrivee, L. S., & Catts, H. W. (1999). Early reading achievement in children with expressive phonological disorders. *American Journal of Speech-Language Pathology, 8*, 118–128.

LaSasso, C. J., Crain, K., & Leybaert, J. (2003). Rhyme generation in deaf students: The effect of exposure to Cued Speech. *Journal of Deaf Studies and Deaf Education, 8*, 250–271.

LaSasso, C. J., & Metzger, M. A. (1998). An alternate route for preparing deaf children for BiBi programs: The home language as L1 and Cued Speech for conveying traditionally spoken languages. *Journal of Deaf Studies and Deaf Education, 3*(4), 265–289.

Law, N., Ki, W. W., Chung, A. L. S., Ko, P. Y., & Lam, H. C. (1998). Children's stroke sequence errors in writing Chinese characters. *Reading and Writing, 10,* 267–292.

Lawrence, V. W., & Shipley, E. F. (1996). Parental speech to middle- and working-class children from two racial groups in three settings. *Applied Psycholinguistics, 17,* 233–255.

Le, E. (2002). Themes and hierarchical structures of written text. In M. Louwerse & W. V. Peer (eds.), *Thematics: Interdisciplinary studies* (pp. 171–188). Amsterdam: Benjamins.

Leach, J. M., Scarborough, H. S., & Rescorla, L. (2003). Late-emerging reading disabilities. *Journal of Educational Psychology, 95,* 211–224.

Leather, C. V., & Henry, L. A. (1994). Working memory span and phonological awareness tasks as predictors of early reading ability. *Journal of Experimental Child Psychology, 58,* 88–11.

Lee, H. W., Rayner, K., & Pollatsek, A. (1999). The time course of phonological, semantic, and orthographic coding in reading: Evidence from the fast priming technique. *Psychonomic Bulletin and Review, 6,* 624–634.

Lee, H. W., Rayner, K., & Pollatsek, A. (2001). The relative contribution of consonants and vowels to word identification during reading. *Journal of Memory and Language, 44,* 189–205.

Lee, J. R. (1997, September). Phonological awareness and Chinese character acquisition in Taiwan dyslexic children: Reading ability control design research. Paper presented at The International Symposium on Cognitive Processes of the Chinese Language, University of Hong Kong.

Leff, A., Crewes, H., Plant, G., Scott, S., Kennard, C., & Wise, R. (2001a). The functional anatomy of single-word reading in patients with hemianopic and pure alexia. *Brain, 124,* 510–521.

Leff, A., Scott, S., Rothwell, J., & Wise, R. (2001b). The planning and guiding of reading saccades: A repetitive transcranial magnetic stimulation study. *Cerebral Cortex, 11,* 918–923.

Lehmkuhle, S., Garzia, R. P., Turner, L., Hash, T., & Baro, J. A. (1993). A defective visual pathway in children with reading disability. *New England Journal of Medicine, 328*(14), 989–996.

Leitao, S., Hogben, J., & Fletcher, J. (1997). Phonological processing skills in speech and language impaired children. *European Journal of Disorders of Communication, 32,* 73–93.

Leong, C. K. (1997). Paradigmatic analysis of Chinese word reading: Research findings and classroom practices. In C. K. Leong & R. Malatesha Joshi (Eds.), *Applied research in reading and spelling in different languages* (pp. 379–417). Dordrecht, the Netherlands: Kluwer Academic.

Lepola, J., Salonen, P., & Vauras, M. (2000). The development of motivational orientations as a function of divergent reading careers from pre-school to the second grade. *Learning and Instruction, 10,* 153–177.

Lesch, M. F., & Pollatsek, A. (1993). Automatic access of semantic information by phonological codes in visual word recognition. *Journal of Experimental Psychology: Learning, Memory, and Cognition, 19,* 285–294.

Lesch, M. F., & Pollatsek, A. (1998). Evidence for the use of assembled phonology in accessing the meaning of printed words. *Journal of Experimental Psychology: Learning, Memory, and Cognition, 24,* 573–592.

Leseman, P. P. M., & de Jong, P. F. (1998). Home literacy: Opportunity, instruction, cooperation, and social-emotional quality predicting early reading achievement. *Reading Research Quarterly, 33,* 294–318.

Leventhal, T., & Brooks-Gunn, J. (2000). The neighborhoods they live in: The effects of neighborhood residence on child and adolescent outcomes. *Psychological Bulletin, 126,* 309–337.

Levin, I., & Freedman, N. (2003). Letter name and letter sound in Hebrew. Unpublished raw data.

Levin, I., & Tolchinsky Landsmann, L. (1989). Becoming literate: Referential and phonetic strategies in early reading and writing. *International Journal of Behavioural Development, 12,* 369–384.

Lewis, B. A. (1990). Familial phonological disorders: Four pedigrees. *Journal of Speech and Hearing Disorders, 55,* 160–170.

Lewis, B. A. (1992). Pedigree analysis of children with phonology disorders. *Journal of Learning Disabilities, 25,* 586–597.

Lewis, B. A., Ekelman, B., & Aram, D. (1989). A family study of severe phonological disorders. *Journal of Speech and Hearing Research, 32,* 713–724.

Lewis, B. A., & Thompson, L. A. (1992). A study of developmental speech and language disorders in twins. *Journal of Speech and Hearing Research, 35,* 1086–1094.

Lewitter, F. L., DeFries, J. C., & Elston, R. C. (1980). Genetic models of reading disability. *Behavior Genetics, 10*(1), 9–30.

Leybaert, J. (1993). Reading in the deaf: The roles of phonological codes. In M. Marschark & D. Clark (Eds.), *Psychological perspectives on deafness* (pp. 269–309). Hillsdale, NJ: Erlbaum.

Leybaert, J. (2000). Phonology acquired through the eyes and spelling in deaf children. *Journal of Experimental Child Psychology, 75,* 291–318.

Leybaert, J., & Alegria, J. (1993). Is word processing involuntary in deaf children? *British Journal of developmental psychology, 11,* 1–29.

Leybaert, J., & Alegria, J. (1995). Spelling development in hearing and deaf children: Evidence for the use of morpho-phonological regularities in French. *Reading and Writing, 7,* 89–109.

Leybaert, J., & D'Hondt, M. (2003). Neurolinguistic development in deaf children: The effect of early experience. *International Journal of Audiology, 42,* S34–S40.

Leybaert, J., & Lechat, J. (2001a). Phonological similarity effects in memory for serial order of cued-speech. *Journal of Speech, Language and Hearing Research, 44,* 949–963.

Leybaert, J., & Lechat, J. (2001b). Variability in deaf children's spelling: The effect of language experience. *Journal of Educational Psychology, 93,* 554–562.

Li, C., & Thompson, S. (1981). *Mandarin Chinese: A functional reference grammar.* Berkeley: University of California Press.

Li, H. T. (1977). *The history of Chinese characters.* Taipei: Lian-Jian.

Li, H. T., & Rao, N. (2000). Parental influences on Chinese literacy development: A comparison of pre-schoolers in Beijing, Hong Kong, and Singapore. *International Journal of Behavioral Development, 24,* 82–90.

Liberman, A. M. (1992). The relation of speech to reading and writing. In R. Frost and L. Katz (Eds.), *Orthography, phonology, morphology, and meaning* (pp. 167–178). Amsterdam: Elsevier.

Liberman, A. M. (1999). The reading researcher and the reading teacher need the right theory of speech. *Scientific Studies of Reading, 3,* 95–112.

Liberman, I. Y., Liberman, A. M., Mattingly, I. G., & Shankweiler, D. (1980). Orthography and the beginning reader. In J. F. Kavanagh & R. L. Venezky (Eds.), *Orthography, reading, and dyslexia* (pp. 137–153). Austin, TX: Pro-Ed.

Liberman, I. Y., & Shankweiler, D. (1979). Speech, the alphabet and teaching to read. In L. Resnick & P. Weaver (Eds.), *Theory and practice of early reading* (Vol. 2, pp. 109–132). Hillsdale, NJ: Erlbaum.

Liberman, I. Y., & Shankweiler, D. (1991). Phonology and beginning reading — a tutorial. In L. Rieben & C. Perfetti (Eds.), *Learning to read: Basic research and its implications* (pp. 3–17). Hillsdale, NJ: Erlbaum.

Liberman, I. Y., Shankweiler, D., Fischer, F. W., & Carter, B. (1974). Explicit syllable and phoneme segmentation in the young child. *Journal of Experimental Child Psychology, 18,* 201–212.

Liberman, I. Y., Shankweiler, D., & Liberman, A. M. (1989). The alphabetic principle and learning to read. In D. Shankweiler & I. Y. Liberman (Eds.), *Phonology and reading disability: Solving the reading puzzle* (pp. 1–33). Ann Arbor: University of Michigan Press.

Lichacz, F. M., Herdman, C. M., LeFevre, J.-A., & Baird, B. (1999). Polysemy effects in word naming. *Canadian Journal of Experimental Psychology, 53*, 189–193.

Lichtenstein, E. H. (1985). Deaf working memory processes and English language skills. In D. S. Martin (Ed.), *Cognition, education, and deafness: Directions for research and instruction* (pp. 111–114). Washington, DC: Gallaudet University Press.

Lichtenstein, E. H. (1998). The relationships between reading processes and English skills for deaf students. *Journal of Deaf Studies and Deaf Education, 3*, 80–134.

Light, J., & DeFries, J. (1995). Comorbidity of reading and mathematics disabilities: Genetic and environmental etiologies. *Journal of Learning Disabilities, 28*, 96–106.

Lima, S. D. (1987). Morphological analysis in sentence reading. *Journal of Memory and language, 26*, 84–99.

Lima, S. D., & Inhoff, A. W. (1985). Lexical access during eye fixations in reading: Effects of word-initial letter sequences. *Journal of Experimental Psychology: Human Perception and Performance, 11*, 272–285.

Lindamood, P., & Lindamood, P. (1998). *The Lindamood Phoneme Sequencing Program for Reading, Spelling, and Speech* (3rd ed.). Austin, TX: Pro-Ed.

Liversedge, S. P., Patterson, K. B., & Pickering, M. J. (1998). Eye movements and measures of reading time. In G. Underwood (Ed.), *Eye guidance in reading and scene perception* (pp. 55–76). Oxford: Elsevier.

Liversedge, S. P., Rayner, K., White, S. J., Vergilino-Perez, D., Findlay, J. M., & Kentridge, R. W. (2004). Eye movements when reading disappearing text: Is there a gap effect in reading? *Vision Reseach, 44*, 1013–1024.

Livingstone, M. S., Rosen, G. D., Drislane, F. W., & Galaburda, A. M. (1991). Physiological and anatomical evidence for a magnocellular defect in developmental dyslexia. *Proceedings of the National Academy of Science, 88*, 7943–7947.

Long, D. L., & De Ley, L. (2000). Implicit causality and discourse focus: The interaction of text and reader characteristics in pronoun resolution. *Journal of Memory and Language, 42*, 526–570.

Long, D. L., Oppy, B. J., & Seely, M. R. (1997). Individual differences in reader's sentence- and text-level representations. *Journal of Memory and Language, 36*, 129–145.

Long, D. L., Seely, M. R., & Oppy, B. J. (1999). The strategic nature of less skilled readers' suppression problems. *Discourse Processes, 27*, 281–302.

Longley, E. (1852). *Furst fonetic redur.* Boston: Otis Clapp.

Lonigan, C. J. (1994). Reading to preschoolers exposed: Is the emperor really naked? *Developmental Review, 14*, 303–323.

Lonigan, C. J. (2004). Family literacy and emergent literacy programs. In B. Wasik (Ed.), *Handbook on family literacy: Research and services* (pp. 57–81). Hillsdale, NJ: Erlbaum.

Lonigan, C. J., Burgess, S. R., & Anthony, J. L. (2000). Development of emergent literacy and early reading skills in preschool children: Evidence from a latent variable longitudinal study. *Developmental Psychology, 36*, 596–613.

Lonigan, C. J., Burgess, S. R., Anthony, J. L., & Barker, T. A. (1998). Development of phonological sensitivity in two- to five-year-old children. *Journal of Educational Psychology, 90*, 294–311.

Lonigan, C. J., Dyer, S. M., & Anthony, J. L. (1996, April). The influence of the home literacy environment on the development of literacy skills in children from diverse racial and economic backgrounds. Paper presented at the Annual Convention of the American Educational Research Association, New York, NY.

Lonigan, C. J., & Whitehurst, G. J. (1998). Examination of the relative efficacy of parent and teacher involvement in a shared-reading intervention for preschool children from low-income backgrounds. *Early Childhood Research Quarterly, 17,* 265–292.

Lorch, R. F., Jr., Lorch, E. P., & Inman, W. E. (1993). Effects of signaling topic structure on text recall. *Journal of Educational Psychology, 85,* 281–290.

Louwerse, M. (2002). Computational retrieval of texts. In M. Louwerse & W. V. Peer (Eds.), *Thematics: Interdisciplinary studies* (pp. 189–216). Amsterdam: Benjamins.

Lovegrove, W., Martin, F., & Slaghuis, W. (1986). A theoretical and experimental case for a visual deficit in specific reading disability. *Cognitive Neuropsychology, 3,* 225–267.

Lovett, M. W. (1984). A developmental perspective on reading dysfunction: Accuracy and rate criteria in the subtyping of dyslexic children. *Brain and Language, 22,* 67–91.

Lovett, M. W., Bordon, S. L., Lacerenza, L., Benson, N. J., & Brackstone, D. (1994). Treating the core deficits of developmental dyslexia: Evidence of transfer of learning after phonologically-and strategy-based reading training programs. *Journal of Educational Psychology, 30,* 805–822.

Lovett, M. W., Lacerenza, L., Bordon, S. L., Frijters, J. C., Steinbach, K. A., & DePalma, M. (2000). Components of effective remediation for developmental reading disabilities: combining phonological and strategy-based instruction to improve outcomes. *Journal of Educational Psychology, 92,* 263–283.

Lovett, M. W., Ransby, M. J., & Barron, R. W. (1988). Treatment, subtype, and word type effects in dyslexic children's response to remediation. *Brain and Language, 34,* 328–349.

Lovett, M. W., Steinbach, K. A., & Frijters, J. C. (2000). Remediating the core deficits of reading disability: A double-deficit perspective. *Journal of Learning Disabilities, 33,* 334–358.

Lukatela, K., Carello, Shankweiler, D., & Liberman, I. Y. (1995). Phonological awareness in illiterates: Observations from Serbo-Croatian. *Applied Psycholinguistics, 16,* 463–487.

Lukatela, G., Feldman, L. B., Turvey, M. T., Carello, C., & Katz, L. (1989). Context effects in bi-alphabetical word perception. *Journal of Memory and Language, 28,* 214–236.

Lukatela, G., Frost, S. J., & Turvey, M. T. (1998). Phonological priming by masked nonword primes in the lexical decision task. *Journal of Memory and Language, 39,* 666–683.

Lukatela, G., Popadic, D., Ognjenovic, P., & Turvey, M. T. (1980). Lexical decision in a phonologically shallow orthography. *Memory and Cognition, 8,* 415–423.

Lukatela, G., Savic, M., Gligorjevic, B., Ognjenovic, P., & Turvey, M. T. (1978). Bi-alphabetical lexical decision. *Language and Speech, 21,* 142–165.

Lukatela, G., & Turvey, M. T. (1994a). Visual access is initially phonological: 1. Evidence from associative priming by words, homophones, and pseudohomophones. *Journal of Experimental Psychology: General, 123,* 107–128.

Lukatela, G., & Turvey, M. T. (1994b). Visual access is initially phonological: 2. Evidence from associative priming by homophones and pseudohomophones. *Journal of Experimental Psychology: General, 123,* 331–353.

Lukatela, G., & Turvey, M. T. (1998). Reading in two alphabets, *American Psychologist, 53,* 1057–1072.

Lukatela, G., & Turvey, M. T. (2000). An evaluation of the two-cycles model of phonology assembly. *Journal of Memory and Language, 42,* 183–207.

Lundberg, I. (1985). Longitudinal studies of reading and reading difficulties in Sweden. *Reading research: Advances in theory and practice* (vol. 4, pp. 65–105). New York: Academic.

Lundberg, I., Frost, J., & Petersen, O. (1988). Effects of an extensive program for stimulating phonological awareness in preschool children. *Reading Research Quarterly, 23,* 263–284.

Lundberg, I., Olofsson, A., & Wall, S. (1980). Reading and spelling skills in the first school years predicted from phonemic awareness skills in kindergarten. *Scandinavian Journal of Psychology, 21,* 159–173.

Lupker, J. S. (1984). Semantic priming without association: A second look. *Journal of Verbal Learning and Verbal Behavior, 23*, 709–733.

Lupker, S. J., & Colombo, L. (1994). Inhibitory effects in form priming: Evaluating a phonological competition explanation. *Journal of Experimental Psychology: Human Perception and Performance, 20*, 437–451.

Luria, A. R. (1976). *Cognitive development. Its cultural and social foundations.* Cambridge, MA: Harvard University Press.

Luster, T., & McAdoo H. (1996). Family and child influences on educational attainment: A secondary analysis of the High Scope/Perry Preschool data. *Developmental Psychology, 32*, 26–39.

Lyon, G. R. (1995). Towards a definition of dyslexia. *Annals of Dyslexia, 45*, 3–27.

Lyon, G. R., Fletcher, J. M., & Barnes, M. (2002). Learning disabilities. In E. J. Marsh & R. A. Barkley (Eds.), *Child Psychopathology* (2nd ed., pp. 520–588). New York: Guilford.

Lyon, G. R., Fletcher, J. M., Shaywitz, S. E., Shaywitz, B. A., Torgesen, J. K., Wood, F. B., et al. (2001). Rethinking learning disabilities. In C. E. Finn, Jr., R. A. J. Rotherham, & C. R. Hokanson, Jr. (Eds.), *Rethinking special education for a new century* (pp. 259–287). Washington, DC: Thomas B. Fordham Foundation and Progressive Policy Institute.

Lyytinen, H., Leinonen, S., Nikula, M., Aro, M., & Leiwo, M. (1995). In search of the core features of dyslexia: Observations concerning dyslexia in the highly orthographically regular Finnish language. In V. Berninger (Ed.), *The varieties of orthographic knowledge II: Relationships to phonology, reading and writing* (pp. 177–204). Dordrecht, the Netherlands: Kluwer Academic.

Magliano, J. P., Baggett, W. B., Johnson, B. K., & Graesser, A. C. (1993). The time course of generating causal antecedent and causal consequence inferences. *Discourse Processes, 16*, 35–53.

Mair, V. H. (1996). Modern Chinese writing. In P. T. Daniels & W. Bright (Eds.), *The world's writing systems* (pp. 200–208). Oxford: Oxford University Press.

Majsterek, D. J., & Ellenwood, A. E. (1995). Phonological awareness and beginning reading: Evaluation of a school-based screening procedure. *Journal of Learning Disabilities, 28*, 449–456.

Manelis, J. (1977). Frequency and meaningfulness in tachistoscopic word perception. *American Journal of Psychology, 99*, 269–280.

Manis, F. R., Doi, L. M., & Bhadha, B. (2000). Naming speed, phonological awareness, and orthographic knowledge in second graders. *Journal of Learning Disabilities, 33*, 325–333.

Manis, F. R., McBride-Chang, C., Seidenberg, M. S., Keating, P., Doi, L. M., Munson, B., et al. (1997). Are speech perception deficits associated with developmental dyslexia? *Journal of Experimental Child Psychology, 66*, 211–235.

Manis, F. R., Seidenberg, M. S., Doi, L. M., McBride-Chang, C., & Petersen, A. (1996). On the bases of two subtypes of developmental dyslexia. *Cognition, 58*(2), 157–195.

Mann, H. (1842). A lecture on the best mode of preparing and using spelling-books. Boston: American Institute of Instruction Lecture Series, XII, 1–40.

Mann, V. A., & Liberman, I. Y. (1984). Phonological awareness and verbal short-term memory. *Journal of Learning Disabilities, 17*, 592–599.

Mann, V. A., & Wimmer, H. (2002). Phoneme awareness and pathways into literacy: A comparison of German and American children. *Reading and Writing, 15*, 653–682.

Mansfield, A. F. (1977). Semantic organization in the young child: Evidence for the development of the semantic feature systems. *Journal of Experimental Child Psychology, 23*, 57–77.

Marcel, A. J. (1983). Conscious and unconscious perception: Experiments on visual masking and word recognition. *Cognitive Psychology, 15*, 197–237.

Marcus, G. F. (1998). Rethinking eliminative connectionism. *Cognitive Psychology, 37*, 243–282.

Maris, E. (2002). The role of orthographic and phonological codes in the word and the pseudo-word superiority effect: An analysis by means of multinomial processing tree models. *Journal of Experimental Psychology: Human Perception and Performance, 28,* 1409–1431.

Markman, A. B., & Dietrich, E. (2000). In defense of representation. *Cognitive Psychology, 40,* 138–171.

Markman, E. M. (1984). The acquisition and hierarchical organisation of categories by children. In C. Sophian (Ed.), *Origins of cognitive skills* (pp. 371–406). Hillsdale, NJ: Erlbaum.

Marschark, M. (1993). *Psychological development of deaf children.* New York: Oxford University Press.

Marschark, M., & Harris, M. (1996). Success and failure in learning to read: The special case (?) of deaf children. In C. Cornoldi & J. Oakhill (Eds.), *Reading comprehension difficulties: Processes and intervention* (pp. 279–300). Mahwah, NJ: Erlbaum.

Marschark, M., Lepoutre, D., & Bement, L. (1998). Mouth movement and signed communication. In R. Campbell, B. Dodd, & D. Burnham (Eds.), *Hearing by eye* (Vol. 2, pp. 245–266). Hove, UK: Psychology Press.

Marsh, G., Friedman, M., Welch, V., & Desberg, P. (1981). A cognitive-developmental theory of reading acquisition. In G. MacKinnon & T. Waller (Eds.), *Reading research: Advances in theory and practice* (pp. 199–221). New York: Academic.

Marshall, C. M., & Nation, K. (2003). Individual differences in semantic and structural errors in children's memory for sentences. *Educational and Child Psychology, 20,* 7–18.

Marshall, J. C., & Newcombe, F. (1973). Patterns of paralexia: A psycholinguistic approach. *Journal of Psycholinguistic Research, 2,* 175–199.

Martin, F., & Lovegrove, W. (1984). The effects of field size and luminance on contrast sensitivity differences between specifically reading disabled and normal children. *Neuropsychologia, 22,* 73–77.

Martin, R. C., & Jensen, C. R. (1988). Phonological priming in the lexical decision task: A failure to replicate. *Memory and Cognition, 16,* 505–521.

Mason, J. (1980). When *do* children learn to read: An exploration of four-year old children's letter and word reading competencies. *Reading Research Quarterly, 15,* 202–227.

Masonheimer, P., Drum, P., & Ehri, L. C. (1984). Does environmental print identification lead children into word reading? *Journal of Reading Behavior, 16,* 257–272.

Massaro, D. W. (1975). *Experimental psychology and information processing.* Chicago: Rand-McNally.

Massaro, D. W. (1988). Some criticisms of connectionist models of human performance. *Journal of Memory and Language, 27,* 213–234.

Masson, M. E. J. (1991). A distributed memory model of context effects in word identification. In D. Besner & G. W. Humphreys (Eds.), *Basic processes in reading: Visual word recognition* (pp. 233–263). Hillsdale, NJ: Erlbaum.

Masson, M. E. J. (1995). A distributed memory model of semantic priming. *Journal of Experimental Psychology: Learning, Memory, and Cognition, 21,* 3–23.

Masurkiewicz, A. J., & Tanyzer, H. J. (1963). *Early-to-read: I/t/a/program.* New York: Initial Teaching Alphabet.

Mathews, M. (1966). *Teaching to read.* Chicago: University of Chicago Press.

Mattingly, I. G. (1972). Reading, the linguistic process, and linguistic awareness. In J. F. Kavanagh & I. G. Mattingly (Eds.), *Language by ear and by eye: The relationship between speech and reading* (pp. 133–147). Cambridge, MA: MIT Press.

Mattingly, I. G. (1992). Linguistic awareness and orthographic form. In R. Frost & L. Katz (Eds.), *Orthography, phonology, morphology, and meaning* (pp. 11–26). Advances in Psychology. Amsterdam: Elsevier.

May, D. C., & Kundert, D. K. (1997). School readiness practices and children at risk: Examining the issues. *Psychology in the Schools, 34*, 73–84.

May, D. C., Kundert, D. K., Nikoloff, O., Welch, E., Garrett, M., & Brent, D. (1994). School readiness: An obstacle to intervention and inclusion. *Journal of Early Intervention, 18*, 290–301.

Mayringer, H., & Wimmer, H. (2000). Pseudoname learning by German-speaking children with dyslexia: Evidence for a phonological learning deficit. *Journal of Experimental Child Psychology, 75*, 116–133.

McBride-Chang, C., Bialystok, E., Chong, K., & Li, Y. (2004). Levels of phonological awareness in three cultures. *Journal of Experimental Child Psychology, 89*, 93–111.

McBride-Chang, C., & Ho, C. S. H. (2000). Cross-cultural similarities in the predictors of reading acquisition. *Journal of Educational Psychology, 92*, 50–55.

McBride-Chang, C., & Kail, R. V. (2002). Cross-cultural similarities in the predictors of reading acquisition. *Child Development, 73*, 1392–1407.

McBride-Chang, C., Shu, H., Zhou, A. B., Wat, C. P., & Wagner, R. K. (2003). Morphological knowledge uniquely predicts young children's Chinese character recognition. *Journal of Educational Psychology, 95*, 743–751.

McBride-Chang, C., & Treiman, R. (2003). Hong Kong Chinese kindergartners learn to read English analytically. *Psychological Science, 14*, 138–143.

McBride-Chang, C., & Zhong, Y. (2003). A longitudinal study of phonological processing, visual skills, and speed of processing on Chinese character acquisition among Hong Kong Chinese kindergartners. In C. McBride-Chang & H. C. Chen (Eds.), *Reading development in Chinese children* (pp. 33–46). Westport, CT: Praeger.

McCandliss, B. D., Cohen, L., & Dehaene, S. (2003). The visual word form area: Expertise for reading in the fusiform gyrus. *Trends in Cognitive Sciences, 7*, 293–299.

McCann, R., & Besner, D. (1987). Reading pseudohomophones: Implications for models of pronunciation assembly and the locus of word-frequency effects in naming. *Journal of Experimental Psychology: Human Perception and Performance, 13*, 14–24.

McCarthy, R., & Warrington, E. K. (1986). Phonological reading: Phenomena and paradoxes. *Cortex, 22*, 359–380.

MacLean, M., Bryant, P., & Bradley, L. (1987). Rhymes, nursery rhymes, and reading in early childhood. *Merrill-Palmer Quarterly, 33*, 255–281.

McClelland, J. L. (1979). On the time relations of mental processes: An examination of systems of processing in cascade. *Psychological Review, 86*, 287–330.

McClelland, J. L. (1991). Stochastic interactive processes and the effect of context on perception. *Cognitive Psychology, 23*, 1–44.

McClelland, J. L., & Johnston, J. C. (1977). The role of familiar units in perception of words and nonwords. *Perception and Psychophysics, 22*, 243–261.

McClelland, J. L., & Rumelhart, D. E. (1981). An interactive activation model of context effects in letter perception. Part 1: An account of basic findings. *Psychological Review, 88*, 375–407.

McClelland, J. L., & Seidenberg, M. S. (2000). Why do kids say goed and brang? Review of S. Pinker, Rules and Words. *Science, 287*, 47–48.

McConkie, G. W., Kerr, P. W., Reddix, M. D., & Zola, D. (1988). Eye movement control during reading: I. The location of initial eye fixations in words. *Vision Research, 28*, 1107–1118.

McConkie, G. W., & Rayner, K. (1975). The span of effective stimulus during a fixation in reading. *Perception and Psychophysics, 17*, 578–586.

McConkie, G. W., & Yang, S. (2003). Basic assumptions concerning eye movement control during reading. *Behavioral and Brain Sciences, 26*, 493–494.

McConkie, G. W., & Zola, D. (1979). Is visual information integrated across successive fixations in reading? *Perception and Psychophysics, 25*, 221–224.

McConkie, G. W., Zola, D., Grimes, J., Kerr, P. W., Bryant, N. R., & Wolff, P. M. (1991). Children's eye movements during reading. In J. F. Stein (Ed.), *Vision and visual dyslexia* (pp. 251–262). London: Macmillan.

McCormick, C. E., & Mason, J. M. (1986). Intervention procedures for increasing preschool children's interest in and knowledge about reading. In W. H. Teale & E. Sulzby (Eds.), *Emergent literacy: Writing and reading* (pp. 90–115). Norwood, NJ: Ablex.

McCracken, G., & Walcutt, C. (1963). *Lippincott Basic Reading Program.* Philadelphia: Lippincott.

McCrory, E. (2001). *The neurocognitive basis of developmental dyslexia.* PhD dissertation, University College London.

McCutchen, D., & Perfetti, C. A. (1982). The visual tongue-twister effect: Phonological activation in silent reading. *Journal of Verbal Learning and Verbal Behavior, 21*, 672–687.

McDermott, K. B., Petersen, S. E., Watson, J. M., & Ojemann, J. G. (2003). A procedure for identifying regions preferentially activated by attention to semantic and phonological relations using functional magnetic resonance imaging. *Neuropsychologia, 41*(3), 293–303.

McDonald, J. L., & MacWhinney, B. (1995). The time course of anaphor resolution: Effects of implicit verb causality and gender. *Journal of Memory and Language, 34*, 543–566.

McDonald, S. A., & Shillcock, R. C. (2003a). Eye movements reveal the on-line computation of lexical probabilities during reading. *Psychological Science, 14*, 648–652.

McDonald, S. A., & Shillcock, R. C. (2003b). Low-level predictive inference in reading: The influence of transitional probabilities on eye movements. *Vision Research, 43*, 1735–1751.

McDougall, S., Hulme, C., Ellis, A. W., & Monk, A. (1994). Learning to read: The role of short-term memory and phonological skills. *Journal of Experimental Child Psychology, 58*, 112–123.

McGill-Franzen, A., Langford, C., & Adams, E. (2002). Learning to be literate: A comparison of five urban early childhood programs. *Journal of Educational Psychology, 94*, 443–464.

McGuffey, W. H. (1879). *McGuffey's first eclectic reader.* New York: American Book.

McGuinness, C., McGuinness, D., & McGuinness, G. (1996). Phono-Graphix: A new method for remediating reading difficulties. *Annals of Dyslexia, 46*, 73–96.

McKeeff, T. J., & Behrmann, M. (2004). Pure alexia and covert reading: Evidence from stroop tasks. *Cognitive Neuropsychology, 2–4*, 443–458.

McKinney, J. D. (1990). Longitudinal research on the behavioral characteristics of children with learning disabilities. In J. Torgesen (Ed.), *Cognitive and behavioral characteristics of children with learning disabilities* (pp. 165–172). Austin, TX.: PRO-ED.

McKoon, G., & Ratcliff, R. (1992). Inference during reading. *Psychological Review, 99*, 440–446.

McNeill, D. (1970). *The acquisition of language: The study of developmental psycholinguistics.* New York: Harper & Row.

McRae, K., Seidenberg, M. S., & de Sa, V. R. (1997). On the nature and scope of featural representations of word meaning. *Journal of Experimental Psychology: General, 126*, 99–130.

MacSweeney, M., Campbell, R., Calvert, G. A., McGuire, P. K., David, A. S., Suckling, J., et al. (2001). Dispersed activation in the left temporal cortex for speech-reading in congenitally deaf people. *Proceedings of the Royal Society of London, 268*, 451–457.

Mechelli, A., Gorno-Tempini, M.-L., & Price C. J. (2003). Neuroimaging studies of word and pseudoword reading: Consistencies, inconsistencies and limitations. *Journal of Cognitive Neuroscience, 15*, 260–271.

Menard, M. T., Kosslyn, S. M., Thompson, W. L., Alpert, N. M., & Rauch, S. L. (1996). Encoding words and pictures: A positron emission tomography study. *Neuropsychologia, 34*(3), 185–194.

Merrills, J. D., Underwood, G., & Wood, D. J. (1994). The word recognition skills of profoundly, prelingually deaf children. *British Journal of Developmental Psychology, 12,* 365–384.

Mervis, C. B., & Bertrand, J. (1997). Developmental relations between cognition and language: Evidence from Williams syndrome. In L. B. Adamson & M. A. Romski (Eds.), *Research on communication and language disorders: Contributions to theories of language development* (pp. 75–106). New York: Brookes.

Meseguer, E., Carreiras, M., & Clifton, C. (2002). Overt reanalysis strategies and eye movements during the reading of mild garden path sentences. *Memory and Cognition, 30,* 551–561.

Metsala, J. L., Stanovich, K. E., & Brown, G. D. A. (1998). Regularity effects and the phonological deficit model of reading disabilities: A meta-analytic review. *Journal of Educational Psychology, 90,* 279–293.

Metsala, J. L., & Walley, A. C. (1998). Spoken vocabulary growth and the segmental restructuring of lexical representations: Precursors to phonemic awareness and early reading ability. In J. L. Metsala & L. C. Ehri (Eds.), *Word recognition in beginning literacy* (pp. 89–120). Mahwah, NJ: Erlbaum.

Metzger, M. A., & Fleetwood, E. (1991). *Becoming a proficient cuer.* Silver Spring, MD: Calliope Press.

Meyer, D. E., & Schvaneveldt, R. W. (1971). Facilitation in recognizing pairs of words: Evidence of a dependence between retrieval operations. *Journal of Experimental Psychology, 90,* 227–234.

Meyer, M. S., & Felton, R. H. (1999). Repeated reading to enhance fluency: Old approaches and new directions. *Annals of Dyslexia, 49,* 283–306.

Miellet, S., & Sparrow, L. (2004). Phonological codes are assembled before word fixation: Evidence from a boundary paradigm in sentence reading. *Brain and Language, 90,* 299–310.

Miller, G. A. (1990). WordNet: An on-line lexical database. *International Journal of Lexicography, 3,* 235–312.

Millis, M. L., & Button, S. B. (1989). The effect of polysemy on lexical decision time: Now you see it, now you don't. *Memory and Cognition, 17,* 141–147.

Minsky, M., & Papert, S. (1969). *Perceptrons: An introduction to computational geometry.* Cambridge, MA: MIT Press.

Miozzo, M., & Caramazza, A. (1998). Varieties of pure alexia: The case of failure to access graphemic representations. *Cognitive Neuropsychology, 15,* 203–238.

Moats, L. (2001, summer). Overcoming the language gap. *American Educator,* 5–9.

Mody, M., Studdert-Kennedy, M., & Brady, S. (1997). Speech perception deficits in poor readers: Auditory processing or phonological coding? *Journal of Experimental Child Psychology, 64,* 199–231.

Monsell, S. (1991). The nature and locus of words frequency effects in reading. In D. Besner & G. W. Humphreys (Eds.), *Basic processes in reading: Visual word recognition* (pp. 148–197). Hillsdale, NJ: Erlbaum.

Monsell, S., Doyle, M. C., & Haggard, P. N. (1989). Effects of frequency on words recognition tasks: Where are they? *Journal of Experimental Psychology: General, 118,* 43–71.

Montant, M., & Ziegler, J. C. (2001). Can orthographic rimes facilitate naming? *Psychonomic Bulletin and Review, 8,* 351–356.

Moore, C. J., & Price, C. J. (1999). Three distinct ventral occipitotemporal regions for reading and object naming. *NeuroImage, 10*(2), 181–192.

Morais, J. (1990). Phonological awareness: A bridge between language and literacy. In D. J. Sawyer & B. J. Fox (Eds.), *Phonological awareness in reading* (pp. 31–71). New York: Springer-Verlag.

Morais, J. (1991a). Phonological awareness: A bridge between language and literacy. In D. J. Sawyer & B. J. Fox (Eds.), *Phonological awareness in reading: The evolution of current perspectives* (pp. 31–71). Berlin: Springer-Verlag.

Morais, J. (1991b). Constraints on the development of phonological awareness. In S. Brady & D. Shankweiler (Eds.), *Phonological processes in literacy: A tribute to Isabelle Y. Liberman.* (pp. 5–27). Hillsdale, NJ: Erlbaum.

Morais, J., Alegria, J., & Content, A. (1987a). The relationships between segmental analysis and alphabetic literacy: An interactive view. *Cahiers de Psychologie Cognitive, 7,* 415–438.

Morais, J., Bertelson, P., Cary, L., & Alegria, J. (1986). Literacy training and speech analysis. *Cognition, 24,* 45–64.

Morais, J., Carey, L., Alegria, J., & Bertelson, P. (1979). Does awareness of speech as a sequence of phones arise spontaneously? *Cognition, 7,* 323–331.

Morais, J., Castro, S. L., Scliar-Cabral, L., Kolinsky, R., & Content, A. (1987b). The effects of literacy on the recognition of dichotic words. *Quarterly Journal of Experimental Psychology, 39A,* 451–465.

Morais, J., Content, A., Bertelson, P., Cary, L., & Kolinsky, R. (1988). Is there a critical period for the acquisition of segmental analysis? *Cognitive Neuropsychology, 5,* 347–352.

Morais, J., & Kolinsky, R. (1994). Perception and awareness in phonological processing: The case of the phoneme. *Cognition, 50,* 287–297.

Morais, J., & Kolinsky, R. (2002a). Literacy effects on language and cognition. In L. Bäckman & C. von Hofsten (Eds.), *Psychology at the turn of the millennium* (Vol. 1, pp. 507–530). Hove, UK: Psychology Press.

Morais, J., & Kolinsky, R. (2002b). Pourquoi étudier les illettrés? *Le Langage et l'Homme, 37,* 191–208.

Morais, J., Kolinsky, R., Alegria, J., & Scliar-Cabral, L. (1998). Alphabetical literacy and phonological structure. *Letras de Hoje, 33,* 61–79.

Morais, J., Macedo, C., Grimm-Cabral, L., & Kolinsky, R. (in preparation, a). *Semantic retrieval from short-term memory in illiterate adults.*

Morais, J., Macedo, C., Grimm-Cabral, L., Larochelle, S., & Kolinsky, R. (in preparation, b). *The knowledge of semantic relations in illiterate adults.*

Morais, J., & Mousty, P. (1992). The causes of phonemic awareness. In J. Alegria, D. Holender, J. Morais, & M. Radeau (Eds.), *Analytic approaches to human cognition* (pp. 193–212). Amsterdam: Elsevier.

Morris, R. D., Steubing, K. K., Fletcher, J. M., Shaywitz, S. E., Lyon, G. R., Shankweiler, D. P., et al. (1998). Subtypes of reading disability: Variability around a phonological core. *Journal of Educational Psychology, 90,* 347–373.

Morrison, C. M., & Ellis, A. W. (1995). Roles of word frequency and age of acquisition in word naming and lexical decision. *Journal of Experimental Psychology: Learning, Memory, and Cognition, 21,* 116–133.

Morrison, F. J., Griffith, E. M., & Alberts, D. M. (1997). Nature—nurture in the classroom: Entrance age, school readiness, and learning in children. *Developmental Psychology, 33,* 254–262.

Morrison, R. E. (1984). Manipulation of stimulus onset delay in reading: Evidence for parallel programming of saccades. *Journal of Experimental Psychology: Human Perception and Performance, 10,* 667–682.

Morrison. R. E., & Rayner, K. (1981). Saccade size in reading depends upon character spaces and not visual angle. *Perception and Psychophysics, 30,* 395–396.

Morrow, D. G., Greenspan, S. L., & Bower, G. H. (1987). Accessibility and situation models in narrative comprehension. *Journal of Memory and Language, 26,* 165–187.

Morton, J. (1969). Interaction of information in word recognition. *Psychological Review, 76,* 165–178.

Morton, J., & Frith, U. (1995). Causal modelling: A structural approach to developmental psychopathology. In D. Cicchetti & D. J. Cohen (Eds.), *Manual of Developmental Psychopathology* (pp. 357–390). New York: Wiley.

Morton, J., & Patterson, K. E. (1980). A new attempt at an interpretation, or, an attempt at a new interpretation. In M. Coltheart, K. E. Patterson, & J. C. Marshall (Eds.), *Deep dyslexia* (pp. 91–118). London: Routledge & Kegan Paul.

Movellan, J. R., & McClelland, J. L. (2001). The Morton–Massaro law of information integration: Implications for models of perception. *Psychological Review, 108,* 113–148.

Mozer, M. C. (1983). Letter migration in word perception. *Journal of Experimental Psychology: Human Perception and Performance, 9,* 531–546.

Mozer, M. C. (1991). *The perception of multiple objects: A connectionist approach.* Cambridge, MA: MIT Press.

Mozer, M. C., & Behrmann, M. (1990). On the interaction of selective attention and lexical knowledge: A connectionist account of neglect dyslexia. *Journal of Cognitive Neuroscience, 2,* 96–123.

Müller, K., & Brady, S. (2001). Correlates of early reading performance in a transparent orthography. *Reading and Writing, 14,* 757–799.

Mummery, C. J., Patterson, K., Hodges, J. R., & Price, C. J. (1998). Functional neuroanatomy of the semantic system: Divisible by what? *Journal of Cognitive Neuroscience, 10*(6), 766–777.

Mummery, C. J., Patterson, K., Price, C. J., Ashburner, J., Frackowiak, R. S. J., & Hodges, J. R. (2000). A voxel-based morphometry study of semantic dementia: Relationship between temporal lobe atrophy and semantic memory. *Annals of Neurology, 47*(1), 36–45.

Mummery, C. J., Patterson, K., Wise, R. J., Vandenbergh, R., Price, C. J., & Hodges, J. R. (1999). Disrupted temporal lobe connections in semantic dementia. *Brain, 122,* 61–73.

Murphy, L., & Pollatsek, A. (1994). Developmental dyslexia: Heterogeneity without discrete subgroups. *Annals of Dyslexia, 44,* 120–146.

Murray, W. S. (1998). Paraoveal pragmatics. In G. Underwood (Ed.), *Eye guidance in reading and scene perception* (pp. 181–199). Oxford: Elsevier.

Muter, V., Hulme, C., Snowling, M. J., & Stevenson, J. (2004). Phonemes, rimes, vocabulary and grammatical skills as foundations of early reading development: Evidence from a longitudinal study. *Developmental Psychology, 40*(5), 665–681.

Muter, V., Hulme, C., Snowling, M., & Taylor, S. (1998). Segmentation, not rhyming, predicts early progress in learning to read. *Journal of Experimental Child Psychology, 71,* 3–27.

Mycroft, R. H., Behrmann, M., & Kay, J. (in press). Evidence for a causal role of a visual processing impairment in letter-by-letter reading? *Cognitive Neuropsychology.*

Myers, J. L., & O'Brien, E. J. (1998). Accessing the discourse representation during reading. *Discourse Processes, 26,* 131–157.

Myklebust, H. R. (1960). *The psychology of deafness.* New York: Grune & Stratton.

Nagy, W. E., & Anderson, R. C. (1984). How many words are there in printed school English? *Reading Research Quarterly, 19,* 304–330.

Nagy, W. E., & Herman, P. A. (1987). Breadth and depth of vocabulary knowledge: Implications for acquisition and instruction. In M. McKeown & M. E. Curtis (Eds.), *The nature of vocabulary acquisition* (pp. 19–36). Hillsdale NJ: Erlbaum.

Nagy, W. E., & Scott, J. A. (2000). Vocabulary processes. In M. L. Kamil, P. B. Mosenthal, P. David Pearson, & R. Barr (Eds.), *Handbook of reading research* (Vol. 3, pp. 69–284). Mahwah, NJ: Erlbaum.

Naslund, J. C., & Schneider, W. (1996). Kindergarten letter knowledge, phonological skills, and memory processes: Relative effects on early literacy. *Journal of Experimental Child Psychology, 62,* 30–59.

Nathan, L., Stackhouse, J., Goulandris, N., & Snowling, M. J. (2004). The development of early literacy skills among children with speech difficulties: A test of the "Critical Age Hypothesis." *Journal of Speech, Language and Hearing Research, 47*, 377–391.

Nation, K. (1999). Reading skills in hyperlexia: A developmental perspective. *Psychological Bulletin, 125*, 338–355.

Nation, K., Adams, J. W., Bowyer-Crane, C., & Snowling, M. J. (1999). Working memory deficits in poor comprehenders reflect underlying impairments. *Journal of Experimental Child Psychology, 73*, 139–158.

Nation, K., Clarke, P., Marshall, C. M., & Durand, M. (2004). Hidden language impairments in children: Parallels between poor reading comprehension and specific language impairment. *Journal of Speech, Hearing and Language Research, 41*(1), 199–211.

Nation, K., Clarke, P., & Snowling, M. J. (2002). General cognitive ability in children with poor reading comprehension. *British Journal of Educational Psychology, 72*, 549–560.

Nation, K., Marshall, C. M., & Altmann, G. T. M. (2003). Investigating individual differences in children's real-time sentence comprehension using language-mediated eye movements. *Journal of Experimental Child Psychology, 86*(4), 314–329.

Nation, K., Marshall, C., & Snowling, M. J. (2001). Phonological and semantic contributions to children's picture naming skill. *Language and Cognitive Processes, 16*, 241–259.

Nation, K., & Snowling, M. J. (1997). Assessing reading difficulties: The validity and utility of current measures of reading skill. *British Journal of Educational Psychology, 67*, 359–370.

Nation, K., & Snowling, M. J. (1998a). Semantic processing and the development of word recognition skills: Evidence from children with reading comprehension difficulties. *Journal of Memory and Language, 39*, 85–101.

Nation, K., & Snowling, M. J. (1998b). Individual differences in contextual facilitation: Evidence from dyslexia and poor reading comprehension. *Child Development, 69*, 996–1011.

Nation, K., & Snowling, M. J. (1999). Developmental differences in sensitivity to semantic relations among good and poor comprehenders: Evidence from semantic priming. *Cognition, 70*, B1–B13.

National Institute of Child Health and Human Development (2000). *Report of the National Reading Panel. Teaching children to read: An evidence-based assessment of the scientific research literature on reading and its implications for reading instruction* (NIH Publication No. 00–4769). Washington, DC: US Government Printing Office.

National Reading Panel (2000). Teaching children to read: An evidence-based assessment of the scientific research literature on reading and its implications for reading instruction. Washington, DC: National Institute for Child Health and Human Development.

National Research Council (1998). *Preventing reading difficulties in young children.* In C. E. Snow, M. S. Burns, & P. Griffin (Eds.). Washington, DC: National Academy.

Neale, M. C., & Cardon, L. R. (1992). *Methodology for genetic studies of twins and families.* Dordrecht, the Netherlands: Kluwer Academic.

Neale, M. C., & Kendler, K. S. (1995). Models of comorbidity for multifactorial disorders. *American Journal of Human Genetics, 57*, 935–953.

Neale, M. D. (1997). *Neale Analysis of Reading Ability-Revised (NARA-II).* Windsor, UK: NFER.

Nebes, R. D. (1989). Semantic memory in Alzheimer's disease. *Psychological Bulletin, 106*, 377–394.

Neely, J. H. (1977). Semantic priming and retrieval from lexical memory: Roles of inhibitionless spreading activation and limited-capacity attention. *Journal of Experimental Psychology: General, 106*, 226–254.

Neely, J. H. (1991). Semantic priming effects in visual word recognition: A selective review of current findings and theories. In D. Besner & G. W. Humphreys (Eds.), *Basic processes in reading: Visual word recognition* (pp. 264–336). Hillsdale, NJ: Erlbaum.

Neuhaus, G. F., Foorman, B. R., Francis, D. J., & Carlson, C. D. (2001). Measures of information processing in Rapid Automatized Naming (RAN) and their relation to reading. *Journal of Experimental Child Psychology, 78*, 359–373.

Neuhaus, G. F., & Swank, P. R. (2002). Understanding the relations between RAN letter subtest components and word reading in first-grade students. *Journal of Learning Disabilities, 35*, 158–174.

Neuman, S., Copple, C., & Bredekamp, S. (2000). *Learning to read and write: Developmentally appropriate practices for young children.* Washington, DC: National Association for the Education of Young Children. New York: Wiley.

Neville, H. J. (1991). Whence the specialization of language hemisphere? In I. G. Mattingly & M. Studdert-Kennedy (Eds.), *Modularity and theory of speech perception* (pp. 269–295). Hillsdale, NJ: Erlbaum.

Neville, H., & Bavelier, D. (2001). Specificity of developmental neuroplasticity in humans: Evidence from sensory deprivation and altered language experience. In C. A. Shaw & J. C. McEachern (Eds.), *Toward a theory of neuroplasticity* (pp. 261–274). Hove, UK: Psychology Press.

Neville, H. J., & Mills, D. L. (1997). Epigenesis of language. *Mental Retardation and Developmental disabilities, 3*, 282–292.

Neville, H. J., Mills, D. L., & Lawson, D. (1992). Fractionating language: Different neural subsystems with different sensitive periods. *Cerebral Cortex, 2*, 244–258.

Newcombe, F., & Marshall, J. C. (1985). Reading and writing by letter sounds. In K. E. Patterson, J. C. Marshall, & M. Coltheart (Eds.), *Surface dyslexia: Neuropsychological and cognitive studies of phonological reading* (pp. 35–51). London: LEA.

Newell, A., & Simon, H. A. (1972). *Human problem solving.* Englewood Cliffs, NJ: Prentice-Hall.

Newton, P. K., & Barry, C. (1997). Concreteness effects in word production but not word comprehension in deep dyslexia. *Cognitive Neuropsychology, 14*, 481–509.

Nielsen, D. C., & Monson, D. L. (1996). Effects of literacy environment on literacy development of kindergarten children. *Journal of Educational Research, 89*, 259–271.

Niessen, M., Frith, U., Reitsma, P., & Öhngren, B. (2000). *Learning disorders as a barrier to human development 1995–1999.* Evaluation Report. Technical Committee, COST Social Sciences.

Niswander, E., Pollatsek, A., & Rayner, K. (2000). The processing of derived and suffixed words during reading. *Language and Cognitive Processes, 15*, 389–420.

Nittrouer, S. (1999). Do temporal processing deficits cause phonological processing problems? *Journal of Speech, Language, and Hearing Research, 42*, 925–942.

Noppeney, U., & Price, C. J. (2003). Functional imaging of the semantic system: Retrieval of sensory experienced and verbally-learnt knowledge. *Brain and Language, 84*, 120–133.

Norbury, C. F., & Bishop, D. V. M. (2002). *International Journal of Language and Communication Disorders, 37*, 227–251.

Norris, D. (1994). A quantitative multiple-levels model of reading aloud. *Journal of Experimental Psychology: Human Perception and Performance, 20*, 1212–1232.

Norris, D., McQueen, J. M., & Cutler, A. (2000). Merging information in speech recognition: Feedback is never necessary. *Behavioral and Brain Sciences, 23*, 299–324.

Nöthan, M. M., Schulte-Körne, G., Grimm, T., Cichon, S., Vogt, I. R., Müller-Myhsok, B., et al. (1999). Genetic linkage analysis with dyslexia: Evidence for linkage of spelling disability to chromosome 15. *European Child and Adolescent Psychiatry, 8*, 56–59.

Nunes, T., Bryant, P., & Bindman, M. (1997). Morphological spelling strategies: Developmental stages and processes. *Developmental Psychology, 33*, 637–649.

O'Brien, E. J., Shank, D. M., Myers, J. L., & Rayner, K. (1988). Elaborative inferences during reading: Do they occur on-line? *Journal of Experimental Psychology: Learning, Memory, and Cognition, 14*, 410–420.

O'Donnell, R. C. (1974). Syntactic differences between speech and writing. *American Speech, 49*, 102–110.

O'Regan, J. K. (1979). Eye guidance in reading: Evidence for the linguistic control hypothesis. *Perception and Psychophysics, 25*, 501–509.

O'Regan, J. K. (1990). Eye movements and reading. In E. Kowler (Ed.), *Eye movements and their role in visual and cognitive processes* (pp. 395–453). Amsterdam: Elsevier.

O'Regan, J. K. (1992). Optimal viewing position in words and the strategy-tactics theory of eye movements in reading. In K. Rayner (Ed.), *Eye movements and visual cognition: Scene perception and reading* (pp. 333–354). New York: Springer-Verlag.

O'Regan, J. K., & Lévy-Schoen, A. (1987). Eye movement strategy and tactics in word recognition and reading. In M. Coltheart (Ed.), *Attention and performance.* Vol 12: *The psychology of reading* (pp. 363–383). Hillsdale, NJ: Erlbaum.

O'Regan, J. K., Lévy-Schoen, A., & Jacobs, A. M. (1983). The effect of visibility on eye movement parameters in reading. *Perception and Psychophysics, 34*, 457–464.

O'Reilly, R. C. (1996). Biologically plausible error-driven learning using local activation differences: The generalized recirculation algorithm. *Neural Computation, 8*, 895–938.

Oakhill, J. V. (1982). Constructive processes in skilled and less-skilled comprehenders' memory for sentences. *British Journal of Psychology, 73*, 13–20.

Oakhill, J. V. (1983). Instantiation in skilled and less-skilled comprehenders. *Quarterly Journal of Experimental Psychology, 35A*, 441–450.

Oakhill, J. V. (1984). Inferential and memory skills in children's comprehension of stories. *British Journal of Educational Psychology, 54*, 31–39.

Oakhill, J. V. (1993). Children's difficulties in reading comprehension. *Educational Psychology Review, 5*, 223–237.

Oakhill, J. V. (1994). Individual differences in children's text comprehension. In M. A. Gernsbacher (Ed.), *Handbook of psycholinguistics* (pp. 821–848). San Diego, CA: Academic.

Oakhill, J. V., Cain, K. E., & Bryant, P. E. (2003a). The dissociation of word reading and text comprehension: Evidence from component skills. *Language and Cognitive Processes, 18*, 443–468.

Oakhill, J. V., Cain, K. E., & Bryant, P. E. (2003b). Prediction of comprehension skill in the primary school years. Paper presented at the biennial meeting of the Society for Research in Child Development, Tampa.

Oakhill, J. V., & Garnham, A. (1988). *Becoming a skilled reader.* New York: Blackwell.

Oakhill, J. V., & Yuill, N. (1986). Pronoun resolution in skilled and less-skilled comprehenders: Effects of memory load and inferential complexity. *Language and Speech, 29*, 25–36.

Oakhill, J. V., & Yuill, N. (1996). Higher order factors in comprehension disability: Processes and remediation. In C. Cornoldi and J. V. Oakhill (Eds.), *Reading comprehension difficulties* (pp. 69–92). Mahwah, NJ: Erlbaum.

Oakhill, J. V., Yuill, N., & Parkin, A. (1986). On the nature of differences between skilled and less-skilled comprehenders. *Journal of Research in Reading, 9*, 80–91.

Ogbu, J. U. (1990). Minority education in comparative perspective. *Journal of Negro Education, 59*, 45–57.

Ogbu, J. U. (1999). Beyond language: Ebonics, proper English, and identity in a Black-American speech community. *American Educational Research Journal, 36*, 147–184.

Okagaki, L., & Sternberg, R. J. (1993). Parental beliefs and children's school performance. *Child Development, 64*, 36–56.

Olson, A. C., & Caramazza, A. (1994). Representation and connectionist models: The NETspell experience. In G. D. A. Brown & N. C. Ellis (Eds.), *Handbook of Spelling* (pp. 337–363). Chichester: Wiley.

Olson, A. C., & Caramazza, A. (2004). Orthographic structure and deaf spelling errors: Syllables, letter frequency and speech. *Quarterly Journal of Experimental Psychology, 57A*(3), 385–417.

Olson, A. C., & Nickerson, J. F. (2001). Syllabic organization and deafness: Orthographic structure or letter frequency in reading? *Quarterly Journal of Experimental Psychology, 54A*, 421–438.

Olson, D. R. (1977). From utterance to text: The bias of language in speech and writing. *Harvard Educational Review, 47*, 257–281.

Olson, R. K. (1985). Disabled reading processes and cognitive profiles. In D. Gray & J. Kavanagh (Eds.), *Biobehavioral measures of dyslexia* (pp. 215–244). Parkton, MD: York.

Olson, R. K., Datta, H., Gayan, J., & DeFries, J. C. (1999). A behavioral-genetic analysis of reading disabilities and component processes. In R. M. Klein & P. A. McMullen (Eds.), *Converging methods for understanding reading and dyslexia* (pp. 133–153). Cambridge, MA: MIT Press.

Olson, R. K., Forsberg, H., & Wise, B. (1994). Genes, environment, and the development of orthographic skills. In V. W. Berninger (Ed.), *The varieties of orthographic knowledge.* Vol. 1: *Theoretical and developmental issues* (pp. 27–71). Dordrecht, the Netherlands: Kluwer Academic.

Olson, R. K., & Gayan, J. (2001). Brains, genes, and environment in reading development. In S. B. Neuman & D. K. Dickinson (Eds.), *Handbook of early literacy research* (pp. 81–94). New York: Guilford.

Olson, R. K., Kliegl, R., & Davidson, B. J. (1983). Dyslexic and normal readers' eye movements. *Journal of Experimental Psychology: Human Perception and Performance, 9*, 816–825.

Olson, R. K., Kliegl, R., Davidson, B. J., & Foltz, G. (1985). Individual and developmental differences in reading disability. In G. E. MacKinnon & T. G. Waller (Eds.), *Reading research: Advances in theory and practice* (Vol. 4, pp. 1–64). New York: Academic.

Olson, R. K., Wise, B., Conners, F., Rack, J., and Fulker, D. (1989). Specific deficits in component reading and language skills: Genetic and environmental influences. *Journal of Learning Disabilities, 22*(6), 339–348.

Olson, R. K., Wise, B., & Ring, J. (1999). Training phonological awareness with and without explicit attention to articulation. *Journal of Experimental Child Psychology, 72*, 271–304.

Olson, S. L., Bates, J. E., & Bayles, K. (1984). Mother—infant interaction and the development of individual differences in children's cognitive competence. *Developmental Psychology, 20*, 166–179.

Öney, B., & Goldman, S. R. (1984). Decoding and comprehension skills in Turkish and English: Effects of the regularity of grapheme—phoneme correspondences. *Journal of Educational Psychology, 76*, 557–567.

O'Regan, J. K. & Lévy-Schoen, A. (1987) Eye movement strategy and tactics in word recognition and reading. In M. Coltheart (Ed.), *Attention and performance: vol. 12. The psychology of reading* (pp. 363–383). Hillsdale, NJ: Erlbaum.

Orton, S. T. (1925). "Word-blindness" in school children. *Archives of Neurology and Psychiatry, 14*, 581–615.

Osaka, N. (1987). Effect of peripheral visual field size upon eye movements during Japanese text processing. In J. K. O'Regan & A. Lévy-Schoen (Eds.), *Eye movements: From physiology to cognition* (pp. 421–429). Amsterdam: Elsevier.

Osaka, N. (1992). Size of saccade and fixation duration of eye movements during reading: Psychophysics of Japanese text processing. *Journal of the Optical Society of America, 9*, 5–13.

Ostrosky-Solis, F., Ardila, A., Rosselli, M., Lopez-Arango, G., & Uriel-Mendoza, V. (1998). Neuropsychological test performance in illiterate subjects. *Archives of Clinical Neuropsychology, 13*, 645–660.

Otero, J., & Kintsch, W. (1992). Failures to detect contradictions in a text: What readers believe versus what they read. *Psychological Science, 3*, 229–235.

Owen, F. W., Adams, P. A., Forrest, T., Stolz, L. M., & Fisher, S. (1971). Leaning disorders in children: Sibling studies. *Monographs of the Society for Research in Child Development, 36*(4), 1–77.

Paap, K. R., Chun, E., & Vonnahme, P. (1999). Discrete threshold versus continuous strength models of perceptual recognition. *Canadian Journal of Experimental Psychology, 53*, 277–293.

Paap, K. R., & Johansen, L. S. (1994). The case of the vanishing frequency effect: A retest of the verification model. *Journal of Experimental Psychology: Human Perception and Performance, 20*, 1129–1157.

Paap, K. R., Johansen, L. S., Chun, E., & Vonnahme, P. (2000). Neighborhood frequency does affect performance in the Reicher task: Encoding or decision? *Journal of Experimental Psychology: Human Perception and Performance, 26*, 1691–1720.

Paap, K. R., & Newsome, S. L. (1980). A perceptual-confusion account of the WSE in the target search paradigm. *Perception and Psychophysics, 27*, 444–456.

Paap, K. R., Newsome, S. L., McDonald, J. E., & Schvaneveldt, R. W. (1982). An activation-verification model for letter and word recognition: The word-superiority effect. *Psychological Review, 89*, 573–594.

Paap, K. R., & Noel, R. W. (1991). Dual-route models of print to sound: Still a good horse race. *Psychological Research, 53*, 13–24.

Paap, K. R., Noel, R. W., & Johansen, L. S. (1992). Dual-route models of print to sound: Red herrings and real horses. In R. Frost & L. Katz (Eds.), *Orthography, phonology, morphology, and meaning* (pp. 293–318). Advances in Psychology. Amsterdam: Elsevier.

Pacton, S., Fayol, M., & Perruchet, P. (2002). The acquisition of untaught orthographic regularities in French. In L. Verhoeven, C. Elbro, & P. Reitsma (Eds.), *Precursors of functional literacy* (pp. 121–137). Dordrecht, the Netherlands: Kluwer Academic.

Pacton, S., Perruchet, P., Cleeremans, A., & Fayol, M. (2001). Implicit learning in real world context: The case of orthographic regularities. *Journal of Experimental Psychology: General, 130*(3), 401–426.

Padden, C. A., & Hanson, V. L. (1999). Search for the missing link: The development of skilled reading in deaf children. In H. Lane & K. Emmorey (Eds.), *The signs of language revisited: An anthology to honor Ursula Bellugi and Edward Klima* (pp. 435–449). Hillsdale, NJ: Erlbaum.

Padden, C. A., & Le Master, B. (1985). An alphabet on the hand: The acquisition of fingerspelling by deaf children. *Sign Language Studies, 47*, 161–172.

Padden, C. A., & Ramsey, C. (2000). American sign language and reading ability in deaf children. In C. Chamberlain, J. P. Morford, & R. I. Mayberry (Eds.), *Language acquisition by eye* (pp. 165–189). Mahwah, NJ: Erlbaum.

Page, M. (2000). Connectionist modelling in psychology: A localist manifesto. *Behavioral and Brain Sciences, 23*, 443–467.

Pagon, R., Bennett, M., LaVeck, B., Stewart, K., & Johnson, J. (1987). Williams syndrome: Features in late childhood and adolescence. *Pediatrics, 80*, 85–91.

Papanicalaou, A. C., Simos, P. G., Fletcher, J. M., Francis, D. J., Foorman, B., Castillo, E. M., et al. (2003). Early development and plasticity of neuro-physiological processes involved in reading. In B. Foorman (Ed.), *Preventing and remediating reading difficulties: Bringing science to scale* (pp. 3–22). Baltimore: York.

Parkin, A. J. (1993). Progressive aphasia without dementia: A clinical and cognitive neuropsychological analysis. *Brain and Language, 44*, 201–220.

Partnership for Reading (2001). Put reading first: The research building blocks for teaching children to read. University of Michigan: Center for the Improvement of Early Reading Achievement.

Patel, T., Snowling, M., & de Jong, P. (2004). A cross-linguistic comparison of children learning to read in English and in Dutch. *Journal of Educational Psychology, 96*, 785–797.

Patterson, K., & Behrmann, M. (1997). Frequency and consistency effects in a pure surface dyslexic patient. *Journal of Experimental Psychology: Human Perception and Performance, 23*, 1217–1231.

Patterson, K., & Coltheart, V. (1987). Phonological processes in reading: A tutorial review. In M. Coltheart (Ed.), *Attention and Performance XII* (pp. 421–447). Hillsdale, NJ: Erlbaum.

Patterson, K., Coltheart, M., & Marshall, J. C. (Eds.) (1985). *Surface dyslexia.* Hillsdale, NJ: Erlbaum.

Patterson, K., & Hodges, J. R. (1992). Deterioration of word meaning: Implications for reading. *Neuropsychologia, 30*, 1025–1040.

Patterson, K., & Kay, J. (1982). Letter-by-letter reading: Psychological descriptions of a neurological syndrome. *Quarterly Journal of Experimental Psychology Human Experimental Psychology, 34A*, 411–441.

Patterson, K., & Lambon Ralph, M. A. (1999). Selective disorders of reading? *Current Opinion in Neurobiology, 9*, 235–239.

Patterson, K., Lambon Ralph, M. A., Hodges, J. R., & McClelland, J. L. (2001). Deficits in irregular past-tense verb morphology associated with degraded semantic knowledge. *Neuropsychologia, 39*, 709–724.

Patterson, K., & Marcel, A. (1992). Phonological ALEXIA or PHONOLOGICAL alexia? In J. Alegria, D. Holender, J. Juncas de Morais, & M. Radeau (Eds.), *Analytic approaches to human cognition* (pp. 259–274). Amsterdam: Elsevier.

Patterson, K., Seidenberg, M. S., & McClelland, J. L. (1989). Connections and disconnections: Acquired dyslexia in a computational model of reading processes. In R. G. M. Morris (Ed.), *Parallel distributed processing: Implications for psychology and neurobiology* (pp. 131–181). Oxford: Oxford University Press.

Patterson, K., Suzuki, T., & Wydell, T. N. (1996). Interpreting a case of Japanese phonological alexia: The key is in phonology. *Cognitive Neuropsychology, 13*, 803–822.

Patterson, K. E. (1982). The relation between reading and phonological coding: Further neuropsychological observations. In A. W. Ellis (Ed.), *Normality and pathology in cognitive functions* (pp. 77–111). London: Academic.

Patterson, K. E., Graham, N., & Hodges, J. R. (1994). The impact of semantic memory loss on phonological representations. *Journal of Cognitive Neuroscience, 6*, 57–69.

Patterson, K. E., Marshall, J. C., & Coltheart, M. (1985). *Surface dyslexia: Cognitive and neuropsychological studies of phonological reading.* Hove, UK: Erlbaum.

Paulesu, E., Demonet, J. F., Fazio, F., McCrory, E., Chanoine, V., Brunswick, N., et al. (2001). Dyslexia: Cultural diversity and biological unity. *Science, 291*(5511), 2165–2167.

Paulesu, E., Frith, C. D., & Frackowiak, R. S. (1993). The neural correlates of the verbal component of working memory. *Nature, 362*(6418), 342–345.

Paulesu, E., McCrory, E., Fazio, F., Menoncello, L., Brunswick, N., Cappa, S. F., et al. (2000). A cultural effect on brain function. *Nature Neuroscience, 3*, 91–96.

Payne, A. C., Whitehurst, G. J., and Angell, A. L. (1994). The role of literacy environment in the language development of children from low-income families. *Early Childhood Research Quarterly, 9*, 427–440.

Pearson, P. D., & Taylor, B. (1998). Schools that beat the odds [on-line]. Available: http://www.ciera.org.

Pecher, D. (2001). Perception is a two-way junction: Feedback semantics in word recognition. *Psychonomic Bulletin and Review, 8*, 545–551.

Pedhazur, E. J. (1982). *Multivariate regression in behavioral research: Explanation and prediction* (2nd ed.). New York: Holt, Rinehart, & Winston.

Peereman, R., Content, & Bonin, P. (1998). Is perception a two-way street? The case of feedback consistency in visual word recognition. *Journal of Memory and Language, 39*, 151–174.

Peisner-Feinberg, E., Burchinal, M., R., Clifford, R. M., Culkin, M. L., Howes, C., Kagan, S. L., et al. (2001). The relation of preschool child-care quality to children's cognitive and social developmental trajectories through second grade. *Child Development, 72*, 1534–1553.

Pellegrini, A. D., Perlmutter, J. C., Galda, L., & Brody, G. H. (1990). Joint reading between Black Head Start children and their mothers. *Child Development, 61*, 443–453.

Pelletier, P. M., Ahmad, S. A., & Rourke, B. P. (2001). Classification rules for basic phonological processing disabilities and nonverbal learning difficulties: formulation and external validity. *Child Neuropsychology, 7*, 84–98.

Pennington, B. F. (1997). Using genetics to dissect cognition [invited editorial]. *American Journal of Human Genetics, 60*, 13–16.

Pennington, B. F., Bender, B., Puck, M., Salbenblatt, J., & Robinson, A. (1982). Learning disabilities in children with sex chromosome anomalies. *Child Development, 53*, 1182–1192.

Pennington, B. F., Gilger, J., Pauls, D., Smith, S. A., Smith, S. D., & DeFries, J. C. (1991). Evidence for major gene transmission of developmental dyslexia. *Journal of the American Medical Association, 266*(11), 1527–1534.

Pennington, B. F., & Lefly, D. L. (2001). Early reading development in children at family risk for dyslexia. *Child Development, 72*, 816–833.

Pennington, B. F., Puck, M., & Robinson, A. (1980). Language and cognitive development in 47, XXX females followed since birth. *Behavior Genetics, 10*(1), 31–41.

Pennington, B. F., & Smith, S. D. (1983). Genetic influences on learning disabilities and speech and language disorders. *Child Development, 54*, 369–387.

Pennington, B. F., van Orden, G. C., Smith, S. D., Green, P. A., & Haith, M. (1990). Phonological processing skills and deficits in adult dyslexics. *Child Development, 61*, 1753–1778.

Perea, M., & Carreiras, M. (1998). Effects of syllable frequency and neighborhood syllable frequency in visual word recognition. *Journal of Experimental Psychology: Human Perception and Performance, 24*, 1–11.

Perea, M., & Lupker, S. J. (2003). Does judge activate COURT? Transposed-letter similarity effects in masked associative priming. *Memory and Cognition, 31*, 829–841.

Perfetti, C. A. (1985). *Reading ability*. New York: Oxford University Press.

Perfetti, C. A. (1991). Representations and awareness in the acquisition of reading competence. In L. Rieben & C. A. Perfetti (Eds.), *Learning to read: Basic research and its implications* (pp. 33–44). Hillsdale, NJ: Erlbaum.

Perfetti, C. A. (1992). The representation problem in reading acquisition. In P. Gough, L. Ehri, & R. Treiman (Eds.), *Reading acquisition* (pp. 107–143). Hillsdale, NJ: Erlbaum.

Perfetti, C. A. (1994). Psycholinguistics and reading ability. In M. A. Gernsbacher (Ed.), *Handbook of psycholinguistics* (pp. 849–894). San Diego, CA: Academic.

Perfetti, C. A., Beck, I., Bell, L. C., & Hughes, C. (1987). Phonemic knowledge and learning to read are reciprocal: A longitudinal study of first-grade children. *Merrill-Palmer Quarterly, 33*, 283–319.

Perfetti, C. A., Bell, L. C., & Delaney, S. M. (1988). Automatic (prelexical) phonetic activation in silent word reading: Evidence from backward masking. *Journal of Memory and Language, 27,* 59–70.

Perfetti, C. A., & Goldman, S. R. (1976). Discourse memory and reading comprehension skill. *Journal of Verbal Learning and Verbal Behavior, 14,* 33–42.

Perfetti, C. A., & Hart, L. (2001). The lexical basis of comprehension skill. In D. S. Gorfein (Ed.), *On the consequences of meaning selection* (pp. 67–86). Washington, DC: American Psychological Association.

Perfetti, C. A., & Hart, L. (2002). The lexical quality hypothesis. In L. Vehoeven, C. Elbro, & P. Reitsma (Eds.), *Precursors of functional literacy* (pp. 189–213). Amsterdam/Philadelphia: Benjamins.

Perfetti, C. A., & Hogaboam, T. W. (1975). The relationship between single word decoding and reading comprehension skill. *Journal of Educational Psychology, 67,* 461–469.

Perfetti, C. A., & Lesgold, A. M. (1977). Discourse comprehension and sources of individual differences. In P. A. Carpenter & M. A. Just (Eds.), *Cognitive processes in comprehension* (pp. 141–183). Hillsdale, NJ: Erlbaum.

Perfetti, C. A., Liu, Y., & Tan, L. H. (2005). The lexical constituency model: Some implications of research on chinese for general theories of reading. *Psychological Review, 112,* 43–59.

Perfetti, C. A., Marron, M. A., & Foltz, P. W. (1996). Sources of comprehension failure: Theoretical perspectives and case studies. In C. Cornoldi & J. Oakhill (Eds.), *Reading comprehension difficulties: Processes and intervention* (pp. 137–165). Mahwah, NJ: Erlbaum.

Perfetti, C. A., & Roth, S. F. (1981). Some of the interactive processes in reading and their role in reading skill. In A. M. Lesgold & C. A. Perfetti (Eds.), *Interactive processes in reading* (pp. 269–297). Hillsdale, NJ: Erlbaum.

Perfetti, C. A., & Sandak, R. (2000). How do children who can't hear learn to read an alphabetic script? A review of the literature on reading and deafness. *Journal of Deaf Studies and Deaf Education, 5*(1), 32–51.

Perfetti, C. A., & Tan, L. H. (1999). The consistency model of Chinese word identification. In J. Wang, A. Imhoff, A. W. Chen, & H. C. Chen (Eds.), *Reading Chinese script: A cognitive analysis* (pp. 115–134). Mahwah, NJ: Erlbaum.

Perfetti, C. A., Zhang, S., & Berent, I. (1992). Reading in English and Chinese: Evidence for a universal phonological principle. In R. Frost & L. Katz (Eds.), *Orthography, phonology, morphology, and meaning* (pp. 227–248). Advances in Psychology. Amsterdam: Elsevier.

Périer, O. (1987). L'enfant à audition déficiente: Aspects médicaux, éducatifs, sociologiques et psychologiques. *Acta Oto-Rhino-Laryngologica Belgica, 41,* 125–420.

Perry, C. (2003). A phoneme–grapheme feedback consistency effect. *Psychonomic Bulletin and Review, 10,* 392–397.

Perry, C., & Ziegler, J. C. (2002). On the nature of phonological assembly: Evidence from backward masking. *Language and Cognitive Processes, 17,* 31–59.

Petersen, S. E., Fox, P. T., Posner, M. I., Mintun, M., & Raichle, M. E. (1988). Positron emission tomographic studies of the cortical anatomy of single-word processing. *Nature, 331*(6157), 585–589.

Peterson, C., & Anderson, J. R. (1987). A mean field theory learning algorithm for neural nets. *Complex Systems, 1,* 995–1019.

Petersson, K. M., Reis, A., & Ingvar, M. (2001). Cognitive processing in literate and illiterate subjects: A review of some recent behavioral and functional neuroimaging data. *Scandinavian Journal of Psychology, 42,* 251–267.

Petryshen, T. L., Kaplan, B. J., Liu, M. F., & Field, L. L. (2000). Absence of significant linkage between phonological coding dyslexia and chromosome 6p23–21.3, as determined by use of quantitative-trait methods: Confirmation of qualitative analyses. *American Journal of Human Genetics, 66*(2), 708–714.

Pexman, P. M., Hino, Y., & Lupker, S. J. (2002). Semantic ambiguity and the process of generating meaning from print. Paper presented at the forty-third Annual Meeting of the Psychonomic Society, Kansas City, MO.

Pexman, P. M., Hino Y., & Lupker, S. (2004) Semantic ambiguity and the problem of generating meaning from print. *Journal of Experimental Psychology: Learning, Memory, and Cognition, 30,* 1252–1270.

Pexman, P. M., & Lupker, S. J. (1999). Ambiguity and visual word recognition: Can feedback explain both homophone and polysemy effects? *Canadian Journal of Experimental Psychology, 53,* 323–334.

Pexman, P. M., Lupker, S. J., & Hino, Y. (2002). The impact of feedback semantics in visual word recognition: Number-of-features effects in lexical decision and naming tasks. *Psychonomic Bulletin and Review, 9,* 542–549.

Pexman, P. M., Lupker, S. J., & Jared, D. (2001). Homophone effects in lexical decision. *Journal of Experimental Psychology: Learning, Memory, and Cognition, 27,* 139–156.

Pexman, P. M., Lupker, S. J., & Reggin, L. D. (2002). Investigating the impact of feedback phonology in visual word recognition. *Journal of Experimental Psychology: Learning, Memory, and Cognition, 28,* 572–584.

Phillips, J., Noppeney, U., Humphreys, G. W., & Price, C. J. (2002). Can segregation within the semantic system account for category-specific deficits? *Brain, 125,* 2067–2080.

Piaget, J. (1952). *The origins of intelligence in children.* New York: International Universities Press.

Piercey, C. D., & Joordens, S. (2000). Turning an advantage into a disadvantage: Ambiguity effects in lexical decision versus reading tasks. *Memory and Cognition, 28,* 657–666.

Pilgrim, L. K., Fadili, J., Fletcher, P., & Tyler, L. K. (2002). Overcoming confounds of stimulus blocking: An event-related fMRI design of semantic processing. *Neuroimage, 16*(3 Pt 1), 713–723.

Pinker, S. (1979). Formal models of language acquisition. *Cognition, 7,* 217–283.

Pinker, S. (1999). *Words and rules: The ingredients of language.* New York: Basic; London: Weidenfeld & Nicolson.

Pinnell, G. S. (1989). Reading recovery: Helping at risk children learn to read. *Elementary School Journal, 90,* 161–184.

Plaut, D. C. (1995a). Double dissociation without modularity: Evidence from connectionist neuropsychology. *Journal of Clinical and Experimental Neuropsychology, 17,* 291–321.

Plaut, D. C. (1995b). Semantic and associative priming in a distributed attractor network. *Proceedings of the Seventeenth Annual Conference of the Cognitive Science Society, 17,* 37–42.

Plaut, D. C. (1996). Relearning after damage in connectionist networks: Toward a theory of rehabilitation. *Brain and Language, 52,* 25–82.

Plaut, D. C. (1997). Structure and function in the lexical system: Insights from distributed models of word reading and lexical decision. *Language and Cognitive Processes, 12,* 765–805.

Plaut, D. C. (1999). A connectionist approach to word reading and acquired dyslexia: Extension to sequential processing. *Cognitive Science, 23,* 543–568.

Plaut, D. C., & Booth, J. R. (2000). Individual and developmental differences in semantic priming: Empirical and computational support for a single-mechanism account of lexical processing. *Psychological Review, 107,* 786–823.

Plaut, D. C., & McClelland, J. L. (2000). Stipulating versus discovering representations [commentary on M. Page, Connectionist modelling in psychology: A localist manifesto]. *Behavioral and Brain Sciences, 23,* 489–491.

Plaut, D. C., McClelland, J. L., Seidenberg, M. S., & Patterson, K. (1996). Understanding normal and impaired word reading: Computational principles in quasi-regular domains. *Psychological Review, 103,* 56–115.

Plaut, D. C., & Shallice, T. (1993). Deep dyslexia: A case study of connectionist neuropsychology. *Cognitive Neuropsychology, 10,* 377–500.

Plomin, R., & Crabbe, J. (2000). DNA. *Psychological Bulletin, 126,* 806–828.

Plomin, R., DeFries, J. C., Craig, I. W., & McGuffin, P. (2003). *Behavioral genetics in the post-genomic era.* Washington, DC: American Psychological Association.

Pollard, R. (n. d.). *Synthetic method of reading and spelling.* New York: American Book.

Pollatsek, A., Bolozky, S., Well, A. D., & Rayner, K. (1981). Asymmetries in the perceptual span for Israeli readers. *Brain and Language, 14,* 174–180.

Pollatsek, A., Hyönä, J., & Bertram, R. (2000). The role of morphological constituents in reading Finnish compound words. *Journal of Experimental Psychology: Human Perception and Performance, 26,* 820–833.

Pollatsek, A., Lesch, M., Morris, R. K., & Rayner, K. (1992). Phonological codes are used in integrating information across saccades in word identification and reading. *Journal of Experimental Psychology: Human Perception and Performance, 18,*148–162.

Pollatsek, A., & Rayner, K. (2003). Perceptual aspects of reading: Word identification and eye movements. In K. Lamberts & R. Goldstone (Eds.), *Handbook of Cognition.* Oxford: Sage.

Pollatsek, A., Rayner, K., & Balota, D. A. (1986). Inferences about eye movement control from the perceptual span in reading. *Perception and Psychophysics, 40,* 123–130.

Pollatsek, A., Reichle, E. D., & Rayner, K. (2003). Modeling eye movements in reading: Extensions of the E-Z Reader model. In J. Hyönä, R. Radach, & H. Deubel (Eds.), *The mind's eye: Cognitive and applied aspects of eye movement research* (pp. 361–390). Oxford: Elsevier.

Porpodas, C. D. (1999). Patterns of phonological and memory processing in beginning readers and spellers of Greek. *Journal of Learning Disabilities, 32,* 406–416.

Posteraro, L., Zinelli, P., & Mazzucchi, A. (1988). Selective impairment of the graphemic buffer in acquired dysgraphia: A case study. *Brain and Language, 35,* 274–286.

Pressley, M., Wharton-McDonald, R., Allington, R., Block, C., Morrow, L., Tracey, D., et al. (2001). A study of effective first-grade literacy instruction. *Scientific Studies of Reading, 5,* 35–58.

Price, C. J. (2000). The anatomy of language: Contributions from functional neuroimaging. *Journal of Anatomy, 197,* 335–359.

Price, C. J., & Devlin, J. T. (2003). The myth of the visual word form area. *NeuroImage, 19,* 478–481.

Price, C. J., & Friston, K. J. (2002). Degeneracy and cognitive anatomy. *Trends in Cognitive Science, 6*(10), 416–421.

Price, C. J., Gorno-Tempini, M. L., Graham, K. S., Biggio, N., Mechelli, A., Patterson, K., et al. (2003). Normal and pathological reading: Converging data from lesion and imaging studies. *NeuroImage, 20,* Supplement 1: S30–41.

Price, C. J., Moore, C. J., & Frackowiak, R. S. J. (1996a). The effect of varying stimulus rate and duration on brain activity during reading. *NeuroImage, 3*(1), 40–52.

Price, C. J., Noppeney, U., Phillips, J., A., & Devlin, J. T. (2003b). How is the fusiform gyrus related to category specificity? *Cognitive Neuropsychology, 20,* 561–574.

Price, C. J., Wise, R. J. S., & Frackowiak, R. S. J. (1996b). Demonstrating the implicit processing of visually presented words and pseudowords. *Cerebral Cortex, 6*(1), 62–70.

Price, C. J., Wise, R. J. S., Warburton, E. A., Moore, C. J., Howard, D., Patterson, K., et al. (1996c). Hearing and saying – The functional neuro-anatomy of auditory word processing. *Brain, 119*(Pt 3), 919–931.

Pringle-Morgan, W. (1896). A case of congenital word-blindness (inability to learn to read). *British Medical Journal, 2,* 1543–1544.

Purcell-Gates, V. (1996). Stories, coupons, and the TV Guide: Relationships between home literacy experiences and emergent literacy knowledge. *Reading Research Quarterly, 31,* 406–428.

Pynte, J., Kennedy, A., & Ducrot, S. (2004). The influence of parafoveal typographical errors on eye movements in reading. *European Journal of Cognitive Psychology, 16,* 178–202.

Qualls, C. D. (2001). Public and personal meanings of literacy. In J. L. Harris, A. G. Kamhi, & K., E. Pollock (Eds.), *Literacy in African American Communities* (pp. 1–19). Mahweh, NJ: Erlbaum.

Rack, J. P., Hulme, C., and Snowling, M. J. (1993). Learning to read: A theoretical synthesis. In H. Reese (Ed.), *Advances in child development and behavior* (pp. 100–132). San Diego, CA: Academic.

Rack, J. P., Hulme, C., Snowling, M. J., & Wightman, J. (1994). The role of phonology in young children's learning of sight words: The direct-mapping hypothesis. *Journal of Experimental Child Psychology, 57,* 42–71.

Rack, J. P., Snowling, M. J., & Olson, R. K. (1992). The nonword reading deficit in developmental dyslexia: A review. *Reading Research Quarterly, 27*(1), 28–53.

Radach, R., & Heller, D. (2000). Relations between spatial and temporal aspects of eye movement control. In A. Kennedy, R. Radach, D. Heller, & J. Pynte (Eds.), *Reading as a perceptual process* (pp. 165–192). Oxford: Elsevier.

Radach, R., Inhoff, A., & Heller, D. (2004). Orthographic regularity gradually modulates saccade amplitudes in reading. *European Journal of Cognitive Psychology, 16,* 27–51.

Radach, R., & Kennedy, A. (2004). Theoretical perspectives on eye movements in reading: Past controversies, current issues, and an agenda for future research. *European Journal of Cognitive Psychology, 16,* 3–26.

Raitano, N. A., Pennington, B. F. Tunick, R. A., Boada, R., & Shriberg, L. D. (2004). Preliteracy skills of subgroups of children with speech sound disorders. *Journal of Child Psychology and Psychiatry, 45,* 821–835.

Ramus, F., Nespor, M., & Mehler, J. (1999). Correlates of linguistic rhythm in the speech signal. *Cognition, 73,* 265–292.

Rapin, I., & Allen, P. (1987). *Developmental dysphasia and autism in pre-school children: Characteristics and subtypes.* First international symposium on speech and language disorders in children. London, Association for All Speech Impaired Children.

Rapp, B., & Caramazza, A. (1993). On the dissociation between deficits of access and deficits of storage: A question of theory. *Cognitive Neuropsychology, 10,* 113–141.

Rashotte, C. A., MacPhee, K., & Torgesen, J. K. (2001). The effectiveness of a group reading instruction program with poor readers in multiple grades. *Learning Disability Quarterly, 24,* 119–134.

Ratcliff, G., Ganguli, M., Chandra, V., Sharma, S., Belle, S., Seaberg, E., et al. (1998). Effects of literacy and education on measures of word fluency. *Brain and Language, 61,* 115–122.

Ratcliff, R. (1981). A theory of order relations in perceptual matching. *Psychological Review, 88,* 552–572.

Rayman, J., & Zaidel, E. (1991). Rhyming and the right hemisphere. *Brain and Language, 40,* 89–105.

Raymer, A. M., & Berndt, R. S. (1994). Models of word reading: Evidence from Alzheimer's disease. *Brain and Language, 47,* 479–482.

Raymer, A. M., & Berndt, R. S. (1996). Reading lexically without semantics: Evidence from patients with probable Alzheimer's disease. *Journal of the International Neuropsychological Society, 2,* 340–349.

Rayner, K. (1975). The perceptual span and peripheral cues in reading. *Cognitive Psychology, 7,* 65–81.

Rayner, K. (1978). Eye movements in reading and information processing. *Psychological Bulletin, 85,* 618–660.

Rayner, K. (1979). Eye guidance in reading: Fixation locations within words. *Perception, 8,* 21–30.

Rayner, K. (1986). Eye movements and the perceptual span in beginning and skilled readers. *Journal of Experimental Child Psychology, 41,* 211–236.

Rayner, K. (1995). Eye movements and cognitive processes in reading, visual search, and scene perception. In J. M. Findlay, R. Walker, & R. W. Kentridge (Eds.), *Eye movement research: Mechanisms, processes and applications* (pp. 3–22). Amsterdam: Elsevier.

Rayner, K. (1998). Eye movements in reading and information processing: 20 years of research. *Psychological Bulletin, 124,* 372–422.

Rayner, K., Ashby, J., Pollatsek, A., & Reichle, E. D. (2004). The effects of word frequency and predictability on eye movements in reading: Implications for the E-Z Reader model. *Journal of Experimental Psychology: Human Perception and Performance, 30,* 720–732.

Rayner, K., Balota, D. A., & Pollatsek, A. (1986). Against parafoveal semantic preprocessing during eye fixations in reading. *Canadian Journal of Psychology, 40,* 473–483.

Rayner, K., & Bertera, J. H. (1979). Reading without a fovea. *Science, 206,* 468–469.

Rayner, K., & Duffy, S. A. (1986). Lexical complexity and fixation times in reading: Effects of word frequency, verb complexity, and lexical ambiguity. *Memory and Cognition, 14,* 191–201.

Rayner, K., & Fischer, M. H. (1996). Mindless reading revisited: Eye movements during reading and scanning are different. *Perception and Psychophysics, 58,* 734–747.

Rayner, K., Fischer, M. H., & Pollatsek, A. (1998). Unspaced text interferes with both word identification and eye movement control. *Vision Research, 38,* 1129–1144.

Rayner, K., Foorman, B. R., Perfetti, C. A., Pesetsky, D., & Seidenberg, M. S. (2001). How psychological science informs the teaching of reading. *Psychological Science in the Public Interest, 2,* 31–74.

Rayner, K., Inhoff, A. W., Morrison, R., Slowiaczek, M. L., & Bertera, J. H. (1981). Masking of foveal and parafoveal vision during eye fixations in reading. *Journal of Experimental Psychology: Human Perception and Performance, 7,* 167–179.

Rayner, K., & Juhasz, B. J. (2004). Eye movements in reading: Old questions and new directions. *European Journal of Cognitive Psychology, 16,* 340–352.

Rayner, K., Juhasz, B., Ashby, J., & Clifton, C. (2003). Inhibition of saccade return in reading. *Vision Research, 43,* 1027–1034.

Rayner, K., Kambe, G., & Duffy, S. A. (2000). The effect of clause wrap-up on eye movements during reading. *Quarterly Journal of Experimental Psychology, 53A,* 1061–1080.

Rayner, K., & Liversedge, S. P. (2004). Visual and linguistic processing during eye fixations in reading. In J. M. Henderson & F. Ferreira (Eds.), *The interface of language, vision, and action* (pp. 59–104). New York: Psychology Press.

Rayner, K., Liversedge, S. P., White, S. J., and Vergilino-Perez, D. (2003). Reading disappearing text: Cognitive control of eye movements. *Psychological Science, 14,* 385–388.

Rayner, K., & McConkie, G. W. (1976). What guides a reader's eye movements. *Vision Research, 16,* 829–837.

Rayner, K., & Morris, R. K. (1992). Eye movement control in reading: Evidence against semantic preprocessing. *Journal of Experimental Psychology: Human Perception and Performance, 18,* 163–172.

Rayner, K., Murphy, L. A., Henderson, J. M., & Pollatsek, A. (1989). Selective attentional dyslexia. *Cognitive Neuropsychology, 6,* 357–378.

Rayner, K., Pollatsek, A., & Binder, K. S. (1998). Phonological codes and eye movements in reading. *Journal of Experimental Psychology: Learning, Memory, and Cognition, 24,* 476–497.

Rayner, K., Pollatsek, A., & Reichle, E. D. (2003). Eye movements in reading: Models and data. *Behavioral and Brain Sciences, 26,* 507–526.

Rayner, K., & Raney, G. E. (1996). Eye movement control in reading and visual search: Effects of word frequency. *Psychonomic Bulletin and Review, 3,* 245–248.

Rayner, K., Reichle, E. D., & Pollatsek, A. (1998). Eye movement control in reading: An overview and model. In G. Underwood (Ed.), *Eye guidance in reading and scene perception* (pp. 243–268). Oxford: Elsevier.

Rayner, K., & Sereno, S. C. (1994a). Eye movements in reading: Psycholinguistic studies. In M. Gernsbacher (Ed.), *Handbook of psycholinguistics* (pp. 57–82). New York: Academic.

Rayner, K., & Sereno, S. C. (1994b). Regression-contingent analyses: A reply to Altmann. *Memory and Cognition, 22,* 291–292.

Rayner, K., Sereno, S. C., Lesch, M. F., & Pollatsek, A. (1995). Phonological codes are automatically activated during reading: Evidence from an eye movement priming paradigm. *Psychological Science, 6,* 26–32.

Rayner, K., Sereno, S. C., Morris, R. K., Schmauder, A. R., & Clifton, C. (1989). Eye movements and on-line language comprehension processes. *Language and Cognitive Processes, 4,* 21–49.

Rayner, K., Sereno, S. C., & Raney, G. E. (1996). Eye movement control in reading: A comparison of two types of models. *Journal of Experimental Psychology: Human Perception and Performance, 22,* 1188–1200.

Rayner, K., & Well, A. D. (1996). Effects of contextual constraint on eye movements in reading: A further examination. *Psychonomic Bulletin and Review, 3,* 504–509.

Raz, I. S., & Bryant, P. (1990). Social background, phonological awareness and children's reading. *British Journal of Developmental Psychology, 8,* 209–225.

Read, C. (1975). *Children's categorization of speech sounds in English* (NCTE Research Report No. 17). Urbana, IL: National Council of Teachers of English.

Read, C. (1980). Writing is not the inverse of reading for young children. In C. H. Frederiksen, M. F. Whiteman, & G. Dominique (Eds.), *Writing: The nature, development and teaching of written communication* (pp. 105–117). Hillsdale, NJ: Erlbaum.

Read, C., Zhang, Y.-F., Nie, H.-Y., & Ding, B.-Q. (1986). The ability to manipulate speech sounds depends on knowing alphabetic writing. *Cognition, 24,* 31–45.

Reber, A. S. (1967). Implicit learning of artificial grammars. *Journal of Verbal Learning and Verbal Behavior, 6,* 855–863.

Reed, M. A. (1989). Speech perception and the discrimination of brief auditory cues in reading disabled children. *Journal of Experimental Child Psychology, 48,* 270–292.

Reese, E. (1995). Predicting children's literacy from mother–child conversations. *Cognitive Development, 10,* 381–405.

Reicher, G. M. (1969). Perceptual recognition as a function of meaningfulness of stimulus material. *Journal of Experimental Psychology, 81,* 274–280.

Reichle, E. D, Pollatsek, A., Fisher, D. L., & Rayner, K. (1998). Toward a model of eye movement control in reading. *Psychological Review, 105,* 125–157.

Reichle, E. D., Rayner, K., & Pollatsek, A. (2003). The E-Z Reader model of eye movement control in reading: Comparisons to other models. *Behavioral and Brain Sciences, 26,* 445–476.

Reilly, R. G., & Radach, R. (2003). Foundations of an interactive activation model of eye movement control in reading. In J. Hyönä, R. Radach, & H. Deubel (Eds.), *The mind's eye: Cognitive and applied aspects of eye movement research* (pp. 429–457). Oxford: Elsevier

Reis, A., & Castro-Caldas, A. (1997). Illiteracy: A bias for cognitive development. *Journal of the International Neuropsychological Society, 3,* 444–450.

Reitsma, P. (1983). Printed word learning in beginning readers. *Journal of Experimental Child Psychology, 75,* 321–339.

Resnick, L. B. (1979). Theories and prescriptions for early reading instruction. In L. B. Resnick & P. A. Weaver (Eds.), *Theory and practice of early reading* (Vol. 2, pp. 321–338). Hillsdale, NJ: Erlbaum.

Reuter-Lorenz, P. A., & Brunn, J. L. (1990). A prelexical basis for letter-by-letter reading: A case study. *Cognitive Neuropsychology, 7,* 1–20.

Reynolds, A. J., & Gill, S. (1994). The role of parental perspectives in the school adjustment of inner-city Black children. *Journal of Youth and Adolescence, 23,* 671–694.

Ricciuti, H. N. (1999). Single parenthood and school readiness in White, Black, and Hispanic 6- and 7-year-olds. *Journal of Family Psychology, 13*, 450–465.

Riley, J. L. (1995). The relationship between adjustment to school and success in reading by the end of the reception year. *Early Child Development and Care, 114*, 25–38.

Roberts, T. (2003). Effects of alphabet letter instruction on young children's word recognition. *Journal of Educational Psychology, 95*, 41–51.

Robinson, H., Monroe, M., & Artley, A. S. (1946). *The new basic readers curriculum foundation series.* Chicago: Scott, Foresman.

Rodd, J. (2004). The effect of semantic ambiguity on reading aloud: A twist in the tail. *Psychonomic Bulletin and Review, 11*, 440–445.

Rodd, J., Gaskell, G., & Marslen-Wilson, W. (2002). Making sense of semantic ambiguity: Semantic competition in lexical access. *Journal of Memory and Language, 46*, 245–266.

Rodda, M., & Grove, C. (1987). *Language, cognition, and deafness.* Hillsdale, NJ: Erlbaum.

Rodgers, B. (1983). The identification and prevalence of specific reading retardation. *British Journal of Educational Psychology, 53*, 369–373.

Roeltgen, D. P. (1985). Agraphia. In K. M. Heilman & E. Valestein (Eds.), *Clinical Neuropsychology* (2nd ed., pp. 63–89). New York: Oxford University Press.

Roeltgen, D. P., Sevush, S., & Heilman, K. M. (1983). Phonological agraphia: Writing by the lexical-semantic route. *Neurology, 33*, 755–765.

Rogers, T. T., Hocking, J., Mechelli, A., Patterson, K., & Price, C. J. (2005). Fusiform activation to animals is driven by the process not the stimulus. *Journal of Cognitive Neuroscience, 17*, 434–445.

Rogers, T. T., Lambon Ralph, M. A., Hodges, J. R., & Patterson, K. (2003). Object recognition under semantic impairment: The effects of conceptual regularities on perceptual decisions. *Language and Cognitive Processes, 18*, 625–662.

Rogers, T. T., Lambon Ralph, M. A., Hodges, J. R., & Patterson, K. (2004). Natural selection: The impact of semantic impairment on lexical and object decision. *Cognitive Neuropsychology, 21*, 331–352.

Rogosa, D. R, & Willett, J. B. (1985). Understanding the correlates of change by modeling individual differences in growth. *Psychometrika, 50*, 203–228.

Romani, C., Di Betta, A. M, & Olson, A. (in preparation). Lexical and non-lexical processing in developmental dyslexia: A case for different impairments.

Romani, C., Olson, A., Semenza, C., & Grana', A. (2002). Phonological errors in two aphasic patients: A phonological vs. an articulatory locus of impairment. *Cortex, 38*, 541–567.

Romani, C., Olson, A., & Ward, J. (1999). A case of developmental dyslexia: A problem with order? *Quarterly Journal of Experimental Psychology, 52A*, 97–128.

Romani, C., Olson, A., Ward, J., & Ercolani, M. G. (2002). Formal lexical paragraphias in a single case study: How "masterpiece" becomes "misterpieman" and "curiosity" "suretoy". *Brain and Language, 83*, 300–334.

Rosch, E., Mervis, C., Gray, W., Johnson, D., & Boyes-Braem, P. (1976). Basic objects in natural categories. *Cognitive Psychology, 8*, 382–439.

Rosen, R. (2000). *Essays on life itself.* New York: Columbia University Press.

Rosinski, R., Golinkoff, R., & Kukish, K. (1975). Automatic semantic processing in a picture–word interference task. *Child Development, 46*, 243–253.

Roskies, A. L., Fiez, J. A., Balota, D. A., Raichle, M. A., & Petersen, S. E. (2001). Task-dependent modulation of regions in the left inferior frontal cortex during semantic processing. *Journal of Cognitive Neuroscience, 13*(6), 829–843.

Rosner, J. (1979). *Helping children overcome learning disabilities.* New York: Walker.

Rosson, M. (1985). The interaction of pronunciation rules and lexical representations in reading aloud. *Memory and Cognition, 13*, 90–99.

Rourke, B. P. (1975). Brain-behavior relationships in children with learning disabilities: A research programme. *American Psychologist, 30*, 911–920.

Rozin, P., Poritsky, S., & Sotsky, R. (1971). American children with reading problems can easily learn to read English represented in Chinese characters. *Science, 171*, 1264–1267.

Rubenstein, H., Garfield, L., & Millikan, J. A. (1970). Homographic entries in the internal lexicon. *Journal of Verbal Learning and Verbal Behavior, 9*, 487–494.

Rubenstein, H., Lewis, S. S., & Rubenstein, M. A. (1971a). Evidence for phonemic recoding in visual word recognition. *Journal of Verbal Learning and Verbal Behavior, 10*, 645–657.

Rubenstein, H., Lewis, S. S., & Rubenstein, M. A. (1971b). Homographic entries in the internal lexicon: Effects of systematicity and relative frequency of meanings. *Journal of Verbal Learning and Verbal Behavior, 10*, 57–62.

Rumelhart, D. E., Hinton, G. E., & Williams, R. J. (1986). Learning representations by back-propagating errors. *Nature, 323*, 533–536.

Rumelhart, D. E., & McClelland, J. L. (1982). An interactive activation model of context effects in letter perception. Part 2: The contextual enhancement effect and some tests and extensions of the model. *Psychological Review, 89*, 60–94.

Rumsey, J. M., Horwitz, B., Donohue, B. C., Nace, K. L., Maisog, J. M., & Andreason, P. (1997a). Phonological and orthographic components of word recognition: A PET-rCBF study. *Brain, 120*(5), 739–759.

Rumsey, J. M., Horwitz, B., Donohue, B. C., Nace, K. L., Maisog, J. M., & Andreason, P. (1999). A functional lesion in developmental dyslexia: Left angular gyral blood flow predicts severity. *Brain and Language, 70*, 187–204.

Rumsey, J. M., Nace, K., Donohue, B. C., Wise, D., Maisog, J. M., & Andreason, P. (1997b). A positron emission tomographic study of impaired word recognition and phonological processing in dyslexic men. *Archives of Neurology, 54*, 562–573.

Saffran, E. M., Bogyo, L. C., Schwartz, M. F., & Marin, O. S. M. (1980). Does deep dyslexia reflect right-hemisphere reading? In M. Coltheart, K. Patterson, & J. C. Marshall (Eds.), *Deep dyslexia* (pp. 381–406). London: Routledge & Kegan Paul.

Saffran, E. M., & Coslett, H. B. (1998). Implicit vs. letter-by-letter reading in pure alexia: A tale of two systems. *Cognitive Neuropsychology, 15*, 141–166.

Saffran, J. R. (2003). Statistical language learning: Mechanisms and constraints. *Current Directions in Psychological Science, 12*, 110–114.

Sampson, G. (1987). *Writing systems: A linguistic introduction.* Stanford, CA: Stanford University Press.

Samuels, S. J. (1971). Letter-name versus letter-sound knowledge in learning to read. *Reading Teacher, 24*, 606–608, 662.

Samuels, S. J., & Kamil, M. (1984). Models of the reading process. In P. D. Pearson (Ed.), *Handbook of Reading Research* (pp. 185–224). New York: Longman.

Samuels, S. J., LaBerge, D., & Bremer, D. (1978). Units of word recognition: Evidence for developmental changes. *Journal of Verbal Learning and Verbal Behavior, 17*, 715–720.

Sanders, R. J., & Caramazza, A. (1990). Operation of the phoneme-to-grapheme conversion mechanisms in a brain injured patient. *Reading and Writing, 2*, 61–82.

Sasanuma, S., Sakuma, N., & Kitano, K. (1992). Reading Kanji without semantics: Evidence from a longitudinal study of dementia. *Cognitive Neuropsychology, 9*, 465–586.

Satz, P., Buka, S., Lipsitt, L., & Seidman, L. (1998). The long-term prognosis of learning disabled children: A review of studies (1954–1993). In B. K. Shapiro, P. J. Accardo, & A. J. Capute (Eds.), *Specific reading disability: A view of the spectrum* (pp. 223–250). New York: York.

Savage, R., Stuart, M., & Hill, V. (2001). The role of scaffolding errors in reading development: Evidence from a longitudinal and a correlational study. *British Journal of Educational Psychology, 71*, 1–13.

Savin, H. B. (1972). What the child knows about speech when he starts to learn to read. In J. F. Kavanagh & I. G. Mattingly (Eds.), *Language by ear and by eye* (pp. 319–326). Cambridge, MA: MIT Press.

Scanlon, D. M., & Vellutino, F. R. (1996). Prerequisite skills, early instruction, and success in first grade reading: Selected results from a longitudinal study. *Mental Retardation and Development Disabilities, 2,* 54–63.

Scanlon, D. M., Vellutino, F. R., Small, S. G. & Fanuele, D. P. (2000, April). Severe reading difficulties: Can they be prevented? A comparison of prevention and intervention approaches. Paper presented at the Annual Conference of The American Educational Research Association, New Orleans.

Scarborough, H. S. (1990). Very early language deficits in dyslexic children. *Child Development, 61,* 1728–1743.

Scarborough, H. S., & Dobrich, W. (1990). Development of children with early delay. *Journal of Speech and Hearing Research, 33,* 70–83.

Scarborough, H. S., & Dobrich, W. (1994). On the efficacy of reading to preschoolers. *Developmental Review, 14,* 245–30.

Schatschneider, C., Carlson, C. D., Francis, D. J., Foorman, B. R., & Fletcher, J. M. (2002). Relationships of rapid automatized naming and phonological awareness in early reading development: Implications for the double deficit hypothesis. *Journal of Learning Disabilities, 35,* 245–256.

Schatschneider, C., Fletcher, J. M., Francis, D. J., Carlson, C. D., & Foorman, B. R. (2004). Kindergarten prediction of reading skills: A longitudinal comparative analysis. *Journal of Educational Psychology, 96,* 265–282.

Schatschneider, C., Francis, D. J., Foorman, B. R., Fletcher, J. M., & Mehta, P. (1999). The dimensionality of phonological awareness: An application of item response theory. *Journal of Educational Psychology, 91,* 439–449.

Schiller, N. O., Greenhall, J. A., Shelton, J. R., & Caramazza, A. (2001). Serial order effects in spelling errors: Evidence from two dysgraphic patients. *Neurocase, 7,* 1–14.

Schilling, H. E., Rayner, K., & Chumbley, J. I. (1998). Comparing naming, lexical decision, and eye fixation times: Word frequency effects and individual differences. *Memory and Cognition, 26,* 1270–1281.

Schmalhofer, F., McDaniel, M. A., & Keefe, D. (2002). A unified model for predictive and bridging inferences. *Discourse Processes, 33,* 105–132.

Schneider, W., Kuspert, P., Roth, E., & Vise, M. (1997). Short- and long-term effects of training phonological awareness in kindergarten: Evidence from two German studies. *Journal of Experimental Child Psychology, 66,* 311–340.

Schneider, W., Roth, E., & Ennemoser, M. (2000). Training phonological skills and letter knowledge in children at risk for dyslexia: A comparison of three kindergarten intervention programs. *Journal of Educational Psychology, 92,* 284–295.

Schonauer, K., & Denes, G. (1994). Graphemic jargon: A case report. *Brain and Language, 47,* 279–299.

Schulte-Körne, G. (2001). Annotation: Genetics of reading and spelling disorder. *Journal of Child Psychology and Psychiatry, 42,* 985–997.

Schumaker, J. B., Deshler, D. D., & Ellis, E. S. (1986). Intervention issues related to the education of learning disabled adolescents. In J. K. Torgesen & B. Y. L. Wong (Eds.), *Psychological and Educational Perspectives on Learning Disabilities* (pp. 329–365). New York: Academic.

Schwanenflugel, P. J., Harnishfeger, K. K., & Stowe, R. W. (1988). Context availability and lexical decisions for abstract and concrete words. *Journal of Memory and Language, 27,* 499–520.

Schwartz, M. F., Saffran, M., & Marin, O. S. M. (1980a). Dissociations of language function in dementia: A case study. *Brain and Language,* 10, 249–262.

Schwartz, M. F., Saffran, E. M., & Marin, O. S. M. (1980b). Fractionating the reading process in dementia: Evidence for word-specific print-to-sound associations. In M. Coltheart, K. Patterson, & J. C. Marshall (Eds.), *Deep dyslexia* (pp. 259–269). London: Routledge & Kegan Paul.

Scliar-Cabral, L., Morais, J., Nepomuceno, L., & Kolinsky, R. (1997). The awareness of phonemes: So close – so far away. *International Journal of Psycholinguistics,* 13, 211–240.

Scott, J., & Ehri, L. C. (1989). Sight word reading in prereaders: Use of logographic vs. alphabetic access routes. *Journal of Reading Behavior,* 22, 149–166.

Scribner, S. (1974). Developmental aspects of categorized recall in a West African society. *Cognitive Psychology,* 6, 475–494.

Scribner, S., & Cole, M. (1981). *The psychology of literacy.* Cambridge, MA: Harvard University Press.

Sears, C. R., Hino, Y., & Lupker, S. J. (1995). Neighborhood size and neighborhood frequency effects in word recognition. *Journal of Experimental Psychology: Human Perception and Performance,* 21, 876–900.

Sears, C. R., Lupker, S. J., & Hino, Y. (1999). Orthographic neighborhood effects in perceptual identification and semantic categorization tasks: A test of the multiple read-out model. *Perception and Psychophysics,* 61, 1537–1554.

Segui, J., & Grainger, J. (1990). Prime word recognition with orthographic neighbors: Effects of relative prime-target frequency. *Journal of Experimental Psychology: Human Perception and Performance,* 16, 65–76.

Seidenberg, M. S. (1985). The time course of phonological code activation in two writing systems. *Cognition,* 19, 1–30.

Seidenberg, M. S. (1992). Beyond orthographic depth: Equitable division of labor. In R. Frost & K. Katz (Eds.), *Orthography, phonology, morphology, and meaning* (pp. 85–118). Amsterdam: Elsevier.

Seidenberg, M. S. (2002). Using connectionist models to understand reading and dyslexia. In R. Stainthorpe & P. Tomlinson (Eds.), *Learning and teaching reading. British Journal of Educational Psychology Monograph Series II; Psychological Aspects of Education – Current Trends,* 1, 75–88.

Seidenberg, M. S., & McClelland, J. L. (1989). A distributed, developmental model of word recognition. *Psychological Review,* 96, 523–568.

Seidenberg, M. S., & McClelland, J. L. (1990). More words but still no lexicon: Reply to Besner et al. *Psychological Review,* 97, 477–452.

Seidenberg, M. S., Petersen, A., MacDonald, M. C., & Plaut, D. C. (1996). Pseudohomophone effects and models of word recognition. *Journal of Experimental Psychology: Learning, Memory, and Cognition,* 22, 48–62.

Seidenberg, M. S., & Plaut, D. C. (1998). Evaluating word-reading models at the item level: Matching the grain of theory and data. *Psychological Science,* 9, 234–237.

Seidenberg, M. S., Plaut, D. C., Petersen, A. S., McClelland, J. L., & McRae, K. (1994). Nonword pronunciation and models of word recognition. *Journal of Experimental Psychology: Human Perception and Performance,* 20, 1177–1196.

Seidenberg, M. S., & Tanenhaus, M. K. (1979). Orthographic effects on rhyme monitoring. *Journal of Experimental Psychology: Human Learning and Memory,* 5, 546–554.

Seidenberg, M. S., Waters, G. S., Barnes, M. A., & Tanenhaus, M. K. (1984). When does irregular spelling or pronunciation influence word recognition? *Journal of Verbal Learning and Verbal Behaviour,* 23, 383–404.

Seigneuric, A. S., Ehrlich, M. F., Oakhill, J. V., & Yuill, N. M. (2000). Working memory resources and children's reading comprehension. *Reading and Writing, 13*, 81–103.

Sejnowski, T. J., & Rosenberg, C. R. (1987). Parallel networks that learn to pronounce English text. *Complex Systems, 1*, 145–168.

Sénéchal, M., & Cornell, E. H. (1993). Vocabulary acquisition through shared reading experiences. *Reading Research Quarterly, 28*, 360–375.

Sénéchal, M., Cornell, E. H., & Broda, L. S. (1995). Age-related differences in the organization of parent–infant interactions during picture-book reading. *Early Childhood Research Quarterly, 10*, 317–337.

Sénéchal, M., & LeFevre, J. (2002). Parental involvement in the development of children's reading skill: A five-year longitudinal study. *Child Development, 73*, 445–460.

Sénéchal, M., LeFevre, J., Hudson, E., & Lawson, E. P. (1996). Knowledge of storybooks as a predictor of young children's vocabulary. *Journal of Educational Psychology, 88*, 520–536.

Sénéchal, M., LeFevre, J., Thomas, E. M., & Daley, K. E. (1998). Differential effects of home literacy experiences on the development of oral and written language. *Reading Research Quarterly, 13*, 96–116.

Serpell, R. Sonnenschein, S., Baker, L., & Ganapathy, H. (2002). Intimate culture of families in the early socialization of literacy. *Journal of Family Psychology, 16*, 391–405.

Sevostianov, A., Horwitz, B., Nechaev, V., Williams, R., Fromm, S., & Braum, A. R. (2002). fMRI study comparing names versus pictures of objects. *Human Brain Mapping, 16*, 168–175.

Seymour, P. H. K. (1986). *Cognitive analysis of dyslexia*. London: Routledge & Kegan Paul.

Seymour, P. H. K. (1990). Developmental dyslexia. In M. W. Eysenck (Ed.), *Cognitive psychology: An international review* (pp. 135–196). Chichester: Wiley.

Seymour, P. H. K. (1993). Un modèle de développement orthographique à double fondation. In J.-P. Jaffré, L. Sprenger-Charolles, & M. Fayol (Eds.), *Lecture-Écriture: Acquisition. Les Actes de la Villette* (pp. 57–79). Paris: Nathan Pedagogie.

Seymour, P. H. K. (1997). Foundations of orthographic development. In C. A. Perfetti, L. Rieben, & M. Fayol (Eds.), *Learning to spell* (pp. 319–337). Hillsdale, NJ: Erlbaum.

Seymour, P. H. K. (1999). Cognitive architecture of early reading. In I. Lundberg, F. E. Tønnessen, & I. Austad (Eds.), *Dyslexia: Advances in theory and practice* (pp. 59–73). Dordrecht, the Netherlands: Kluwer Academic.

Seymour, P. H. K., Aro, M., & Erskine, J. M. (2003). Foundation literacy acquisition in European orthographies. *British Journal of Psychology, 94*, 143–174.

Seymour, P. H. K., & Duncan, L. G. (2001). Learning to read in English. *Psychology: The Journal of the Hellenic Psychological Society, 8*, 281–299.

Seymour, P. H. K., & Elder, L. (1986). Beginning reading without phonology. *Cognitive Neuropsychology, 3*, 1–36.

Seymour, P. H. K., & Evans, H. M. (1992). Beginning reading without semantics: A cognitive study of hyperlexia. *Cognitive Neuropsychology, 9*, 89–122.

Seymour, P. H. K., & Evans, H. M. (1994). Levels of phonological awareness and learning to read. *Reading and Writing, 6*, 221–250.

Seymour, P. H. K., & Evans, H. M. (1999). Foundation level dyslexias: Assessment and treatment. *Journal of Learning Disabilities, 32*, 394–405.

Seymour, P. H. K., & J. MacGregor (1984). Developmental dyslexia: A cognitive experimental analysis of phonological, morphemic and visual impairments. *Cognitive Neuropsychology, 1*, 43–82.

Shallice, T. (1981). Phonological agraphia and the lexical route in writing. *Brain, 104*, 413–429.

Shallice, T. (1982). Specific impairments in planning. *Philosophical Transactions of the Royal Society London (Biology), 298*, 199–209.

Shallice, T., & Saffran, E. (1986). Lexical processing in the absence of explicit word identification: Evidence from a letter-by-letter reader. *Cognitive Neuropsychology, 3,* 429–458.

Shallice, T., & Warrington, E. K. (1975). Word recognition in a phonemic dyslexic patient. *Quarterly Journal of Experimental Psychology, 27,* 187–199.

Shallice, T., & Warrington, E. K. (1980). Single and multiple component central dyslexic syndromes. In M. Coltheart, K. Patterson, & J. C. Marshall (Eds.), *Deep dyslexia* (pp. 119–145). London: Routledge & Kegan Paul.

Shallice, T., Warrington, E. K., & McCarthy, R. (1983). Reading without semantics. *Quarterly Journal of Experimental Psychology, 35A,* 111–138.

Shankweiler, D. (1989). How problems of comprehension are related to difficulties in word reading. In D. Shankweiler & I. Y. Liberman (Eds.), *Phonology and reading disability: Solving the reading puzzle* (pp. 35–68). Ann Arbor: University of Michigan Press.

Shankweiler, D., Lundquist, E., Katz, L., Stuebing, K. K., Fletcher, J. M., Brad, S., et al. (1999). Comprehension and decoding: Patterns of association in children with reading difficulties. *Scientific Studies of Reading, 3,* 69–94.

Share, D. L. (1995). Phonological recoding and self-teaching: Sine qua non of reading acquisition. *Cognition, 55,* 151–218.

Share, D. L. (1999). Phonological recoding and orthographic learning: A direct test of the self-teaching hypothesis. *Journal of Experimental Child Psychology, 72,* 95–129.

Share, D. L. (2004). Orthographic learning at a glance: On the time course and developmental onset of self-teaching. *Journal of Experimental Child Psychology, 87,* 267–298.

Share, D. L., & Gur, T. (1999). How reading begins: A study of preschoolers' print identification strategies. *Cognition and Instruction, 17,* 177–213.

Share, D. L., Jorm, A. F., Maclean, R., & Matthews, R. (1984). Sources of individual differences in reading acquisition. *Journal of Educational Psychology, 76,* 1309–1324.

Share, D. L., & Stanovich, K. E. (1995). Cognitive processes in early reading development: Accommodating individual differences into a model of acquisition. *Issues in Education, 1,* 1–57.

Shaywitz, B. A., Shaywitz, S. E., Pugh, K. R., Mencl, W. E., Fulbright, R. K., Skudlarski, P., et al. (2002). Disruption of posterior brain systems for reading in children with developmental dyslexia. *Biological Psychiatry, 52*(2), 101–10.

Shaywitz, S. E., Escobar, M. D., Shaywitz, B. A., Fletcher, J. M., & Makuch, R. (1992). Evidence that dyslexia may represent the lower tail of a normal distribution of reading ability. *New England Journal of Medicine, 326,* 145–150.

Shaywitz, S. E., Fletcher, J. M., Holahan, J. M., Schneider, A. E., Marchione, K. E., Stuebing, K. K., et al. (1999). Persistence of dyslexia: The Connecticut longitudinal study at adolescence. *Pediatrics, 104,* 1351–1359.

Shaywitz, S. E., Shaywitz, B. A., Fulbright, R. K., Skudlarski, P., Mencl, W. E., Constable, R. T., et al. (2003). Neural systems for compensation and persistence: Young adult outcome of childhood reading disability. *Biological Psychiatry, 54*(1), 25–33.

Shaywitz, S. E., Shaywitz, B. A., Pugh, K. R., Fulbright, R. K., Constable, R.T., Menci, W.B., et al. (1998). Functional disruption in the organisation of the brain for reading in dyslexia. *Proceedings of the National Academy of Sciences, USA, 95,* 2636–2641.

Shelton, J. R., & Martin, R. C. (1992). How semantic is automatic semantic priming? *Journal of Experimental Psychology: Learning, Memory, and Cognition, 18,* 1191–1210.

Shen, D., & Forster, K. I. (1999). Masked phonological priming in reading Chinese words depends on the task. *Language and Cognitive Processes, 14,* 429–459.

Shen, H., & Bear, D. R. (2000). Development of orthographic skills in Chinese children. *Reading and Writing, 13,* 197–236.

Shepard, L. A. (1997). Children not ready to learn? The invalidity of school readiness testing. *Psychology in the Schools, 34*, 85–97.

Shibahara, N., Zorzi, M., Hill, M. P., Wydell, T., & Butterworth, B. (2003). Semantic effects in word naming: Evidence from English and Japanese Kanji. *Quarterly Journal of Experimental Psychology, 56*, 263–286.

Shimamura, A. (1987). Word comprehension and naming: An analysis of English and Japanese orthographies. *American Journal of Psychology, 100*, 15–40.

Shu, H., & Anderson, R. C. (1997). Role of radical awareness in the character and word acquisition of Chinese children. *Reading Research Quarterly, 32*(1), 78–89.

Shu, H., & Anderson, R. C. (1999). Learning to read Chinese: The development of metalinguistic awareness. In J. Wang, A. Imhoff, A. W. Chen, & H. C. Chen (Eds.), *Reading Chinese script: A cognitive analysis* (pp. 1–18). Mahwah, NJ: Erlbaum.

Shu, H., Anderson, R. C., & Wu, N. (2000). Phonetic awareness: Knowledge of orthography–phonology relationships in the character acquisition of Chinese children. *Journal of Educational Psychology, 92*, 56–62.

Shu, H., Chen, X., Anderson, R. C., Wu, N., & Xuan, Y. (2003). Properties of school Chinese: Implications for learning to read. *Child Development, 74*(1), 27–47.

Siakaluk, P. D., Sears, C. R., & Lupker, S. J. (2002). Orthographic neighborhood effects in lexical decision: The effects of nonword orthographic neighborhood size. *Journal of Experimental Psychology: Learning, Memory, and Cognition, 28*, 661–681.

Silva, P. A., McGee, R., & Williams, S. (1985). Some characteristics of 9-year-old boys with general reading backwardness or specific reading retardation. *Journal of Child Psychology and Psychiatry, 26*, 407–421.

Simpson, G. B., & Kang, H. (1994). The flexible use of phonological information in word recognition in Korean. *Journal of Memory and Language, 33*, 319–331.

Singer Harris, N. G., Bellugi, U., Bates, E., Jones W., & Rossen, M. (1997). Contrasting profiles of language development in children with Williams and Down syndromes. *Developmental Neuropsychology, 13*, 345–370.

Singer, M. (1994). Discourse inference processes. In M. A. Gernsbacher (Ed.), *Handbook of psycholinguistics* (pp. 479–515). San Diego, CA: Academic.

Singer, M., Halldorson, M., Lear, J. C., & Andrusiak, P. (1992). Validation of causal bridging inferences in discourse understanding. *Journal of Memory and Language, 31*, 507–524.

Siok, W. T., & Fletcher, P. (2001). The role of phonological awareness and visual-orthographic skills in Chinese reading acquisition. *Developmental Psychology, 37*, 886–899.

SLI Consortium (2002). A genomewide scan identifies two novel loci involved in specific language impairment. *American Journal of Human Genetics, 70*, 384–398.

Smiley, S. S., Oakley, D. D., Worthen, D., Campione, J. C., & Brown, A. L. (1977). Recall of thematically relevant material by adolescent good and poor readers as a function of written versus oral presentation. *Journal of Educational Psychology, 69*, 381–387.

Smith E. E., & Spoehr, K. T. (1974). The perception of printed English: A theoretical perspective. In B. H. Kantowitz (Ed.), *Human information processing: Tutorials in performance and cognition* (pp. 231–275). Potomac, MD: Erlbaum.

Smith, F. (1971). *Understanding reading: A psycholinguistic analysis of reading and learning to read.* New York: Holt, Rinehart, & Winston.

Smith, F. (1973). *Psycholinguistics and reading.* New York: Holt, Rinehart, & Winston.

Smith, F. (1978). *Understanding reading: A psycholinguistic analysis of reading and learning to read* (2nd ed.). New York: Holt, Rinehart, & Winston.

Smith, K. E., Landry, S. H., & Swank, P. R. (2000). The influence of early patterns of positive parenting on children's preschool outcomes. *Early Education and Development, 11*, 147–169.

Smith, M. K. (1941). Measurement of the size of general English vocabulary through the elementary grades and high school. *Genetic Psychological Monographs, 24,* 311–345.

Smith, S. D., Deffenbacher, K. E., Boada, R., Tunick, R. A., Raitano, N., & Pennington, B. F. (2003). Speech sound disorder is linked to dyslexia risk loci on chromosome 6 and 15. Paper presented at the American Society for Human Genetics.

Smith, S. D., Gilger, J. W., & Pennington, B. F. (2001). Dyslexia and other specific learning disorders. In D. L. Rimoin, J. M. Conner, & R. E. Pyeritz (Eds.), *Emery and Rimoin's principles and practice of medical genetics* (4th ed., pp. 2827–2865). New York: Churchill Livingstone.

Smith, S. D., Kimberling, W. J., Pennington, B. F., & Lubs, H. A. (1983). Specific reading disability: Identification of an inherited form through linkage analysis. *Science, 219,* 1345–1347.

Smith, S. S., & Dixon, R. G. (1995). Literacy concepts of low- and middle-class four-year-olds entering preschool. *Journal of Educational Research, 88,* 243–253.

Snow, C. E., Barnes, W., Chandler, J. Goodman, & Hemphill, L. (1991). *Unfulfilled expectations: Home and school influences on literacy.* Cambridge, MA: Harvard University Press.

Snow, C. E., Burns, M. S., & Griffin, P. (1998). *Preventing reading difficulties in young children.* Washington, DC: National Academy Press.

Snow, C. E., & Tabors, P. O. (1993). Language skills that relate to literacy development. In B. Spodek & O. Saracho (Eds.), *Yearbook in early childhood education* (Vol. 4, pp. 1–20). New York: Teachers College.

Snowden, J. S., Goulding, P. J., & Neary, D. (1989). Semantic dementia: A form of circumscribed cerebral atrophy. *Behavioural Neurology, 2,* 167–182.

Snowling, M. J. (1980). The development of grapheme–phoneme correspondence in normal and dyslexic readers. *Journal of Experimental Child Psychology, 29,* 294–305.

Snowling, M. J. (1981). Phonemic deficits in developmental dyslexia. *Psychological Research, 43,* 219–234.

Snowling, M. J. (1983). A comparison of acquired and developmental disorders of reading. *Cognition, 14,* 105–118.

Snowling, M. J. (2000a). *Dyslexia* (2nd ed.). Oxford: Blackwell.

Snowling, M. J. (2000b). Language and literacy skills: Who is at risk and why? In L. B. Leonard & D. V. M. Bishop (Eds.), *Speech and language impairments in children: Causes, characteristics, intervention and outcome* (pp. 245–259). Philadelphia: Psychology Press.

Snowling, M., Bishop, D. V. M., & Stothard, S. E. (2000). Do language-impaired preschoolers turn into dyslexic adolescents? *Journal of Child Psychology and Psychiatry, 41,* 587–600.

Snowling, M., Bryant, P. E., & Hulme, C. (1996). Theoretical and methodological pitfalls in making comparisons between developmental and acquired dyslexias: Some comments on A. Castles & M. Coltheart (1993). *Reading and writing, 8,* 443–451.

Snowling, M., Chiat, S., & Hulme, C. (1991). Words, nonwords, and phonological processes: Some comments on Gathercole, Willis, Emslie, and Baddeley. *Applied Psycholinguistics, 12,* 369–373.

Snowling, M. J., & Frith, U. (1986). Comprehension in "hyperlexic" readers. *Journal of Experimental Child Psychology, 42,* 392–415.

Snowling, M. J., Gallagher, A., & Frith, U. (2003). Family risk of dyslexia is continuous: Individual differences in the precursors of reading skill. *Child Development, 74,* 358–373.

Snowling, M., Goulandris, N., Bowlby, M., & Howell, P. (1986). Segmentation and speech perception in relation to reading skill: A developmental analysis. *Journal of Experimental Child Psychology, 41,* 489–507.

Snowling, M. J., & Hulme, C. (1989). A longitudinal case study of developmental phonological dyslexia. *Cognitive Neuropsychology, 6,* 379–401.

Snowling, M. J., & Hulme, C. (1994a). The development of phonological skills. *Philosophical Transactions of the Royal Society, B 346*, 21–28.

Snowling, M. J., & Hulme, C. (Eds.) (1994b). *Reading development and dyslexia.* London: Whurr.

Snowling, M., Hulme, C., & Goulandris, N. (1994). Word recognition and development: A connectionist interpretation. *Quarterly Journal of Experimental Psychology, 47A*, 895–916.

Snowling, M. J., Hulme, C., & Mercer, R. C. (2002). A deficit in rime awareness in children with Down syndrome. *Reading and Writing, 15*, 471–495.

Snowling, M. J., Stackhouse, J., & Rack, J. (1986). Phonological dyslexia and dysgraphia: A developmental analysis. *Cognitive Neuropsychology, 3*, 309–339.

Snowling, M. J., Stothard, S. E., & McLean, J. (1996). *The Graded Nonword Reading Test.* Reading: Thames Valley Test Company.

So, D., & Siegel, L. (1997). Learning to read Chinese: Semantic, syntactic, phonological and working memory skills in normally achieving and poor Chinese readers. *Reading and Writing, 9*, 1–21.

Solan, H. A., Feldman, J., & Tujak, L. (1995). Developing visual and reading efficiency in older adults. *Optometry and Vision Science, 72*, 139–145.

Sonnenschein, S., & Munsterman, K. (2002). The influence of home-based reading interactions on 5-year-olds' reading motivations and early literacy development. *Early Childhood Research Quarterly, 17*, 318–337.

Sparks, R. L. (1995). Phonemic awareness in hyperlexic children. *Reading and Writing, 7*, 217–235.

Sparks, R. L. (2001). Phonemic awareness and reading skill in hyperlexic children: A longitudinal study. *Reading and Writing, 14*, 333–360.

Spear-Swerling, L., & Sternberg, R. J. (1994). The road not taken: An integrative theoretical model for reading disability. *Journal of Learning Disabilities, 27*, 91–103, 122.

Spear-Swerling, L., & Sternberg, R. J. (1996). *Off track: When your readers become "learning disabled."* Denver: Westview Press.

Spector, J. E. (1992). Predicting progress in beginning reading: Dynamic assessment of phonemic awareness. *Journal of Educational Psychology, 84*, 353–363.

Spencer, L. H., & Hanley, J. R. (2003). Effects of orthographic transparency on reading and phoneme awareness in children learning to read in Wales. *British Journal of Psychology, 94*, 1–28.

Spieler, D. H., & Balota, D. A. (1997). Bringing computational models of word naming down to the item level. *Psychological Science, 8*, 411–416.

Spilich, G. J., Vesonder, G. T., Chiesi, H. L., & Voss, J. F. (1979). Text processing of domain related information for individuals with high and low domain knowledge. *Journal of Verbal Learning and Verbal Behavior, 18*, 275–290.

Sprenger-Charolles, L., Colle, P., Lacert, P., & Serniclaes, W. (2000). On subtypes of developmental dyslexia: Evidence from processing time and accuracy scores. *Canadian Journal of Experimental Psychology, 54*, 87–103.

Sprenger-Charolles, L., Siegel, L. S., & Béchennec, D. (1997). Beginning reading and spelling acquisition in French: A longitudinal study. In C. A. Perfetti, L. Rieben, & M. Fayol (Eds.), *Learning to spell: Research, theory, and practice across languages* (pp. 339–359). Mahwah, NJ: Erlbaum.

Sprenger-Charolles, L., Siegel, L. S., Béchennec, D., & Serniclaes, W. (2003). Development of phonological and orthographic processing in reading aloud, in silent reading, and in spelling: A four-year longitudinal study. *Journal of Experiemental Child Psychology, 84*, 194–217.

Stackhouse, J. (1982). An investigation of reading and spelling performance in speech disordered children. *British Journal of Disorders of Communicaion, 17*, 53–60.

Stackhouse, J., & Snowling, M. J. (1992). Barriers to literacy development in two cases of developmental verbal dyspraxia. *Cognitive Neuropsychology, 9*, 273–299.

Stahl, S. A., & Murray, B. A. (1994). Defining phonological awareness and its relationship to early reading. *Journal of Educational Psychology, 86,* 221–234.

Stanley, G., Smith, G. A., & Howell, E. A. (1983). Eye movements and sequential tracking in dyslexic and control children. *British Journal of Psychology, 74,* 181–187.

Stanners, R. F., & Forbach, G. B. (1973). Analysis of letter strings in word recognition. *Journal of Experimental Psychology, 98,* 31–35.

Stanovich, K. E. (1980). Toward an interactive-compensatory model of individual differences in the development of reading fluency. *Reading Research Quarterly, 16,* 32–71.

Stanovich, K. E. (1986). Mathew effects in reading: Some consequences of individual differences in the acquisition of reading. *Reading Research Quarterly, 21,* 360–407.

Stanovich, K. E. (1988). Explaining the differences between the dyslexic and the garden-variety poor reader: The phonological core-variable difference model. *Journal of Learning Disabilities, 21,* 590–604.

Stanovich, K. E. (1991). Discrepancy definitions of reading disability: Has intelligence led us astray? *Reading Research Quarterly, 26,* 7–29.

Stanovich, K. E. (1992). Speculations on the causes and consequences of individual differences in reading acquisition. In P. Gough, L. Ehri, & R. Treiman (Eds.), *Reading acquisition* (pp. 307–342). Hillsdale, NJ: Erlbaum.

Stanovich, K. E. (1993). The construct validity of discrepancy definitions of reading disability. In G. R. Lyon, D. B. Gray, J. F. Kavanagh, & N. A. Krasnegor (Eds.), *Better understanding learning disabilities* (pp. 273–308). Baltimore: Brooks.

Stanovich, K. E. (2000). *Progress in understanding reading: Scientific foundations and new frontiers.* New York: Guilford.

Stanovich, K. E., Cunningham, A. E., & Freeman, D. J. (1984). Relation between early reading acquisition and word decoding with and without context: A longitudinal study of first grade children. *Journal of Educational Psychology, 76,* 668–677.

Stanovich, K. E., Feeman, D. J., & Cunningham, A. E. (1983). The development of the relation between letter-naming speed and reading ability. *Bulletin of the Psychonomic Society, 21,* 199–202.

Stanovich, K. E., Nathan, R. G., & Zolman, J. E. (1988). The developmental lag hypothesis in reading: Longitudinal and matched reading level comparisons. *Child Development, 59,* 71–86.

Stanovich, K. E., & Siegel, L. S. (1994). The phenotypic performance profile of reading-disabled children: A regression-based test of the phonological-core variable-difference model. *Journal of Educational Psychology, 86,* 24–53.

Stanovich, K. E., Siegel, L. S., & Gottardo, A. (1997). Converging evidence for phonological and surface subtypes of reading disability. *Journal of Educational Psychology, 89,* 114–127.

Stanovich, K. E., & Stanovich, P. J. (1995). How research might inform the debate about early reading acquisition. *Journal of Research in Reading, 18,* 87–105.

Stanovich, K. E., & West, R. F. (1989). Exposure to print and orthographic processing. *Reading Research Quarterly, 24,* 402–433.

Starr, M. S., & Inhoff, A. W. (2004). Attention allocation to the right and left of a fixated word: Use of orthographic information from multiple words during reading. *European Journal of Cognitive Psychology, 16,* 203–225.

Starr, M. S., & Rayner, K. (2001). Eye movements during reading: Some current controversies. *Trends in Cognitive Sciences, 5,* 156–163.

Stein, C. L., Cairns, J. S., & Zurif, E. B. (1984). Sentence comprehension limitations related to syntactic deficits in reading-disabled children. *Applied Psycholinguistics, 5,* 305–322.

Stein, J. F. (2001). The sensory basis of reading problems. *Developmental Neuropsychology, 20,* 509–534.

Stein, M., & L. D'Amico. (2002). Inquiry at the crossroads of policy and learning: a study of a district-wide literacy initiative. *Teachers College Record, 104,* 1313–1344.

Stein, N. L., & Albro, E. R. (1997). The emergence of narrative understanding: Evidence for rapid learning in personally relevant contexts. *Contemporary Issues in Education, 60,* 83–98.

Stein, N. L., & Glenn, C. G. (1979). An analysis of story comprehension in elementary school children. In R. O. Freedle (Ed.), *New directions in discourse processing* (pp. 53–120). Hillsdale, NJ: Erlbaum.

Stephenson, S. (1907). Six cases of congenital word-blindness affecting three generations of one family. *Ophthalmoscope, 5,* 482–484.

Sternberg, R. J. (1981). Testing and cognitive psychology. *American Psychologist, 36,* 1181–1189.

Sternberg, R. J., & Powell, J. S. (1983). Comprehending verbal comprehension. *American Psychologist, 38,* 878–893.

Sterne, A. (1996). *Phonological awareness, memory, and reading in deaf children.* Cambridge: University of Cambridge.

Sterne, A., & Goswami, U. (2000). Phonological awareness of syllables, rhymes, and phonemes in deaf children. *Journal of Child Psychology and Psychiatry, 41*(5), 609–625.

Stevens, E., Blake, J., Vitale, G., & Macdonald, S. (1998). Mother–infant object involvement at 9 and 15 months: Relation to infant cognition and early vocabulary. *First Language, 18,* 203–222.

Stevens, T., & Karmiloff-Smith, A. (1997). Word learning in a special population: Do individuals with Williams syndrome obey lexical constraints? *Journal of Child Language, 24,* 737–765.

Stevenson, H. W., & Newman, R. S. (1986). Long-term prediction of achievement and attitudes in mathematics and reading. *Child Development, 57,* 646–659.

Stevenson, H. W., Parker, T., Wilkinson, A., Hegion, A., & Fish, E. (1976). Longitudinal study of individual differences in cognitive development and scholastic achievement. *Journal of Educational Psychology, 68,* 377–340.

Stevenson, H. W., Stigler, J. W., Lucker, G. W., Lee, S., Hsu, C., & Kitamura, S. (1982). Reading disabilities: The case of Chinese, Japanese, and English. *Child Development, 53,* 1164–1181.

Stevenson, J. (1991). Which aspects of processing text mediate genetic effects? *Reading and Writing, 3,* 249–269.

Stevenson, J., Pennington, B. F., Gilger, J. W., DeFries, J. C., & Gillis, J. J. (1993). Hyperactivity and spelling disability: testing for shared genetic etiology. *Journal of Child Psychology and Psychiatry, 34,* 1137–1152.

Stevenson, R., Knott, A., Oberlander, J., & McDonald, S. (2000). Interpreting pronouns and connectives: Interactions among focusing, thematic roles and coherence relations. *Language and Cognitive Processes, 15,* 225–262.

Stewart, A. J., Pickering, M. J., & Sanford, A. J. (2000). The time course of the influence of implicit causality information: Focusing versus integration accounts. *Journal of Memory and Language, 42,* 423–443.

Sticht, T., & James, J. (1984). Listening and reading. In P. Pearson (Ed.), *Handbook of research on reading* (pp. 293–317). New York: Longman.

Stigler, J., & Hiebert, J. (1999). *The teaching gap.* New York: Free Press.

Stipek, D. (2002). At what age should children enter kindergarten? A question for policy makers and parents. *Social Policy Report, 16*(2), 3–16.

Stipek, D., & Byler, P. (2001). Academic achievement and social behaviors associated with age of entry into kindergarten. *Applied Developmental Psychology, 22,* 175–189.

Stipek, D., Feiler, R., Daniels, D., & Milburn, S. (1995). Effects of different instructional approaches on young children's achievement and motivation. *Child Development, 66,* 209–223.

Stipek, D., Milburn, S., Clements, D., & Daniels, D. H. (1992). Parents' beliefs about appropriate education for young children. *Journal of Applied Developmental Psychology, 13,* 293–310.

Stokoe, W. C. (1978). *Sign language structure.* Silver Spring: Linstok.

Stone, G. O., Vanhoy, M. D., & Van Orden, G. C. (1997). Perception is a two-way street: Feed-forward and feedback phonology in visual word recognition. *Journal of Memory and Language, 36,* 337–359.

Stone, G. O., & Van Orden, G. C. (1993). Strategic control of processing in word recognition. *Journal of Experimental Psychology: Human Perception and Performance, 19,* 744–774.

Stone, G. O., & Van Orden, G. C. (1994). Building a resonance framework for words recognition using design and system principles. *Journal of Experimental Psychology: Human Perception and Performance, 20,* 1248–1268.

Storch, S. A., & Whitehurst, G. J. (2001). The role of family and home in the literacy development of children from low-income backgrounds. In P. R. Britto & J. Brooks-Gunn (Eds.), *The role of family literacy environments in promoting young children's emerging literacy skills.* New directions for child and adolescent development (pp. 53–71). San Francisco: Jossey-Bass.

Storch, S. A., & Whitehurst, G. J. (2002). Oral language and code-related precursors to reading: Evidence from a longitudinal structural model. *Developmental Psychology, 38,* 934–947.

Stothard, S. E., & Hulme, C. (1992). Reading comprehension difficulties in children: The role of language comprehension and working memory skills. *Reading and Writing, 4,* 245–256.

Stothard, S. E., & Hulme, C. (1995). A comparison of reading comprehension and decoding difficulties in children. *Journal of Child Psychology and Psychiatry, 36,* 399–408.

Stothard, S. E., Snowling, M. J., Bishop, D. V. M., Chipchase, B., & Kaplan, C. (1998). Language impaired pre-schoolers: A follow-up in adolescence. *Journal of Speech, Language, and Hearing Research, 41,* 407–418.

Stothard, S. E., Snowling, M. J., & Hulme, C. (1996). Deficits in phonology but not dyslexic? *Cognitive Neuropsychology, 13,* 641–672.

Strain, E., Patterson, K., Graham, N., & Hodges, J. R. (1998). Word reading in Alzheimer's disease: Cross-sectional and longitudinal analyses of response time and accuracy data. *Neuropsychologia, 36,* 155–171.

Strain, E., Patterson, K., & Seidenberg, M. S. (1995). Semantic effects in single-word naming. *Journal of Experimental Psychology: Learning, Memory, and Cognition, 21,* 1140–1154.

Strickland, D., Snow, C., Griffin, P., Burns, M. S., & McNamara, P. (2002). *Preparing our teachers: Opportunities for better reading instruction.* Washington, DC: Henry.

Strong, M., & Prinz, P. (1997). A study of the relationship between American Sign Language and English literacy. *Journal of Deaf Studies and Deaf Education, 2,* 37–46.

Strong, M., & Prinz, P. (2000). Is American Sign Language skill related to English literacy? In C. Chamberlain, J. P. Morford, & R. I. Mayberry (Eds.), *Language acquisition by eye* (pp. 131–143). Mahwah, NJ: Erlbaum.

Stuart, M. (2002). Using the dual-route cascade model as a framework for considering reading development. In R. Stainthorpe & P. Tomlinson (Eds.), *Learning and teaching reading. British Journal of Educational Psychology Monograph Series II; Psychological Aspects of Education – Current Trends, 1,* 45–60.

Stuart, M., & Coltheart, M. (1988). Does reading develop in a sequence of stages? *Cognition, 30,* 139–181.

Stuart, M., & Masterson, J. (1992). Patterns of reading and spelling in 10-year-old children related to prereading phonological abilities. *Journal of Experimental Child Psychology, 54,* 168–187.

Stuart, M., Masterson, J., Dixon, M., & Quinlan, P. (1999). Inferring sublexical correspondences from sight vocabulary: Evidence from 6- and 7-year-olds. *The Quarterly Journal of Experimental Psychology, 52,* 353–366.

Stuckless, E. R., & Birch, J. W. (1966b). The influence of early manual communication on the linguistic development of deaf children. *American Annals of the Deaf, 111,* 499–504.

Studdert-Kennedy, M., & Mody, M. (1995). Auditory-temporal perception deficits in the reading-impaired: A critical review of the evidence. *Psychonomic Bulletin and Review, 2*, 508–514.

Stuebing, K. K., Fletcher, J. M., LeDoux, J. M., Lyon, G. R., Shaywitz, S. E., & Shaywitz, B. A. (2002). Validity of IQ-discrepancy classifications of reading disabilities: A meta-analysis. *American Educational Research Journal, 39*, 469–518.

Sulzby, E. (1998). Early reading achievement [on-line]. Available: www.ciera.org

Sulzby, E., & Teale, W. (1991). Emergent literacy. In R. Barr, M. Kamil, P. Mosenthal, & P. D. Pearson (Eds.), *Handbook of reading research* (Vol. 2, pp. 727–758). New York: Longman.

Surber, J. R. (2001). Effect of topic label repetition and importance on reading time and recall of text. *Journal of Educational Psychology, 93*, 279–287.

Sutcliffe, A., Dowker, A., & Campbell, R. (1999). Deaf children's spelling: Does it show sensitivity to phonology? *Journal of Deaf Studies and Deaf Education, 4*(2), 111–123.

Sutton, R. S. (1988). Learning to predict by the method of temporal differences. *Machine Learning, 3*, 9–44.

Swan, D., & Goswami, U. (1997a). Phonological awareness deficits in developmental dyslexia and the phonological representations hypothesis. *Journal of Experimental Child Psychology, 66*, 18–41.

Swan, D., & Goswami, U. (1997b). Picture naming deficits in developmental dyslexia: The phonological representation hypothesis. *Brain and Language, 56*, 334–353.

Tabors, P. O., & Snow, C. E. (2001). Young bilingual children and early literacy development. In S. B. Neuman & D. K. Dickinson (Eds.), *Handbook of early literacy research* (pp. 159–178). New York: Guilford.

Tabossi, P., & Laghi, L. (1992). Semantic priming in the pronunciation of words in two writing systems: Italian and English. *Memory and Cognition, 20*, 303–313.

Taft, M., & Tamaoka, K. (1994). Is the smallest unit in phonological processing equivalent to the smallest unit in orthographic processing? Lexical judgements of Katakana nonwords. *Japanese Journal of Psychology, 65*, 377–382 (in Japanese).

Taft, M., & van Graan, G. (1998). Lack of phonological mediation in a semantic categorization task. *Journal of Memory and Language, 38*, 203–224.

Tagamets, M. A., Novick, J. M., Chalmers, M. L., & Friedman, R. B. (2001). A parametric approach to orthographic processing in the brain: An fMRI study. *Journal of Cognitive Neuroscience, 12*, 281–297.

Tainturier, M. J. (1996). Phonologically-based errors and their implications in the specification of phonology to orthography conversion processes. *Brain and Cognition, 32*, 148–151.

Tainturier, M. J., & Rapp, B. (2000). The spelling process. In B. Rapp (Ed.), *The handbook of cognitive neuropsychology* (pp. 263–289). Ann Arbor: Edwards.

Taipale, M., Kaminen, N., Napola-Hemmi, J., Haltia, T., Myllyluoma, B., Lyytinen, H., et al. (2003). A candidate gene for developmental dyslexia encodes a nuclear tetratricopepeptide repeat domain protein dynamically regulated in the brain. PNAS Early Edition, www.pnas.org/cgi/doi/10.1073/pnas.1833911100.

Talairach, J., & Tournoux, P. (1988). *A co-planar stereotactic atlas of the human brain.* Stuttgart: Thieme.

Tallal, P. (1980). Auditory temporal perception, phonics, and reading disabilities in children. *Brain and Language, 9*, 182–198.

Tallal, P. (2003). Language learning disabilities: Integrating research approaches. *Current Directions in Psychological Science, 12*, 206–211.

Tallal, P., & Percy, M. (1973). Developmental aphasia: Impaired rate of nonverbal processing as a function of sensory modality. *Neuropsychologia, 11*, 389–398.

Tang, Y.-P., Shimizu, E., Dube, G. R., Rampon, C., Kerchner, G. A., Zhuo, M., et al. (1999). Genetic enhancement of learning and memory in mice. *Nature, 401,* 63–69.

Taraban, R., & McClelland, J. L. (1987). Conspiracy effects in word recognition. *Journal of Memory and Language, 26,* 608–631.

Taylor, B., Pearson, P. D., Clark, K., & Walpole, S. (2000). Effective schools and accomplished teachers: Lessons about primary-grade reading instruction in low-income schools. *Elementary School Journal, 101,* 121–166.

Teale, W. H., & Sulzby, E. (Eds.) (1986). *Emergent literacy: Writing and reading.* Norwood, NJ: Ablex.

Temple, C. M. (1986). Developmental dysgraphias. *Quarterly Journal of Experimental Psychology, 38A,* 77–110.

Temple, C. M., & Carney, R. (1996). Reading skills in children with Turner's Syndrome: An analysis of hyperlexia. *Cortex, 32,* 335–345.

Temple, C. M., & Marshall J. C. (1983). A case study of developmental phonological dyslexia. *British Journal of Psychology, 74,* 517–533.

Temple, E., Poldrack, R. A., Salidis, J., Deutsch, G. K., Tallal, P., Merzenich, M. M., et al. (2001). Disrupted neural responses to phonological and orthographic processing in dyslexic children: An fMRI study. *Neuroreport, 12*(2), 299–307.

Tfouni, L. V. (1988). Adultos não alfabetizados: o avesso do avesso. Campinas: Pontes Editores.

Theios, J., & Muise, J. G. (1977). The word identification process in reading. In N. J. Castillan, D. Pisoni, & G. R. Potts (Eds.), *Cognitive theory* (pp. 281–298). Hillsdale, NJ: Erlbaum.

Thomas, C. J. (1905). Congenital word-blindness and its treatment. *Ophthalmoscope, 3,* 380–385.

Thompson, G. B., Cottrell, D., & Fletcher-Flinn, C. (1996). Sublexical orthographic–phonological relations early in the acquisition of reading: The knowledge sources account. *Journal of Experimental Child Psychology, 62,* 190–222.

Thompson, G. B., Fletcher-Finn, C. M., & Cottrell, D. S. (1999). Learning correspondences between letters and phonemes without explicit instruction. *Applied Psycholinguistics, 20,* 21–50.

Tiedemann, J., & Faber, G. (1992). Preschoolers' maternal support and cognitive competencies as predictors of elementary achievement. *Journal of Educational Research, 85,* 348–354.

Tivnan, T., & Hemphill, L. (2004). Comparing literacy reform models in high poverty schools: Patterns of first grade achievement. Manuscript submitted for publication, Harvard Graduate School of Education.

Tolchinsky, L. (2003). *The cradle of culture and what children know about writing and numbers before being taught.* Mahwah, NJ: Erlbaum.

Torgesen, J. K. (1993). Variations on theory in learning disabilities. In R. Lyon, D. Gray, N. Krasnegor, & J. Kavenagh (Eds.), *Better understanding learning disabilities: Perspectives on classification, identification, and assessment and their implications for education and policy* (pp. 153–170). Baltimore: Brookes.

Torgesen, J. K. (1999). Phonologically based reading disabilities: Toward a coherent theory of one kind of learning disability. In R. J. Sternberg & L. Spear-Swerling (Eds.), *Perspectives on learning disabilities* (pp. 231–262). New Haven: Westview.

Torgesen, J. K. (2002). The prevention of reading difficulties. *Journal of School Psychology, 40,* 7–26.

Torgesen, J. K., Alexander, A. W., Wagner, R. K., Rashotte, C. A., Voeller, K., Conway, T., et al. (2001a). Intensive remedial instruction for children with severe reading disabilities: Immediate and long-term outcomes from two instructional approaches. *Journal of Learning Disabilities, 34,* 33–58.

Torgesen, J. K., & Burgess, S. R. (1998). Consistency of reading-related phonological processes throughout early childhood: Evidence from longitudinal-correlational and instructional studies.

In J. L. Metsala & L. C. Ehri (Eds.), *Word recognition in beginning literacy* (pp. 161–188). Hillsdale, NJ: Erlbaum.

Torgesen, J. K., & Hecht, S. A. (1996). Preventing and remediating reading disabilities: Instructional variables that make a difference for special students. In M. F. Graves, P. van den Broek, & B. M. Taylor (Eds.), *The first R: Every child's right to read* (pp. 133–159). New York: Teacher's College.

Torgesen, J. K., Rashotte, C. A., & Alexander, A. (2001b). Principles of fluency instruction in reading: Relationships with established empirical outcomes. In M. Wolf (Ed. ), *Dyslexia, fluency, and the brain* (pp. 333–355). Parkton, MD: York.

Torgesen, J. K., Rashotte, C. A., Alexander, A., Alexander, J., & MacPhee, K. (2003a). Progress towards understanding the instructional conditions necessary for remediating reading difficulties in older children. In B. Foorman (Ed.), *Preventing and remediating reading difficulties: Bringing science to scale* (pp. 275–298). Parkton, MD: York.

Torgesen, J. K., Rose, E., Lindamood, P., Conway, T., & Garvan C. (1999). Preventing reading failure in young children with phonological processing disabilities: Group and individual responses to instruction. *Journal of Educational Psychology, 91,* 579–594.

Torgesen, J. K., & Wagner, R. K. (1995, May). Alternative diagnostic approaches for specific developmental reading disabilities. Manuscript presented, for the National Research Council's Board on Testing and Assessment, at a workshop on IQ testing and educational decision making, Washington, DC [cited by Torgesen & Burgess, 1998].

Torgesen, J. K., Wagner, R. K., & Rashotte, C. A. (1999). *Test of Word Reading Efficiency (TOWRE).* Austin, TX: Pro-ed.

Torgesen, J. K., Wagner, R. K., Rashotte, C. A., Burgess, S., & Hecht, S. (1997). Contributions of phonological awareness and rapid automatic naming ability to the growth of word-reading skills in second to fifth grade children. *Scientific Studies of Reading, 1,* 161–185.

Torgesen, J. K., Wagner, R. K., Rashotte, C. A., & Herron, J. (2003b). Summary of outcomes from first grade study with *read, write, and type* and *auditory discrimination in depth* instruction and software with at-risk children. Technical Report #3, Florida Center for Reading Research, Tallahassee, FL.

Torgesen, J. K., Wagner, R. K., Rashotte, C. A., Rose, E., Lindamood, P., Conway, T., et al. (1999). Preventing reading failure in young children with phonological processing disabilities: Group and individual responses to instruction. *Journal of Educational Psychology, 91,* 579–593.

Trabasso, T., & Suh, S. (1993). Understanding text: Achieving explanatory coherence through online inferences and mental operations in working memory. *Discourse Processes, 16,* 3–34.

Tracey, D. H., & Morrow, L. M. (1998). Motivating contexts for young children's literacy development: Implications for word recognition. In J. L Metsala & L. C. Ehri (Eds.), *Word recognition in beginning literacy* (pp. 341–356). Mahwah, NJ: Erlbaum.

Transler, C., Gombert, J. E., & Leybaert, J. (2001). Phonological decoding in severely and profoundly deaf children: Similarity judgment between written pseudowords. *Applied Psycholinguistics, 22,* 61–82.

Transler, C., & Reitsma, P. (submitted). Deaf children develop normal orthotactic sensitivity: Evidence from spelling errors and word-likeness judgments.

Traxler, C. (2000). The Stanford achievement test, 9th edition: National norming and performance standards for deaf and hard-of-hearing students. *Journal of Deaf Studies and Deaf Education, 5,* 337–348.

Treiman, R. (1985). Onsets and rimes as units of spoken syllables: Evidence from children. *Journal of Experimental Child Psychology, 39,* 161–181.

Treiman, R. (1993). *Beginning to spell: A study of first-grade children.* New York: Oxford University Press.

Treiman, R., Berch, D., & Weatherston, S. (1993). Children's use of phoneme–grapheme correspondences in spelling: Roles of position and stress. *Journal of Educational Psychology, 85,* 466–477.

Treiman, R., & Broderick, V. (1998). What's in a name: Children's knowledge about the letters in their own names. *Journal of Experimental Child Psychology, 70,* 97–116.

Treiman, R., Cassar, M., & Zukowski, A. (1994). What types of linguistic information do children use in spelling? The case of flaps. *Child Development, 65,* 1310–1329.

Treiman, R., & Kessler, B. (2003). The role of letter names in the acquisition of literacy. In R. Kail (Ed.), *Advances in child development and behavior* (Vol. 31, pp. 105–135). San Diego, CA: Academic.

Treiman, R., Kessler, B., & Bick, S. (2003). Influence of consonantal context on the pronunciation of vowels: A comparison of human readers and computational models. *Cognition, 88,* 49–78.

Treiman, R., Mullennix, J., Bijeljac-Babic, R., & Richmond-Welty, E. D. (1995). The special role of rimes in the description, use, and acquisition of English orthography. *Journal of Experimental Psychology: General, 124,* 107–136.

Treiman, R., & Rodriguez, K. (1999). Young children use letter names in learning to read words. *Psychological Science, 10,* 334–338.

Treiman, R., Sotak, L., & Bowman, M. (2001). The roles of letter names and letter sounds in connecting print and speech. *Memory and Cognition, 29,* 860–873.

Treiman, R., Tincoff, R., & Richmond-Welty, E. D. (1996). Letter names help children to connect print and speech. *Developmental Psychology, 32,* 505–514.

Treiman, R., Tincoff, R., Rodriguez, K., Mouzaki, A., & Francis, D. J. (1998). The foundations of literacy: Learning the sounds of letters. *Child Development, 69,* 1524–1540.

Treiman, R., Weatherstone, S., & Berch, D. (1994). The role of letter names in children's learning of phoneme–grapheme relations. *Applied Psycholinguistics, 15,* 97–122.

Treiman, R., & Zukowski, A. (1991). Levels of phonological awareness. In S. A. Brady & D. P. Shankweiler (Eds.), *Phonological processes in literacy: A tribute to Isabelle Y Liberman* (pp. 67–83). Hillsdale, NJ: Erlbaum.

Truch, S. (1994). Stimulating basic reading processes using auditory discrimination in depth. *Annals of Dyslexia, 44,* 60–80.

Truch, S. (2003). Comparing remedial outcomes using LIPS and Phono-Graphix: An in-depth look from a clinical perspective. Unpublished manuscript. Reading Foundation, Calgary, Alberta, Canada.

Tsai, K. C., & Nunes, T. (2003). The role of character schema in learning novel Chinese characters. In C. McBride-Chang & H. C. Chen (Eds.), *Reading development in Chinese children* (pp. 104–119). Westport, CT: Praeger.

Tzeng, O. J. L. (2002). Current issues in learning to read Chinese. In W. Li, J. S. Gaffney, & J. L. Packard (Eds.), *Chinese children's reading acquisition: Theoretical and pedagogical issues* (pp. 3–15). Boston: Kluwer Academic.

Tzeng, O. J. L., Lin, Z. H., Hung, D. L., & Lee, W. L. (1995). Learning to be a conspirator: A tale of becoming a good Chinese reader. In B. de Gelder & J. Morais (Eds.), *Speech and reading: A comparative approach* (pp. 227–244). Hove, UK: Erlbaum.

Tzeng, O. J. L., Zhong, H. L., Hung, D. L., & Lee, W. L. (1995). Learning to be a conspirator: A tale of becoming a good Chinese reader. In B. de Gelder & J. Morais (Eds.), *Speech and reading: A comparative approach* (pp. 22–246). Hove, UK: Erlbaum.

Tunick, R. A., & Pennington, B. F. (2002). The etiological relationship between reading disability and phonological disorder. *Annals of Dyslexia, 52,* 75–95.

Tunmer, W. E. (1989). The role of language related factors in reading disability. In D. Shankweiler & I. Y. Liberman (Eds.), *Phonology and reading disability: Solving the reading puzzle* (pp. 91–131). Ann Arbor: University of Michigan Press.

Tunmer, W. E., & Chapman, J. (1998). Language prediction skill, phonological recording ability, and beginning reading. In C. Hulme & R. Joshi (Eds.), *Reading and spelling: Development and disorders* (pp. 33–68). Mahwah, NJ: Erlbaum.

Tunmer, W. E., & Hoover, W. A. (1992). Cognitive and linguistic factors in learning to read. In P. B. Gough, L. C. Ehri, & R. Treiman (Eds.), *Reading acquisition* (pp. 175–214). Hillsdale, NJ: Erlbaum.

Turkeltaub, P. E., Eden, G. F., Jones, K. M., & Zeffiro, T. A. (2002). Meta-analysis of the functional neuroanatomy of single word reading: Method and validation. *NeuroImage, 16,* 765–780.

Turkheimer, E., Haley, A., Waldron, M., D'Onofrio, B., Gottesman, I. I. (2003). Socioeconomic status modifies heritability of IQ in young children. *Psychological Science, 14,* 623–628.

Turvey, M. T., Feldman. L. B., & Lukatela, G. (1984). The Serbo-Croatian orthography constrains the reader to a phonologically analytic strategy. In L. Henderson (Ed.), *Orthographies and reading: Perspectives from cognitive psychology, neuropsychology, and linguistics* (pp. 81–89). Hillsdale, NJ: Erlbaum.

Uhry, J., & Shepherd, J. (1993). Segmentation/spelling instruction as a part of a first-grade reading program: Effects on several measures of reading. *Reading Research Quarterly, 28,* 218–233.

Ullman, M. T., Corkin, S., Coppola, M., Hickok, G., Growdon, J. H., Koroshetz, W. J., et al. (1997). A neural dissociation within language: Evidence that the mental dictionary is part of declarative memory, and that grammatical rules are processed by the procedural system. *Journal of Cognitive Neuroscience, 9,* 266–276.

Underwood, G., Bloomfield, R., & Clews, S. (1988). Information influences the pattern of eye fixations during sentence comprehension. *Perception, 17,* 267–278.

Underwood, N. R., & McConkie, G. W. (1985). Perceptual span for letter distinctions during reading. *Reading Research Quarterly, 20,* 153–162.

Unsworth, S. J., & Pexman, P. M. (2003). The impact of reader skill on phonological processing in visual word recognition. *Quarterly Journal of Experimental Psychology Section A: Human Experimental Psychology, 56,* 63–81.

Vandenberghe, R., Price, C. J., Wise, R., Josephs, O., & Frackowiak, R. S. J. (1996). Functional anatomy of a common semantic system for words and pictures. *Nature, 383,* 254–256.

van den Broek, P., Risden, K., Fletcher, C. R., & Thurlow, R. (1996). A "landscape" view of reading: Fluctuating patterns of activation and the construction of a stable memory representation. In B. K. Britton & A. C. Graesser (Eds.), *Models of understanding text* (pp. 165–187). Mahwah, NJ: Erlbaum.

Van Dijk, T. A., & Kintsch, W. (1983). *Strategies of discourse comprehension.* New York: Academic.

Vanhoy, M., & Van Orden, G. C. (2001). Pseudohomophones and word recognition. *Memory and Cognition, 29,* 522–529.

Van Orden, G. C. (1987). A ROWS is a ROSE: Spelling, sound, and reading. *Memory and Cognition, 15,* 181–198.

Van Orden, G. C., & Goldinger, S. D. (1994). Interdependence of form and function in cognitive systems explains perception of printed words. *Journal of Experimental Psychology: Human Perception and Performance, 20,* 1269–1291.

Van Orden, G. C., & Holden, J. G. (2002). Intentional contents and self control. *Ecological Psychology, 14,* 87–109.

Van Orden, G. C., Holden, J. G., Podgornik, M. N., & Aitchison, C. S. (1999). What swimming says about reading: Coordination, context, and homophone errors. *Ecological Psychology, 11,* 45–79.

Van Orden, G. C., Holden, J. G., & Turvey, M. T. (2003). Self-organization of cognitive perfor- mance. *Journal of Experimental Psychology: General, 132*, 331–350.

Van Orden, G. C., Moreno, M. A., & Holden, J. G. (2003). A proper metaphysics for cognitive performance. *Nonlinear Dynamics, Psychology, and Life Sciences, 7*, 47–58.

Van Orden, G. C., Pennington, B. F., & Stone, G. O. (1990). Word identification in reading and the promise of subsymbolic psycholinguistics. *Psychological Review, 97*, 488–522.

Van Orden, G. C., Pennington, B. F., & Stone, G. O. (2001). What do double dissociations prove? *Cognitive Science, 25*, 111–172.

Vellutino, F. R. (1979). *Dyslexia: Theory and research.* Cambridge, MA: MIT Press.

Vellutino, F. R., Fletcher, J. M., Snowling, M. J., & Scanlon, D. M. (2004). Specific reading dis- ability (dyslexia): What have we learned in the past four decades? *Journal of Child Psychology and Psychiatry, 45*(1), 2–40.

Vellutino, F. R., & Scanlon, D. M. (1982). Verbal processing in poor and normal readers. In C. J. Brainerd & M. Pressley (Eds.), *Verbal processes in children* (pp. 189–264). New York: Springer-Verlag.

Vellutino, F. R., & Scanlon, D. M., (1987). Phonological coding, phonological awareness, and reading ability: Evidence from a longitudinal and experimental study. *Merrill-Palmer Quarterly, 33*, 321–363.

Vellutino, F. R., Scanlon, D. M., & Lyon, G. R. (2000). Differentiating between difficult-to- remediate and readily remediated poor readers: More evidence against the IQ-achievement discrepancy definition of reading disability. *Journal of Learning Disabilities, 33*, 223–238.

Vellutino, F. R., Scanlon, D. M., Sipay, E., Small, S., Pratt, A., Chen, R., et al. (1996). Cognitive profiles of difficult-to-remediate and readily-remediated poor readers: Early intervention as a vehicle for distinguishing between cognitive and experiential deficits as basic causes of specific reading disability. *Journal of Educational Psychology, 88*, 601–638.

Vellutino, F. R., Scanlon, D. M., & Spearing, D. (1995). Semantic and phonological coding in poor and normal readers. *Journal of Experimental Child Psychology, 59*, 76–123.

Vellutino, F. R., Scanlon, D. M., & Tanzman, M. S. (1988). Lexical memory in poor and normal readers: Developmental differences in the use of category cues. *Canadian Journal of Psychology, 42*, 216–241.

Vellutino, F. R., Scanlon, D. M., & Tanzman, M. S. (1994). Components of reading ability: Issues and problems in operationalizing word identification, phonological coding, and orthographic coding. In G. R. Lyon (Ed.), *Frames of reference for the assessment of learning disabilities: New views on measurement issues* (pp. 279–324). Baltimore: Brookes.

Venezky, R. L. (1967). English orthography: Its graphical structure and its relation to sound. *Reading Research Quarterly, 2*, 75–106.

Ventura, P., Kolinsky, R., Brito-Mendes, C., & Morais, J. (2001). Mental representations of the syllable internal structure are influenced by orthography. *Language and Cognitive Processes, 16*, 393–418.

Ventura, P., Morais, J., Pattamadilok, C., & Kolinsky, R. (2004). The locus of the orthographic consistency effect in auditory word recognition. *Language and Cognitive Processes, 19*, 57–95.

Verhaeghe, A. (1999). L'influence de la scolarisation et de l'alphabétisation sur les capacités de traitement visuel. PhD dissertation, University of Lisbon.

Verhaeghe, A., & Kolinsky, R. (1992). Discriminação entre figuras orientadas em espelho em função do modo de apresentacão em adultos escolarisados e adultos iletrados. *Las Jornadas de Estudo dos Processos Cognitivos da Sociedade Portuguesa de Psicologia* (pp. 51–67). Lisbon: Astoria.

Verstaen, A., Humphreys, G. W., Olson, A., & D'Ydewalle, G. (1995). Are phonemic effects in backward masking evidence for automatic prelexical phonemic activation in visual word recog- nition? *Journal of Memory and Language, 34*, 335–356.

Vitu, F. (2003). The basic assumptions of E-Z Reader are not well founded. *Behavioral and Brain Sciences, 26*, 506–507.

Vitu, F., McConkie, G. W., Kerr, P., & O'Regan, J. K. (2001). Fixation location effects on fixation durations during reading: An inverted optimal viewing position effect. *Vision Research, 41*, 3513–3533.

Volterra, V., Capirci, O., Pezzini, G., Sabbadini, L., & Vicari, S. (1996). Linguistic abilities in Italian children with Williams syndrome. *Cortex, 32*, 663–677.

Vosniadou, S., Pearson, P. D., & Rogers, T. (1988). What causes children's failures to detect inconsistencies in texts? Representation versus comparison difficulties. *Journal of Educational Psychology, 80*, 27–39.

Waber, D. P., Weiler, M. D., Wolff, P. H., Bellinger, D., Marcus, D. J., Ariel, R., et al. (2001). Processing of rapid auditory stimuli in school-age children referred for evaluation of learning disorders. *Child Development, 72*, 37–49.

Wadsworth, S. J., Knopik, V. S., & DeFries, J. C. (2000). Reading disability in boys and girls: No evidence for a differential genetic etiology. *Reading and Writing, 13*, 133–145.

Wadsworth, S. J., Olson, R. K., Pennington, B. F., & DeFries, J. C. (2000). Differential genetic etiology of reading disability as a function of IQ. *Journal of Learning Disabilities, 33*, 192–199.

Wagner, R. K., & Torgesen, J. K. (1987). The nature of phonological processing and its causal role in the acquisition of reading skills. *Psychological Bulletin, 101*, 192–212.

Wagner, R. K., Torgesen, J. K., Laughon, P., Simmons, K., & Rashotte, C. A. (1993). Development of young children's phonological processing abilities. *Journal of Educational Psychology, 85*, 83–103.

Wagner, R. K., Torgesen, J. K., & Rashotte, C. A. (1994). Development of reading-related phonological processing abilities: New evidence of bidirectional causality from a latent variable longitudinal study. *Developmental Psychology, 30*, 73–87.

Wagner, R. K., Torgesen, J. K., & Rashotte, C. A. (1999). *Comprehensive Test of Phonological Processes*. Austin, TX: Pro-ed.

Wagner, R. K., Torgesen, J. K., Rashotte, C. A., Hecht, S. A., Barker, T. A., Burgess, S. R., et al. (1997). Changing relations between phonological processing abilities and word-level reading as children develop from beginning to skilled readers: A 5-year longitudinal study. *Developmental Psychology, 33*, 468–479.

Walker, D., Greenwood, C., Hart, B., & Carta, J. (1994). Prediction of school outcomes based on early language production and socioeconomic factors. *Child Development, 65*, 606–621.

Walker, I., & Hulme, C. (1999). Concrete words are easier to recall than abstract words: Evidence for a semantic contribution to short-term serial recall. *Journal of Experimental Psychology: Learning, Memory and Cognition, 25*, 1256–1271.

Walley, A. (1993). The role of vocabulary development in children's spoken word recognition and segmentation ability. *Developmental Review, 13*, 286–350.

Walsh, D. J., Price, G. G., & Gillingham, M. G. (1988). The critical but transitory importance of letter naming. *Reading Research Quarterly, 23*, 108–122.

Wang, M., and Geva, E. (2003b). Spelling acquisition of novel English phonemes in Chinese children. *Reading and Writing, 16*, 325–348.

Wang, M., Perfetti, C. A., & Liu, Y. (2003). Alphabetic readers quickly acquire orthographic structure in learning to read Chinese. *Scientific Studies of Reading, 7*, 183–208.

Wang, P. P., & Bellugi, U. (1994). Evidence from two genetic syndromes for a dissociation between verbal and visuo-spatial short-term memory. *Journal of Clinical and Experimental Neuropsychology, 16*, 317–322.

Wang, W. S. Y. (1973). The Chinese language. *Scientific American, 228*, 50–63.

Warburton, E., Wise, R. J. S., Price, C. J., Weiller, C., Hadar, U., Ramsay, S., et al. (1996). Noun and verb retrieval by normal subjects studies with PET. *Brain, 119*(Pt 1), 159–179.

Ward, J., & Romani, C. (1998). Serial position effects and lexical activation in spelling: Evidence from a single case study. *Neurocase, 4*, 189–206.

Ward, J., & Romani, C. (2000). Consonant–vowel encoding and ortho-syllables in a case of acquired dysgraphia. *Cognitive Neuropsychology, 17*(7), 641–663.

Warrington, E. K. (1975). The selective impairment of semantic memory. *Quarterly Journal of Experimental Psychology, 27*, 635–657.

Warrington, E. K. (1981). Concrete word dyslexia. *British Journal of Psychology, 72*, 175–196.

Warrington, E. K., Cipolotti, L., & McNeil, J. (1993). Attentional dyslexia: A single case study. *Neuropsychologia, 31*, 871–885.

Warrington, E. K., & Shallice, T. (1979). Semantic access dyslexica. *Brain, 102*, 43–63.

Waters, G. S., & Doehring, D. G. (1990). Reading acquisition in congenitally deaf children who communicate orally: Insights from an analysis of component reading, language, and memory skills. In T. H. Carr & B. A. Levy (Eds.), *Reading and its development: Component skills approaches* (pp. 323–373). San Diego, CA: Academic.

Waters, G. S., & Seidenberg, M. S. (1985). Spelling-sound effects in reading: Time course and decision criteria. *Memory and Cognition, 13*, 557–572.

Weber, H. (1997). *Die Sprache der Nicht-Sprechenden*. Retrieved Jan. 18, 2007, from http://www.uni-kl.de/FB-SoWi/LS-Zink/BLISS/article.html

Wechsler, D. (1945). A standardized memory scale for clinical use. *Journal of Psychology, 19*, 87–95.

Wechsler, D. (1992). *The Wechsler Intelligence Scale for Children* (3rd UK ed.). London: Psychological Corporation.

Weekes, B., & Coltheart, M. (1996). Surface dyslexia and surface dysgraphia: Treatment studies and their theoretical implications. *Cognitive Neuropsychology, 13*, 277–315.

Weizman, Z. O., & Snow, C. E. (2001). Lexical input as related to children's vocabulary acquisition: Effects of sophisticated exposure and support for meaning. *Developmental Psychology, 37*, 265–279.

Welbourne, S. R., & Lambon Ralph, M. A. (in press). Subtracting subtractivity? A connectionist account of recovery in single word reading following brain damage. *Cognitive Neuropsychology*.

Wheeler, D. (1970). Processes in word recognition. *Cognitive Psychology, 1*, 59–85.

Wesseling, R., & Reitsma, P. (2000). The transient role of explicit phonological recoding for reading acquisition. *Reading and Writing, 13*, 313–336.

Whaley, C. P. (1978). Word–nonword classification time. *Journal of Verbal Learning and Verbal Behavior, 17*, 143–154.

Wheeler, D. D. (1970). Processes in word recognition. *Cognitive Psychology, 1*, 59–85.

White, S. J., & Liversedge, S. P. (2004). Orthographic familiarity influences initial eye fixation positions in reading. *European Journal of Cognitive Psychology, 16*, 52–78.

Whitehurst, G. J. (1997). Language processes in context: Language learning in children reared in poverty. In L. B. Adamson & M. A. Romski (Eds.), *Research on communication and language disorders: Contribution to theories of language development* (pp. 233–266). Baltimore: Brookes.

Whitehurst, G. J., Arnold, D. H., Epstein, J. N., Angell, A. L., Smith, M., & Fischel, J. E. (1994). A picture book reading intervention in daycare and home for children from low-income families. *Developmental Psychology, 30*, 679–689.

Whitehurst, G. J., & Lonigan, C. J. (1998). Child development and emergent literacy. *Child Development, 68*, 848–872.

Whitehurst, G. J., & Lonigan, C. J. (2001). Emergent literacy: Development from prereaders to readers. In S. B Neuman & D. K. Dickensen (Eds.), *Handbook of early literacy research* (pp. 11–29). New York: Guilford.

Whitney, C. (2001). How the brain encodes the order of letters in a printed word: The SERIOL model and selective literature review. *Psychonomic Bulletin and Review, 8,* 221–243.

Wickelgren, W. A. (1969). Context-sensitive coding, associative memory, and serial order in (speech) behavior. *Psychological Review, 76,* 1–15.

Wickens, D. D., Dalezman, R. E., & Eggemeier, F. T. (1976). Multiple encoding of word attributes in memory. *Memory and Cognition, 4,* 307–310.

Wiederholt, J. L., & Bryant, B. R. (1992). *Gray Oral Reading Tests-III.* Austin, TX: Pro-ed.

Willcutt, E. G., & Pennington, B. F. (2000). Psychiatric comorbidity in children and adolescents with reading disability. *Journal of Child Psychology and Psychiatry, 41,* 1039–1048.

Willcutt, E. G., Pennington, B. F., DeFries, J. C. (2000). A twin study of the etiology of comorbidity between reading disability and attention-deficit/hyperactivity disorder. *American Journal of Medical Genetics (Neuropsychiatric Genetics), 96,* 293–301.

Willcutt, E. G., Pennington, B. F., Smith, S. D., Cardon, L. R., Gayan, J., Knopik, V. S., et al. (2002). Quantitative trait locus for reading disability on chromosome 6p is pleiotropic for attention-deficit/hyperactivity disorder. *American Journal of Medical Genetics: Neuropsychiatric Genetics, 114,* 260–268.

Williams, J. N. (1996). Is automatic priming semantic? *European Journal of Cognitive Psychology, 8,* 113–161.

Williams, R. J., & Peng, J. (1990). An efficient gradient-based algorithm for on-line training of recurrent network trajectories. *Neural Computation, 2,* 490–501.

Williams, R. S., & Morris, R. K. (2004). Eye movements, word familiarity, and vocabulary acquisition. *European Journal of Cognitive Psychology, 16,* 285–311.

Wilson, R. A. (2003). Pluralism, entwinement, and the levels of selection. *Philosophy of Science, 70,* 531–552.

Wimmer, H. (1993). Characteristics of developmental dyslexia in a regular writing system. *Applied Psycholinguistics, 14,* 1–33.

Wimmer, H. (1996a). The early manifestation of developmental dyslexia: Evidence from German children. *Reading and Writing, 8,* 171–188.

Wimmer, H. (1996b). The non-word reading deficit in developmental dyslexia: Evidence from children learning to read German. *Journal of Experimental Child Psychology, 61,* 80–90.

Wimmer, H., & Goswami, U. (1994). The influence of orthographic consistency on reading development: Word recognition in English and German children. *Cognition, 51,* 91–103.

Wimmer, H., & Hummer, P. (1990). How German-speaking first graders read and spell: Doubts on the importance of the logographic stage. *Applied Psycholinguistics, 11,* 349–368.

Wimmer, H., Landerl, K., Linortner, R., & Hummer, P. (1991). The relationship of phonemic awareness to reading acquisition: More consequence than precondition but still important. *Cognition, 40,* 219–249.

Wimmer, H., & Mayringer, H. (2002). Dysfluent reading in the absence of spelling difficulties: A specific disability in regular orthographies. *Journal of Educational Psychology, 94*(2), 272–277.

Wimmer, H., Mayringer, H., & Landerl, K. (2000). The double-deficit hypothesis and difficulties in learning to read a regular orthography. *Journal of Educational Psychology, 92,* 668–680.

Windfuhr, K. L., & Snowling, M. J. (2001). The relationship between paired associate learning and phonological skills in normally developing readers. *Journal of Experimental Child Psychology, 80,* 160–173.

Wing, A. M., & Baddeley, A. D. (1980). Spelling errors in handwriting: A corpus and a distributional analysis. In U. Frith (Ed.), *Cognitive processes in spelling* (pp. 251–285). London: Academic.

Wise, B. W., Ring, J., & Olson, R. K. (1999). Training phonological awareness with and without explicit attention to articulation. *Journal of Experimental Child Psychology, 72,* 271–304.

Wise, B. W., Ring, J., & Olson, R. K. (2000). Individual differences in gains from computer-assisted remedial reading with more emphasis on phonological analysis or accurate reading in context. *Journal of Experimental Child Psychology, 77,* 197–235.

Wolf, M. (1991). Naming speed and reading: The contribution of the cognitive neurosciences. *Reading Research Quarterly, 26,* 123–141.

Wolf, M., Bally, H., & Morris, R. (1986). Automaticity, retrieval processes, and reading: Longitudinal study in average and impaired readers. *Child Development, 57,* 988–1005.

Wolf, M., & Bowers, P. G. (1999). The double deficit hypothesis for the developmental dyslexias. *Journal of Educational Psychology, 91,* 415–438.

Wolf, M., Bowers, P. G., & Biddle, K. (2000). Naming-speed processes, timing, and reading: A conceptual overview. *Journal of Learning Disabilities, 33,* 387–407.

Wolf, M., & Goodglass, H. (1986). Dyslexia, dysnomia, and lexical retrieval: A longitudinal investigation. *Brain and Language, 28,* 154–168.

Wolf, M., Miller, L., & Donnelly, K. (2000). Retrieval, Automaticity, Vocabulary Elaboration, Orthography (RAVE-O): A comprehensive, fluency-based reading intervention program. *Journal of Learning Disabilities, 33,* 322–324.

Wolf, M., Pfeil, C., Lotz, R., & Biddle, K. (1994). Towards a more universal understanding of the developmental dyslexias: The contribution of orthographic factors. In V. Berninger (Ed.), *The varieties of orthographic knowledge* (Vol. 1, pp. 137–171). Dordrecht, the Netherlands: Kluwer Academic.

Wolff, P. H., Michel, G. F., & Ovrut, M. (1990). Rate variables and automatized naming in developmental dyslexia. *Brain and Language, 39,* 556–575.

Wolverton, G. S., & Zola, D. (1983). The temporal characteristics of visual information extraction during reading. In K. Rayner (Ed.), *Eye movements in reading: Perceptual and language processes* (pp. 41–52). New York: Academic.

Woo, E. Y., & Hoosain, R. (1984). Visual and auditory functions of Chinese dylsexics. *Psychologia, 27,* 164–170.

Woodcock, R. W. (1987). *Woodcock Reading Mastery Tests-Revised.* Circle Pines, MN: American Guidance Service.

Wydell, T. N., Butterworth, B., & Patterson, K. (1995). The inconsistency of consistency effects in reading: The case of Japanese Kanji. *Journal of Experimental Psychology: Learning, Memory, and Cognition, 21,* 1169–1185.

Wydell, T. N., Patterson, K., & Humphreys, G. W. (1993). Phonologically mediated access to meaning for Kanji: Is a ROWS still a ROSE in Japanese Kanji? *Journal of Experimental Psychology: Learning, Memory, and Cognition, 19,* 491–514.

Xu, B., Grafman, J., Gaillard, W. D., Ishii, K., Vega-Bermudez, F., Pietrini, P., et al. (2001). Conjoint and extended neural networks for the computation of speech codes: The neural basis of selective impairment in reading words and pseudowords. *Cerebral Corte, 11,* 267–277.

Xu, B., & Perfetti, C. A. (1999). Nonstrategic subjective thresholds effects in phonemic masking. *Memory and Cognition, 27,* 26–36.

Yang, S.-N., & McConkie, G. W. (2001). Eye movements during reading: A theory of saccade initiation times. *Vision Research, 41,* 3567–3585.

Yang, S.-N., & McConkie, G. W. (2004). Saccade generation during reading: Are words necessary? *European Journal of Cognitive Psychology, 16,* 226–261.

Yuill, N., & Joscelyne, T. (1988). Effects of organizational cures and strategies on good and poor comprehenders' story understanding. *Journal of Educational Psychology, 80,* 152–158.

Yuill, N., & Oakhill, J. V. (1988). Effects on inference awareness training of poor reading comprehension. *Applied Cognitive Psychology, 2,* 33–45.

Yuill, N., & Oakhill, J. V. (1991). *Children's problems in text comprehension.* Cambridge: Cambridge University Press.

Yuill, N., Oakhill, J. V., & Parkin, A. (1989). Working memory, comprehension ability and the resolution of text anomaly. *British Journal of Psychology, 80,* 351–361.

Zabell, C., & Everatt, J. (2002). Surface and phonological subtypes of adult developmental dyslexia. *Dyslexia, 8,* 160–177.

Zayas, L. H., & Solari, F. (1994). Early childhood socialization practices in Hispanic families: Context, culture, and practical implications. *Professional Psychology: Research and Practice, 25,* 200–206.

Zerbin-Rudin, E. (1967). Congenital word-blindness. *Bulletin of the Orton Society, 17,* 47–56.

Zhou, Y. G. (1978). To what extent are the "phonetics" of present-day Chinese characers still phonetic. *Zhonggou Yuwen, 146,* 172–177.

Ziegler, J. C., & Ferrand, L. (1998). Orthography shapes the perception of speech: The consistency effect in auditory word recognition. *Psychonomic Bulletin and Review, 5,* 683–689.

Ziegler, J. C., Ferrand, L., Jacobs, A. M., Rey, A., & Grainger, J. (2000). Visual and phonological codes in letter and word recognition: Evidence from incremental priming. *Quarterly Journal of Experimental Psychology Section A: Human Experimental Psychology, 53,* 671–692.

Ziegler, J. C., & Jacobs, A. M. (1995). Phonological information provides early sources of constraint in the processing of letter strings. *Journal of Memory and Language, 34,* 567–593.

Ziegler, J. C., Jacobs, A. M., & Stone, G. O. (1996). Statistical analysis of the bi-directional inconsistency of spelling and sound in French. *Behavior Research Methods, Instruments and Computers, 28,* 504–515.

Ziegler, J. C., Montant, M., & Jacobs, A. M. (1997). The feedback consistency effect in lexical decision and naming. *Journal of Memory and Language, 37,* 533–554.

Ziegler, J. C., Muneaux, M., & Grainger, J. (2003). Neighborhood effects in auditory word recognition: Phonological competition and orthographic facilitation. *Journal of Memory and Language, 48,* 779–793.

Ziegler, J. C., Perry, C., Jacobs, A. M., & Braun, M. (2001). Identical words are read differently in different languages. *Psychological Science, 12,* 379–384.

Ziegler, J. C., Perry, C., Ma-Wyatt, A., Ladner, D., & Schulte-Körne, G. (2003). Developmental dyslexia in different languages: Language-specific or universal? *Journal of Experimental Child Psychology, 86,* 169–193.

Ziegler, J. C., Stone, G. O., & Jacobs, A. M. (1997). What is the pronunciation for – *ough* and the spelling for /u/? A database for computing feedforward and feedback consistency in English. *Behavior Research Methods, Instruments and Computers, 29,* 600–618.

Ziegler, J. C., Tan, L. H., Perry, C., & Montant, M. (2000). Phonology matters: The phonological frequency effect in written Chinese. *Psychological Science, 11,* 234–238.

Ziegler, J. C., Van Orden, G. C., & Jacobs, A. M. (1997). Phonology can help or hurt the perception of print. *Journal of Experimental Psychology: Human Perception and Performance, 23,* 845–860.

Zigler, E., & Styfco, S. J. (1994). Head Start: Criticisms in a constructive context. *American Psychologist, 49,* 127–132.

Zorzi, M., Houghton, G., & Butterworth, B. (1998). Two routes or one in reading aloud? A connectionist dual-process model. *Journal of Experimental Psychology: Human Perception and Performance, 24,* 1131–1161.

Zwaan, R. A. (1996). Processing narrative time shifts. *Journal of Experimental Psychology: Learning, Memory, and Cognition, 22,* 1196–1207.

Zwaan, R. A., Langston, M. C., & Graesser, A. C. (1995). The construction of situation models in narrative comprehension: An event-indexing model. *Psychological Science, 6,* 292–297.

Zwaan, R. A., Magliano, J. P., & Graesser, A. C. (1995). Dimensions of situation model construction in narrative comprehension. *Journal of Experimental Psychology: Learning, Memory, and Cognition, 21*, 386–397.

Zwaan, R. A., & Radvansky, G. A. (1998). Situation models in language comprehension and memory. *Psychological Bulletin, 123*, 162–185.

# Author Index

# Subject Index